CW00798885

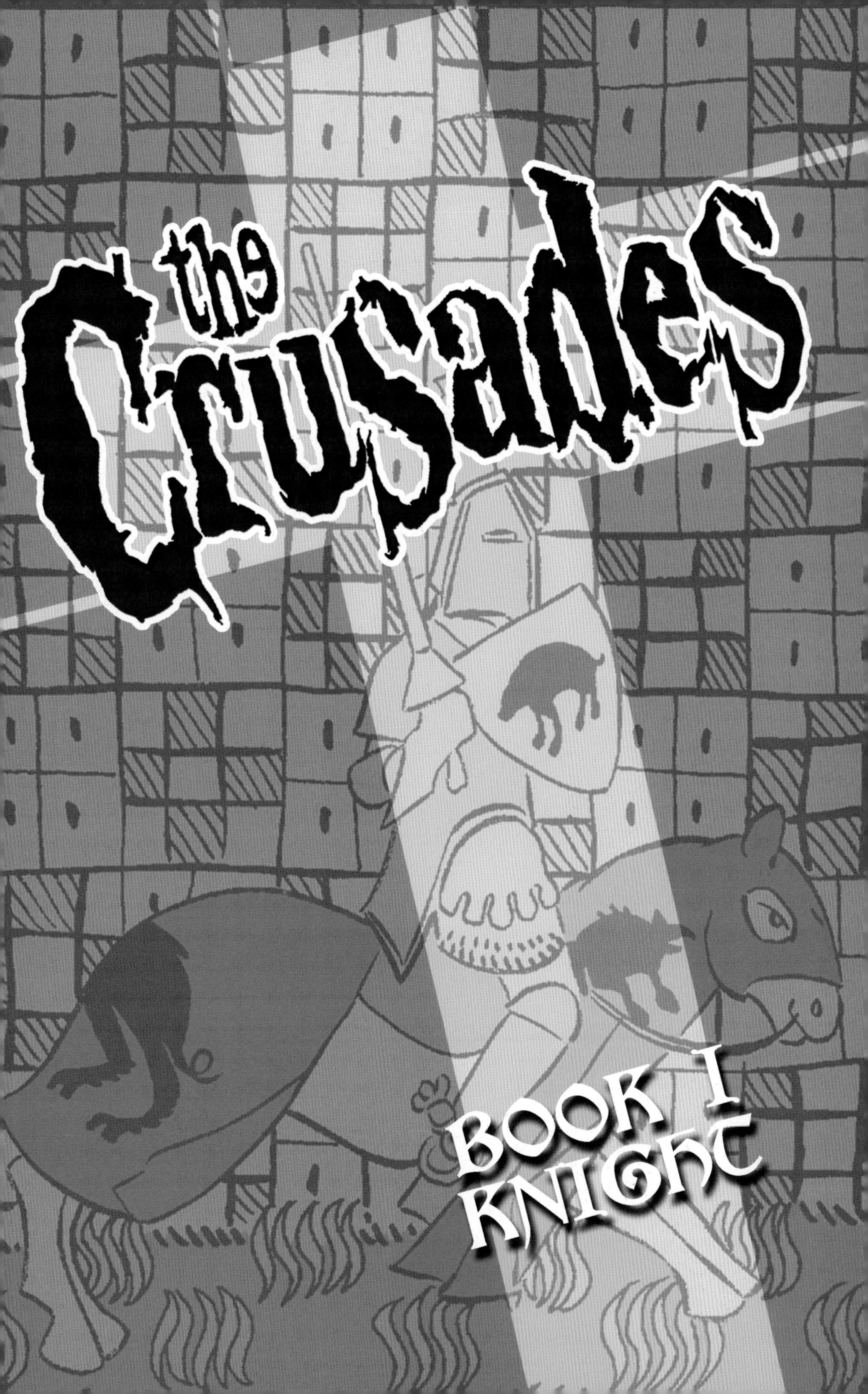
the Crusades
BOOK I
KNIGHT

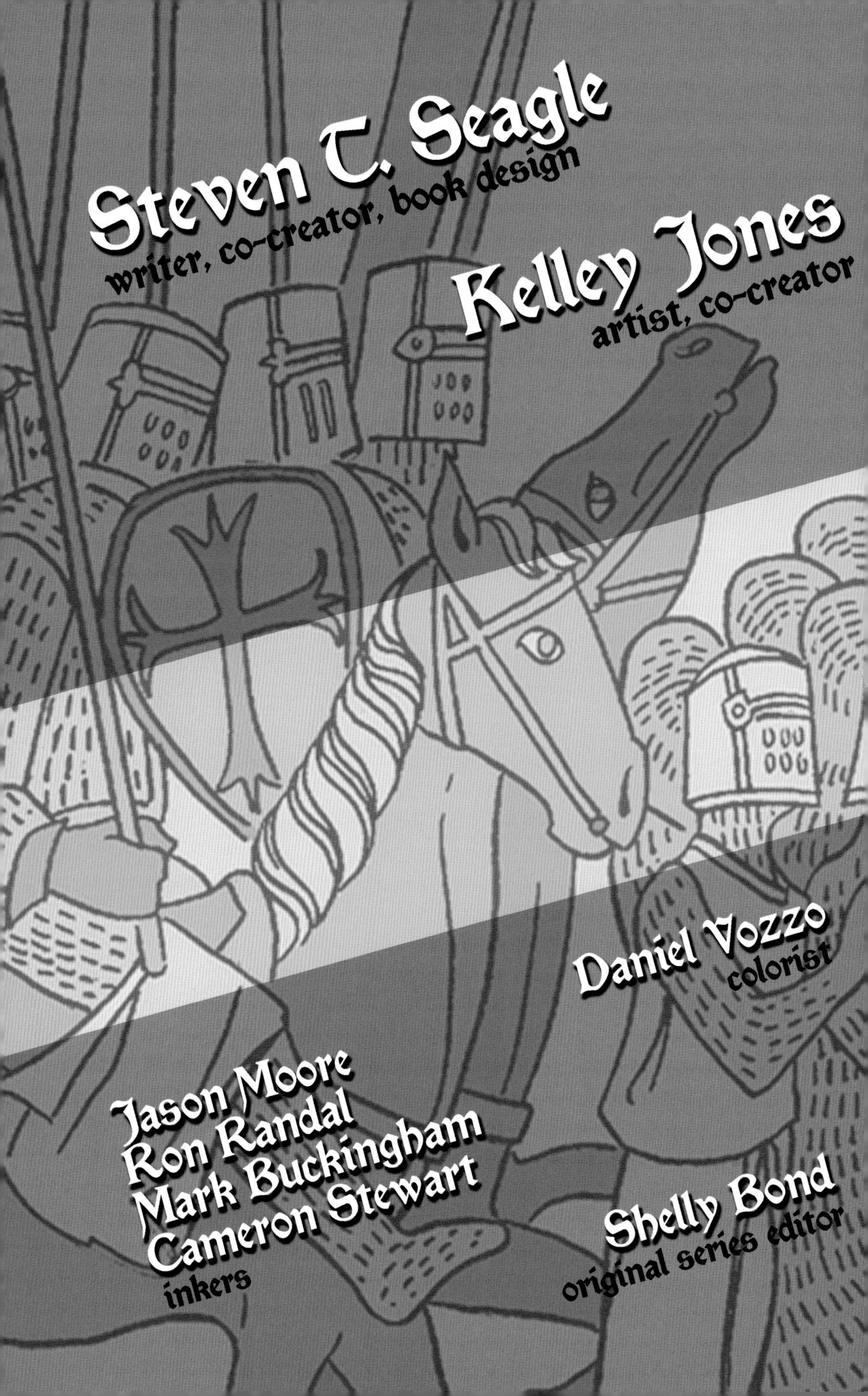

Steven T. Seagle
writer, co-creator, book design

Kelley Jones
artist, co-creator

Daniel Vozzo
colorist

Jason Moore
Ron Randal
Mark Buckingham
Cameron Stewart
inkers

Shelly Bond
original series editor

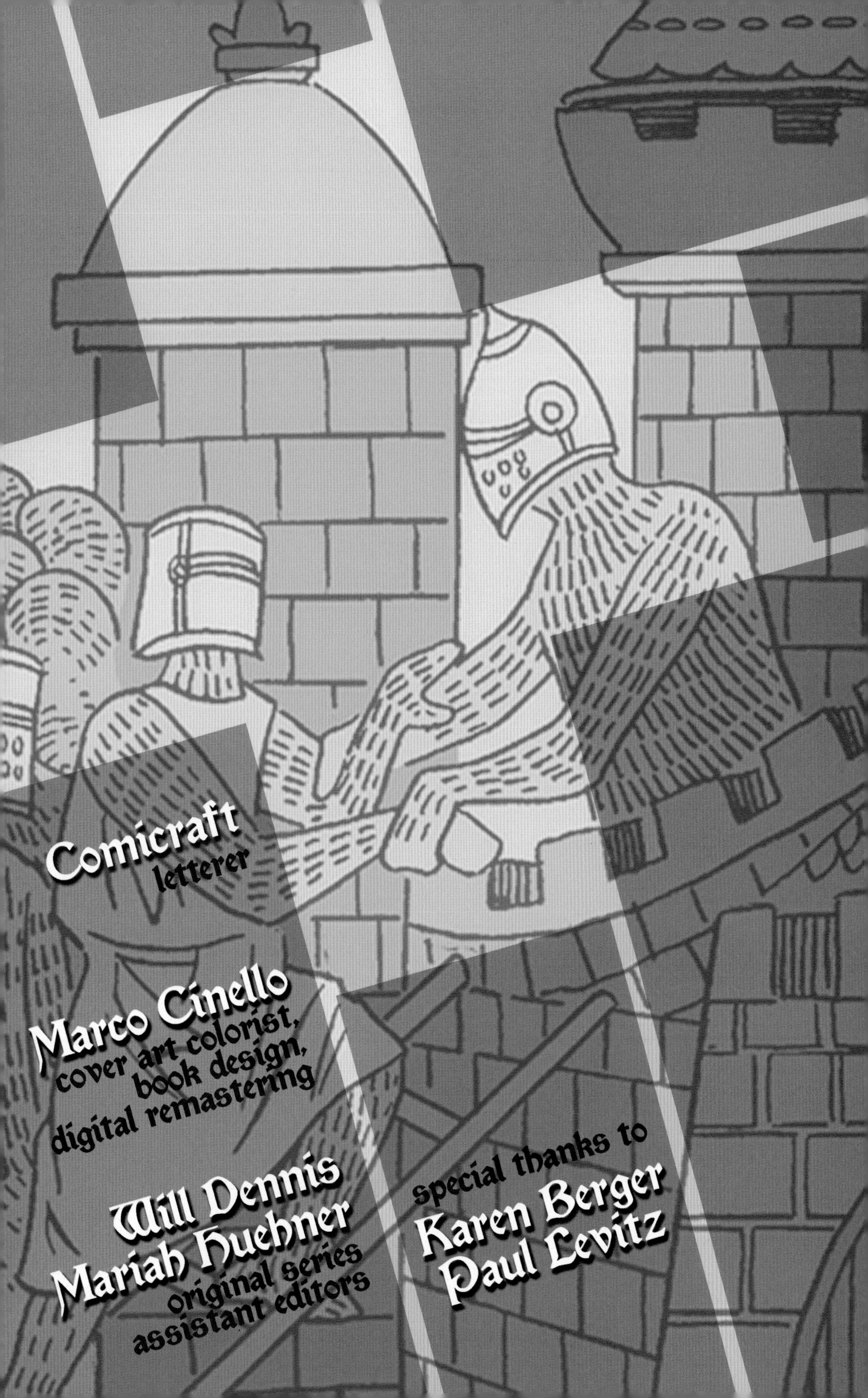

Comicraft
letterer

Marco Cinello
cover art colorist,
book design,
digital remastering

Will Dennis
Mariah Huehner
original series
assistant editors

special thanks to
Karen Berger
Paul Levitz

THE CRUSADES

STEVEN T. SEAGLE *Writer, Co-Creator, Designer*
KELLEY JONES   *Artist, Co-Creator*

WWW.MANOFACTION.TV

THE CRUSADES, BOOK ONE: KNIGHT HC
ISBN: 978-1-60706-288-2

First Printing

Published by Image Comics, Inc.
Office of publication:
2134 Allston Way, 2nd Floor,
Berkeley, California 94704, U.S.A.

PRINTED IN SOUTH KOREA

International Rights Representative:
Christine Jensen - christine@gfloystudio.com

IMAGE COMICS, INC.

chief operating officer : Robert Kirkman
chief financial officer : Erik Larsen
president : Todd McFarlane
chief executive officer : Marc Silvestri
vice-president : Jim Valentino

publisher : Eric Stephenson
sales & licensing coordinator : Todd Martinez
pr & marketing coordinator : Betsy Gomez
accounts manager : Branwyn Bigglestone
administrative assistant : Sarah deLaine
production manager : Tyler Shainline
art director : Drew Gill
production artist : Jonathan Chan
production artist : Monica Howard
production artist : Vincent Kukua
www.imagecomics.com

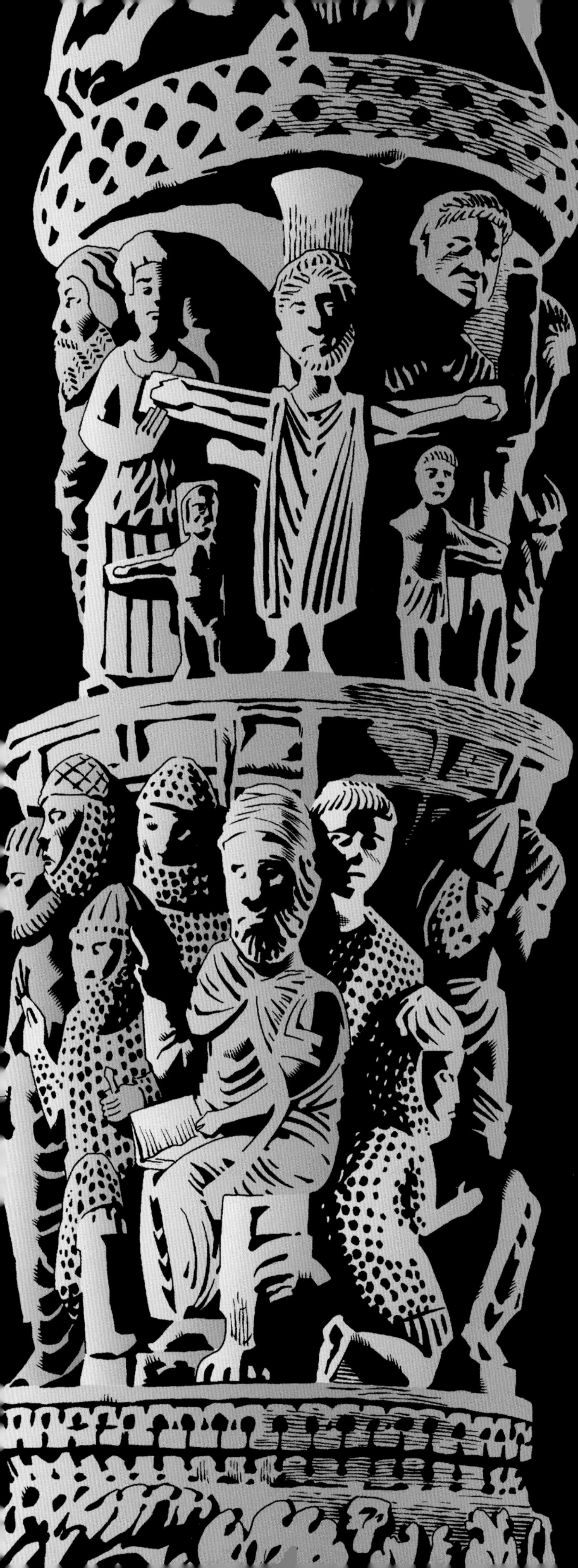

All that is
noble is of
a quiet nature
and appears
to sleep until
it is aroused
and summoned
forth by
contrast.

—Goethe

"...IT WAS LIKE
HE COME OUTTA
NOWHERE..."

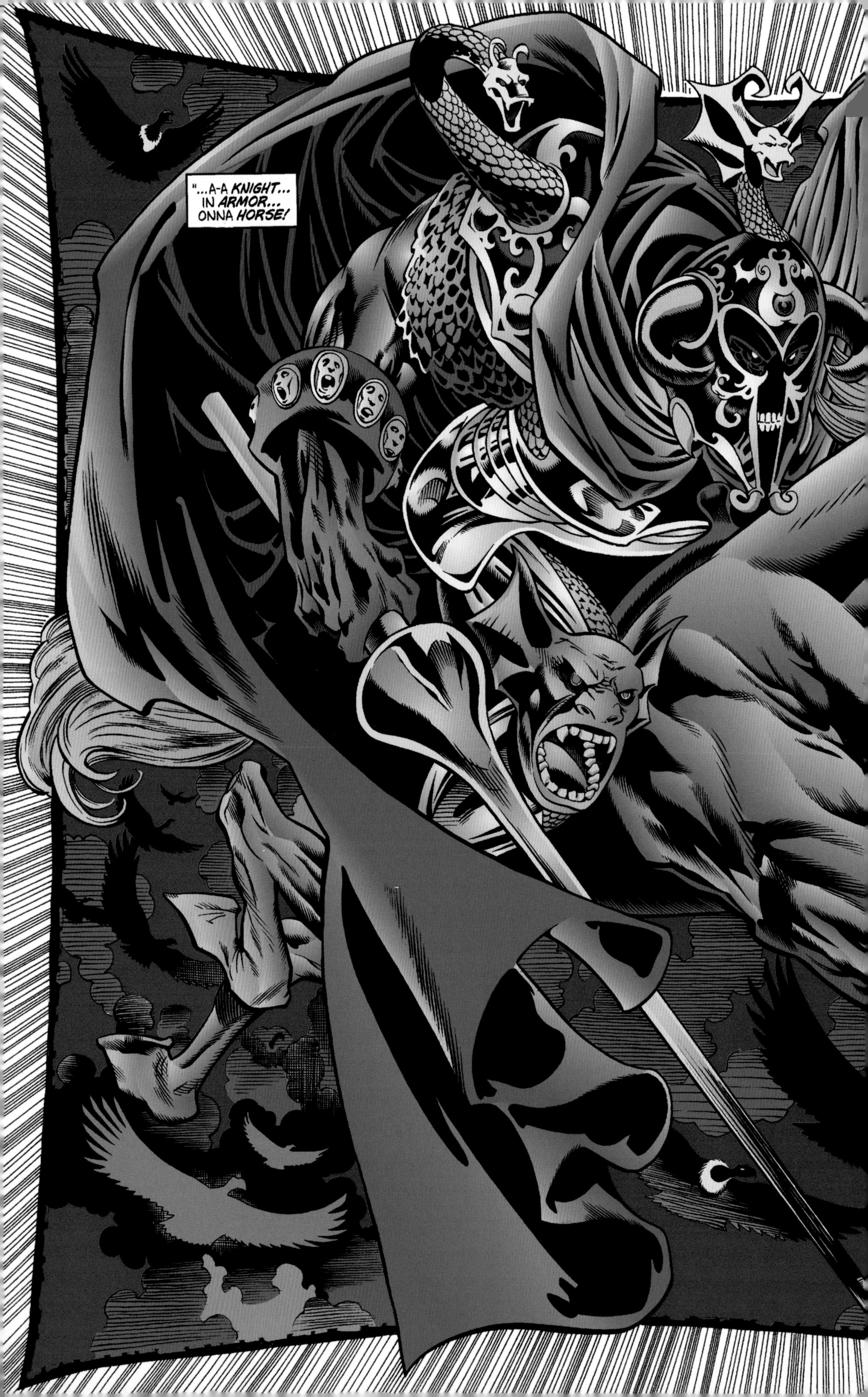
"...A-A KNIGHT... IN ARMOR... ONNA HORSE!

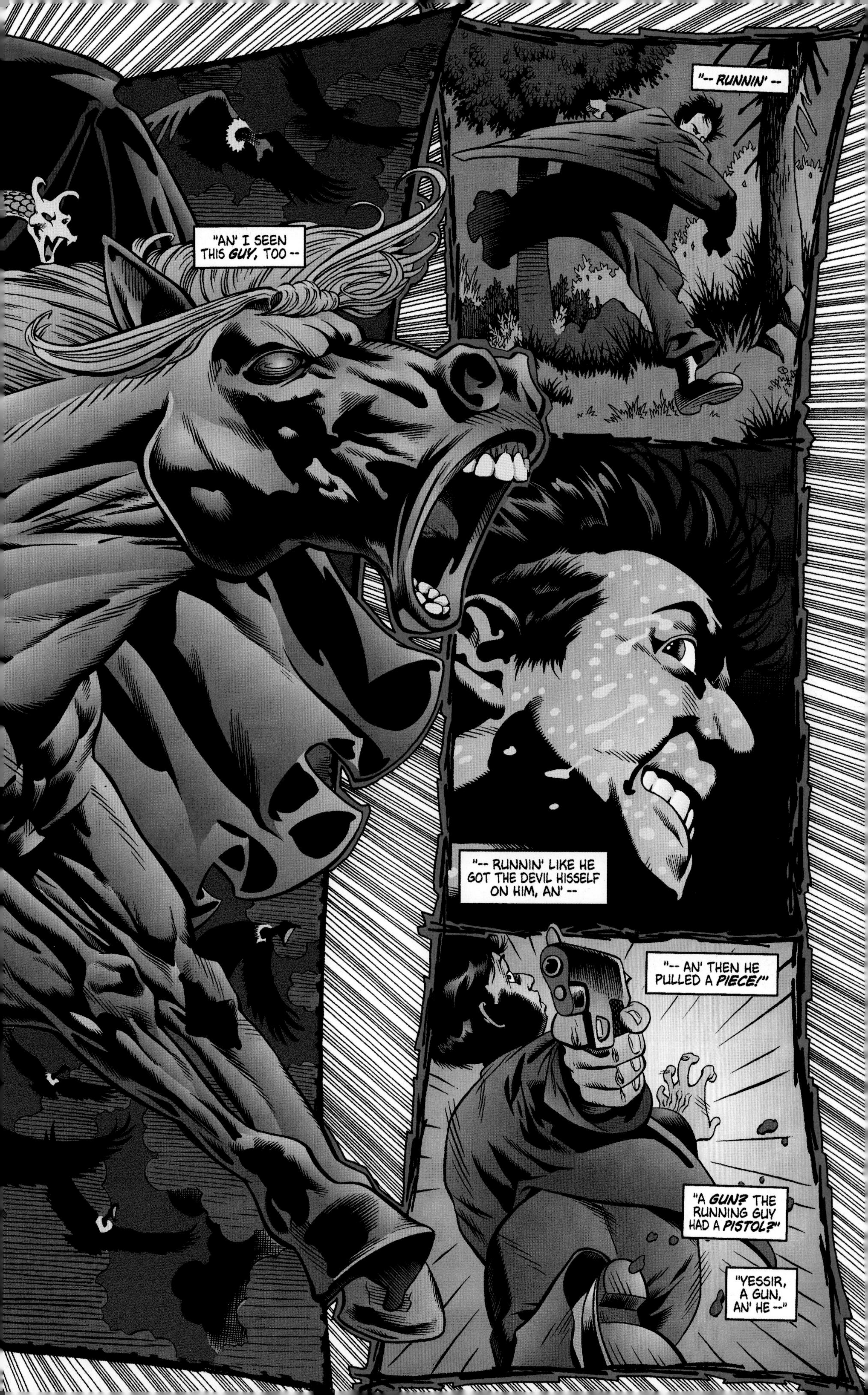
"AN' I SEEN THIS GUY, TOO --
"-- RUNNIN' --
"-- RUNNIN' LIKE HE GOT THE DEVIL HISSELF ON HIM, AN' --
"-- AN' THEN HE PULLED A PIECE!"
"A GUN? THE RUNNING GUY HAD A PISTOL?"
"YESSIR, A GUN, AN' HE --"

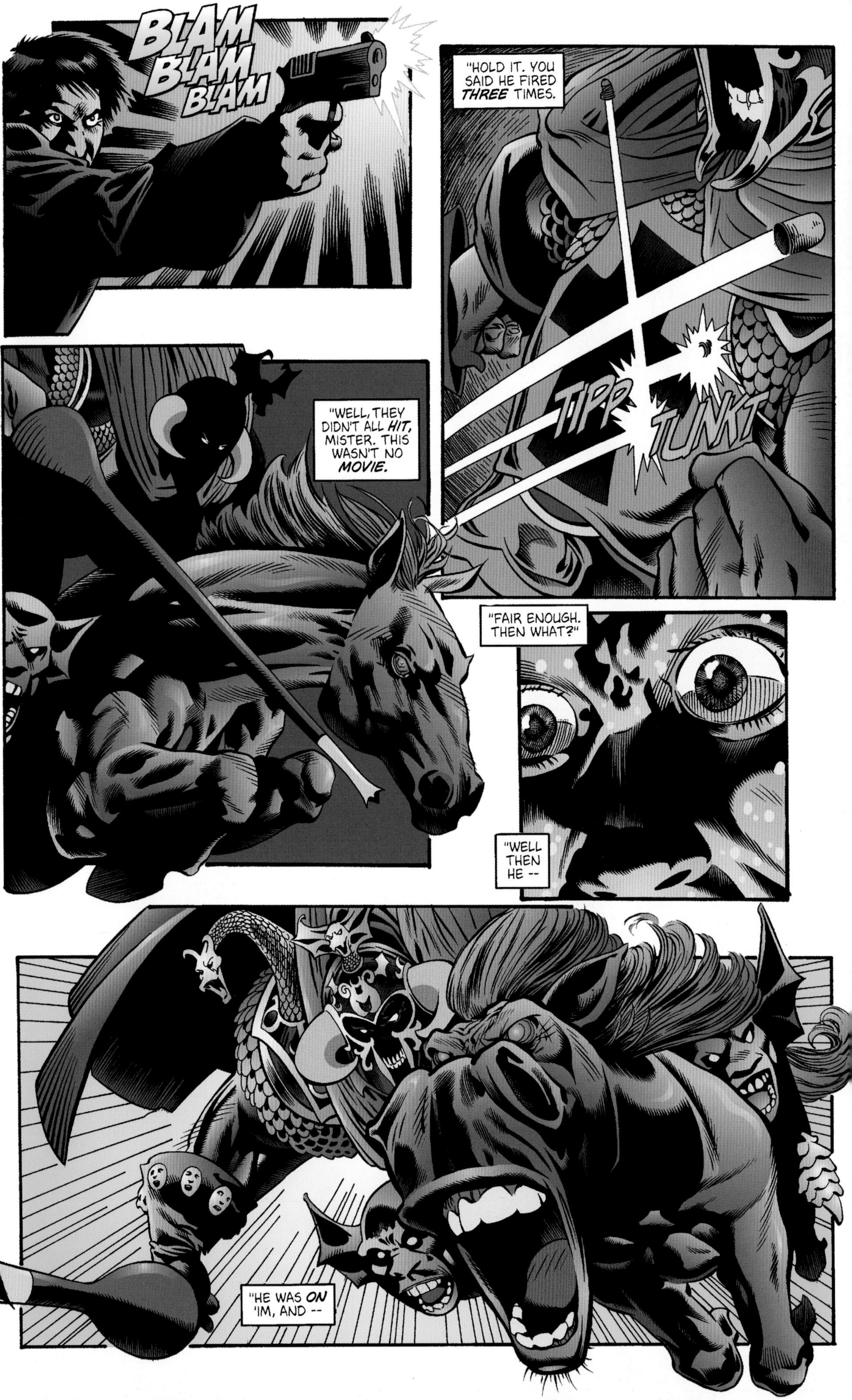
BLAM BLAM BLAM
"HOLD IT. YOU SAID HE FIRED THREE TIMES.
"WELL, THEY DIDN'T ALL HIT, MISTER. THIS WASN'T NO MOVIE.
TIPP
TUNK!
"FAIR ENOUGH. THEN WHAT?"
"WELL THEN HE --
"HE WAS ON 'IM, AND --

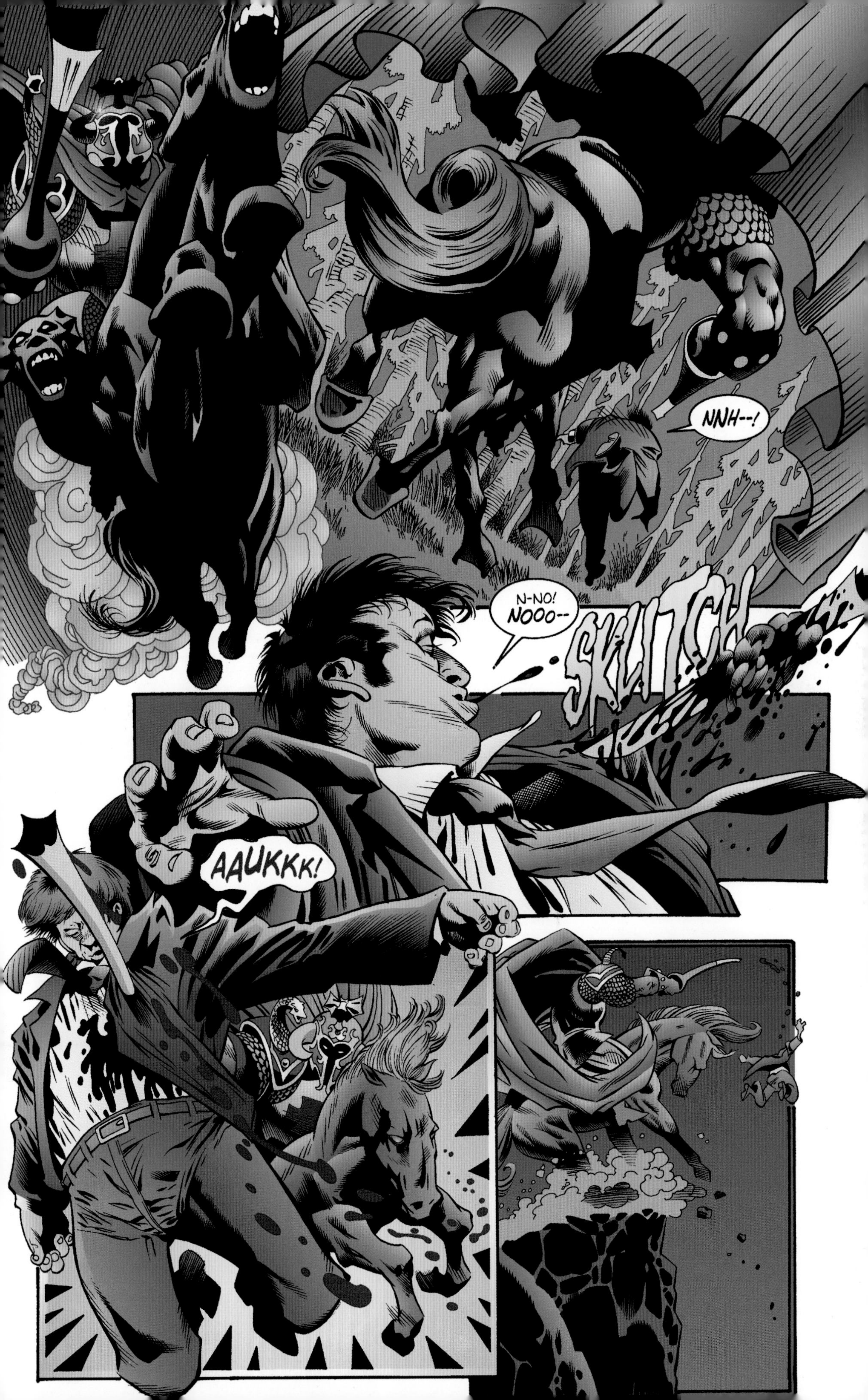
NNH--!
N-NO! NOOO--
SKLITCH
AAUKKK!

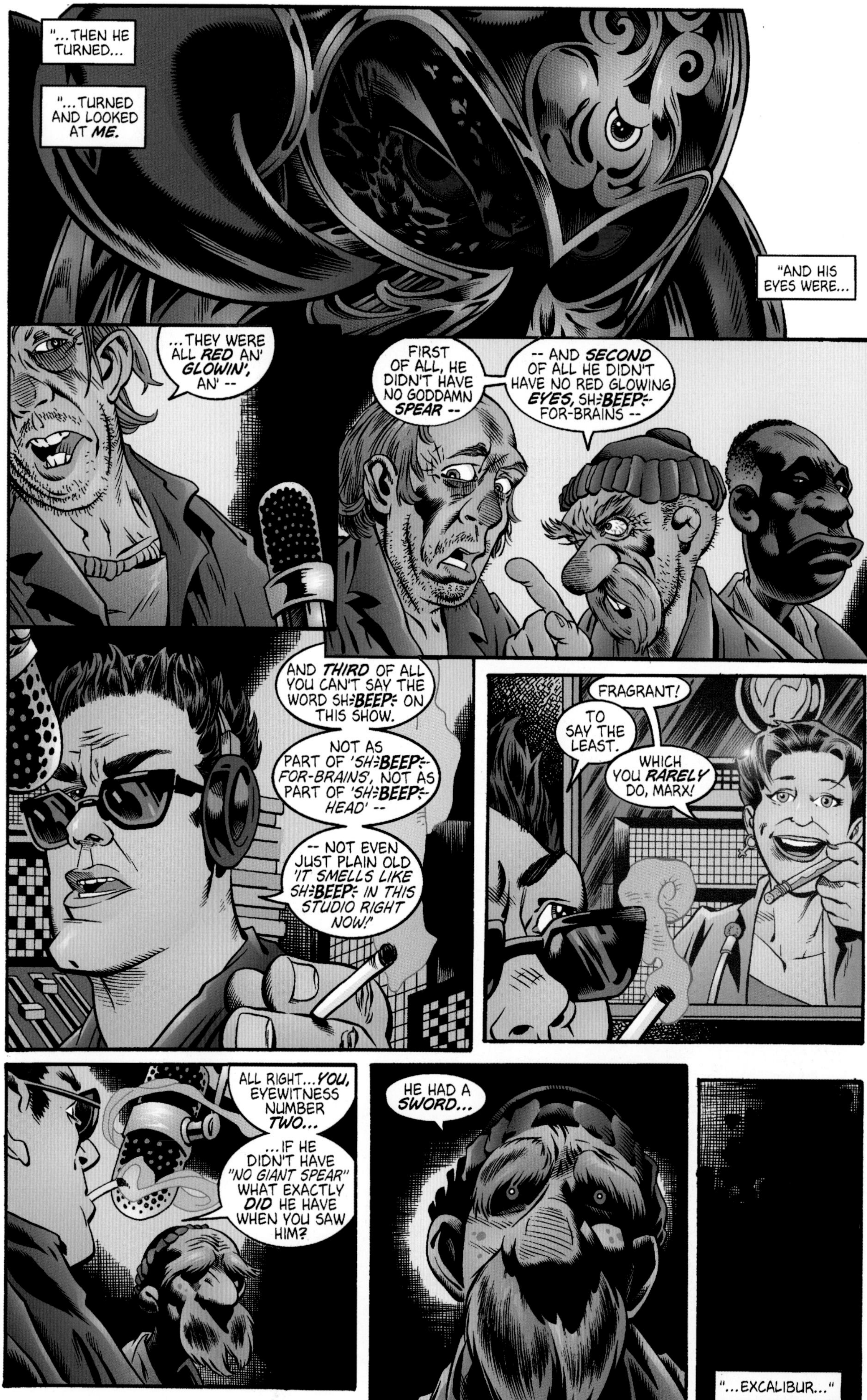
"...THEN HE TURNED...
"...TURNED AND LOOKED AT *ME.*
"AND HIS EYES WERE...
...THEY WERE ALL *RED* AN' *GLOWIN',* AN' --
FIRST OF ALL, HE DIDN'T HAVE NO GODDAMN *SPEAR* --
-- AND *SECOND* OF ALL HE DIDN'T HAVE NO RED GLOWING *EYES,* SH-*BEEP*-FOR-BRAINS --
AND *THIRD* OF ALL YOU CAN'T SAY THE WORD SH-*BEEP*- ON THIS SHOW.
NOT AS PART OF *'SH-BEEP-FOR-BRAINS',* NOT AS PART OF *'SH-BEEP-HEAD'* --
-- NOT EVEN JUST PLAIN OLD *'IT SMELLS LIKE SH-BEEP- IN THIS STUDIO RIGHT NOW!'*
FRAGRANT!
TO SAY THE LEAST.
WHICH YOU *RARELY* DO, MARX!
ALL RIGHT...*YOU,* EYEWITNESS NUMBER *TWO...*
...IF HE DIDN'T HAVE *"NO GIANT SPEAR"* WHAT EXACTLY *DID* HE HAVE WHEN YOU SAW HIM?
HE HAD A *SWORD...*
"...EXCALIBUR..."

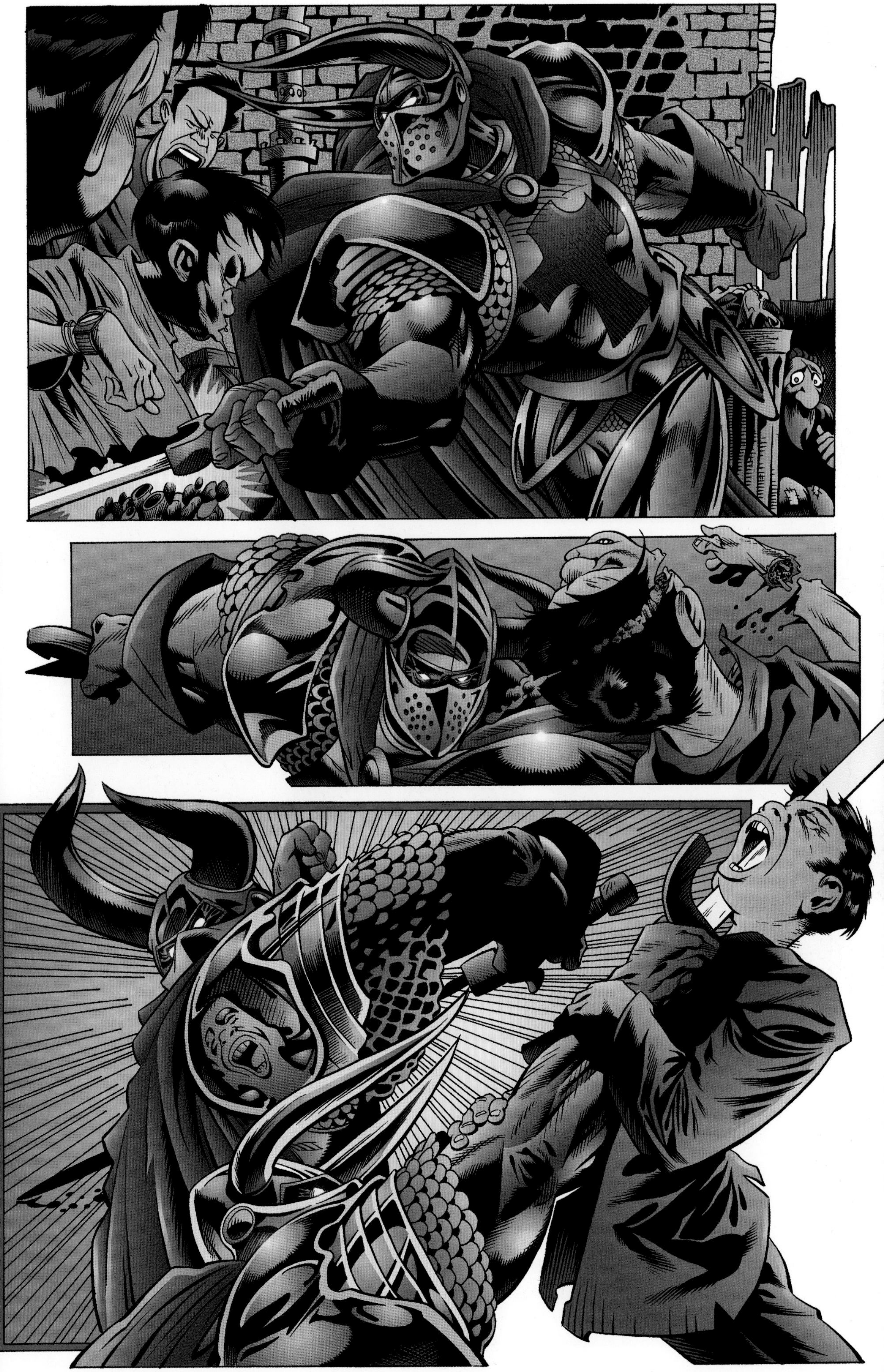

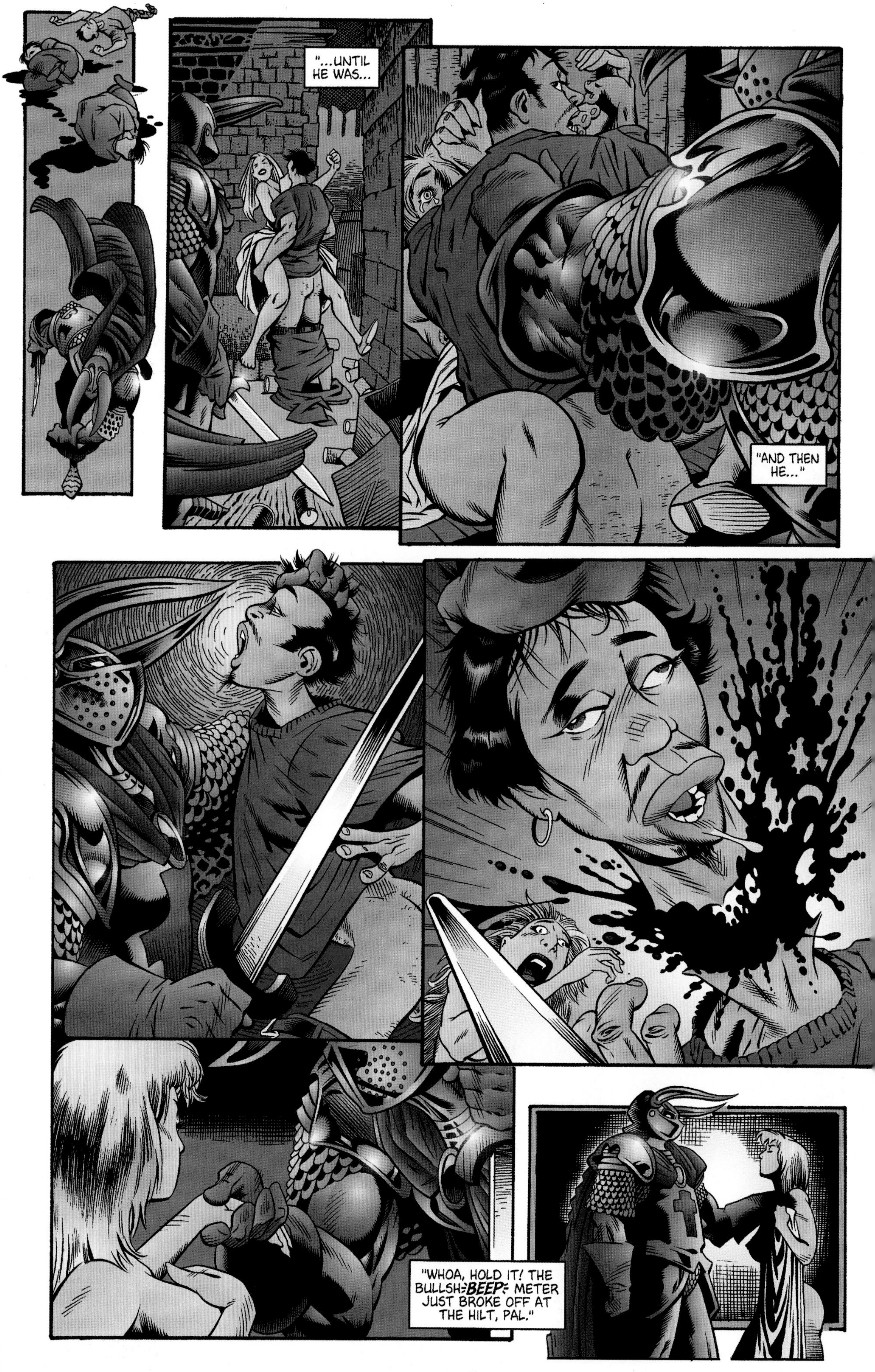
"...UNTIL HE WAS...
"AND THEN HE..."
"WHOA, HOLD IT! THE BULLSH-BEEP- METER JUST BROKE OFF AT THE HILT, PAL."

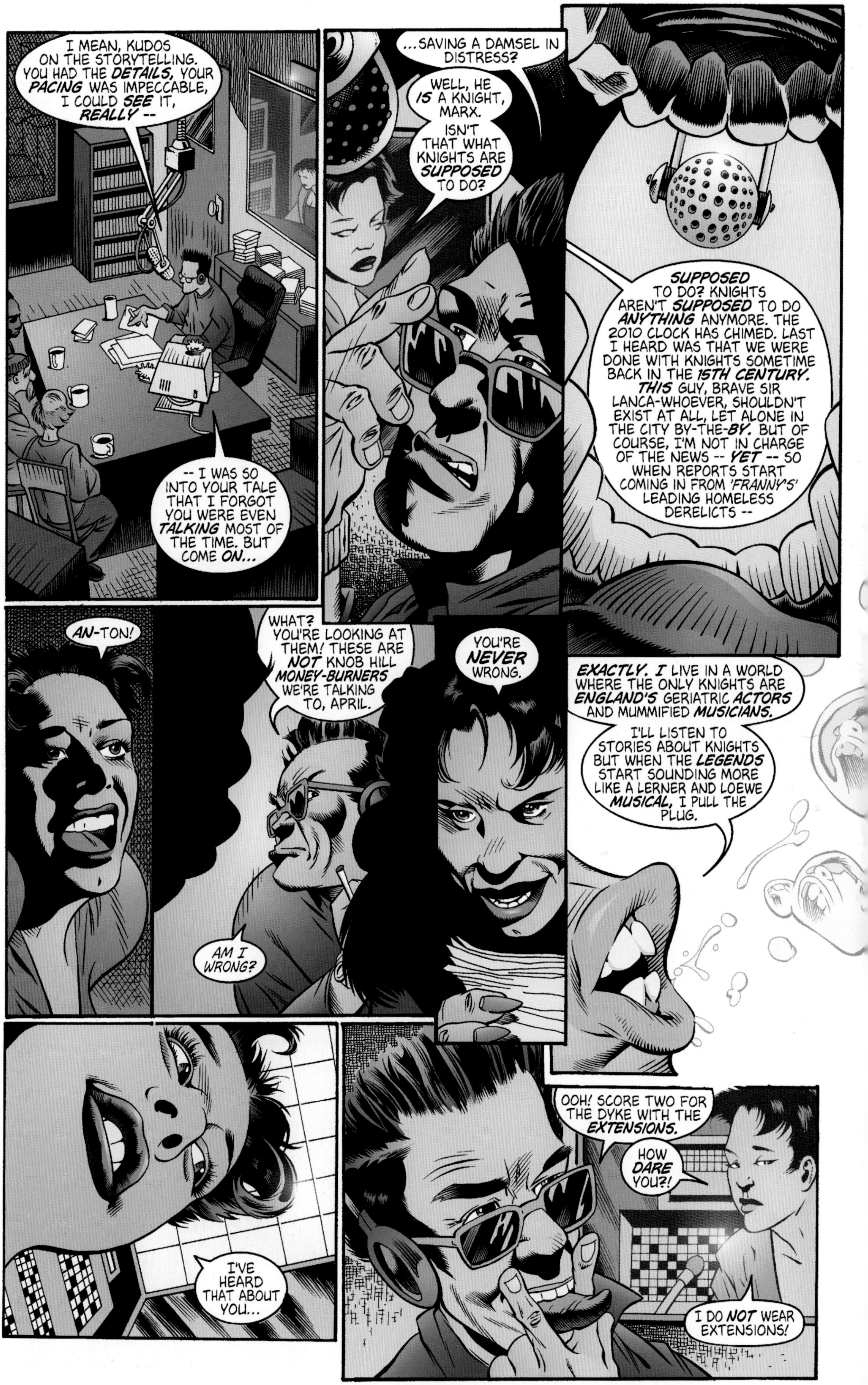
I MEAN, KUDOS ON THE STORYTELLING. YOU HAD THE DETAILS, YOUR PACING WAS IMPECCABLE, I COULD SEE IT, REALLY --
-- I WAS SO INTO YOUR TALE THAT I FORGOT YOU WERE EVEN TALKING MOST OF THE TIME. BUT COME ON...
...SAVING A DAMSEL IN DISTRESS?
WELL, HE IS A KNIGHT, MARX.
ISN'T THAT WHAT KNIGHTS ARE SUPPOSED TO DO?
SUPPOSED TO DO? KNIGHTS AREN'T SUPPOSED TO DO ANYTHING ANYMORE. THE 2010 CLOCK HAS CHIMED. LAST I HEARD WAS THAT WE WERE DONE WITH KNIGHTS SOMETIME BACK IN THE 15TH CENTURY. THIS GUY, BRAVE SIR LANCA-WHOEVER, SHOULDN'T EXIST AT ALL, LET ALONE IN THE CITY BY-THE-BY. BUT OF COURSE, I'M NOT IN CHARGE OF THE NEWS -- YET -- SO WHEN REPORTS START COMING IN FROM 'FRANNY'S' LEADING HOMELESS DERELICTS --
AN-TON!
WHAT? YOU'RE LOOKING AT THEM! THESE ARE NOT KNOB HILL MONEY-BURNERS WE'RE TALKING TO, APRIL.
AM I WRONG?
YOU'RE NEVER WRONG.
EXACTLY. I LIVE IN A WORLD WHERE THE ONLY KNIGHTS ARE ENGLAND'S GERIATRIC ACTORS AND MUMMIFIED MUSICIANS.
I'LL LISTEN TO STORIES ABOUT KNIGHTS BUT WHEN THE LEGENDS START SOUNDING MORE LIKE A LERNER AND LOEWE MUSICAL, I PULL THE PLUG.
I'VE HEARD THAT ABOUT YOU...
OOH! SCORE TWO FOR THE DYKE WITH THE EXTENSIONS.
HOW DARE YOU?!
I DO NOT WEAR EXTENSIONS!

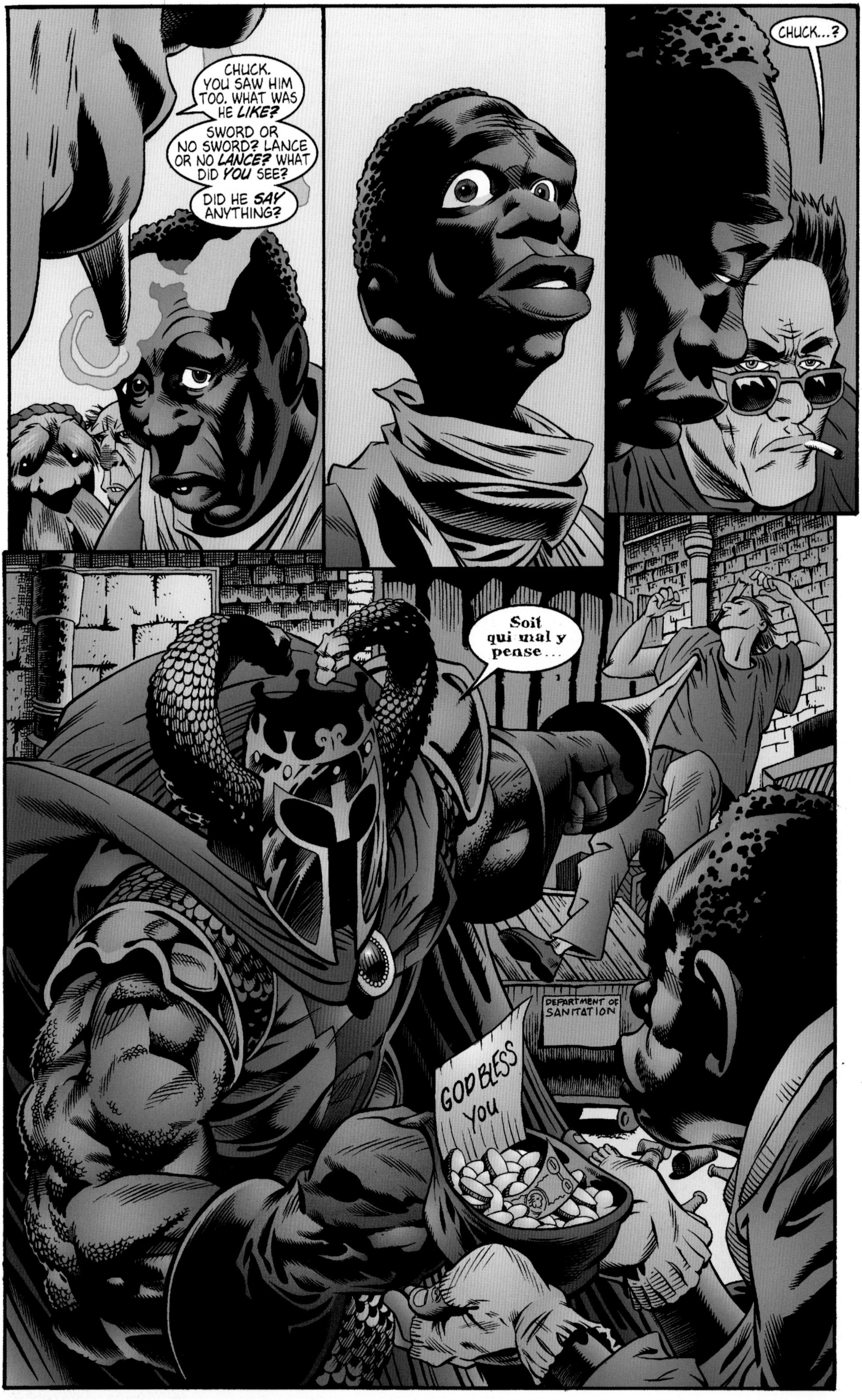
CHUCK. YOU SAW HIM TOO. WHAT WAS HE LIKE?
SWORD OR NO SWORD? LANCE OR NO LANCE? WHAT DID YOU SEE?
DID HE SAY ANYTHING?
CHUCK...?
Soit qui mal y pense...
DEPARTMENT OF SANITATION
GOD BLESS YOU

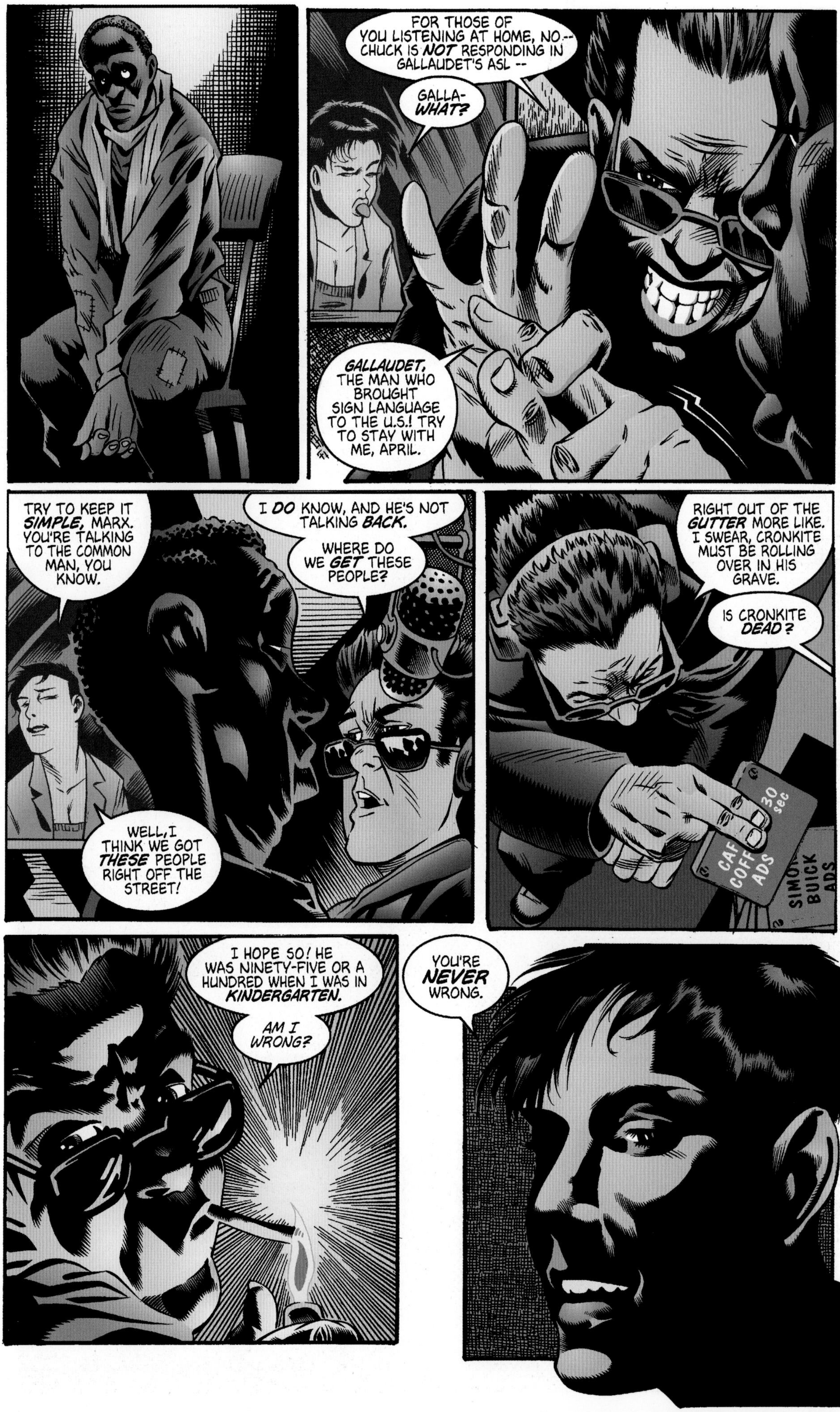

FOR THOSE OF YOU LISTENING AT HOME, NO.-- CHUCK IS *NOT* RESPONDING IN GALLAUDET'S ASL --
GALLA-*WHAT?*
GALLAUDET, THE MAN WHO BROUGHT SIGN LANGUAGE TO THE U.S.! TRY TO STAY WITH ME, APRIL.
TRY TO KEEP IT *SIMPLE,* MARX. YOU'RE TALKING TO THE COMMON MAN, YOU KNOW.
I *DO* KNOW, AND HE'S NOT TALKING *BACK.*
WHERE DO WE *GET* THESE PEOPLE?
WELL, I THINK WE GOT *THESE* PEOPLE RIGHT OFF THE STREET!
RIGHT OUT OF THE *GUTTER* MORE LIKE. I SWEAR, CRONKITE MUST BE ROLLING OVER IN HIS GRAVE.
IS CRONKITE *DEAD?*
30 sec
I HOPE SO! HE WAS NINETY-FIVE OR A HUNDRED WHEN I WAS IN *KINDERGARTEN.*
AM I WRONG?
YOU'RE *NEVER* WRONG.

EXACTLY. ANYWAY, IF YOU'RE ALIVE AND AWAKE, YOU SAW IT ON THE COVER OF *THE GUARDIAN* -- THE CITY'S "*RESPECTABLE*" PAPER -- THIS MORNING.

"*KNIGHT KNOCKS KNOB.*" MEANING?

MEANING THAT FOR THE FIRST TIME IN *WEEKS*, THE LEAD HEADLINE'S BEEN GRABBED AWAY FROM THE TUG OF WAR BETWEEN THE CITY'S FAVORITE ORGANIZED CRIMINALS --

-- TONY QUETONE AND THE NOT SO RELIGIOUS "*POPE.*"

MEANING THAT THE LEGITIMATE PRESS IS SUDDENLY ACCEPTING STORIES OF A "*KNIGHT*" ON THE LOOSE IN OUR FAIR BAY-OPOLIS --

-- STORIES *DISMISSED* AS THE ADDLED BANTER OF DT-SUFFERING *DROPOUTS* LIKE OUR *GUESTS* THIS MORNING --

-- WHO WE'D LIKE TO THANK FOR SHARING, EXCEPT *CHUCK*, WHO WE'D JUST LIKE TO GIVE A SWIFT KICK IN THE *ASS* TO --

AN-TON!

-- BUT *NOTICE* THAT OUR URBANE URBAN *LEGENDS* REMAIN JUST *THAT* -- STORIES WHISPERED BY THE CITY'S HOMELESS, IGNORED, ONLY *UNTIL* THOSE MYTHS START GALLOPING THROUGH HIGH-RENT DISTRICTS, LIKE *KNOB-HILL.*

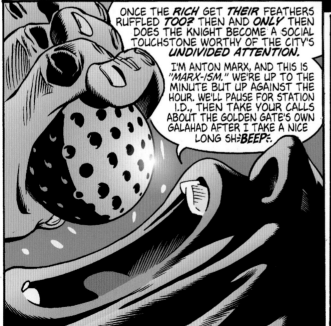

ONCE THE *RICH* GET *THEIR* FEATHERS RUFFLED *TOO?* THEN AND *ONLY* THEN DOES THE KNIGHT BECOME A SOCIAL TOUCHSTONE WORTHY OF THE CITY'S *UNDIVIDED ATTENTION.*

I'M ANTON MARX, AND THIS IS "*MARX-ISM.*" WE'RE UP TO THE MINUTE BUT UP AGAINST THE HOUR. WE'LL PAUSE FOR STATION I.D., THEN TAKE YOUR CALLS ABOUT THE GOLDEN GATE'S OWN GALAHAD AFTER I TAKE A NICE LONG SH≈*BEEP*≈.

SORRY... MUST BE THE COMPANY I'M KEEPING.

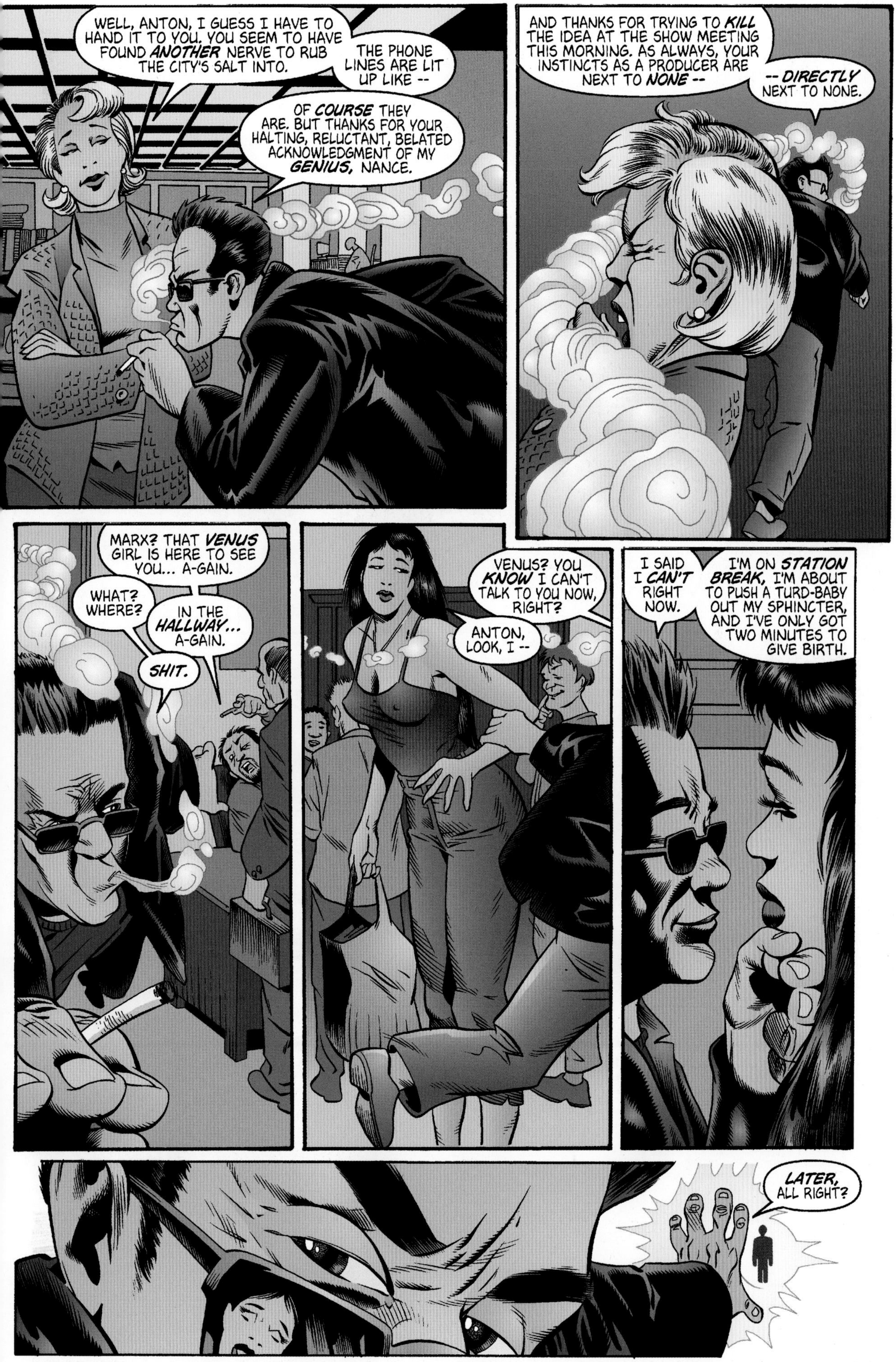
WELL, ANTON, I GUESS I HAVE TO HAND IT TO YOU. YOU SEEM TO HAVE FOUND ANOTHER NERVE TO RUB THE CITY'S SALT INTO.
THE PHONE LINES ARE LIT UP LIKE --
OF COURSE THEY ARE. BUT THANKS FOR YOUR HALTING, RELUCTANT, BELATED ACKNOWLEDGMENT OF MY GENIUS, NANCE.
AND THANKS FOR TRYING TO KILL THE IDEA AT THE SHOW MEETING THIS MORNING. AS ALWAYS, YOUR INSTINCTS AS A PRODUCER ARE NEXT TO NONE --
-- DIRECTLY NEXT TO NONE.
MARX? THAT VENUS GIRL IS HERE TO SEE YOU... A-GAIN.
WHAT? WHERE?
IN THE HALLWAY... A-GAIN.
SHIT.
VENUS? YOU KNOW I CAN'T TALK TO YOU NOW, RIGHT?
ANTON, LOOK, I --
I SAID I CAN'T RIGHT NOW.
I'M ON STATION BREAK, I'M ABOUT TO PUSH A TURD-BABY OUT MY SPHINCTER, AND I'VE ONLY GOT TWO MINUTES TO GIVE BIRTH.
LATER, ALL RIGHT?

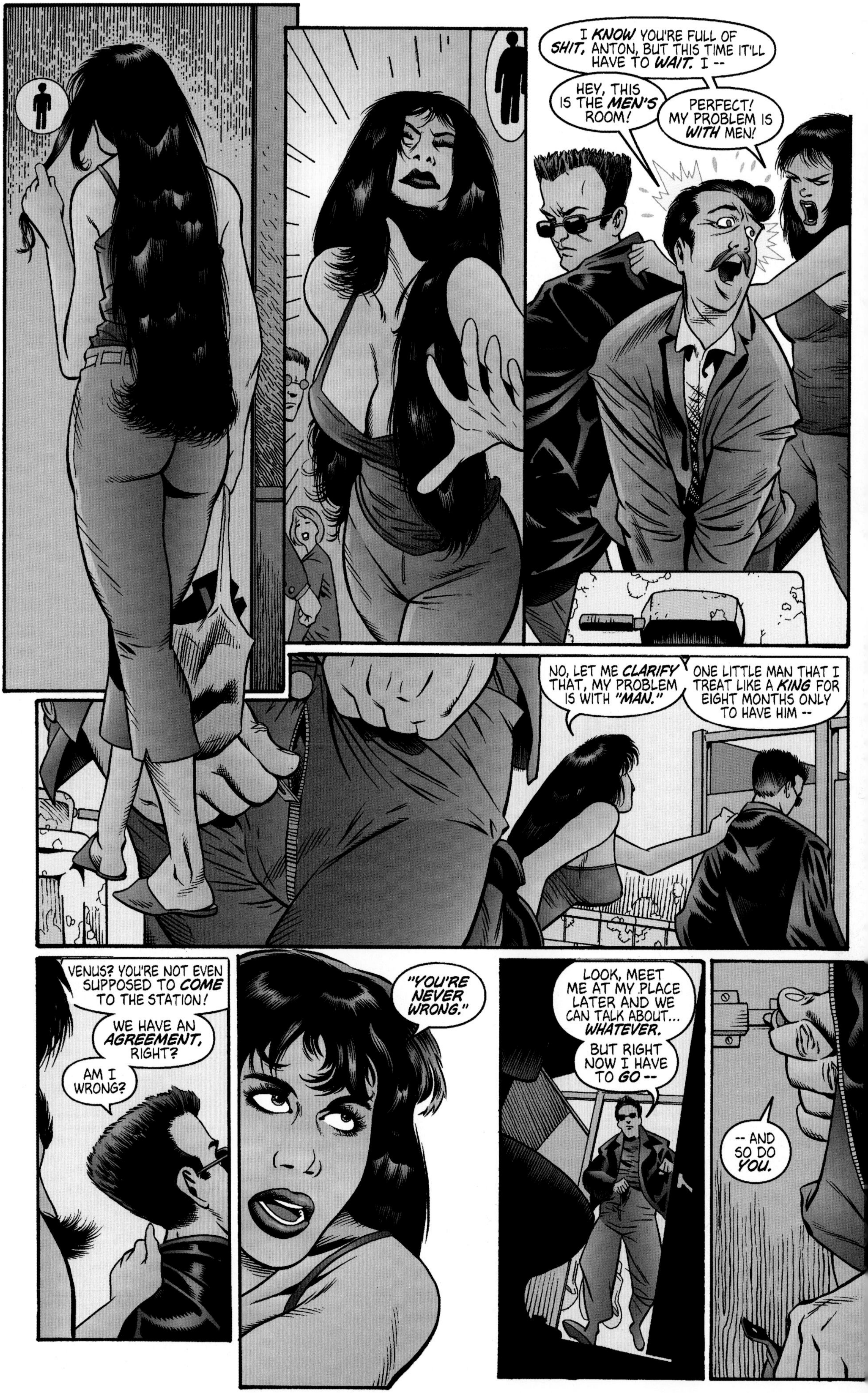
I KNOW YOU'RE FULL OF SHIT, ANTON, BUT THIS TIME IT'LL HAVE TO WAIT. I --
HEY, THIS IS THE MEN'S ROOM!
PERFECT! MY PROBLEM IS WITH MEN!
NO, LET ME CLARIFY THAT, MY PROBLEM IS WITH "MAN."
ONE LITTLE MAN THAT I TREAT LIKE A KING FOR EIGHT MONTHS ONLY TO HAVE HIM --
VENUS? YOU'RE NOT EVEN SUPPOSED TO COME TO THE STATION!
WE HAVE AN AGREEMENT, RIGHT?
AM I WRONG?
"YOU'RE NEVER WRONG."
LOOK, MEET ME AT MY PLACE LATER AND WE CAN TALK ABOUT... WHATEVER.
BUT RIGHT NOW I HAVE TO GO --
-- AND SO DO YOU.

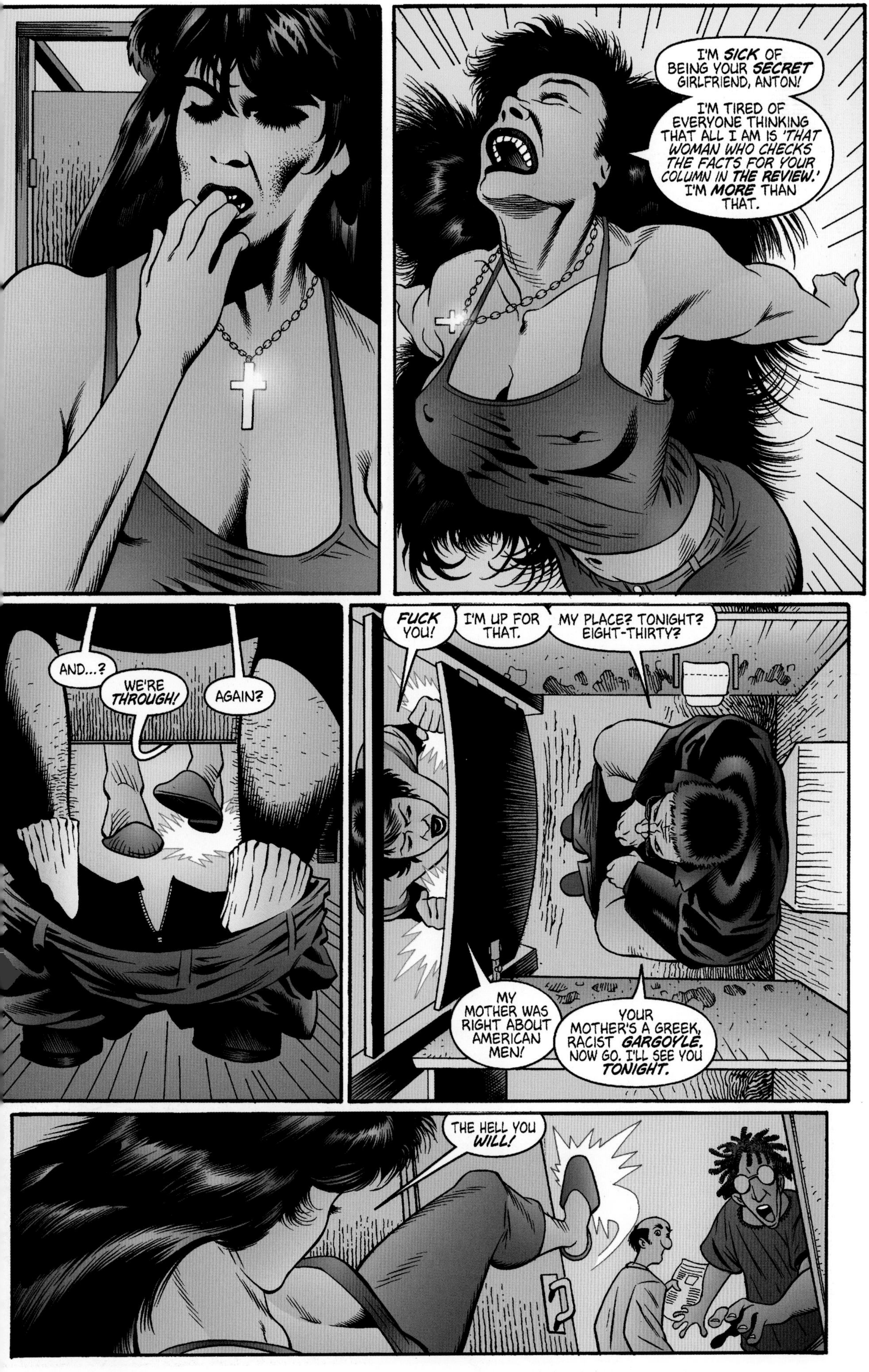
I'M SICK OF BEING YOUR SECRET GIRLFRIEND, ANTON!
I'M TIRED OF EVERYONE THINKING THAT ALL I AM IS 'THAT WOMAN WHO CHECKS THE FACTS FOR YOUR COLUMN IN THE REVIEW.' I'M MORE THAN THAT.
AND...?
WE'RE THROUGH!
AGAIN?
FUCK YOU!
I'M UP FOR THAT.
MY PLACE? TONIGHT? EIGHT-THIRTY?
MY MOTHER WAS RIGHT ABOUT AMERICAN MEN!
YOUR MOTHER'S A GREEK, RACIST GARGOYLE. NOW GO. I'LL SEE YOU TONIGHT.
THE HELL YOU WILL!

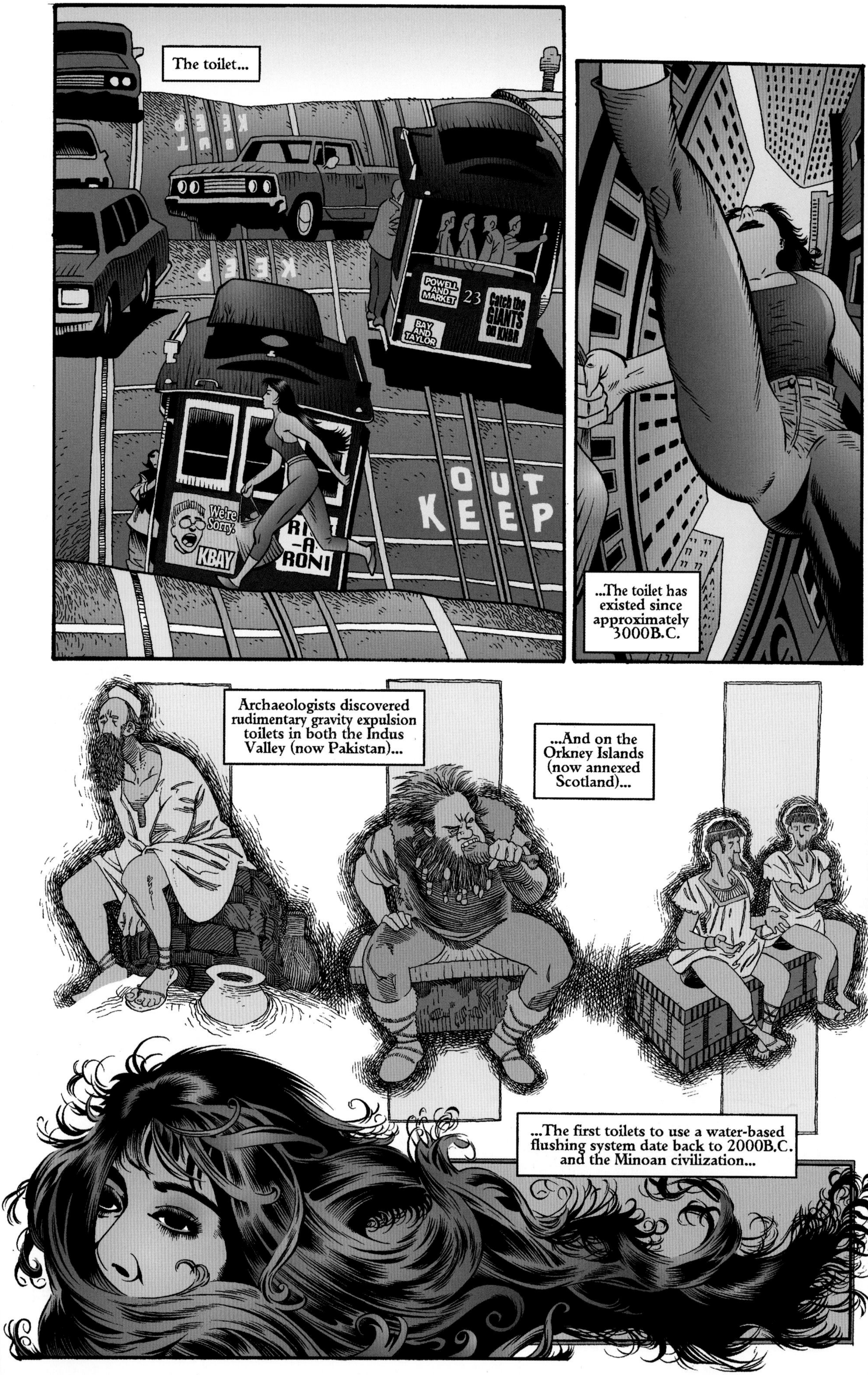
The toilet...
KEEP
OUT
KEEP
POWELL AND MARKET
23
Catch the GIANTS on KNBR
BAY AND TAYLOR
We're Sorry.
KBAY
RICE -A- RONI
OUT
KEEP
...The toilet has existed since approximately 3000B.C.
Archaeologists discovered rudimentary gravity expulsion toilets in both the Indus Valley (now Pakistan)...
...And on the Orkney Islands (now annexed Scotland)...
...The first toilets to use a water-based flushing system date back to 2000B.C. and the Minoan civilization...

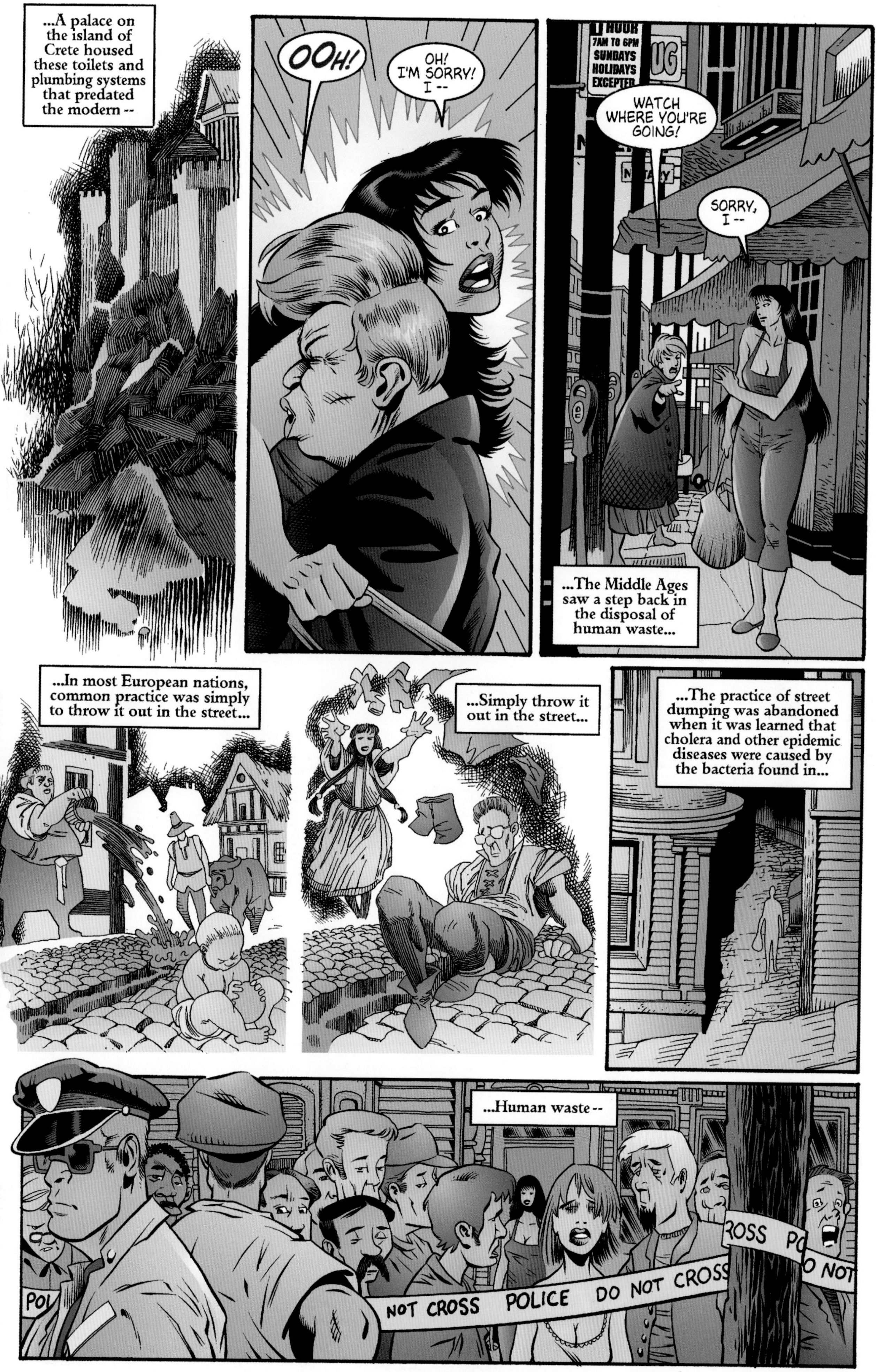
...A palace on the island of Crete housed these toilets and plumbing systems that predated the modern --
OOH!
OH! I'M SORRY! I --
1 HOUR
7AM TO 6PM
SUNDAYS
HOLIDAYS
EXCEPTED
WATCH WHERE YOU'RE GOING!
SORRY, I --
...The Middle Ages saw a step back in the disposal of human waste...
...In most European nations, common practice was simply to throw it out in the street...
...Simply throw it out in the street...
...The practice of street dumping was abandoned when it was learned that cholera and other epidemic diseases were caused by the bacteria found in...
...Human waste --
NOT CROSS POLICE DO NOT CROSS

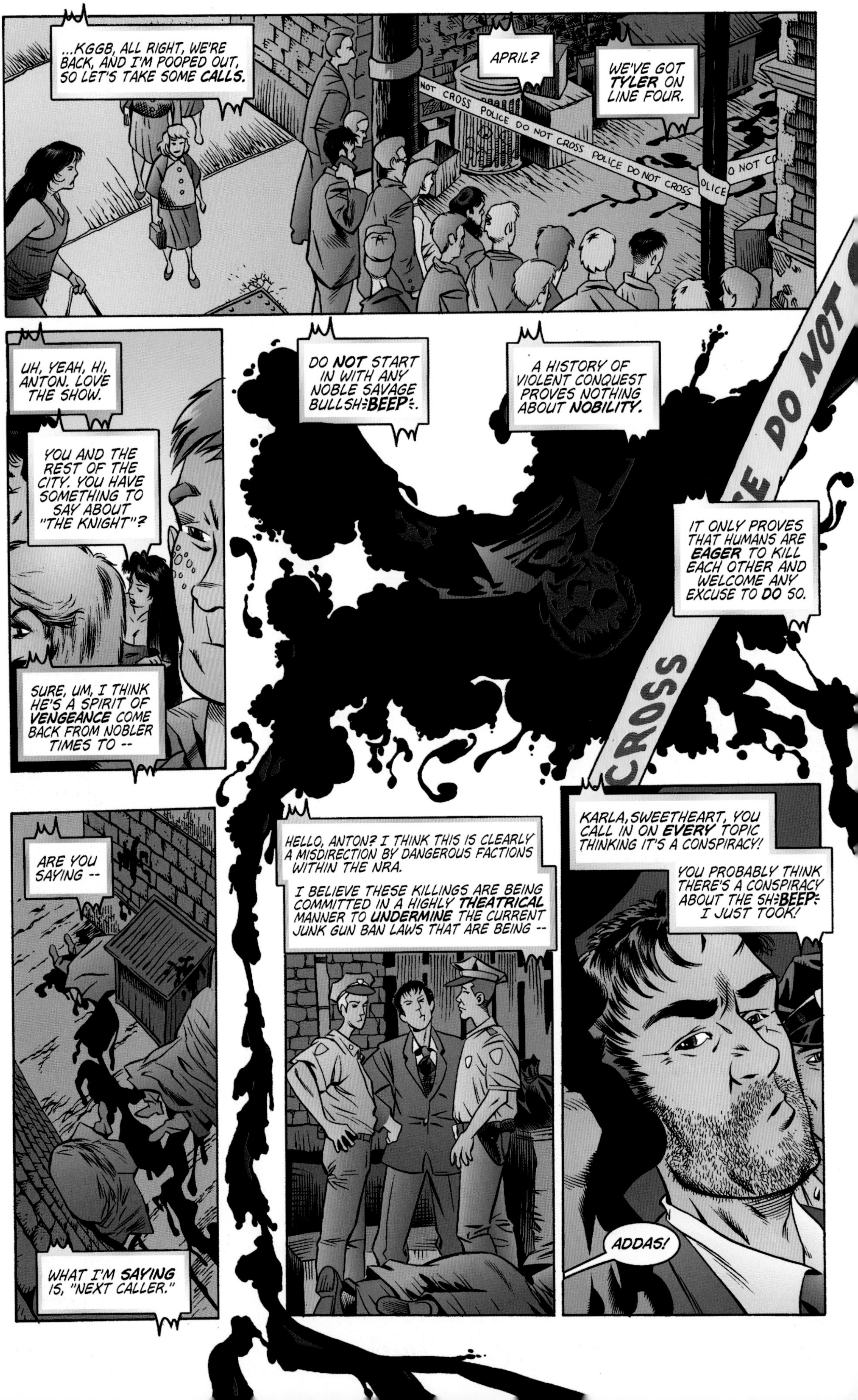
...KGGB, ALL RIGHT, WE'RE BACK, AND I'M POOPED OUT, SO LET'S TAKE SOME CALLS.
APRIL?
WE'VE GOT TYLER ON LINE FOUR.
NOT CROSS POLICE DO NOT CROSS POLICE DO NOT CROSS POLICE DO NOT CROSS
UH, YEAH, HI, ANTON. LOVE THE SHOW.
YOU AND THE REST OF THE CITY. YOU HAVE SOMETHING TO SAY ABOUT "THE KNIGHT"?
SURE, UM, I THINK HE'S A SPIRIT OF VENGEANCE COME BACK FROM NOBLER TIMES TO --
DO NOT START IN WITH ANY NOBLE SAVAGE BULLSH-BEEP-.
A HISTORY OF VIOLENT CONQUEST PROVES NOTHING ABOUT NOBILITY.
IT ONLY PROVES THAT HUMANS ARE EAGER TO KILL EACH OTHER AND WELCOME ANY EXCUSE TO DO SO.
DO NOT
CROSS
ARE YOU SAYING --
WHAT I'M SAYING IS, "NEXT CALLER."
HELLO, ANTON? I THINK THIS IS CLEARLY A MISDIRECTION BY DANGEROUS FACTIONS WITHIN THE NRA.
I BELIEVE THESE KILLINGS ARE BEING COMMITTED IN A HIGHLY THEATRICAL MANNER TO UNDERMINE THE CURRENT JUNK GUN BAN LAWS THAT ARE BEING --
KARLA, SWEETHEART, YOU CALL IN ON EVERY TOPIC THINKING IT'S A CONSPIRACY!
YOU PROBABLY THINK THERE'S A CONSPIRACY ABOUT THE SH-BEEP- I JUST TOOK!
ADDAS!

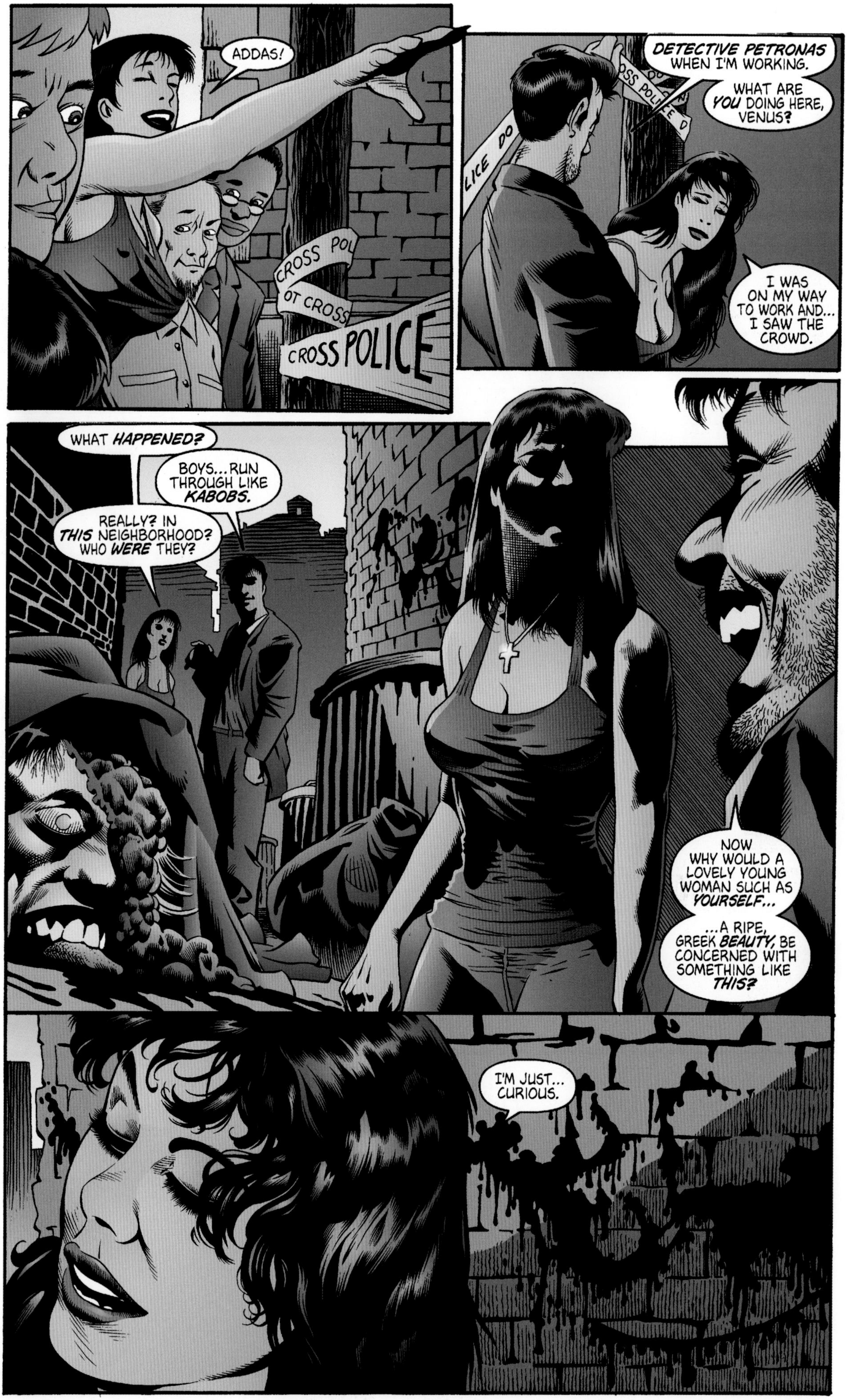

ADDAS!
CROSS POL
OT CROSS
CROSS POLICE
DETECTIVE PETRONAS WHEN I'M WORKING.
WHAT ARE YOU DOING HERE, VENUS?
I WAS ON MY WAY TO WORK AND... I SAW THE CROWD.
WHAT HAPPENED?
BOYS... RUN THROUGH LIKE KABOBS.
REALLY? IN THIS NEIGHBORHOOD? WHO WERE THEY?
NOW WHY WOULD A LOVELY YOUNG WOMAN SUCH AS YOURSELF...
...A RIPE, GREEK BEAUTY, BE CONCERNED WITH SOMETHING LIKE THIS?
I'M JUST... CURIOUS.

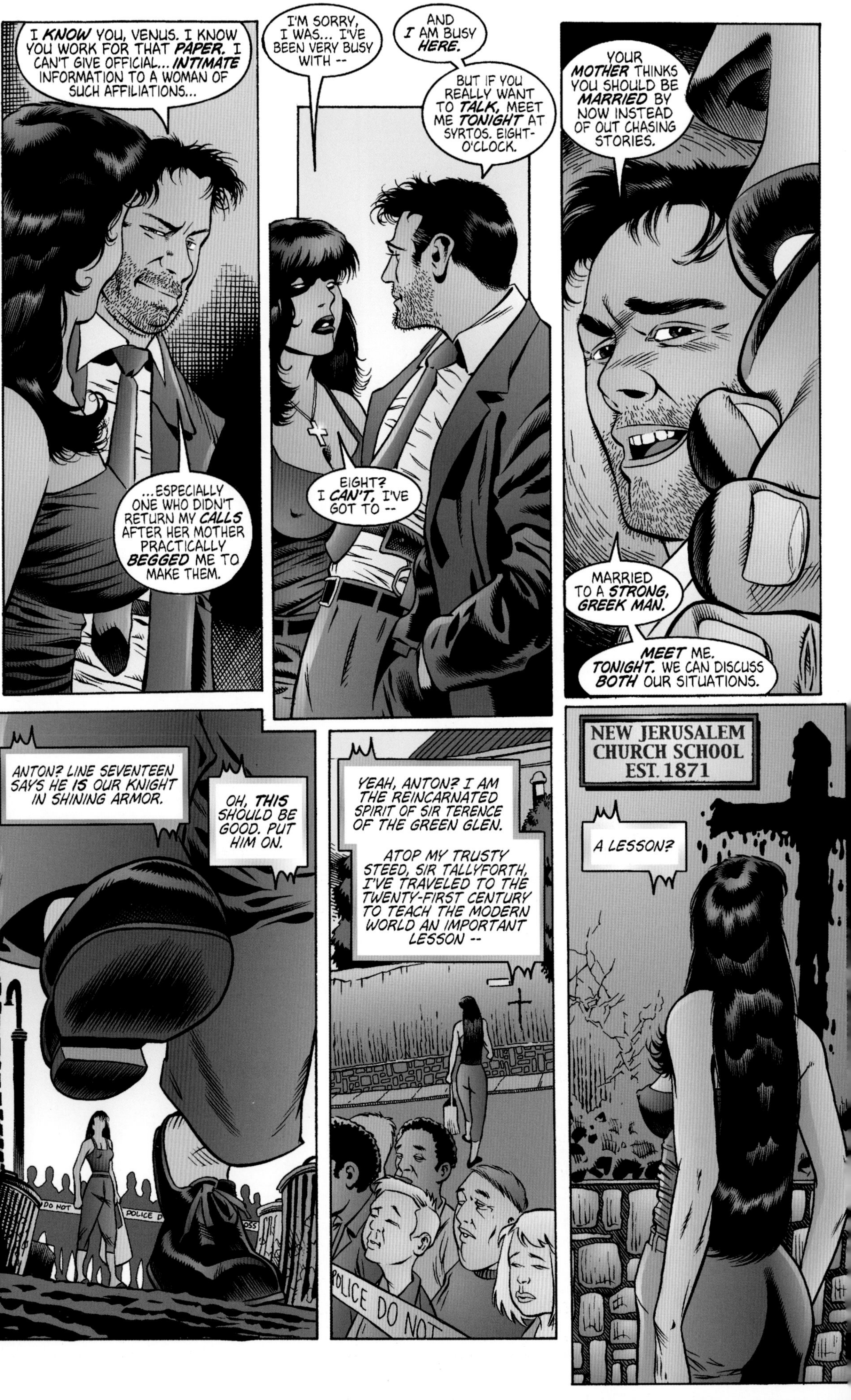
I KNOW YOU, VENUS. I KNOW YOU WORK FOR THAT PAPER. I CAN'T GIVE OFFICIAL... INTIMATE INFORMATION TO A WOMAN OF SUCH AFFILIATIONS...
...ESPECIALLY ONE WHO DIDN'T RETURN MY CALLS AFTER HER MOTHER PRACTICALLY BEGGED ME TO MAKE THEM.
I'M SORRY, I WAS... I'VE BEEN VERY BUSY WITH --
AND I AM BUSY HERE.
BUT IF YOU REALLY WANT TO TALK, MEET ME TONIGHT AT SYRTOS. EIGHT-O'CLOCK.
EIGHT? I CAN'T, I'VE GOT TO --
YOUR MOTHER THINKS YOU SHOULD BE MARRIED BY NOW INSTEAD OF OUT CHASING STORIES.
MARRIED TO A STRONG, GREEK MAN.
MEET ME. TONIGHT. WE CAN DISCUSS BOTH OUR SITUATIONS.
ANTON? LINE SEVENTEEN SAYS HE IS OUR KNIGHT IN SHINING ARMOR.
OH, THIS SHOULD BE GOOD. PUT HIM ON.
YEAH, ANTON? I AM THE REINCARNATED SPIRIT OF SIR TERENCE OF THE GREEN GLEN.
ATOP MY TRUSTY STEED, SIR TALLYFORTH, I'VE TRAVELED TO THE TWENTY-FIRST CENTURY TO TEACH THE MODERN WORLD AN IMPORTANT LESSON --
POLICE DO NOT
NEW JERUSALEM CHURCH SCHOOL EST. 1871
A LESSON?

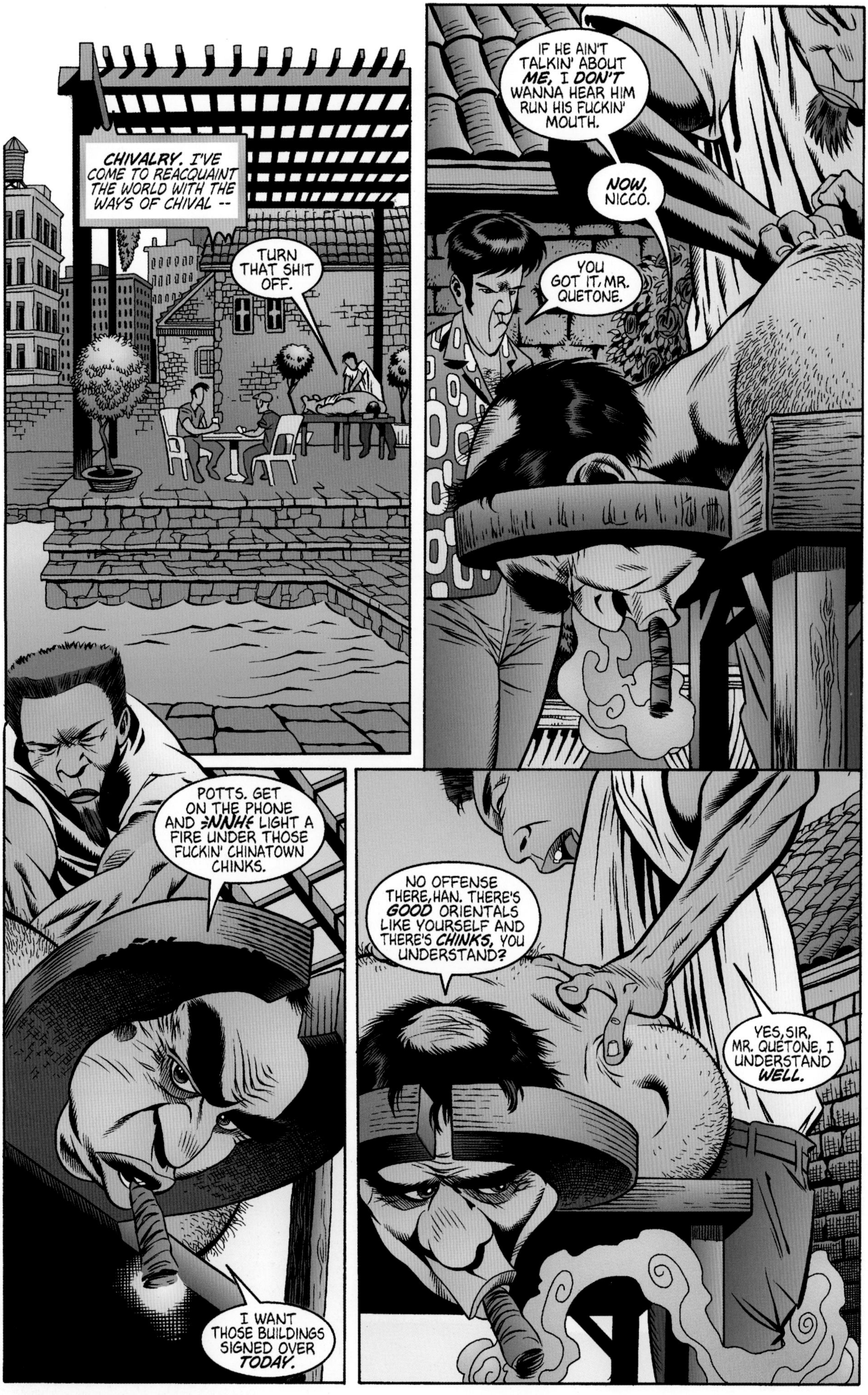
CHIVALRY. I'VE COME TO REACQUAINT THE WORLD WITH THE WAYS OF CHIVAL --
TURN THAT SHIT OFF.
IF HE AIN'T TALKIN' ABOUT ME, I DON'T WANNA HEAR HIM RUN HIS FUCKIN' MOUTH.
NOW, NICCO.
YOU GOT IT, MR. QUETONE.
POTTS. GET ON THE PHONE AND NNH LIGHT A FIRE UNDER THOSE FUCKIN' CHINATOWN CHINKS.
I WANT THOSE BUILDINGS SIGNED OVER TODAY.
NO OFFENSE THERE, HAN. THERE'S GOOD ORIENTALS LIKE YOURSELF AND THERE'S CHINKS, YOU UNDERSTAND?
YES, SIR, MR. QUETONE, I UNDERSTAND WELL.

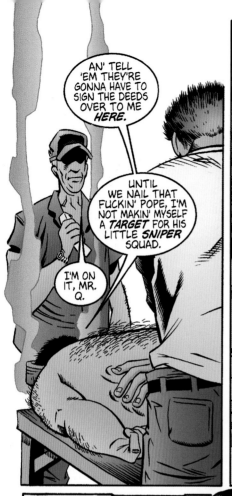

AN' TELL 'EM THEY'RE GONNA HAVE TO SIGN THE DEEDS OVER TO ME *HERE*.

UNTIL WE NAIL THAT FUCKIN' POPE, I'M NOT MAKIN' MYSELF A *TARGET* FOR HIS LITTLE *SNIPER* SQUAD.

I'M ON IT, MR. Q.

BREEEEEE

AHH!

HA! LOOK AT THAT STUPID SHIT!

AFRAID OF HIS OWN FUCKIN' SHADOW!

YOU KISS MY ASS YOU FUCKING SPIC.

HELLO...? *HUH?* YOU BETTER NOT BE *BULLSHITTIN'*... YEAH... UH, OKAY... HANG ON...

IT'S THE POPE.

PUT HIM ON SPEAKER.

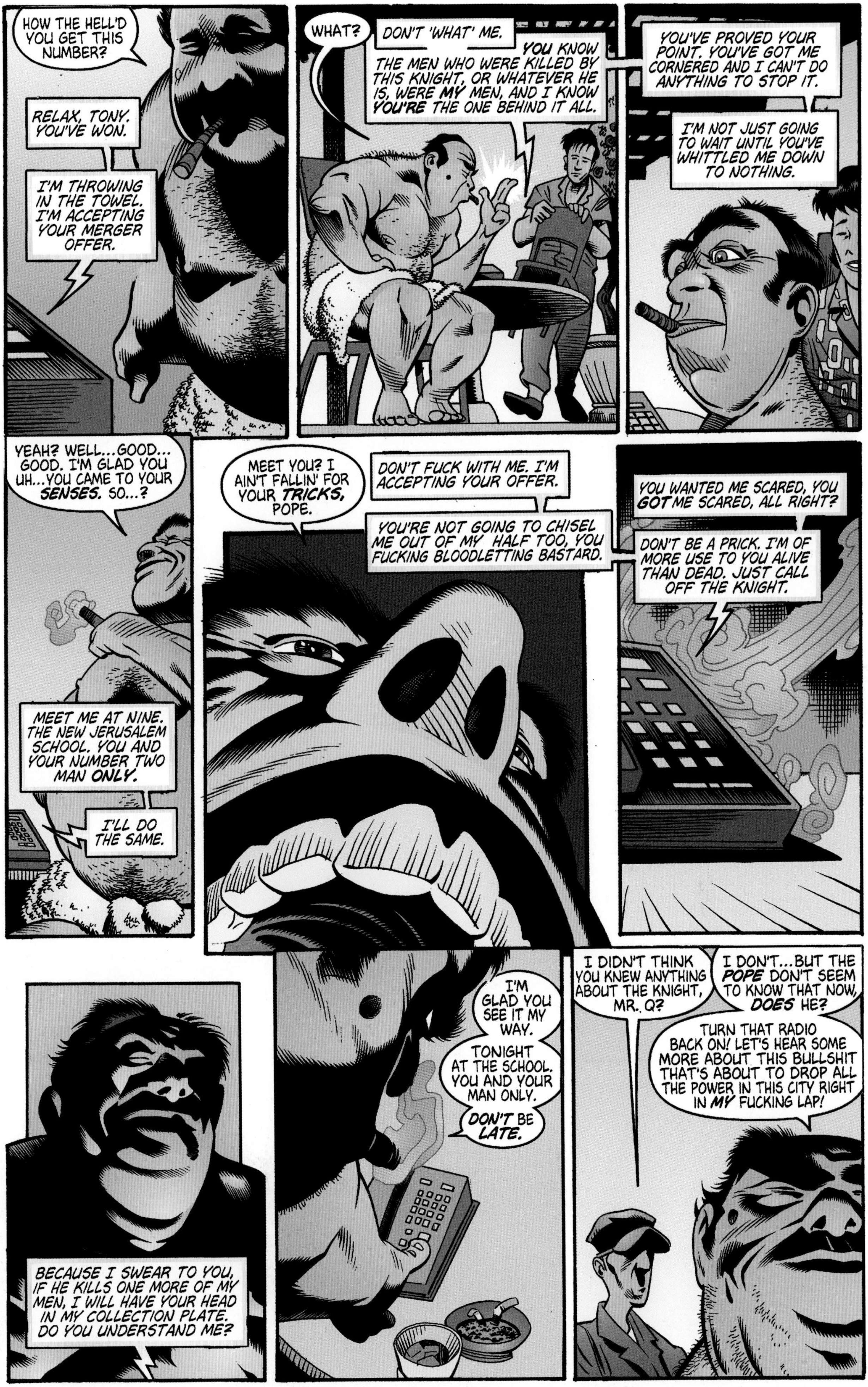

HOW THE HELL'D YOU GET THIS NUMBER?
RELAX, TONY. YOU'VE WON.
I'M THROWING IN THE TOWEL. I'M ACCEPTING YOUR MERGER OFFER.
WHAT?
DON'T 'WHAT' ME.
YOU KNOW THE MEN WHO WERE KILLED BY THIS KNIGHT, OR WHATEVER HE IS, WERE MY MEN, AND I KNOW YOU'RE THE ONE BEHIND IT ALL.
YOU'VE PROVED YOUR POINT. YOU'VE GOT ME CORNERED AND I CAN'T DO ANYTHING TO STOP IT.
I'M NOT JUST GOING TO WAIT UNTIL YOU'VE WHITTLED ME DOWN TO NOTHING.
YEAH? WELL...GOOD... GOOD. I'M GLAD YOU UH...YOU CAME TO YOUR SENSES. SO...?
MEET ME AT NINE. THE NEW JERUSALEM SCHOOL. YOU AND YOUR NUMBER TWO MAN ONLY.
I'LL DO THE SAME.
MEET YOU? I AIN'T FALLIN' FOR YOUR TRICKS, POPE.
DON'T FUCK WITH ME. I'M ACCEPTING YOUR OFFER.
YOU'RE NOT GOING TO CHISEL ME OUT OF MY HALF TOO, YOU FUCKING BLOODLETTING BASTARD.
YOU WANTED ME SCARED, YOU GOT ME SCARED, ALL RIGHT?
DON'T BE A PRICK. I'M OF MORE USE TO YOU ALIVE THAN DEAD. JUST CALL OFF THE KNIGHT.
BECAUSE I SWEAR TO YOU, IF HE KILLS ONE MORE OF MY MEN, I WILL HAVE YOUR HEAD IN MY COLLECTION PLATE. DO YOU UNDERSTAND ME?
I'M GLAD YOU SEE IT MY WAY.
TONIGHT AT THE SCHOOL. YOU AND YOUR MAN ONLY.
DON'T BE LATE.
I DIDN'T THINK YOU KNEW ANYTHING ABOUT THE KNIGHT, MR. Q?
I DON'T...BUT THE POPE DON'T SEEM TO KNOW THAT NOW, DOES HE?
TURN THAT RADIO BACK ON! LET'S HEAR SOME MORE ABOUT THIS BULLSHIT THAT'S ABOUT TO DROP ALL THE POWER IN THIS CITY RIGHT IN MY FUCKING LAP!

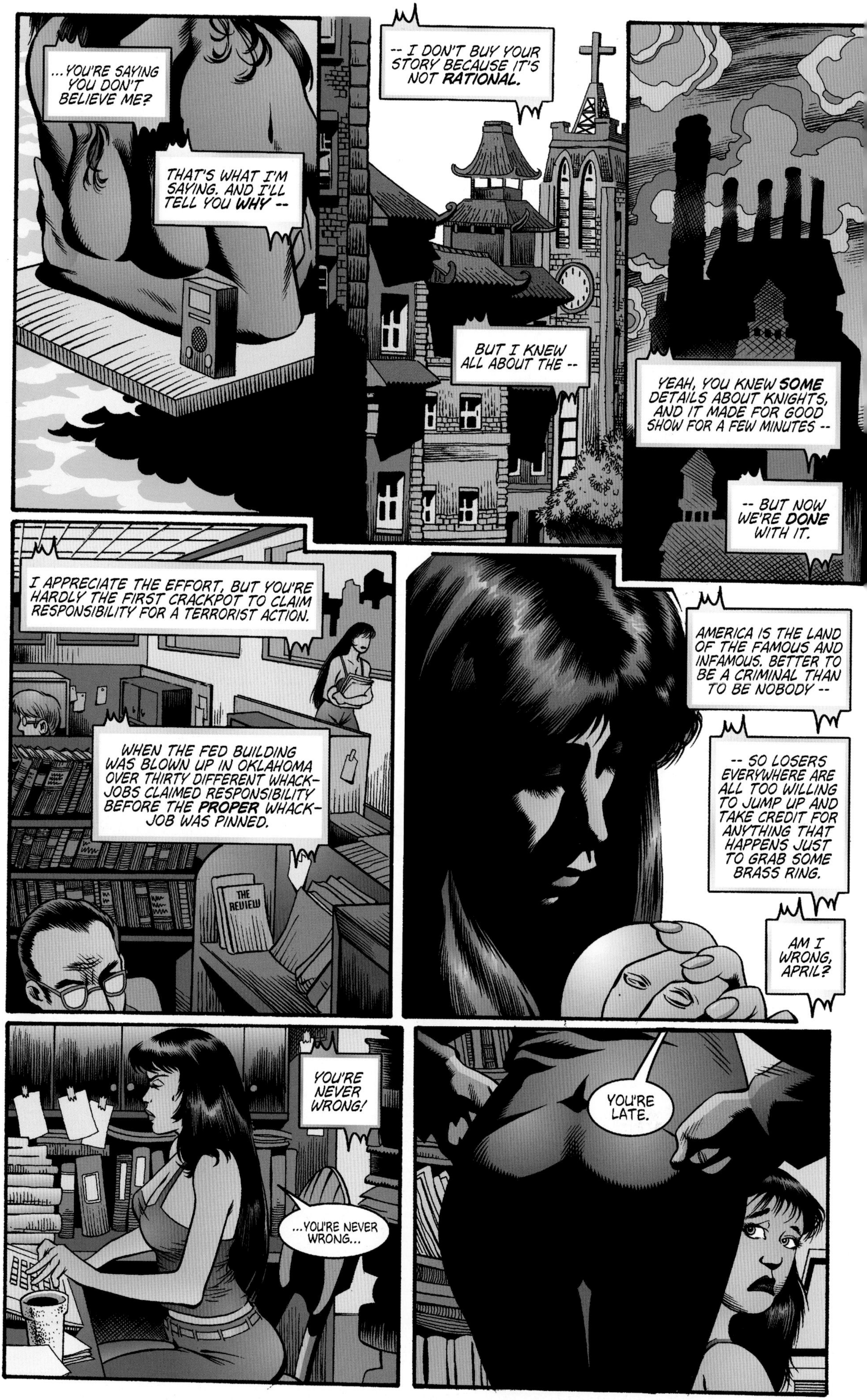

...YOU'RE SAYING YOU DON'T BELIEVE ME?
THAT'S WHAT I'M SAYING. AND I'LL TELL YOU WHY --
-- I DON'T BUY YOUR STORY BECAUSE IT'S NOT RATIONAL.
BUT I KNEW ALL ABOUT THE --
YEAH, YOU KNEW SOME DETAILS ABOUT KNIGHTS, AND IT MADE FOR GOOD SHOW FOR A FEW MINUTES --
-- BUT NOW WE'RE DONE WITH IT.
I APPRECIATE THE EFFORT, BUT YOU'RE HARDLY THE FIRST CRACKPOT TO CLAIM RESPONSIBILITY FOR A TERRORIST ACTION.
WHEN THE FED BUILDING WAS BLOWN UP IN OKLAHOMA OVER THIRTY DIFFERENT WHACK-JOBS CLAIMED RESPONSIBILITY BEFORE THE PROPER WHACK-JOB WAS PINNED.
THE REVIEW
AMERICA IS THE LAND OF THE FAMOUS AND INFAMOUS. BETTER TO BE A CRIMINAL THAN TO BE NOBODY --
-- SO LOSERS EVERYWHERE ARE ALL TOO WILLING TO JUMP UP AND TAKE CREDIT FOR ANYTHING THAT HAPPENS JUST TO GRAB SOME BRASS RING.
AM I WRONG, APRIL?
YOU'RE NEVER WRONG!
...YOU'RE NEVER WRONG...
YOU'RE LATE.

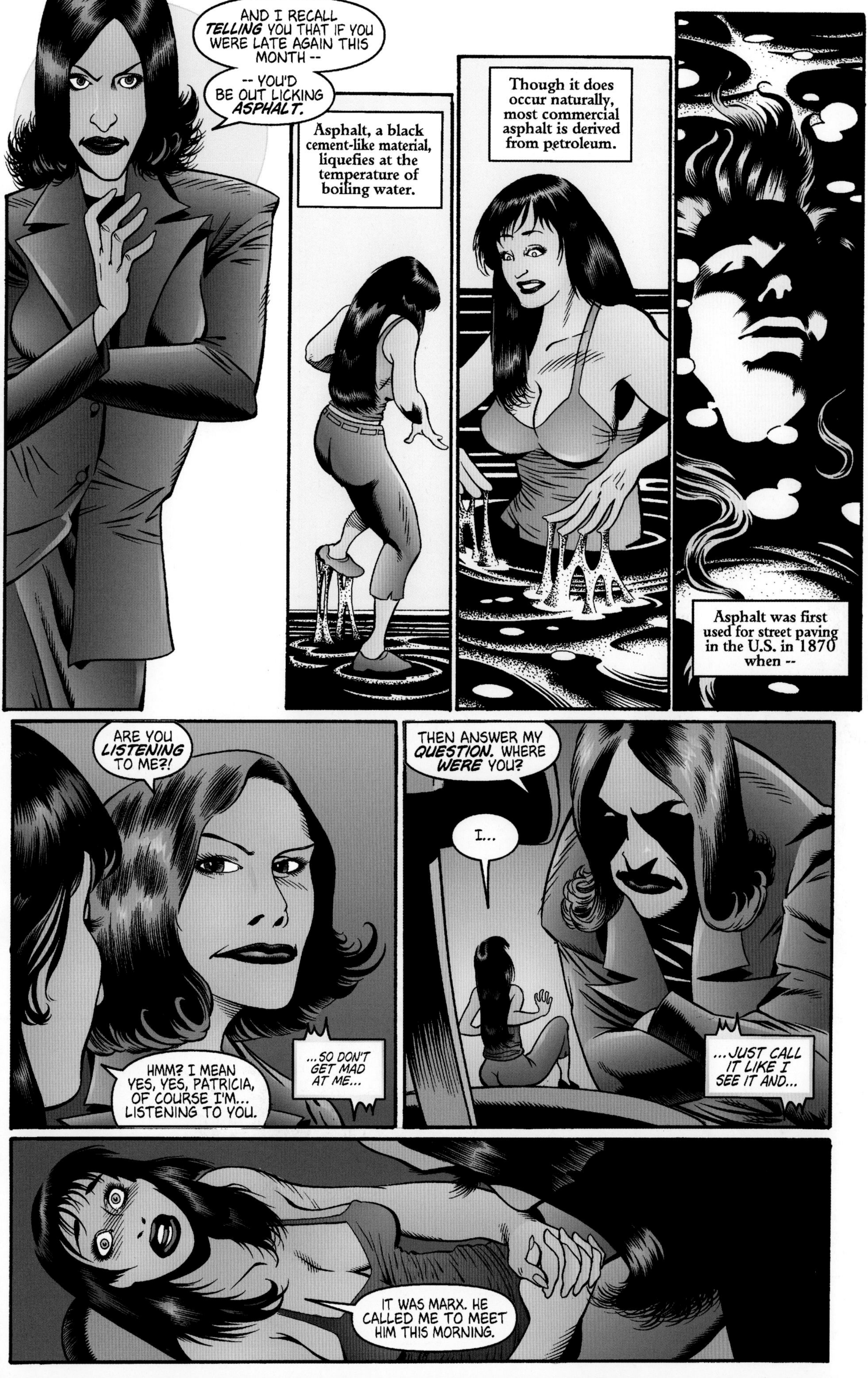
AND I RECALL TELLING YOU THAT IF YOU WERE LATE AGAIN THIS MONTH --
-- YOU'D BE OUT LICKING ASPHALT.
Asphalt, a black cement-like material, liquefies at the temperature of boiling water.
Though it does occur naturally, most commercial asphalt is derived from petroleum.
Asphalt was first used for street paving in the U.S. in 1870 when --
ARE YOU LISTENING TO ME?!
HMM? I MEAN YES, YES, PATRICIA, OF COURSE I'M... LISTENING TO YOU.
...SO DON'T GET MAD AT ME...
THEN ANSWER MY QUESTION. WHERE WERE YOU?
I...
...JUST CALL IT LIKE I SEE IT AND...
IT WAS MARX. HE CALLED ME TO MEET HIM THIS MORNING.

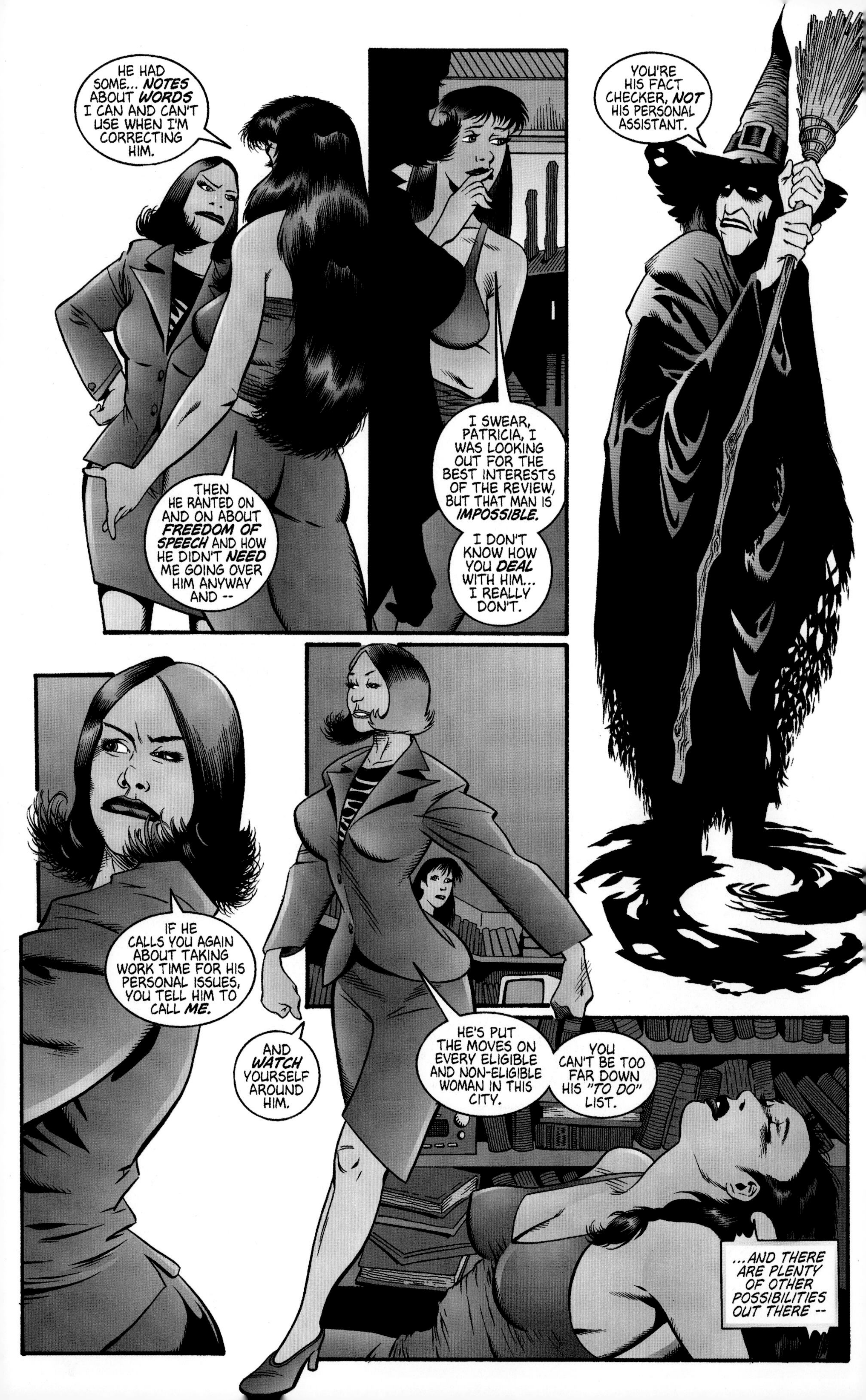
HE HAD SOME... NOTES ABOUT WORDS I CAN AND CAN'T USE WHEN I'M CORRECTING HIM.
THEN HE RANTED ON AND ON ABOUT FREEDOM OF SPEECH AND HOW HE DIDN'T NEED ME GOING OVER HIM ANYWAY AND --
I SWEAR, PATRICIA, I WAS LOOKING OUT FOR THE BEST INTERESTS OF THE REVIEW, BUT THAT MAN IS IMPOSSIBLE.
I DON'T KNOW HOW YOU DEAL WITH HIM... I REALLY DON'T.
YOU'RE HIS FACT CHECKER, NOT HIS PERSONAL ASSISTANT.
IF HE CALLS YOU AGAIN ABOUT TAKING WORK TIME FOR HIS PERSONAL ISSUES, YOU TELL HIM TO CALL ME.
AND WATCH YOURSELF AROUND HIM.
HE'S PUT THE MOVES ON EVERY ELIGIBLE AND NON-ELIGIBLE WOMAN IN THIS CITY.
YOU CAN'T BE TOO FAR DOWN HIS "TO DO" LIST.
...AND THERE ARE PLENTY OF OTHER POSSIBILITIES OUT THERE --

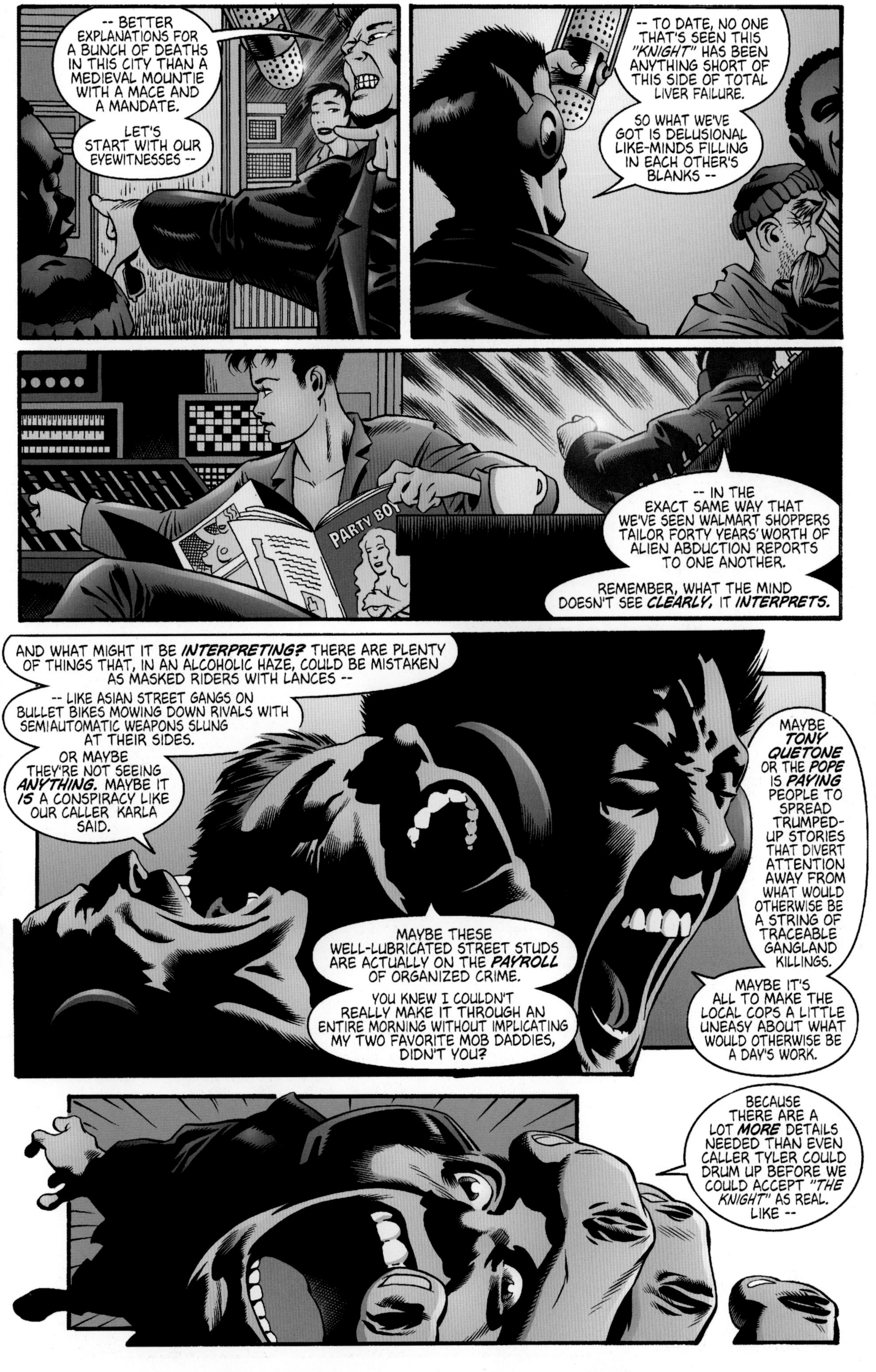
-- BETTER EXPLANATIONS FOR A BUNCH OF DEATHS IN THIS CITY THAN A MEDIEVAL MOUNTIE WITH A MACE AND A MANDATE.
LET'S START WITH OUR EYEWITNESSES --
-- TO DATE, NO ONE THAT'S SEEN THIS "KNIGHT" HAS BEEN ANYTHING SHORT OF THIS SIDE OF TOTAL LIVER FAILURE.
SO WHAT WE'VE GOT IS DELUSIONAL LIKE-MINDS FILLING IN EACH OTHER'S BLANKS --
PARTY BOY
-- IN THE EXACT SAME WAY THAT WE'VE SEEN WALMART SHOPPERS TAILOR FORTY YEARS' WORTH OF ALIEN ABDUCTION REPORTS TO ONE ANOTHER.
REMEMBER, WHAT THE MIND DOESN'T SEE CLEARLY, IT INTERPRETS.
AND WHAT MIGHT IT BE INTERPRETING? THERE ARE PLENTY OF THINGS THAT, IN AN ALCOHOLIC HAZE, COULD BE MISTAKEN AS MASKED RIDERS WITH LANCES --
-- LIKE ASIAN STREET GANGS ON BULLET BIKES MOWING DOWN RIVALS WITH SEMIAUTOMATIC WEAPONS SLUNG AT THEIR SIDES.
OR MAYBE THEY'RE NOT SEEING ANYTHING. MAYBE IT IS A CONSPIRACY LIKE OUR CALLER KARLA SAID.
MAYBE THESE WELL-LUBRICATED STREET STUDS ARE ACTUALLY ON THE PAYROLL OF ORGANIZED CRIME.
YOU KNEW I COULDN'T REALLY MAKE IT THROUGH AN ENTIRE MORNING WITHOUT IMPLICATING MY TWO FAVORITE MOB DADDIES, DIDN'T YOU?
MAYBE TONY QUETONE OR THE POPE IS PAYING PEOPLE TO SPREAD TRUMPED-UP STORIES THAT DIVERT ATTENTION AWAY FROM WHAT WOULD OTHERWISE BE A STRING OF TRACEABLE GANGLAND KILLINGS.
MAYBE IT'S ALL TO MAKE THE LOCAL COPS A LITTLE UNEASY ABOUT WHAT WOULD OTHERWISE BE A DAY'S WORK.
BECAUSE THERE ARE A LOT MORE DETAILS NEEDED THAN EVEN CALLER TYLER COULD DRUM UP BEFORE WE COULD ACCEPT "THE KNIGHT" AS REAL. LIKE --

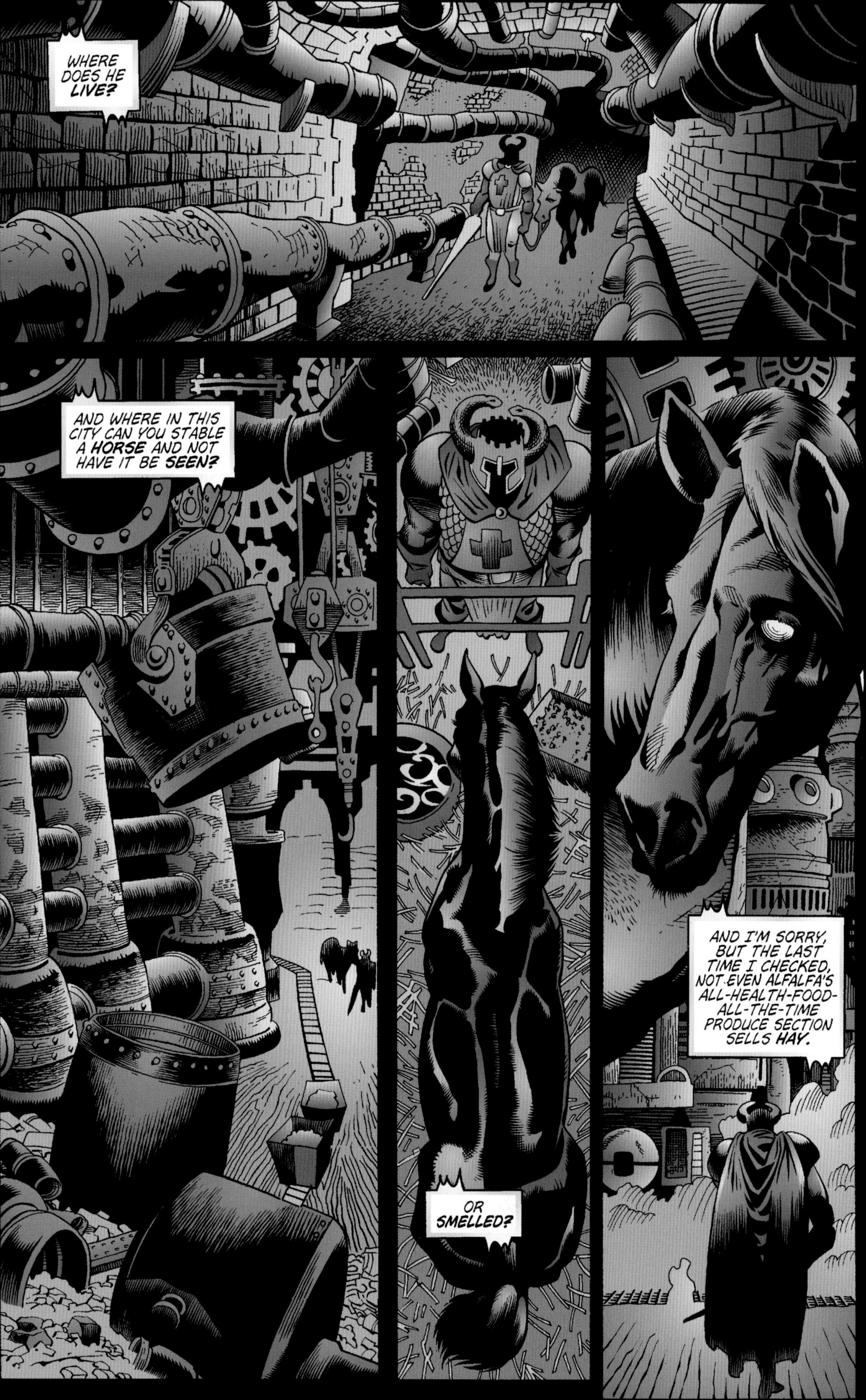
WHERE DOES HE LIVE?
AND WHERE IN THIS CITY CAN YOU STABLE A HORSE AND NOT HAVE IT BE SEEN?
OR SMELLED?
AND I'M SORRY, BUT THE LAST TIME I CHECKED, NOT EVEN ALFALFA'S ALL-HEALTH-FOOD-ALL-THE-TIME PRODUCE SECTION SELLS HAY.

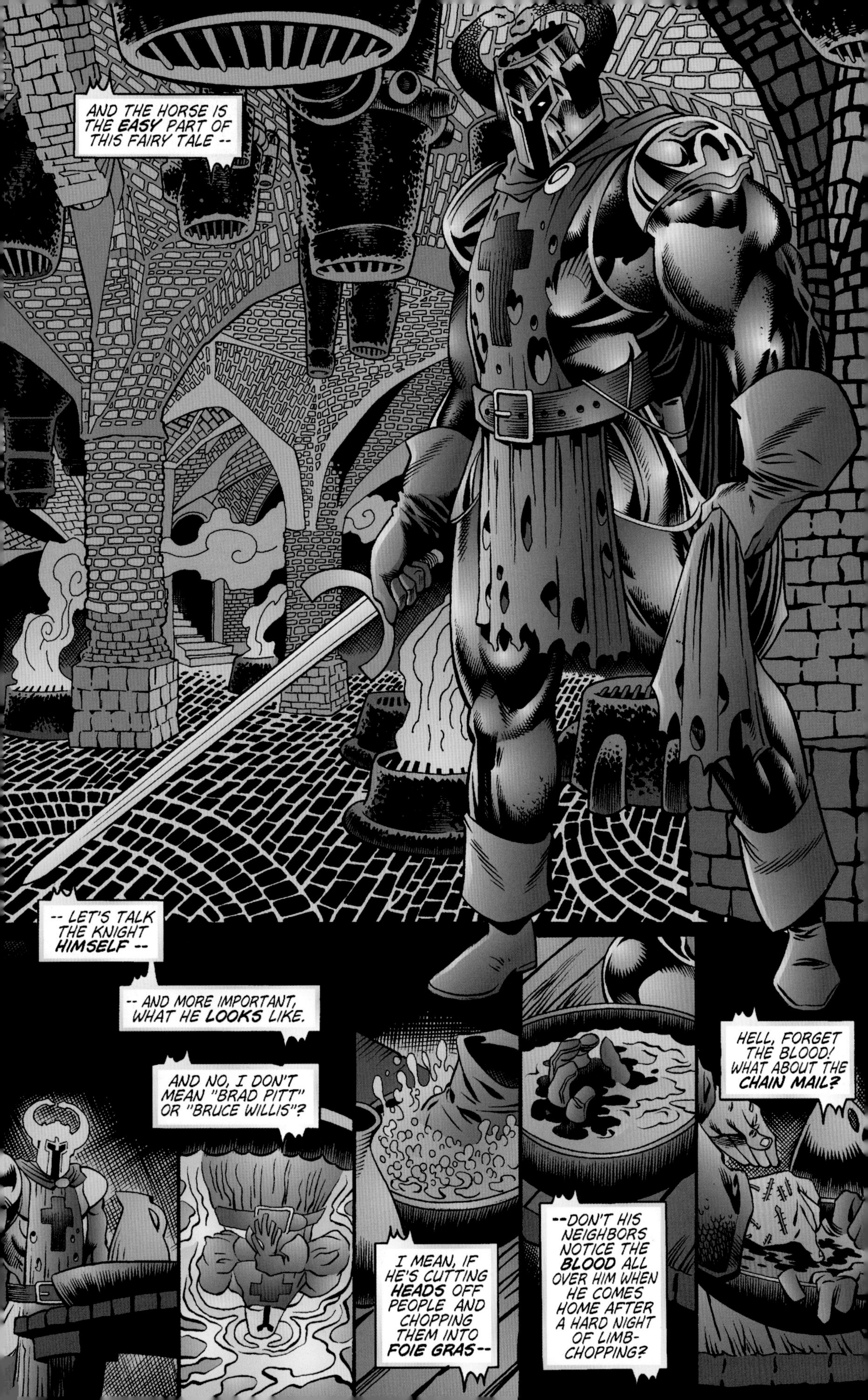
AND THE HORSE IS THE EASY PART OF THIS FAIRY TALE --
-- LET'S TALK THE KNIGHT HIMSELF --
-- AND MORE IMPORTANT, WHAT HE LOOKS LIKE.
AND NO, I DON'T MEAN "BRAD PITT" OR "BRUCE WILLIS"?
I MEAN, IF HE'S CUTTING HEADS OFF PEOPLE AND CHOPPING THEM INTO FOIE GRAS--
--DON'T HIS NEIGHBORS NOTICE THE BLOOD ALL OVER HIM WHEN HE COMES HOME AFTER A HARD NIGHT OF LIMB-CHOPPING?
HELL, FORGET THE BLOOD! WHAT ABOUT THE CHAIN MAIL?

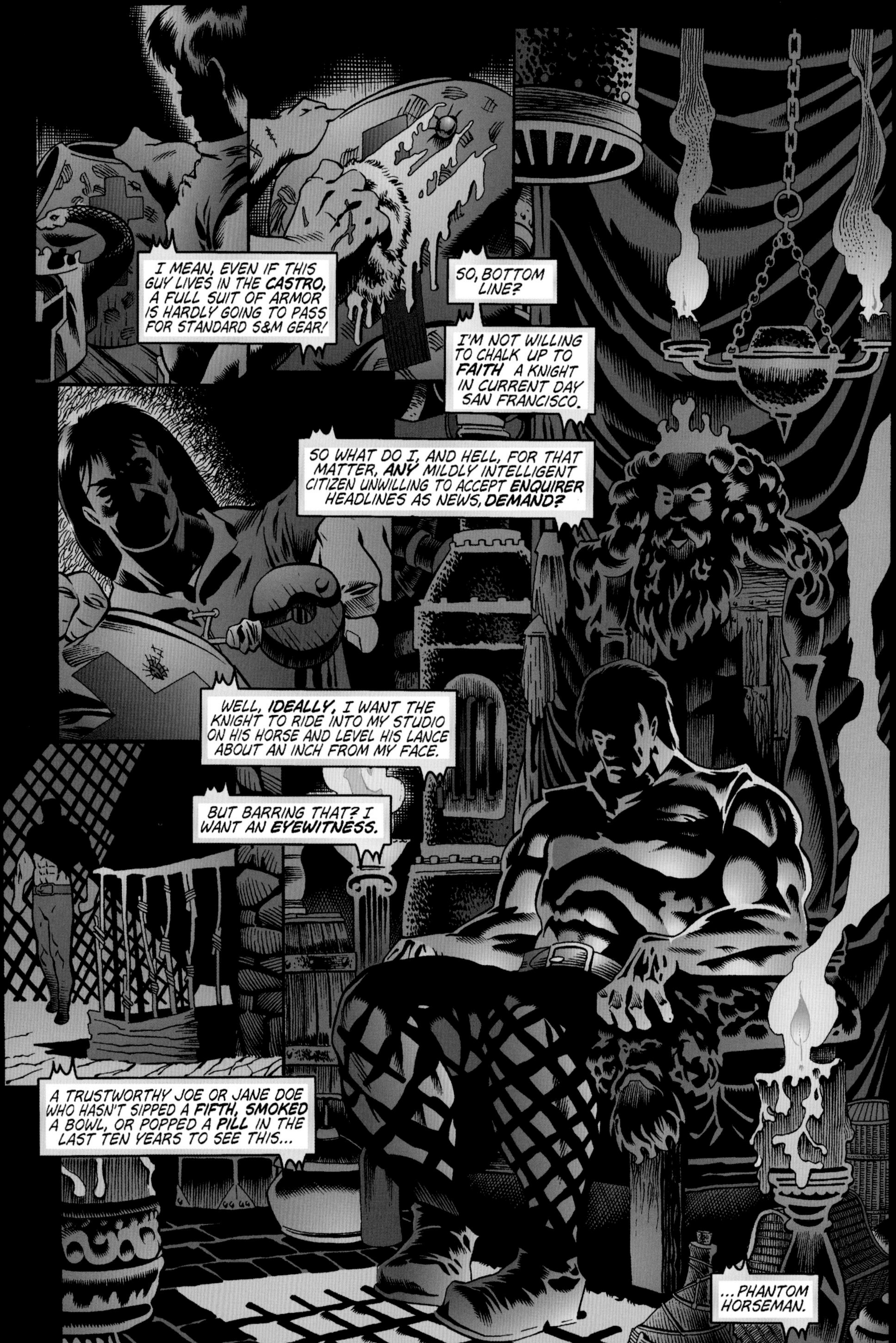
I MEAN, EVEN IF THIS GUY LIVES IN THE CASTRO, A FULL SUIT OF ARMOR IS HARDLY GOING TO PASS FOR STANDARD S&M GEAR!
SO, BOTTOM LINE?
I'M NOT WILLING TO CHALK UP TO FAITH A KNIGHT IN CURRENT DAY SAN FRANCISCO.
SO WHAT DO I, AND HELL, FOR THAT MATTER, ANY MILDLY INTELLIGENT CITIZEN UNWILLING TO ACCEPT ENQUIRER HEADLINES AS NEWS, DEMAND?
WELL, IDEALLY, I WANT THE KNIGHT TO RIDE INTO MY STUDIO ON HIS HORSE AND LEVEL HIS LANCE ABOUT AN INCH FROM MY FACE.
BUT BARRING THAT? I WANT AN EYEWITNESS.
A TRUSTWORTHY JOE OR JANE DOE WHO HASN'T SIPPED A FIFTH, SMOKED A BOWL, OR POPPED A PILL IN THE LAST TEN YEARS TO SEE THIS...
...PHANTOM HORSEMAN.

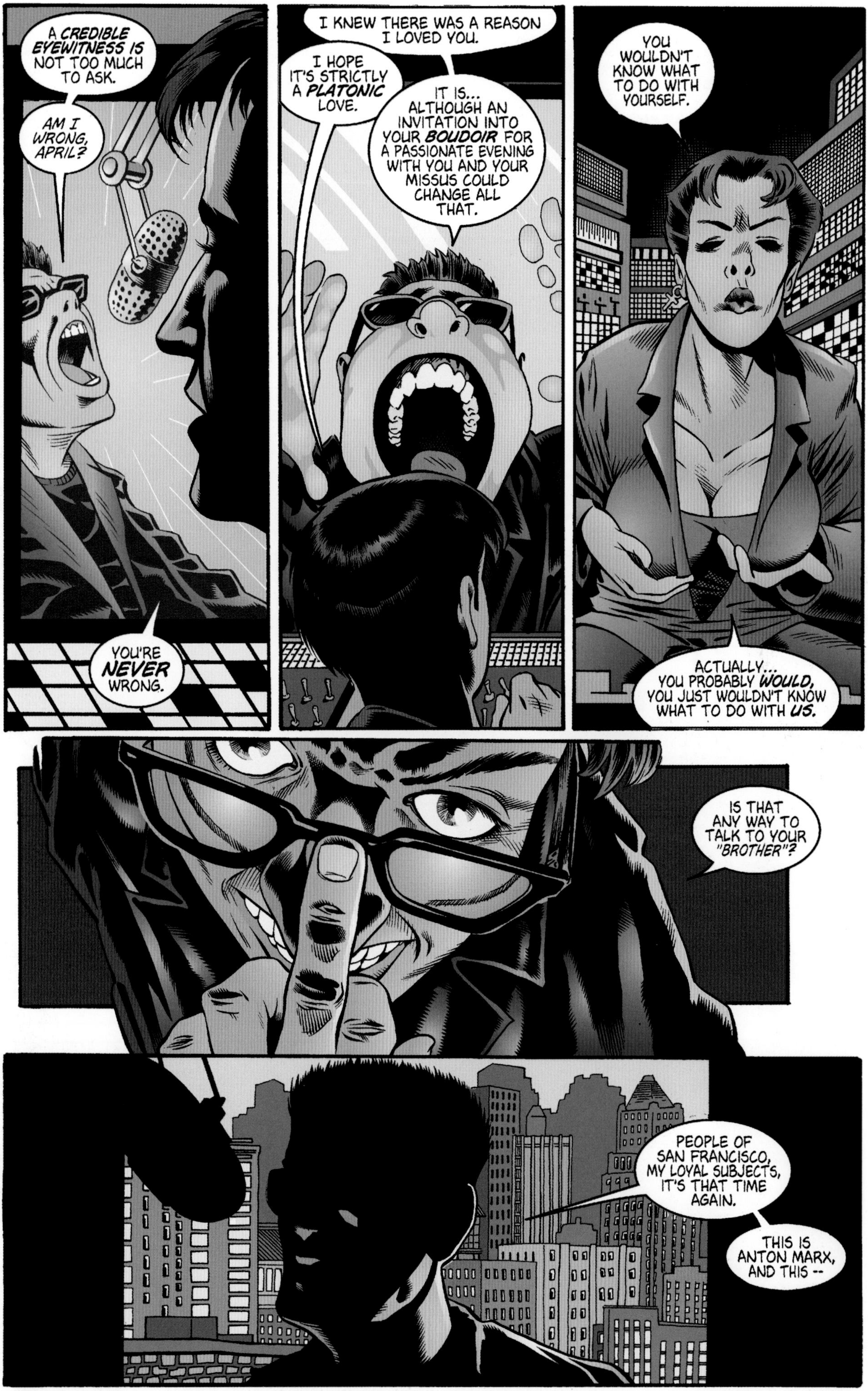
A CREDIBLE EYEWITNESS IS NOT TOO MUCH TO ASK.
AM I WRONG, APRIL?
YOU'RE NEVER WRONG.
I KNEW THERE WAS A REASON I LOVED YOU.
I HOPE IT'S STRICTLY A PLATONIC LOVE.
IT IS... ALTHOUGH AN INVITATION INTO YOUR BOUDOIR FOR A PASSIONATE EVENING WITH YOU AND YOUR MISSUS COULD CHANGE ALL THAT.
YOU WOULDN'T KNOW WHAT TO DO WITH YOURSELF.
ACTUALLY... YOU PROBABLY WOULD, YOU JUST WOULDN'T KNOW WHAT TO DO WITH US.
IS THAT ANY WAY TO TALK TO YOUR "BROTHER"?
PEOPLE OF SAN FRANCISCO, MY LOYAL SUBJECTS, IT'S THAT TIME AGAIN.
THIS IS ANTON MARX, AND THIS --

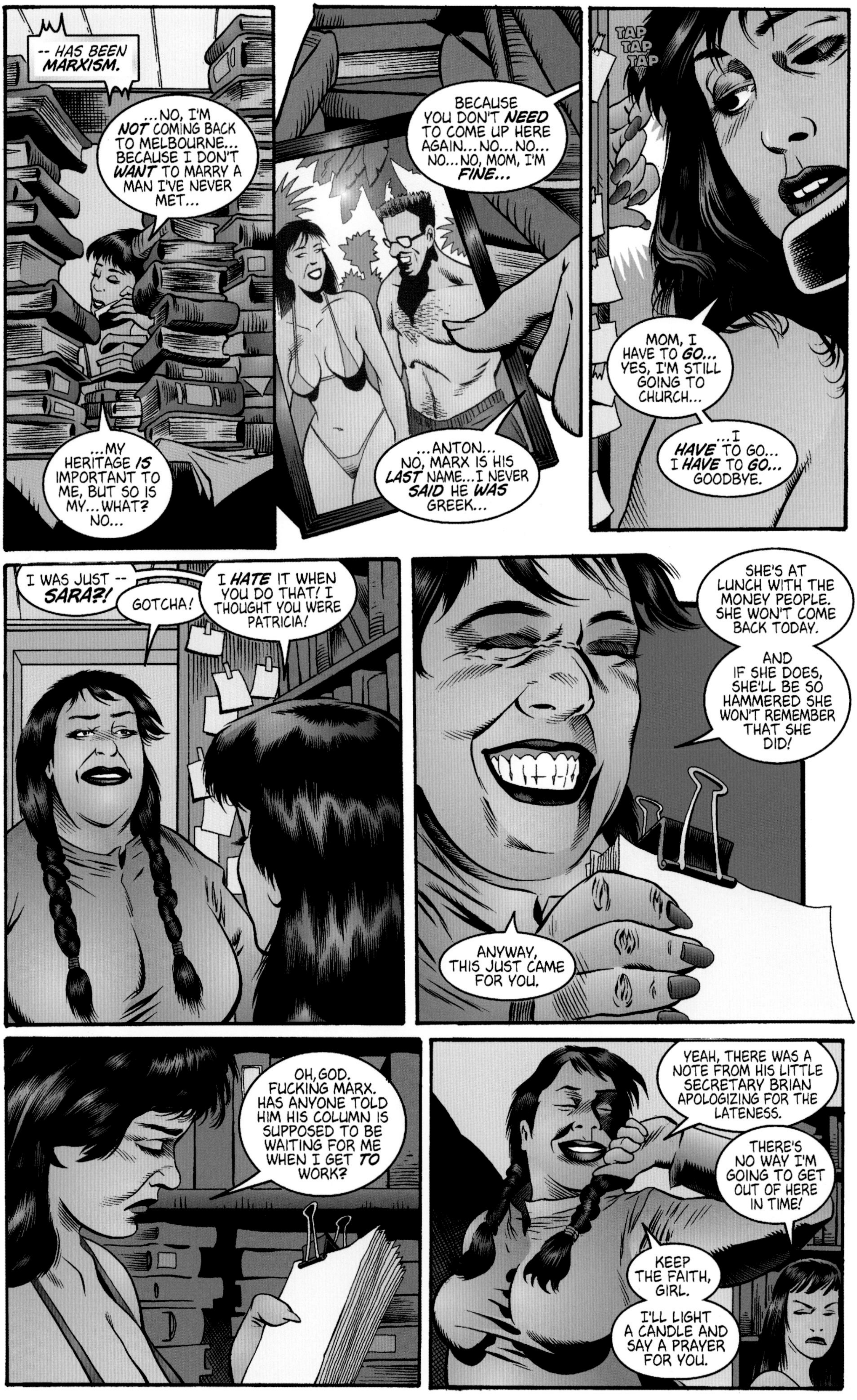
-- HAS BEEN MARXISM.
...NO, I'M NOT COMING BACK TO MELBOURNE... BECAUSE I DON'T WANT TO MARRY A MAN I'VE NEVER MET...
...MY HERITAGE IS IMPORTANT TO ME, BUT SO IS MY...WHAT? NO...
BECAUSE YOU DON'T NEED TO COME UP HERE AGAIN...NO...NO... NO...NO, MOM, I'M FINE...
...ANTON... NO, MARX IS HIS LAST NAME...I NEVER SAID HE WAS GREEK...
TAP TAP TAP
MOM, I HAVE TO GO... YES, I'M STILL GOING TO CHURCH...
...I HAVE TO GO... I HAVE TO GO... GOODBYE.
I WAS JUST -- SARA?!
GOTCHA!
I HATE IT WHEN YOU DO THAT! I THOUGHT YOU WERE PATRICIA!
SHE'S AT LUNCH WITH THE MONEY PEOPLE. SHE WON'T COME BACK TODAY.
AND IF SHE DOES, SHE'LL BE SO HAMMERED SHE WON'T REMEMBER THAT SHE DID!
ANYWAY, THIS JUST CAME FOR YOU.
OH, GOD. FUCKING MARX. HAS ANYONE TOLD HIM HIS COLUMN IS SUPPOSED TO BE WAITING FOR ME WHEN I GET TO WORK?
YEAH, THERE WAS A NOTE FROM HIS LITTLE SECRETARY BRIAN APOLOGIZING FOR THE LATENESS.
THERE'S NO WAY I'M GOING TO GET OUT OF HERE IN TIME!
KEEP THE FAITH, GIRL.
I'LL LIGHT A CANDLE AND SAY A PRAYER FOR YOU.

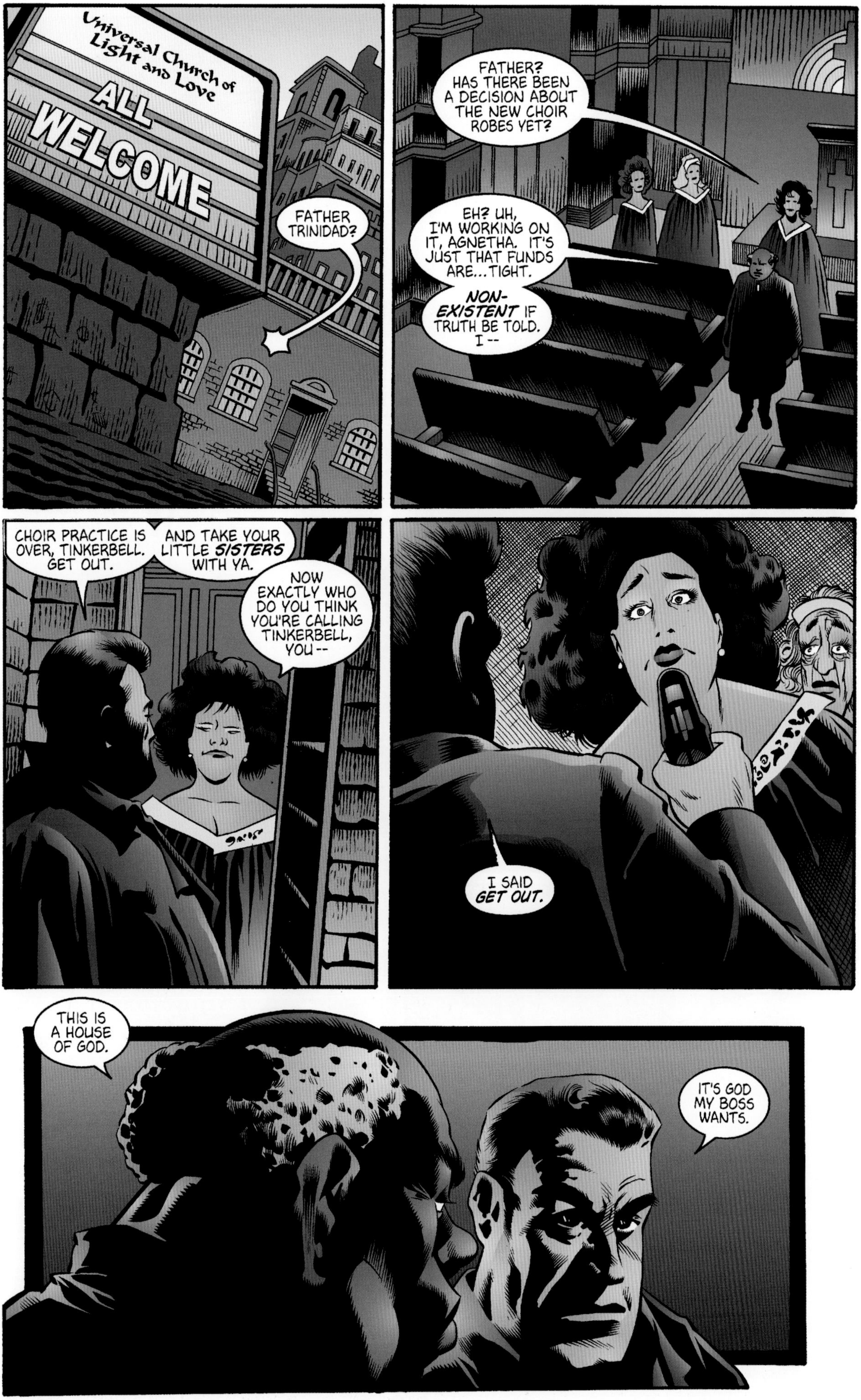
Universal Church of Light and Love
ALL WELCOME
FATHER TRINIDAD?
FATHER? HAS THERE BEEN A DECISION ABOUT THE NEW CHOIR ROBES YET?
EH? UH, I'M WORKING ON IT, AGNETHA. IT'S JUST THAT FUNDS ARE...TIGHT.
NON-EXISTENT IF TRUTH BE TOLD. I --
CHOIR PRACTICE IS OVER, TINKERBELL. GET OUT.
AND TAKE YOUR LITTLE SISTERS WITH YA.
NOW EXACTLY WHO DO YOU THINK YOU'RE CALLING TINKERBELL, YOU --
I SAID GET OUT.
THIS IS A HOUSE OF GOD.
IT'S GOD MY BOSS WANTS.

YOUR... *BOSS?*

YOU CAN CALL HIM THE POPE.

I-I CAN'T CALL A MAN WHO *ISN'T* THE POPE *'THE POPE,'* IT'S *DISRESPECTFUL.*

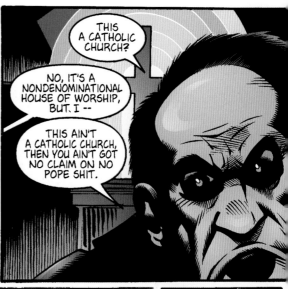

THIS A CATHOLIC CHURCH?

NO, IT'S A NONDENOMINATIONAL HOUSE OF WORSHIP, BUT, I --

THIS AIN'T A CATHOLIC CHURCH, THEN YOU AIN'T GOT NO CLAIM ON NO POPE SHIT.

NOW TELL ME YOU KNOW HOW TO KEEP A *SECRET* AND YOU'LL LIVE TILL SUNDOWN... *AND* MAKE A NICE PENNY TO FIX UP THIS *DUMP.*

TELL ME *OTHERWISE,* AND THE NEXT SERVICES HERE'LL BE *YOURS.*

I-I AM A MAN WHO KNOWS HOW TO KEEP A *CONFIDENCE.*

GOOD, MY BOSS'S LAST PRIEST *WASN'T,* NOW *HE'S* POLISHING ROCKS UNDER THE BAY BRIDGE.

YOU'RE GONNA TAKE *CONFESSION* FROM THE POPE.

ME, I DON'T SEE THE WISENESS IN IT, 'SPECIALLY NOT FREQUENTING SOME FAGGOT CHURCH --

-- BUT *I* DON'T MAKE THE CALLS.

SO YOU *LISTEN,* AN' WHATEVER YOU *HEAR,* YOU TELL HIM IT'S OKAY, AND YOU TAKE IT WITH YOU TO THE *GRAVE* --

-- OR THE GRAVE'S GONNA FIND *YOU* A LOT SOONER THAN YOU MIGHT *LIKE.* GOT IT?

I...YES... I'D *LIKE* TO HELP. HIS SOUL MUST BE VERY TROUBLED IF --

IT AIN'T *HELP.* IT'S A *JOB.*

YOU'LL BE WELL-PAID FOR YOUR WORK. YOU ACCEPT?

THOUGHT SO. I AIN'T MET A RELIGIOUS MAN YET WHO COULDN'T SEE HIS WAY PAST HIS BELIEFS LONG ENOUGH TO GRAB A STACK OF GREEN.

FORGIVE ME, FATHER...

...FOR I *PLAN* TO *SIN...*

SLICE OF HEAVEN

COFFEE

OPEN

I'M HERE!

OH, *HALLELUJAH* --

-- NOW WE CAN ALL STOP SITTING HERE *STARING* AT ONE ANOTHER AS IF WE HAVE NO IDEA WHAT WE'RE DOING --

-- AND COMMENCE WITH LISTENING TO *YOU.*

I NEED YOUR SARCASM LIKE I NEED A RIP IN MY FORESKIN, JASPER.

GO EASY ON HIM, ANTON, HIS NEW SHOW OPENED.

BOMB?

WORSE, A *HUGE* SUCCESS.

UH-OH.

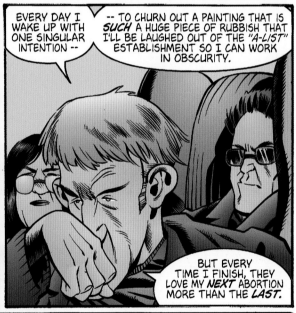

EVERY DAY I WAKE UP WITH ONE SINGULAR INTENTION --

-- TO CHURN OUT A PAINTING THAT IS *SUCH* A HUGE PIECE OF RUBBISH THAT I'LL BE LAUGHED OUT OF THE *"A-LIST"* ESTABLISHMENT SO I CAN WORK IN OBSCURITY.

BUT EVERY TIME I FINISH, THEY LOVE MY *NEXT* ABORTION MORE THAN THE *LAST.*

YEAH, INFALLIBLE SUCCESS *IS* A DRAG, I CAN DEFINITELY RELATE --

-- EXCEPT FOR THE *DOWNSIDE* PART.

BLACK COFFEE WITH SUGAR, GABRIELLE?

NO THANKS, I'M NOT THIRSTY.

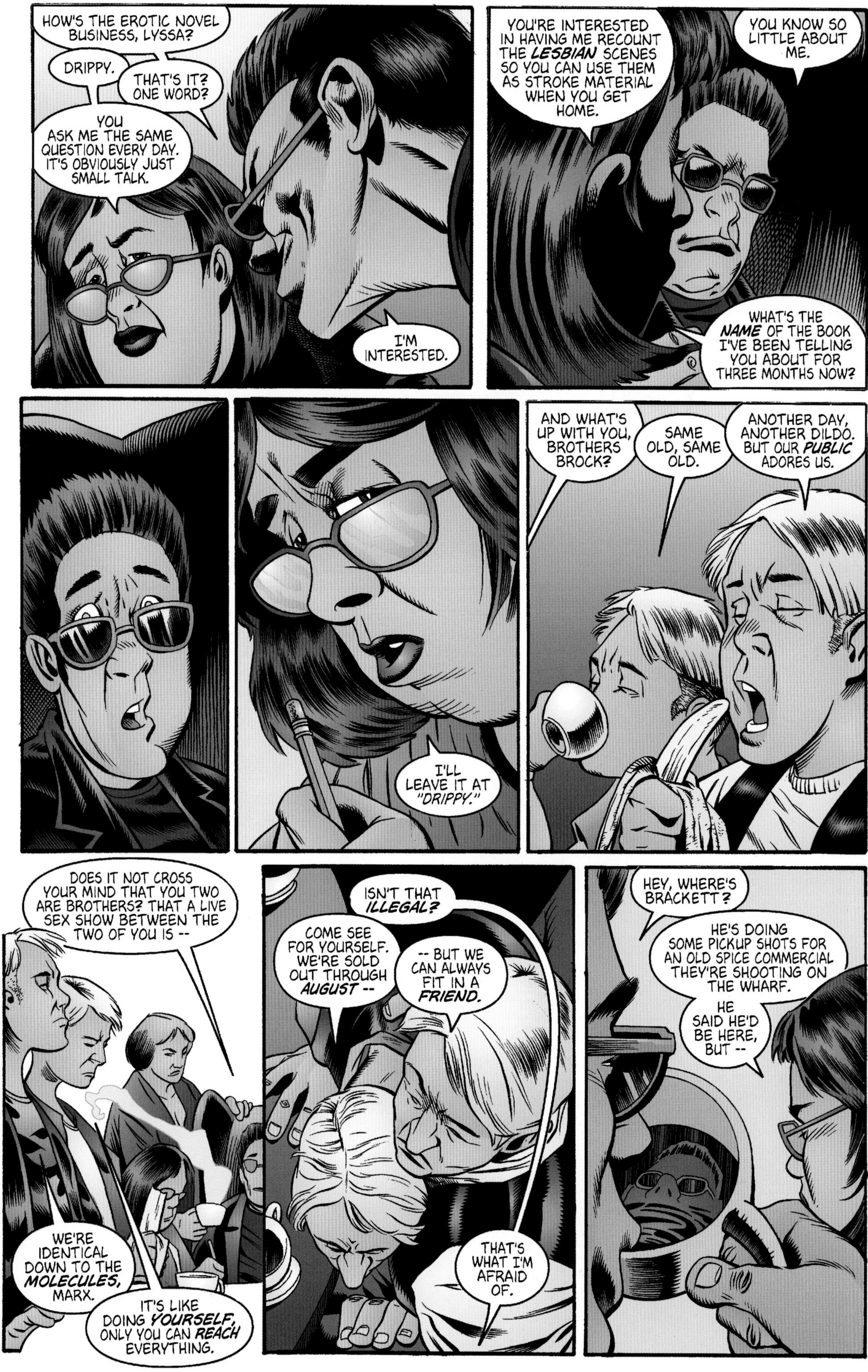
HOW'S THE EROTIC NOVEL BUSINESS, LYSSA?
DRIPPY.
THAT'S IT? ONE WORD?
YOU ASK ME THE SAME QUESTION EVERY DAY. IT'S OBVIOUSLY JUST SMALL TALK.
I'M INTERESTED.
YOU'RE INTERESTED IN HAVING ME RECOUNT THE LESBIAN SCENES SO YOU CAN USE THEM AS STROKE MATERIAL WHEN YOU GET HOME.
YOU KNOW SO LITTLE ABOUT ME.
WHAT'S THE NAME OF THE BOOK I'VE BEEN TELLING YOU ABOUT FOR THREE MONTHS NOW?
I'LL LEAVE IT AT "DRIPPY."
AND WHAT'S UP WITH YOU, BROTHERS BROCK?
SAME OLD, SAME OLD.
ANOTHER DAY, ANOTHER DILDO. BUT OUR PUBLIC ADORES US.
DOES IT NOT CROSS YOUR MIND THAT YOU TWO ARE BROTHERS? THAT A LIVE SEX SHOW BETWEEN THE TWO OF YOU IS --
WE'RE IDENTICAL DOWN TO THE MOLECULES, MARX.
IT'S LIKE DOING YOURSELF, ONLY YOU CAN REACH EVERYTHING.
ISN'T THAT ILLEGAL?
COME SEE FOR YOURSELF. WE'RE SOLD OUT THROUGH AUGUST --
-- BUT WE CAN ALWAYS FIT IN A FRIEND.
THAT'S WHAT I'M AFRAID OF.
HEY, WHERE'S BRACKETT?
HE'S DOING SOME PICKUP SHOTS FOR AN OLD SPICE COMMERCIAL THEY'RE SHOOTING ON THE WHARF.
HE SAID HE'D BE HERE, BUT --

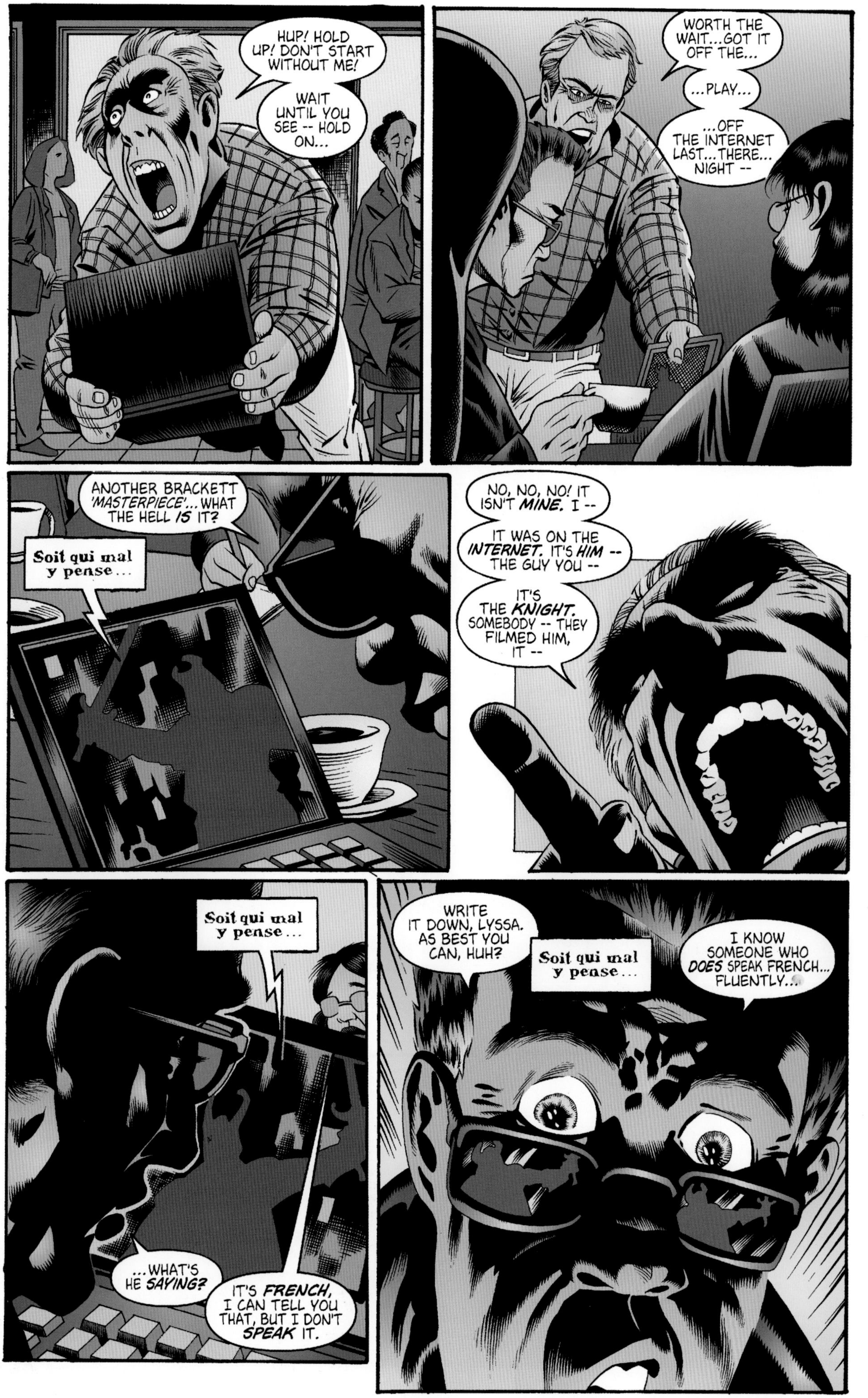
HUP! HOLD UP! DON'T START WITHOUT ME!
WAIT UNTIL YOU SEE -- HOLD ON...
WORTH THE WAIT...GOT IT OFF THE...
...PLAY...
...OFF THE INTERNET LAST...THERE... NIGHT --
ANOTHER BRACKETT 'MASTERPIECE'... WHAT THE HELL *IS* IT?
Soit qui mal y pense...
NO, NO, NO! IT ISN'T *MINE.* I --
IT WAS ON THE *INTERNET.* IT'S *HIM* -- THE GUY YOU --
IT'S THE *KNIGHT.* SOMEBODY -- THEY FILMED HIM, IT --
Soit qui mal y pense...
...WHAT'S HE *SAYING?*
IT'S *FRENCH,* I CAN TELL YOU THAT, BUT I DON'T *SPEAK* IT.
WRITE IT DOWN, LYSSA. AS BEST YOU CAN, HUH?
Soit qui mal y pense...
I KNOW SOMEONE WHO *DOES* SPEAK FRENCH... FLUENTLY...

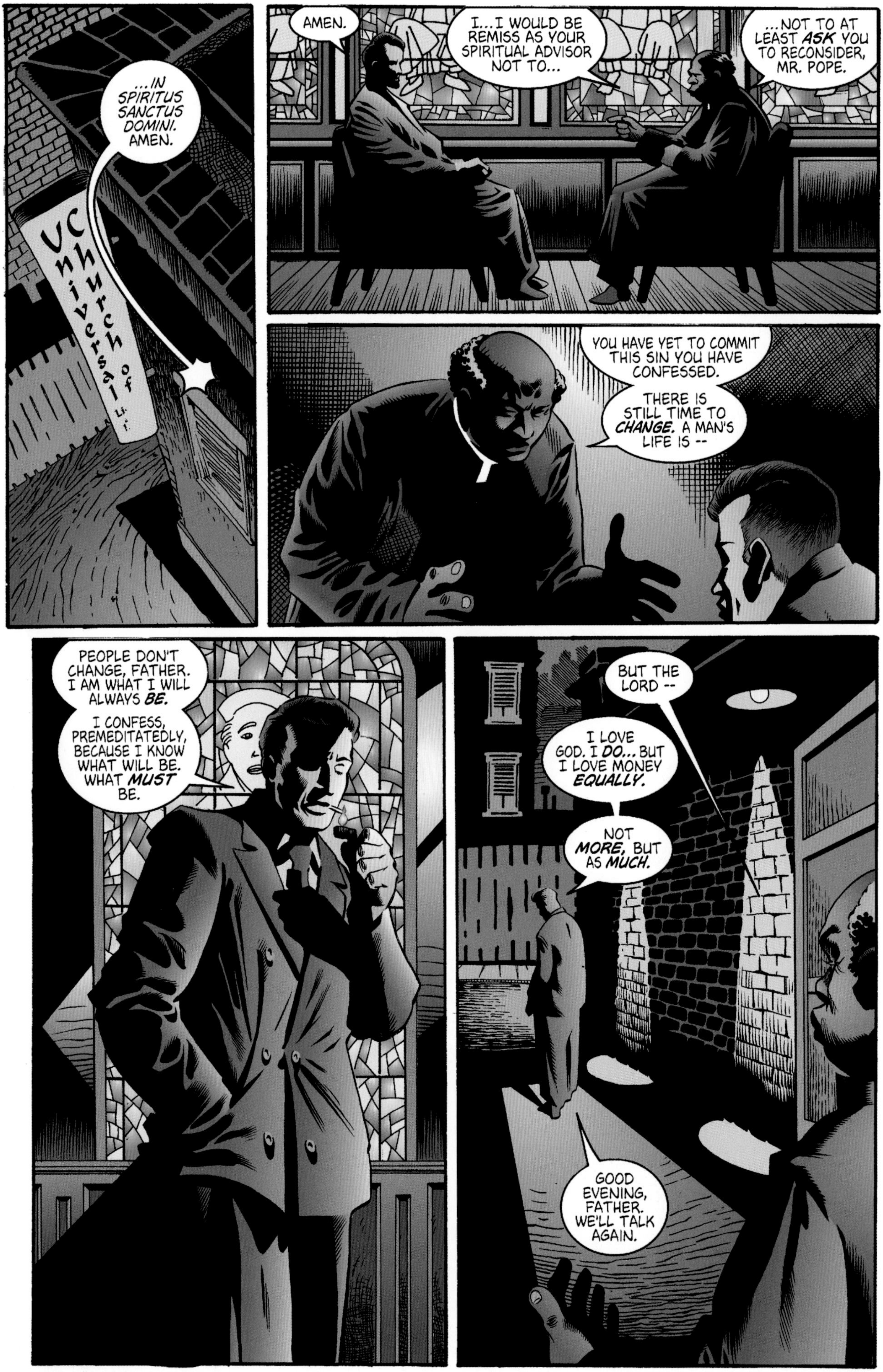
...IN SPIRITUS SANCTUS DOMINI. AMEN.
Universal Church of
AMEN.
I... I WOULD BE REMISS AS YOUR SPIRITUAL ADVISOR NOT TO...
...NOT TO AT LEAST ASK YOU TO RECONSIDER, MR. POPE.
YOU HAVE YET TO COMMIT THIS SIN YOU HAVE CONFESSED.
THERE IS STILL TIME TO CHANGE. A MAN'S LIFE IS --
PEOPLE DON'T CHANGE, FATHER. I AM WHAT I WILL ALWAYS BE.
I CONFESS, PREMEDITATEDLY, BECAUSE I KNOW WHAT WILL BE. WHAT MUST BE.
BUT THE LORD --
I LOVE GOD. I DO... BUT I LOVE MONEY EQUALLY.
NOT MORE, BUT AS MUCH.
GOOD EVENING, FATHER. WE'LL TALK AGAIN.

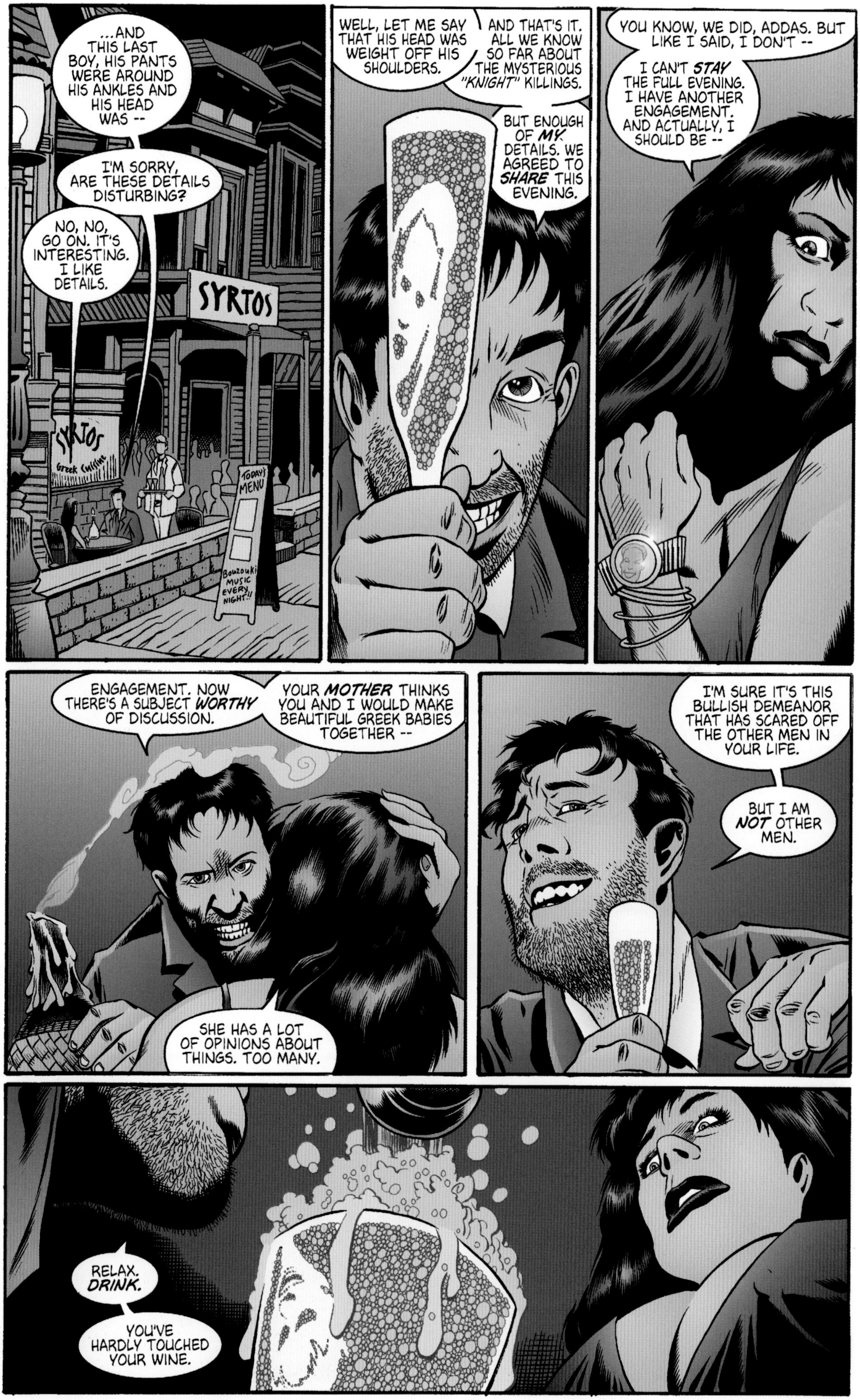
...AND THIS LAST BOY, HIS PANTS WERE AROUND HIS ANKLES AND HIS HEAD WAS --
I'M SORRY, ARE THESE DETAILS DISTURBING?
NO, NO, GO ON. IT'S INTERESTING. I LIKE DETAILS.
SYRTOS
SYRTOS Greek Cuisine
TODAY'S MENU
BOUZOUKI MUSIC EVERY NIGHT!!
WELL, LET ME SAY THAT HIS HEAD WAS WEIGHT OFF HIS SHOULDERS.
AND THAT'S IT. ALL WE KNOW SO FAR ABOUT THE MYSTERIOUS "KNIGHT" KILLINGS.
BUT ENOUGH OF MY DETAILS. WE AGREED TO SHARE THIS EVENING.
YOU KNOW, WE DID, ADDAS. BUT LIKE I SAID, I DON'T --
I CAN'T STAY THE FULL EVENING. I HAVE ANOTHER ENGAGEMENT. AND ACTUALLY, I SHOULD BE --
ENGAGEMENT. NOW THERE'S A SUBJECT WORTHY OF DISCUSSION.
YOUR MOTHER THINKS YOU AND I WOULD MAKE BEAUTIFUL GREEK BABIES TOGETHER --
SHE HAS A LOT OF OPINIONS ABOUT THINGS. TOO MANY.
I'M SURE IT'S THIS BULLISH DEMEANOR THAT HAS SCARED OFF THE OTHER MEN IN YOUR LIFE.
BUT I AM NOT OTHER MEN.
RELAX. DRINK.
YOU'VE HARDLY TOUCHED YOUR WINE.

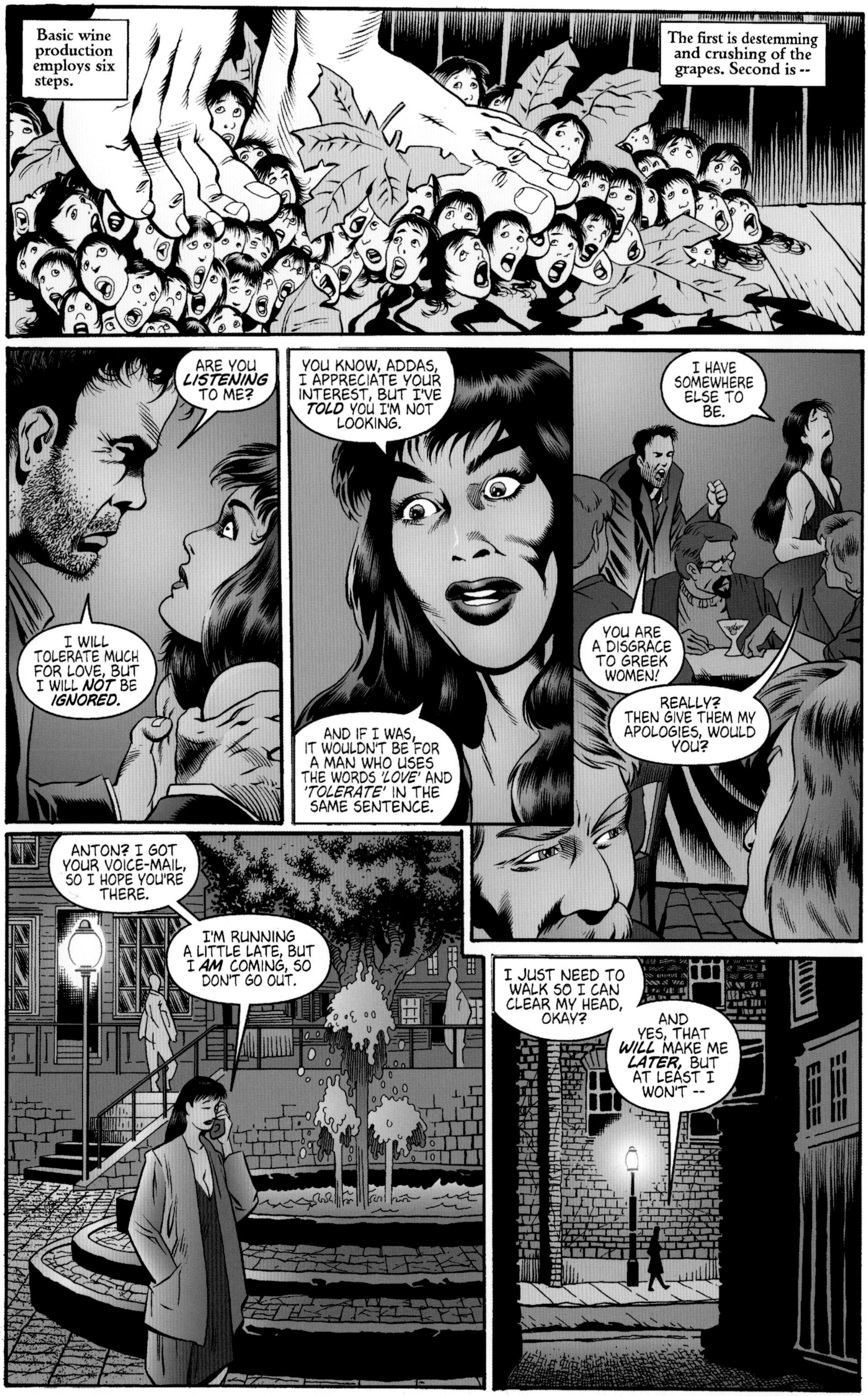
Basic wine production employs six steps.
The first is destemming and crushing of the grapes. Second is --
ARE YOU LISTENING TO ME?
I WILL TOLERATE MUCH FOR LOVE, BUT I WILL NOT BE IGNORED.
YOU KNOW, ADDAS, I APPRECIATE YOUR INTEREST, BUT I'VE TOLD YOU I'M NOT LOOKING.
AND IF I WAS, IT WOULDN'T BE FOR A MAN WHO USES THE WORDS 'LOVE' AND 'TOLERATE' IN THE SAME SENTENCE.
I HAVE SOMEWHERE ELSE TO BE.
YOU ARE A DISGRACE TO GREEK WOMEN!
REALLY? THEN GIVE THEM MY APOLOGIES, WOULD YOU?
ANTON? I GOT YOUR VOICE-MAIL, SO I HOPE YOU'RE THERE.
I'M RUNNING A LITTLE LATE, BUT I AM COMING, SO DON'T GO OUT.
I JUST NEED TO WALK SO I CAN CLEAR MY HEAD, OKAY?
AND YES, THAT WILL MAKE ME LATER, BUT AT LEAST I WON'T --

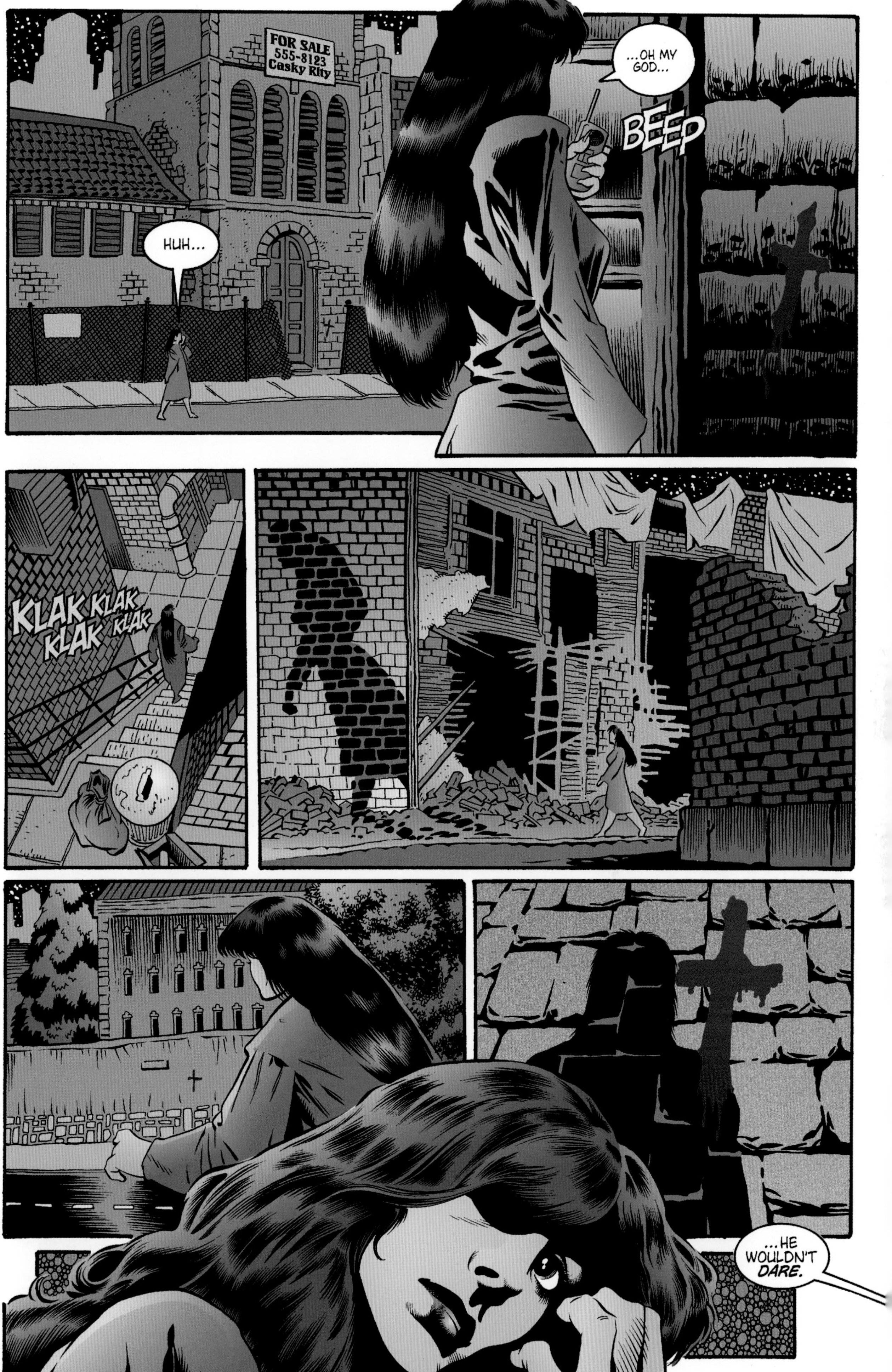
FOR SALE
555-8123
Casky Rlty
HUH...
...OH MY GOD...
BEEP
KLAK KLAK
KLAK KLAK
...HE WOULDN'T *DARE.*

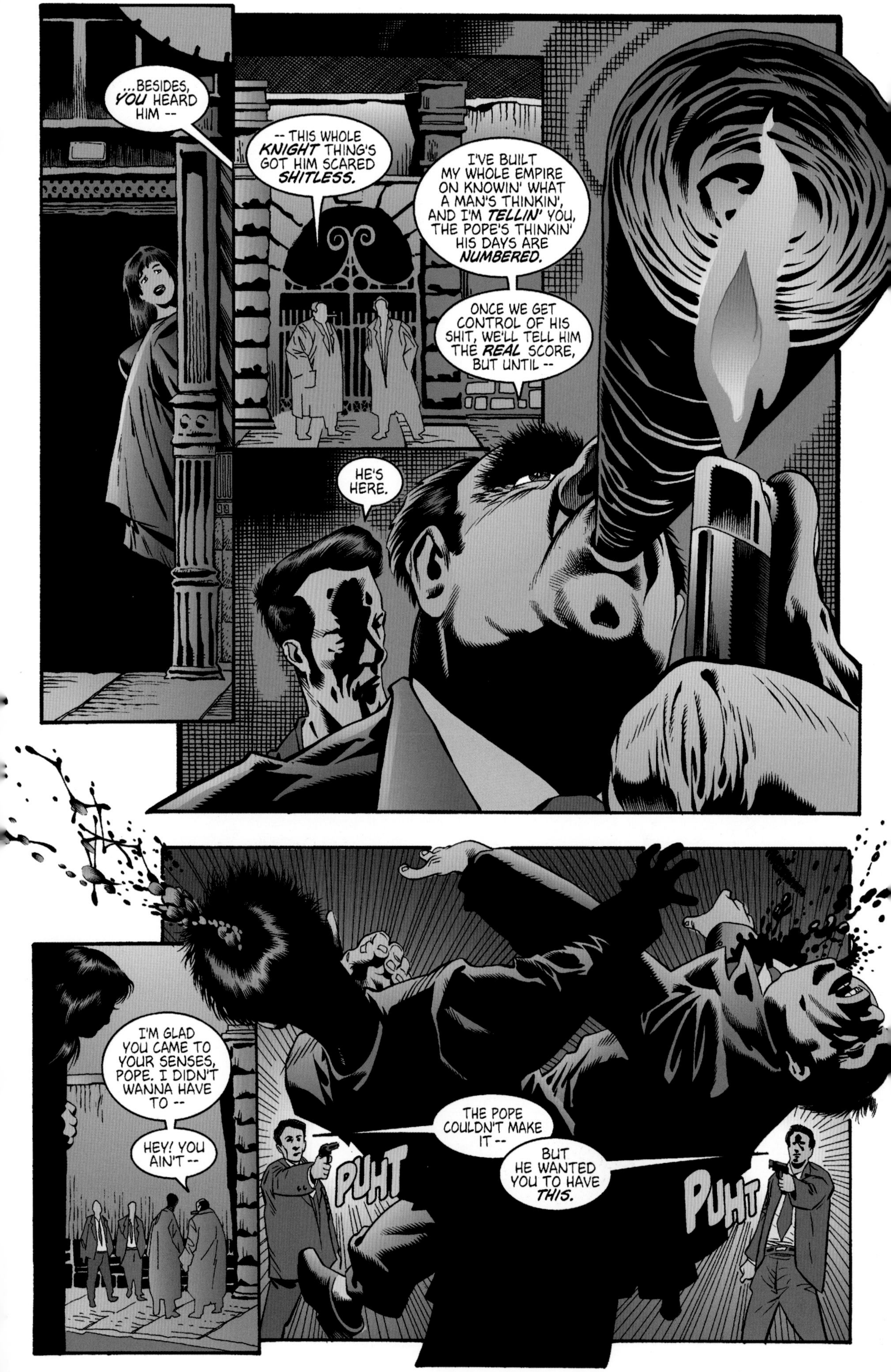
...BESIDES, YOU HEARD HIM --
-- THIS WHOLE KNIGHT THING'S GOT HIM SCARED SHITLESS.
I'VE BUILT MY WHOLE EMPIRE ON KNOWIN' WHAT A MAN'S THINKIN', AND I'M TELLIN' YOU, THE POPE'S THINKIN' HIS DAYS ARE NUMBERED.
ONCE WE GET CONTROL OF HIS SHIT, WE'LL TELL HIM THE REAL SCORE, BUT UNTIL --
HE'S HERE.
I'M GLAD YOU CAME TO YOUR SENSES, POPE. I DIDN'T WANNA HAVE TO --
HEY! YOU AIN'T --
THE POPE COULDN'T MAKE IT --
BUT HE WANTED YOU TO HAVE THIS.
PUHT
PUHT

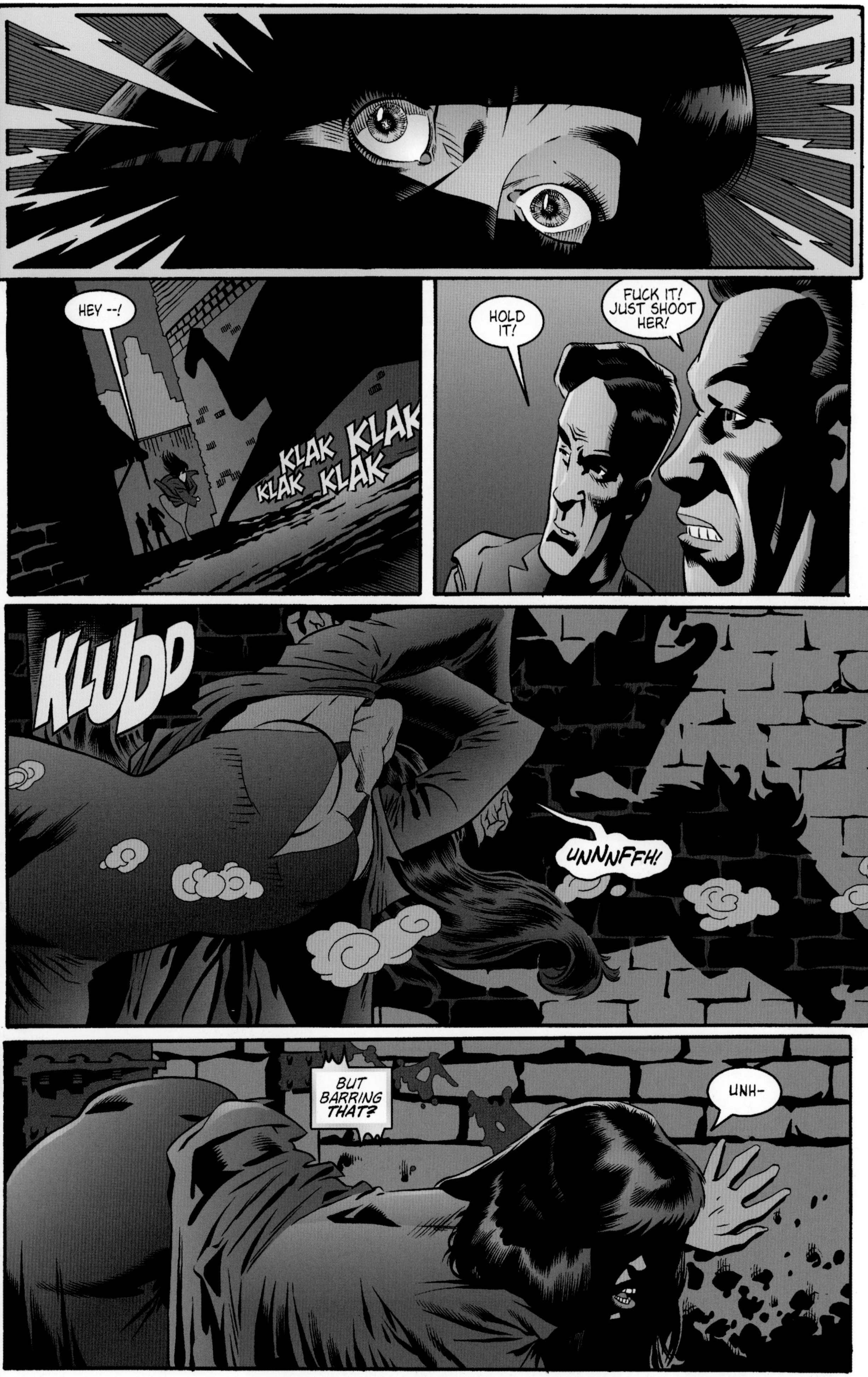
HEY --!
KLAK KLAK
KLAK KLAK
HOLD IT!
FUCK IT! JUST SHOOT HER!
KLUDD
UNNNFFH!
BUT BARRING THAT?
UNH-

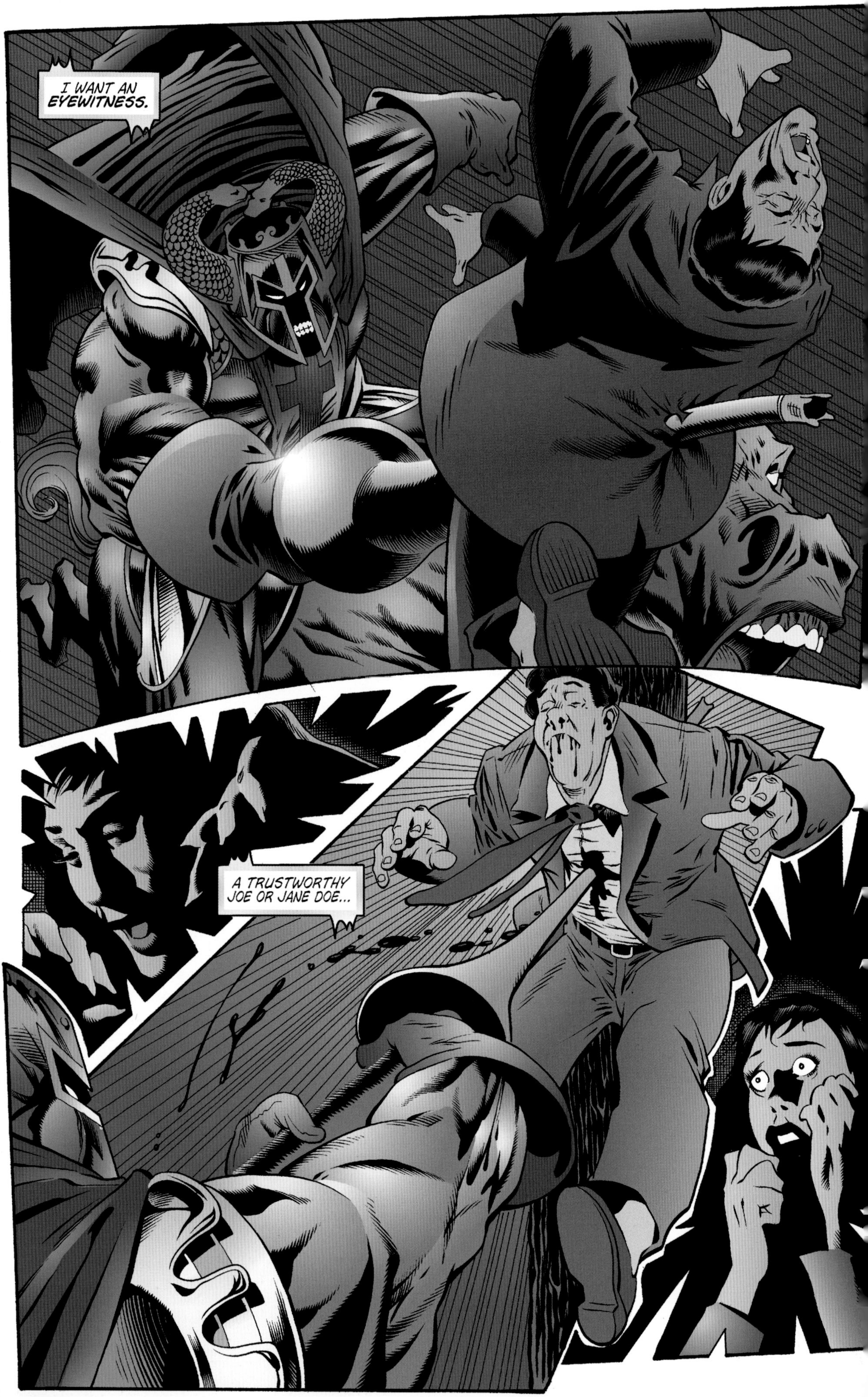
I WANT AN EYEWITNESS.
A TRUSTWORTHY JOE OR JANE DOE...

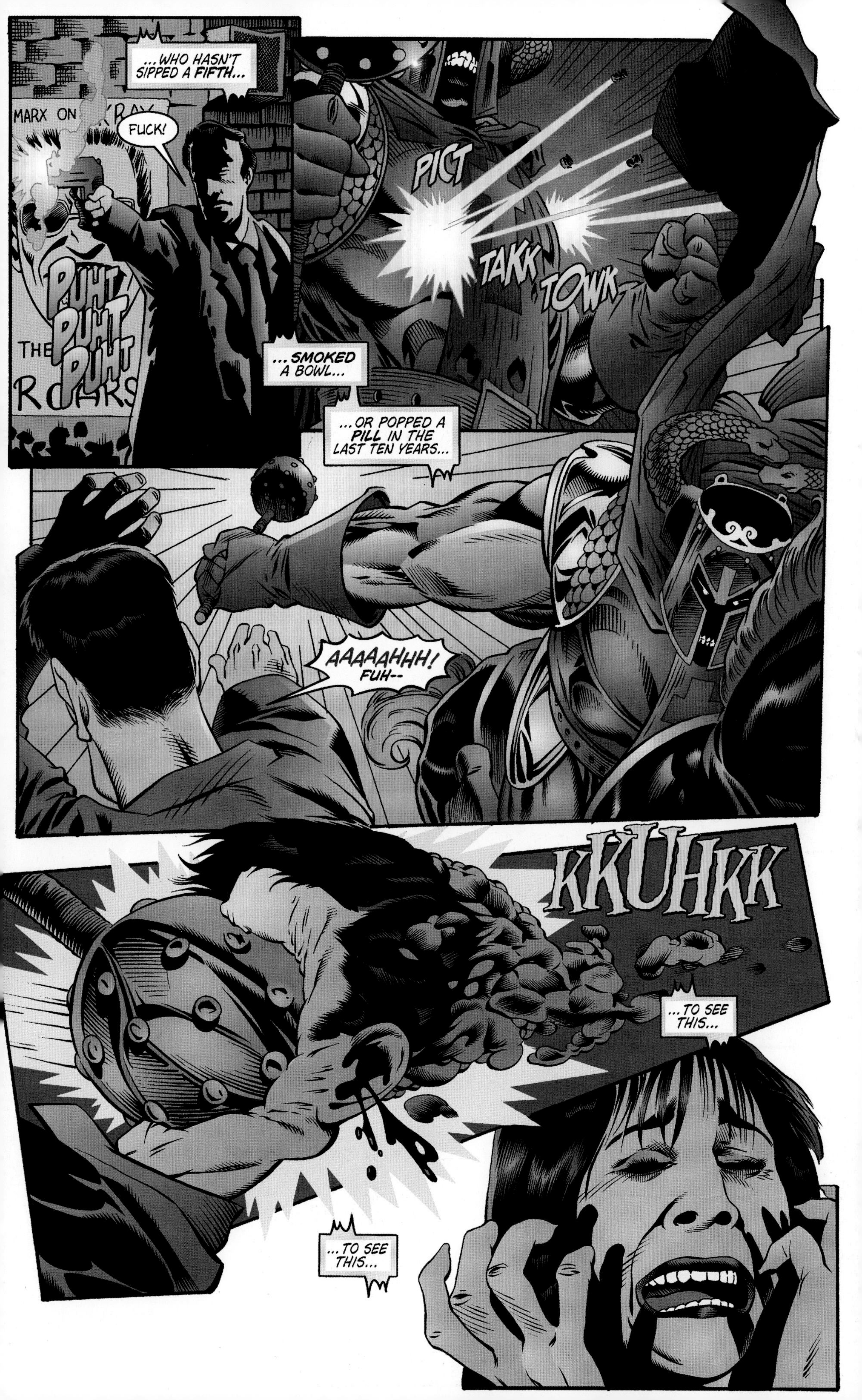
...WHO HASN'T SIPPED A FIFTH...
FUCK!
PUHT PUHT PUHT
...SMOKED A BOWL...
PICT
TAKK
TOWK
...OR POPPED A PILL IN THE LAST TEN YEARS...
AAAAAHHH! FUH--
KKUHKK
...TO SEE THIS...
...TO SEE THIS...

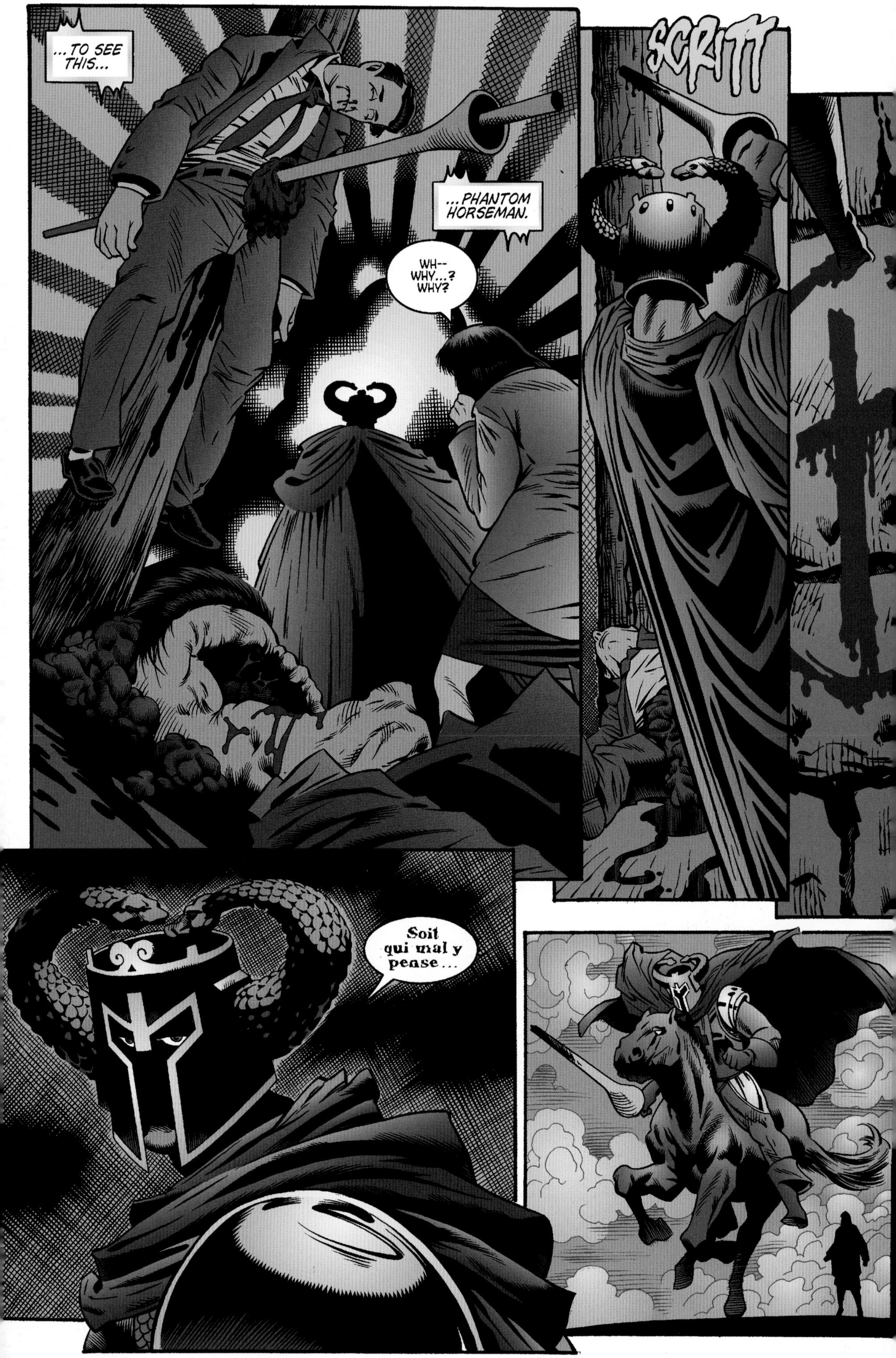
...TO SEE THIS...
...PHANTOM HORSEMAN.
WH-- WHY...? WHY?
SCRITT
Soit qui mal y pense...

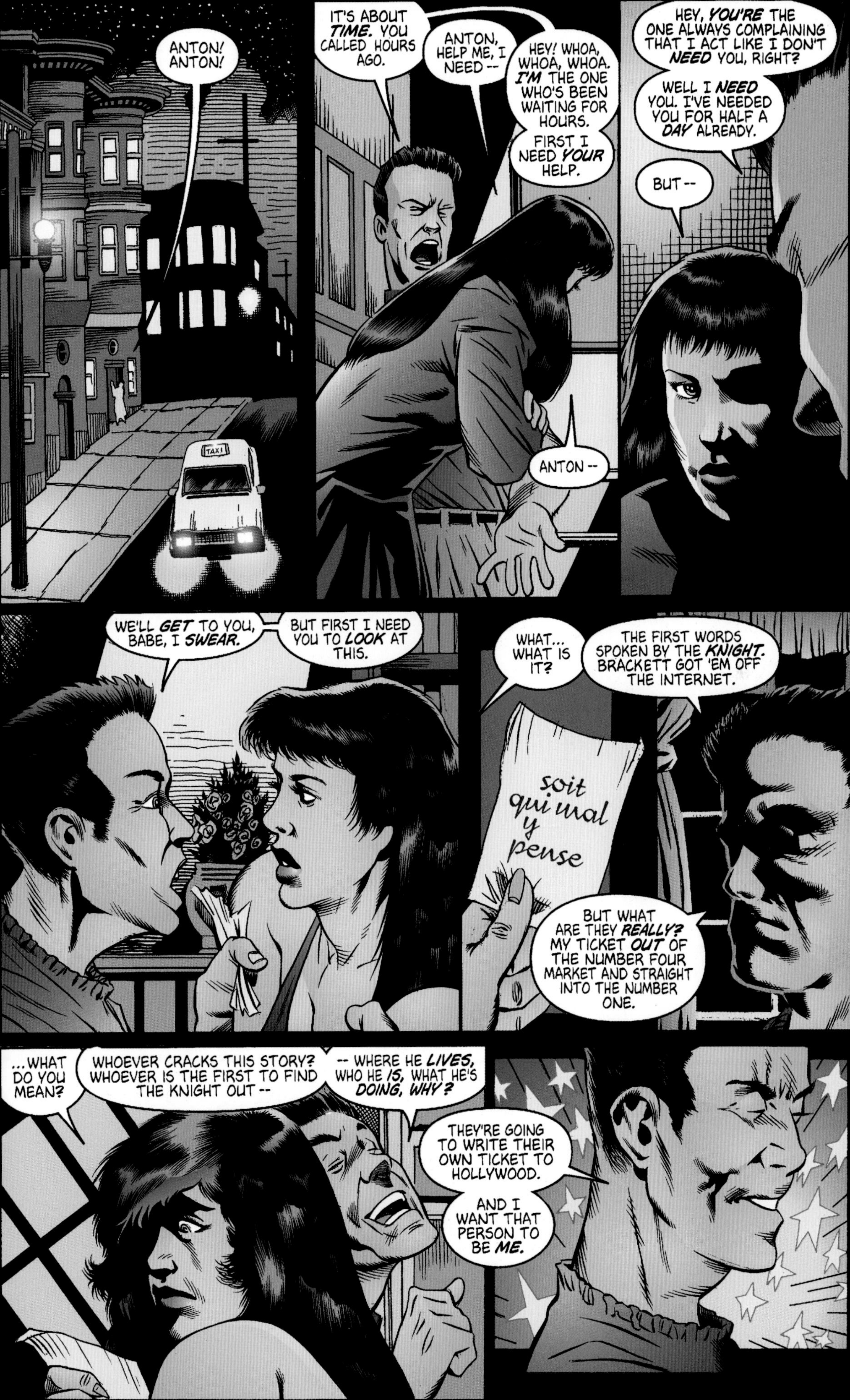

ANTON! ANTON!
IT'S ABOUT TIME. YOU CALLED HOURS AGO.
ANTON, HELP ME, I NEED --
HEY! WHOA, WHOA, WHOA. I'M THE ONE WHO'S BEEN WAITING FOR HOURS.
FIRST I NEED YOUR HELP.
ANTON --
HEY, YOU'RE THE ONE ALWAYS COMPLAINING THAT I ACT LIKE I DON'T NEED YOU, RIGHT?
WELL I NEED YOU. I'VE NEEDED YOU FOR HALF A DAY ALREADY.
BUT --
WE'LL GET TO YOU, BABE, I SWEAR.
BUT FIRST I NEED YOU TO LOOK AT THIS.
WHAT... WHAT IS IT?
THE FIRST WORDS SPOKEN BY THE KNIGHT. BRACKETT GOT 'EM OFF THE INTERNET.
soit qui mal y pense
BUT WHAT ARE THEY REALLY? MY TICKET OUT OF THE NUMBER FOUR MARKET AND STRAIGHT INTO THE NUMBER ONE.
...WHAT DO YOU MEAN?
WHOEVER CRACKS THIS STORY? WHOEVER IS THE FIRST TO FIND THE KNIGHT OUT --
-- WHERE HE LIVES, WHO HE IS, WHAT HE'S DOING, WHY?
THEY'RE GOING TO WRITE THEIR OWN TICKET TO HOLLYWOOD.
AND I WANT THAT PERSON TO BE ME.

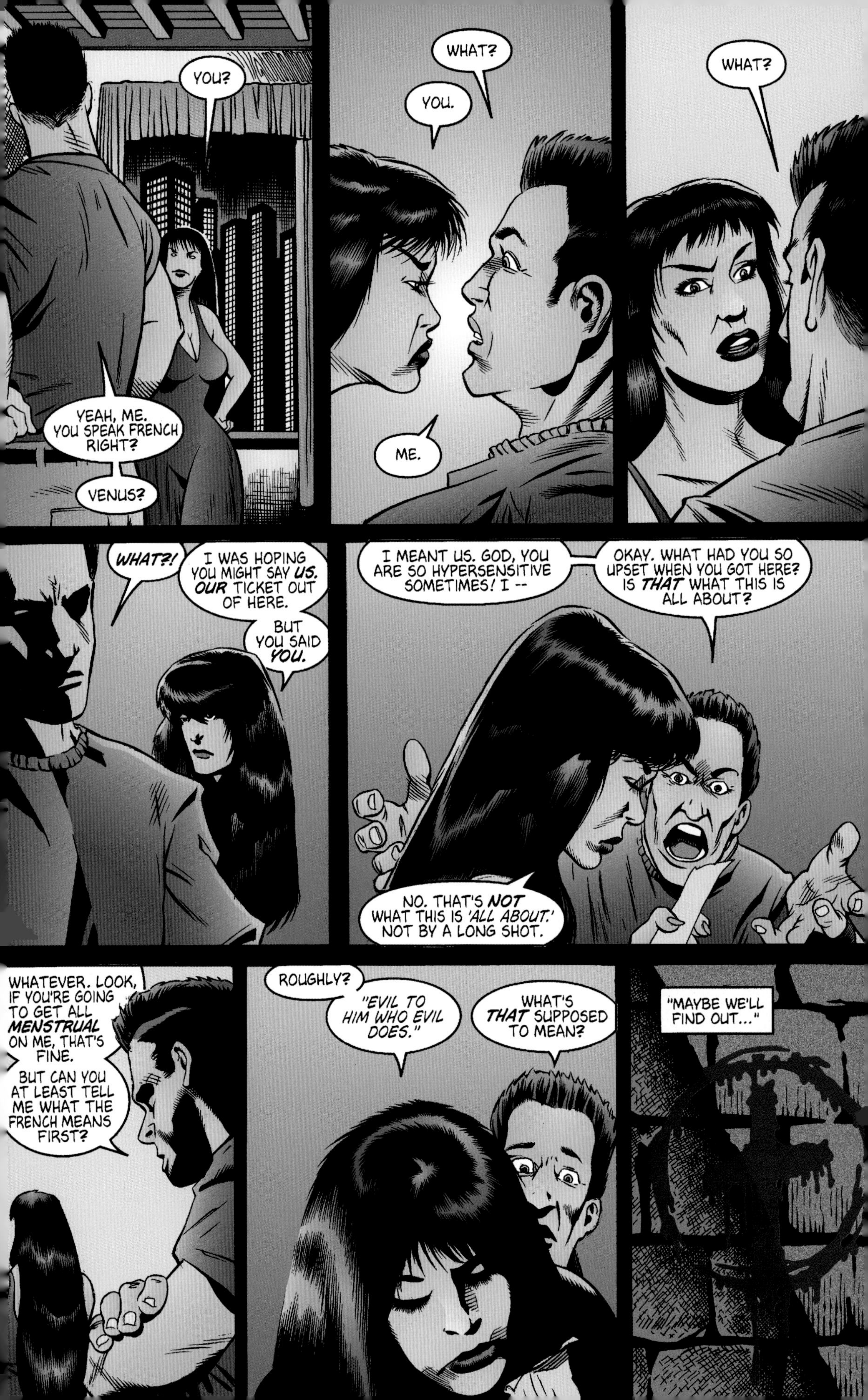
YOU?
YEAH, ME. YOU SPEAK FRENCH RIGHT?
VENUS?
WHAT?
YOU.
ME.
WHAT?
WHAT?!
I WAS HOPING YOU MIGHT SAY US. OUR TICKET OUT OF HERE.
BUT YOU SAID YOU.
I MEANT US. GOD, YOU ARE SO HYPERSENSITIVE SOMETIMES! I --
OKAY. WHAT HAD YOU SO UPSET WHEN YOU GOT HERE? IS THAT WHAT THIS IS ALL ABOUT?
NO. THAT'S NOT WHAT THIS IS 'ALL ABOUT.' NOT BY A LONG SHOT.
WHATEVER. LOOK, IF YOU'RE GOING TO GET ALL MENSTRUAL ON ME, THAT'S FINE.
BUT CAN YOU AT LEAST TELL ME WHAT THE FRENCH MEANS FIRST?
ROUGHLY?
"EVIL TO HIM WHO EVIL DOES."
WHAT'S THAT SUPPOSED TO MEAN?
"MAYBE WE'LL FIND OUT..."

"Children are natural mythologists; they beg to be told tales, and they love not only to invent, but to enact falsehoods."
— George Santayana

"SAY IT LIKE
I TOLD YOU --"

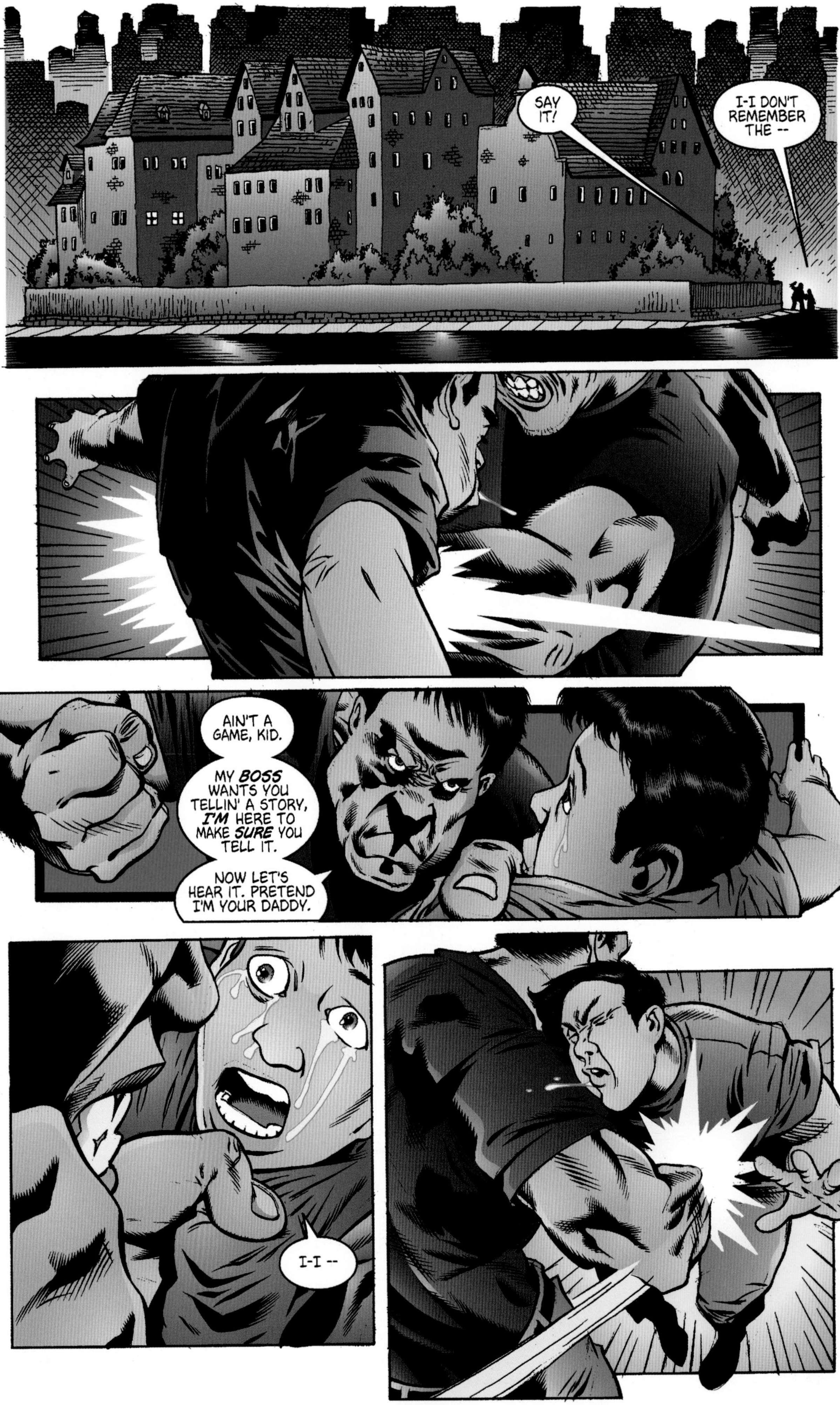
SAY IT!
I-I DON'T REMEMBER THE --
AIN'T A GAME, KID.
MY BOSS WANTS YOU TELLIN' A STORY, I'M HERE TO MAKE SURE YOU TELL IT.
NOW LET'S HEAR IT. PRETEND I'M YOUR DADDY.
I-I --

I AIN'T A PLAYGROUND BULLY GONNA MESS YOU UP A LITTLE EVERY DAY.
YOU DO WHAT I SAY, OR I'LL DUMP YOUR BONY ASS IN THE BAY FIVE MINUTES FROM NOW.
I-I'M SUPPOSED TO SAY THAT I --
-- I DON'T WANNA GO TO SCHOOL HERE ANYMORE 'CAUSE -- 'CAUSE THE GANGS ARE BAD, AN --
THE ASIAN GANGS. DON'T FORGET THAT PART.
WHAT ELSE?
THAT THE GUYS -- THE ASIAN GUYS THAT HIT ME SAID THEY'D KILL ME IF I C-COME BACK HERE TOMORROW.
GOOD JOB, TWIG. YOU LEARN QUICK. MUST BE A STRAIGHT-A STUDENT.
YOU A STRAIGHT-A STUDENT?

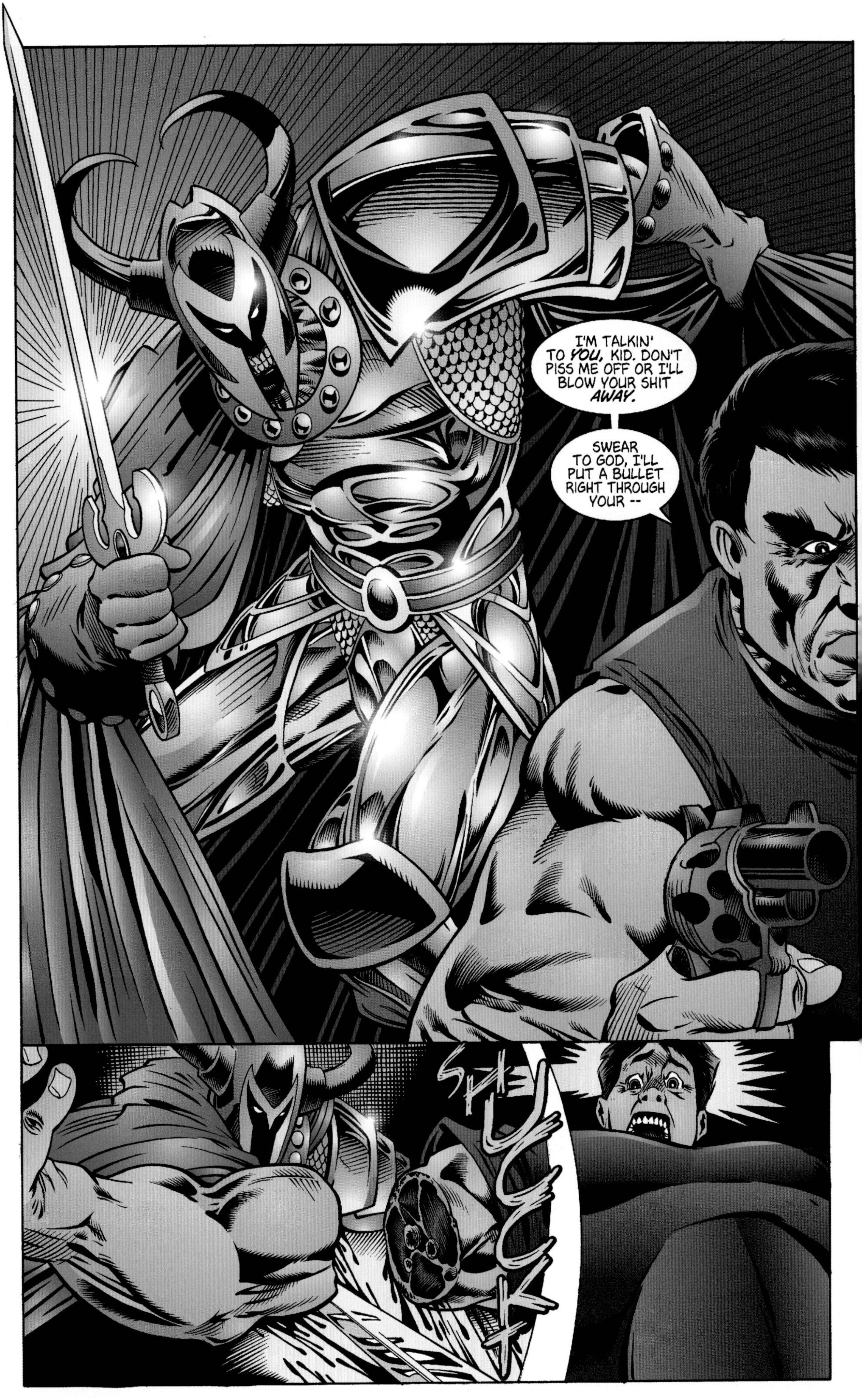
I'M TALKIN' TO *YOU*, KID. DON'T PISS ME OFF OR I'LL BLOW YOUR SHIT *AWAY*.
SWEAR TO GOD, I'LL PUT A BULLET RIGHT THROUGH YOUR --

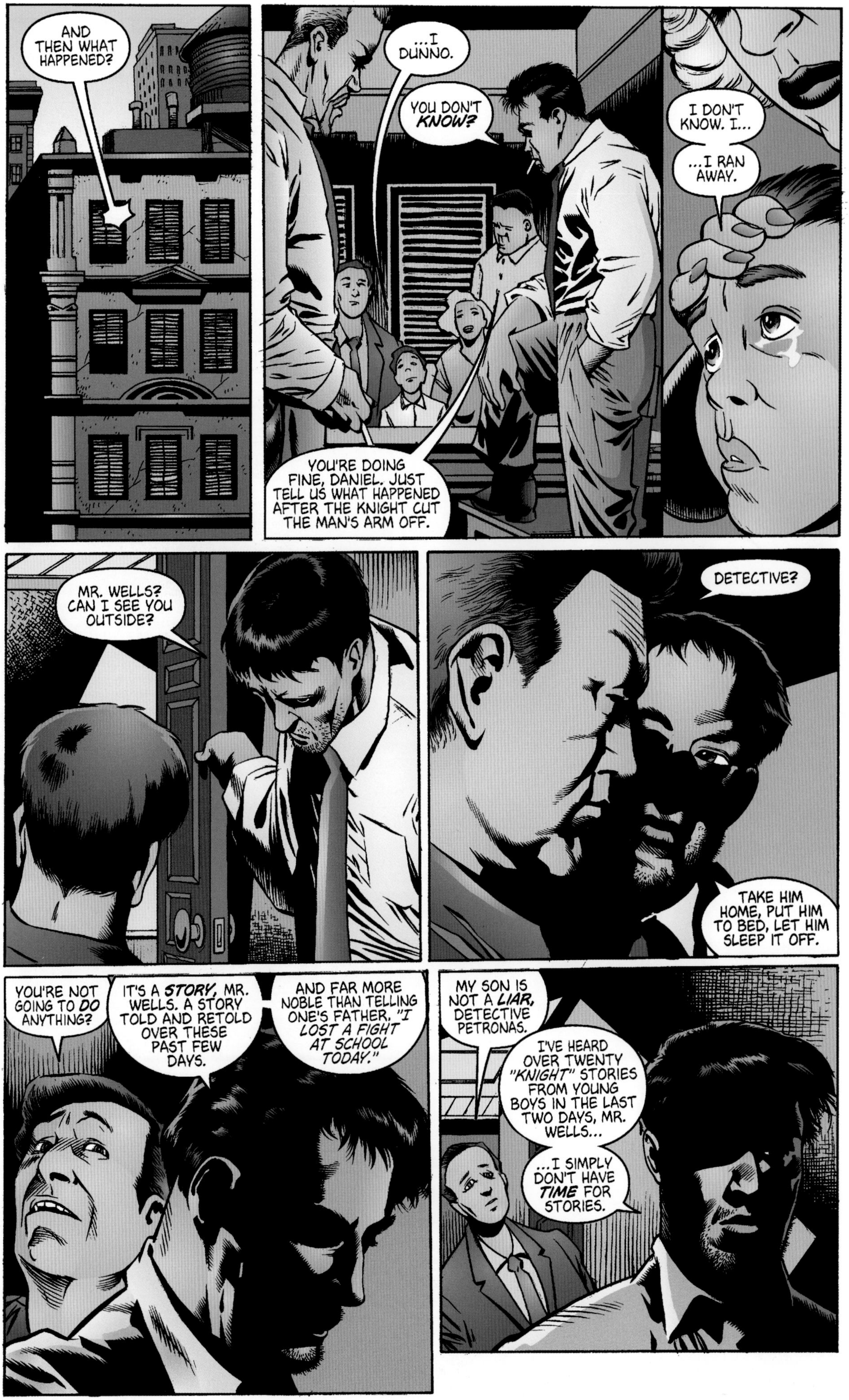
AND THEN WHAT HAPPENED?
...I DUNNO.
YOU DON'T KNOW?
YOU'RE DOING FINE, DANIEL. JUST TELL US WHAT HAPPENED AFTER THE KNIGHT CUT THE MAN'S ARM OFF.
I DON'T KNOW. I...
...I RAN AWAY.
MR. WELLS? CAN I SEE YOU OUTSIDE?
DETECTIVE?
TAKE HIM HOME, PUT HIM TO BED, LET HIM SLEEP IT OFF.
YOU'RE NOT GOING TO DO ANYTHING?
IT'S A STORY, MR. WELLS. A STORY TOLD AND RETOLD OVER THESE PAST FEW DAYS.
AND FAR MORE NOBLE THAN TELLING ONE'S FATHER, "I LOST A FIGHT AT SCHOOL TODAY."
MY SON IS NOT A LIAR, DETECTIVE PETRONAS.
I'VE HEARD OVER TWENTY "KNIGHT" STORIES FROM YOUNG BOYS IN THE LAST TWO DAYS, MR. WELLS...
...I SIMPLY DON'T HAVE TIME FOR STORIES.

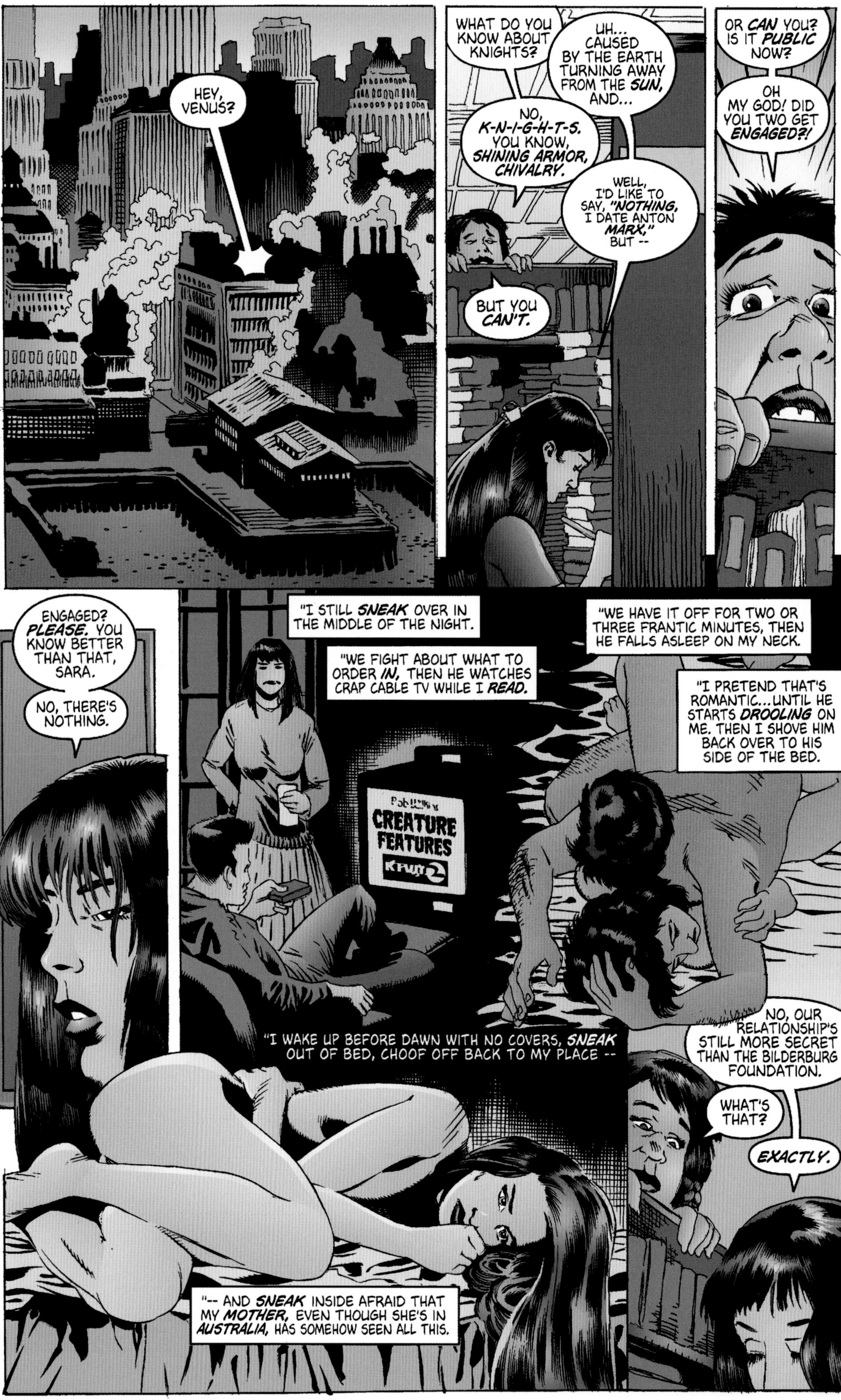
HEY, VENUS?
WHAT DO YOU KNOW ABOUT KNIGHTS?
UH... CAUSED BY THE EARTH TURNING AWAY FROM THE SUN, AND...
NO, K-N-I-G-H-T-S. YOU KNOW, SHINING ARMOR, CHIVALRY.
WELL, I'D LIKE TO SAY, "NOTHING, I DATE ANTON MARX," BUT --
BUT YOU CAN'T.
OR CAN YOU? IS IT PUBLIC NOW?
OH MY GOD! DID YOU TWO GET ENGAGED?!
ENGAGED? PLEASE. YOU KNOW BETTER THAN THAT, SARA.
NO, THERE'S NOTHING.
"I STILL SNEAK OVER IN THE MIDDLE OF THE NIGHT.
"WE FIGHT ABOUT WHAT TO ORDER IN, THEN HE WATCHES CRAP CABLE TV WHILE I READ.
CREATURE FEATURES
"WE HAVE IT OFF FOR TWO OR THREE FRANTIC MINUTES, THEN HE FALLS ASLEEP ON MY NECK.
"I PRETEND THAT'S ROMANTIC...UNTIL HE STARTS DROOLING ON ME. THEN I SHOVE HIM BACK OVER TO HIS SIDE OF THE BED.
"I WAKE UP BEFORE DAWN WITH NO COVERS, SNEAK OUT OF BED, CHOOF OFF BACK TO MY PLACE --
"-- AND SNEAK INSIDE AFRAID THAT MY MOTHER, EVEN THOUGH SHE'S IN AUSTRALIA, HAS SOMEHOW SEEN ALL THIS.
NO, OUR RELATIONSHIP'S STILL MORE SECRET THAN THE BILDERBURG FOUNDATION.
WHAT'S THAT?
EXACTLY.

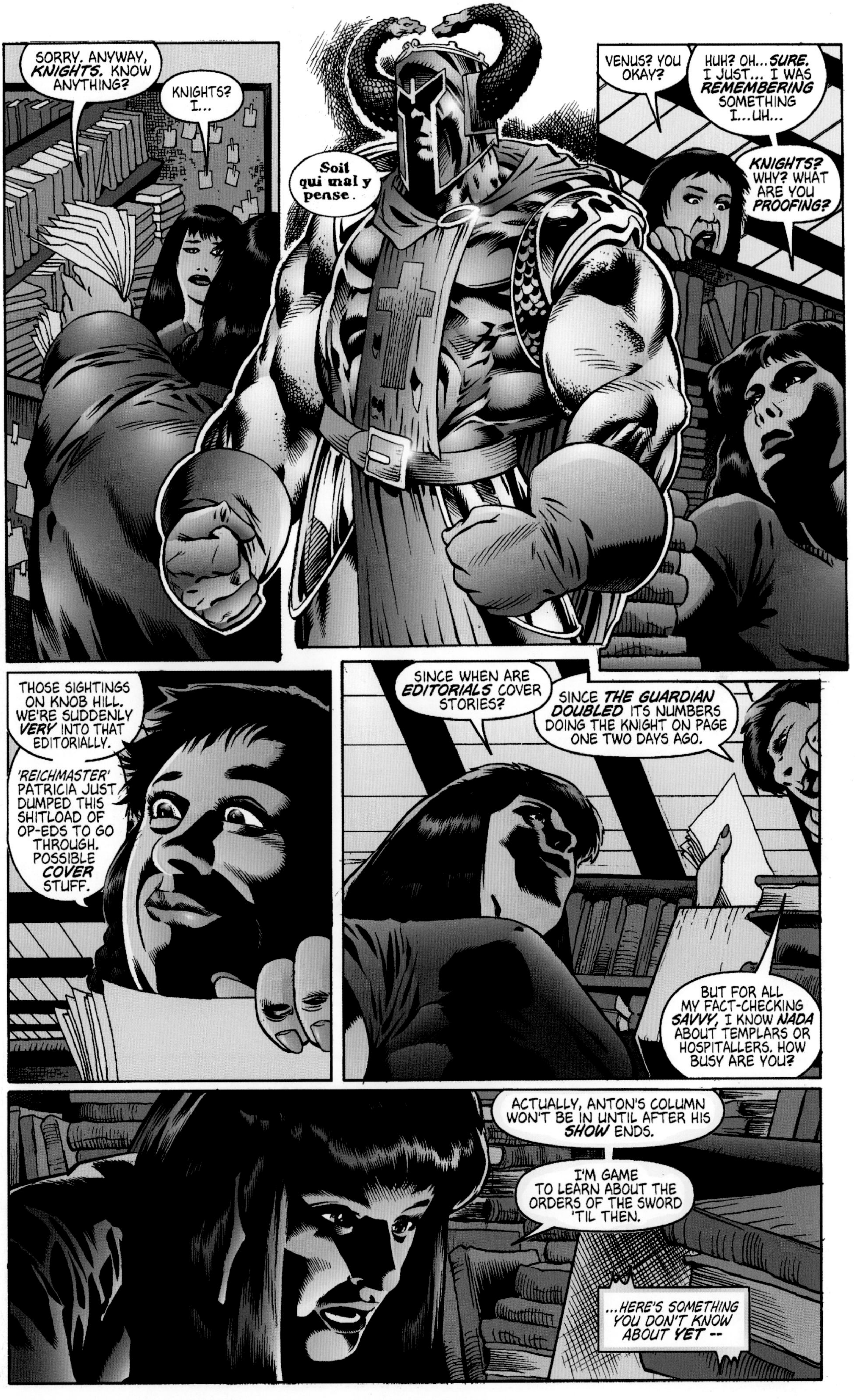

SORRY. ANYWAY, KNIGHTS. KNOW ANYTHING?
KNIGHTS? I...
Soit qui mal y pense.
VENUS? YOU OKAY?
HUH? OH...SURE. I JUST... I WAS REMEMBERING SOMETHING I...UH...
KNIGHTS? WHY? WHAT ARE YOU PROOFING?
THOSE SIGHTINGS ON KNOB HILL. WE'RE SUDDENLY VERY INTO THAT EDITORIALLY.
'REICHMASTER' PATRICIA JUST DUMPED THIS SHITLOAD OF OP-EDS TO GO THROUGH. POSSIBLE COVER STUFF.
SINCE WHEN ARE EDITORIALS COVER STORIES?
SINCE THE GUARDIAN DOUBLED ITS NUMBERS DOING THE KNIGHT ON PAGE ONE TWO DAYS AGO.
BUT FOR ALL MY FACT-CHECKING SAVVY, I KNOW NADA ABOUT TEMPLARS OR HOSPITALLERS. HOW BUSY ARE YOU?
ACTUALLY, ANTON'S COLUMN WON'T BE IN UNTIL AFTER HIS SHOW ENDS.
I'M GAME TO LEARN ABOUT THE ORDERS OF THE SWORD 'TIL THEN.
...HERE'S SOMETHING YOU DON'T KNOW ABOUT YET --

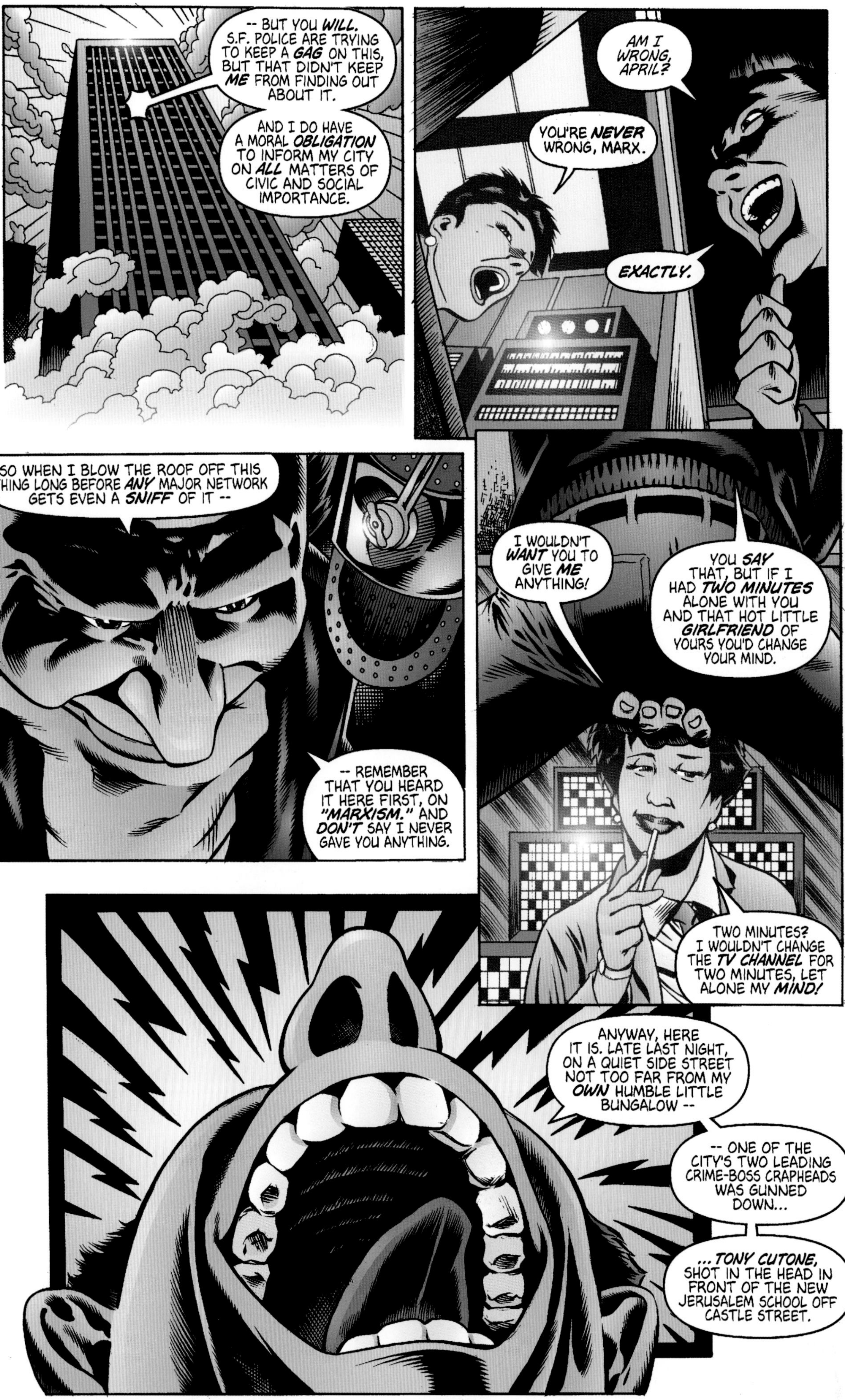
-- BUT YOU WILL. S.F. POLICE ARE TRYING TO KEEP A GAG ON THIS, BUT THAT DIDN'T KEEP ME FROM FINDING OUT ABOUT IT.
AND I DO HAVE A MORAL OBLIGATION TO INFORM MY CITY ON ALL MATTERS OF CIVIC AND SOCIAL IMPORTANCE.
AM I WRONG, APRIL?
YOU'RE NEVER WRONG, MARX.
EXACTLY.
SO WHEN I BLOW THE ROOF OFF THIS THING LONG BEFORE ANY MAJOR NETWORK GETS EVEN A SNIFF OF IT --
-- REMEMBER THAT YOU HEARD IT HERE FIRST, ON "MARXISM." AND DON'T SAY I NEVER GAVE YOU ANYTHING.
I WOULDN'T WANT YOU TO GIVE ME ANYTHING!
YOU SAY THAT, BUT IF I HAD TWO MINUTES ALONE WITH YOU AND THAT HOT LITTLE GIRLFRIEND OF YOURS YOU'D CHANGE YOUR MIND.
TWO MINUTES? I WOULDN'T CHANGE THE TV CHANNEL FOR TWO MINUTES, LET ALONE MY MIND!
ANYWAY, HERE IT IS. LATE LAST NIGHT, ON A QUIET SIDE STREET NOT TOO FAR FROM MY OWN HUMBLE LITTLE BUNGALOW --
-- ONE OF THE CITY'S TWO LEADING CRIME-BOSS CRAPHEADS WAS GUNNED DOWN...
...TONY CUTONE, SHOT IN THE HEAD IN FRONT OF THE NEW JERUSALEM SCHOOL OFF CASTLE STREET.

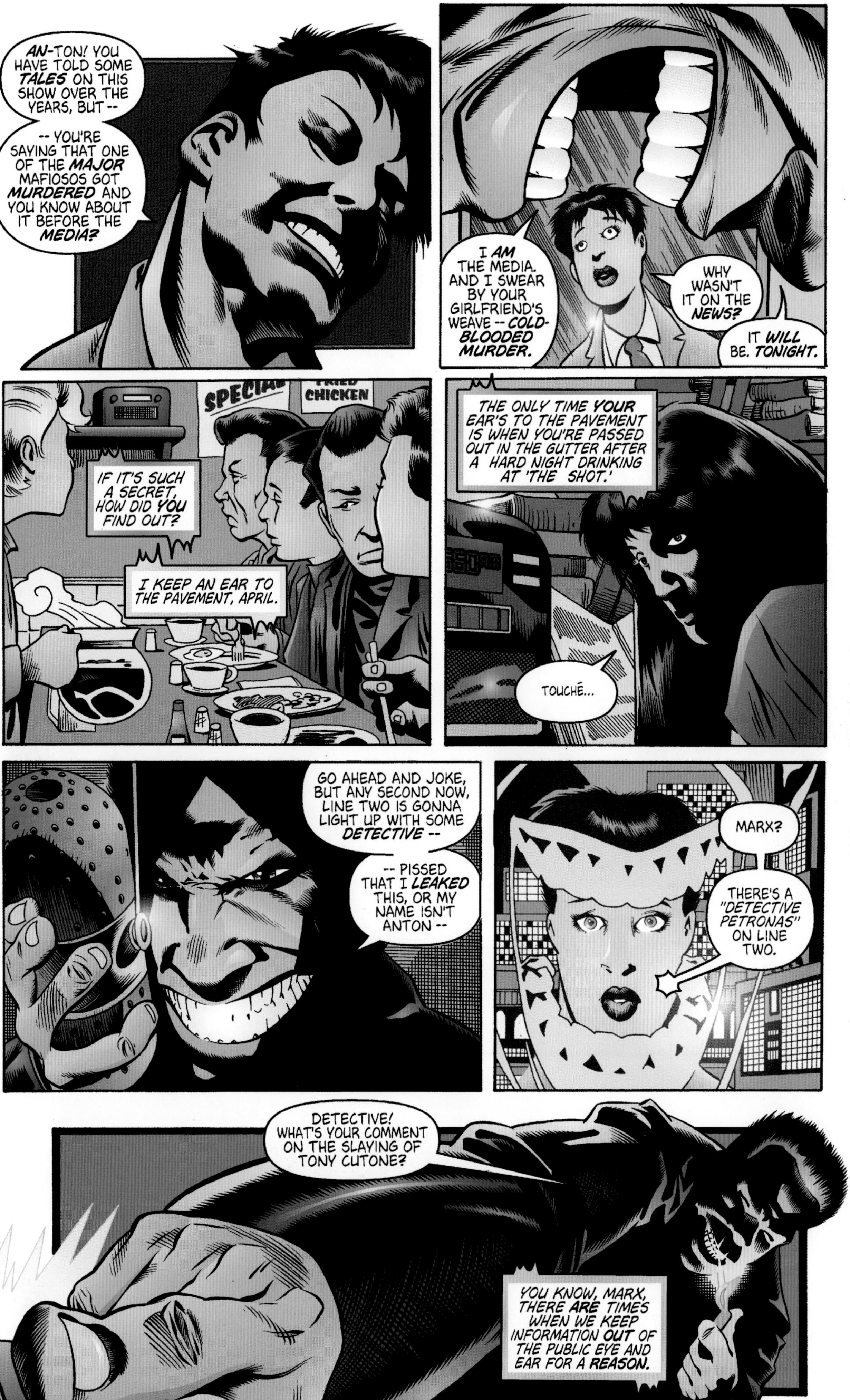

AN-TON! YOU HAVE TOLD SOME TALES ON THIS SHOW OVER THE YEARS, BUT --
-- YOU'RE SAYING THAT ONE OF THE MAJOR MAFIOSOS GOT MURDERED AND YOU KNOW ABOUT IT BEFORE THE MEDIA?
I AM THE MEDIA. AND I SWEAR BY YOUR GIRLFRIEND'S WEAVE -- COLD-BLOODED MURDER.
WHY WASN'T IT ON THE NEWS?
IT WILL BE. TONIGHT.
SPECIAL
CHICKEN
IF IT'S SUCH A SECRET, HOW DID YOU FIND OUT?
I KEEP AN EAR TO THE PAVEMENT, APRIL.
THE ONLY TIME YOUR EAR'S TO THE PAVEMENT IS WHEN YOU'RE PASSED OUT IN THE GUTTER AFTER A HARD NIGHT DRINKING AT 'THE SHOT.'
TOUCHÉ...
GO AHEAD AND JOKE, BUT ANY SECOND NOW, LINE TWO IS GONNA LIGHT UP WITH SOME DETECTIVE --
-- PISSED THAT I LEAKED THIS, OR MY NAME ISN'T ANTON --
MARX?
THERE'S A "DETECTIVE PETRONAS" ON LINE TWO.
DETECTIVE! WHAT'S YOUR COMMENT ON THE SLAYING OF TONY CUTONE?
YOU KNOW, MARX, THERE ARE TIMES WHEN WE KEEP INFORMATION OUT OF THE PUBLIC EYE AND EAR FOR A REASON.

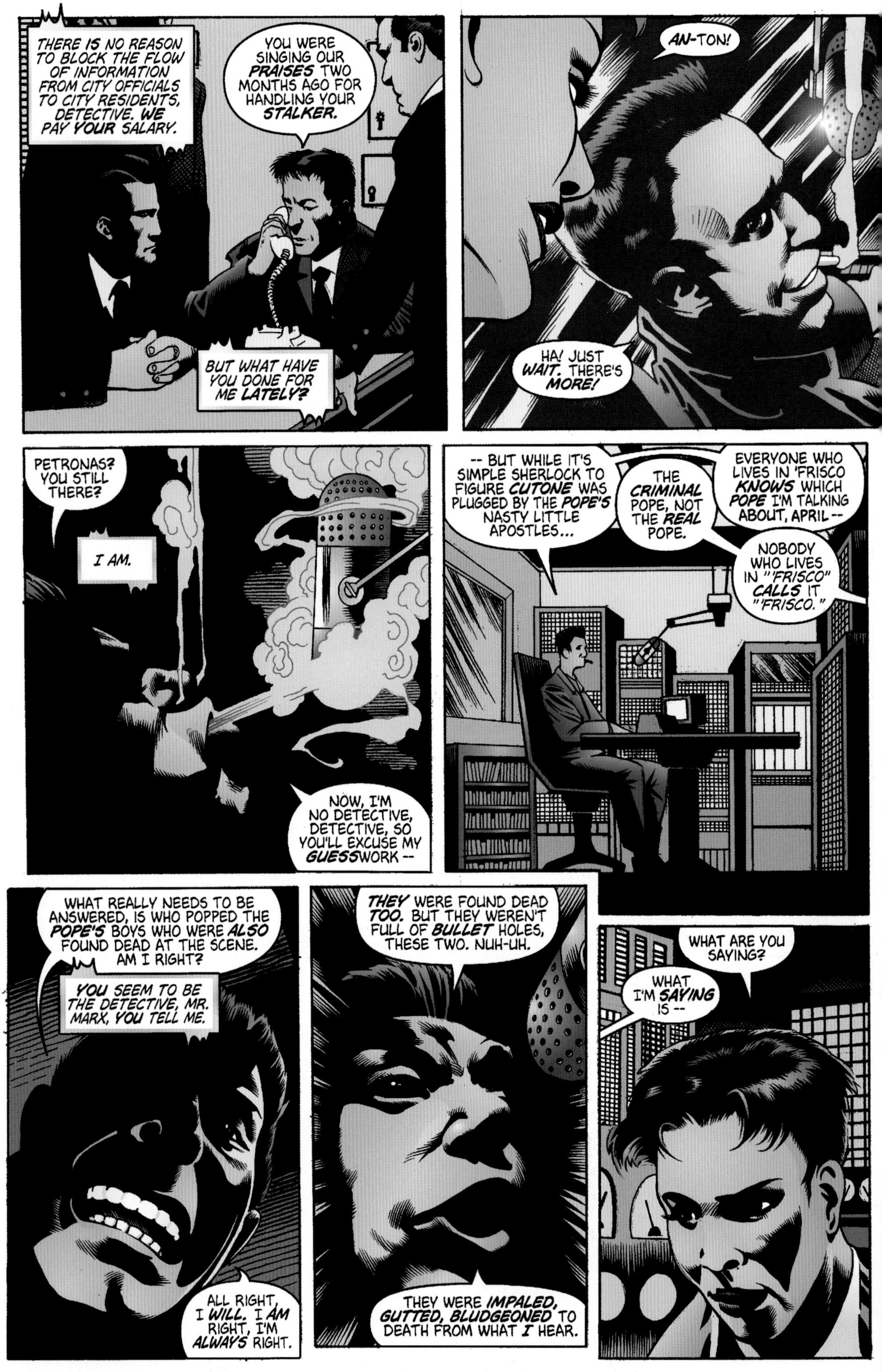
THERE IS NO REASON TO BLOCK THE FLOW OF INFORMATION FROM CITY OFFICIALS TO CITY RESIDENTS, DETECTIVE. WE PAY YOUR SALARY.
YOU WERE SINGING OUR PRAISES TWO MONTHS AGO FOR HANDLING YOUR STALKER.
BUT WHAT HAVE YOU DONE FOR ME LATELY?
AN-TON!
HA! JUST WAIT. THERE'S MORE!
PETRONAS? YOU STILL THERE?
I AM.
NOW, I'M NO DETECTIVE, DETECTIVE, SO YOU'LL EXCUSE MY GUESSWORK --
-- BUT WHILE IT'S SIMPLE SHERLOCK TO FIGURE CUTONE WAS PLUGGED BY THE POPE'S NASTY LITTLE APOSTLES...
THE CRIMINAL POPE, NOT THE REAL POPE.
EVERYONE WHO LIVES IN 'FRISCO KNOWS WHICH POPE I'M TALKING ABOUT, APRIL --
NOBODY WHO LIVES IN "FRISCO" CALLS IT "FRISCO."
WHAT REALLY NEEDS TO BE ANSWERED, IS WHO POPPED THE POPE'S BOYS WHO WERE ALSO FOUND DEAD AT THE SCENE. AM I RIGHT?
YOU SEEM TO BE THE DETECTIVE, MR. MARX, YOU TELL ME.
ALL RIGHT, I WILL. I AM RIGHT, I'M ALWAYS RIGHT.
THEY WERE FOUND DEAD TOO. BUT THEY WEREN'T FULL OF BULLET HOLES, THESE TWO. NUH-UH.
THEY WERE IMPALED, GUTTED, BLUDGEONED TO DEATH FROM WHAT I HEAR.
WHAT ARE YOU SAYING?
WHAT I'M SAYING IS --

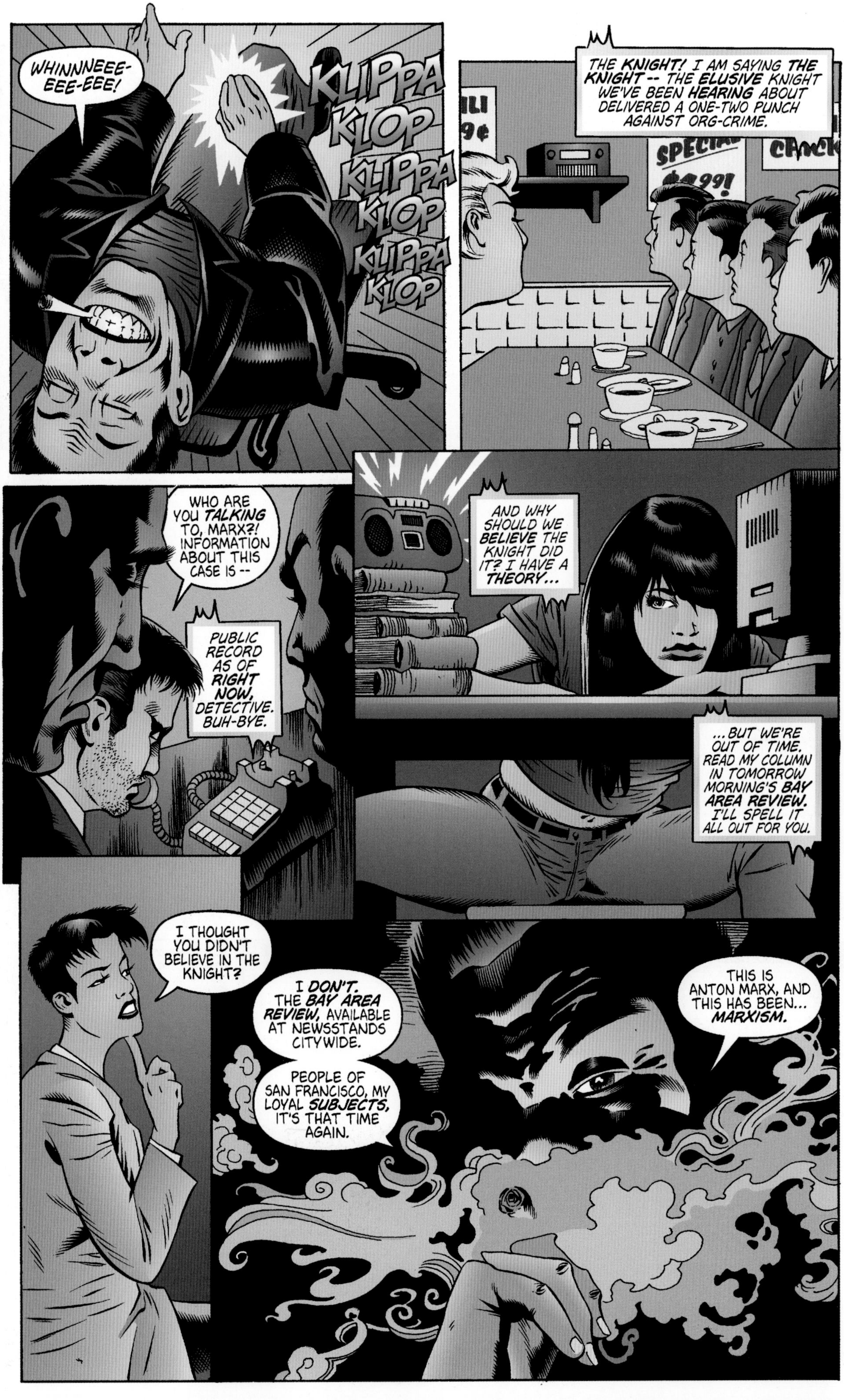

WHINNNEEE-EEE-EEE!
KLIPPA KLOP KLIPPA KLOP KLIPPA KLOP
THE KNIGHT! I AM SAYING THE KNIGHT -- THE ELUSIVE KNIGHT WE'VE BEEN HEARING ABOUT DELIVERED A ONE-TWO PUNCH AGAINST ORG-CRIME.
SPECIAL
WHO ARE YOU TALKING TO, MARX?! INFORMATION ABOUT THIS CASE IS --
PUBLIC RECORD AS OF RIGHT NOW, DETECTIVE. BUH-BYE.
AND WHY SHOULD WE BELIEVE THE KNIGHT DID IT? I HAVE A THEORY...
...BUT WE'RE OUT OF TIME. READ MY COLUMN IN TOMORROW MORNING'S BAY AREA REVIEW. I'LL SPELL IT ALL OUT FOR YOU.
I THOUGHT YOU DIDN'T BELIEVE IN THE KNIGHT?
I DON'T. THE BAY AREA REVIEW, AVAILABLE AT NEWSSTANDS CITYWIDE.
PEOPLE OF SAN FRANCISCO, MY LOYAL SUBJECTS, IT'S THAT TIME AGAIN.
THIS IS ANTON MARX, AND THIS HAS BEEN... MARXISM.

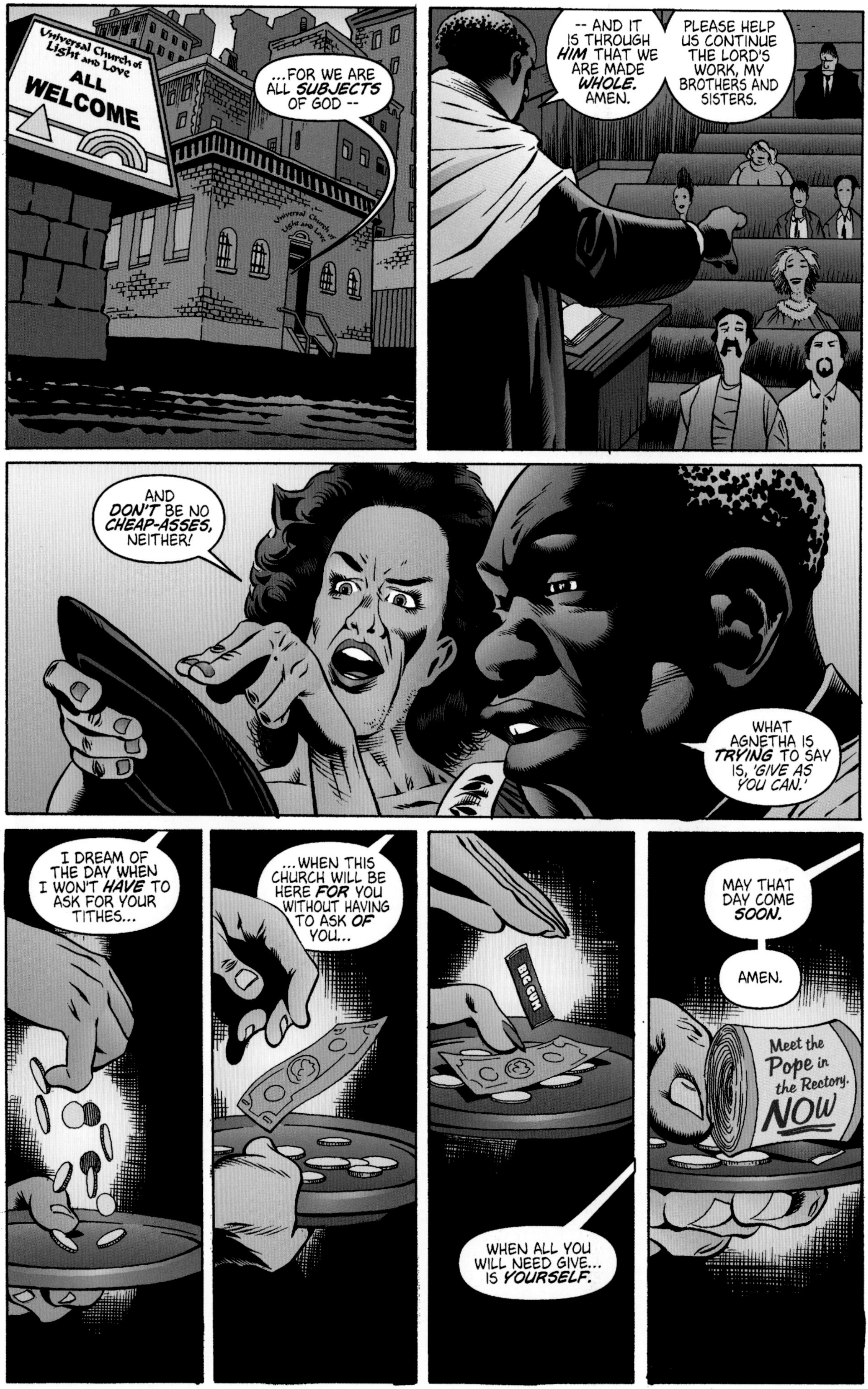
Universal Church of Light and Love
ALL WELCOME
...FOR WE ARE ALL SUBJECTS OF GOD --
Universal Church of Light and Love
-- AND IT IS THROUGH HIM THAT WE ARE MADE WHOLE. AMEN.
PLEASE HELP US CONTINUE THE LORD'S WORK, MY BROTHERS AND SISTERS.
AND DON'T BE NO CHEAP-ASSES, NEITHER!
WHAT AGNETHA IS TRYING TO SAY IS, 'GIVE AS YOU CAN.'
I DREAM OF THE DAY WHEN I WON'T HAVE TO ASK FOR YOUR TITHES...
...WHEN THIS CHURCH WILL BE HERE FOR YOU WITHOUT HAVING TO ASK OF YOU...
BIG GUM
WHEN ALL YOU WILL NEED GIVE... IS YOURSELF.
MAY THAT DAY COME SOON.
AMEN.
Meet the Pope in the Rectory. NOW

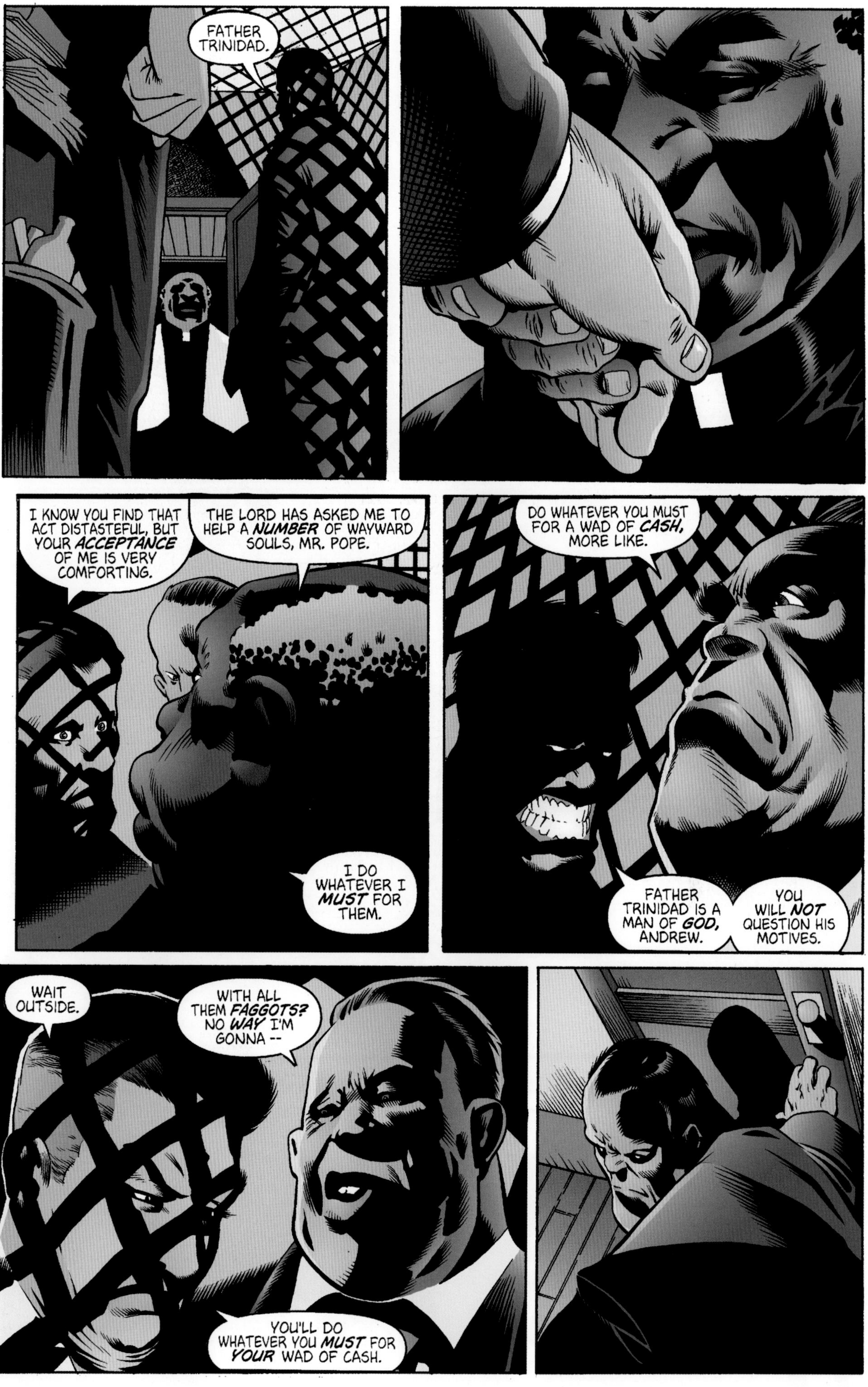
FATHER TRINIDAD.
I KNOW YOU FIND THAT ACT DISTASTEFUL, BUT YOUR ACCEPTANCE OF ME IS VERY COMFORTING.
THE LORD HAS ASKED ME TO HELP A NUMBER OF WAYWARD SOULS, MR. POPE.
I DO WHATEVER I MUST FOR THEM.
DO WHATEVER YOU MUST FOR A WAD OF CASH, MORE LIKE.
FATHER TRINIDAD IS A MAN OF GOD, ANDREW.
YOU WILL NOT QUESTION HIS MOTIVES.
WAIT OUTSIDE.
WITH ALL THEM FAGGOTS? NO WAY I'M GONNA --
YOU'LL DO WHATEVER YOU MUST FOR YOUR WAD OF CASH.

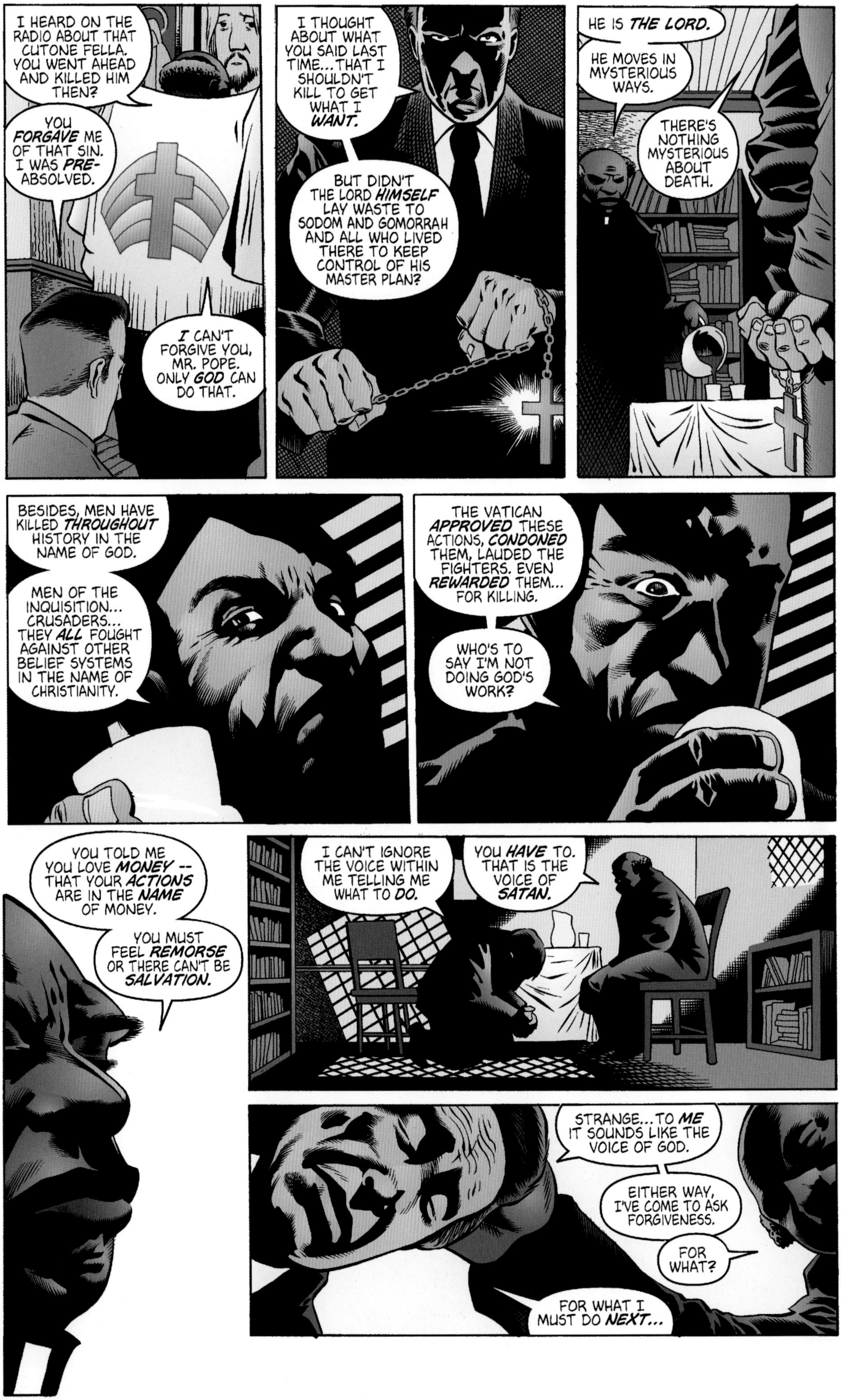
I HEARD ON THE RADIO ABOUT THAT CUTONE FELLA. YOU WENT AHEAD AND KILLED HIM THEN?
YOU FORGAVE ME OF THAT SIN. I WAS PRE-ABSOLVED.
I CAN'T FORGIVE YOU, MR. POPE. ONLY GOD CAN DO THAT.
I THOUGHT ABOUT WHAT YOU SAID LAST TIME...THAT I SHOULDN'T KILL TO GET WHAT I WANT.
BUT DIDN'T THE LORD HIMSELF LAY WASTE TO SODOM AND GOMORRAH AND ALL WHO LIVED THERE TO KEEP CONTROL OF HIS MASTER PLAN?
HE IS THE LORD.
HE MOVES IN MYSTERIOUS WAYS.
THERE'S NOTHING MYSTERIOUS ABOUT DEATH.
BESIDES, MEN HAVE KILLED THROUGHOUT HISTORY IN THE NAME OF GOD.
MEN OF THE INQUISITION... CRUSADERS... THEY ALL FOUGHT AGAINST OTHER BELIEF SYSTEMS IN THE NAME OF CHRISTIANITY.
THE VATICAN APPROVED THESE ACTIONS, CONDONED THEM, LAUDED THE FIGHTERS. EVEN REWARDED THEM... FOR KILLING.
WHO'S TO SAY I'M NOT DOING GOD'S WORK?
YOU TOLD ME YOU LOVE MONEY -- THAT YOUR ACTIONS ARE IN THE NAME OF MONEY.
YOU MUST FEEL REMORSE OR THERE CAN'T BE SALVATION.
I CAN'T IGNORE THE VOICE WITHIN ME TELLING ME WHAT TO DO.
YOU HAVE TO. THAT IS THE VOICE OF SATAN.
STRANGE...TO ME IT SOUNDS LIKE THE VOICE OF GOD.
EITHER WAY, I'VE COME TO ASK FORGIVENESS.
FOR WHAT?
FOR WHAT I MUST DO NEXT...

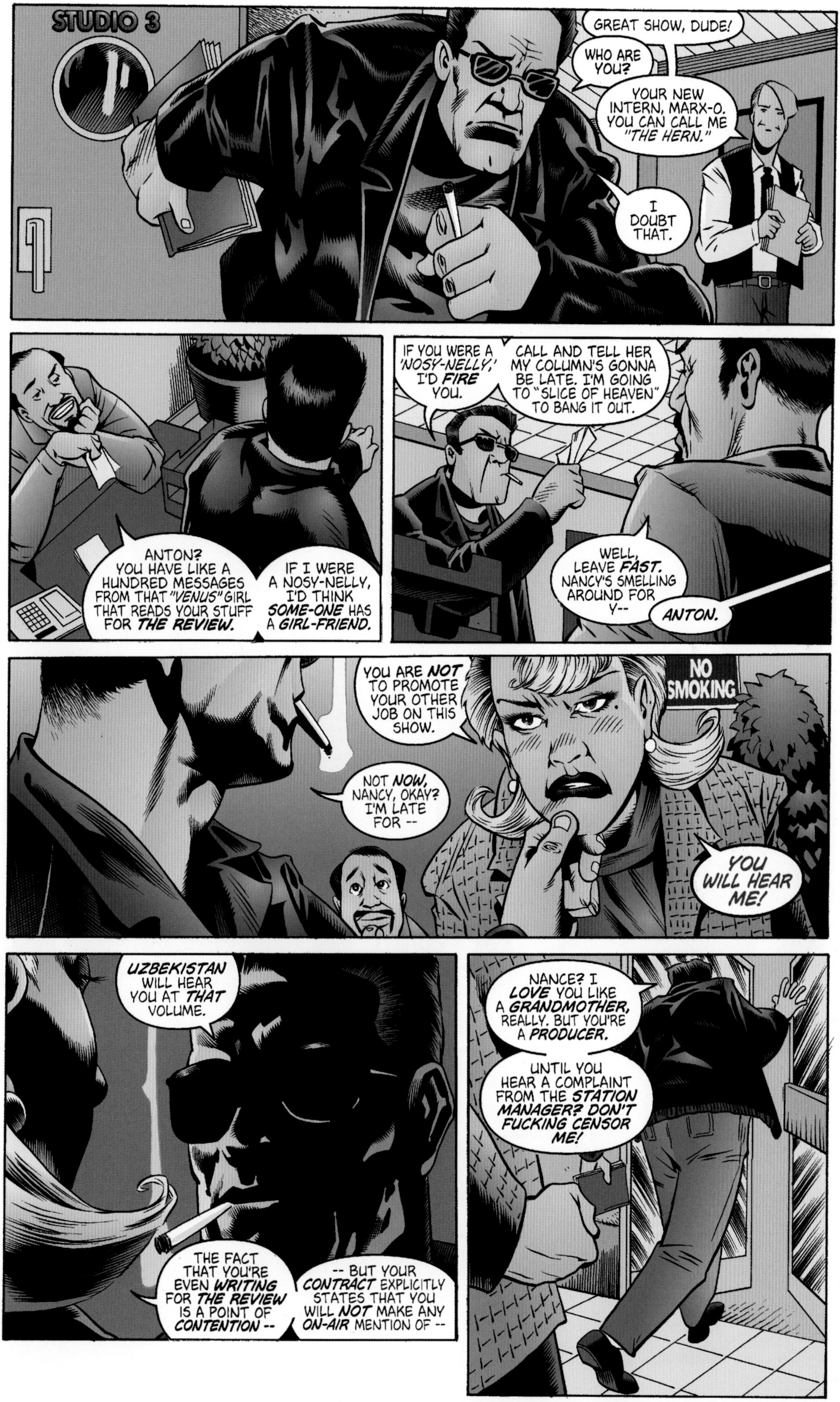
STUDIO 3
GREAT SHOW, DUDE!
WHO ARE YOU?
YOUR NEW INTERN, MARX-O. YOU CAN CALL ME "THE HERN."
I DOUBT THAT.
ANTON? YOU HAVE LIKE A HUNDRED MESSAGES FROM THAT "VENUS" GIRL THAT READS YOUR STUFF FOR THE REVIEW.
IF I WERE A NOSY-NELLY, I'D THINK SOME-ONE HAS A GIRL-FRIEND.
IF YOU WERE A 'NOSY-NELLY,' I'D FIRE YOU.
CALL AND TELL HER MY COLUMN'S GONNA BE LATE. I'M GOING TO "SLICE OF HEAVEN" TO BANG IT OUT.
WELL, LEAVE FAST. NANCY'S SMELLING AROUND FOR Y--
ANTON.
YOU ARE NOT TO PROMOTE YOUR OTHER JOB ON THIS SHOW.
NO SMOKING
NOT NOW, NANCY, OKAY? I'M LATE FOR --
YOU WILL HEAR ME!
UZBEKISTAN WILL HEAR YOU AT THAT VOLUME.
THE FACT THAT YOU'RE EVEN WRITING FOR THE REVIEW IS A POINT OF CONTENTION --
-- BUT YOUR CONTRACT EXPLICITLY STATES THAT YOU WILL NOT MAKE ANY ON-AIR MENTION OF --
NANCE? I LOVE YOU LIKE A GRANDMOTHER, REALLY. BUT YOU'RE A PRODUCER.
UNTIL YOU HEAR A COMPLAINT FROM THE STATION MANAGER? DON'T FUCKING CENSOR ME!

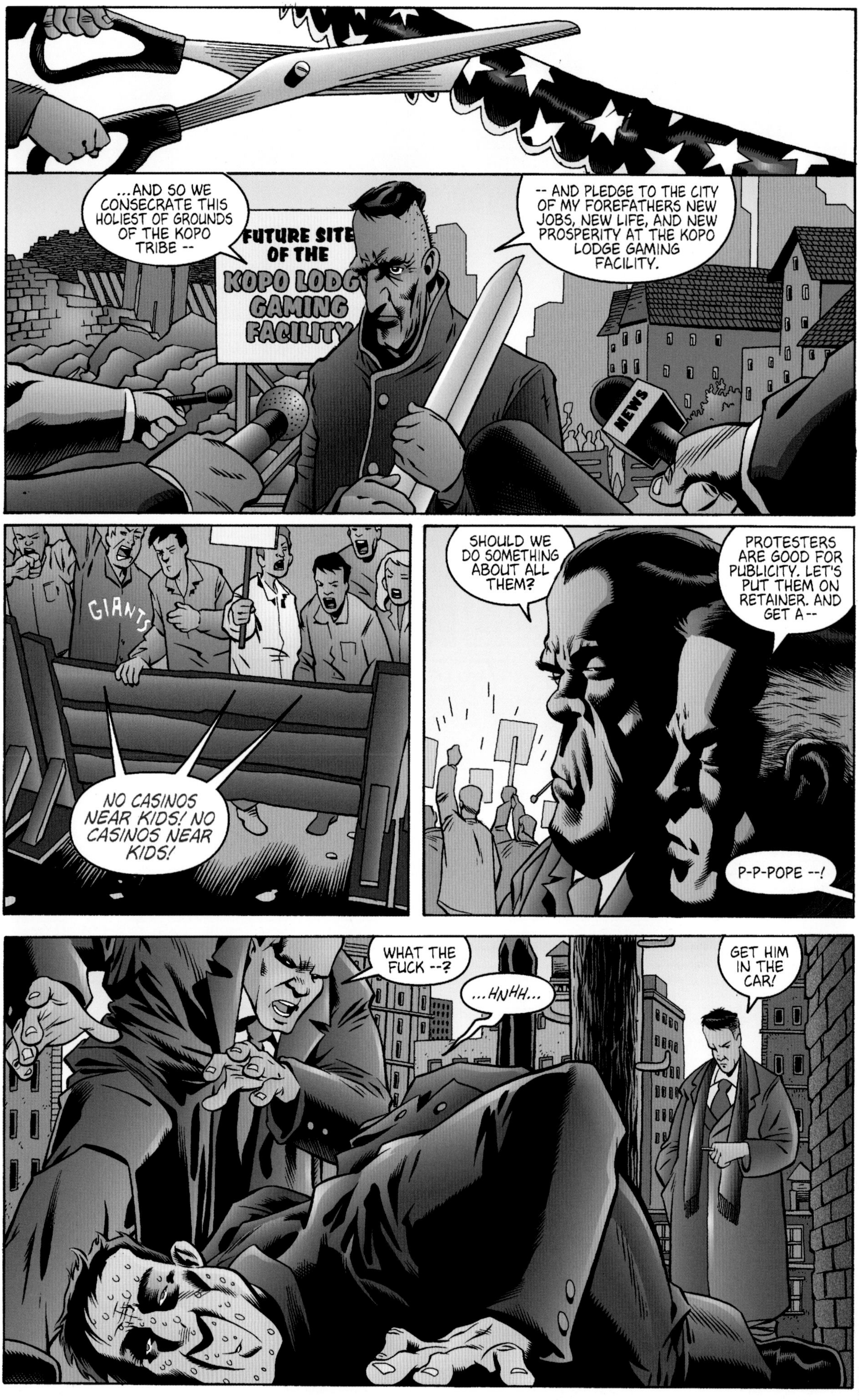

...AND SO WE CONSECRATE THIS HOLIEST OF GROUNDS OF THE KOPO TRIBE --
FUTURE SITE OF THE KOPO LODGE GAMING FACILITY
-- AND PLEDGE TO THE CITY OF MY FOREFATHERS NEW JOBS, NEW LIFE, AND NEW PROSPERITY AT THE KOPO LODGE GAMING FACILITY.
NEWS
GIANTS
NO CASINOS NEAR KIDS! NO CASINOS NEAR KIDS!
SHOULD WE DO SOMETHING ABOUT ALL THEM?
PROTESTERS ARE GOOD FOR PUBLICITY. LET'S PUT THEM ON RETAINER. AND GET A --
P-P-POPE --!
WHAT THE FUCK --?
...HNHH...
GET HIM IN THE CAR!

SLICE OF HEAVEN
COFFEE
SLICE HEA

"SO, THE KNIGHT -- WHAT DO WE KNOW IN THE END?"

"NOTHING FOR CERTAIN. BUT IN A CITY FILLED WITH FALSE FACES AND SECRET AGENDAS..."

"...MARX IS BETTING ON *FRAUD.*"

"IF YOU WANT TO KNOW WHAT'S BEHIND THE FACEPLATE OF THE KNIGHT, LOOK FOR A HORSE IN THE STABLES OF THE POPE."

SO? WHAT DO YOU THINK?

I THINK YOU SHOULDN'T READ THESE THINGS TO US IF YOU REALLY *DON'T* CARE WHAT OUR OPINIONS ARE.

I *DO* CARE, LYSSA. *TALK.*

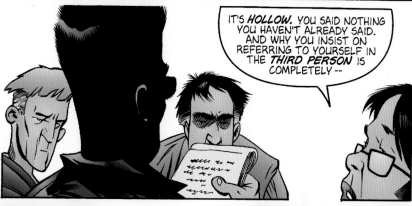

IT'S *HOLLOW.* YOU SAID NOTHING YOU HAVEN'T ALREADY SAID. AND WHY YOU INSIST ON REFERRING TO YOURSELF IN THE *THIRD PERSON* IS COMPLETELY --

YOU WRITE SOFT-CORE PORN FOR HORNY HOUSEWIVES. WHO *CARES* WHAT YOU THINK?

BRAK, WHAT ABOUT YOU? LIKE IT?

LOVED IT.

≥HAKK≤
HOFF
KOFF

A STONER WITH A FAILED FILM CAREER I *DON'T* NEED.

I NEED A CLEAR, LEVEL-HEADED REVIEW. I NEED *MAINSTREAM* AMERICA. I NEED --

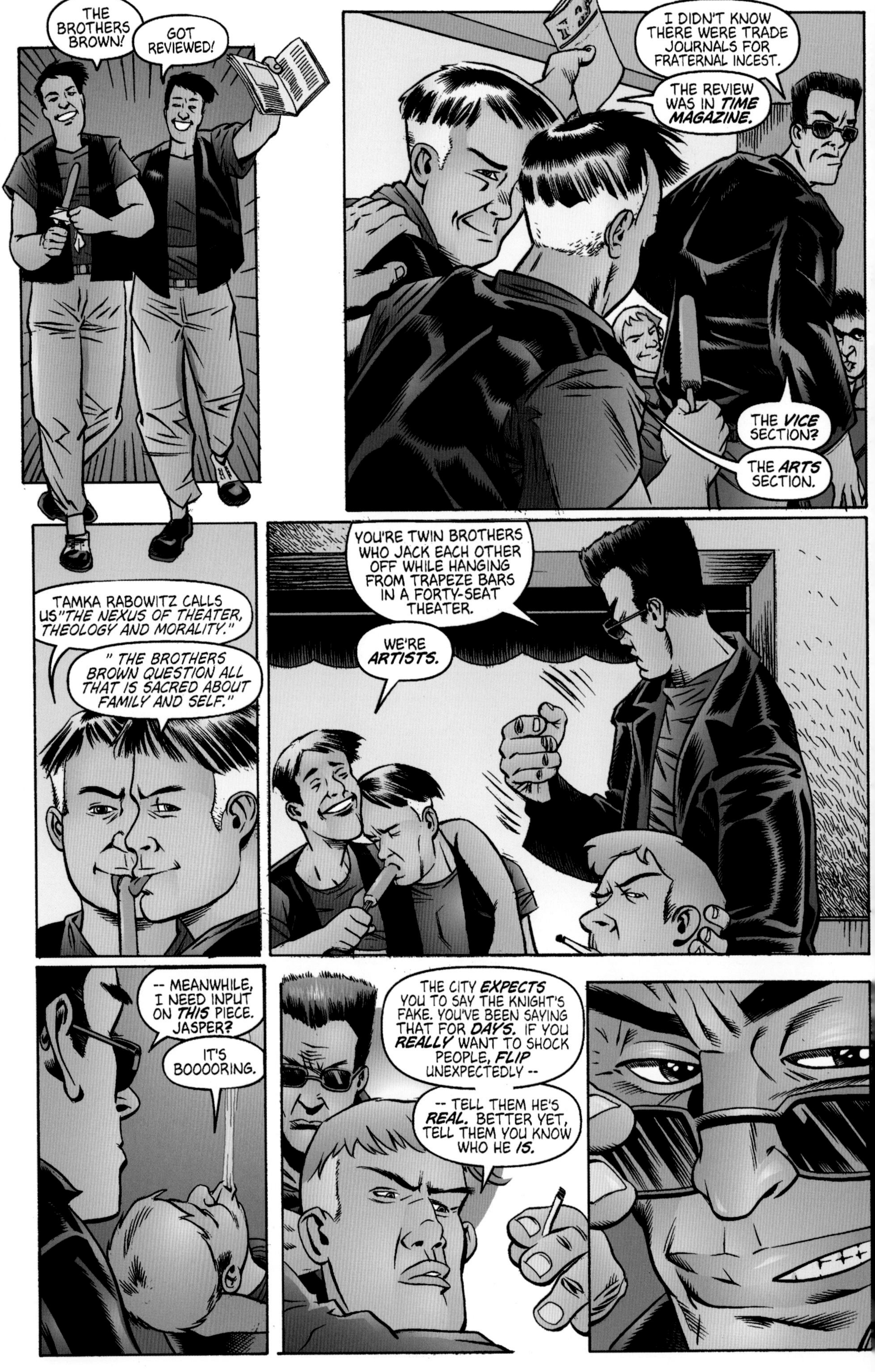
THE BROTHERS BROWN!
GOT REVIEWED!
I DIDN'T KNOW THERE WERE TRADE JOURNALS FOR FRATERNAL INCEST.
THE REVIEW WAS IN *TIME MAGAZINE.*
THE *VICE* SECTION?
THE *ARTS* SECTION.
TAMKA RABOWITZ CALLS US *"THE NEXUS OF THEATER, THEOLOGY AND MORALITY."*
" THE BROTHERS BROWN QUESTION ALL THAT IS SACRED ABOUT FAMILY AND SELF."
YOU'RE TWIN BROTHERS WHO JACK EACH OTHER OFF WHILE HANGING FROM TRAPEZE BARS IN A FORTY-SEAT THEATER.
WE'RE *ARTISTS.*
-- MEANWHILE, I NEED INPUT ON *THIS* PIECE. JASPER?
IT'S BOOOORING.
THE CITY *EXPECTS* YOU TO SAY THE KNIGHT'S FAKE. YOU'VE BEEN SAYING THAT FOR *DAYS.* IF YOU *REALLY* WANT TO SHOCK PEOPLE, *FLIP* UNEXPECTEDLY --
-- TELL THEM HE'S *REAL.* BETTER YET, TELL THEM YOU KNOW WHO HE *IS.*

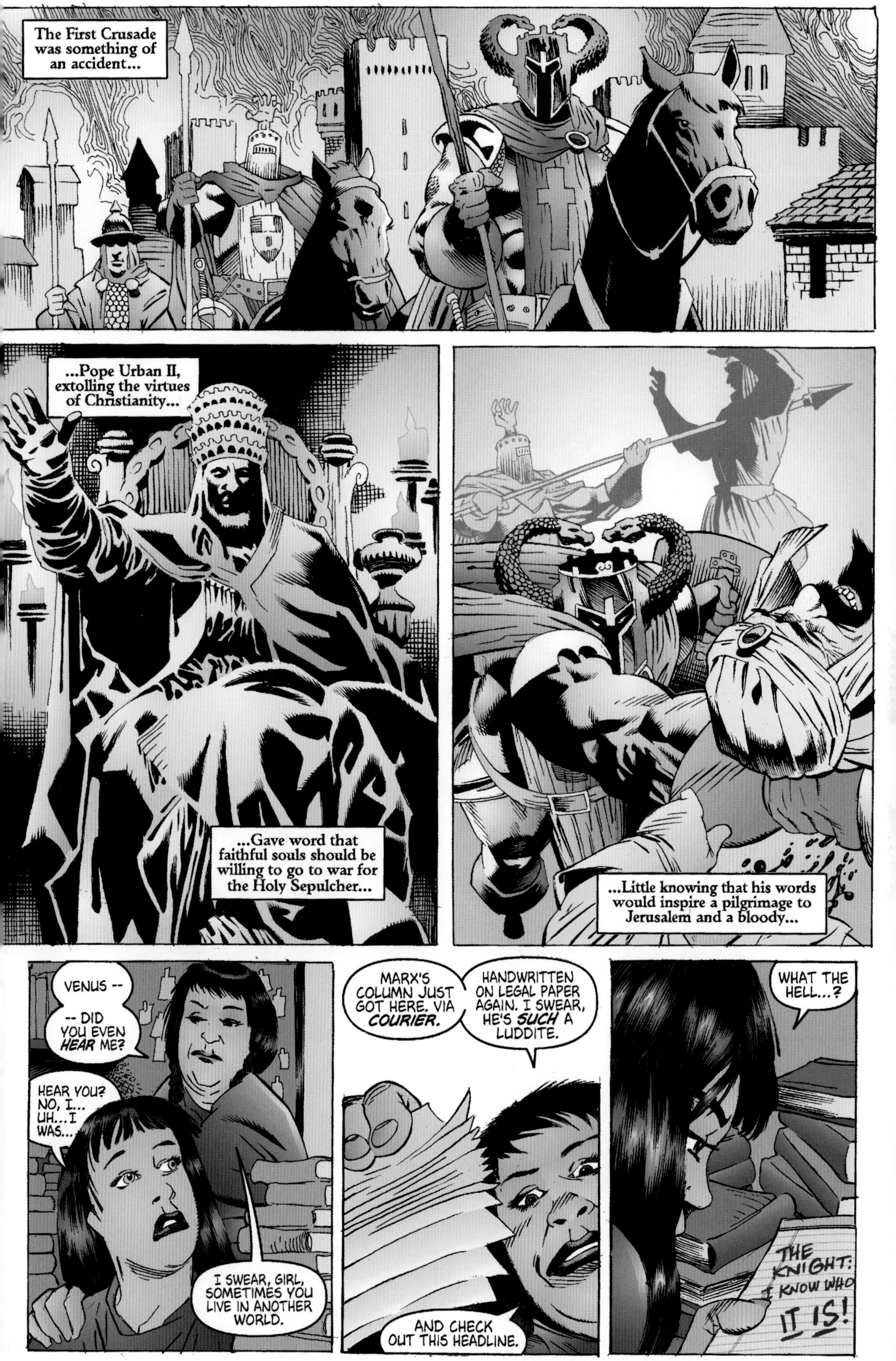
The First Crusade was something of an accident...
...Pope Urban II, extolling the virtues of Christianity...
...Gave word that faithful souls should be willing to go to war for the Holy Sepulcher...
...Little knowing that his words would inspire a pilgrimage to Jerusalem and a bloody...
VENUS --
-- DID YOU EVEN HEAR ME?
HEAR YOU? NO, I... UH... I WAS...
I SWEAR, GIRL, SOMETIMES YOU LIVE IN ANOTHER WORLD.
MARX'S COLUMN JUST GOT HERE. VIA COURIER.
HANDWRITTEN ON LEGAL PAPER AGAIN. I SWEAR, HE'S SUCH A LUDDITE.
AND CHECK OUT THIS HEADLINE.
WHAT THE HELL...?
THE KNIGHT: I KNOW WHO IT IS!

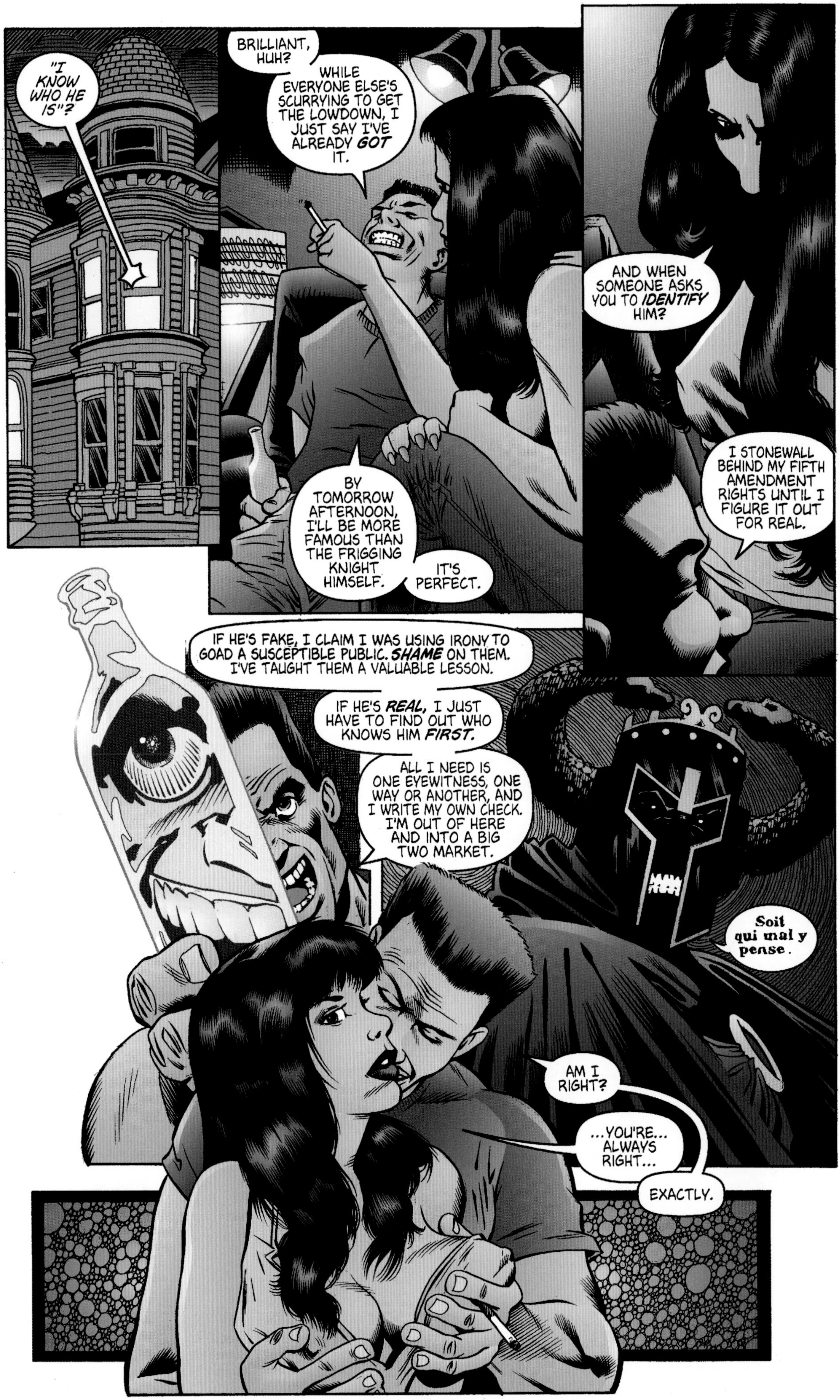
"I KNOW WHO HE IS"?
BRILLIANT, HUH?
WHILE EVERYONE ELSE'S SCURRYING TO GET THE LOWDOWN, I JUST SAY I'VE ALREADY GOT IT.
BY TOMORROW AFTERNOON, I'LL BE MORE FAMOUS THAN THE FRIGGING KNIGHT HIMSELF.
IT'S PERFECT.
AND WHEN SOMEONE ASKS YOU TO IDENTIFY HIM?
I STONEWALL BEHIND MY FIFTH AMENDMENT RIGHTS UNTIL I FIGURE IT OUT FOR REAL.
IF HE'S FAKE, I CLAIM I WAS USING IRONY TO GOAD A SUSCEPTIBLE PUBLIC. SHAME ON THEM. I'VE TAUGHT THEM A VALUABLE LESSON.
IF HE'S REAL, I JUST HAVE TO FIND OUT WHO KNOWS HIM FIRST.
ALL I NEED IS ONE EYEWITNESS, ONE WAY OR ANOTHER, AND I WRITE MY OWN CHECK. I'M OUT OF HERE AND INTO A BIG TWO MARKET.
Soit qui mal y pense.
AM I RIGHT?
...YOU'RE... ALWAYS RIGHT...
EXACTLY.

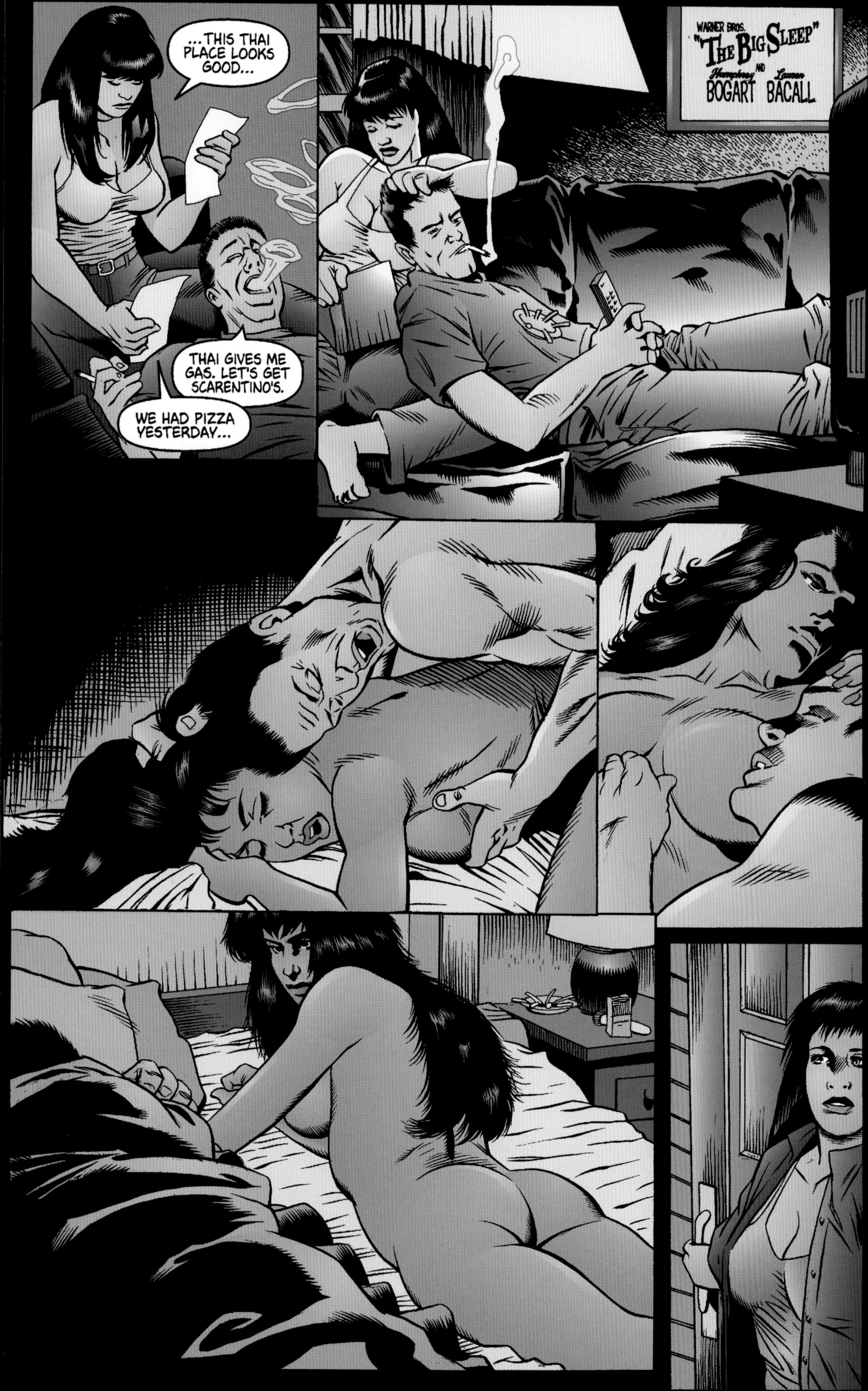
...THIS THAI PLACE LOOKS GOOD...
THAI GIVES ME GAS. LET'S GET SCARENTINO'S.
WE HAD PIZZA YESTERDAY...
WARNER BROS.
"THE BIG SLEEP"
Humphrey AND Lauren
BOGART BACALL

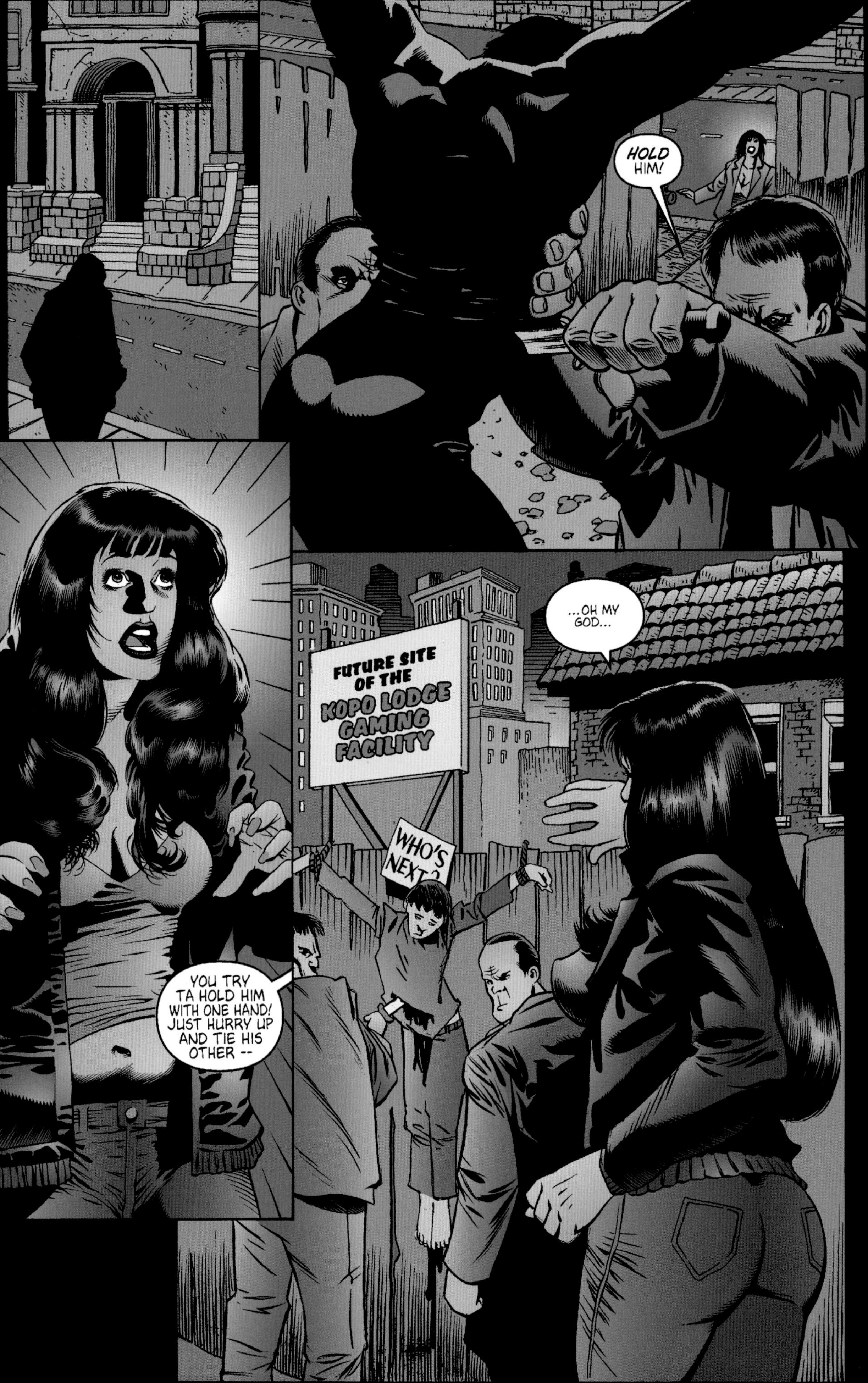
HOLD HIM!
YOU TRY TA HOLD HIM WITH ONE HAND! JUST HURRY UP AND TIE HIS OTHER --
...OH MY GOD...
FUTURE SITE OF THE KOPO LODGE GAMING FACILITY
WHO'S NEXT?

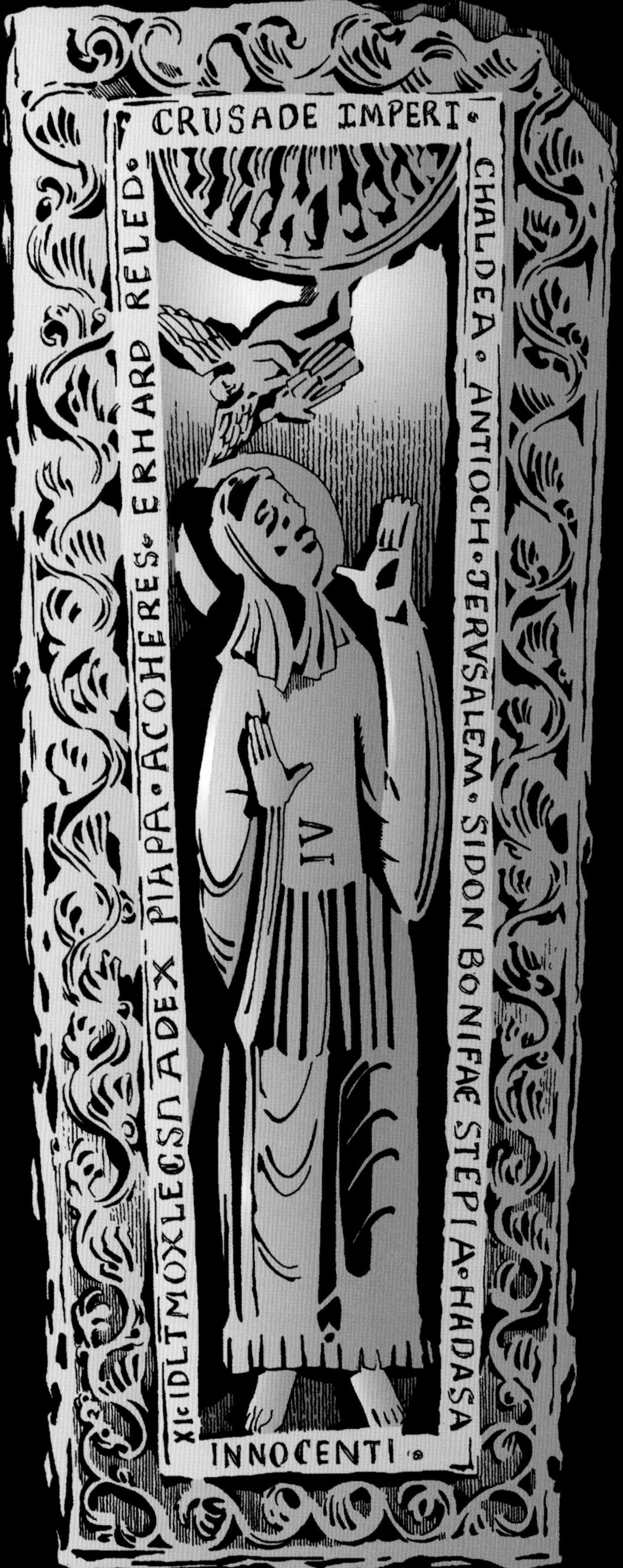
CRUSADE IMPERI
CHALDEA • ANTIOCH • JERUSALEM • SIDON BONIFAE STEPIA • HADASA
INNOCENTI
XI•IDLTMOXLECSN ADEX PIAPA • ACOHERES • ERHARD RELED

"Cruelty, like every
other vice, requires
no motive outside itself;
It only requires
opportunity."

--George Eliot
(aka) Mary Ann Evans

"BRING THEM OUT!"

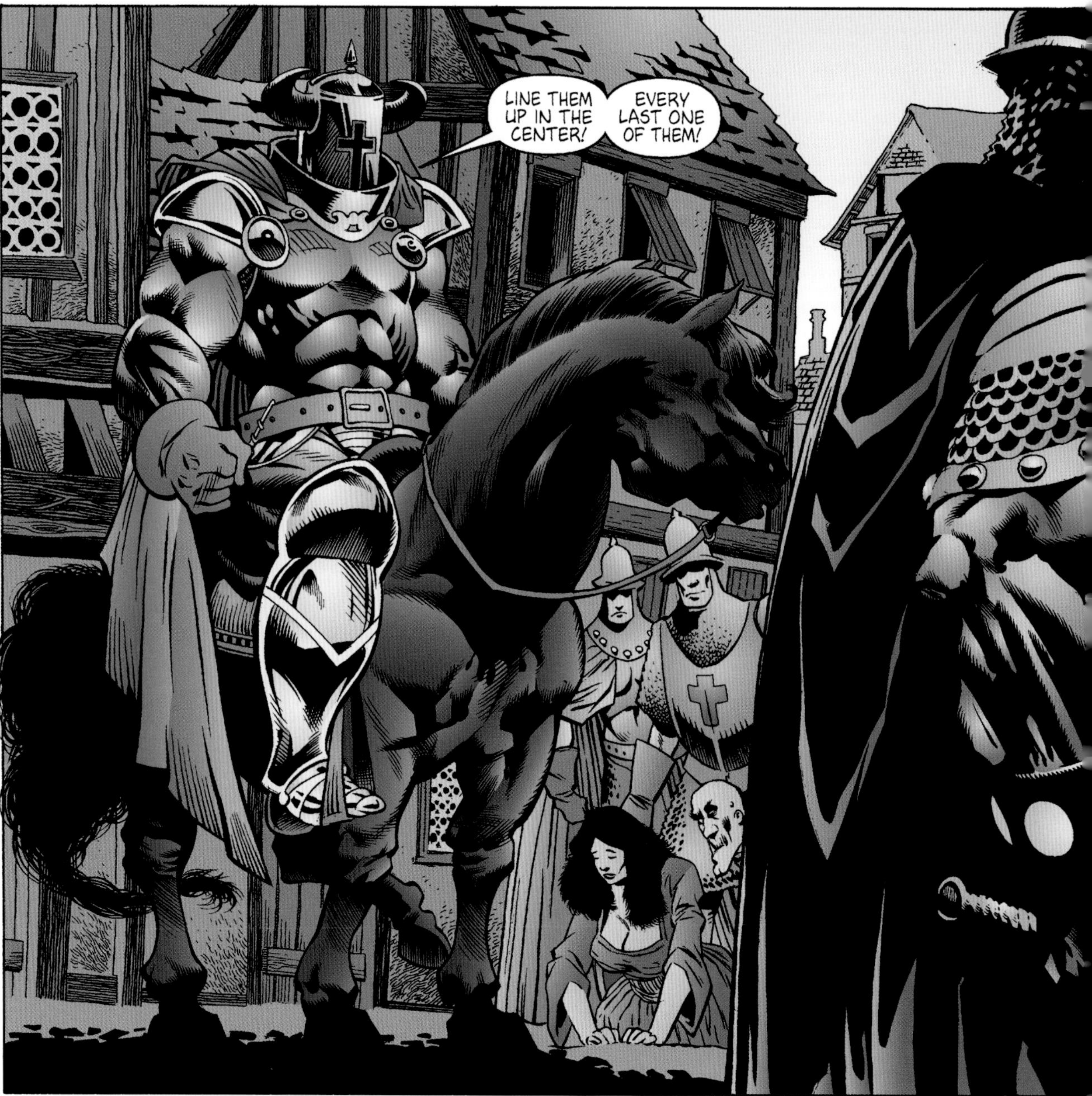
LINE THEM UP IN THE CENTER!
EVERY LAST ONE OF THEM!

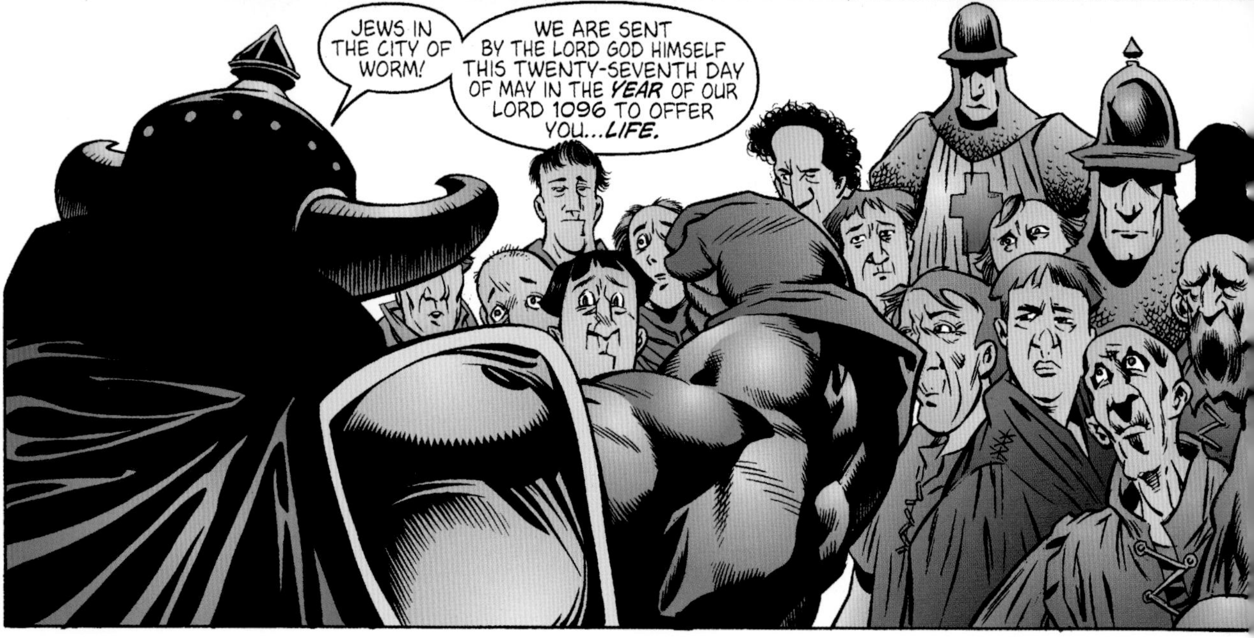
JEWS IN THE CITY OF WORM!
WE ARE SENT BY THE LORD GOD HIMSELF THIS TWENTY-SEVENTH DAY OF MAY IN THE YEAR OF OUR LORD 1096 TO OFFER YOU...LIFE.

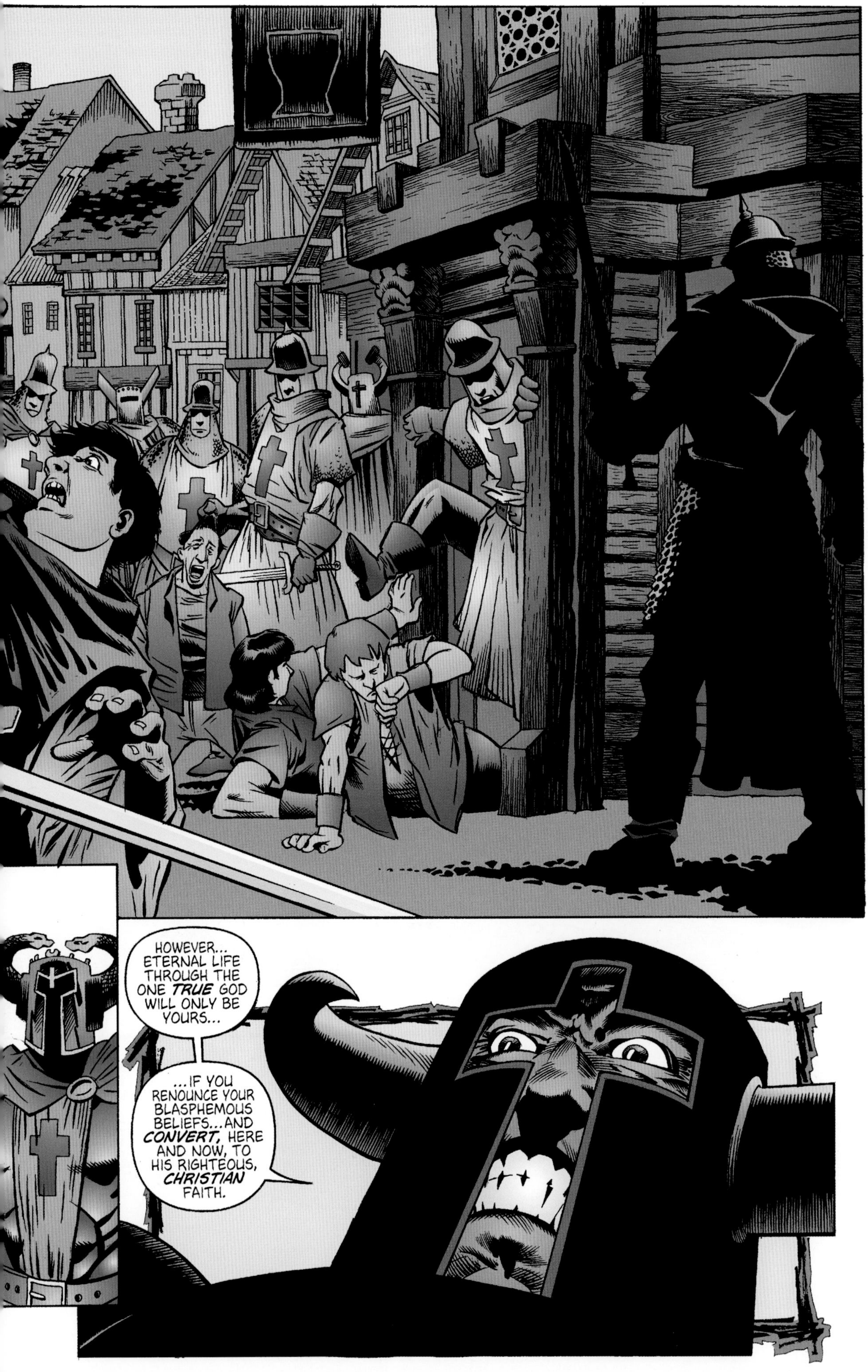
HOWEVER... ETERNAL LIFE THROUGH THE ONE TRUE GOD WILL ONLY BE YOURS...
...IF YOU RENOUNCE YOUR BLASPHEMOUS BELIEFS...AND CONVERT, HERE AND NOW, TO HIS RIGHTEOUS, CHRISTIAN FAITH.

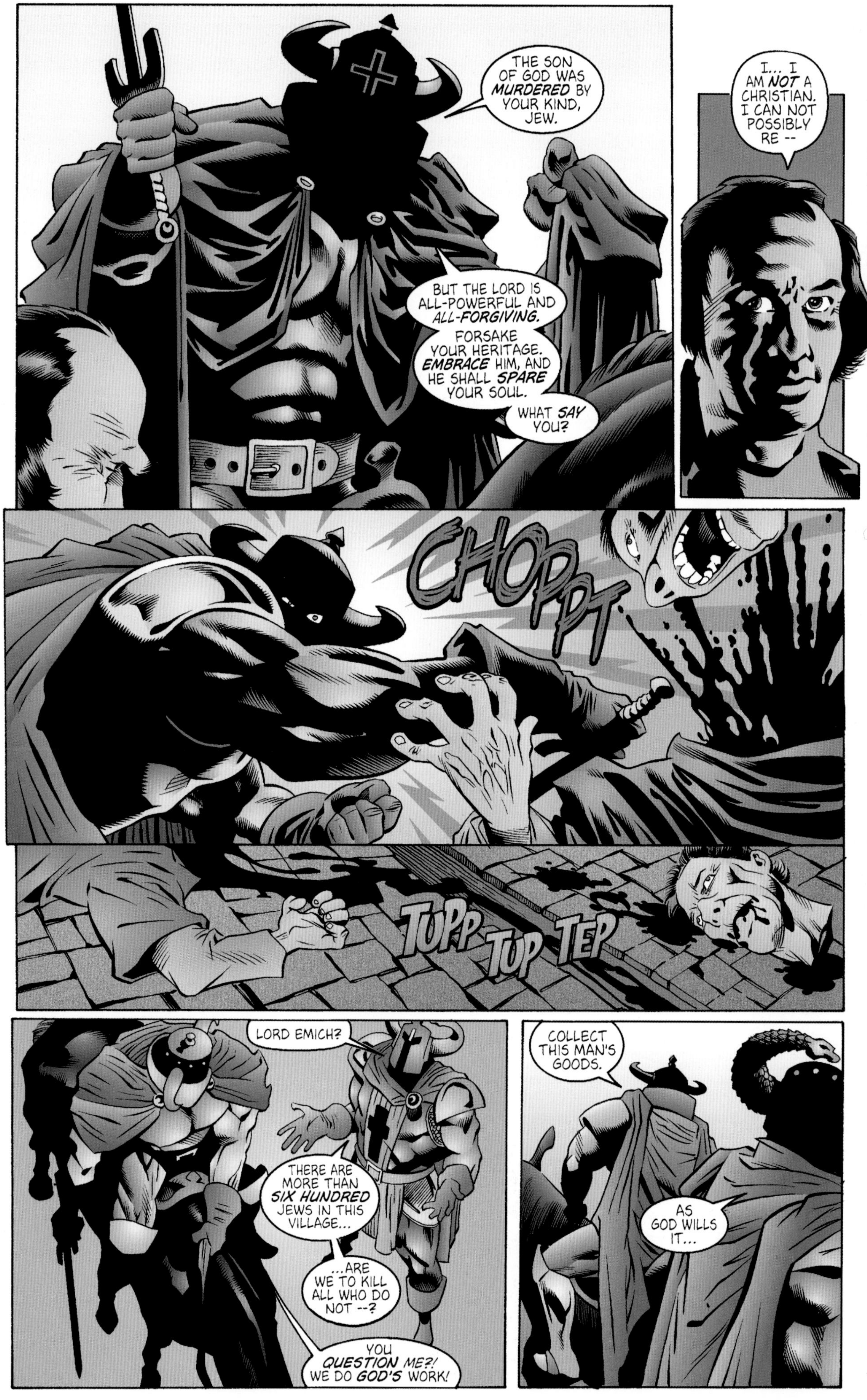
THE SON OF GOD WAS *MURDERED* BY YOUR KIND, JEW.
BUT THE LORD IS ALL-POWERFUL AND *ALL-FORGIVING.*
FORSAKE YOUR HERITAGE. *EMBRACE* HIM, AND HE SHALL *SPARE* YOUR SOUL.
WHAT *SAY* YOU?
I... I AM *NOT* A CHRISTIAN. I CAN NOT POSSIBLY RE --
CHOPPT
TUPP TUP TEP
LORD EMICH?
THERE ARE MORE THAN *SIX HUNDRED* JEWS IN THIS VILLAGE...
...ARE WE TO KILL ALL WHO DO NOT --?
YOU *QUESTION ME?!* WE DO *GOD'S* WORK!
COLLECT THIS MAN'S GOODS.
AS GOD WILLS IT...

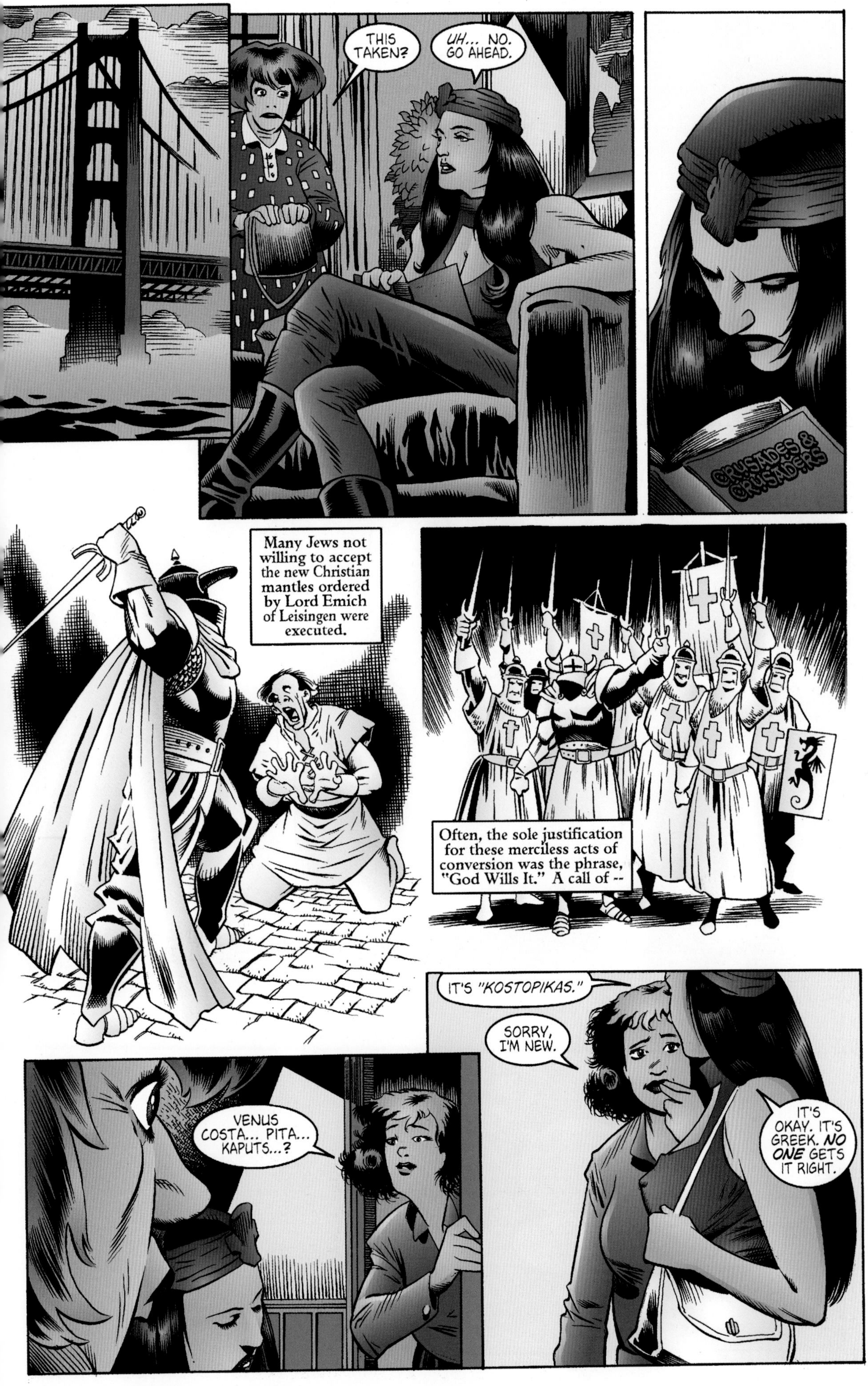
THIS TAKEN?
UH... NO. GO AHEAD.
CRUSADES & CRUSADERS
Many Jews not willing to accept the new Christian mantles ordered by Lord Emich of Leisingen were executed.
Often, the sole justification for these merciless acts of conversion was the phrase, "God Wills It." A call of --
IT'S "KOSTOPIKAS."
SORRY, I'M NEW.
IT'S OKAY. IT'S GREEK. NO ONE GETS IT RIGHT.
VENUS COSTA... PITA... KAPUTS...?

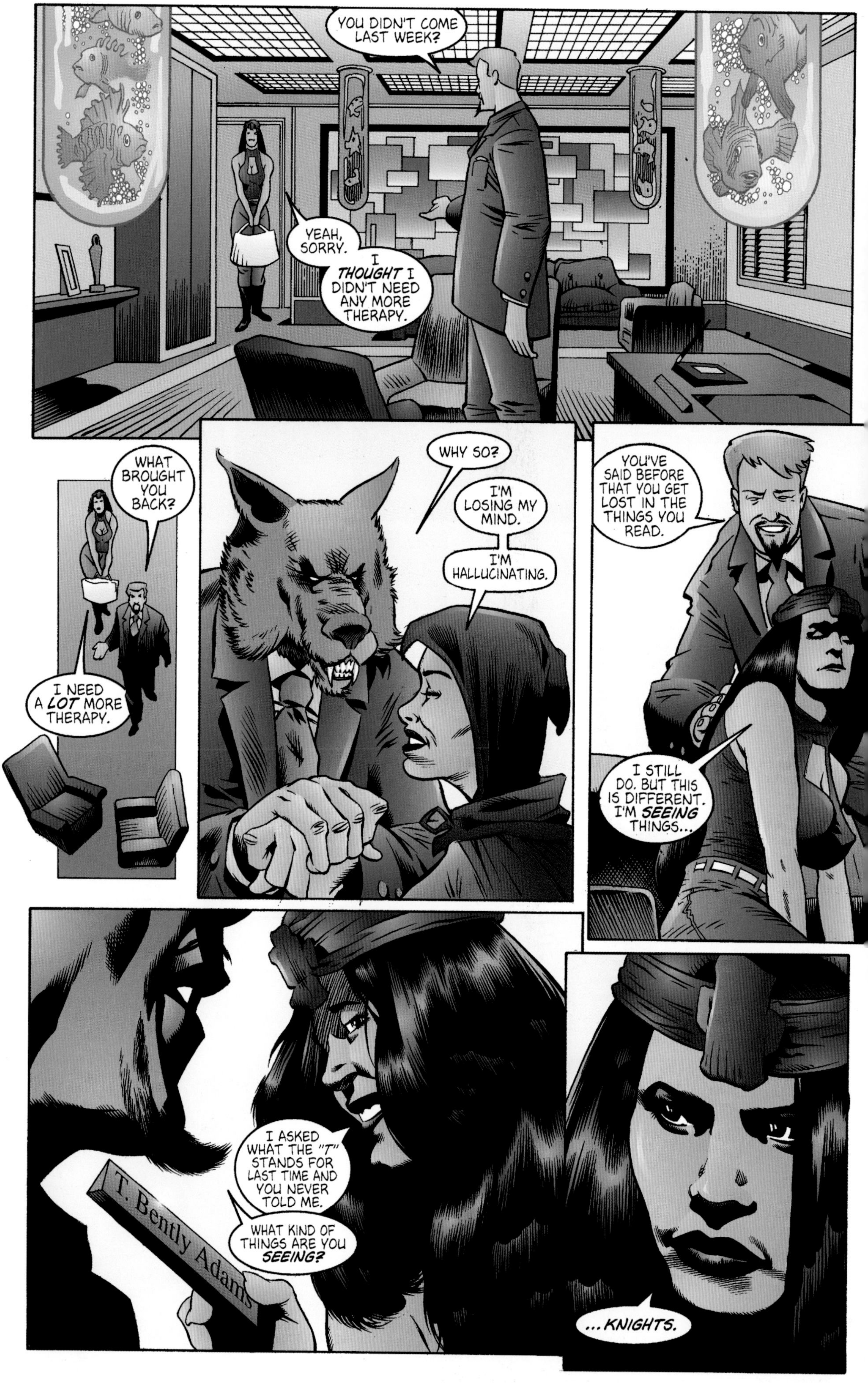
YOU DIDN'T COME LAST WEEK?
YEAH, SORRY.
I THOUGHT I DIDN'T NEED ANY MORE THERAPY.
WHAT BROUGHT YOU BACK?
I NEED A LOT MORE THERAPY.
WHY SO?
I'M LOSING MY MIND.
I'M HALLUCINATING.
YOU'VE SAID BEFORE THAT YOU GET LOST IN THE THINGS YOU READ.
I STILL DO. BUT THIS IS DIFFERENT. I'M SEEING THINGS...
T. Bently Adams
I ASKED WHAT THE "T" STANDS FOR LAST TIME AND YOU NEVER TOLD ME.
WHAT KIND OF THINGS ARE YOU SEEING?
...KNIGHTS.

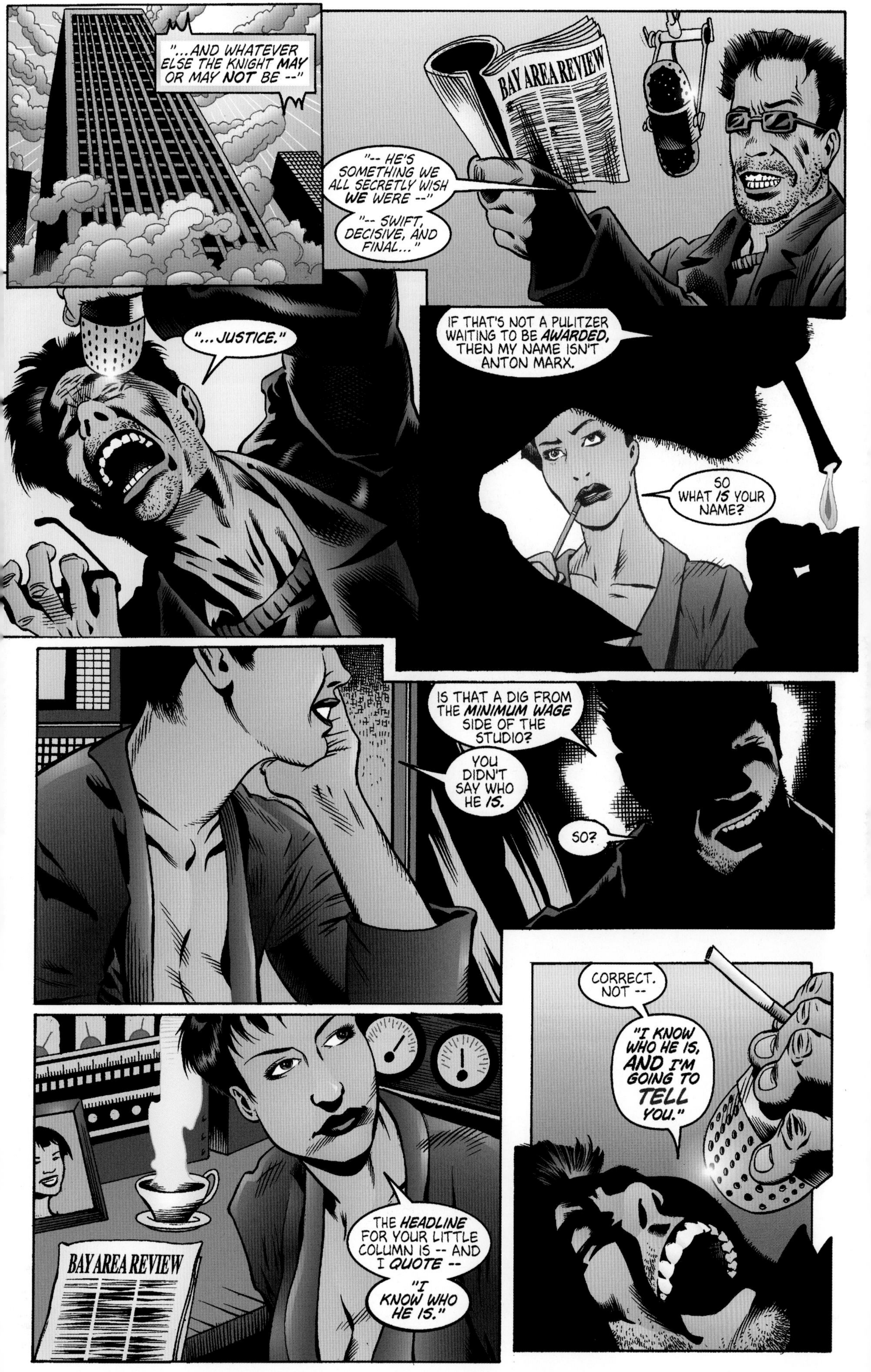
"...AND WHATEVER ELSE THE KNIGHT MAY OR MAY NOT BE --"
BAY AREA REVIEW
"-- HE'S SOMETHING WE ALL SECRETLY WISH WE WERE --"
"-- SWIFT, DECISIVE, AND FINAL..."
"...JUSTICE."
IF THAT'S NOT A PULITZER WAITING TO BE AWARDED, THEN MY NAME ISN'T ANTON MARX.
SO WHAT IS YOUR NAME?
IS THAT A DIG FROM THE MINIMUM WAGE SIDE OF THE STUDIO?
YOU DIDN'T SAY WHO HE IS.
SO?
BAY AREA REVIEW
THE HEADLINE FOR YOUR LITTLE COLUMN IS -- AND I QUOTE --
"I KNOW WHO HE IS."
CORRECT. NOT --
"I KNOW WHO HE IS, AND I'M GOING TO TELL YOU."

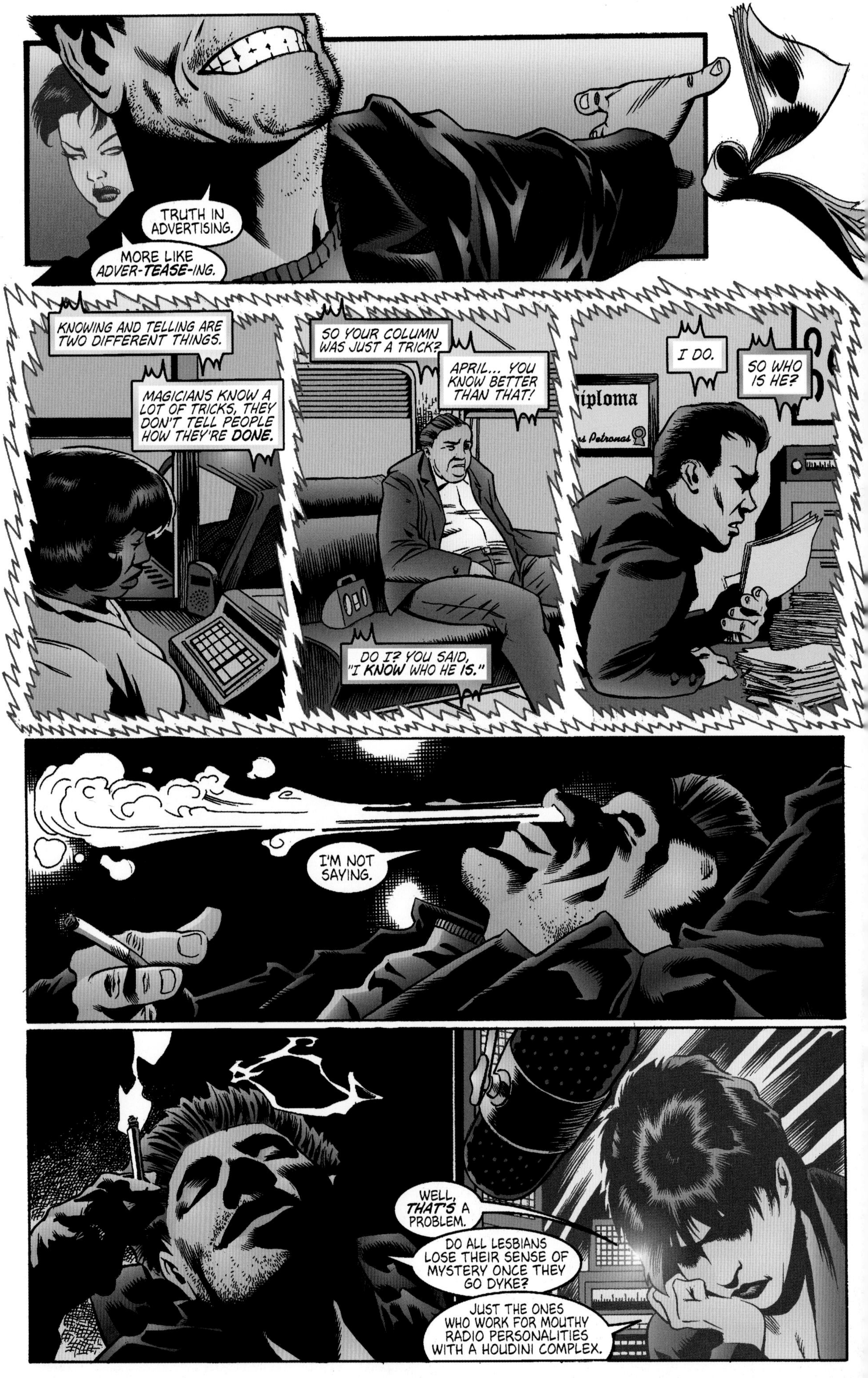
TRUTH IN ADVERTISING.
MORE LIKE ADVER-TEASE-ING.
KNOWING AND TELLING ARE TWO DIFFERENT THINGS.
MAGICIANS KNOW A LOT OF TRICKS, THEY DON'T TELL PEOPLE HOW THEY'RE DONE.
SO YOUR COLUMN WAS JUST A TRICK?
APRIL... YOU KNOW BETTER THAN THAT!
DO I? YOU SAID, "I KNOW WHO HE IS."
I DO.
SO WHO IS HE?
Diploma
I'M NOT SAYING.
WELL, THAT'S A PROBLEM.
DO ALL LESBIANS LOSE THEIR SENSE OF MYSTERY ONCE THEY GO DYKE?
JUST THE ONES WHO WORK FOR MOUTHY RADIO PERSONALITIES WITH A HOUDINI COMPLEX.

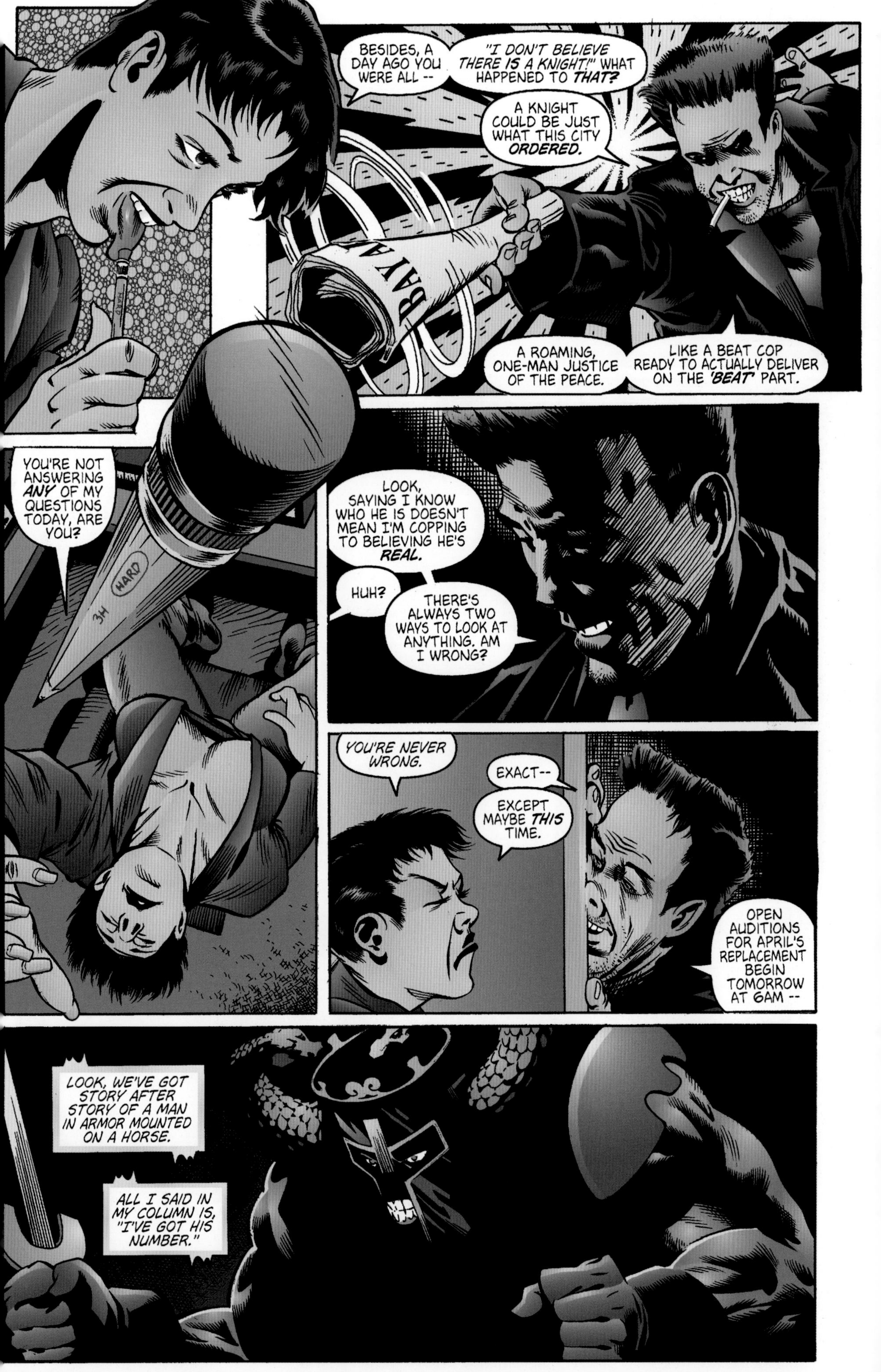
BESIDES, A DAY AGO YOU WERE ALL --
"I DON'T BELIEVE THERE IS A KNIGHT!" WHAT HAPPENED TO THAT?
A KNIGHT COULD BE JUST WHAT THIS CITY ORDERED.
BAY
A ROAMING, ONE-MAN JUSTICE OF THE PEACE.
LIKE A BEAT COP READY TO ACTUALLY DELIVER ON THE 'BEAT' PART.
YOU'RE NOT ANSWERING ANY OF MY QUESTIONS TODAY, ARE YOU?
HARD
3H
LOOK, SAYING I KNOW WHO HE IS DOESN'T MEAN I'M COPPING TO BELIEVING HE'S REAL.
HUH?
THERE'S ALWAYS TWO WAYS TO LOOK AT ANYTHING. AM I WRONG?
YOU'RE NEVER WRONG.
EXACT--
EXCEPT MAYBE THIS TIME.
OPEN AUDITIONS FOR APRIL'S REPLACEMENT BEGIN TOMORROW AT 6AM --
LOOK, WE'VE GOT STORY AFTER STORY OF A MAN IN ARMOR MOUNTED ON A HORSE.
ALL I SAID IN MY COLUMN IS, "I'VE GOT HIS NUMBER."

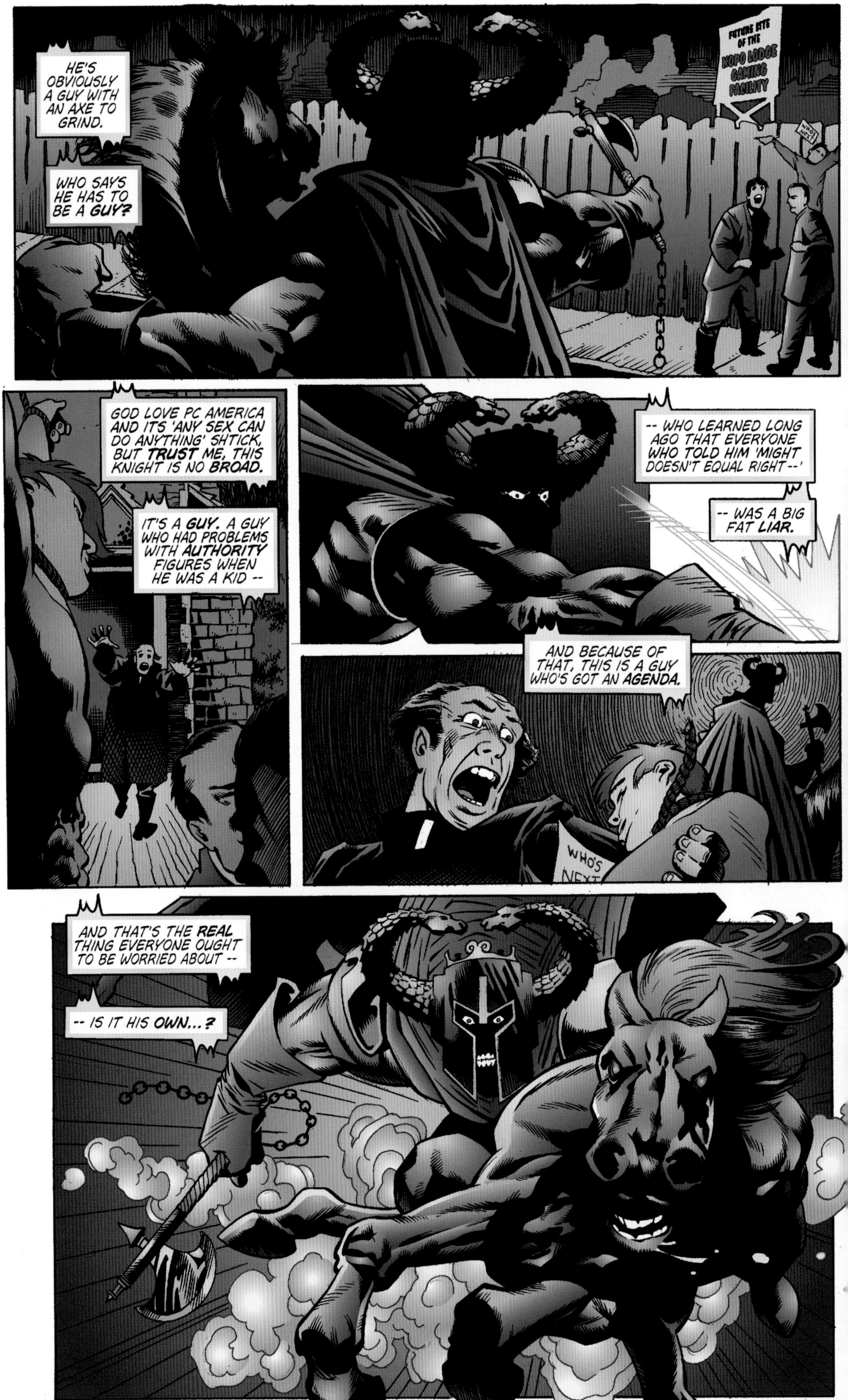

HE'S OBVIOUSLY A GUY WITH AN AXE TO GRIND.
FUTURE SITE OF THE KOPO LODGE GAMING FACILITY
WHO'S NEXT
WHO SAYS HE HAS TO BE A **GUY?**
GOD LOVE PC AMERICA **AND** ITS 'ANY SEX CAN DO ANYTHING' SHTICK, BUT **TRUST** ME, THIS KNIGHT IS NO **BROAD.**
IT'S A **GUY**. A GUY WHO HAD PROBLEMS WITH **AUTHORITY** FIGURES WHEN HE WAS A KID --
-- WHO LEARNED LONG AGO THAT EVERYONE WHO TOLD HIM 'MIGHT DOESN'T EQUAL RIGHT --'
-- WAS A BIG FAT **LIAR.**
AND BECAUSE OF THAT, THIS IS A GUY WHO'S GOT AN **AGENDA.**
WHO'S NEXT
AND THAT'S THE **REAL** THING EVERYONE OUGHT TO BE WORRIED ABOUT --
-- IS IT HIS **OWN...?**

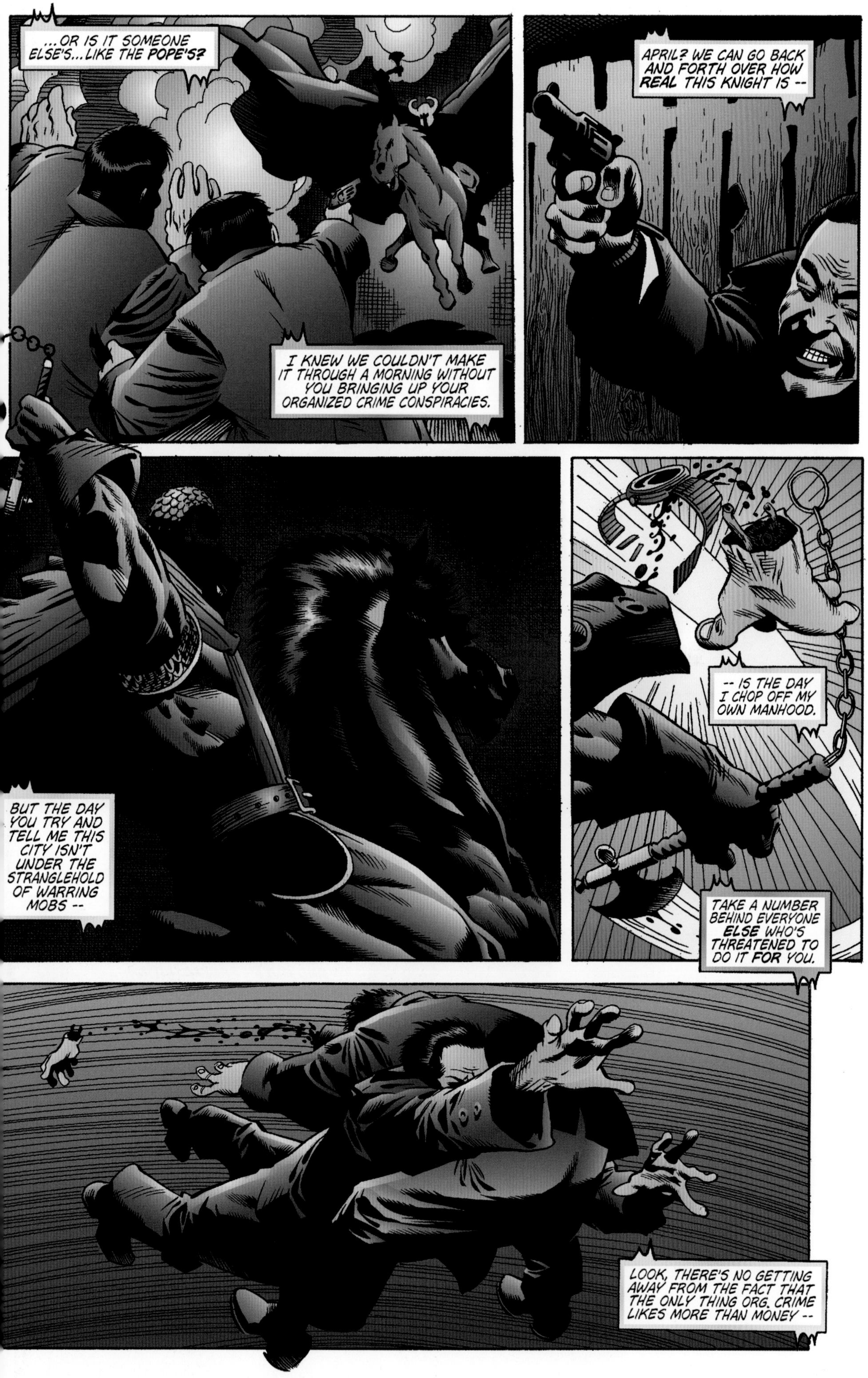

...OR IS IT SOMEONE ELSE'S...LIKE THE **POPE'S?**
I KNEW WE COULDN'T MAKE IT THROUGH A MORNING WITHOUT YOU BRINGING UP YOUR ORGANIZED CRIME CONSPIRACIES.
APRIL? WE CAN GO BACK AND FORTH OVER HOW **REAL** THIS KNIGHT IS --
BUT THE DAY YOU TRY AND TELL ME THIS CITY ISN'T UNDER THE STRANGLEHOLD OF WARRING MOBS --
-- IS THE DAY I CHOP OFF MY OWN MANHOOD.
TAKE A NUMBER BEHIND EVERYONE **ELSE** WHO'S THREATENED TO DO IT **FOR** YOU.
LOOK, THERE'S NO GETTING AWAY FROM THE FACT THAT THE ONLY THING ORG. CRIME LIKES MORE THAN MONEY --

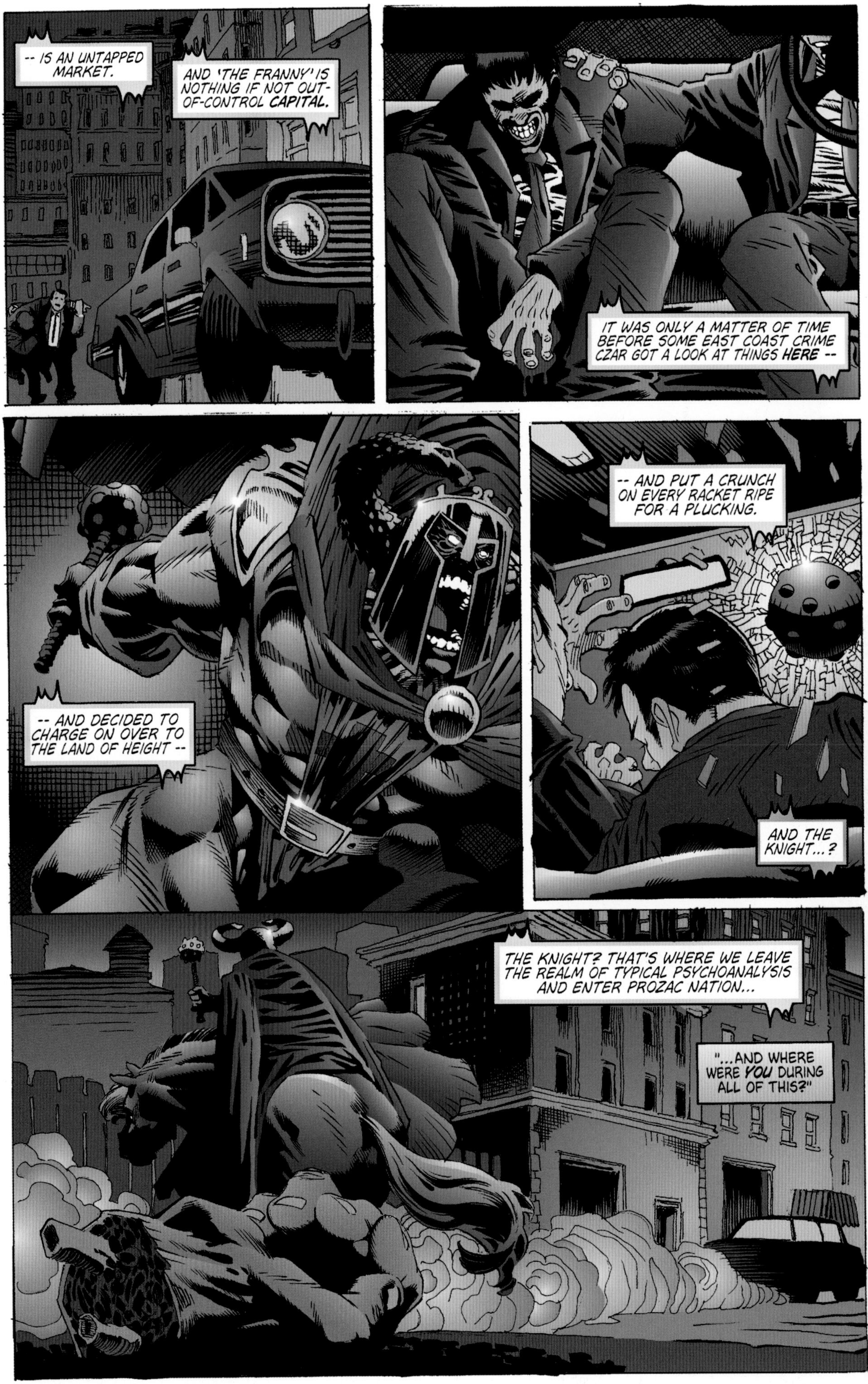
-- IS AN UNTAPPED MARKET.
AND 'THE FRANNY' IS NOTHING IF NOT OUT-OF-CONTROL CAPITAL.
IT WAS ONLY A MATTER OF TIME BEFORE SOME EAST COAST CRIME CZAR GOT A LOOK AT THINGS HERE --
-- AND DECIDED TO CHARGE ON OVER TO THE LAND OF HEIGHT --
-- AND PUT A CRUNCH ON EVERY RACKET RIPE FOR A PLUCKING.
AND THE KNIGHT...?
THE KNIGHT? THAT'S WHERE WE LEAVE THE REALM OF TYPICAL PSYCHOANALYSIS AND ENTER PROZAC NATION...
"...AND WHERE WERE YOU DURING ALL OF THIS?"

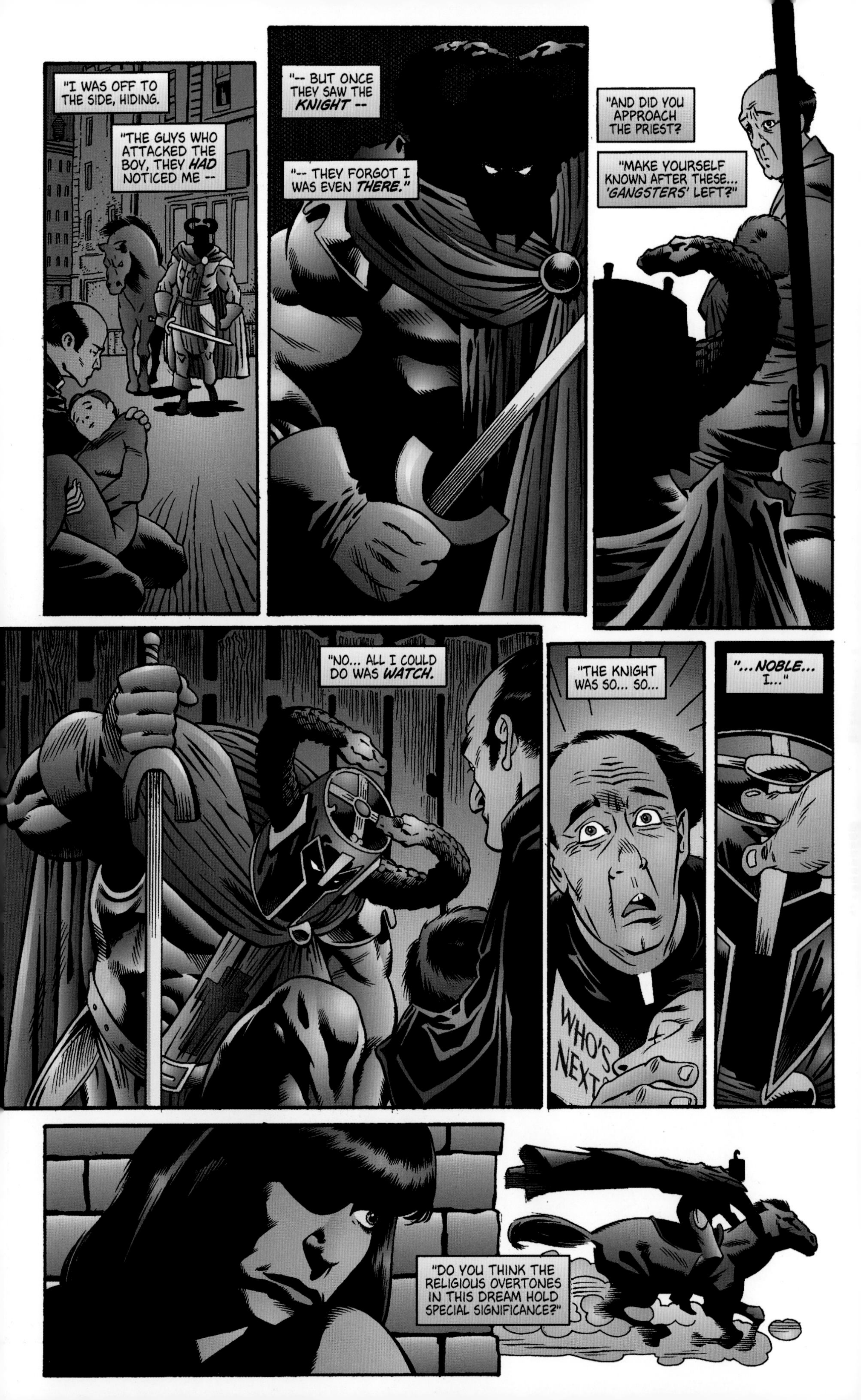
"I WAS OFF TO THE SIDE, HIDING.
"THE GUYS WHO ATTACKED THE BOY, THEY HAD NOTICED ME --
"-- BUT ONCE THEY SAW THE KNIGHT --
"-- THEY FORGOT I WAS EVEN THERE."
"AND DID YOU APPROACH THE PRIEST?
"MAKE YOURSELF KNOWN AFTER THESE... 'GANGSTERS' LEFT?"
"NO... ALL I COULD DO WAS WATCH.
"THE KNIGHT WAS SO... SO...
WHO'S NEXT
"...NOBLE... I..."
"DO YOU THINK THE RELIGIOUS OVERTONES IN THIS DREAM HOLD SPECIAL SIGNIFICANCE?"

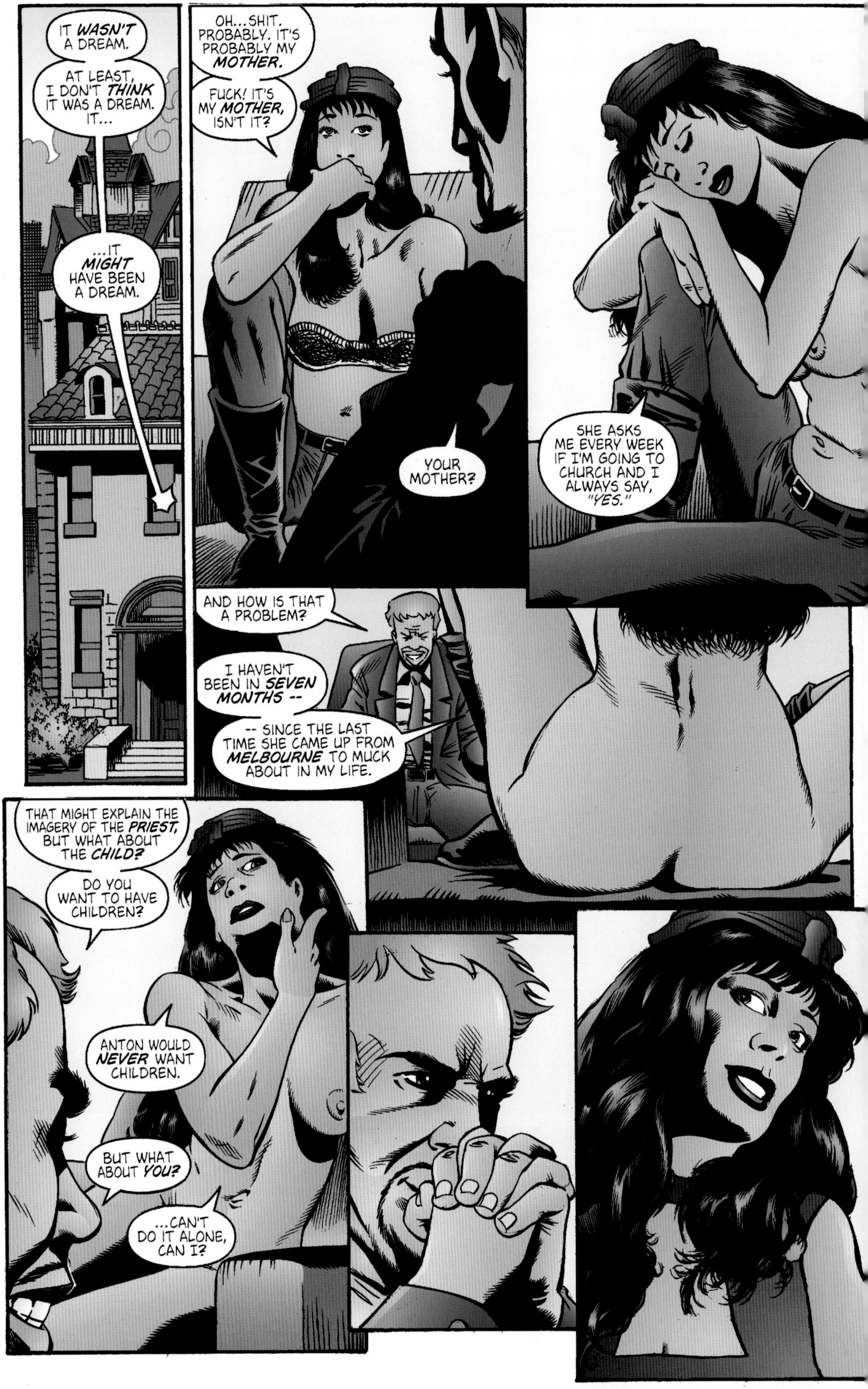
IT WASN'T A DREAM.
AT LEAST, I DON'T THINK IT WAS A DREAM. IT...
...IT MIGHT HAVE BEEN A DREAM.
OH...SHIT. PROBABLY. IT'S PROBABLY MY MOTHER.
FUCK! IT'S MY MOTHER, ISN'T IT?
YOUR MOTHER?
SHE ASKS ME EVERY WEEK IF I'M GOING TO CHURCH AND I ALWAYS SAY, "YES."
AND HOW IS THAT A PROBLEM?
I HAVEN'T BEEN IN SEVEN MONTHS --
-- SINCE THE LAST TIME SHE CAME UP FROM MELBOURNE TO MUCK ABOUT IN MY LIFE.
THAT MIGHT EXPLAIN THE IMAGERY OF THE PRIEST, BUT WHAT ABOUT THE CHILD?
DO YOU WANT TO HAVE CHILDREN?
ANTON WOULD NEVER WANT CHILDREN.
BUT WHAT ABOUT YOU?
...CAN'T DO IT ALONE, CAN I?

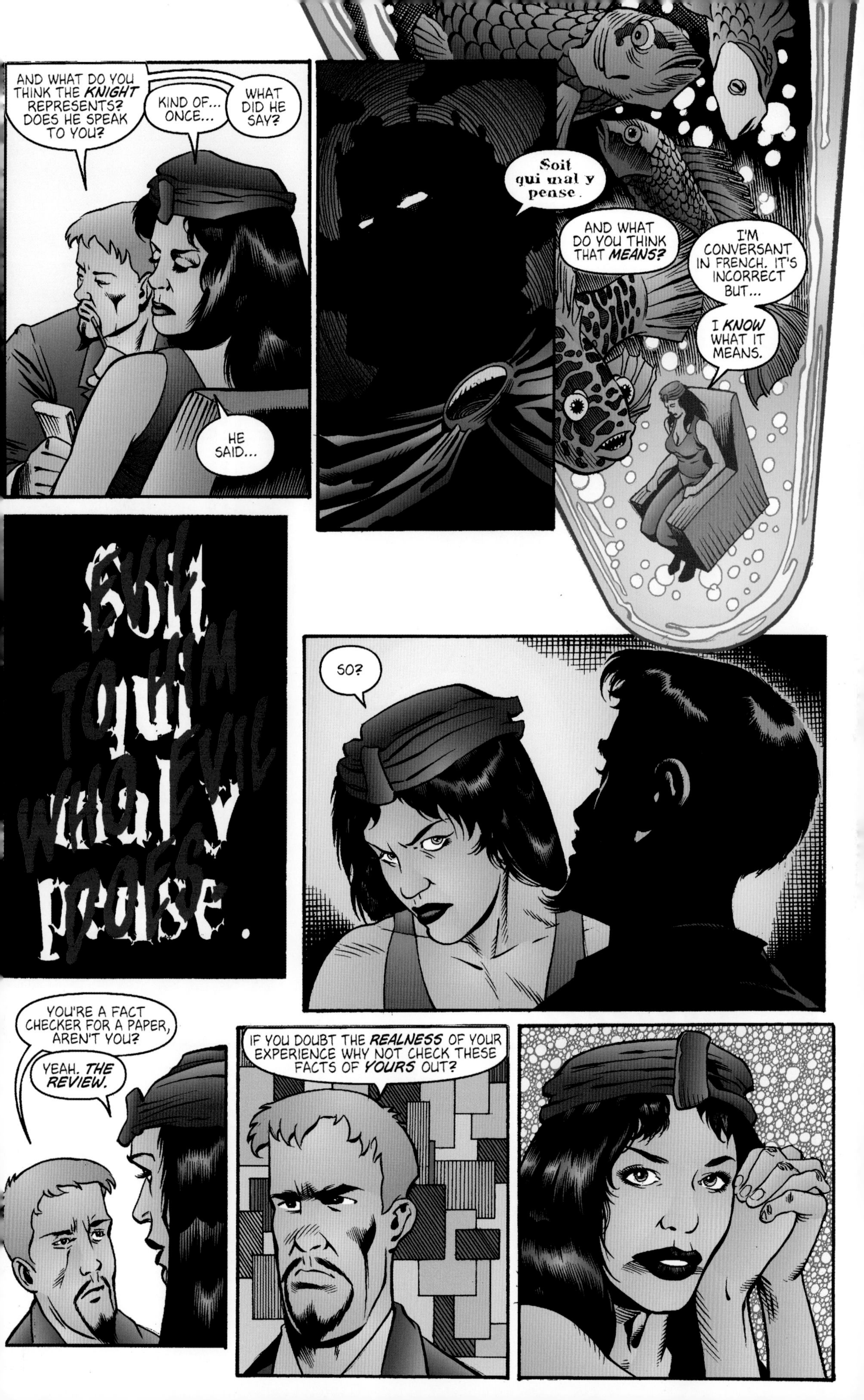

AND WHAT DO YOU THINK THE *KNIGHT* REPRESENTS? DOES HE SPEAK TO YOU?
KIND OF... ONCE...
WHAT DID HE SAY?
HE SAID...
Soit qui mal y pense.
AND WHAT DO YOU THINK THAT *MEANS?*
I'M CONVERSANT IN FRENCH. IT'S INCORRECT BUT...
I *KNOW* WHAT IT MEANS.
SO?
YOU'RE A FACT CHECKER FOR A PAPER, AREN'T YOU?
YEAH. *THE REVIEW.*
IF YOU DOUBT THE *REALNESS* OF YOUR EXPERIENCE WHY NOT CHECK THESE FACTS OF *YOURS* OUT?

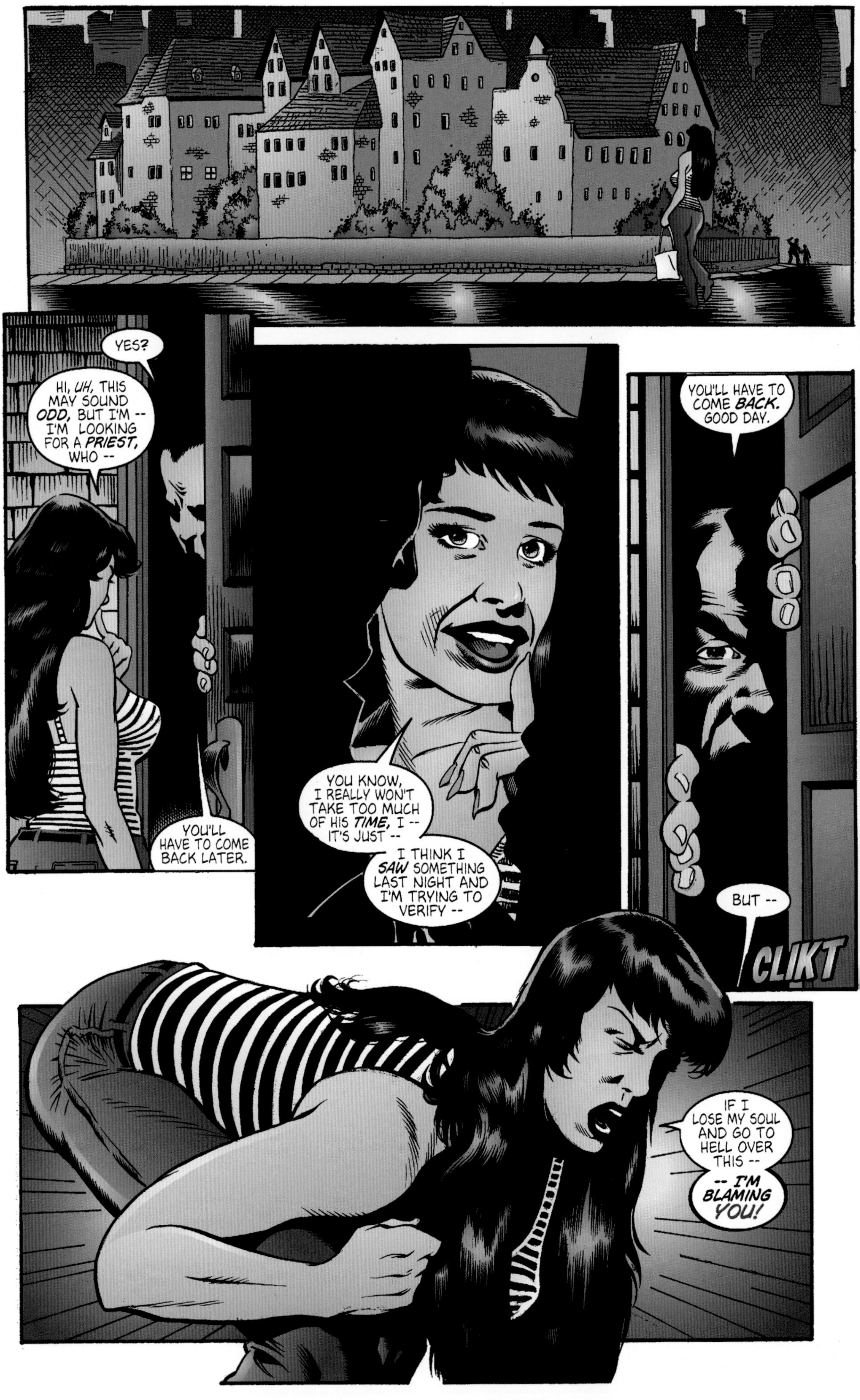

YES?
HI, UH, THIS MAY SOUND ODD, BUT I'M -- I'M LOOKING FOR A PRIEST, WHO --
YOU'LL HAVE TO COME BACK LATER.
YOU KNOW, I REALLY WON'T TAKE TOO MUCH OF HIS TIME, I -- IT'S JUST --
I THINK I SAW SOMETHING LAST NIGHT AND I'M TRYING TO VERIFY --
YOU'LL HAVE TO COME BACK. GOOD DAY.
BUT --
CLIKT
IF I LOSE MY SOUL AND GO TO HELL OVER THIS --
-- I'M BLAMING YOU!

CLIK.T

GOOD JOB, POPS. NOW...

...BACK TO *BUSINESS*.

WALK.

WHO WAS IT?

NOBODY. SOME BROAD. *CUTIE.*

FATHER FRIAR HERE'D FUCK HER!

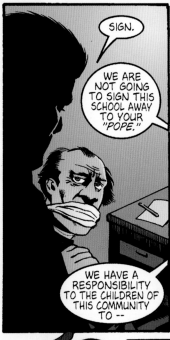

SIGN.

WE ARE NOT GOING TO SIGN THIS SCHOOL AWAY TO YOUR *"POPE."*

WE HAVE A RESPONSIBILITY TO THE CHILDREN OF THIS COMMUNITY TO --

YOU *ARE*, OR YOU'RE GONNA BE *LUNCHIN'* WITH THE *LORD.*

I AM NOT AFRAID TO DIE, YOU --

SIGN.

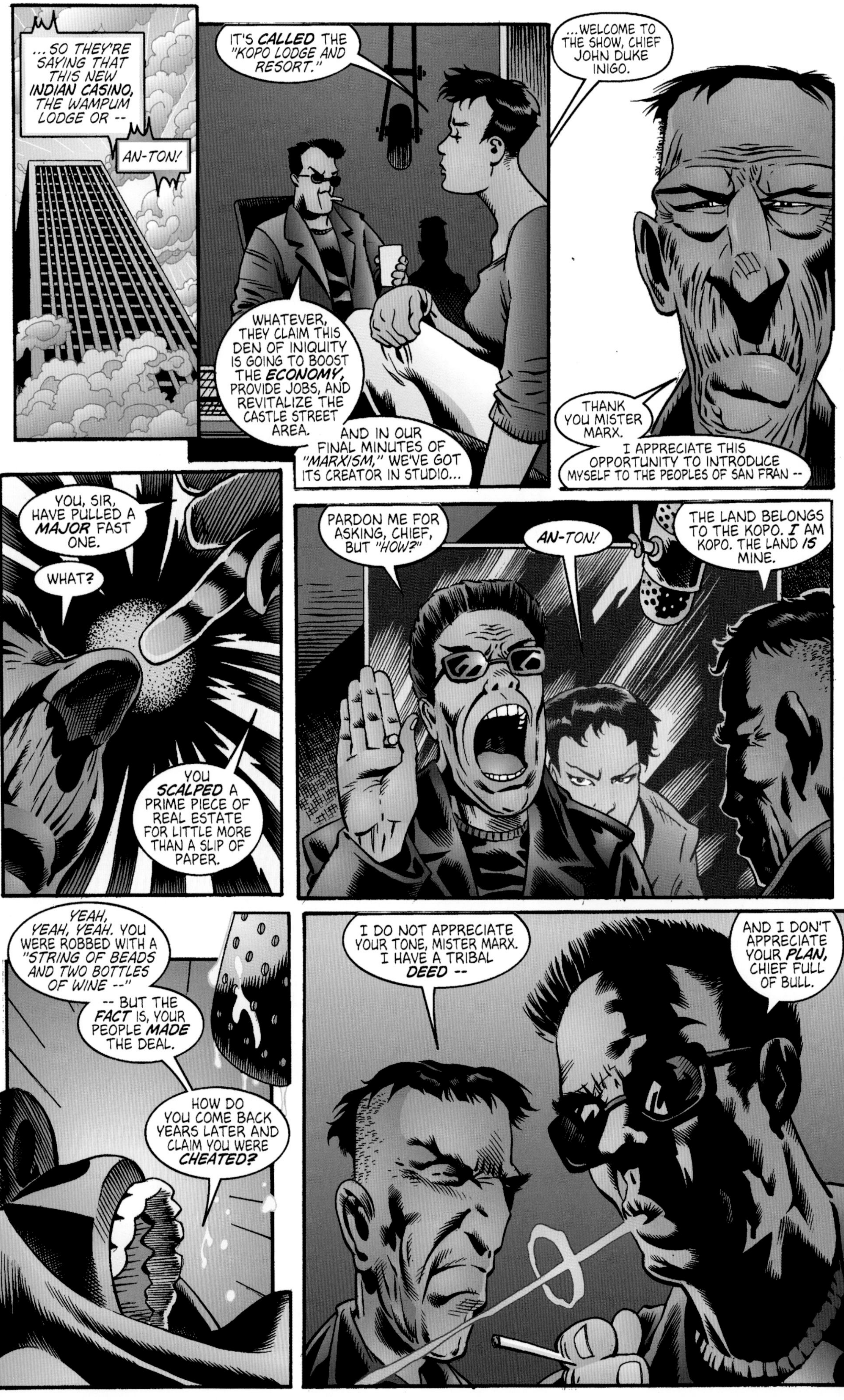
...SO THEY'RE SAYING THAT THIS NEW INDIAN CASINO, THE WAMPUM LODGE OR --
AN-TON!
IT'S CALLED THE "KOPO LODGE AND RESORT."
WHATEVER, THEY CLAIM THIS DEN OF INIQUITY IS GOING TO BOOST THE ECONOMY, PROVIDE JOBS, AND REVITALIZE THE CASTLE STREET AREA.
AND IN OUR FINAL MINUTES OF "MARXISM," WE'VE GOT ITS CREATOR IN STUDIO...
...WELCOME TO THE SHOW, CHIEF JOHN DUKE INIGO.
THANK YOU MISTER MARX.
I APPRECIATE THIS OPPORTUNITY TO INTRODUCE MYSELF TO THE PEOPLES OF SAN FRAN --
YOU, SIR, HAVE PULLED A MAJOR FAST ONE.
WHAT?
YOU SCALPED A PRIME PIECE OF REAL ESTATE FOR LITTLE MORE THAN A SLIP OF PAPER.
PARDON ME FOR ASKING, CHIEF, BUT "HOW?"
AN-TON!
THE LAND BELONGS TO THE KOPO. I AM KOPO. THE LAND IS MINE.
YEAH, YEAH, YEAH. YOU WERE ROBBED WITH A "STRING OF BEADS AND TWO BOTTLES OF WINE --"
-- BUT THE FACT IS, YOUR PEOPLE MADE THE DEAL.
HOW DO YOU COME BACK YEARS LATER AND CLAIM YOU WERE CHEATED?
I DO NOT APPRECIATE YOUR TONE, MISTER MARX. I HAVE A TRIBAL DEED --
AND I DON'T APPRECIATE YOUR PLAN, CHIEF FULL OF BULL.

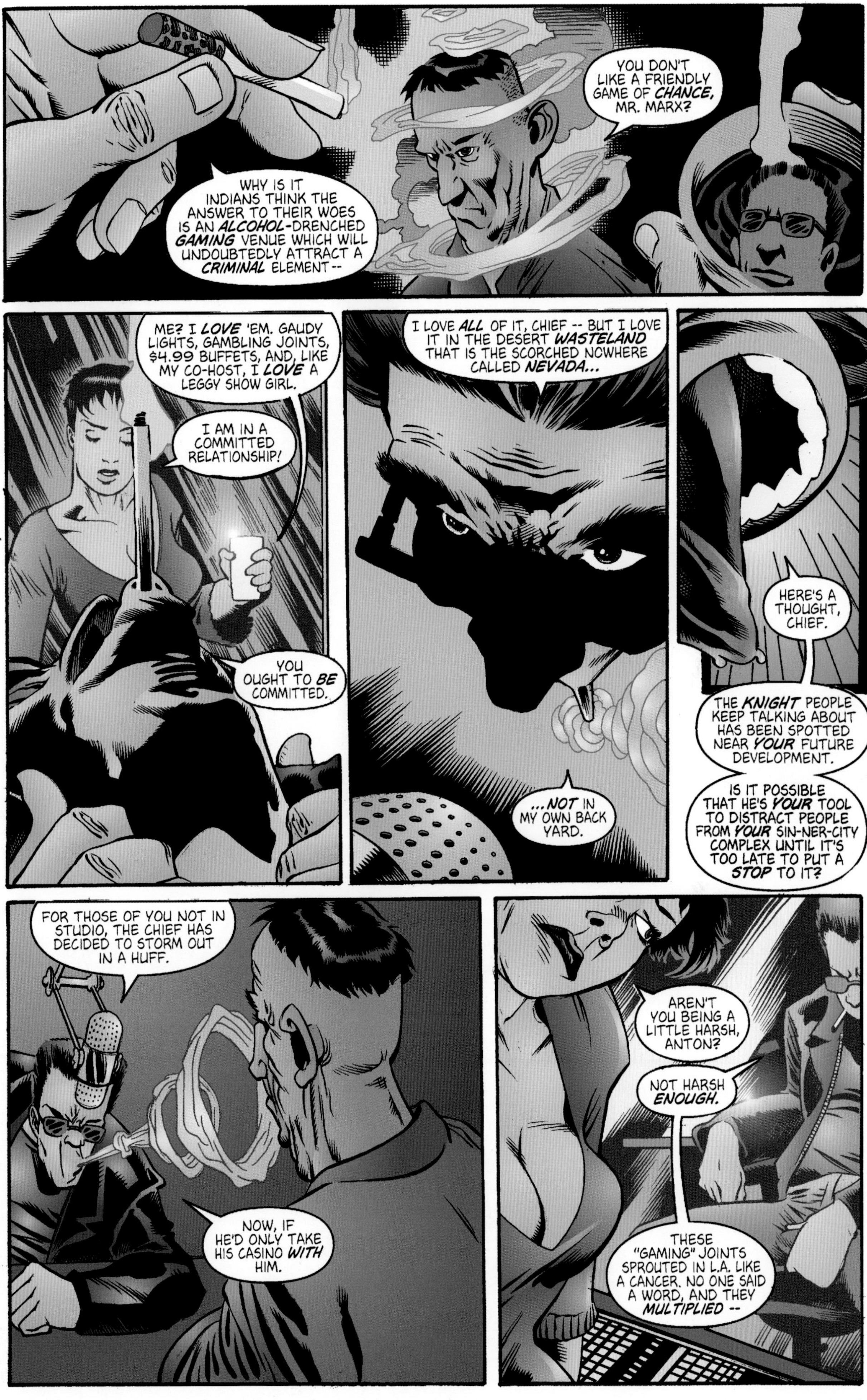
WHY IS IT INDIANS THINK THE ANSWER TO THEIR WOES IS AN ALCOHOL-DRENCHED GAMING VENUE WHICH WILL UNDOUBTEDLY ATTRACT A CRIMINAL ELEMENT --
YOU DON'T LIKE A FRIENDLY GAME OF CHANCE, MR. MARX?
ME? I LOVE 'EM. GAUDY LIGHTS, GAMBLING JOINTS, $4.99 BUFFETS, AND, LIKE MY CO-HOST, I LOVE A LEGGY SHOW GIRL.
I AM IN A COMMITTED RELATIONSHIP!
YOU OUGHT TO BE COMMITTED.
I LOVE ALL OF IT, CHIEF -- BUT I LOVE IT IN THE DESERT WASTELAND THAT IS THE SCORCHED NOWHERE CALLED NEVADA...
...NOT IN MY OWN BACK YARD.
HERE'S A THOUGHT, CHIEF.
THE KNIGHT PEOPLE KEEP TALKING ABOUT HAS BEEN SPOTTED NEAR YOUR FUTURE DEVELOPMENT.
IS IT POSSIBLE THAT HE'S YOUR TOOL TO DISTRACT PEOPLE FROM YOUR SIN-NER-CITY COMPLEX UNTIL IT'S TOO LATE TO PUT A STOP TO IT?
FOR THOSE OF YOU NOT IN STUDIO, THE CHIEF HAS DECIDED TO STORM OUT IN A HUFF.
NOW, IF HE'D ONLY TAKE HIS CASINO WITH HIM.
AREN'T YOU BEING A LITTLE HARSH, ANTON?
NOT HARSH ENOUGH.
THESE "GAMING" JOINTS SPROUTED IN L.A. LIKE A CANCER. NO ONE SAID A WORD, AND THEY MULTIPLIED --

-- NOW THEY'RE COMING TO THE MOST BEAUTIFUL MUNICIPALITY IN THE USA?

NOT IF I HAVE ANYTHING TO SAY ABOUT IT.

MOTHER FUCKIN' FUCK! CUT IT OUT!

DOCTOR SO IS DOING YOU A FAVOR, PHILLIP.

DON'T BITE THE HAND THAT FEEDS.

SORRY, THERE, POPE. BUT IT -- HURTS WORSE'N MY FUCKIN' HAND DID!

YOU SHOULDA SEEN THIS KNIGHT, POPE. LIKE SOME FUCKIN' --

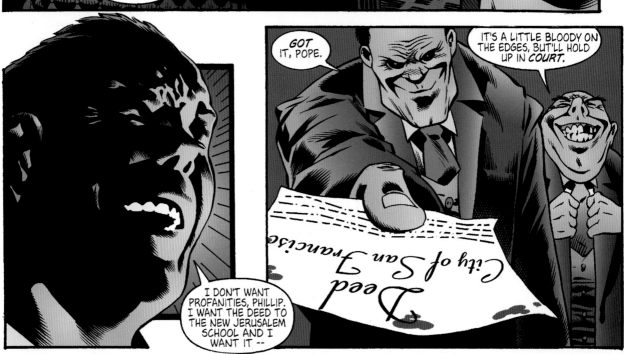

GOT IT, POPE.

IT'S A LITTLE BLOODY ON THE EDGES, BUT'LL HOLD UP IN COURT.

I DON'T WANT PROFANITIES, PHILLIP. I WANT THE DEED TO THE NEW JERUSALEM SCHOOL AND I WANT IT --

Deed City of San Francisco

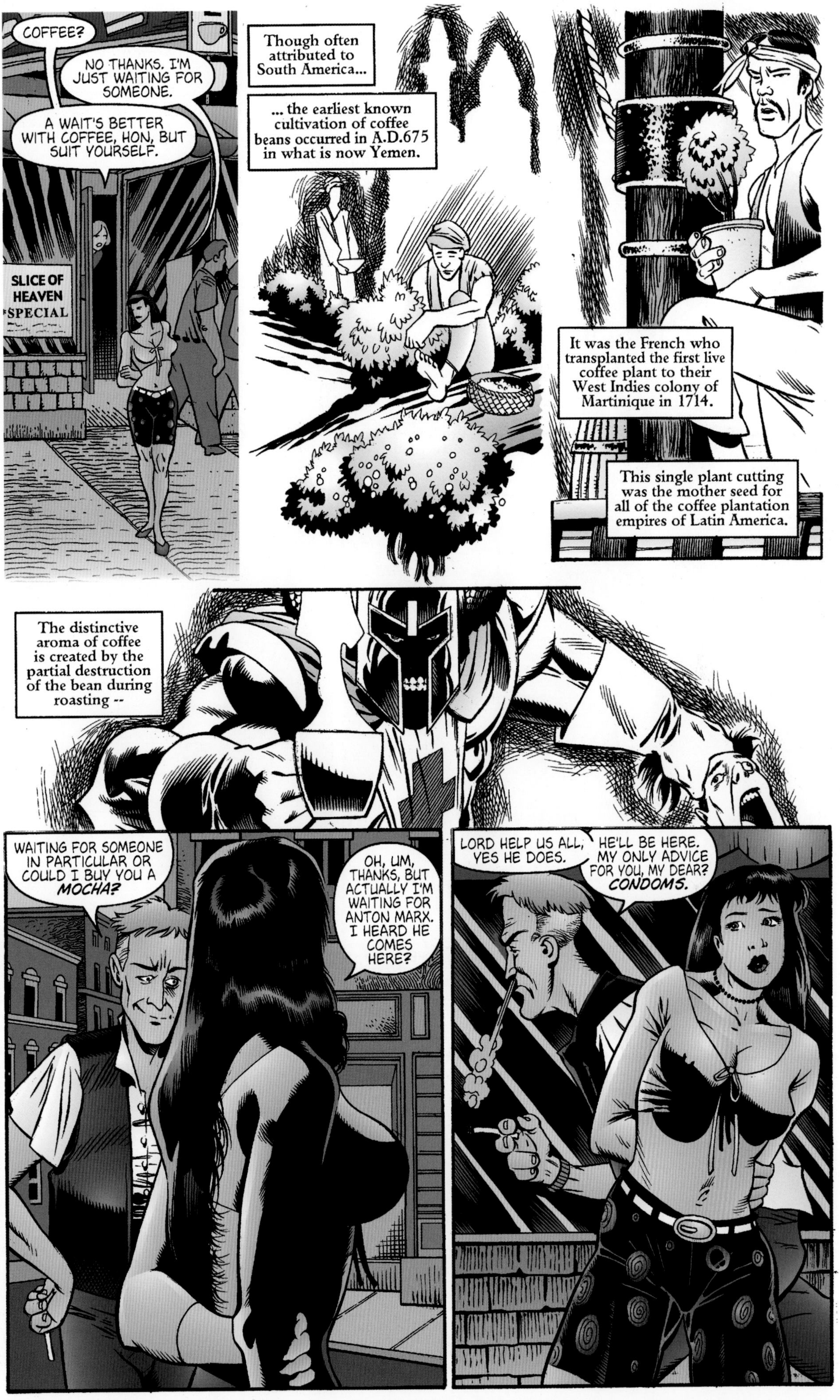
COFFEE?
NO THANKS. I'M JUST WAITING FOR SOMEONE.
A WAIT'S BETTER WITH COFFEE, HON, BUT SUIT YOURSELF.
SLICE OF HEAVEN SPECIAL
Though often attributed to South America...
... the earliest known cultivation of coffee beans occurred in A.D.675 in what is now Yemen.
It was the French who transplanted the first live coffee plant to their West Indies colony of Martinique in 1714.
This single plant cutting was the mother seed for all of the coffee plantation empires of Latin America.
The distinctive aroma of coffee is created by the partial destruction of the bean during roasting --
WAITING FOR SOMEONE IN PARTICULAR OR COULD I BUY YOU A *MOCHA?*
OH, UM, THANKS, BUT ACTUALLY I'M WAITING FOR ANTON MARX. I HEARD HE COMES HERE?
LORD HELP US ALL, YES HE DOES.
HE'LL BE HERE. MY ONLY ADVICE FOR YOU, MY DEAR? *CONDOMS.*

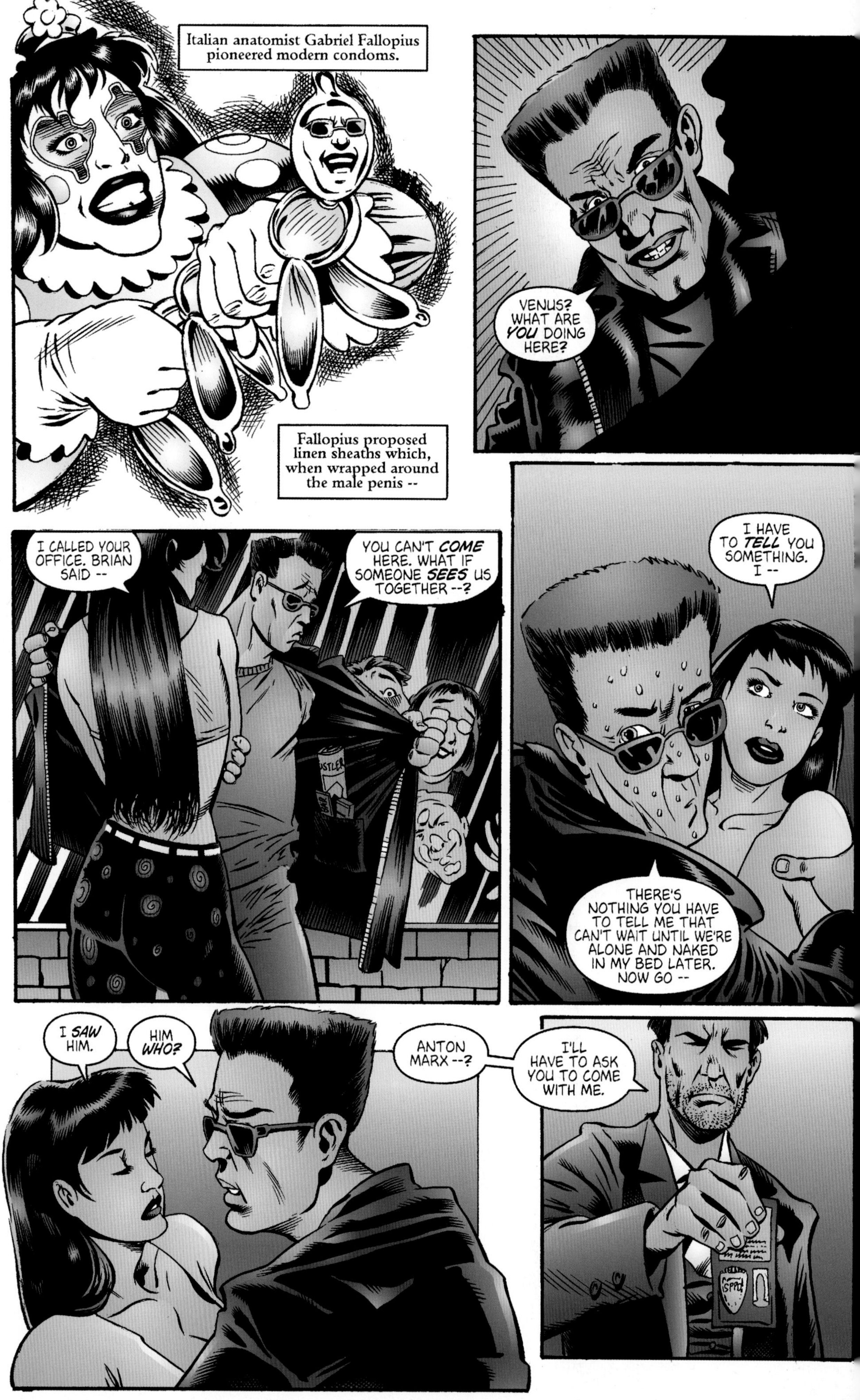
Italian anatomist Gabriel Fallopius pioneered modern condoms.
Fallopius proposed linen sheaths which, when wrapped around the male penis --
VENUS? WHAT ARE YOU DOING HERE?
I CALLED YOUR OFFICE. BRIAN SAID --
YOU CAN'T COME HERE. WHAT IF SOMEONE SEES US TOGETHER --?
I HAVE TO TELL YOU SOMETHING. I --
THERE'S NOTHING YOU HAVE TO TELL ME THAT CAN'T WAIT UNTIL WE'RE ALONE AND NAKED IN MY BED LATER. NOW GO --
I SAW HIM.
HIM WHO?
ANTON MARX --?
I'LL HAVE TO ASK YOU TO COME WITH ME.

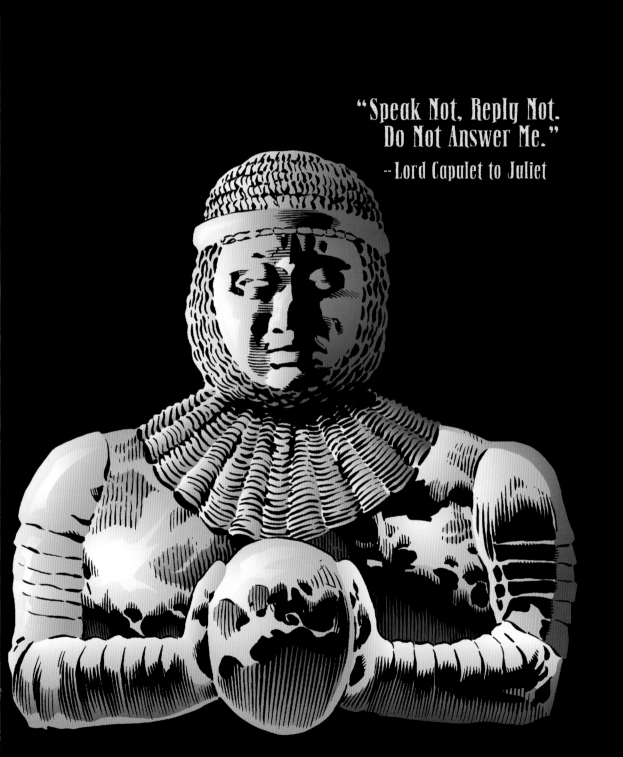

"Speak Not, Reply Not.
Do Not Answer Me."

-- Lord Capulet to Juliet

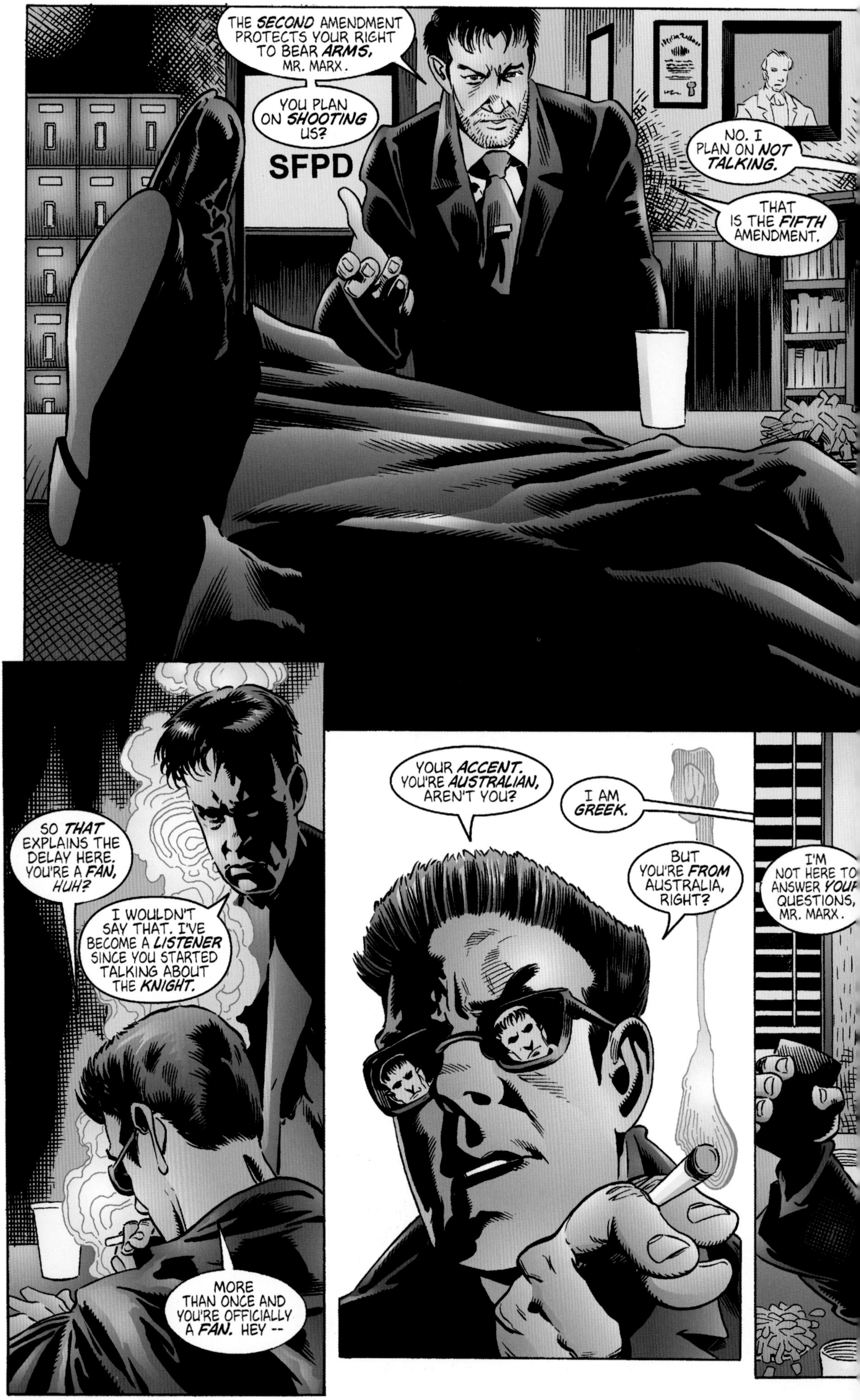
THE SECOND AMENDMENT PROTECTS YOUR RIGHT TO BEAR ARMS, MR. MARX.
YOU PLAN ON SHOOTING US?
SFPD
NO. I PLAN ON NOT TALKING.
THAT IS THE FIFTH AMENDMENT.
SO THAT EXPLAINS THE DELAY HERE. YOU'RE A FAN, HUH?
I WOULDN'T SAY THAT. I'VE BECOME A LISTENER SINCE YOU STARTED TALKING ABOUT THE KNIGHT.
MORE THAN ONCE AND YOU'RE OFFICIALLY A FAN. HEY --
YOUR ACCENT. YOU'RE AUSTRALIAN, AREN'T YOU?
I AM GREEK.
BUT YOU'RE FROM AUSTRALIA, RIGHT?
I'M NOT HERE TO ANSWER YOUR QUESTIONS, MR. MARX.

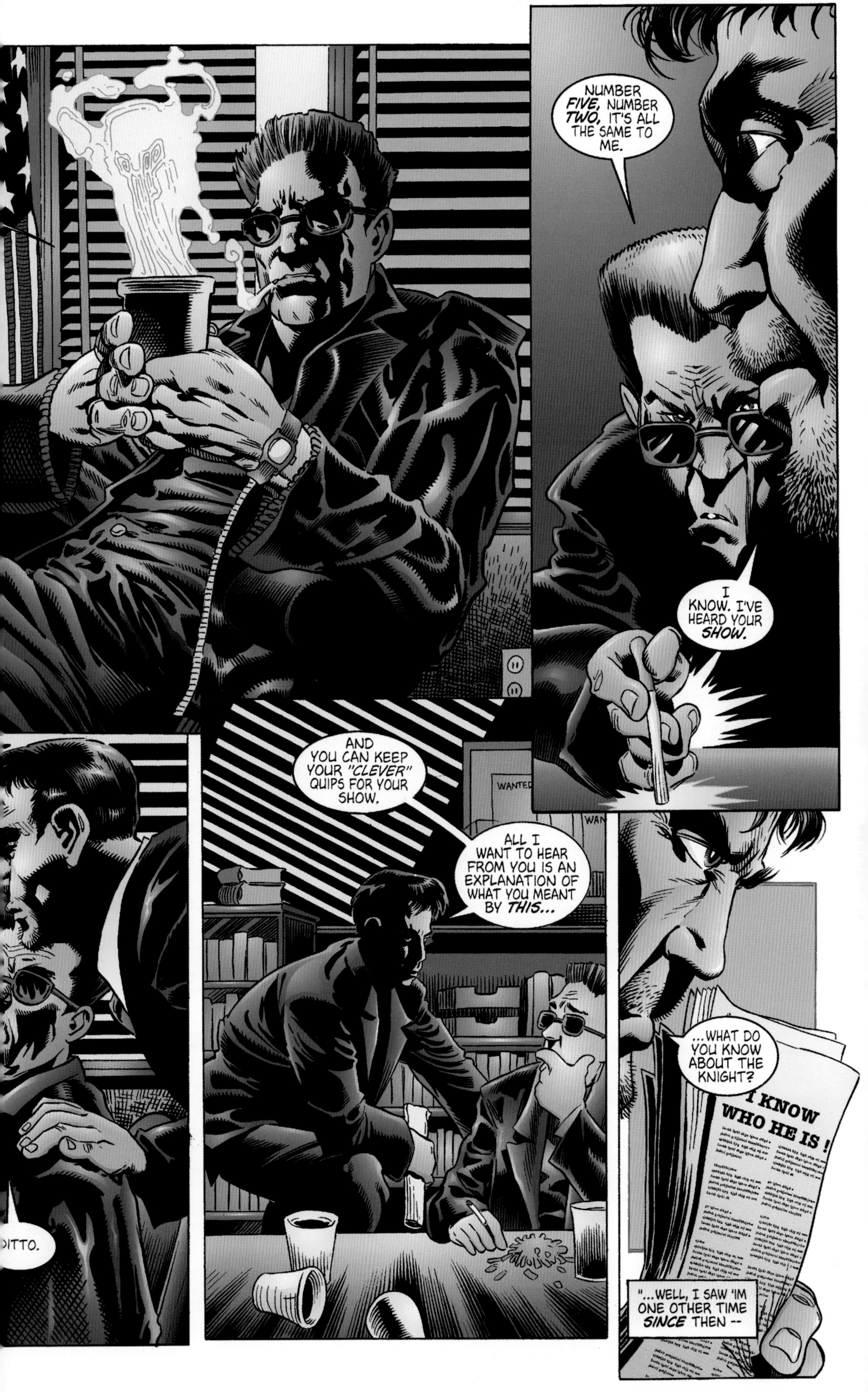
NUMBER FIVE, NUMBER TWO, IT'S ALL THE SAME TO ME.
I KNOW. I'VE HEARD YOUR SHOW.
DITTO.
AND YOU CAN KEEP YOUR "CLEVER" QUIPS FOR YOUR SHOW.
WANTED
ALL I WANT TO HEAR FROM YOU IS AN EXPLANATION OF WHAT YOU MEANT BY THIS...
...WHAT DO YOU KNOW ABOUT THE KNIGHT?
I KNOW WHO HE IS!
"...WELL, I SAW 'IM ONE OTHER TIME SINCE THEN --

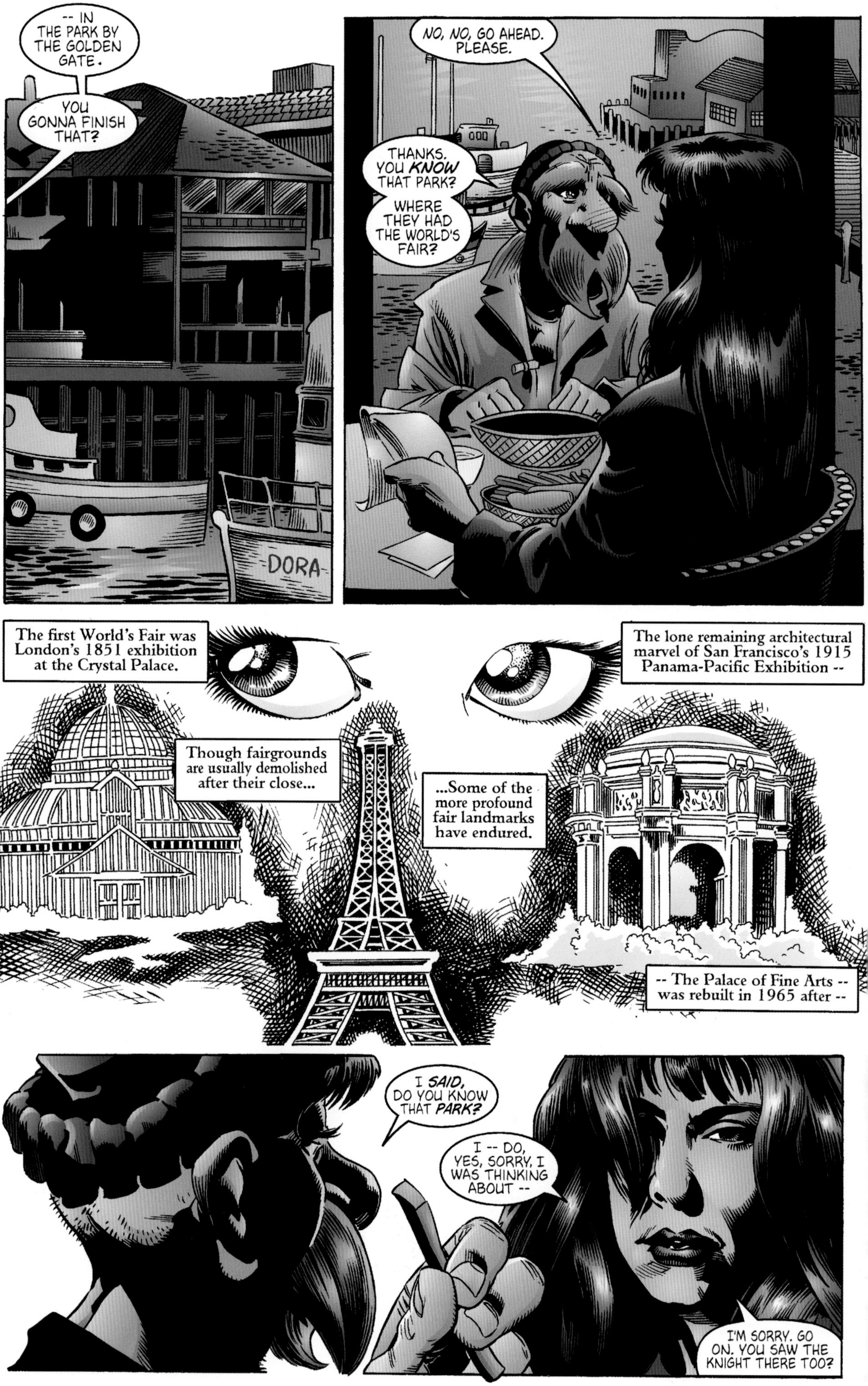
-- IN THE PARK BY THE GOLDEN GATE.
YOU GONNA FINISH THAT?
NO, NO, GO AHEAD. PLEASE.
THANKS. YOU KNOW THAT PARK?
WHERE THEY HAD THE WORLD'S FAIR?
DORA
The first World's Fair was London's 1851 exhibition at the Crystal Palace.
The lone remaining architectural marvel of San Francisco's 1915 Panama-Pacific Exhibition --
Though fairgrounds are usually demolished after their close...
...Some of the more profound fair landmarks have endured.
-- The Palace of Fine Arts -- was rebuilt in 1965 after --
I SAID, DO YOU KNOW THAT PARK?
I -- DO, YES, SORRY, I WAS THINKING ABOUT --
I'M SORRY. GO ON. YOU SAW THE KNIGHT THERE TOO?

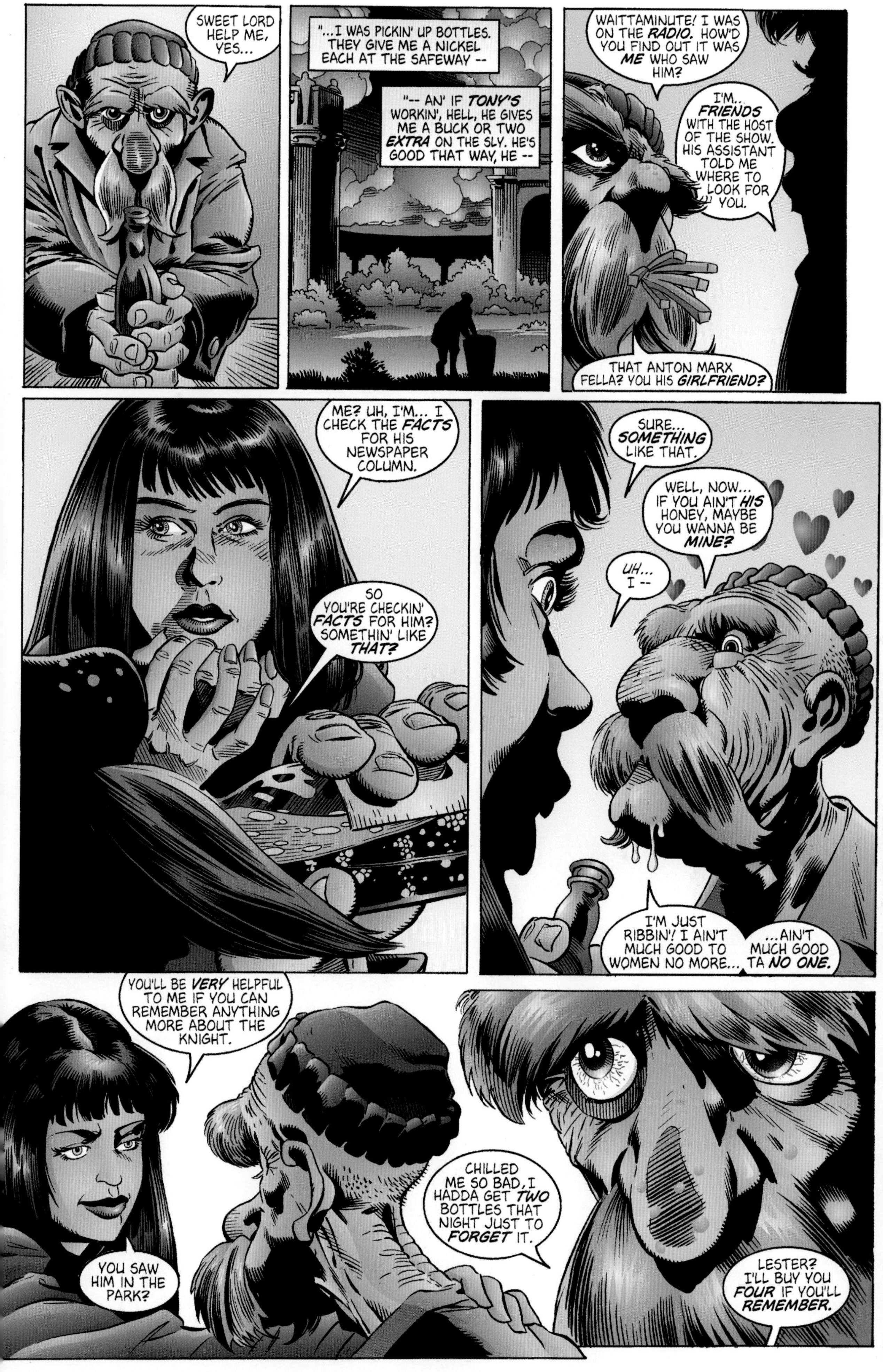
SWEET LORD HELP ME, YES...
"...I WAS PICKIN' UP BOTTLES. THEY GIVE ME A NICKEL EACH AT THE SAFEWAY --
"-- AN' IF TONY'S WORKIN', HELL, HE GIVES ME A BUCK OR TWO EXTRA ON THE SLY. HE'S GOOD THAT WAY, HE --
WAITTAMINUTE! I WAS ON THE RADIO. HOW'D YOU FIND OUT IT WAS ME WHO SAW HIM?
I'M... FRIENDS WITH THE HOST OF THE SHOW. HIS ASSISTANT TOLD ME WHERE TO LOOK FOR YOU.
THAT ANTON MARX FELLA? YOU HIS GIRLFRIEND?
ME? UH, I'M... I CHECK THE FACTS FOR HIS NEWSPAPER COLUMN.
SO YOU'RE CHECKIN' FACTS FOR HIM? SOMETHIN' LIKE THAT?
SURE... SOMETHING LIKE THAT.
WELL, NOW... IF YOU AIN'T HIS HONEY, MAYBE YOU WANNA BE MINE?
UH... I --
I'M JUST RIBBIN'! I AIN'T MUCH GOOD TO WOMEN NO MORE...
...AIN'T MUCH GOOD TA NO ONE.
YOU'LL BE VERY HELPFUL TO ME IF YOU CAN REMEMBER ANYTHING MORE ABOUT THE KNIGHT.
YOU SAW HIM IN THE PARK?
CHILLED ME SO BAD, I HADDA GET TWO BOTTLES THAT NIGHT JUST TO FORGET IT.
LESTER? I'LL BUY YOU FOUR IF YOU'LL REMEMBER.

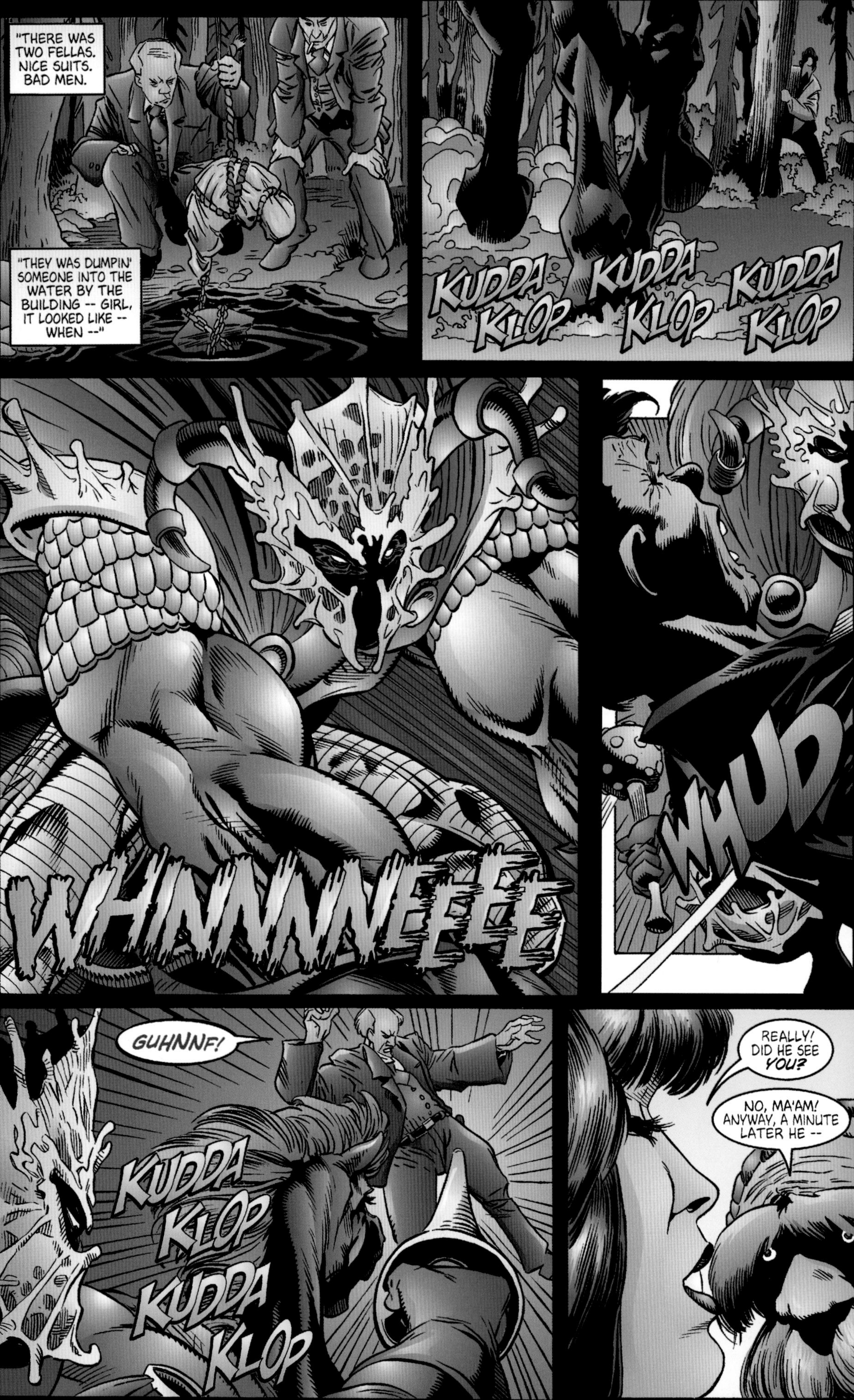
"THERE WAS TWO FELLAS. NICE SUITS. BAD MEN.
"THEY WAS DUMPIN' SOMEONE INTO THE WATER BY THE BUILDING -- GIRL, IT LOOKED LIKE -- WHEN --"
KUDDA KLOP KUDDA KLOP KUDDA KLOP
WHNNNNEEEE
WHUD
GUHNNF!
KUDDA KLOP KUDDA KLOP
REALLY! DID HE SEE YOU?
NO, MA'AM! ANYWAY, A MINUTE LATER HE --

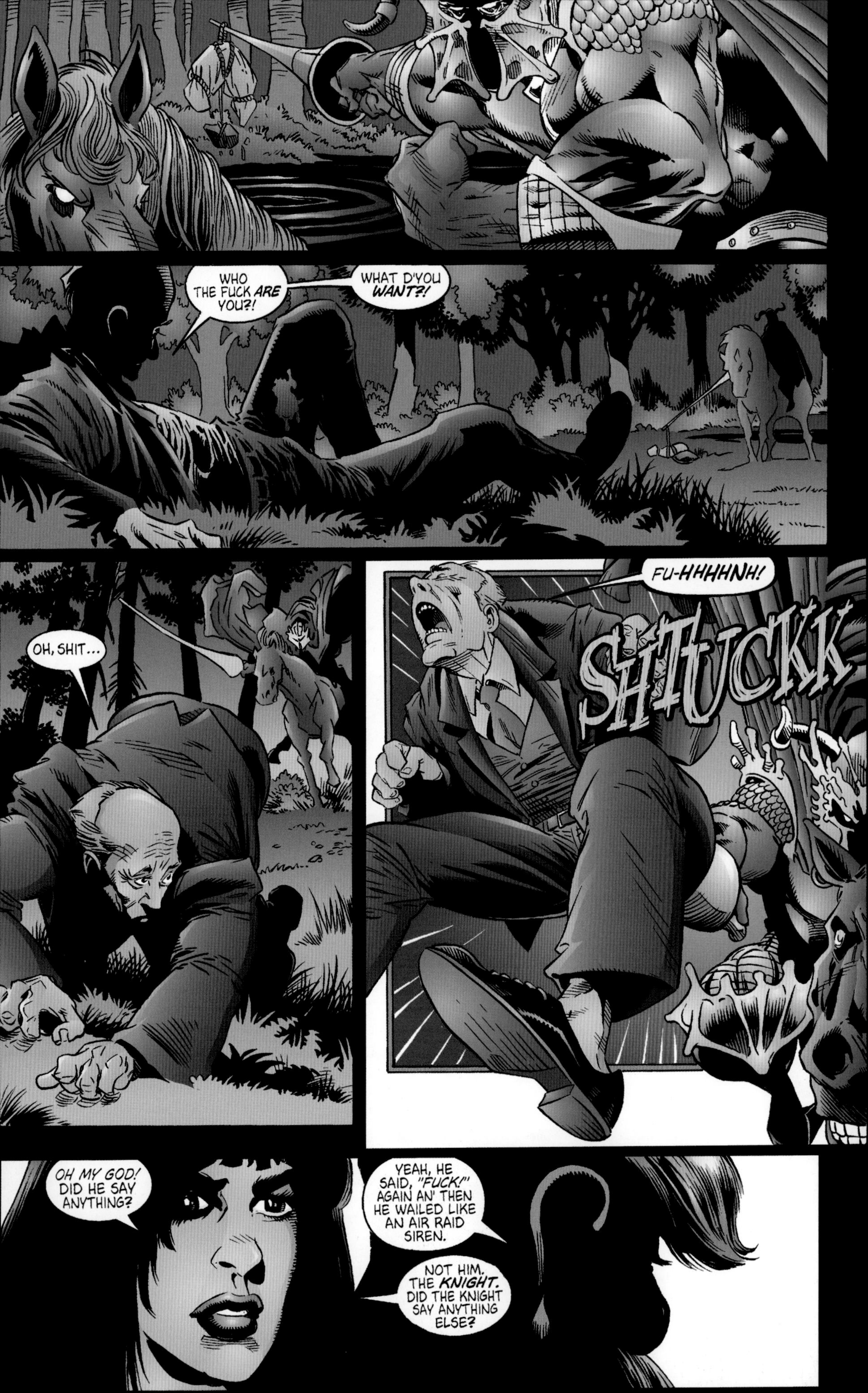
WHO THE FUCK ARE YOU?!
WHAT D'YOU WANT?!
OH, SHIT...
FU-HHHHNH!
SHUCKK
OH MY GOD! DID HE SAY ANYTHING?
YEAH, HE SAID, "FUCK!" AGAIN AN' THEN HE WAILED LIKE AN AIR RAID SIREN.
NOT HIM. THE KNIGHT. DID THE KNIGHT SAY ANYTHING ELSE?

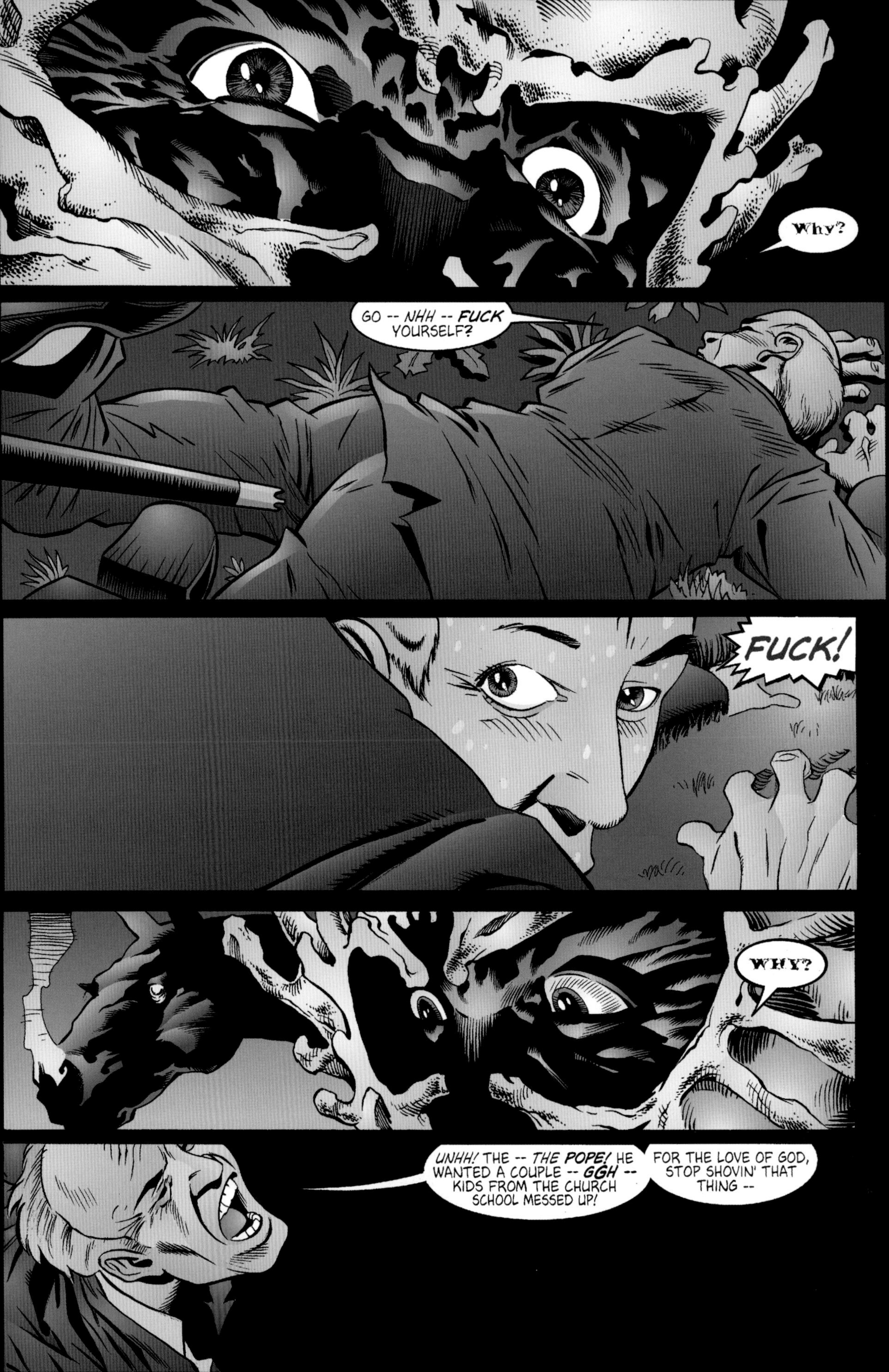

Why?
GO -- NHH -- FUCK YOURSELF?
FUCK!
WHY?
UNHH! THE -- THE POPE! HE WANTED A COUPLE -- GGH -- KIDS FROM THE CHURCH SCHOOL MESSED UP!
FOR THE LOVE OF GOD, STOP SHOVIN' THAT THING --

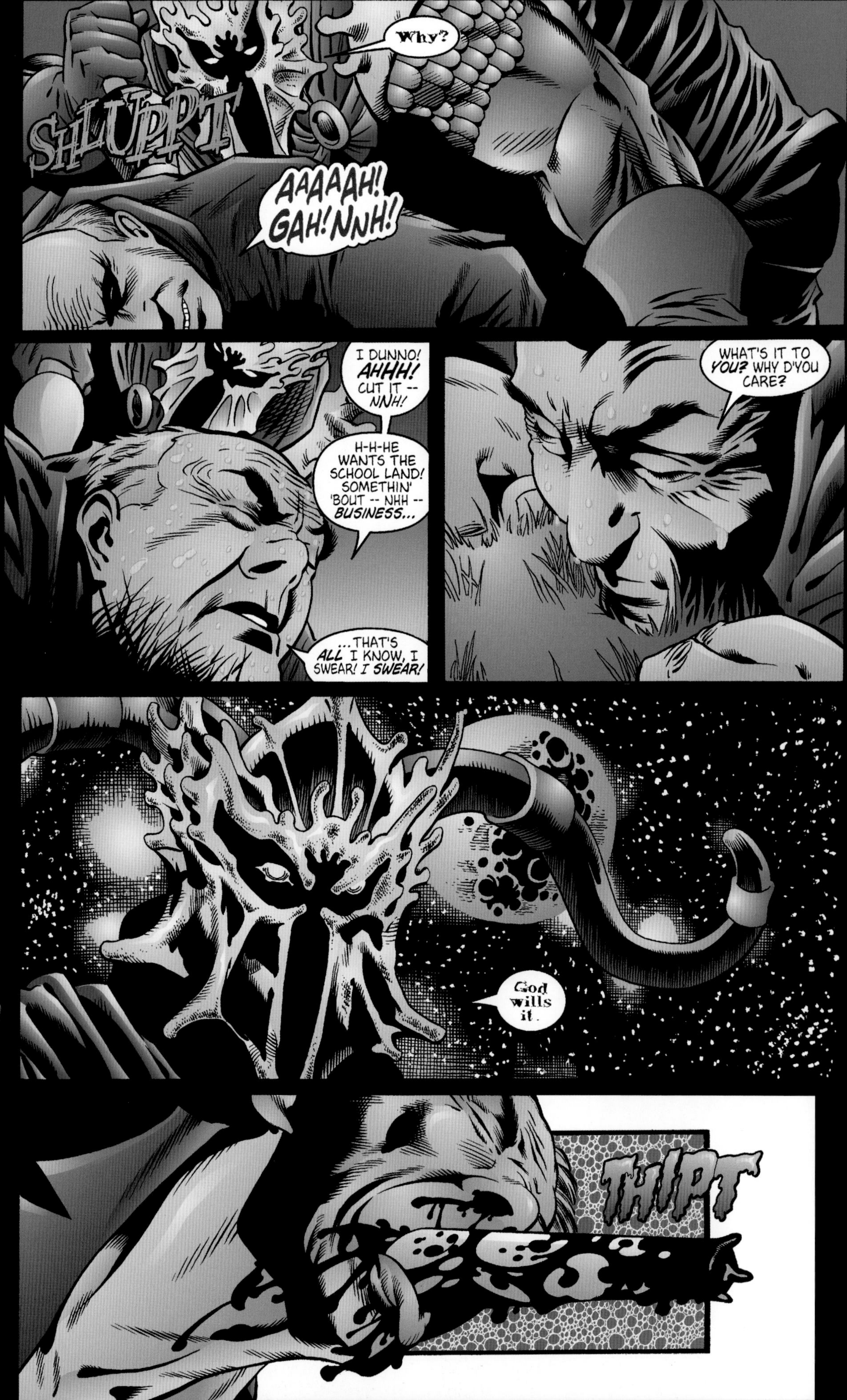
Why?
SHLUPPT
AAAAAH! GAH! NNH!
I DUNNO! AHHH! CUT IT -- NNH!
H-H-HE WANTS THE SCHOOL LAND! SOMETHIN' 'BOUT -- NHH -- BUSINESS...
...THAT'S ALL I KNOW, I SWEAR! I SWEAR!
WHAT'S IT TO YOU? WHY D'YOU CARE?
God wills it.
THPT

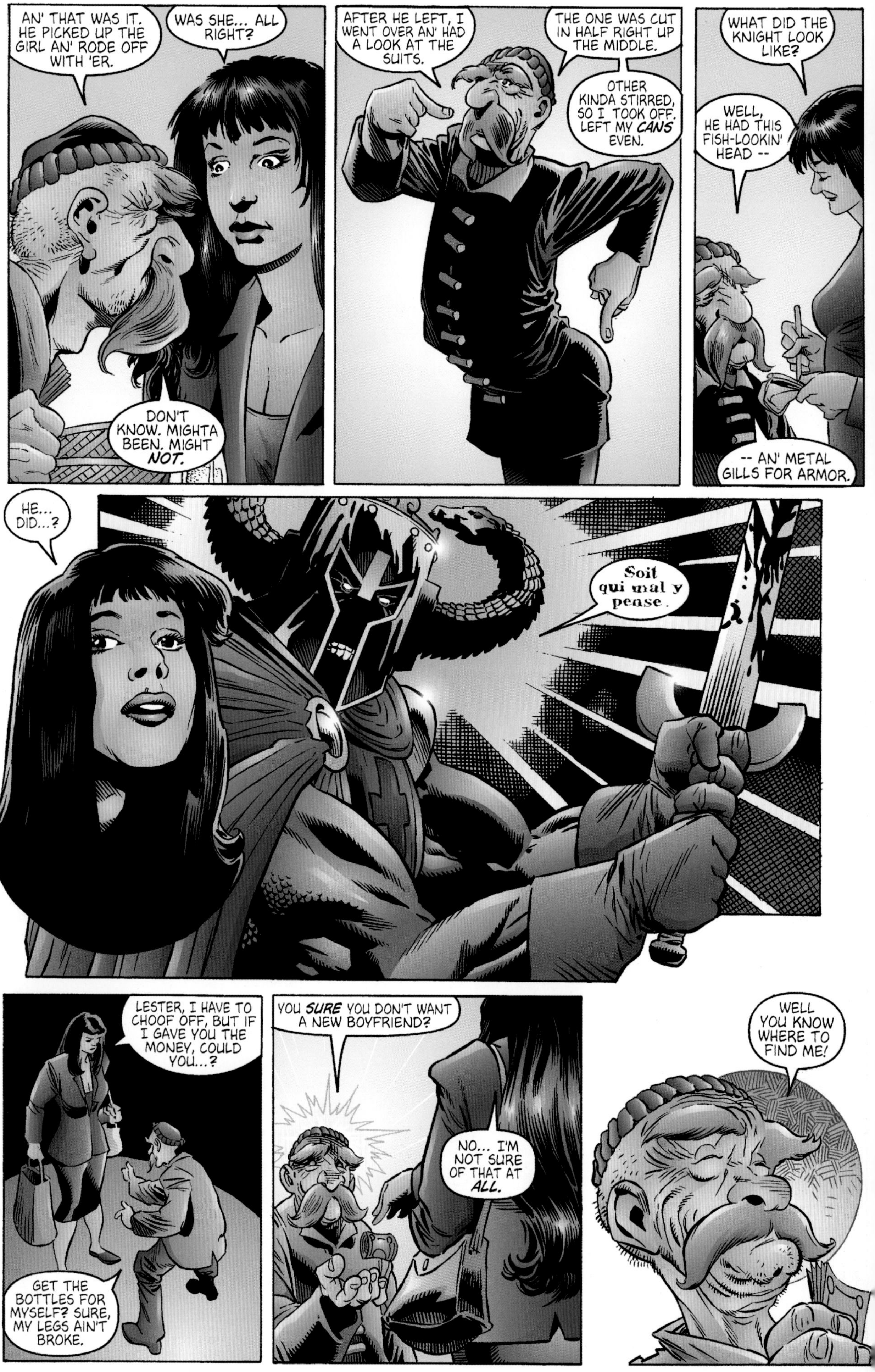
AN' THAT WAS IT. HE PICKED UP THE GIRL AN' RODE OFF WITH 'ER.
WAS SHE... ALL RIGHT?
DON'T KNOW. MIGHTA BEEN. MIGHT NOT.
AFTER HE LEFT, I WENT OVER AN' HAD A LOOK AT THE SUITS.
THE ONE WAS CUT IN HALF RIGHT UP THE MIDDLE.
OTHER KINDA STIRRED, SO I TOOK OFF. LEFT MY CANS EVEN.
WHAT DID THE KNIGHT LOOK LIKE?
WELL, HE HAD THIS FISH-LOOKIN' HEAD --
-- AN' METAL GILLS FOR ARMOR.
HE... DID...?
Soit qui mal y pense.
LESTER, I HAVE TO CHOOF OFF, BUT IF I GAVE YOU THE MONEY, COULD YOU...?
GET THE BOTTLES FOR MYSELF? SURE, MY LEGS AIN'T BROKE.
YOU SURE YOU DON'T WANT A NEW BOYFRIEND?
NO... I'M NOT SURE OF THAT AT ALL.
WELL YOU KNOW WHERE TO FIND ME!

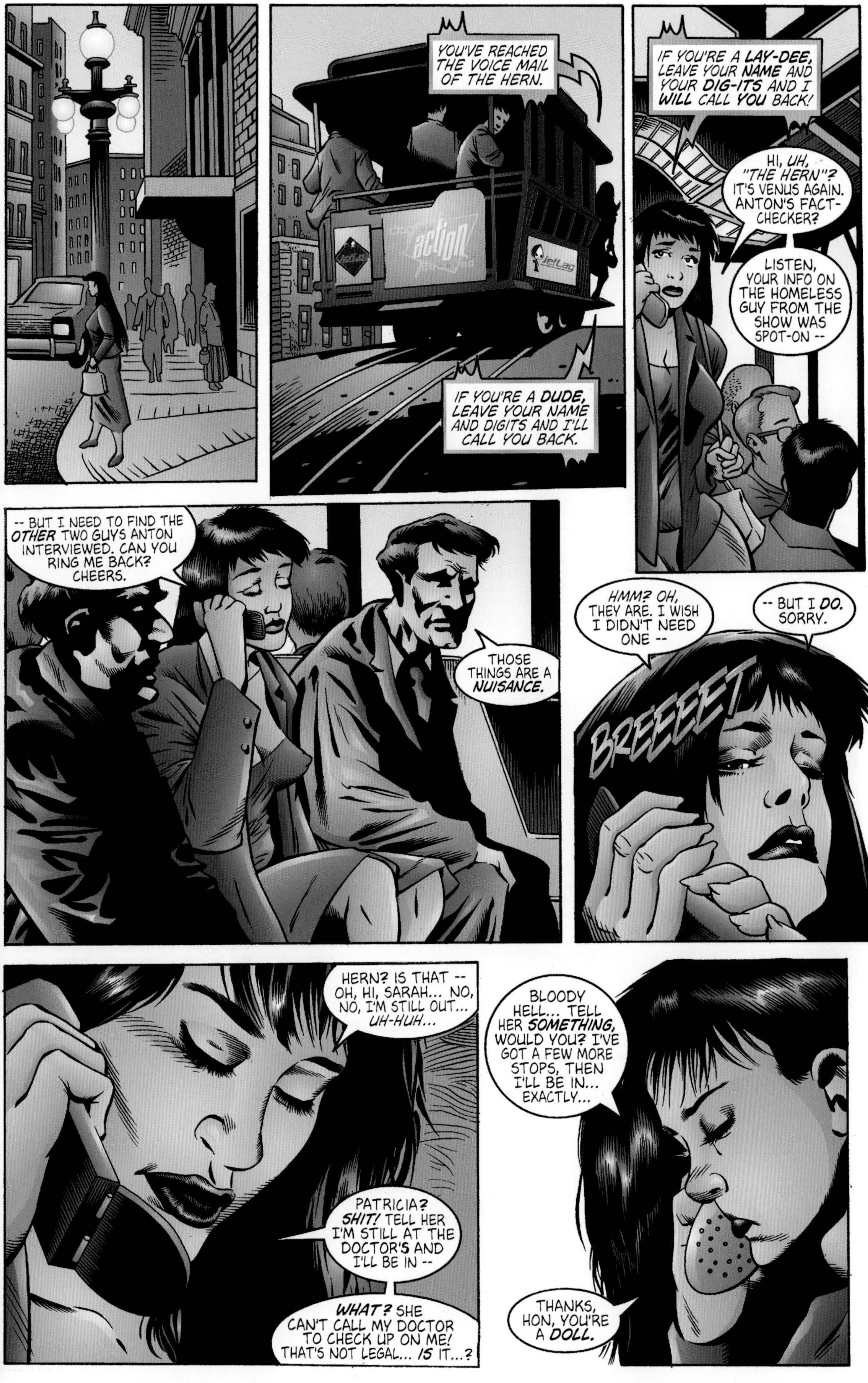
YOU'VE REACHED THE VOICE MAIL OF THE HERN.
IF YOU'RE A DUDE, LEAVE YOUR NAME AND DIGITS AND I'LL CALL YOU BACK.
IF YOU'RE A LAY-DEE, LEAVE YOUR NAME AND YOUR DIG-ITS AND I WILL CALL YOU BACK!
HI, UH, "THE HERN"? IT'S VENUS AGAIN. ANTON'S FACT-CHECKER?
LISTEN, YOUR INFO ON THE HOMELESS GUY FROM THE SHOW WAS SPOT-ON --
-- BUT I NEED TO FIND THE OTHER TWO GUYS ANTON INTERVIEWED. CAN YOU RING ME BACK? CHEERS.
THOSE THINGS ARE A NUISANCE.
HMM? OH, THEY ARE. I WISH I DIDN'T NEED ONE --
-- BUT I DO. SORRY.
BREEEET
HERN? IS THAT -- OH, HI, SARAH... NO, NO, I'M STILL OUT... UH-HUH...
PATRICIA? SHIT! TELL HER I'M STILL AT THE DOCTOR'S AND I'LL BE IN --
WHAT? SHE CAN'T CALL MY DOCTOR TO CHECK UP ON ME! THAT'S NOT LEGAL... IS IT...?
BLOODY HELL... TELL HER SOMETHING, WOULD YOU? I'VE GOT A FEW MORE STOPS, THEN I'LL BE IN... EXACTLY...
THANKS, HON, YOU'RE A DOLL.

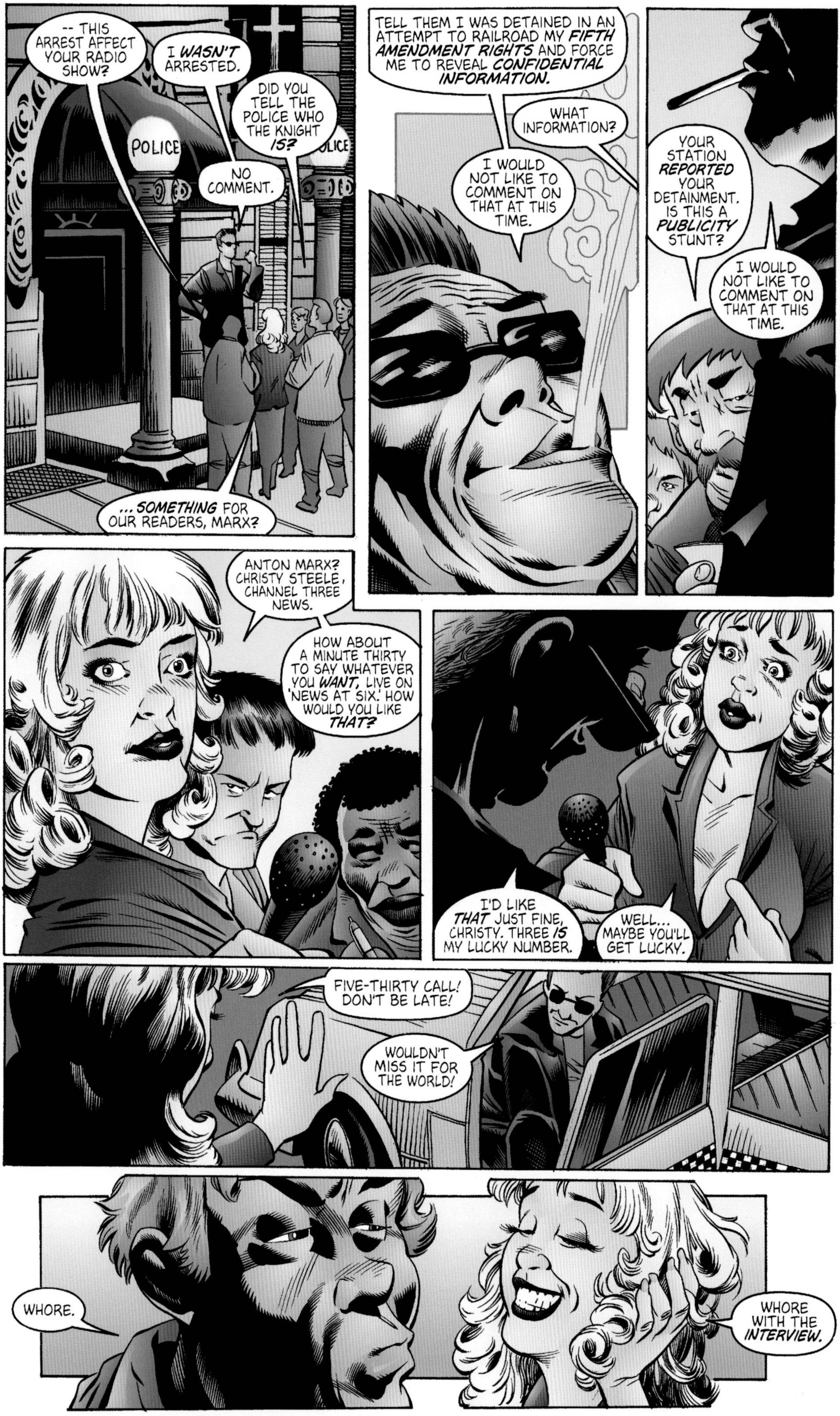

-- THIS ARREST AFFECT YOUR RADIO SHOW?
I WASN'T ARRESTED.
DID YOU TELL THE POLICE WHO THE KNIGHT IS?
POLICE
POLICE
NO COMMENT.
...SOMETHING FOR OUR READERS, MARX?
TELL THEM I WAS DETAINED IN AN ATTEMPT TO RAILROAD MY FIFTH AMENDMENT RIGHTS AND FORCE ME TO REVEAL CONFIDENTIAL INFORMATION.
WHAT INFORMATION?
I WOULD NOT LIKE TO COMMENT ON THAT AT THIS TIME.
YOUR STATION REPORTED YOUR DETAINMENT. IS THIS A PUBLICITY STUNT?
I WOULD NOT LIKE TO COMMENT ON THAT AT THIS TIME.
ANTON MARX? CHRISTY STEELE, CHANNEL THREE NEWS.
HOW ABOUT A MINUTE THIRTY TO SAY WHATEVER YOU WANT, LIVE ON 'NEWS AT SIX.' HOW WOULD YOU LIKE THAT?
I'D LIKE THAT JUST FINE, CHRISTY. THREE IS MY LUCKY NUMBER.
WELL... MAYBE YOU'LL GET LUCKY.
FIVE-THIRTY CALL! DON'T BE LATE!
WOULDN'T MISS IT FOR THE WORLD!
WHORE.
WHORE WITH THE INTERVIEW.

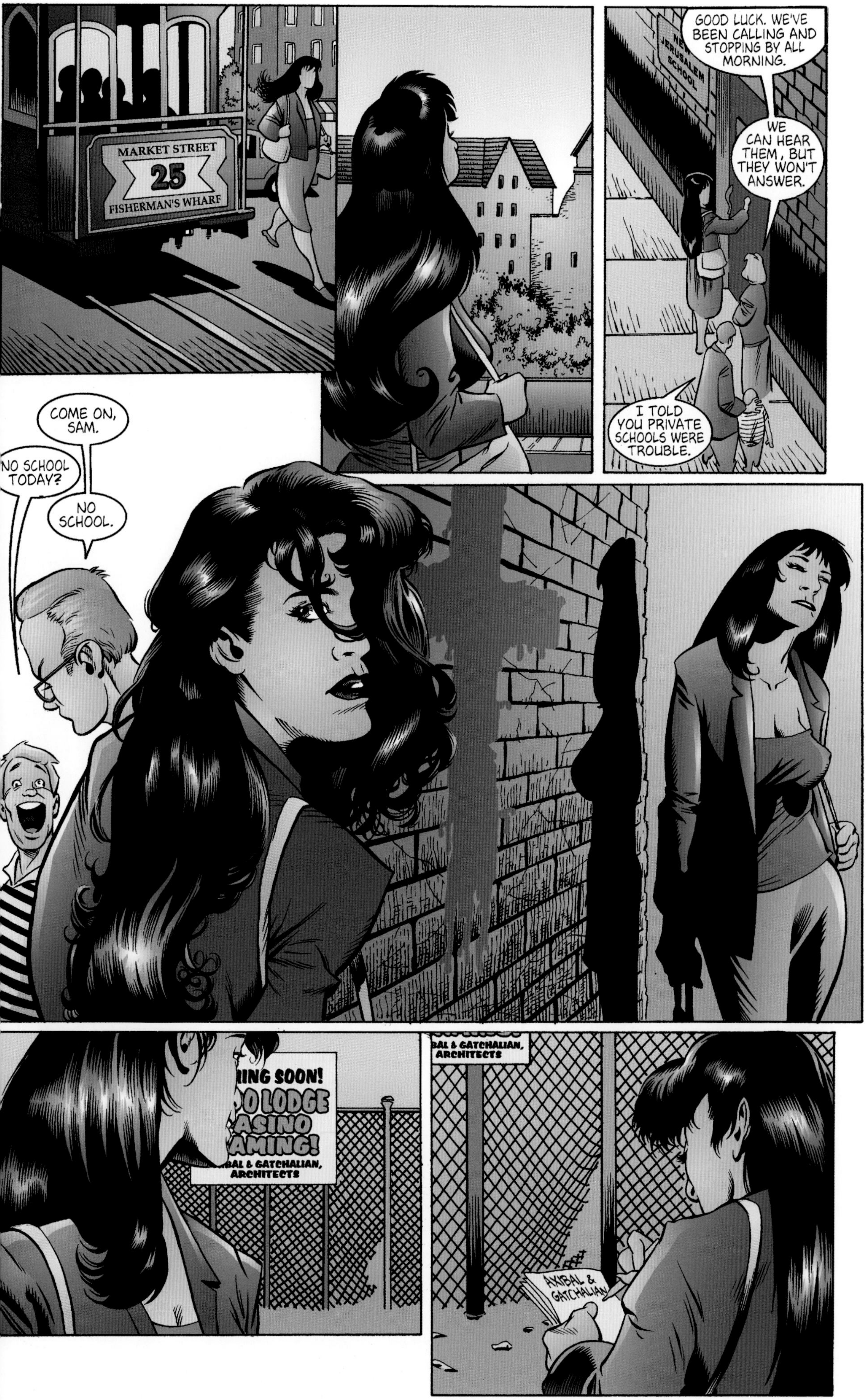

MARKET STREET
25
FISHERMAN'S WHARF
JERUSALEM
SCHOOL
GOOD LUCK. WE'VE BEEN CALLING AND STOPPING BY ALL MORNING.
WE CAN HEAR THEM, BUT THEY WON'T ANSWER.
I TOLD YOU PRIVATE SCHOOLS WERE TROUBLE.
COME ON, SAM.
NO SCHOOL TODAY?
NO SCHOOL.
ING SOON!
O LODGE
ASINO
AMING!
BAL & GATCHALIAN,
ARCHITECTS
BAL & GATCHALIAN,
ARCHITECTS
AXIBAL & GATCHALIAN

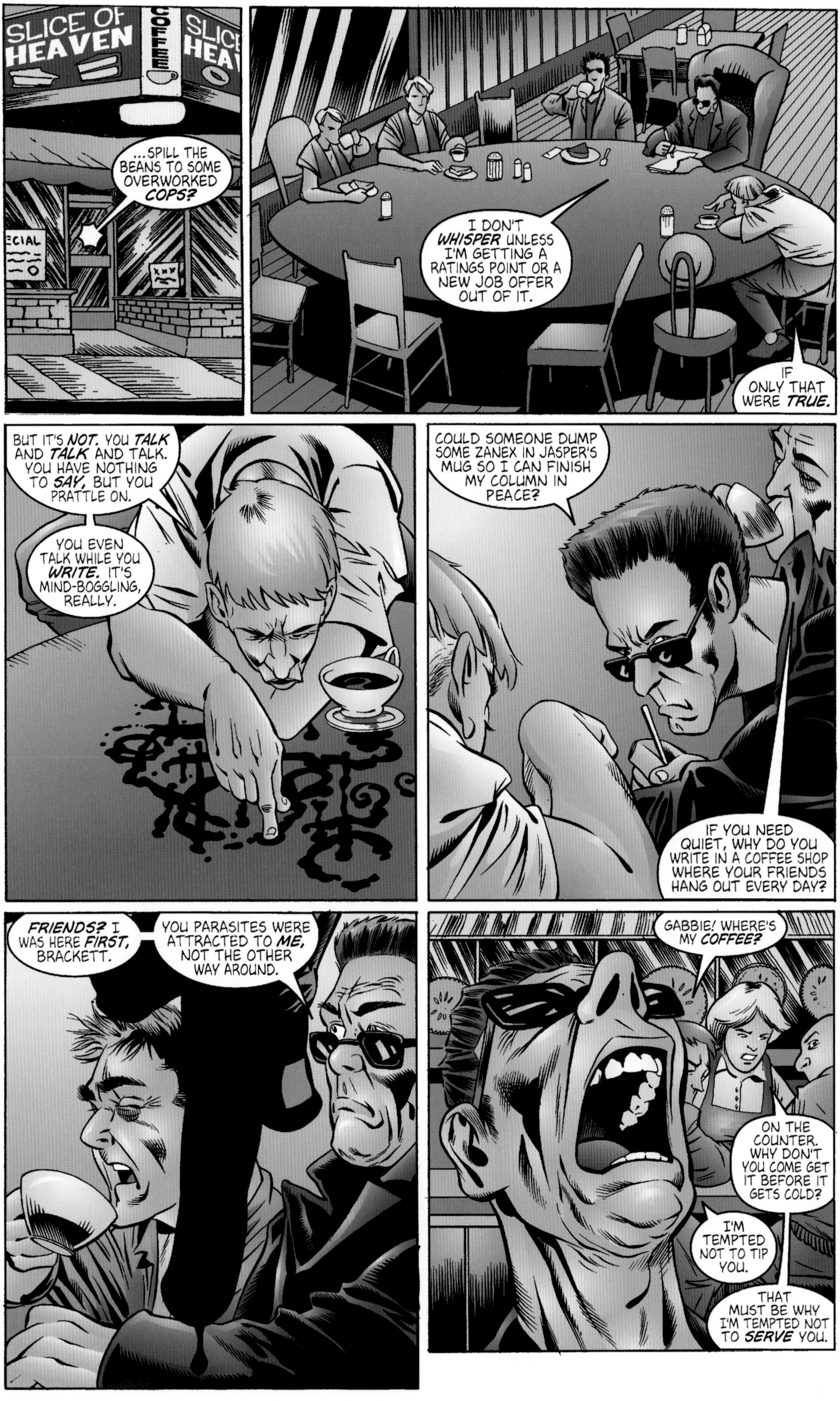
SLICE OF HEAVEN
COFFEE
...SPILL THE BEANS TO SOME OVERWORKED COPS?
I DON'T WHISPER UNLESS I'M GETTING A RATINGS POINT OR A NEW JOB OFFER OUT OF IT.
IF ONLY THAT WERE TRUE.
BUT IT'S NOT. YOU TALK AND TALK AND TALK. YOU HAVE NOTHING TO SAY, BUT YOU PRATTLE ON.
YOU EVEN TALK WHILE YOU WRITE. IT'S MIND-BOGGLING, REALLY.
COULD SOMEONE DUMP SOME ZANEX IN JASPER'S MUG SO I CAN FINISH MY COLUMN IN PEACE?
IF YOU NEED QUIET, WHY DO YOU WRITE IN A COFFEE SHOP WHERE YOUR FRIENDS HANG OUT EVERY DAY?
FRIENDS? I WAS HERE FIRST, BRACKETT.
YOU PARASITES WERE ATTRACTED TO ME, NOT THE OTHER WAY AROUND.
GABBIE! WHERE'S MY COFFEE?
ON THE COUNTER. WHY DON'T YOU COME GET IT BEFORE IT GETS COLD?
I'M TEMPTED NOT TO TIP YOU.
THAT MUST BE WHY I'M TEMPTED NOT TO SERVE YOU.

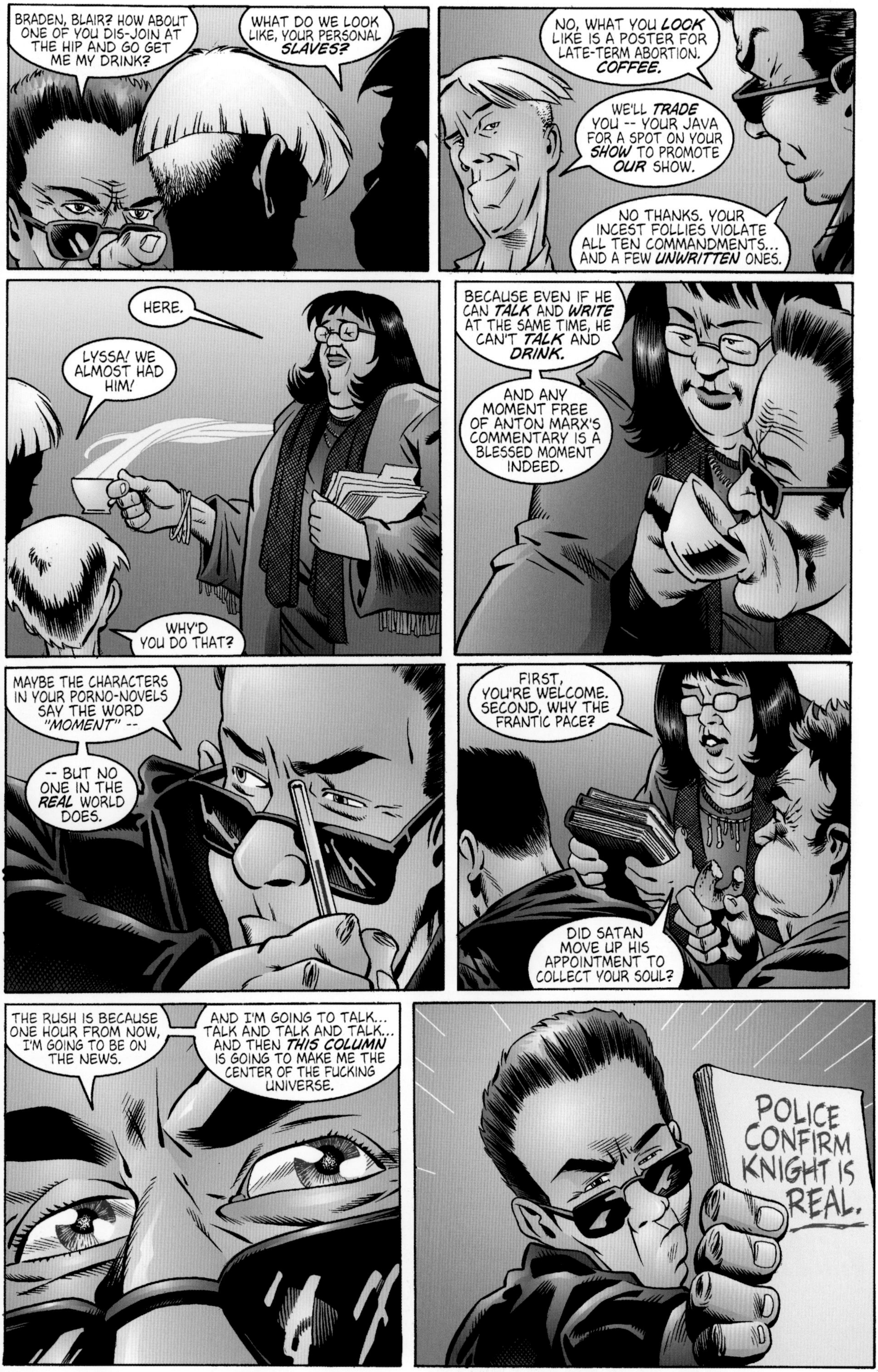
BRADEN, BLAIR? HOW ABOUT ONE OF YOU DIS-JOIN AT THE HIP AND GO GET ME MY DRINK?
WHAT DO WE LOOK LIKE, YOUR PERSONAL SLAVES?
NO, WHAT YOU LOOK LIKE IS A POSTER FOR LATE-TERM ABORTION. COFFEE.
WE'LL TRADE YOU -- YOUR JAVA FOR A SPOT ON YOUR SHOW TO PROMOTE OUR SHOW.
NO THANKS. YOUR INCEST FOLLIES VIOLATE ALL TEN COMMANDMENTS... AND A FEW UNWRITTEN ONES.
HERE.
LYSSA! WE ALMOST HAD HIM!
WHY'D YOU DO THAT?
BECAUSE EVEN IF HE CAN TALK AND WRITE AT THE SAME TIME, HE CAN'T TALK AND DRINK.
AND ANY MOMENT FREE OF ANTON MARX'S COMMENTARY IS A BLESSED MOMENT INDEED.
MAYBE THE CHARACTERS IN YOUR PORNO-NOVELS SAY THE WORD "MOMENT" --
-- BUT NO ONE IN THE REAL WORLD DOES.
FIRST, YOU'RE WELCOME. SECOND, WHY THE FRANTIC PACE?
DID SATAN MOVE UP HIS APPOINTMENT TO COLLECT YOUR SOUL?
THE RUSH IS BECAUSE ONE HOUR FROM NOW, I'M GOING TO BE ON THE NEWS.
AND I'M GOING TO TALK... TALK AND TALK AND TALK... AND THEN THIS COLUMN IS GOING TO MAKE ME THE CENTER OF THE FUCKING UNIVERSE.
POLICE CONFIRM KNIGHT IS REAL.

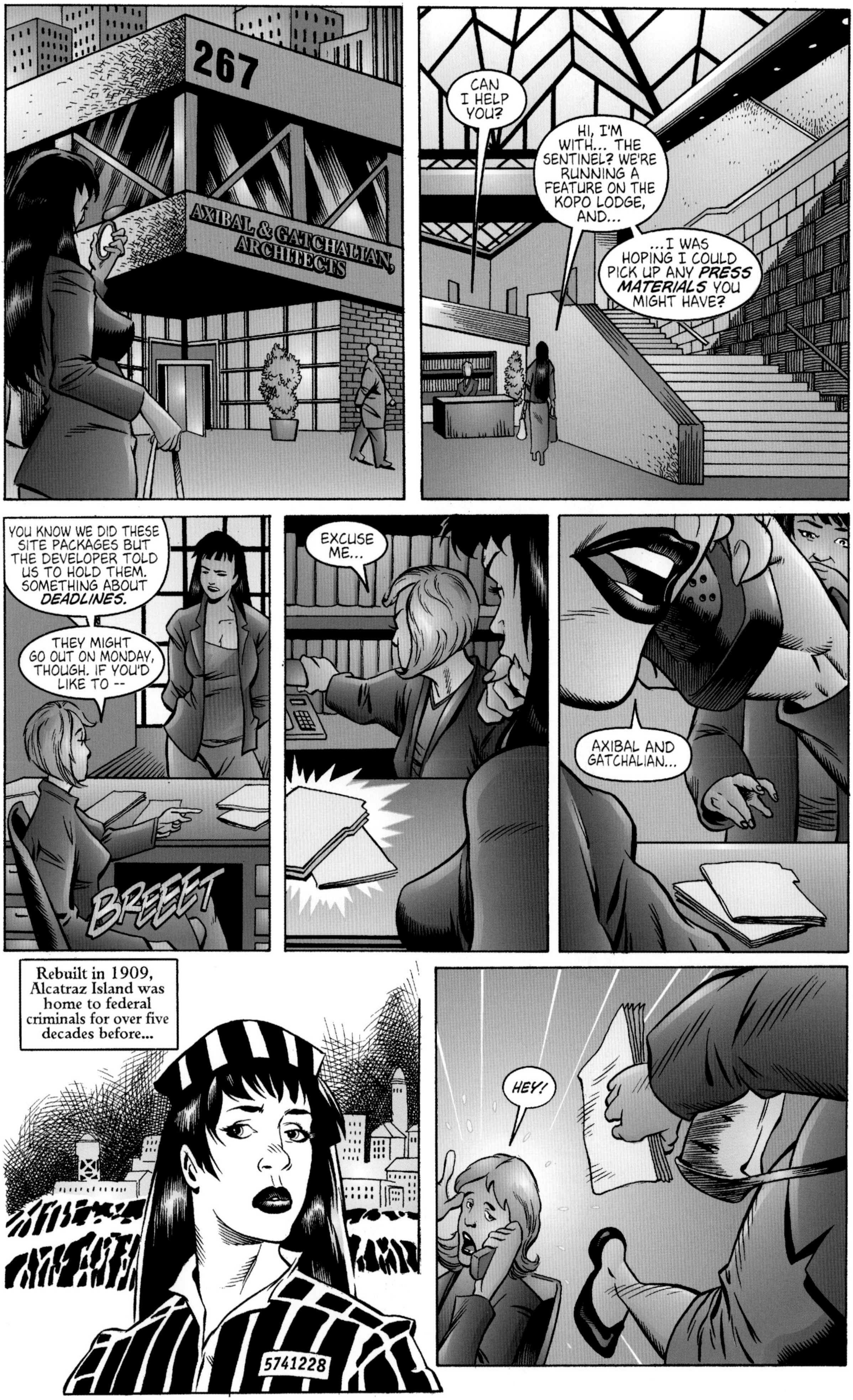
267
AXIBAL & GATCHALIAN, ARCHITECTS
CAN I HELP YOU?
HI, I'M WITH... THE SENTINEL? WE'RE RUNNING A FEATURE ON THE KOPO LODGE, AND...
...I WAS HOPING I COULD PICK UP ANY PRESS MATERIALS YOU MIGHT HAVE?
YOU KNOW WE DID THESE SITE PACKAGES BUT THE DEVELOPER TOLD US TO HOLD THEM. SOMETHING ABOUT DEADLINES.
THEY MIGHT GO OUT ON MONDAY, THOUGH. IF YOU'D LIKE TO --
BREEET
EXCUSE ME...
AXIBAL AND GATCHALIAN...
Rebuilt in 1909, Alcatraz Island was home to federal criminals for over five decades before...
5741228
HEY!

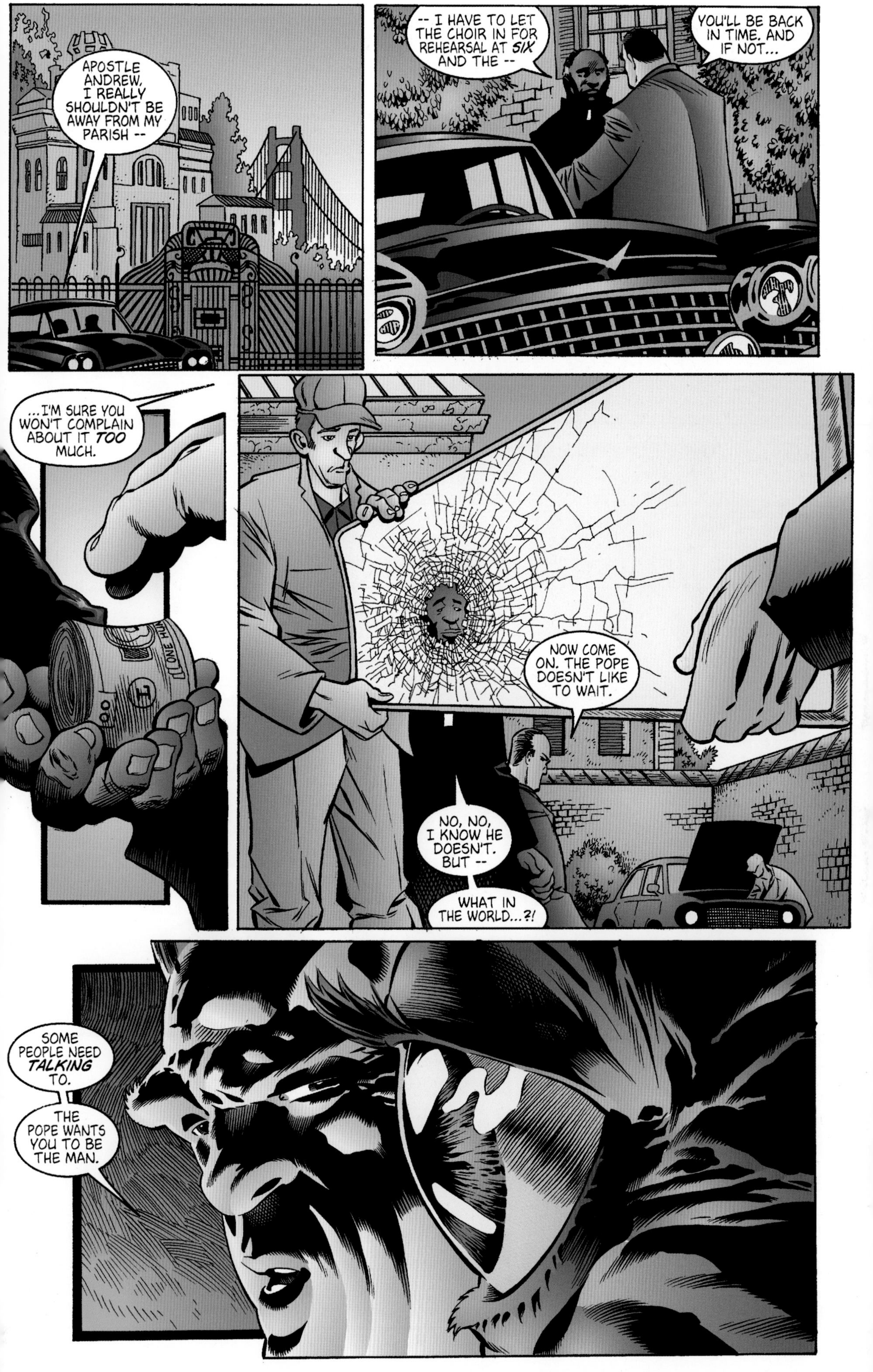
APOSTLE ANDREW, I REALLY SHOULDN'T BE AWAY FROM MY PARISH --
-- I HAVE TO LET THE CHOIR IN FOR REHEARSAL AT SIX AND THE --
YOU'LL BE BACK IN TIME. AND IF NOT...
...I'M SURE YOU WON'T COMPLAIN ABOUT IT TOO MUCH.
NOW COME ON. THE POPE DOESN'T LIKE TO WAIT.
NO, NO, I KNOW HE DOESN'T. BUT --
WHAT IN THE WORLD...?!
SOME PEOPLE NEED TALKING TO.
THE POPE WANTS YOU TO BE THE MAN.

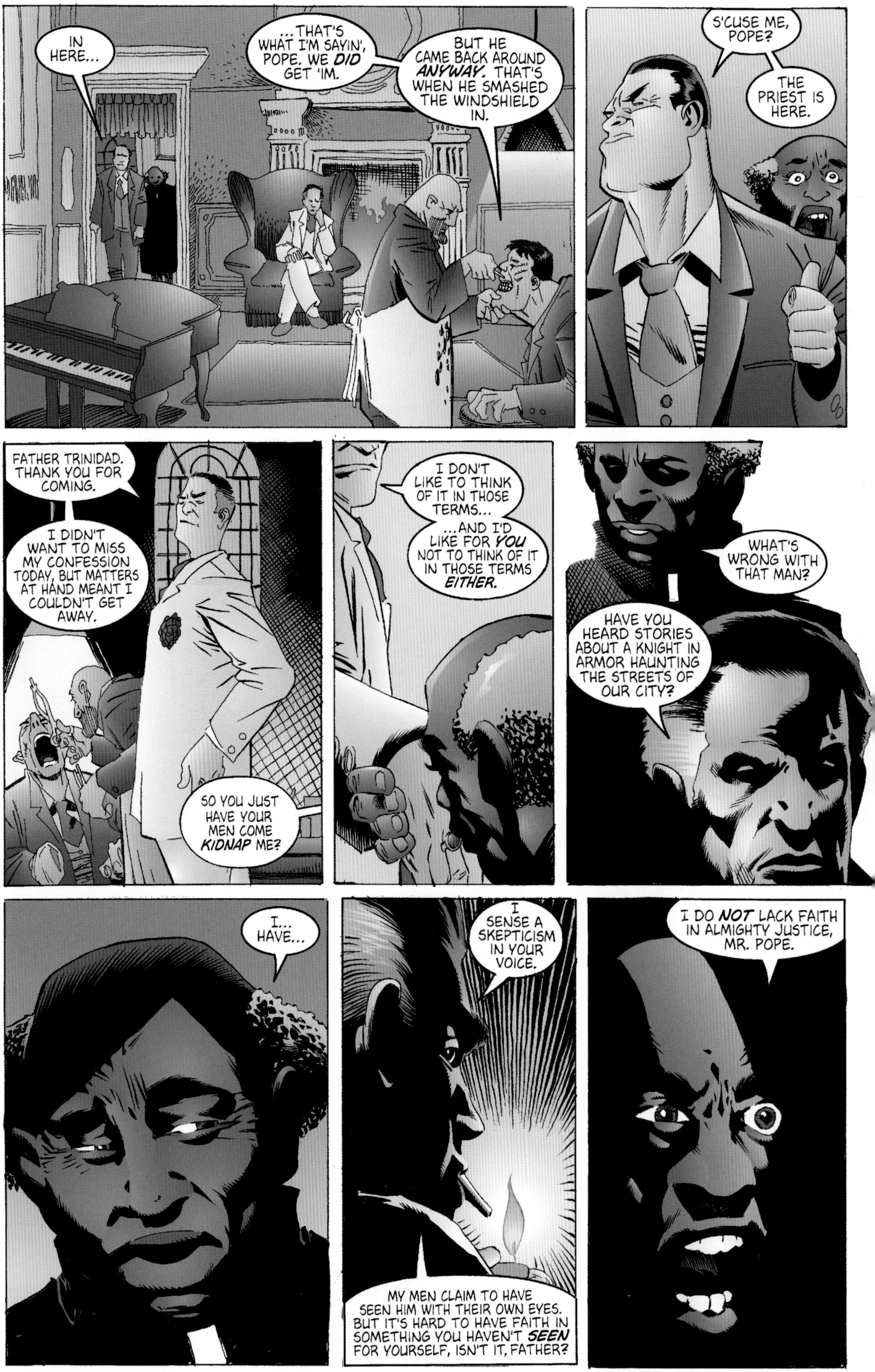
IN HERE...
...THAT'S WHAT I'M SAYIN', POPE. WE DID GET 'IM.
BUT HE CAME BACK AROUND ANYWAY. THAT'S WHEN HE SMASHED THE WINDSHIELD IN.
S'CUSE ME, POPE?
THE PRIEST IS HERE.
FATHER TRINIDAD. THANK YOU FOR COMING.
I DIDN'T WANT TO MISS MY CONFESSION TODAY, BUT MATTERS AT HAND MEANT I COULDN'T GET AWAY.
SO YOU JUST HAVE YOUR MEN COME KIDNAP ME?
I DON'T LIKE TO THINK OF IT IN THOSE TERMS...
...AND I'D LIKE FOR YOU NOT TO THINK OF IT IN THOSE TERMS EITHER.
WHAT'S WRONG WITH THAT MAN?
HAVE YOU HEARD STORIES ABOUT A KNIGHT IN ARMOR HAUNTING THE STREETS OF OUR CITY?
I... HAVE...
I SENSE A SKEPTICISM IN YOUR VOICE.
MY MEN CLAIM TO HAVE SEEN HIM WITH THEIR OWN EYES. BUT IT'S HARD TO HAVE FAITH IN SOMETHING YOU HAVEN'T SEEN FOR YOURSELF, ISN'T IT, FATHER?
I DO NOT LACK FAITH IN ALMIGHTY JUSTICE, MR. POPE.

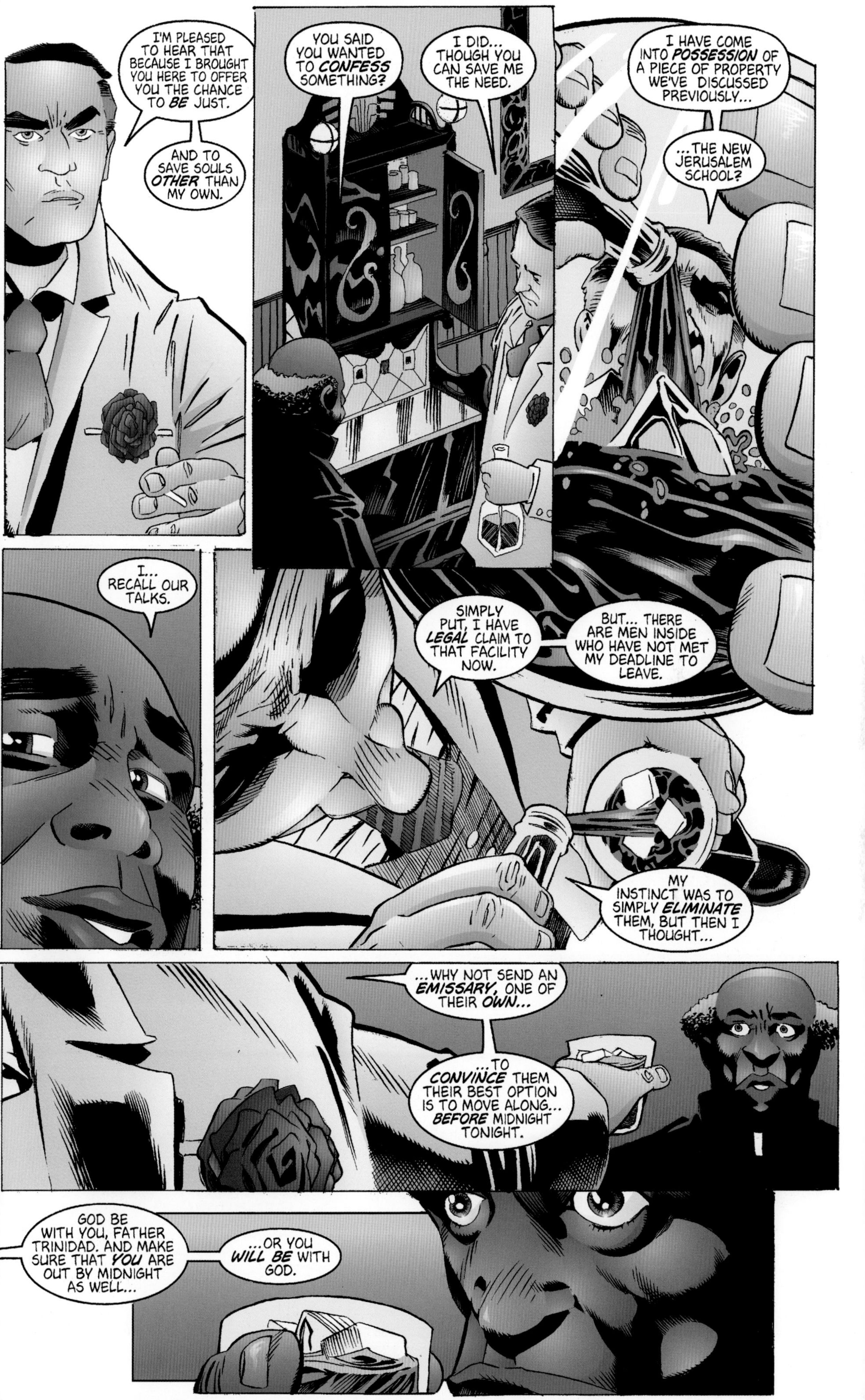
I'M PLEASED TO HEAR THAT BECAUSE I BROUGHT YOU HERE TO OFFER YOU THE CHANCE TO *BE* JUST.
AND TO SAVE SOULS *OTHER* THAN MY OWN.
YOU SAID YOU WANTED TO *CONFESS* SOMETHING?
I DID... THOUGH YOU CAN SAVE ME THE NEED.
I HAVE COME INTO *POSSESSION* OF A PIECE OF PROPERTY WE'VE DISCUSSED PREVIOUSLY...
...THE NEW JERUSALEM SCHOOL?
I... RECALL OUR TALKS.
SIMPLY PUT, I HAVE *LEGAL* CLAIM TO THAT FACILITY NOW.
BUT... THERE ARE MEN INSIDE WHO HAVE NOT MET MY DEADLINE TO LEAVE.
MY INSTINCT WAS TO SIMPLY *ELIMINATE* THEM, BUT THEN I THOUGHT...
...WHY NOT SEND AN *EMISSARY*, ONE OF THEIR *OWN*...
...TO *CONVINCE* THEM THEIR BEST OPTION IS TO MOVE ALONG... *BEFORE* MIDNIGHT TONIGHT.
GOD BE WITH YOU, FATHER TRINIDAD. AND MAKE SURE THAT *YOU* ARE OUT BY MIDNIGHT AS WELL...
...OR YOU *WILL BE* WITH GOD.

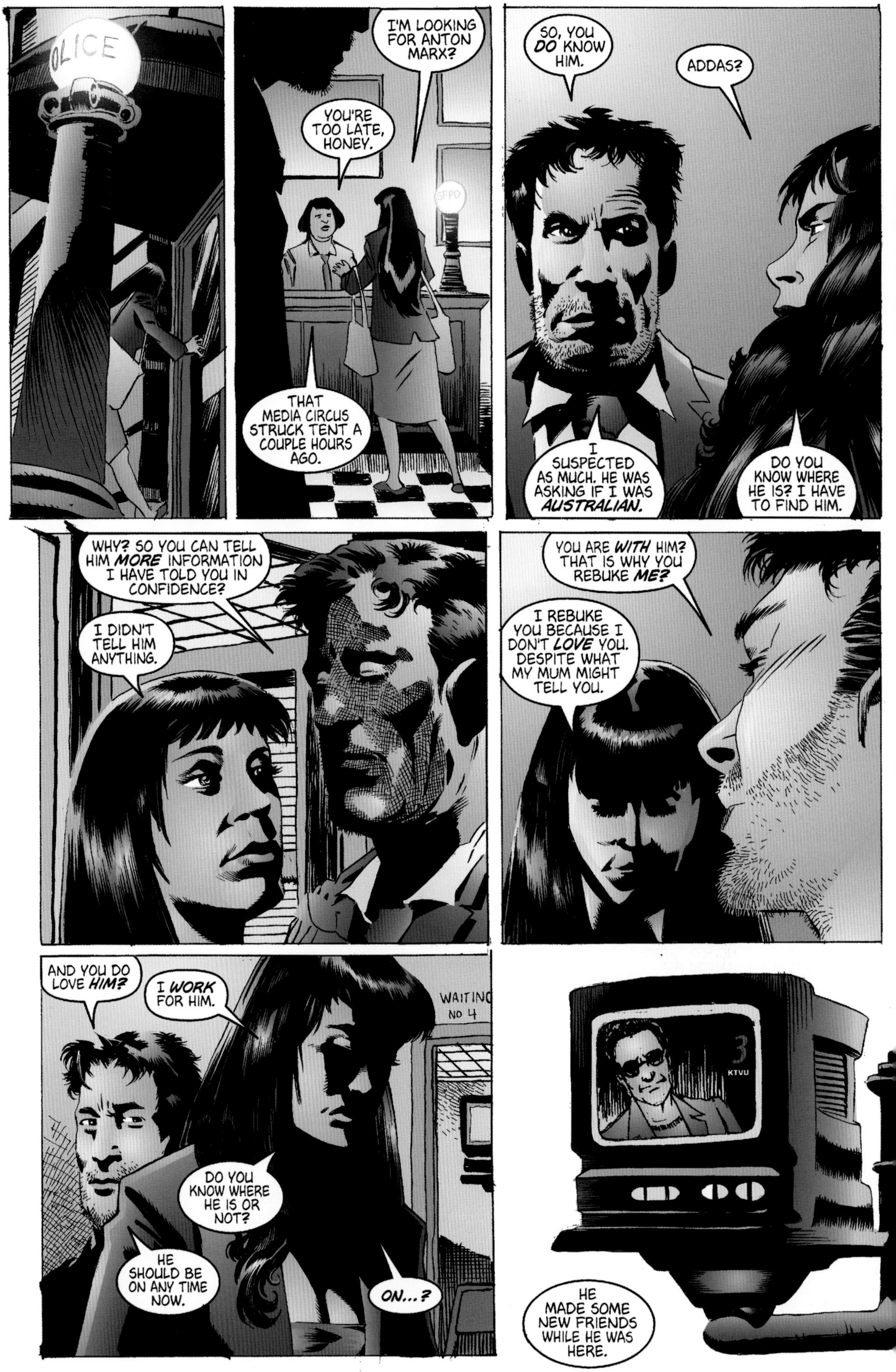
OLICE
I'M LOOKING FOR ANTON MARX?
YOU'RE TOO LATE, HONEY.
SFPD
THAT MEDIA CIRCUS STRUCK TENT A COUPLE HOURS AGO.
SO, YOU *DO* KNOW HIM.
ADDAS?
I SUSPECTED AS MUCH. HE WAS ASKING IF I WAS ***AUSTRALIAN.***
DO YOU KNOW WHERE HE IS? I HAVE TO FIND HIM.
WHY? SO YOU CAN TELL HIM ***MORE*** INFORMATION I HAVE TOLD YOU IN CONFIDENCE?
I DIDN'T TELL HIM ANYTHING.
YOU ARE ***WITH*** HIM? THAT IS WHY YOU REBUKE ***ME?***
I REBUKE YOU BECAUSE I DON'T ***LOVE*** YOU. DESPITE WHAT MY MUM MIGHT TELL YOU.
AND YOU DO LOVE ***HIM?***
I ***WORK*** FOR HIM.
WAITING NO 4
DO YOU KNOW WHERE HE IS OR NOT?
HE SHOULD BE ON ANY TIME NOW.
ON...?
3
KTVU
HE MADE SOME NEW FRIENDS WHILE HE WAS HERE.

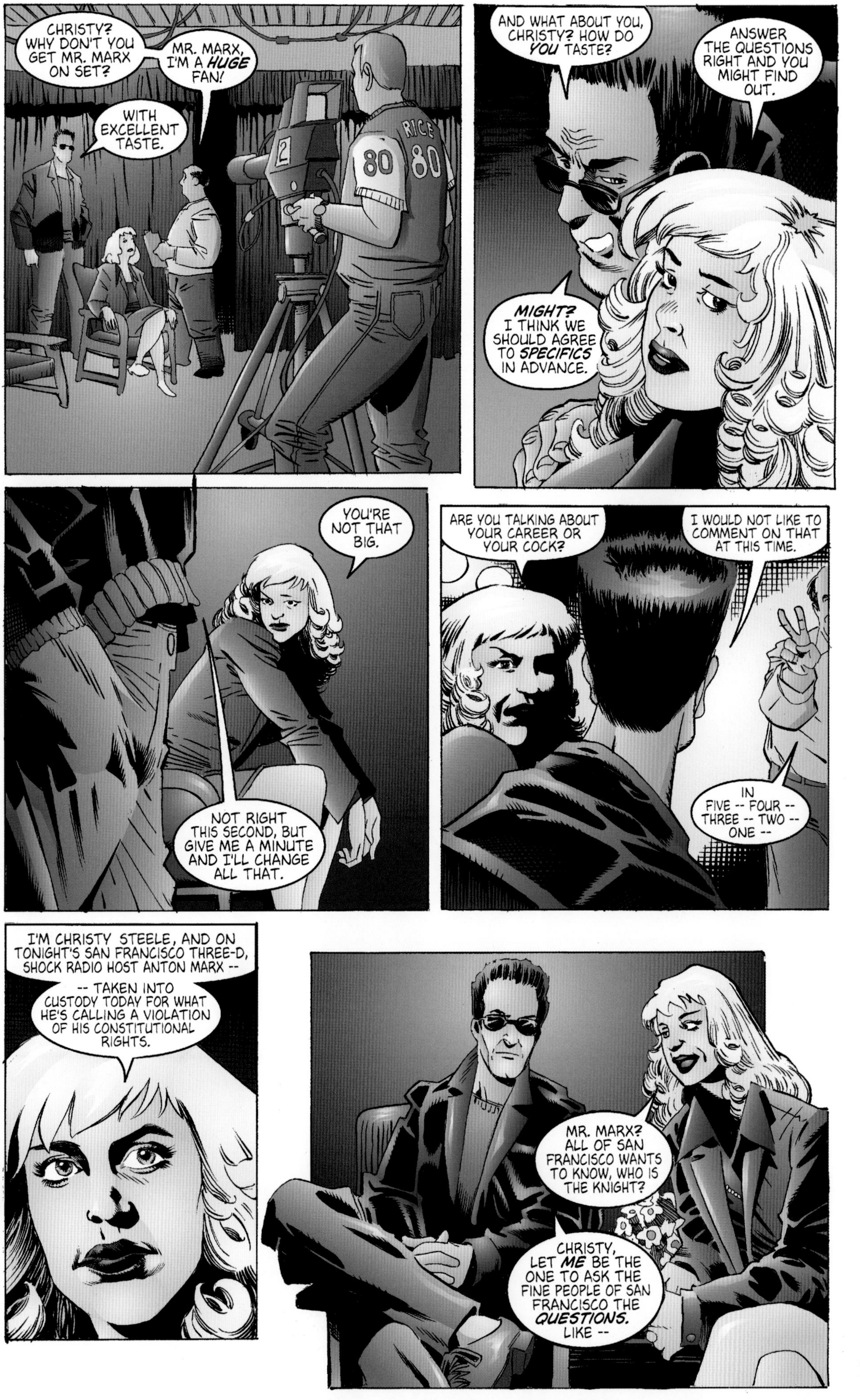
CHRISTY? WHY DON'T YOU GET MR. MARX ON SET?
MR. MARX, I'M A HUGE FAN!
WITH EXCELLENT TASTE.
RICE
80
2
AND WHAT ABOUT YOU, CHRISTY? HOW DO YOU TASTE?
ANSWER THE QUESTIONS RIGHT AND YOU MIGHT FIND OUT.
MIGHT? I THINK WE SHOULD AGREE TO SPECIFICS IN ADVANCE.
YOU'RE NOT THAT BIG.
NOT RIGHT THIS SECOND, BUT GIVE ME A MINUTE AND I'LL CHANGE ALL THAT.
ARE YOU TALKING ABOUT YOUR CAREER OR YOUR COCK?
I WOULD NOT LIKE TO COMMENT ON THAT AT THIS TIME.
IN FIVE -- FOUR -- THREE -- TWO -- ONE --
I'M CHRISTY STEELE, AND ON TONIGHT'S SAN FRANCISCO THREE-D, SHOCK RADIO HOST ANTON MARX --
-- TAKEN INTO CUSTODY TODAY FOR WHAT HE'S CALLING A VIOLATION OF HIS CONSTITUTIONAL RIGHTS.
MR. MARX? ALL OF SAN FRANCISCO WANTS TO KNOW, WHO IS THE KNIGHT?
CHRISTY, LET ME BE THE ONE TO ASK THE FINE PEOPLE OF SAN FRANCISCO THE QUESTIONS. LIKE --

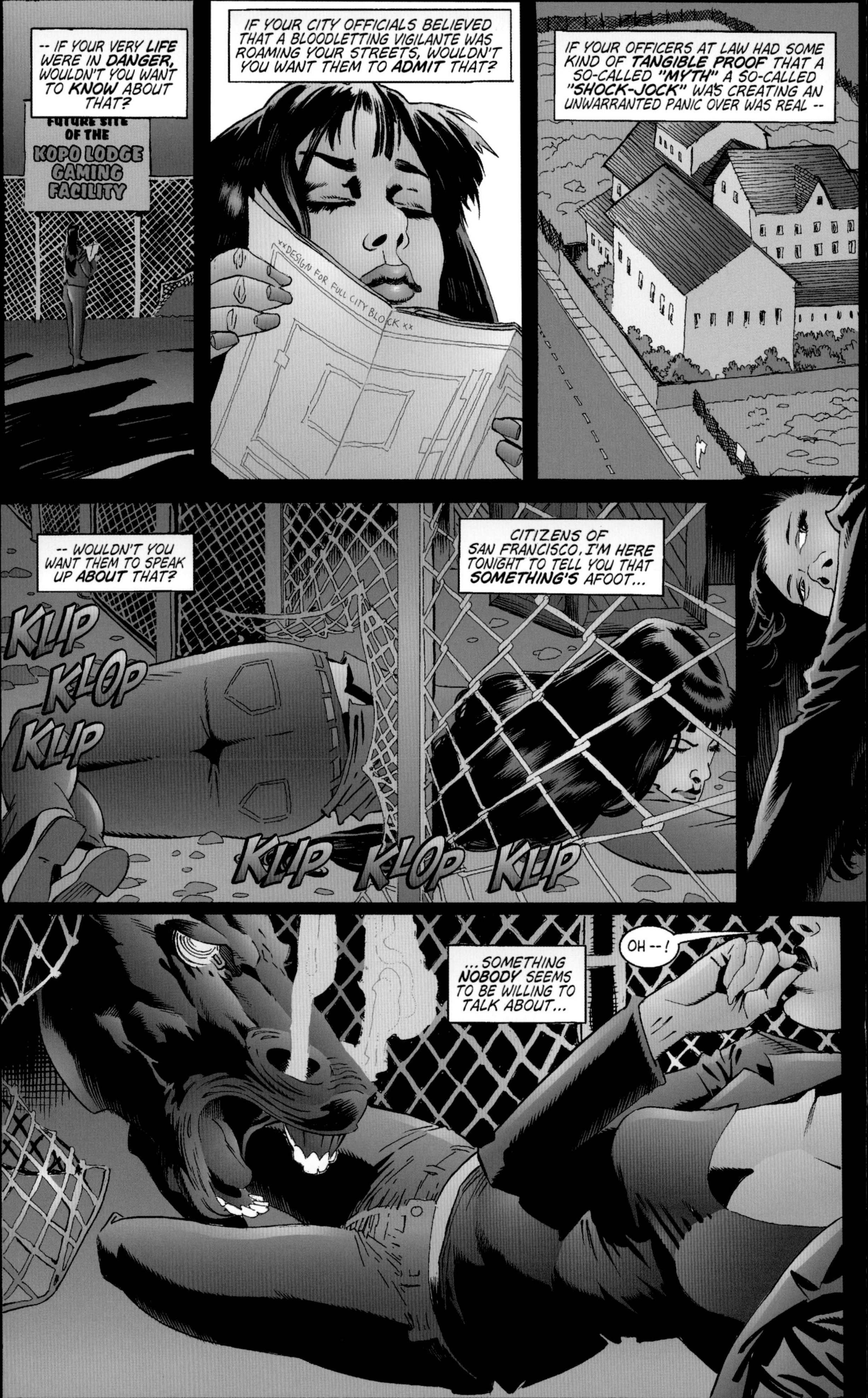
-- IF YOUR VERY LIFE WERE IN DANGER, WOULDN'T YOU WANT TO KNOW ABOUT THAT?
FUTURE SITE OF THE KOPO LODGE GAMING FACILITY
IF YOUR CITY OFFICIALS BELIEVED THAT A BLOODLETTING VIGILANTE WAS ROAMING YOUR STREETS, WOULDN'T YOU WANT THEM TO ADMIT THAT?
xx DESIGN FOR FULL CITY BLOCK xx
IF YOUR OFFICERS AT LAW HAD SOME KIND OF TANGIBLE PROOF THAT A SO-CALLED "MYTH" A SO-CALLED "SHOCK-JOCK" WAS CREATING AN UNWARRANTED PANIC OVER WAS REAL --
-- WOULDN'T YOU WANT THEM TO SPEAK UP ABOUT THAT?
KLIP KLOP KLIP
CITIZENS OF SAN FRANCISCO, I'M HERE TONIGHT TO TELL YOU THAT SOMETHING'S AFOOT...
KLIP KLOP KLIP
...SOMETHING NOBODY SEEMS TO BE WILLING TO TALK ABOUT...
OH --!

"The Freedom of the Press Works in Such a Way
That There is Not Much Freedom From It."
--Princess Grace of Monaco

"STOP RIGHT
THERE...!"

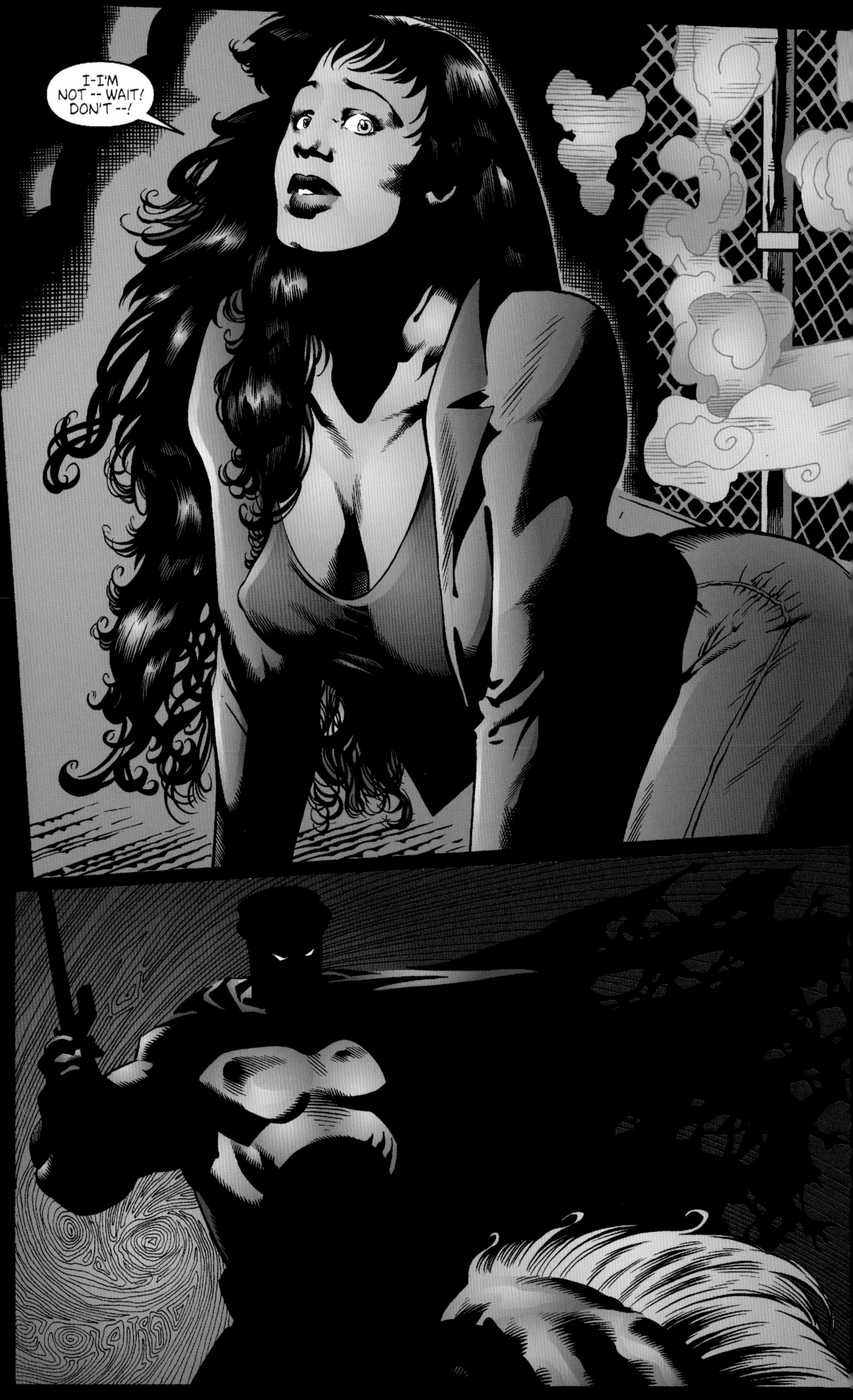
I-I'M NOT -- WAIT! DON'T --!

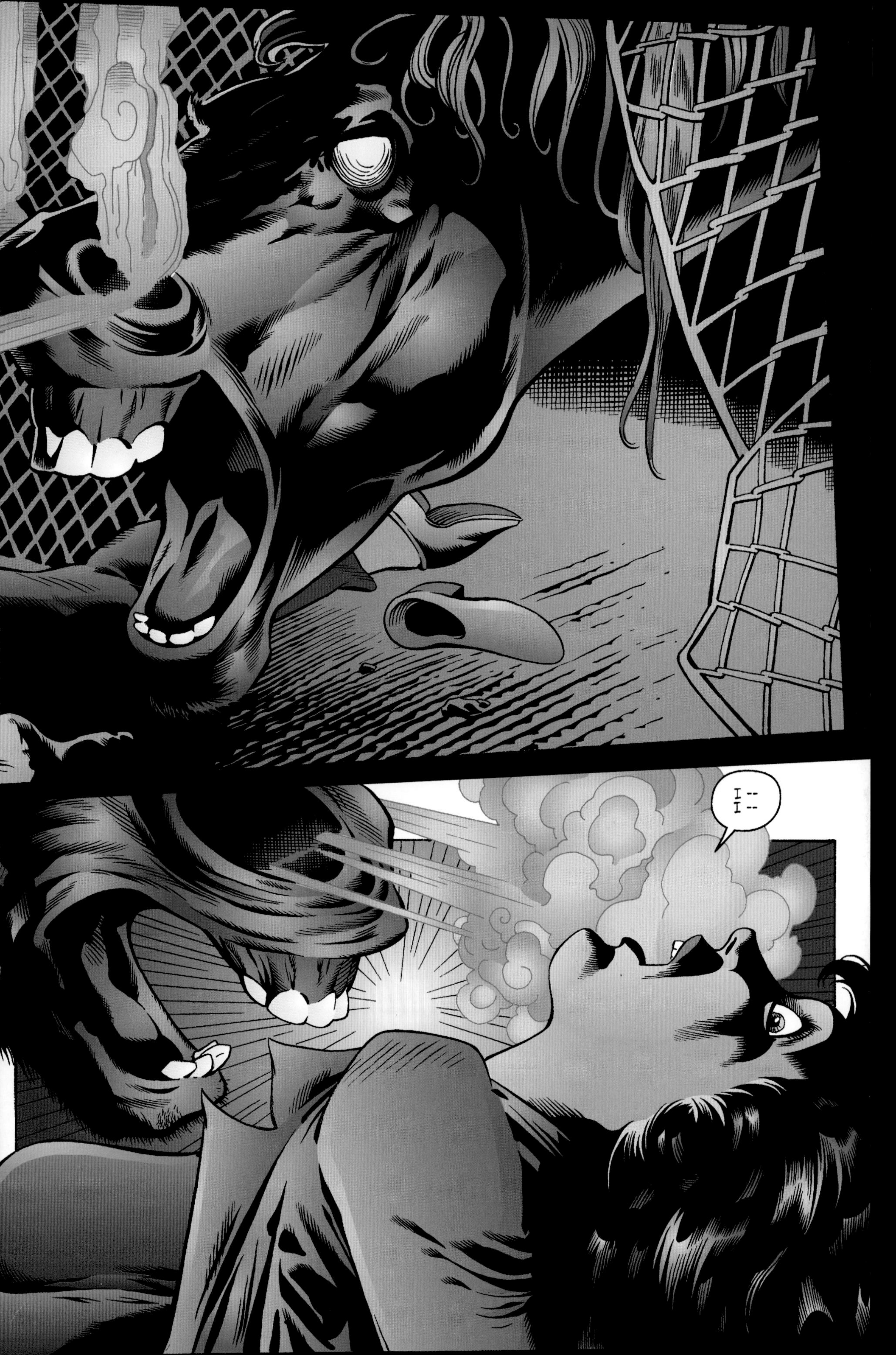
I --
I --

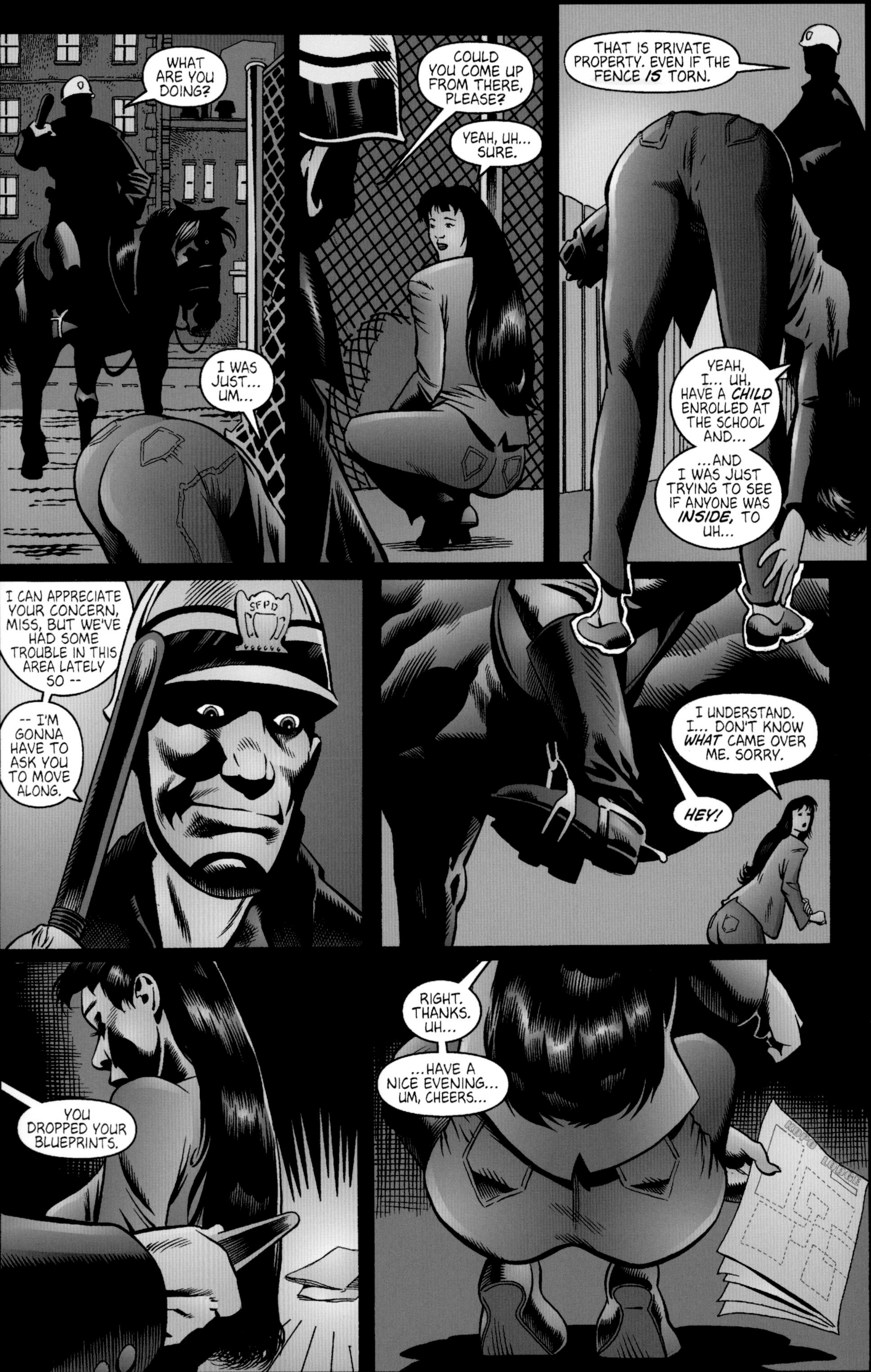
WHAT ARE YOU DOING?
I WAS JUST... UM...
COULD YOU COME UP FROM THERE, PLEASE?
YEAH, UH... SURE.
THAT IS PRIVATE PROPERTY. EVEN IF THE FENCE *IS* TORN.
YEAH, I... UH, HAVE A *CHILD* ENROLLED AT THE SCHOOL AND...
...AND I WAS JUST TRYING TO SEE IF ANYONE WAS *INSIDE,* TO UH...
I CAN APPRECIATE YOUR CONCERN, MISS, BUT WE'VE HAD SOME TROUBLE IN THIS AREA LATELY SO --
-- I'M GONNA HAVE TO ASK YOU TO MOVE ALONG.
SFPD
I UNDERSTAND. I... DON'T KNOW *WHAT* CAME OVER ME. SORRY.
HEY!
YOU DROPPED YOUR BLUEPRINTS.
RIGHT. THANKS. UH...
...HAVE A NICE EVENING... UM, CHEERS...

ANTON MARX, **YOU** CLAIM TO KNOW WHO THE **KNIGHT** IS...

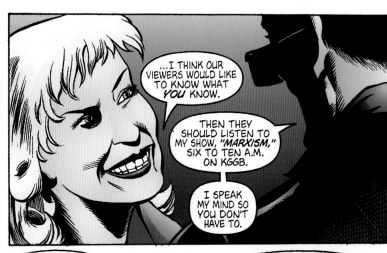

...I THINK OUR VIEWERS WOULD LIKE TO KNOW WHAT **YOU** KNOW.

THEN THEY SHOULD LISTEN TO MY SHOW, "**MARXISM**," SIX TO TEN A.M. ON KGGB.

I SPEAK MY MIND SO YOU DON'T HAVE TO.

YOUR SELF-PROMOTION IS **LEGENDARY** IN MEDIA CIRCLES.

IN FACT, SOME HAVE SPECULATED THAT YOU CLAIMED TO KNOW THE KNIGHT'S IDENTITY PURELY TO GET PUBLICITY FROM WHAT IS, SO FAR, AN **UNCONFIRMED** STORY.

UNCONFIRMED? IF YOU'VE BEEN LISTENING TO "**MARXISM**" SIX TO TEN A.M. ON KGGB --

-- OR READING MY **COLUMN**, DAILY IN THE *BAY AREA REVIEW*, AVAILABLE AT BETTER NEWSSTANDS --

-- YOU'D **KNOW** I'VE BEEN DOING NOTHING BUT **CONFIRMING** THE STORIES OF A KNIGHT RUNNING RAMPANT IN THE STREETS OF SAN FRANCISCO.

IF YOU CALL **PROVING** TO THIS CITY THAT A **REAL** MENACE **IS** REAL "**SELF-PROMOTION**" --

-- THEN **SUE** ME. I'M SELF-PROMOTING.

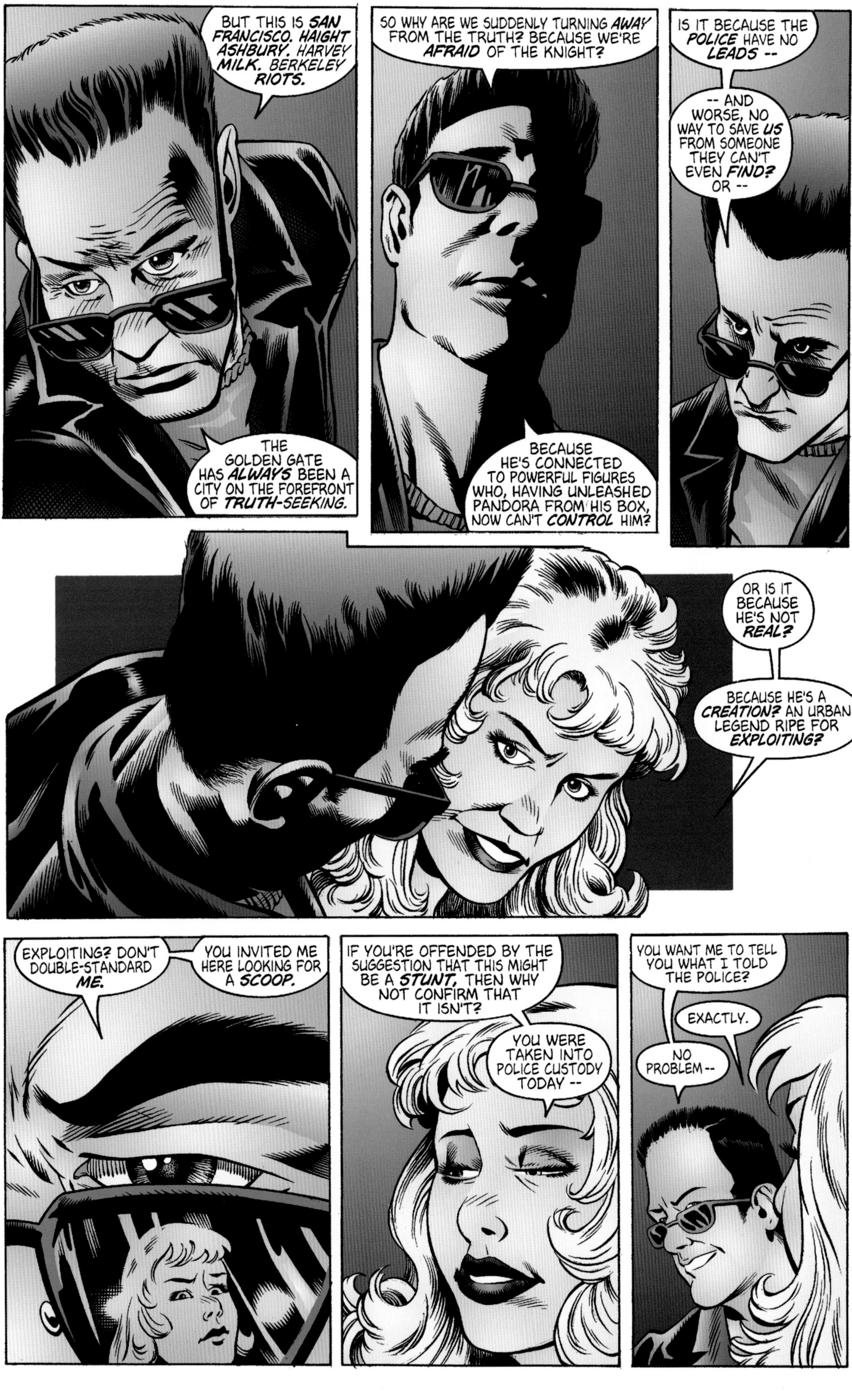
BUT THIS IS SAN FRANCISCO. HAIGHT ASHBURY. HARVEY MILK. BERKELEY RIOTS.
THE GOLDEN GATE HAS ALWAYS BEEN A CITY ON THE FOREFRONT OF TRUTH-SEEKING.
SO WHY ARE WE SUDDENLY TURNING AWAY FROM THE TRUTH? BECAUSE WE'RE AFRAID OF THE KNIGHT?
BECAUSE HE'S CONNECTED TO POWERFUL FIGURES WHO, HAVING UNLEASHED PANDORA FROM HIS BOX, NOW CAN'T CONTROL HIM?
IS IT BECAUSE THE POLICE HAVE NO LEADS --
-- AND WORSE, NO WAY TO SAVE US FROM SOMEONE THEY CAN'T EVEN FIND? OR --
OR IS IT BECAUSE HE'S NOT REAL?
BECAUSE HE'S A CREATION? AN URBAN LEGEND RIPE FOR EXPLOITING?
EXPLOITING? DON'T DOUBLE-STANDARD ME.
YOU INVITED ME HERE LOOKING FOR A SCOOP.
IF YOU'RE OFFENDED BY THE SUGGESTION THAT THIS MIGHT BE A STUNT, THEN WHY NOT CONFIRM THAT IT ISN'T?
YOU WERE TAKEN INTO POLICE CUSTODY TODAY --
YOU WANT ME TO TELL YOU WHAT I TOLD THE POLICE?
EXACTLY.
NO PROBLEM --

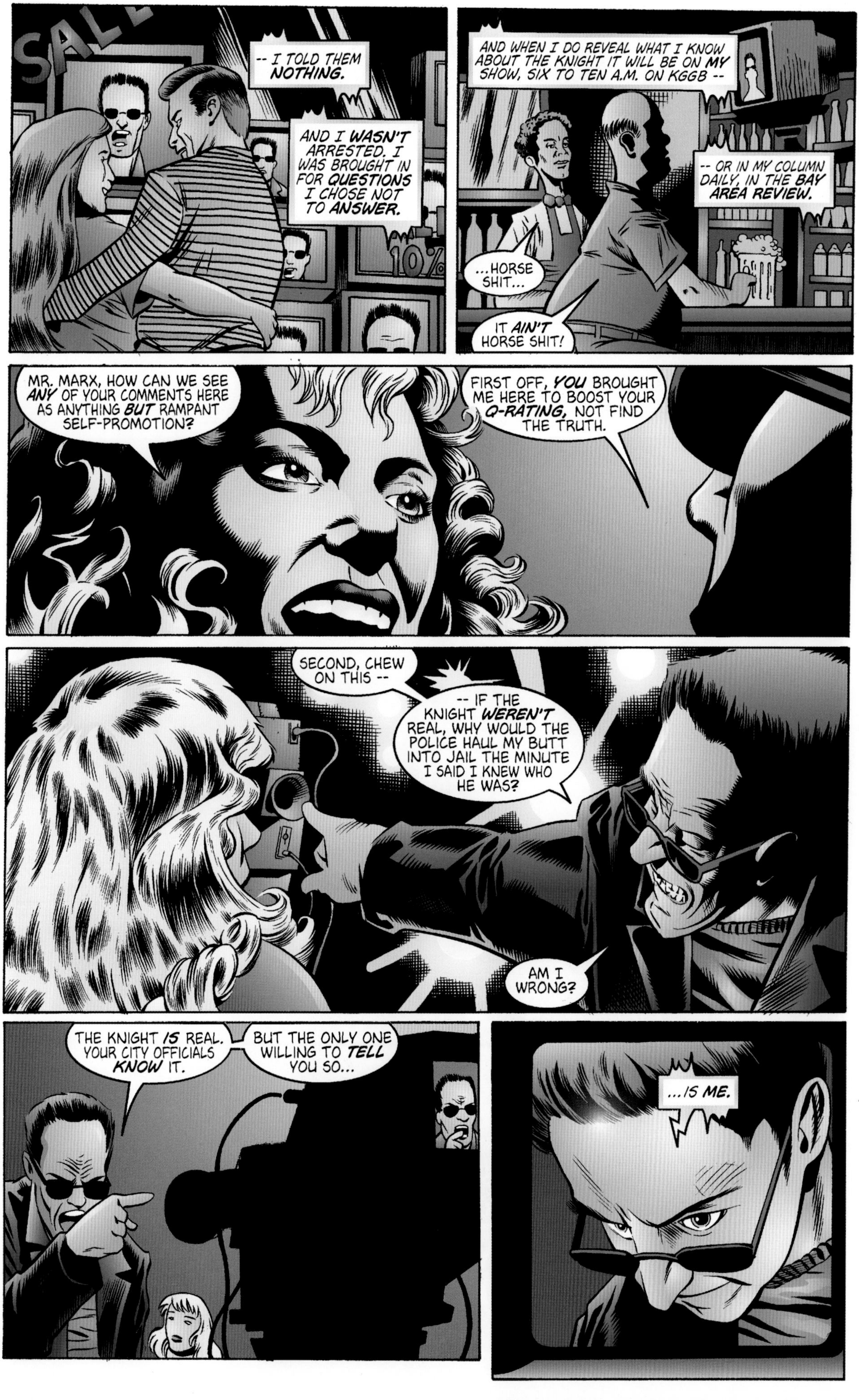
-- I TOLD THEM NOTHING.
AND I WASN'T ARRESTED. I WAS BROUGHT IN FOR QUESTIONS I CHOSE NOT TO ANSWER.
10%
AND WHEN I DO REVEAL WHAT I KNOW ABOUT THE KNIGHT IT WILL BE ON MY SHOW, SIX TO TEN A.M. ON KGGB --
-- OR IN MY COLUMN DAILY, IN THE BAY AREA REVIEW.
...HORSE SHIT...
IT AIN'T HORSE SHIT!
MR. MARX, HOW CAN WE SEE ANY OF YOUR COMMENTS HERE AS ANYTHING BUT RAMPANT SELF-PROMOTION?
FIRST OFF, YOU BROUGHT ME HERE TO BOOST YOUR Q-RATING, NOT FIND THE TRUTH.
SECOND, CHEW ON THIS --
-- IF THE KNIGHT WEREN'T REAL, WHY WOULD THE POLICE HAUL MY BUTT INTO JAIL THE MINUTE I SAID I KNEW WHO HE WAS?
AM I WRONG?
THE KNIGHT IS REAL. YOUR CITY OFFICIALS KNOW IT.
BUT THE ONLY ONE WILLING TO TELL YOU SO...
...IS ME.

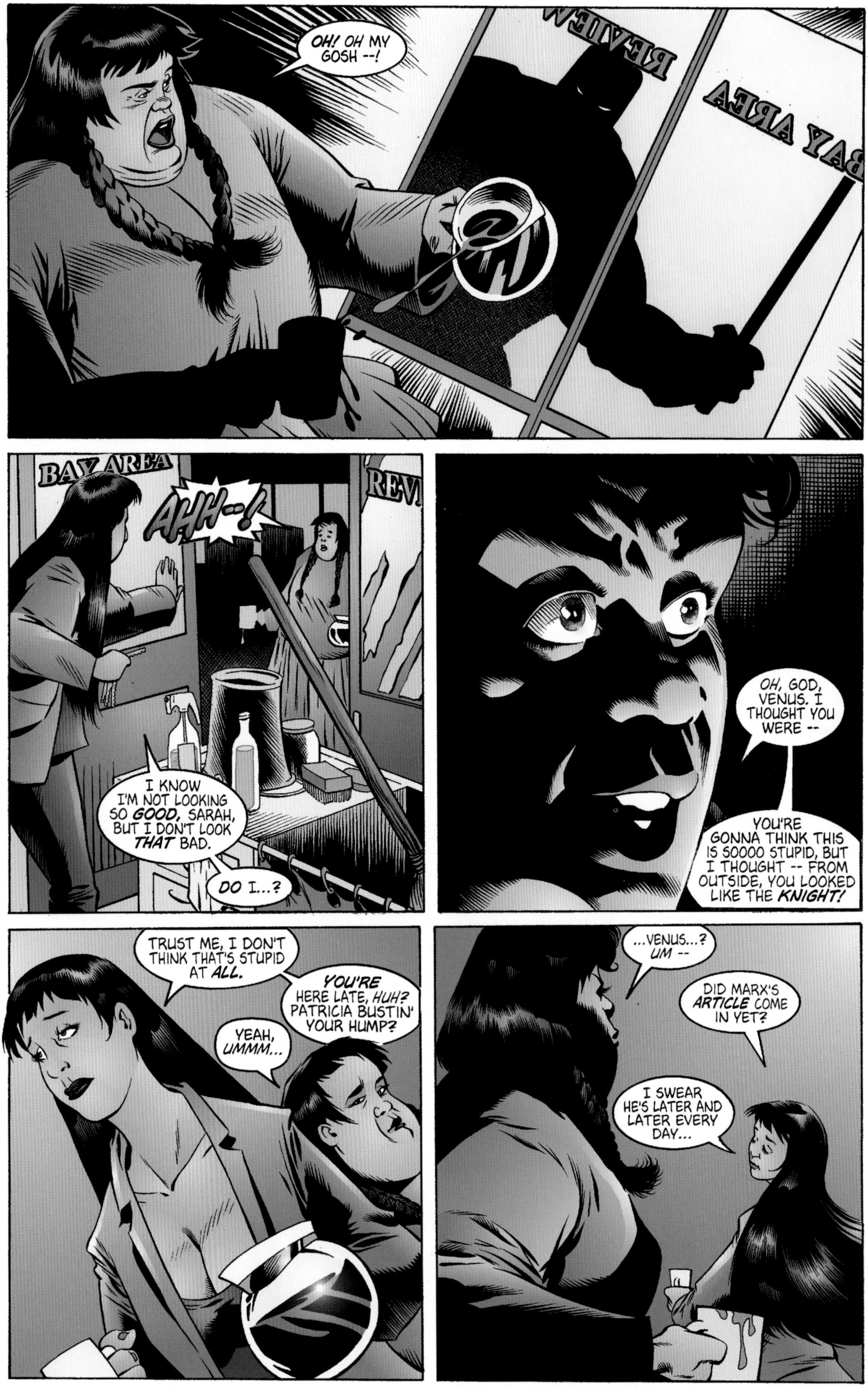
OH! OH MY GOSH --!
REVIEW
BAY AREA
BAY AREA
REVI
AHH--!
I KNOW I'M NOT LOOKING SO GOOD, SARAH, BUT I DON'T LOOK THAT BAD.
DO I...?
OH, GOD, VENUS. I THOUGHT YOU WERE --
YOU'RE GONNA THINK THIS IS SOOOO STUPID, BUT I THOUGHT -- FROM OUTSIDE, YOU LOOKED LIKE THE KNIGHT!
TRUST ME, I DON'T THINK THAT'S STUPID AT ALL.
YOU'RE HERE LATE, HUH? PATRICIA BUSTIN' YOUR HUMP?
YEAH, UMMM...
...VENUS...? UM --
DID MARX'S ARTICLE COME IN YET?
I SWEAR HE'S LATER AND LATER EVERY DAY...

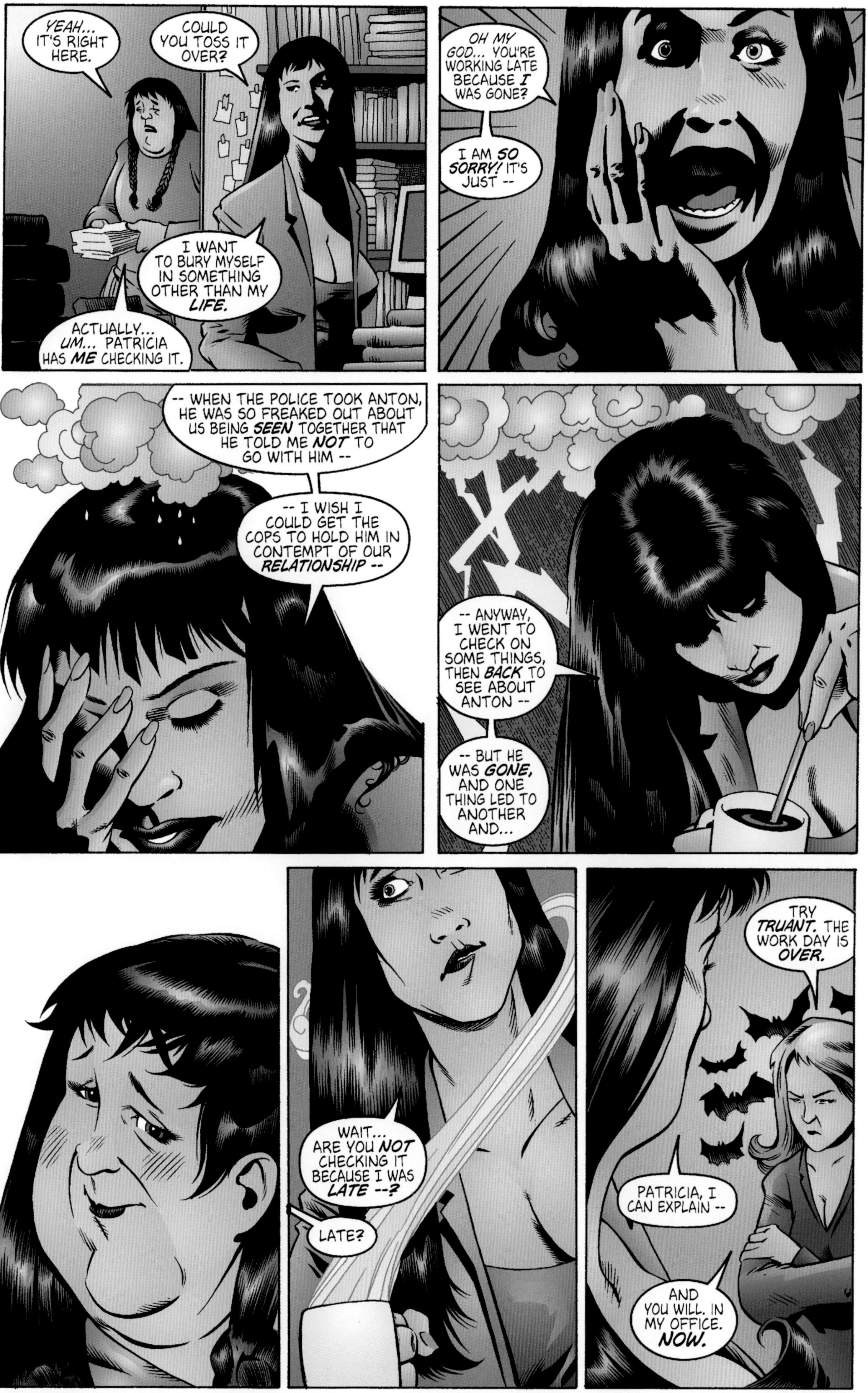
YEAH... IT'S RIGHT HERE.
COULD YOU TOSS IT OVER?
I WANT TO BURY MYSELF IN SOMETHING OTHER THAN MY LIFE.
ACTUALLY... UM... PATRICIA HAS ME CHECKING IT.
OH MY GOD... YOU'RE WORKING LATE BECAUSE I WAS GONE?
I AM SO SORRY! IT'S JUST --
-- WHEN THE POLICE TOOK ANTON, HE WAS SO FREAKED OUT ABOUT US BEING SEEN TOGETHER THAT HE TOLD ME NOT TO GO WITH HIM --
-- I WISH I COULD GET THE COPS TO HOLD HIM IN CONTEMPT OF OUR RELATIONSHIP --
-- ANYWAY, I WENT TO CHECK ON SOME THINGS, THEN BACK TO SEE ABOUT ANTON --
-- BUT HE WAS GONE, AND ONE THING LED TO ANOTHER AND...
WAIT... ARE YOU NOT CHECKING IT BECAUSE I WAS LATE --?
LATE?
TRY TRUANT. THE WORK DAY IS OVER.
PATRICIA, I CAN EXPLAIN --
AND YOU WILL. IN MY OFFICE. NOW.

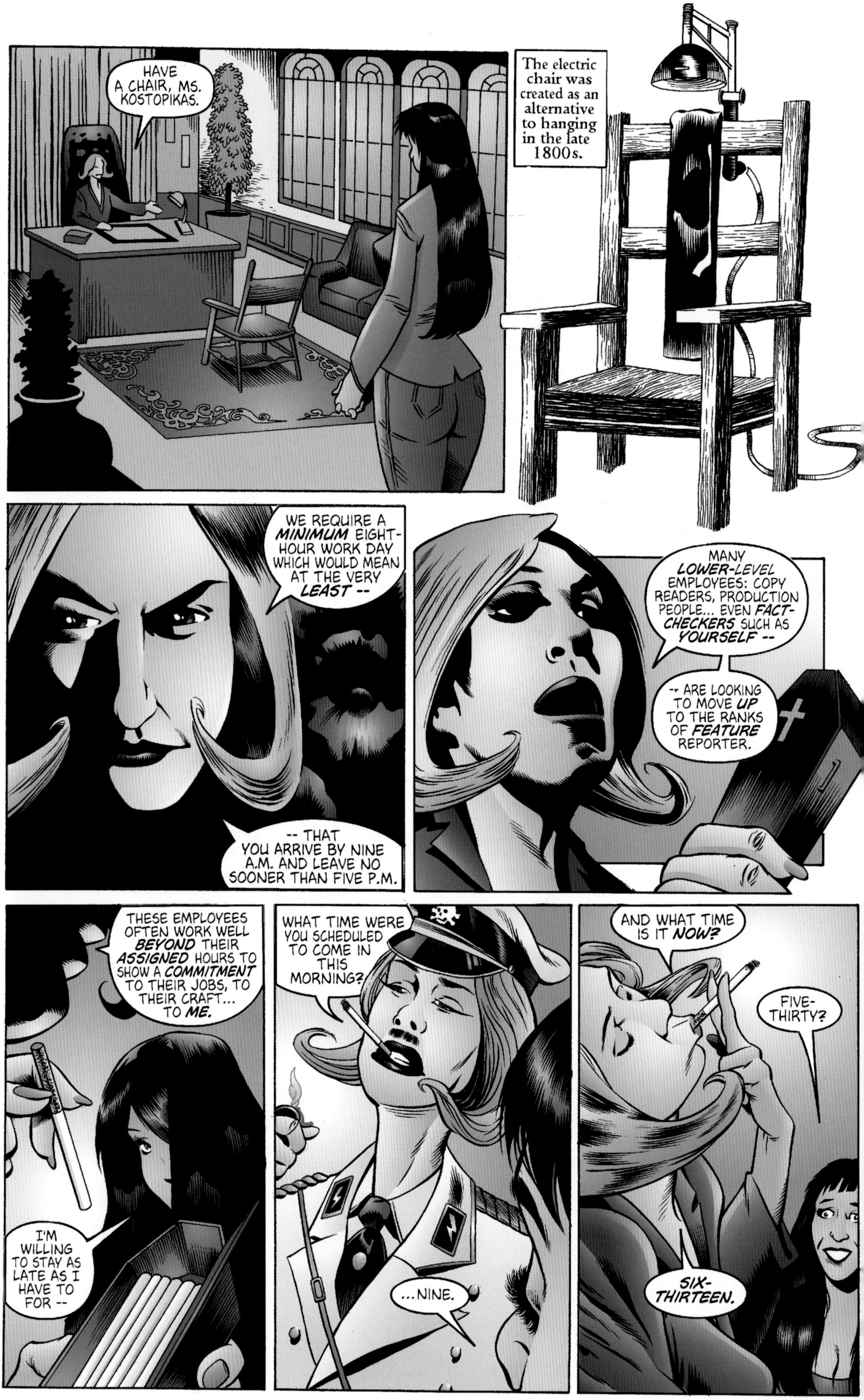
HAVE A CHAIR, MS. KOSTOPIKAS.
The electric chair was created as an alternative to hanging in the late 1800s.
WE REQUIRE A *MINIMUM* EIGHT-HOUR WORK DAY WHICH WOULD MEAN AT THE VERY *LEAST* --
-- THAT YOU ARRIVE BY NINE A.M. AND LEAVE NO SOONER THAN FIVE P.M.
MANY *LOWER-LEVEL* EMPLOYEES: COPY READERS, PRODUCTION PEOPLE... EVEN *FACT-CHECKERS* SUCH AS *YOURSELF* --
-- ARE LOOKING TO MOVE *UP* TO THE RANKS OF *FEATURE* REPORTER.
THESE EMPLOYEES OFTEN WORK WELL *BEYOND* THEIR *ASSIGNED* HOURS TO SHOW A *COMMITMENT* TO THEIR JOBS, TO THEIR CRAFT... TO *ME.*
I'M WILLING TO STAY AS LATE AS I HAVE TO FOR --
WHAT TIME WERE YOU SCHEDULED TO COME IN THIS MORNING?
...NINE.
AND WHAT TIME IS IT *NOW?*
FIVE-THIRTY?
SIX-THIRTEEN.

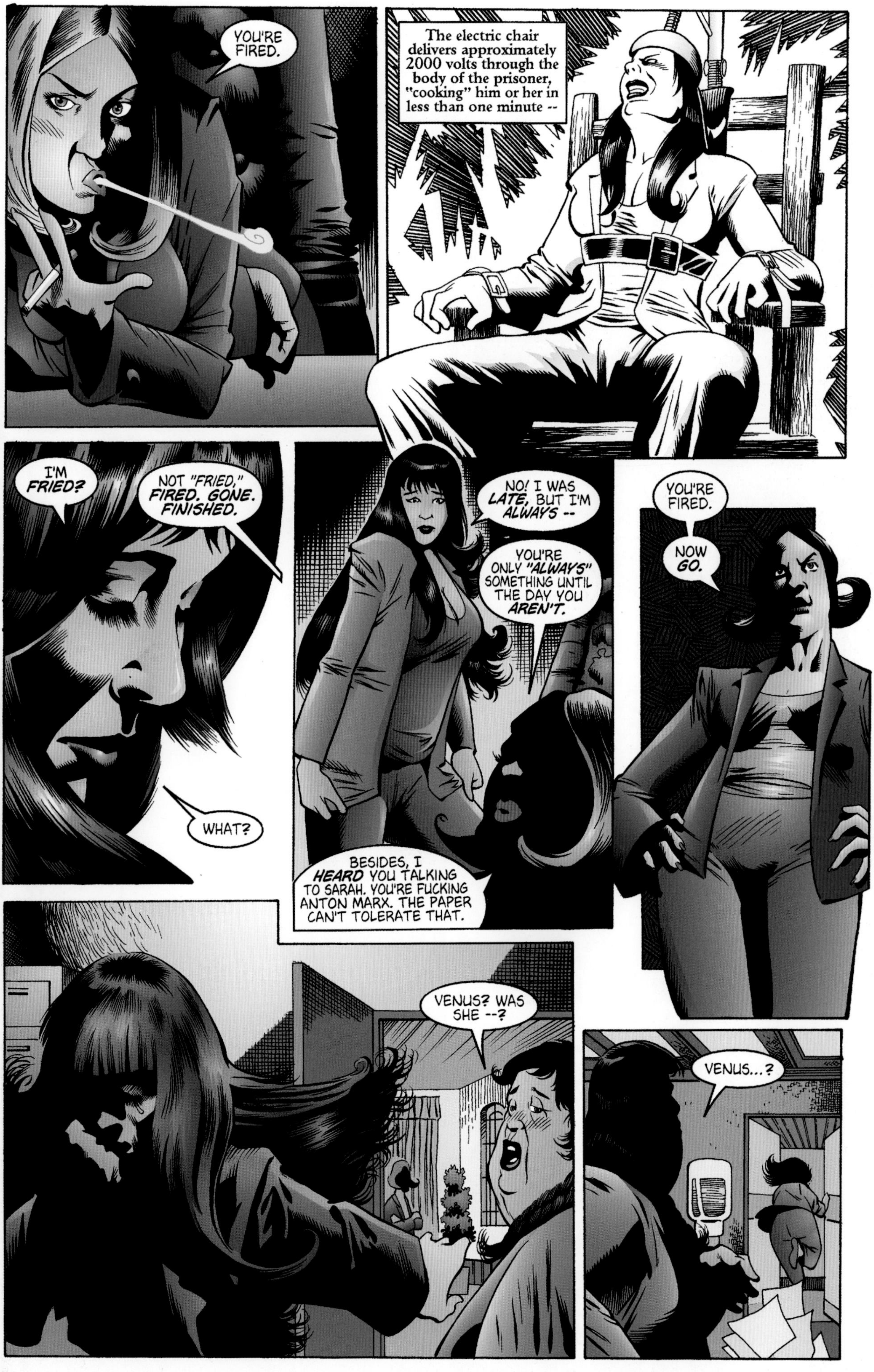
YOU'RE FIRED.
The electric chair delivers approximately 2000 volts through the body of the prisoner, "cooking" him or her in less than one minute --
I'M *FRIED?*
NOT "FRIED," *FIRED. GONE. FINISHED.*
WHAT?
NO! I WAS *LATE,* BUT I'M *ALWAYS* --
YOU'RE ONLY *"ALWAYS"* SOMETHING UNTIL THE DAY YOU *AREN'T.*
BESIDES, I *HEARD* YOU TALKING TO SARAH. YOU'RE FUCKING ANTON MARX. THE PAPER CAN'T TOLERATE THAT.
YOU'RE FIRED.
NOW *GO.*
VENUS? WAS SHE --?
VENUS...?

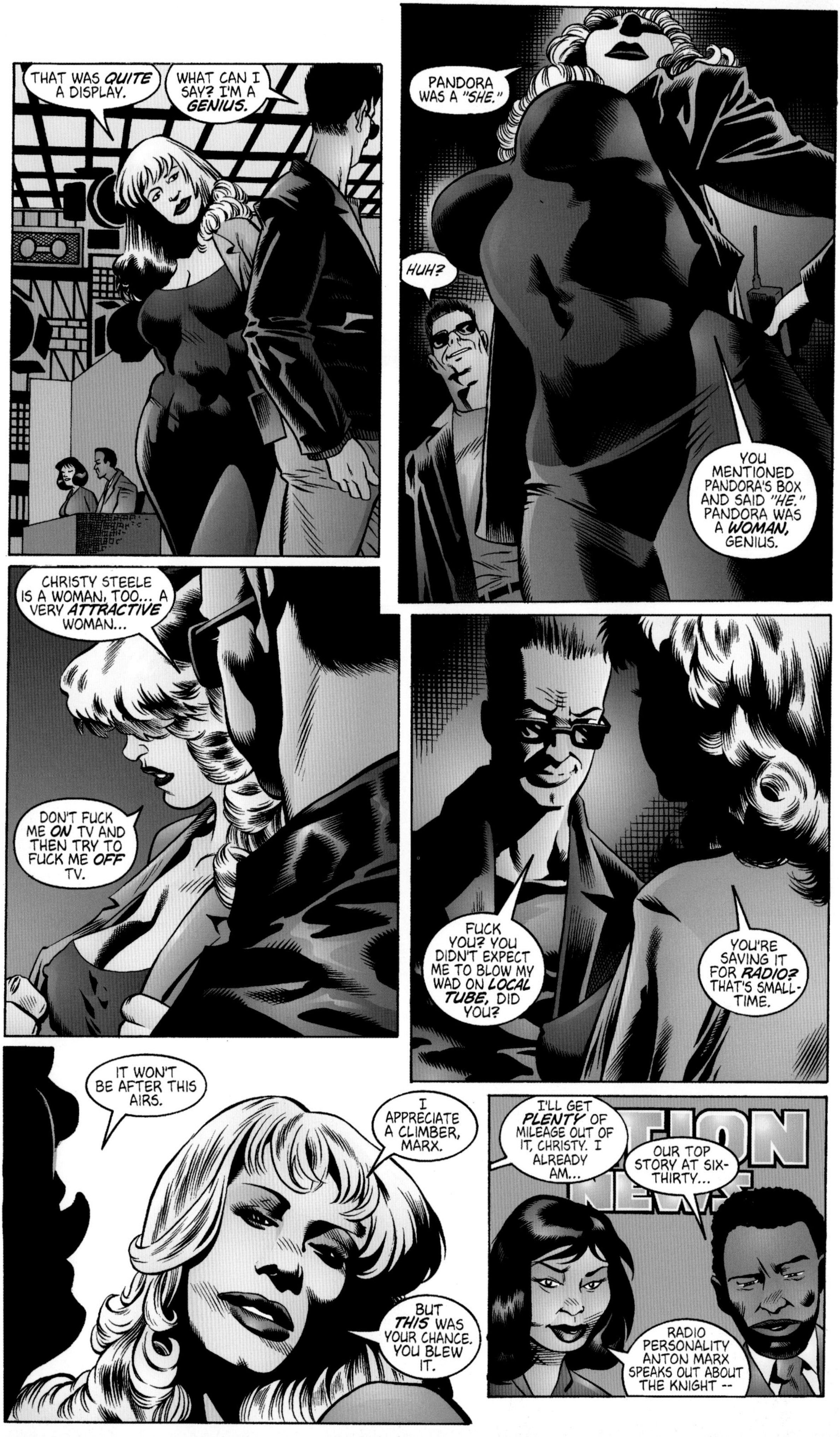
THAT WAS QUITE A DISPLAY.
WHAT CAN I SAY? I'M A GENIUS.
PANDORA WAS A "SHE."
HUH?
YOU MENTIONED PANDORA'S BOX AND SAID "HE." PANDORA WAS A WOMAN, GENIUS.
CHRISTY STEELE IS A WOMAN, TOO... A VERY ATTRACTIVE WOMAN...
DON'T FUCK ME ON TV AND THEN TRY TO FUCK ME OFF TV.
FUCK YOU? YOU DIDN'T EXPECT ME TO BLOW MY WAD ON LOCAL TUBE, DID YOU?
YOU'RE SAVING IT FOR RADIO? THAT'S SMALL-TIME.
IT WON'T BE AFTER THIS AIRS.
I APPRECIATE A CLIMBER, MARX.
BUT THIS WAS YOUR CHANCE. YOU BLEW IT.
I'LL GET PLENTY OF MILEAGE OUT OF IT, CHRISTY. I ALREADY AM...
OUR TOP STORY AT SIX-THIRTY...
RADIO PERSONALITY ANTON MARX SPEAKS OUT ABOUT THE KNIGHT --

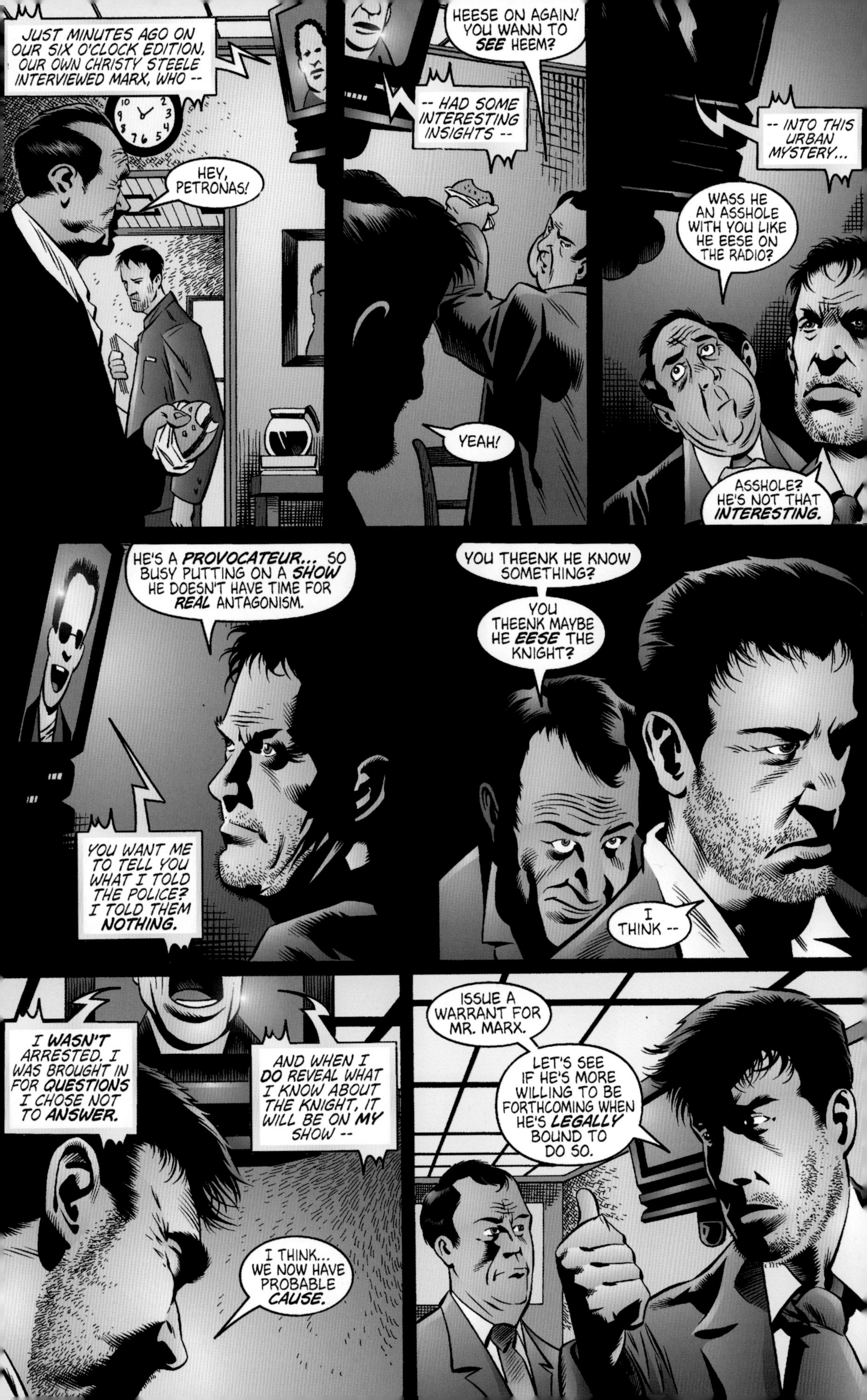
JUST MINUTES AGO ON OUR SIX O'CLOCK EDITION, OUR OWN CHRISTY STEELE INTERVIEWED MARX, WHO --
HEY, PETRONAS!
HEESE ON AGAIN! YOU WANN TO SEE HEEM?
-- HAD SOME INTERESTING INSIGHTS --
YEAH!
-- INTO THIS URBAN MYSTERY...
WASS HE AN ASSHOLE WITH YOU LIKE HE EESE ON THE RADIO?
ASSHOLE? HE'S NOT THAT INTERESTING.
HE'S A PROVOCATEUR... SO BUSY PUTTING ON A SHOW HE DOESN'T HAVE TIME FOR REAL ANTAGONISM.
YOU WANT ME TO TELL YOU WHAT I TOLD THE POLICE? I TOLD THEM NOTHING.
YOU THEENK HE KNOW SOMETHING?
YOU THEENK MAYBE HE EESE THE KNIGHT?
I THINK --
I WASN'T ARRESTED. I WAS BROUGHT IN FOR QUESTIONS I CHOSE NOT TO ANSWER.
AND WHEN I DO REVEAL WHAT I KNOW ABOUT THE KNIGHT, IT WILL BE ON MY SHOW --
I THINK... WE NOW HAVE PROBABLE CAUSE.
ISSUE A WARRANT FOR MR. MARX.
LET'S SEE IF HE'S MORE WILLING TO BE FORTHCOMING WHEN HE'S LEGALLY BOUND TO DO SO.

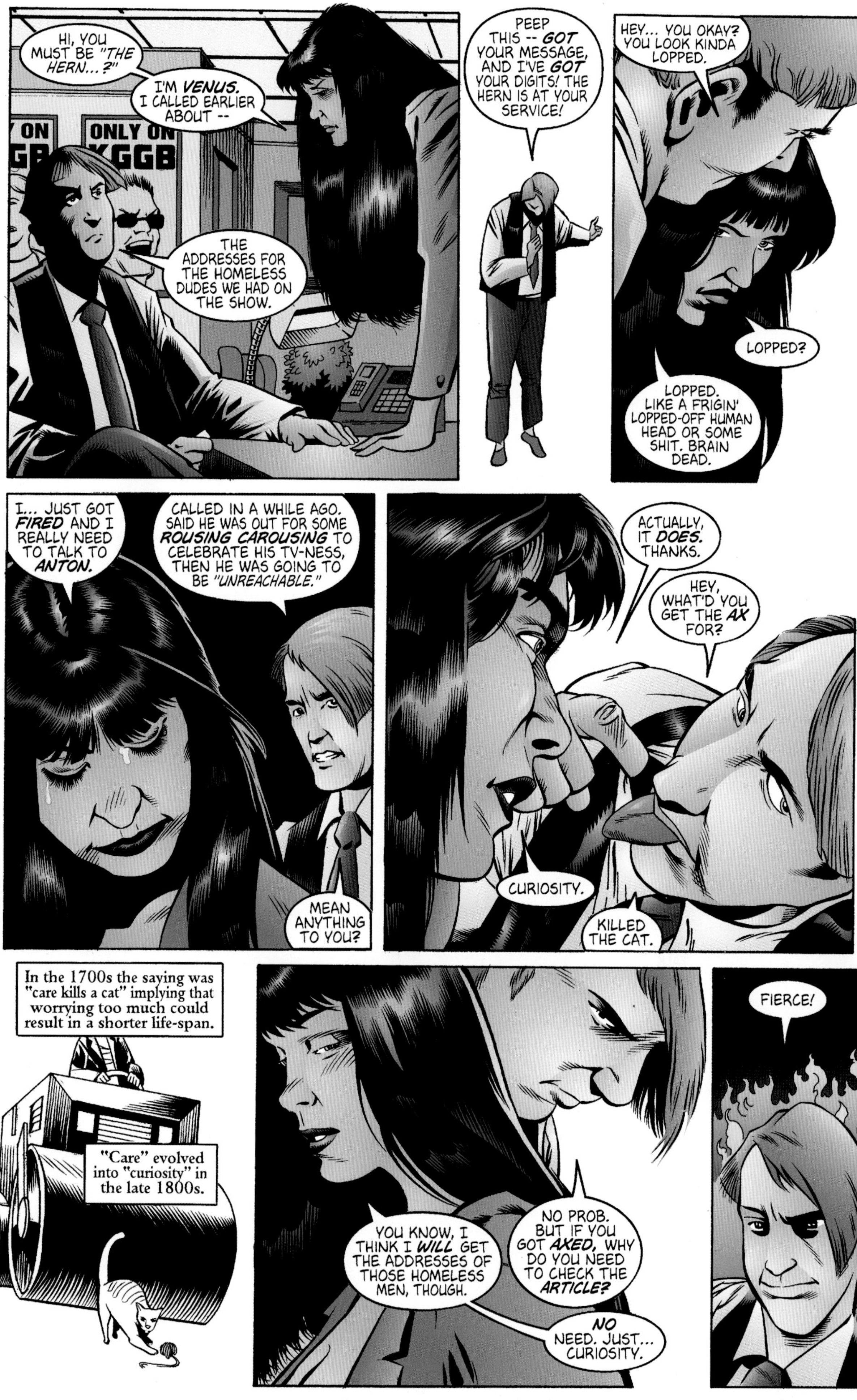
ONLY ON KGGB
HI, YOU MUST BE "THE HERN...?"
I'M VENUS. I CALLED EARLIER ABOUT --
THE ADDRESSES FOR THE HOMELESS DUDES WE HAD ON THE SHOW.
PEEP THIS -- GOT YOUR MESSAGE, AND I'VE GOT YOUR DIGITS! THE HERN IS AT YOUR SERVICE!
HEY... YOU OKAY? YOU LOOK KINDA LOPPED.
LOPPED?
LOPPED. LIKE A FRIGIN' LOPPED-OFF HUMAN HEAD OR SOME SHIT. BRAIN DEAD.
I... JUST GOT FIRED AND I REALLY NEED TO TALK TO ANTON.
CALLED IN A WHILE AGO. SAID HE WAS OUT FOR SOME ROUSING CAROUSING TO CELEBRATE HIS TV-NESS, THEN HE WAS GOING TO BE "UNREACHABLE."
MEAN ANYTHING TO YOU?
ACTUALLY, IT DOES. THANKS.
HEY, WHAT'D YOU GET THE AX FOR?
CURIOSITY.
KILLED THE CAT.
In the 1700s the saying was "care kills a cat" implying that worrying too much could result in a shorter life-span.
"Care" evolved into "curiosity" in the late 1800s.
YOU KNOW, I THINK I WILL GET THE ADDRESSES OF THOSE HOMELESS MEN, THOUGH.
NO PROB. BUT IF YOU GOT AXED, WHY DO YOU NEED TO CHECK THE ARTICLE?
NO NEED. JUST... CURIOSITY.
FIERCE!

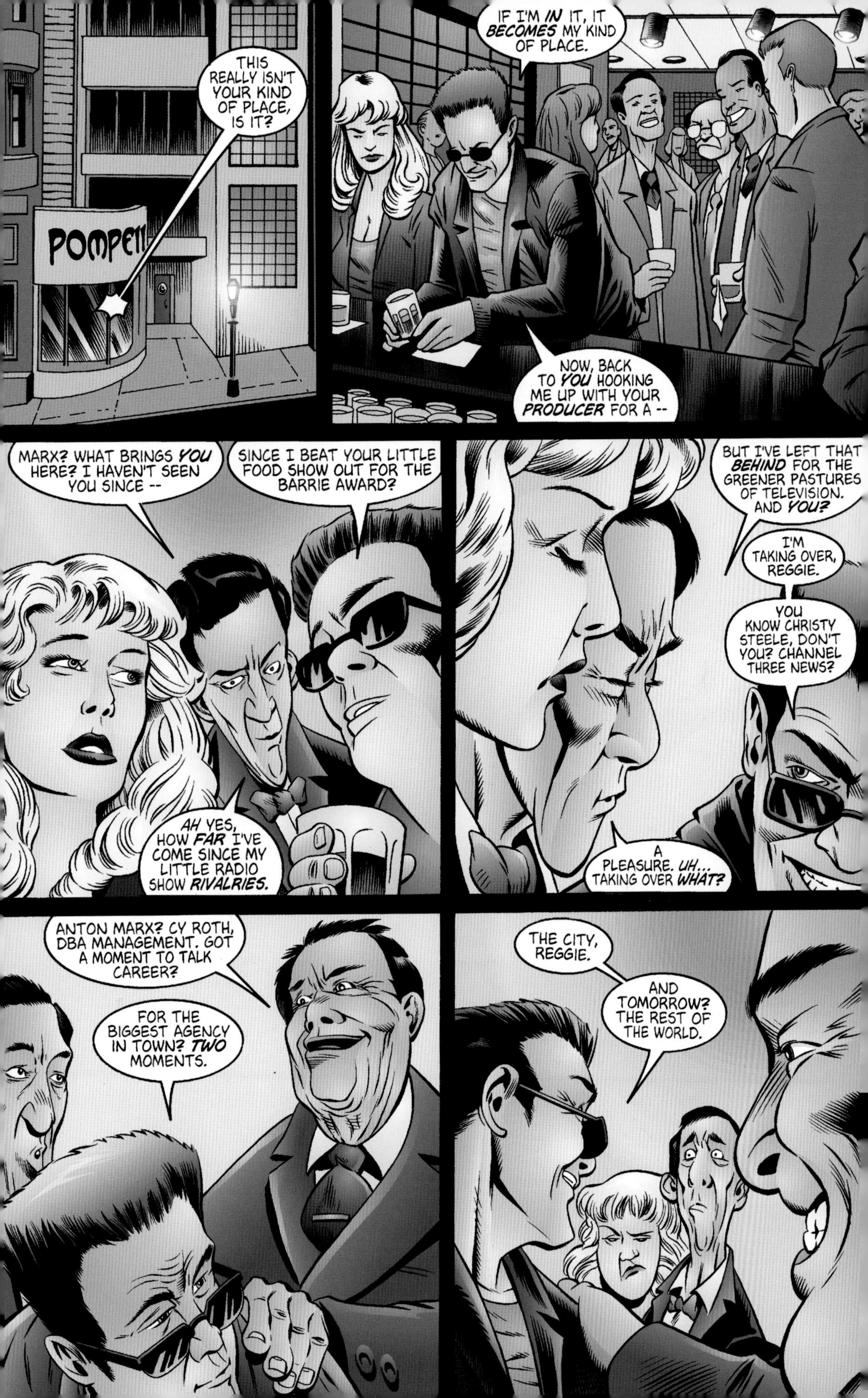
POMPEII
THIS REALLY ISN'T YOUR KIND OF PLACE, IS IT?
IF I'M *IN* IT, IT *BECOMES* MY KIND OF PLACE.
NOW, BACK TO *YOU* HOOKING ME UP WITH YOUR *PRODUCER* FOR A --
MARX? WHAT BRINGS *YOU* HERE? I HAVEN'T SEEN YOU SINCE --
SINCE I BEAT YOUR LITTLE FOOD SHOW OUT FOR THE BARRIE AWARD?
AH YES, HOW *FAR* I'VE COME SINCE MY LITTLE RADIO SHOW *RIVALRIES*.
BUT I'VE LEFT THAT *BEHIND* FOR THE GREENER PASTURES OF TELEVISION. AND *YOU?*
I'M TAKING OVER, REGGIE.
YOU KNOW CHRISTY STEELE, DON'T YOU? CHANNEL THREE NEWS?
A PLEASURE. *UH...* TAKING OVER *WHAT?*
ANTON MARX? CY ROTH, DBA MANAGEMENT. GOT A MOMENT TO TALK CAREER?
FOR THE BIGGEST AGENCY IN TOWN? *TWO* MOMENTS.
THE CITY, REGGIE.
AND TOMORROW? THE REST OF THE WORLD.

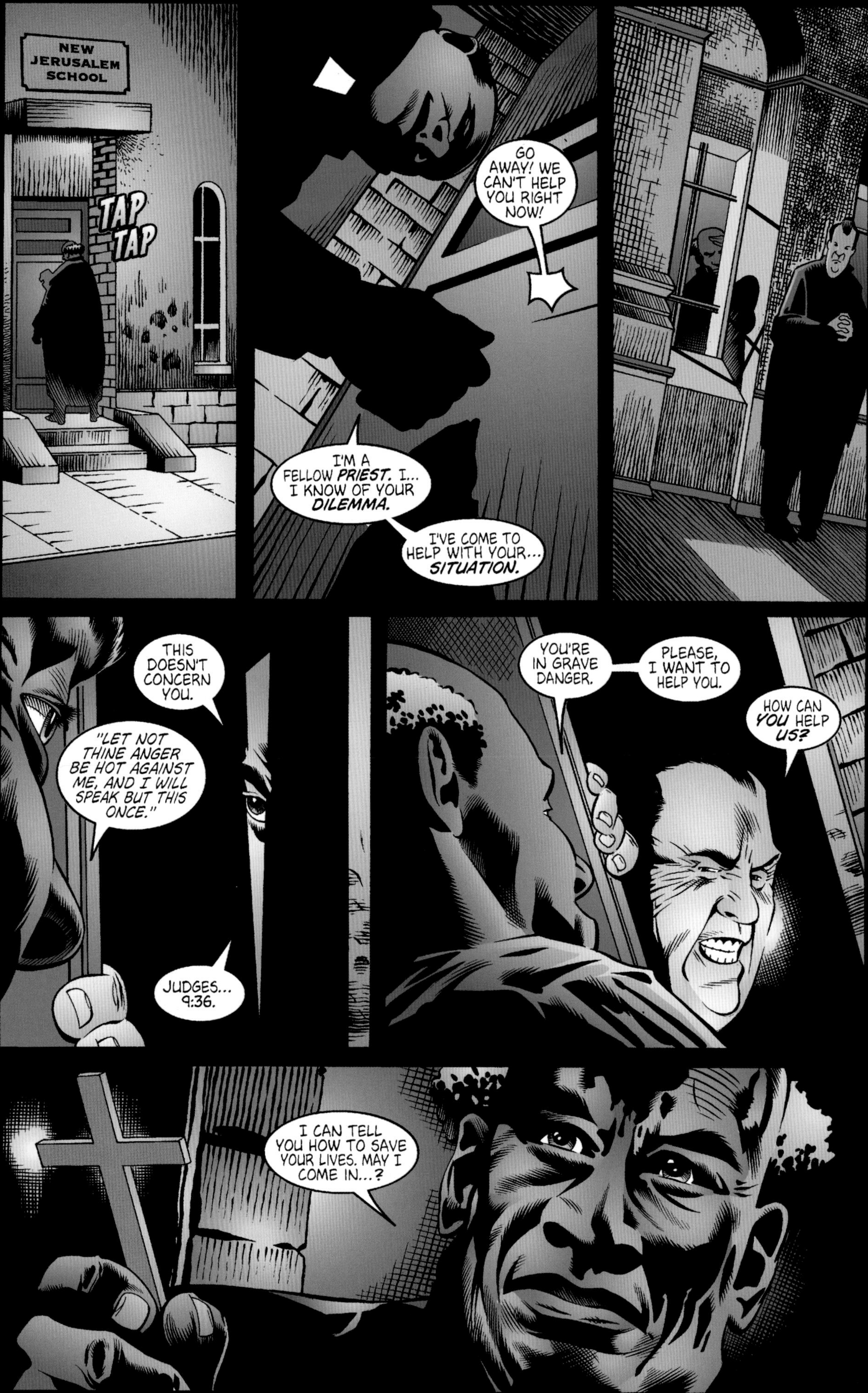
NEW JERUSALEM SCHOOL
TAP TAP
GO AWAY! WE CAN'T HELP YOU RIGHT NOW!
I'M A FELLOW PRIEST. I... I KNOW OF YOUR DILEMMA.
I'VE COME TO HELP WITH YOUR... SITUATION.
THIS DOESN'T CONCERN YOU.
"LET NOT THINE ANGER BE HOT AGAINST ME, AND I WILL SPEAK BUT THIS ONCE."
JUDGES... 9:36.
YOU'RE IN GRAVE DANGER.
PLEASE, I WANT TO HELP YOU.
HOW CAN YOU HELP US?
I CAN TELL YOU HOW TO SAVE YOUR LIVES. MAY I COME IN...?

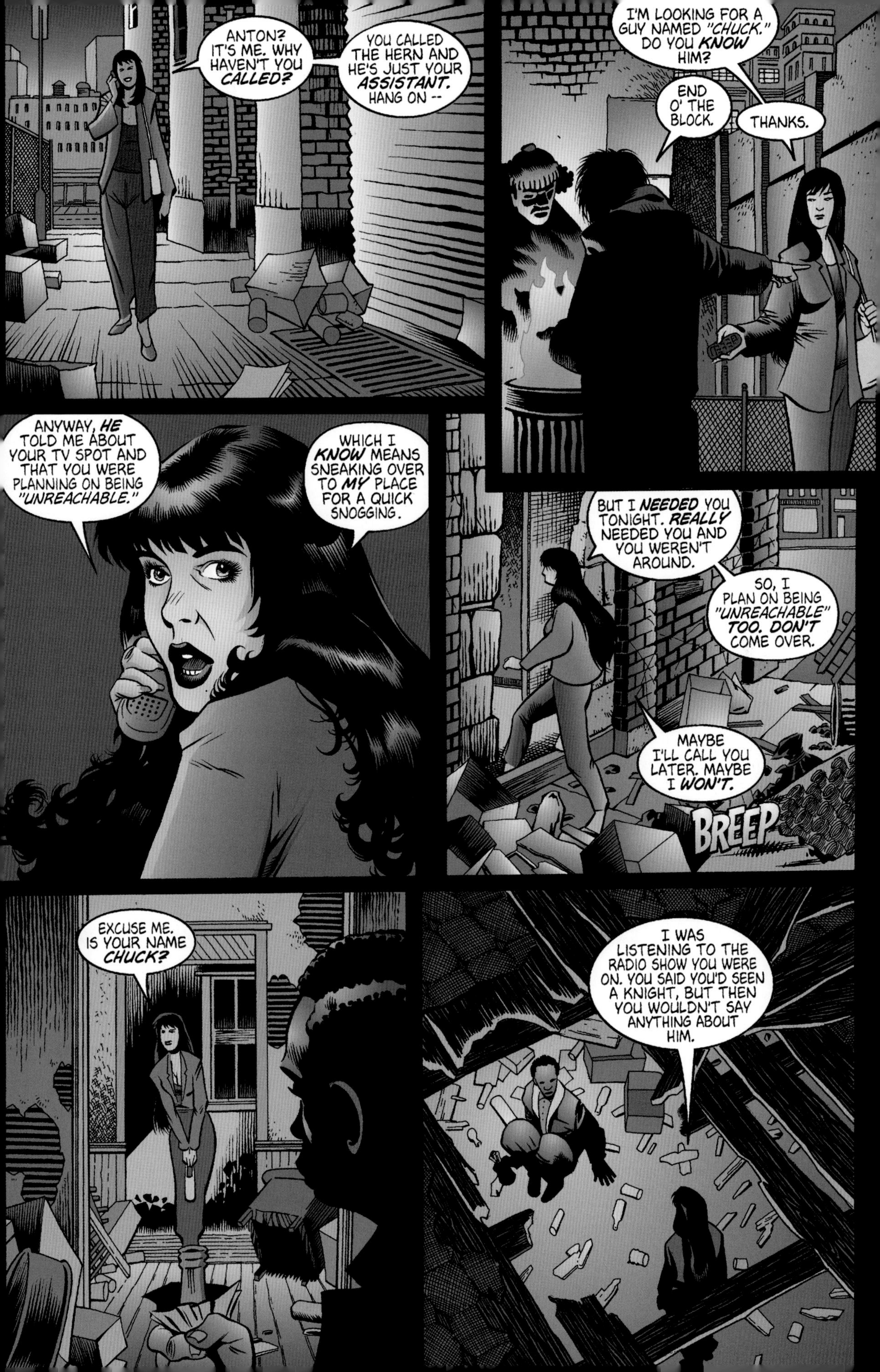
ANTON? IT'S ME. WHY HAVEN'T YOU CALLED?
YOU CALLED THE HERN AND HE'S JUST YOUR ASSISTANT. HANG ON --
I'M LOOKING FOR A GUY NAMED "CHUCK." DO YOU KNOW HIM?
END O' THE BLOCK.
THANKS.
ANYWAY, HE TOLD ME ABOUT YOUR TV SPOT AND THAT YOU WERE PLANNING ON BEING "UNREACHABLE."
WHICH I KNOW MEANS SNEAKING OVER TO MY PLACE FOR A QUICK SNOGGING.
BUT I NEEDED YOU TONIGHT. REALLY NEEDED YOU AND YOU WEREN'T AROUND.
SO, I PLAN ON BEING "UNREACHABLE" TOO. DON'T COME OVER.
MAYBE I'LL CALL YOU LATER. MAYBE I WON'T.
BREEP
EXCUSE ME. IS YOUR NAME CHUCK?
I WAS LISTENING TO THE RADIO SHOW YOU WERE ON. YOU SAID YOU'D SEEN A KNIGHT, BUT THEN YOU WOULDN'T SAY ANYTHING ABOUT HIM.

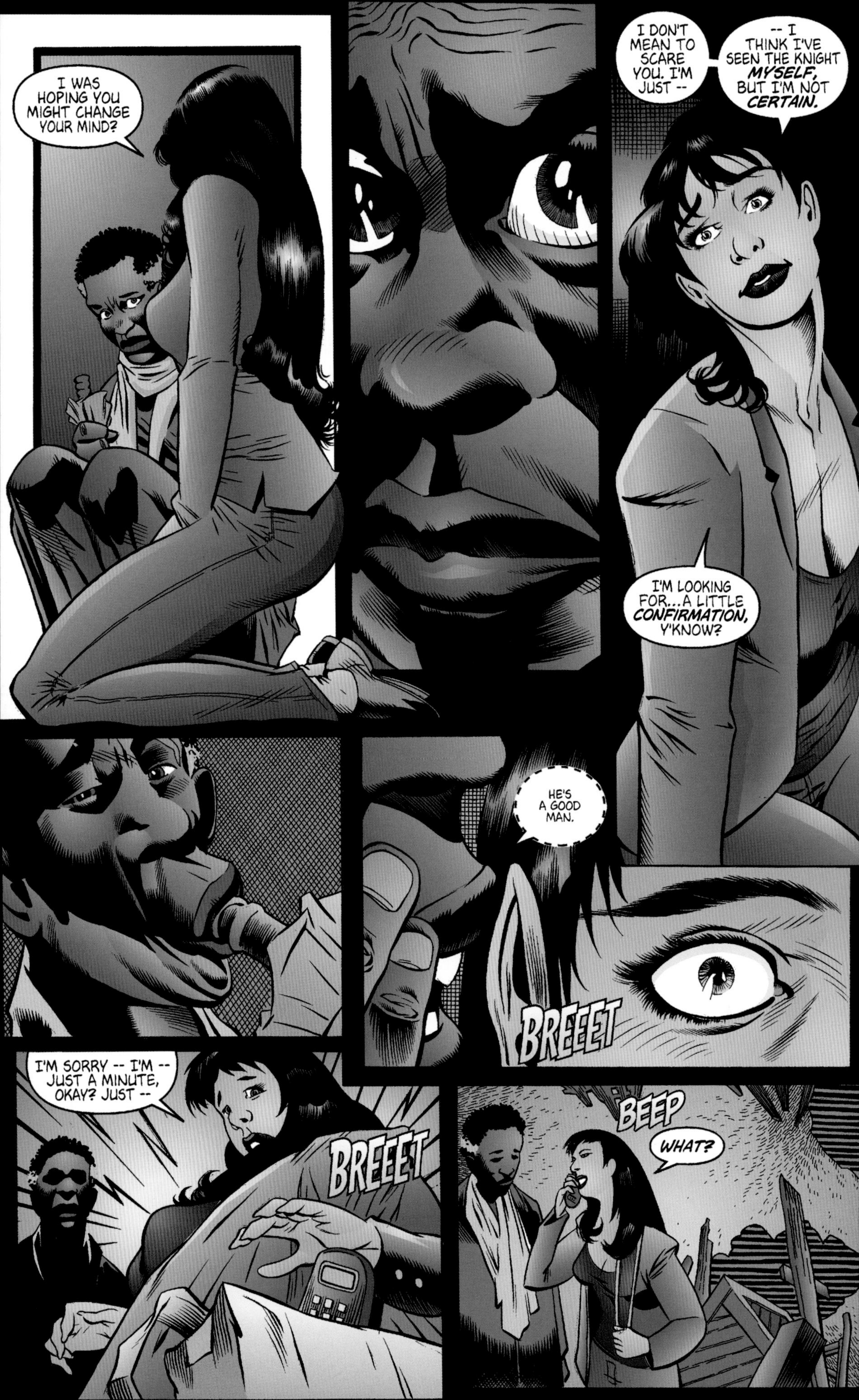
I WAS HOPING YOU MIGHT CHANGE YOUR MIND?
I DON'T MEAN TO SCARE YOU. I'M JUST --
-- I THINK I'VE SEEN THE KNIGHT *MYSELF,* BUT I'M NOT *CERTAIN.*
I'M LOOKING FOR...A LITTLE *CONFIRMATION,* Y'KNOW?
HE'S A GOOD MAN.
BREEET
I'M SORRY -- I'M -- JUST A MINUTE, OKAY? JUST --
BREEET
BEEP
WHAT?

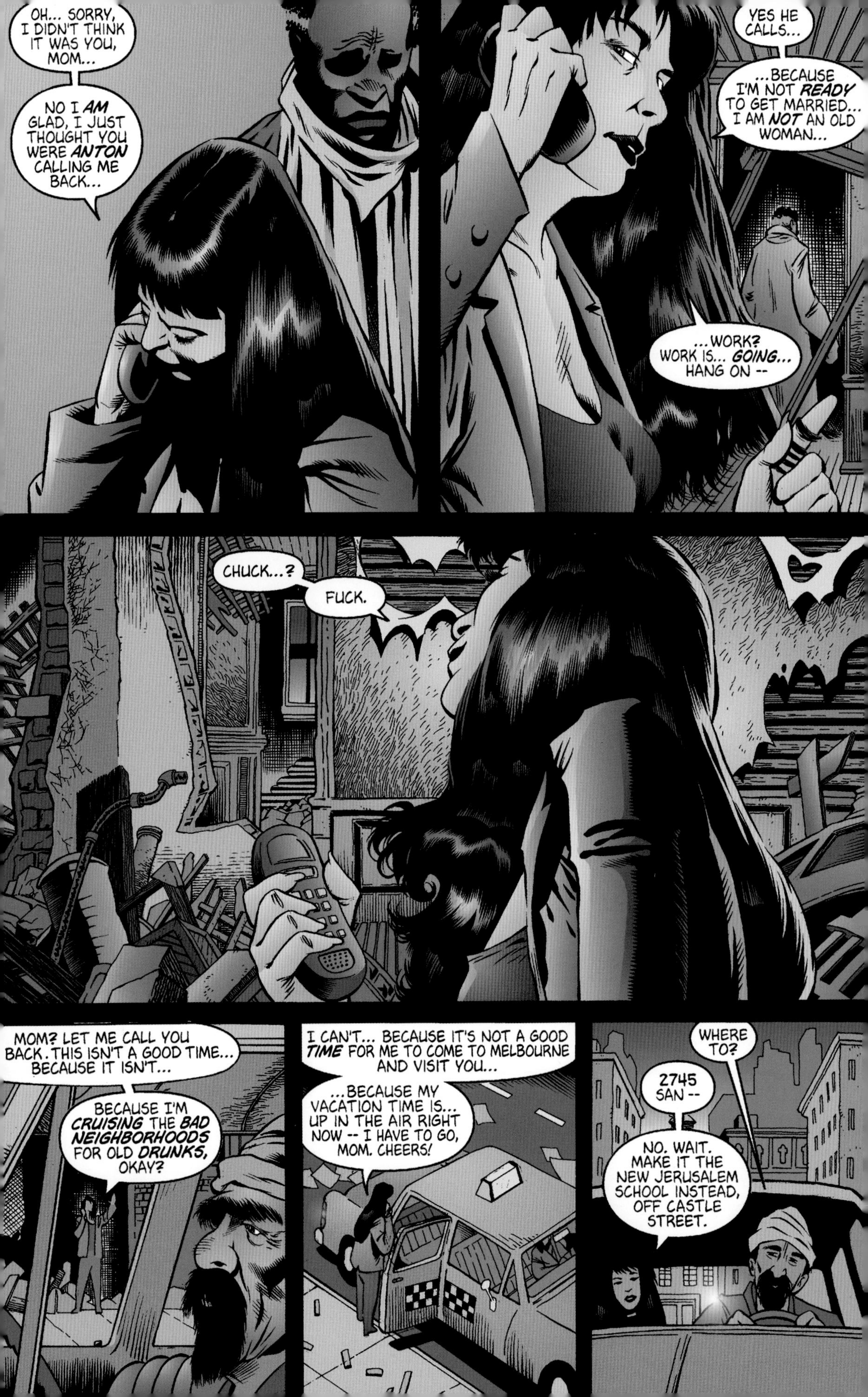
OH... SORRY, I DIDN'T THINK IT WAS YOU, MOM...
NO I **AM** GLAD, I JUST THOUGHT YOU WERE **ANTON** CALLING ME BACK...
YES HE CALLS...
...BECAUSE I'M NOT **READY** TO GET MARRIED... I AM **NOT** AN OLD WOMAN...
...WORK? WORK IS... **GOING...** HANG ON --
CHUCK...?
FUCK.
MOM? LET ME CALL YOU BACK. THIS ISN'T A GOOD TIME... BECAUSE IT ISN'T...
BECAUSE I'M **CRUISING** THE **BAD NEIGHBORHOODS** FOR OLD **DRUNKS,** OKAY?
I CAN'T... BECAUSE IT'S NOT A GOOD **TIME** FOR ME TO COME TO MELBOURNE AND VISIT YOU...
...BECAUSE MY VACATION TIME IS... UP IN THE AIR RIGHT NOW -- I HAVE TO GO, MOM. CHEERS!
WHERE TO?
2745 SAN --
NO. WAIT. MAKE IT THE NEW JERUSALEM SCHOOL INSTEAD, OFF CASTLE STREET.

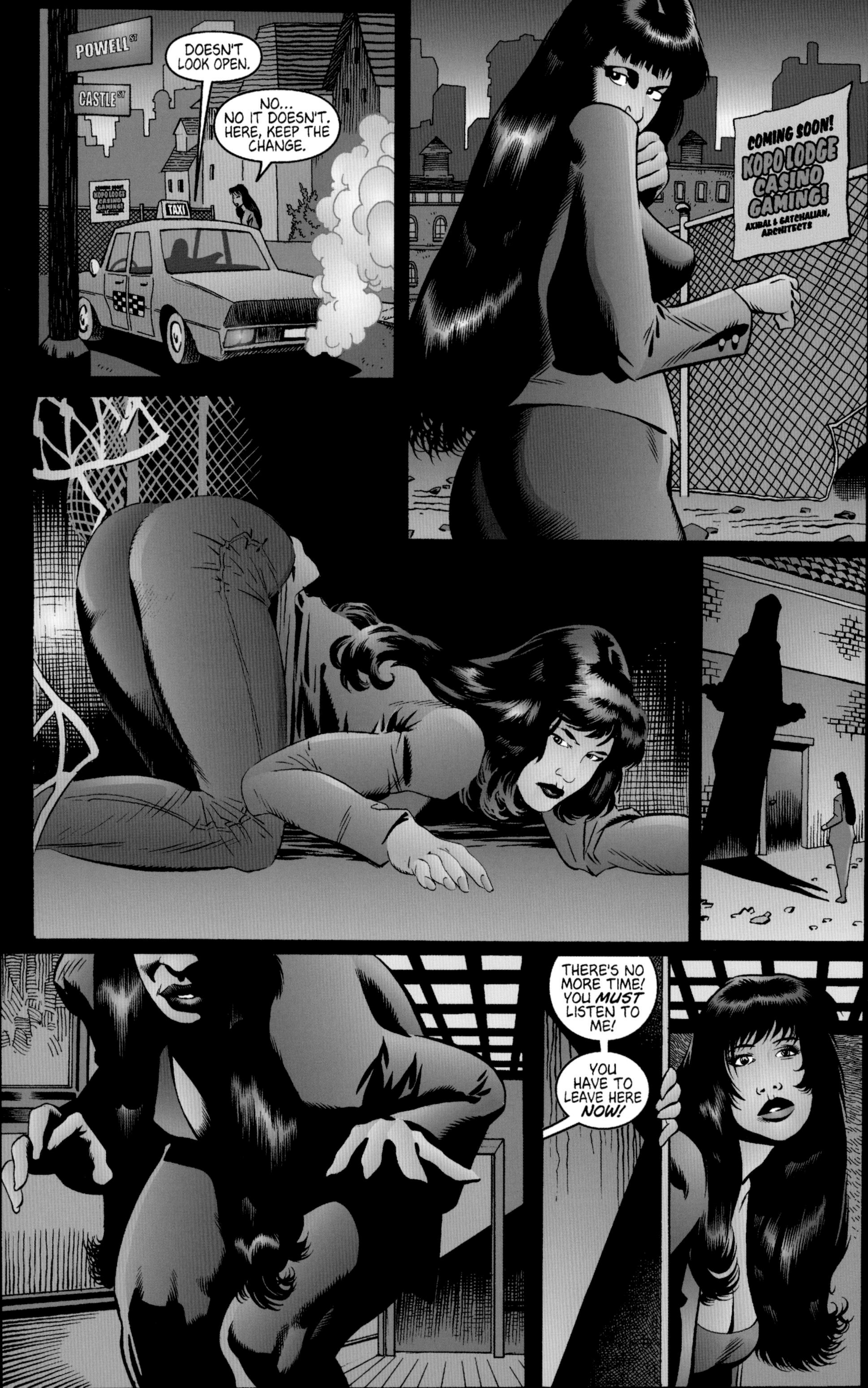

POWELL ST
CASTLE ST
DOESN'T LOOK OPEN.
NO... NO IT DOESN'T. HERE, KEEP THE CHANGE.
TAXI
COMING SOON!
KOPO LODGE CASINO GAMING!
AXIBAL & GATCHALIAN, ARCHITECTS
THERE'S NO MORE TIME! YOU MUST LISTEN TO ME!
YOU HAVE TO LEAVE HERE NOW!

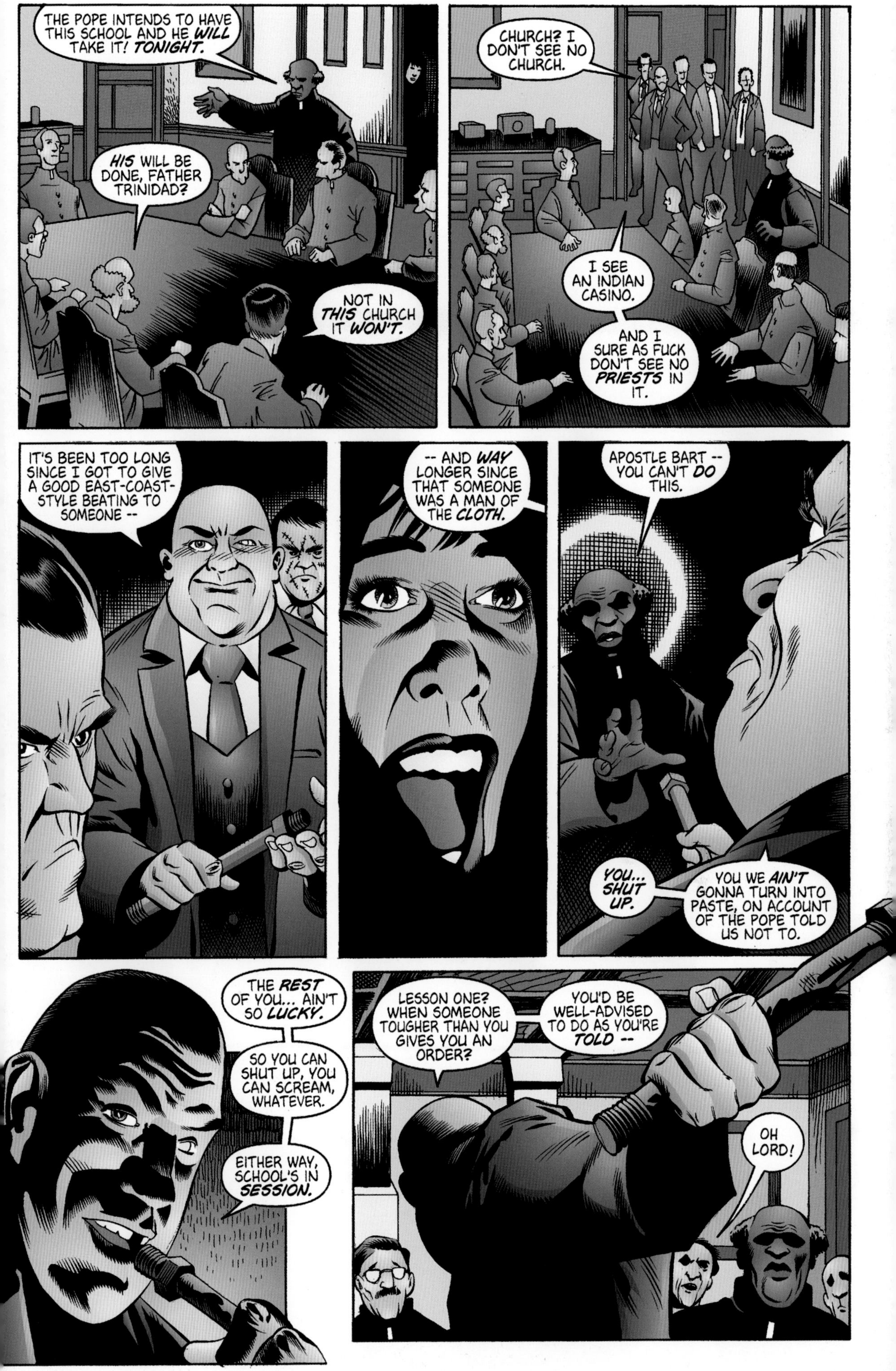
THE POPE INTENDS TO HAVE THIS SCHOOL AND HE WILL TAKE IT! TONIGHT.
HIS WILL BE DONE, FATHER TRINIDAD?
NOT IN THIS CHURCH IT WON'T.
CHURCH? I DON'T SEE NO CHURCH.
I SEE AN INDIAN CASINO.
AND I SURE AS FUCK DON'T SEE NO PRIESTS IN IT.
IT'S BEEN TOO LONG SINCE I GOT TO GIVE A GOOD EAST-COAST-STYLE BEATING TO SOMEONE --
-- AND WAY LONGER SINCE THAT SOMEONE WAS A MAN OF THE CLOTH.
APOSTLE BART -- YOU CAN'T DO THIS.
YOU... SHUT UP.
YOU WE AIN'T GONNA TURN INTO PASTE, ON ACCOUNT OF THE POPE TOLD US NOT TO.
THE REST OF YOU... AIN'T SO LUCKY.
SO YOU CAN SHUT UP, YOU CAN SCREAM, WHATEVER.
EITHER WAY, SCHOOL'S IN SESSION.
LESSON ONE? WHEN SOMEONE TOUGHER THAN YOU GIVES YOU AN ORDER?
YOU'D BE WELL-ADVISED TO DO AS YOU'RE TOLD --
OH LORD!

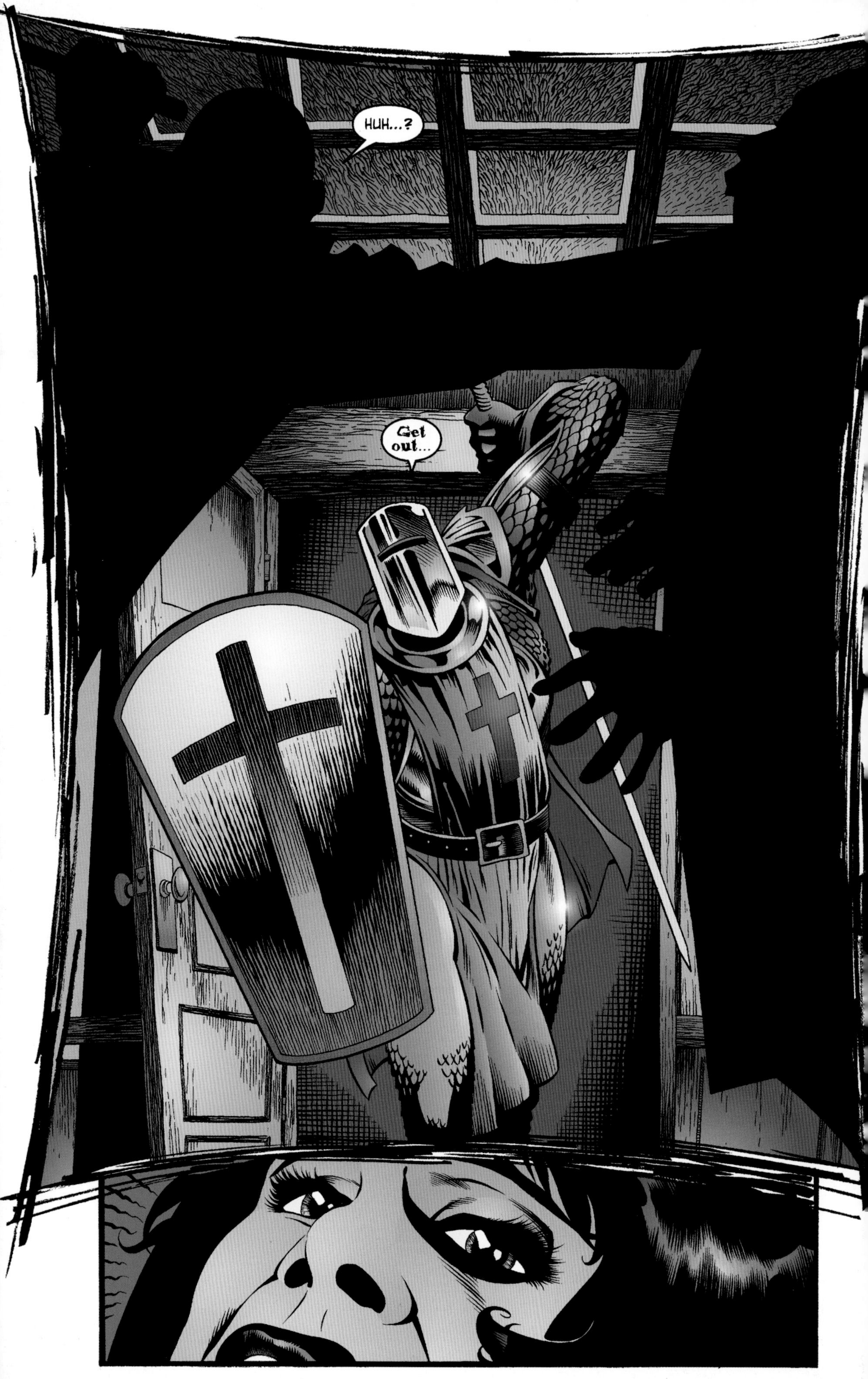
HUH...?
Get out...

"We have heard that some of you desire to go to Jerusalem. Know then that anyone who sets out on that journey is remitted in entirely all penance for all his sins."
-- Pope Urban II, 1095

"...MY GOD..."

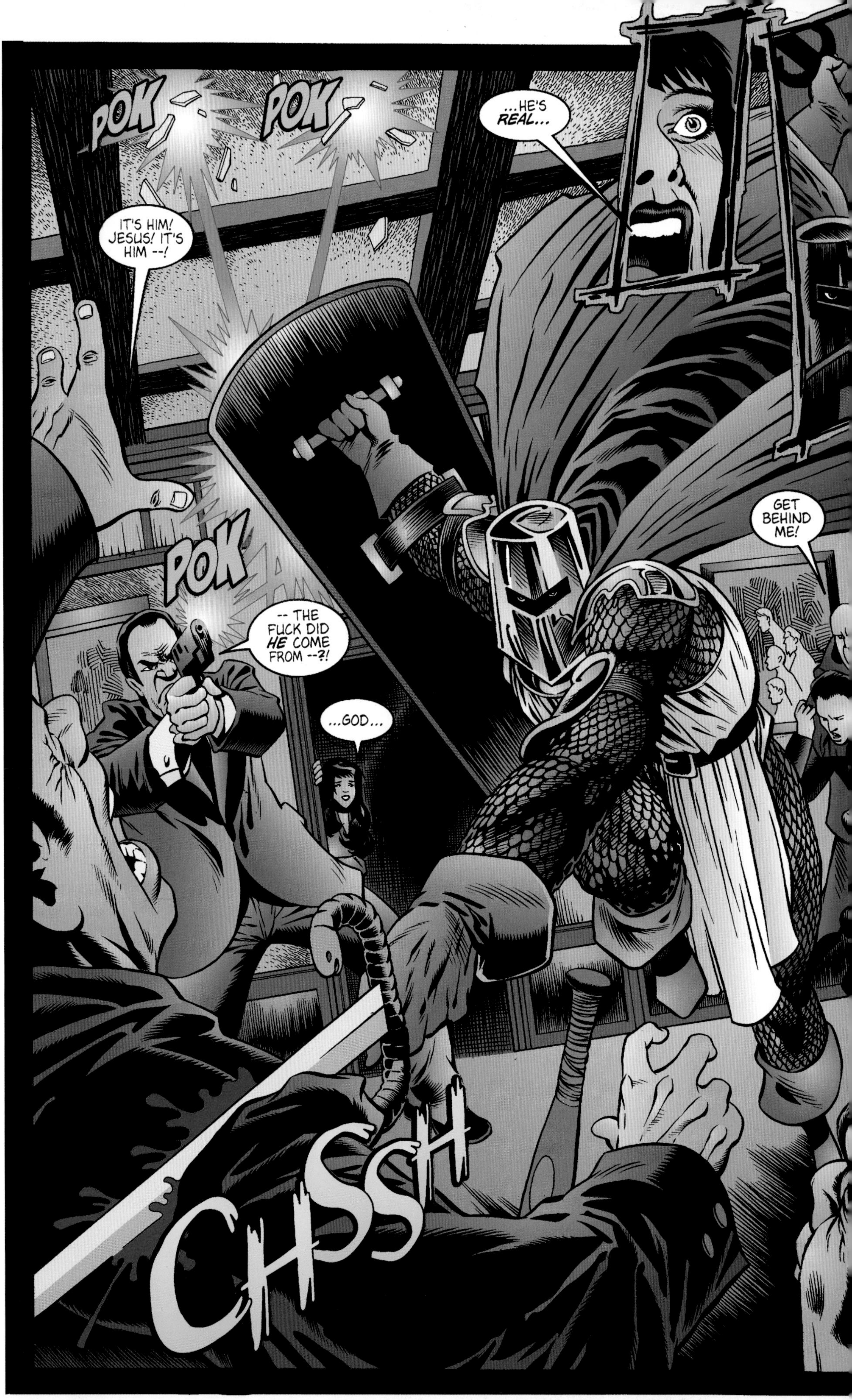
POK
POK
...HE'S REAL...
IT'S HIM! JESUS! IT'S HIM --!
POK
-- THE FUCK DID HE COME FROM --?!
...GOD...
GET BEHIND ME!
CHSSH

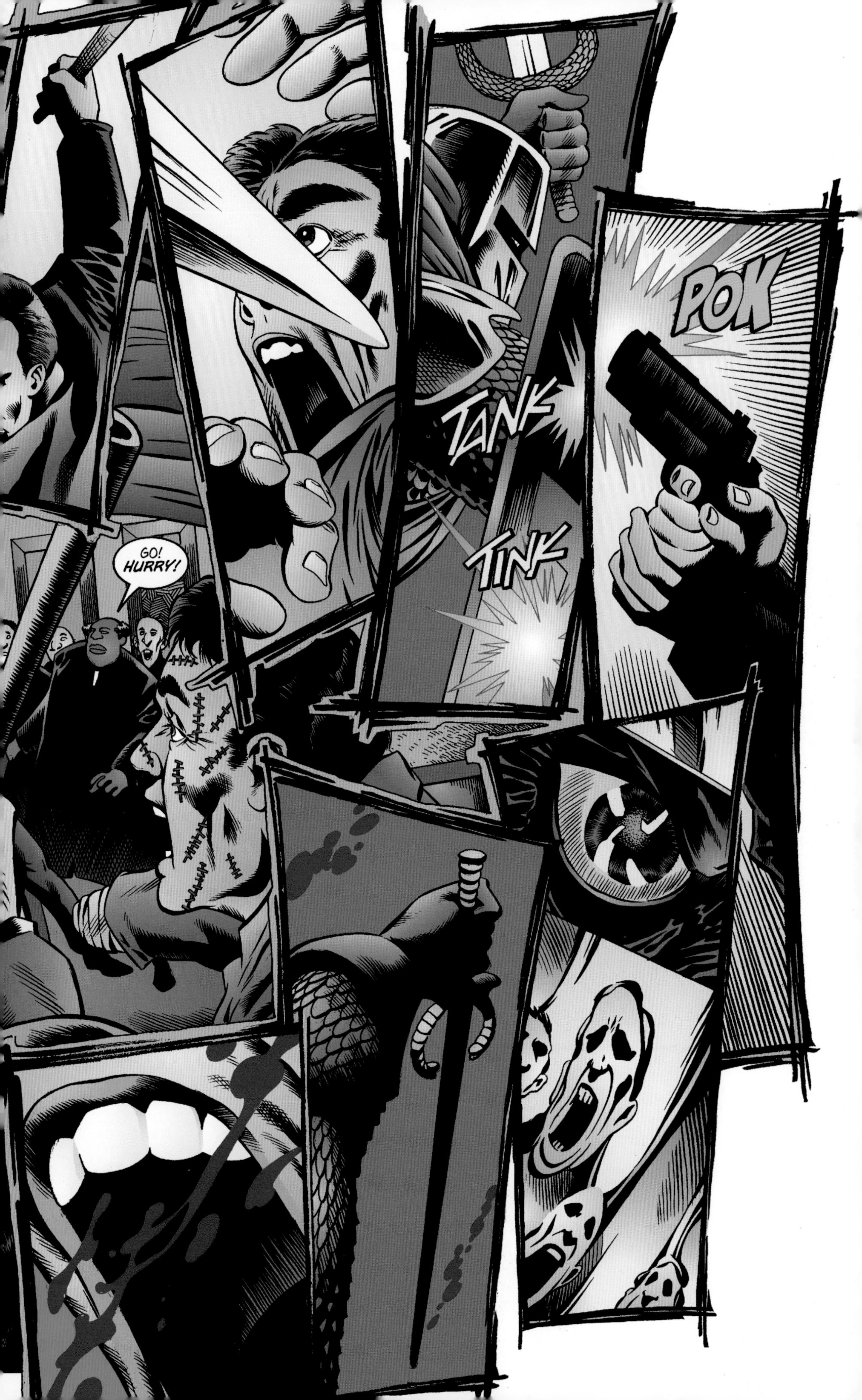
TANK
TINK
POK
GO! HURRY!

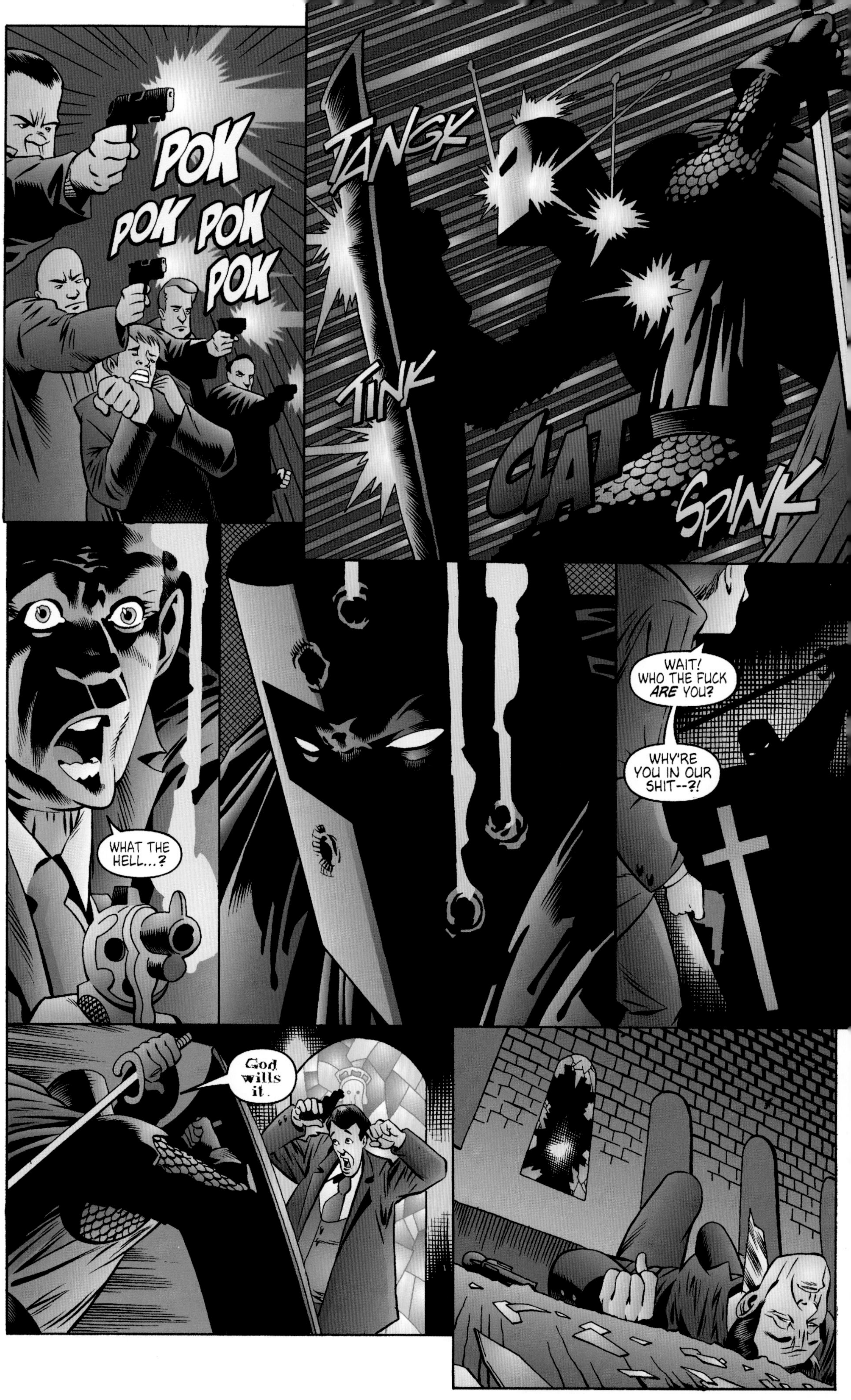
POK
POK POK
POK
TANGK
TINK
CLAT
SPINK
WHAT THE HELL...?
WAIT! WHO THE FUCK ARE YOU?
WHY'RE YOU IN OUR SHIT--?!
God wills it.

QUICKLY!
WHAT IN HEAVEN'S NAME IS GOING ON BACK THERE?!
I WARNED YOU TO LEAVE THIS SCHOOL. YOU SHOULD HAVE LISTENED--
EXIT
WE DON'T EVEN KNOW YOU.
I AM A SON OF THE LORD, LIKE YOURSELVES.
AND I AM TELLING YOU FOR THE LAST TIME. GET OUT.
IT WON'T OPEN! IT'S LOCKED!
IT'S NOT LOCKED. THAT LOCK'S BROKEN.
NEW JERUSALEM SCHOOL
THEN WE'RE TRAPPED! WE -- WE HAVE TO CALL 911!
THE POLICE MIGHT HELP TONIGHT, BUT MORE STUDENTS WILL BE HARMED TOMORROW. THIS MUST END.
THEN WE'LL STAY AND FIGHT!
YOU HAVE A HIGHER POWER FIGHTING FOR YOU. YOU MUST EXIT THIS BUILDING.
WE ARE NOT LYING DOWN AND GIVING UP!
FATHER WAYNE? WHERE'S FATHER SEASHOLTZ...?

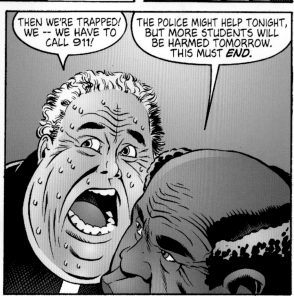

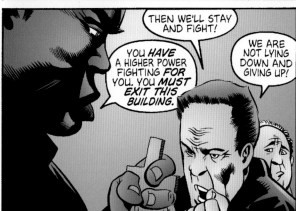

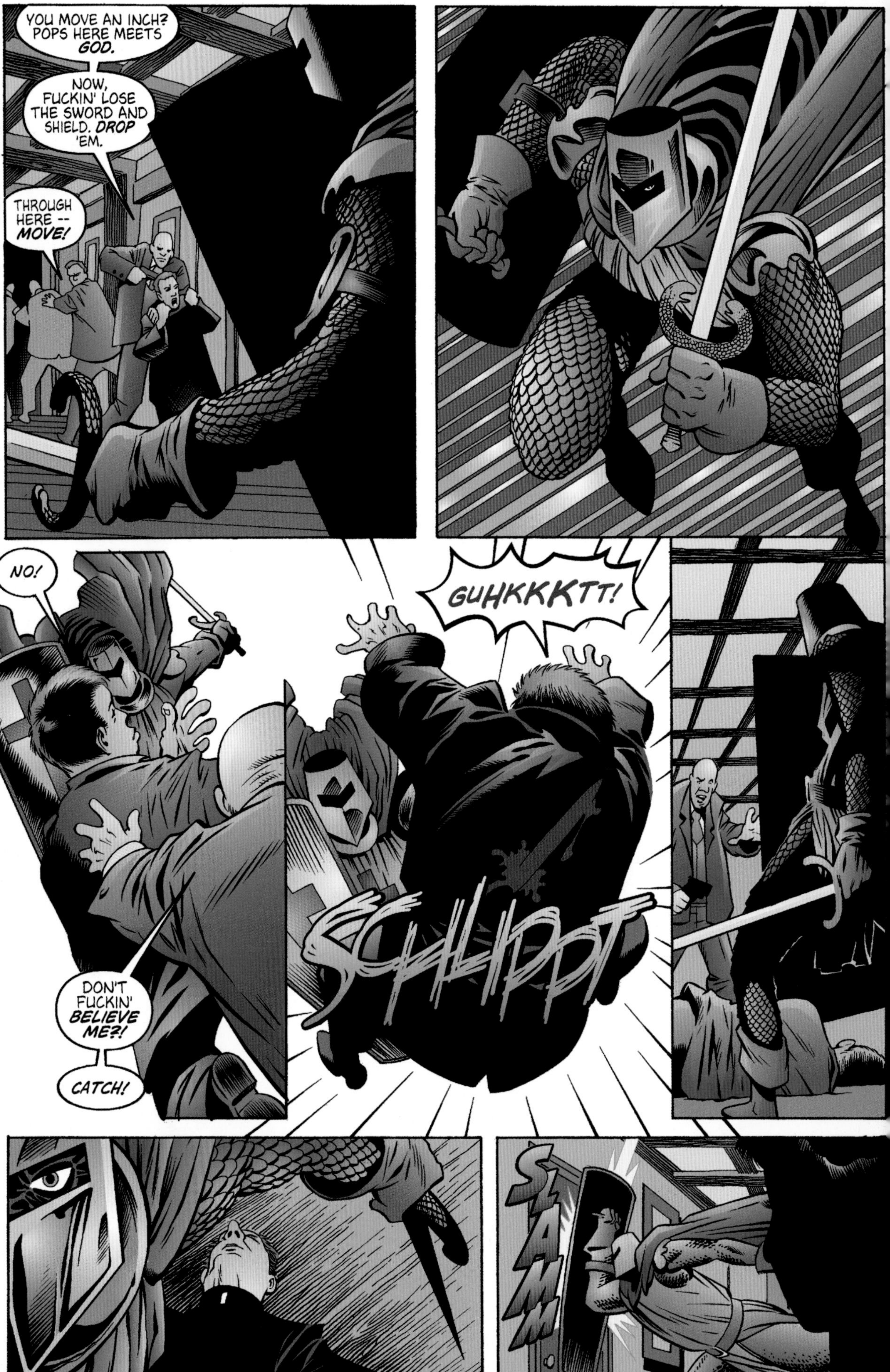
YOU MOVE AN INCH? POPS HERE MEETS GOD.
NOW, FUCKIN' LOSE THE SWORD AND SHIELD. DROP 'EM.
THROUGH HERE -- MOVE!
NO!
DON'T FUCKIN' BELIEVE ME?!
CATCH!
GUHKKKTT!
SCHLIPPT
SLAMM
TINK CLINK SHINK

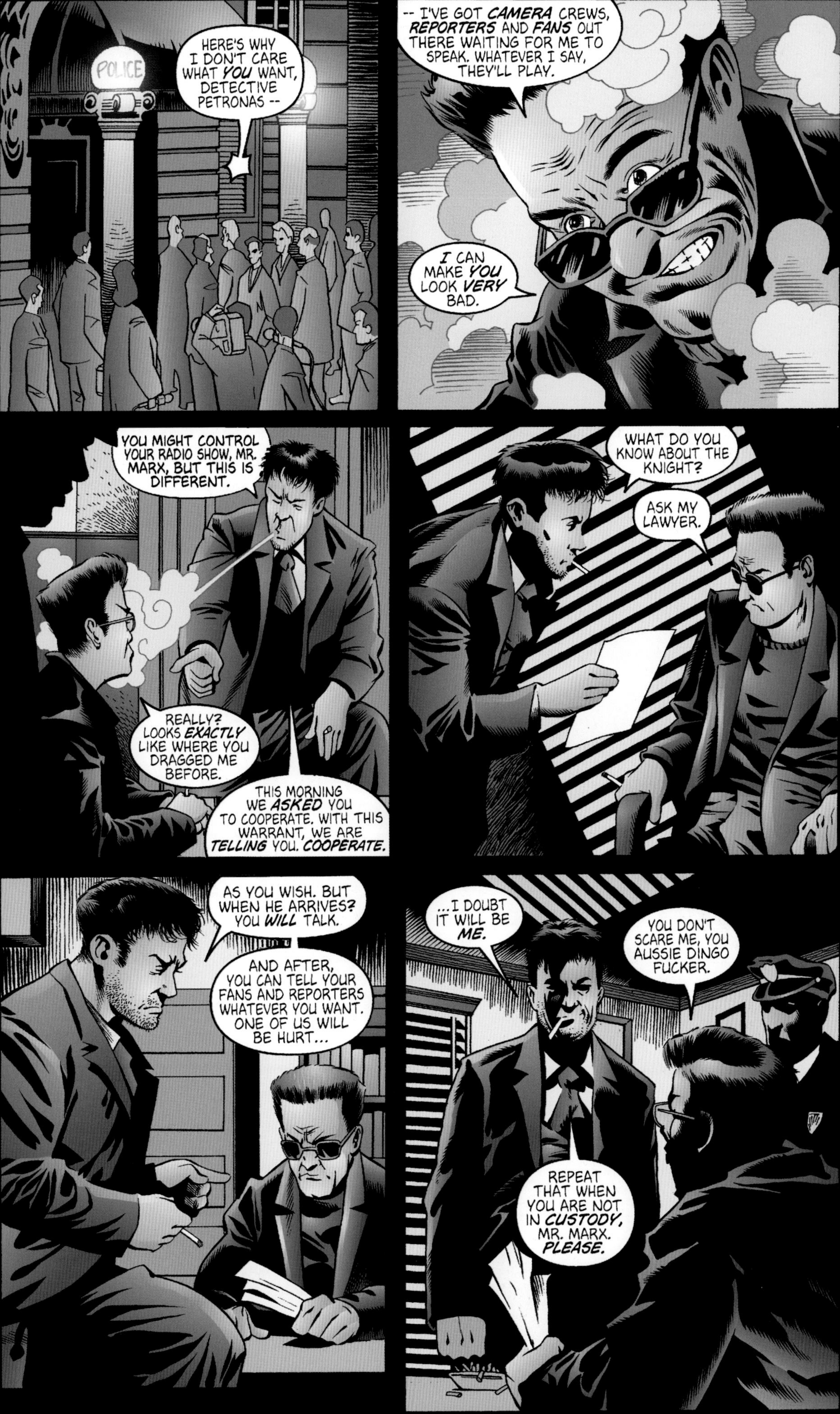
HERE'S WHY I DON'T CARE WHAT YOU WANT, DETECTIVE PETRONAS --
POLICE
-- I'VE GOT CAMERA CREWS, REPORTERS AND FANS OUT THERE WAITING FOR ME TO SPEAK. WHATEVER I SAY, THEY'LL PLAY.
I CAN MAKE YOU LOOK VERY BAD.
YOU MIGHT CONTROL YOUR RADIO SHOW, MR. MARX, BUT THIS IS DIFFERENT.
REALLY? LOOKS EXACTLY LIKE WHERE YOU DRAGGED ME BEFORE.
THIS MORNING WE ASKED YOU TO COOPERATE. WITH THIS WARRANT, WE ARE TELLING YOU. COOPERATE.
WHAT DO YOU KNOW ABOUT THE KNIGHT?
ASK MY LAWYER.
AS YOU WISH. BUT WHEN HE ARRIVES? YOU WILL TALK.
AND AFTER, YOU CAN TELL YOUR FANS AND REPORTERS WHATEVER YOU WANT. ONE OF US WILL BE HURT...
...I DOUBT IT WILL BE ME.
YOU DON'T SCARE ME, YOU AUSSIE DINGO FUCKER.
REPEAT THAT WHEN YOU ARE NOT IN CUSTODY, MR. MARX. PLEASE.

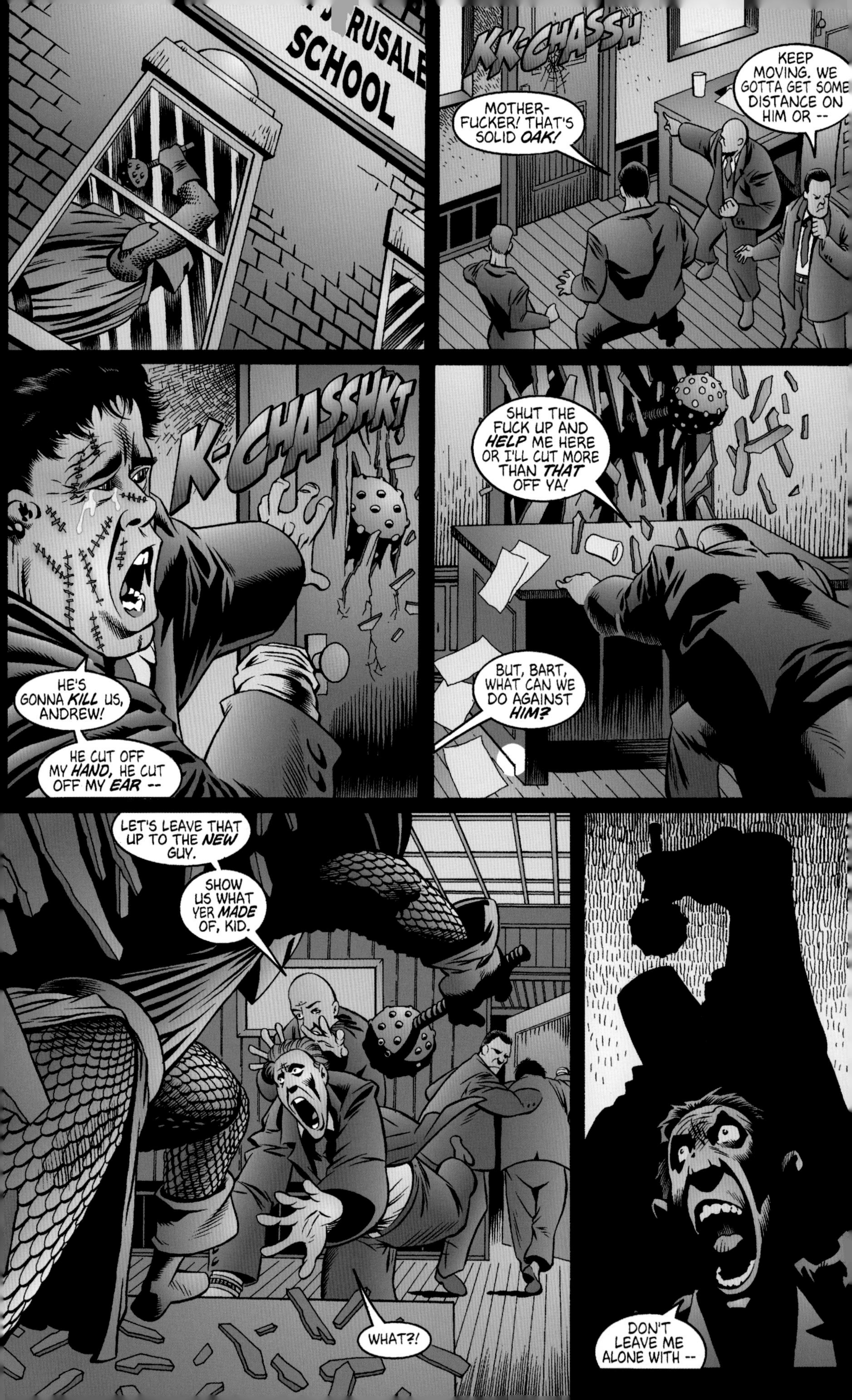
RUSALE
SCHOOL
KK-CHASSH
MOTHER-FUCKER! THAT'S SOLID OAK!
KEEP MOVING. WE GOTTA GET SOME DISTANCE ON HIM OR --
K-CHASSHKT
HE'S GONNA KILL US, ANDREW!
HE CUT OFF MY HAND, HE CUT OFF MY EAR --
SHUT THE FUCK UP AND HELP ME HERE OR I'LL CUT MORE THAN THAT OFF YA!
BUT, BART, WHAT CAN WE DO AGAINST HIM?
LET'S LEAVE THAT UP TO THE NEW GUY.
SHOW US WHAT YER MADE OF, KID.
WHAT?!
DON'T LEAVE ME ALONE WITH --

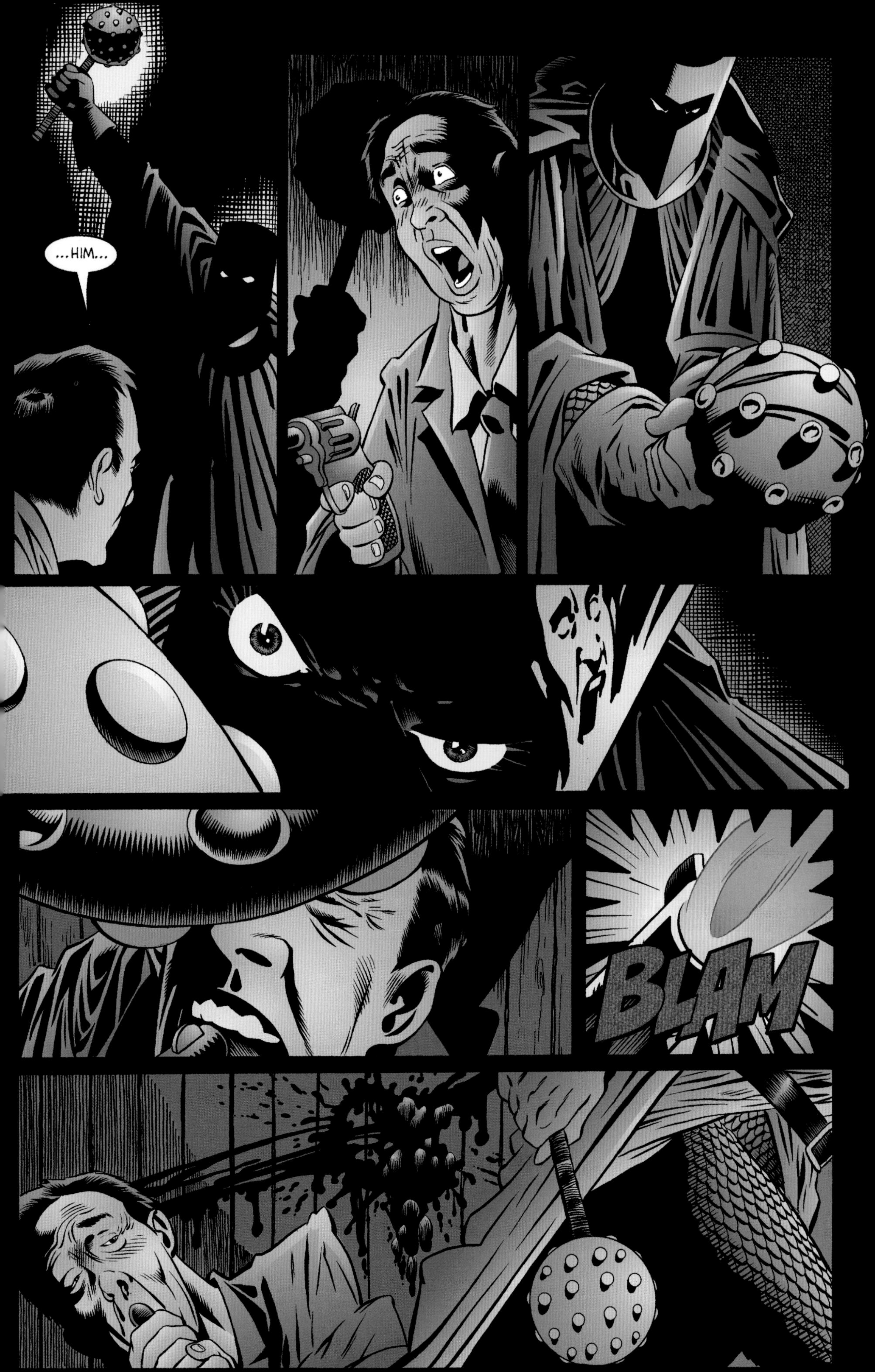
...HIM...
BLAM

OKAY... PLEASE DON'T BE *DEAD*...

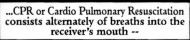

...CPR or Cardio Pulmonary Resuscitation consists alternately of breaths into the receiver's mouth --

-- and compression of the chest cavity.

UH...

...In triage situations, severe bleeding is treated with elevation or tourniquets.

...Severe bleeding that does not stop may require direct pressure of the artery to the nearest bone...

...OH MY GOD... *AHH...*

...To earn a field medical badge, Melbourne Girl Guides must first complete...

CHILD? WHAT ARE YOU *DOING* HERE?

I-I'M TRYING TO THINK OF *ANYTHING* I CAN *REMEMBER* TO -- *HELP* THIS PRIEST, I --

HE'S BEYOND *OUR* HELP.

COME. IT'S NOT *SAFE* FOR YOU HERE.

"OUT OF THE DEPTHS HAVE I CRIED UNTO THEE, O LORD...

"...HEAR MY VOICE: LET THINE EARS BE ATTENTIVE TO THE VOICE OF MY SUPPLICATIONS...

"...IF THOU SHOULDEST MARK INIQUITIES, O LORD, WHO SHALL STAND?

"BUT THERE IS FORGIVENESS WITH THEE, THAT THOU MAYEST BE FEARED..."

"...I WAIT FOR THEE, LORD, MY SOUL DOTH WAIT, AND IN YOUR WORD DO I HOPE."

WOULD YOU SHUT UP?!

I WAS PRAYING FOR US.

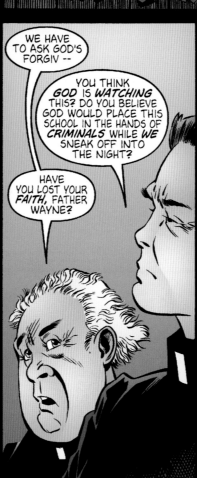

WE HAVE TO ASK GOD'S FORGIV --

YOU THINK GOD IS WATCHING THIS? DO YOU BELIEVE GOD WOULD PLACE THIS SCHOOL IN THE HANDS OF CRIMINALS WHILE WE SNEAK OFF INTO THE NIGHT?

HAVE YOU LOST YOUR FAITH, FATHER WAYNE?

NO. I FOUND MY NERVE. WAIT HERE FOR THAT PRIEST IF YOU WANT.

I'M GOING TO TAKE OUR SCHOOL, OUR CHURCH... BACK.

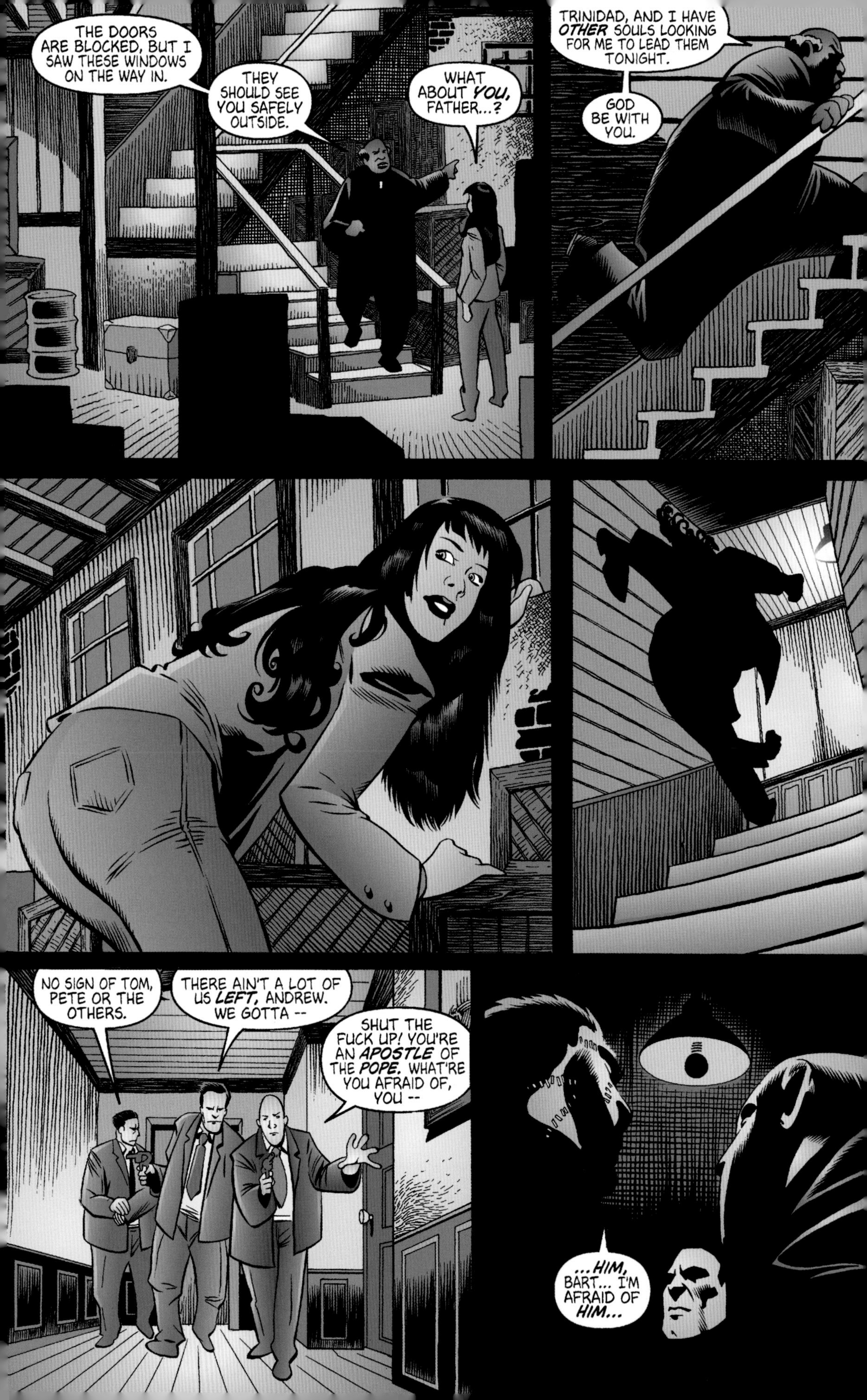
THE DOORS ARE BLOCKED, BUT I SAW THESE WINDOWS ON THE WAY IN.
THEY SHOULD SEE YOU SAFELY OUTSIDE.
WHAT ABOUT *YOU,* FATHER...?
TRINIDAD, AND I HAVE *OTHER* SOULS LOOKING FOR ME TO LEAD THEM TONIGHT.
GOD BE WITH YOU.
NO SIGN OF TOM, PETE OR THE OTHERS.
THERE AIN'T A LOT OF US *LEFT,* ANDREW. WE GOTTA --
SHUT THE FUCK UP! YOU'RE AN *APOSTLE* OF THE *POPE.* WHAT'RE YOU AFRAID OF, YOU --
...*HIM,* BART... I'M AFRAID OF *HIM...*

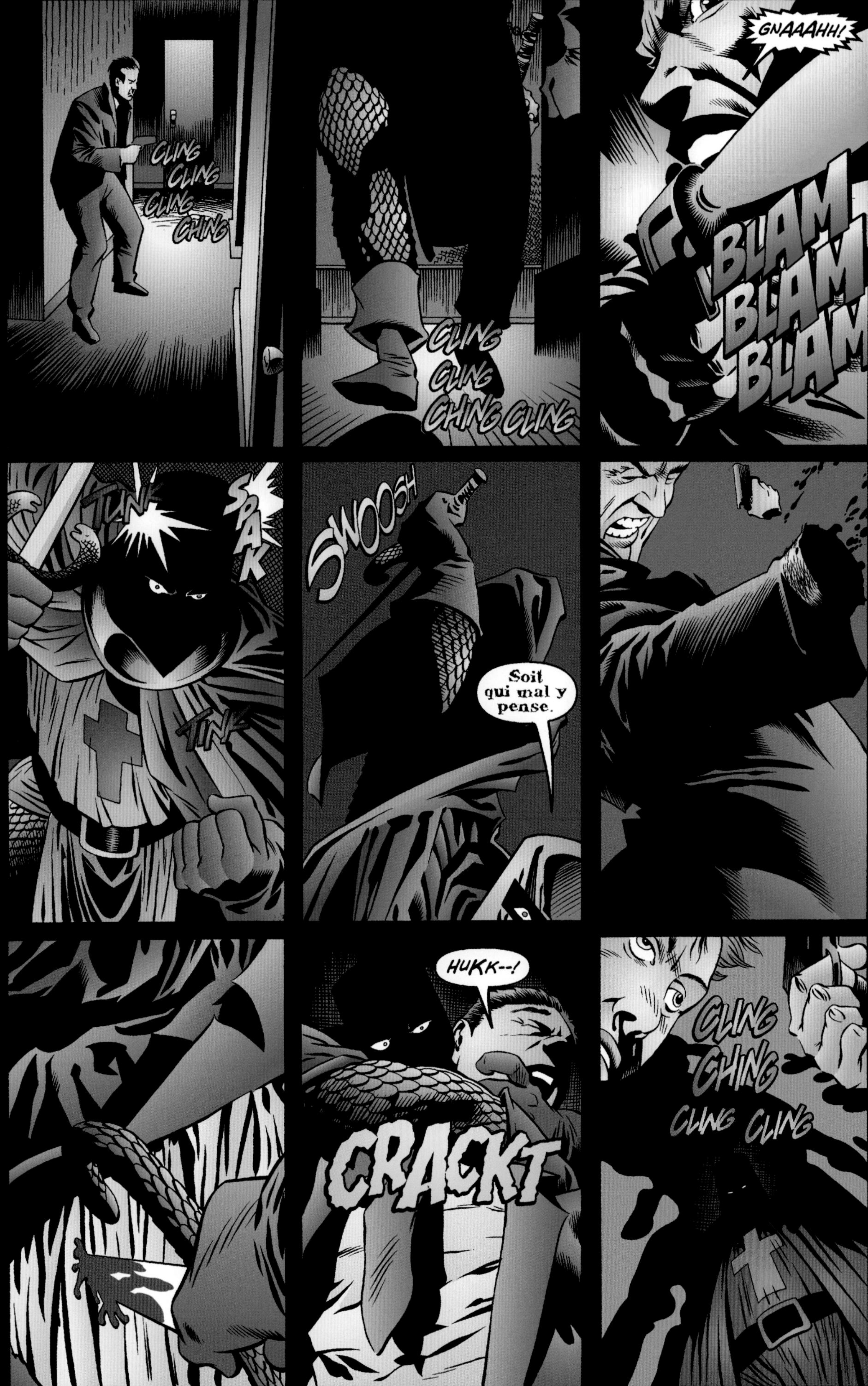
CLING CLING CLING CHING
CLING CLING CHING CLING
GNAAAHH!
BLAM BLAM BLAM
TUNK
SPAK
TINK
SWOOSH
Soit qui mal y pense.
HUKK--!
CRACKT
CLING CHING CLING CLING

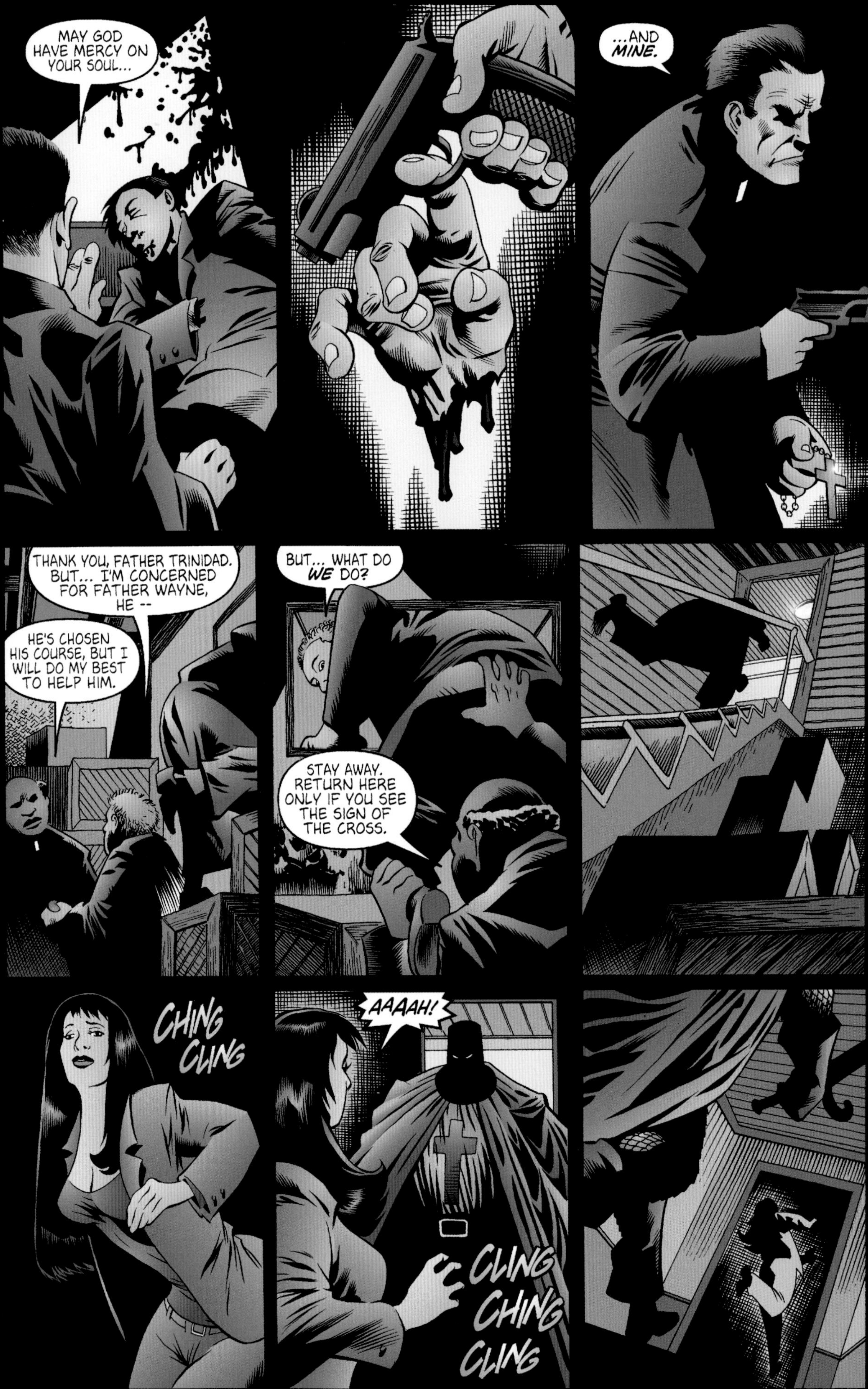
MAY GOD HAVE MERCY ON YOUR SOUL...
...AND MINE.
THANK YOU, FATHER TRINIDAD. BUT... I'M CONCERNED FOR FATHER WAYNE, HE --
HE'S CHOSEN HIS COURSE, BUT I WILL DO MY BEST TO HELP HIM.
BUT... WHAT DO WE DO?
STAY AWAY. RETURN HERE ONLY IF YOU SEE THE SIGN OF THE CROSS.
CHING CLING
AAAAH!
CLING CHING CLING

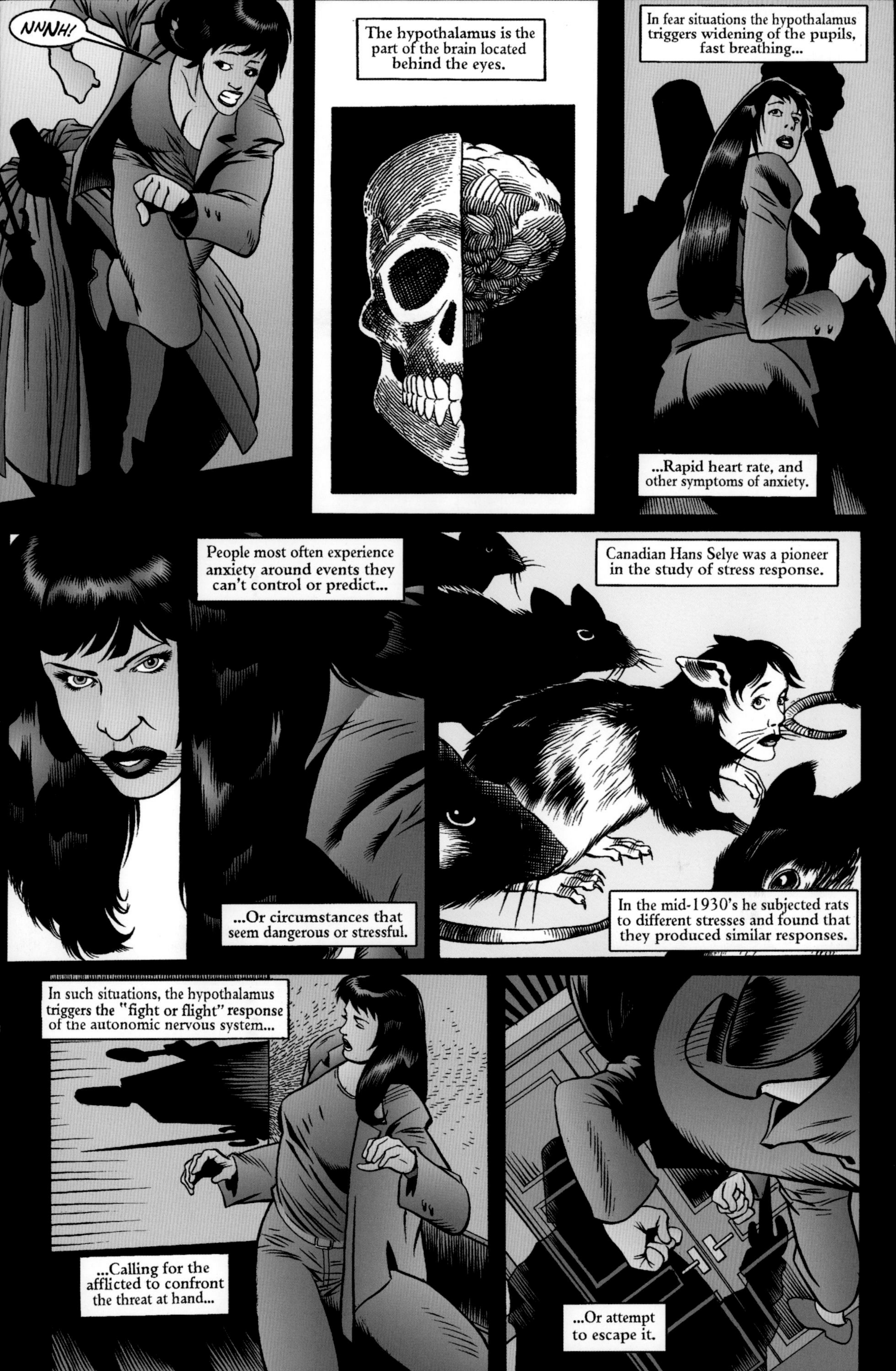
NNNH!
The hypothalamus is the part of the brain located behind the eyes.
In fear situations the hypothalamus triggers widening of the pupils, fast breathing...
...Rapid heart rate, and other symptoms of anxiety.
People most often experience anxiety around events they can't control or predict...
...Or circumstances that seem dangerous or stressful.
Canadian Hans Selye was a pioneer in the study of stress response.
In the mid-1930's he subjected rats to different stresses and found that they produced similar responses.
In such situations, the hypothalamus triggers the "fight or flight" response of the autonomic nervous system...
...Calling for the afflicted to confront the threat at hand...
...Or attempt to escape it.

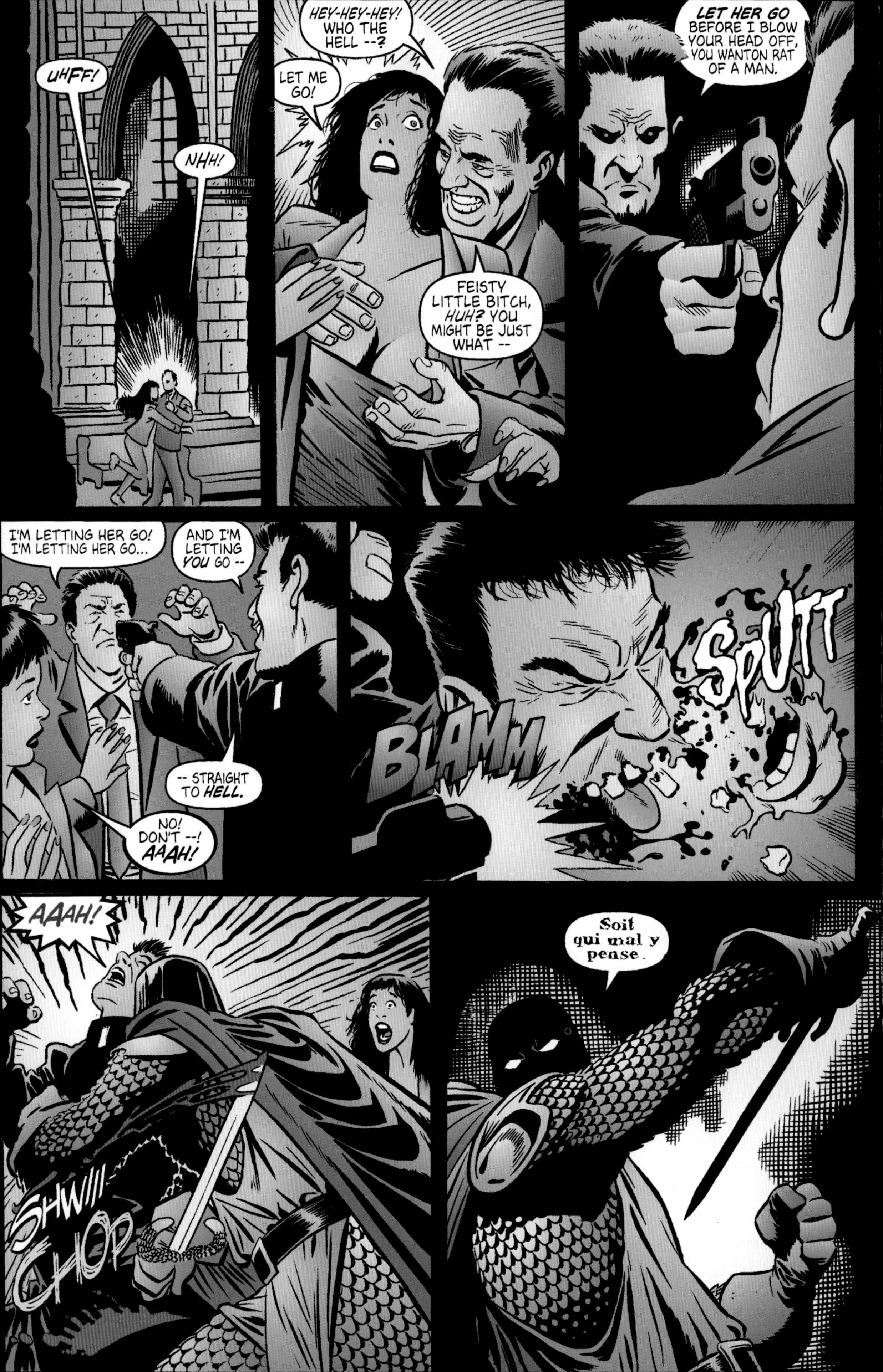
UHFF!
NHH!
HEY-HEY-HEY! WHO THE HELL --?
LET ME GO!
FEISTY LITTLE BITCH, HUH? YOU MIGHT BE JUST WHAT --
LET HER GO BEFORE I BLOW YOUR HEAD OFF, YOU WANTON RAT OF A MAN.
I'M LETTING HER GO! I'M LETTING HER GO...
AND I'M LETTING YOU GO --
-- STRAIGHT TO HELL.
NO! DON'T --! AAAH!
BLAMM
SPUTT
AAAH!
SHWIII
CHOP
Soit qui mal y pense.

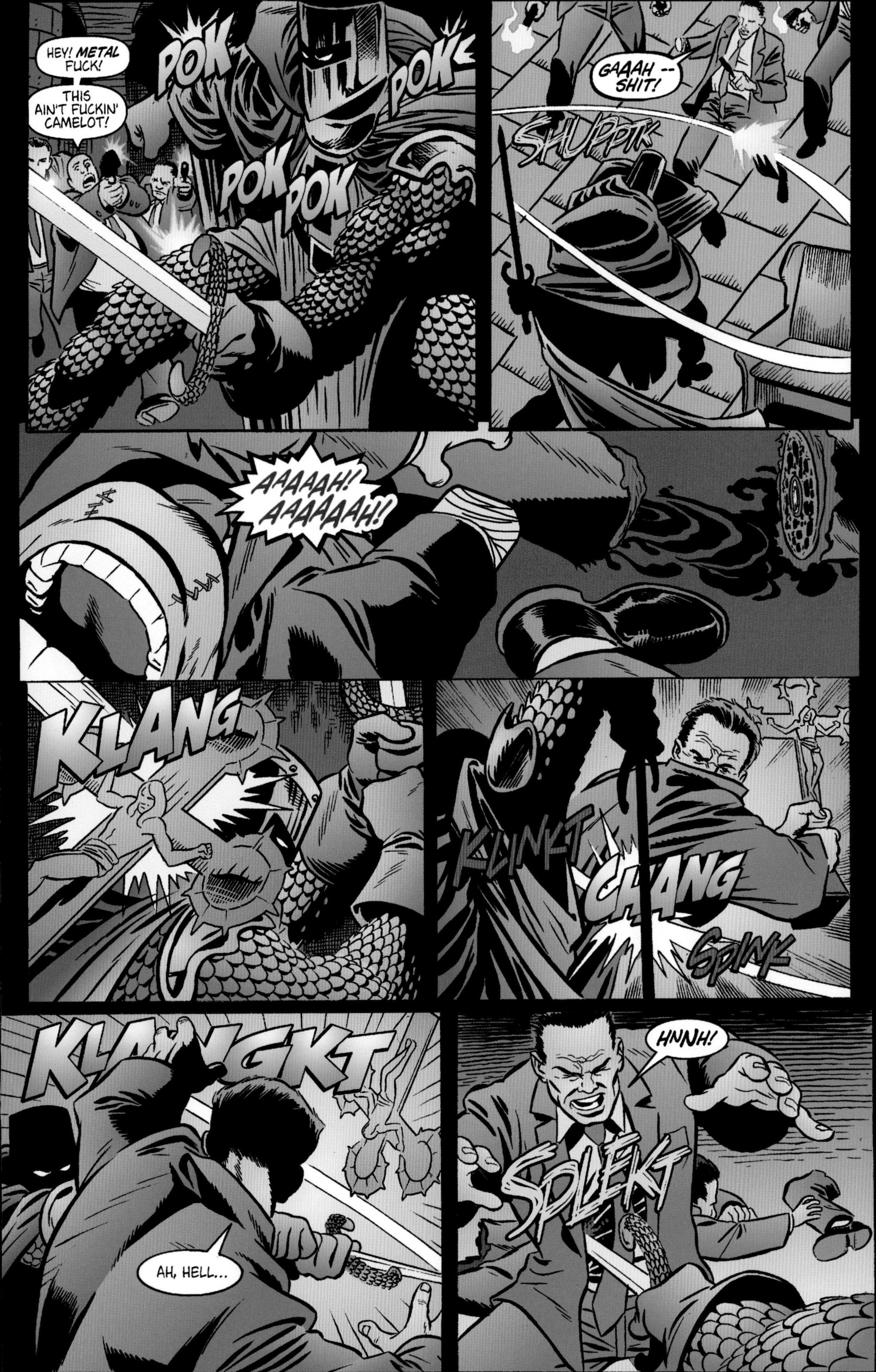
HEY! METAL FUCK!
THIS AIN'T FUCKIN' CAMELOT!
POK
POK
POK
POK
POK
GAAAH -- SHIT!
SPLUPPTK
AAAAAH! AAAAAAH!
KLANG
KLINKT
CHANG
SPINK
KLANGKT
AH, HELL...
HNNH!
SPLEKT

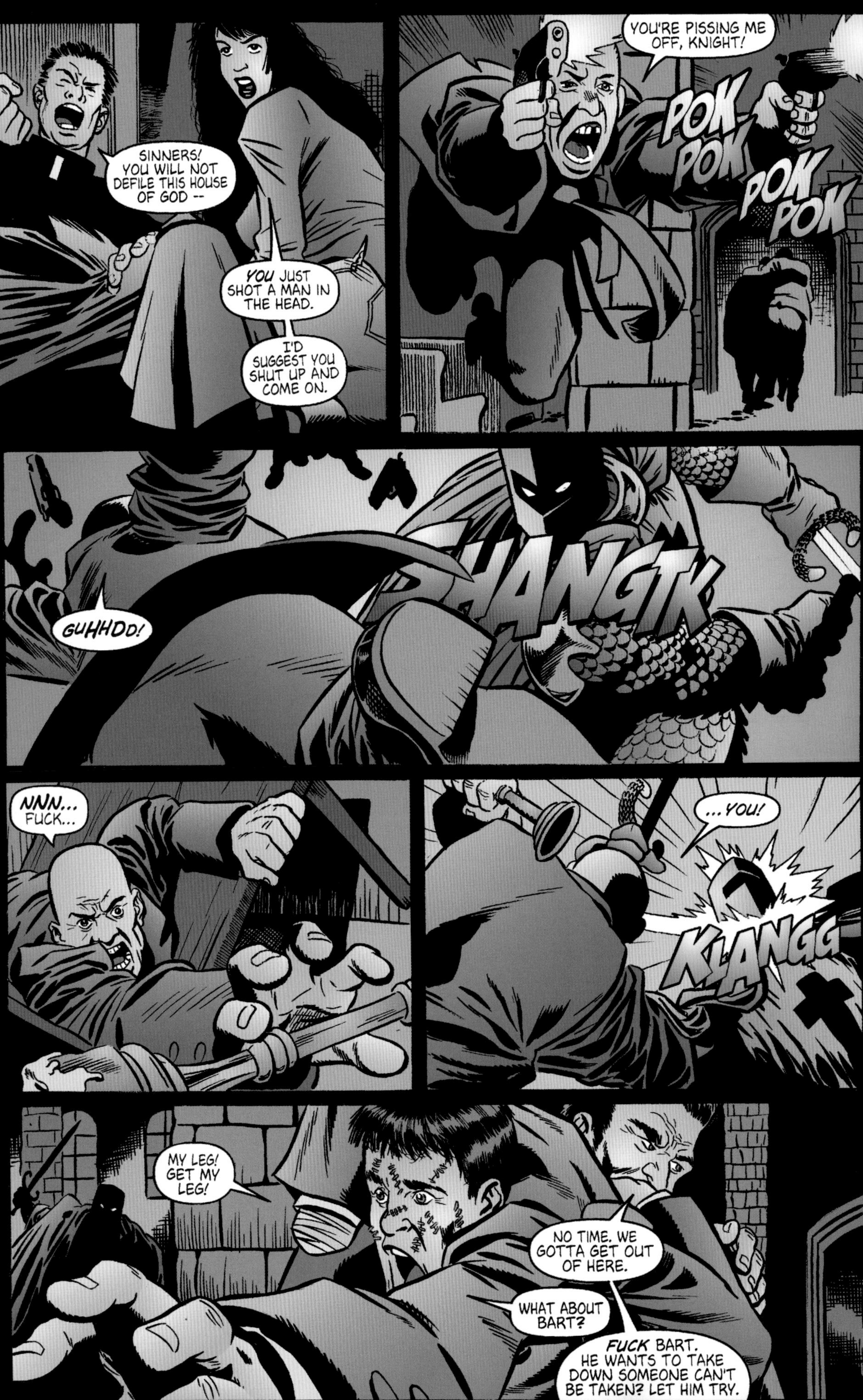
SINNERS! YOU WILL NOT DEFILE THIS HOUSE OF GOD --
YOU JUST SHOT A MAN IN THE HEAD.
I'D SUGGEST YOU SHUT UP AND COME ON.
YOU'RE PISSING ME OFF, KNIGHT!
POK POK POK POK
SHANGTK
GUHHDD!
NNN... FUCK...
...YOU!
KLANGG
MY LEG! GET MY LEG!
NO TIME. WE GOTTA GET OUT OF HERE.
WHAT ABOUT BART?
FUCK BART. HE WANTS TO TAKE DOWN SOMEONE CAN'T BE TAKEN? LET HIM TRY.

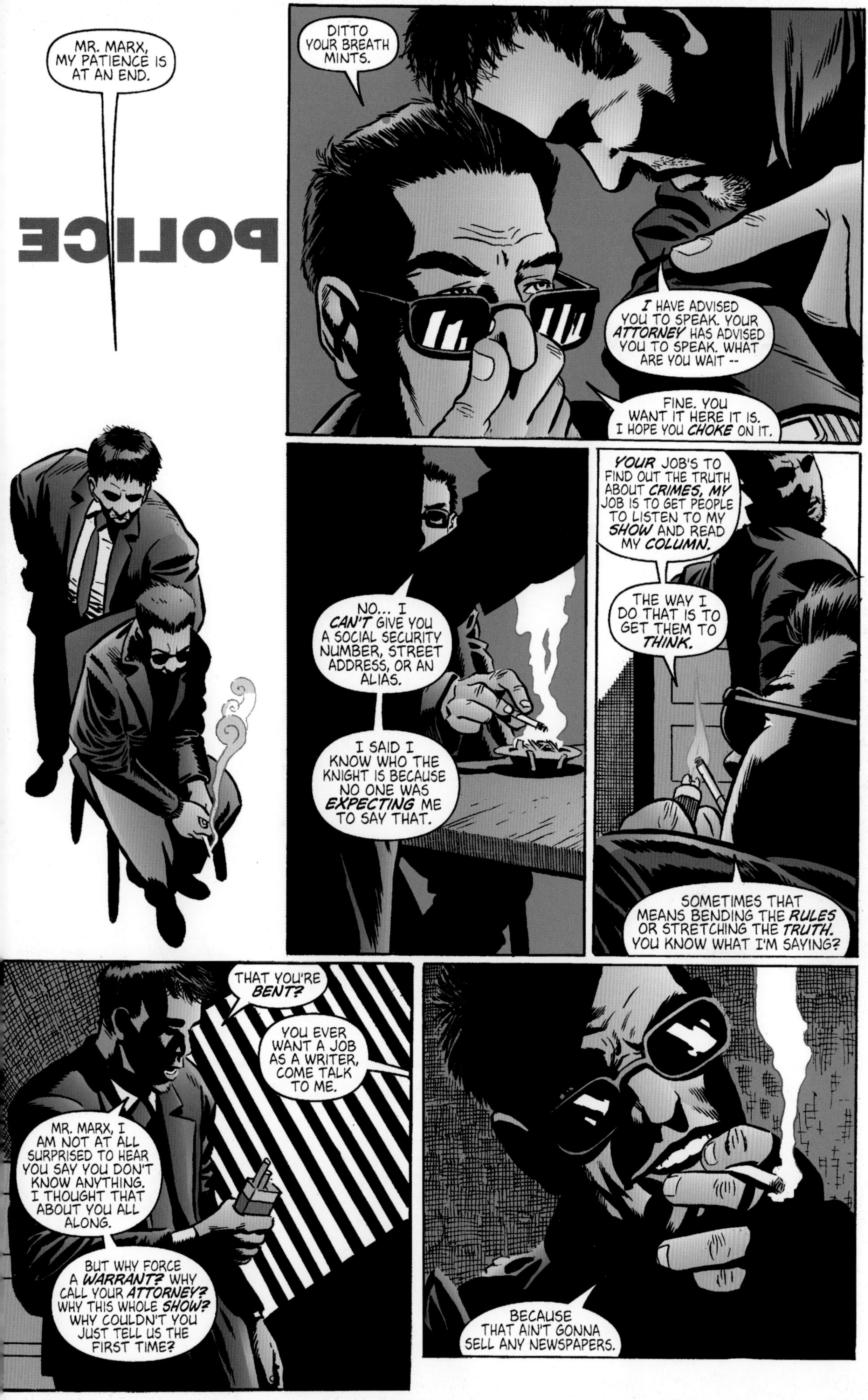
MR. MARX, MY PATIENCE IS AT AN END.
POLICE
DITTO YOUR BREATH MINTS.
I HAVE ADVISED YOU TO SPEAK. YOUR ATTORNEY HAS ADVISED YOU TO SPEAK. WHAT ARE YOU WAIT --
FINE. YOU WANT IT HERE IT IS. I HOPE YOU CHOKE ON IT.
NO... I CAN'T GIVE YOU A SOCIAL SECURITY NUMBER, STREET ADDRESS, OR AN ALIAS.
I SAID I KNOW WHO THE KNIGHT IS BECAUSE NO ONE WAS EXPECTING ME TO SAY THAT.
YOUR JOB'S TO FIND OUT THE TRUTH ABOUT CRIMES, MY JOB IS TO GET PEOPLE TO LISTEN TO MY SHOW AND READ MY COLUMN.
THE WAY I DO THAT IS TO GET THEM TO THINK.
SOMETIMES THAT MEANS BENDING THE RULES OR STRETCHING THE TRUTH. YOU KNOW WHAT I'M SAYING?
THAT YOU'RE BENT?
YOU EVER WANT A JOB AS A WRITER, COME TALK TO ME.
MR. MARX, I AM NOT AT ALL SURPRISED TO HEAR YOU SAY YOU DON'T KNOW ANYTHING. I THOUGHT THAT ABOUT YOU ALL ALONG.
BUT WHY FORCE A WARRANT? WHY CALL YOUR ATTORNEY? WHY THIS WHOLE SHOW? WHY COULDN'T YOU JUST TELL US THE FIRST TIME?
BECAUSE THAT AIN'T GONNA SELL ANY NEWSPAPERS.

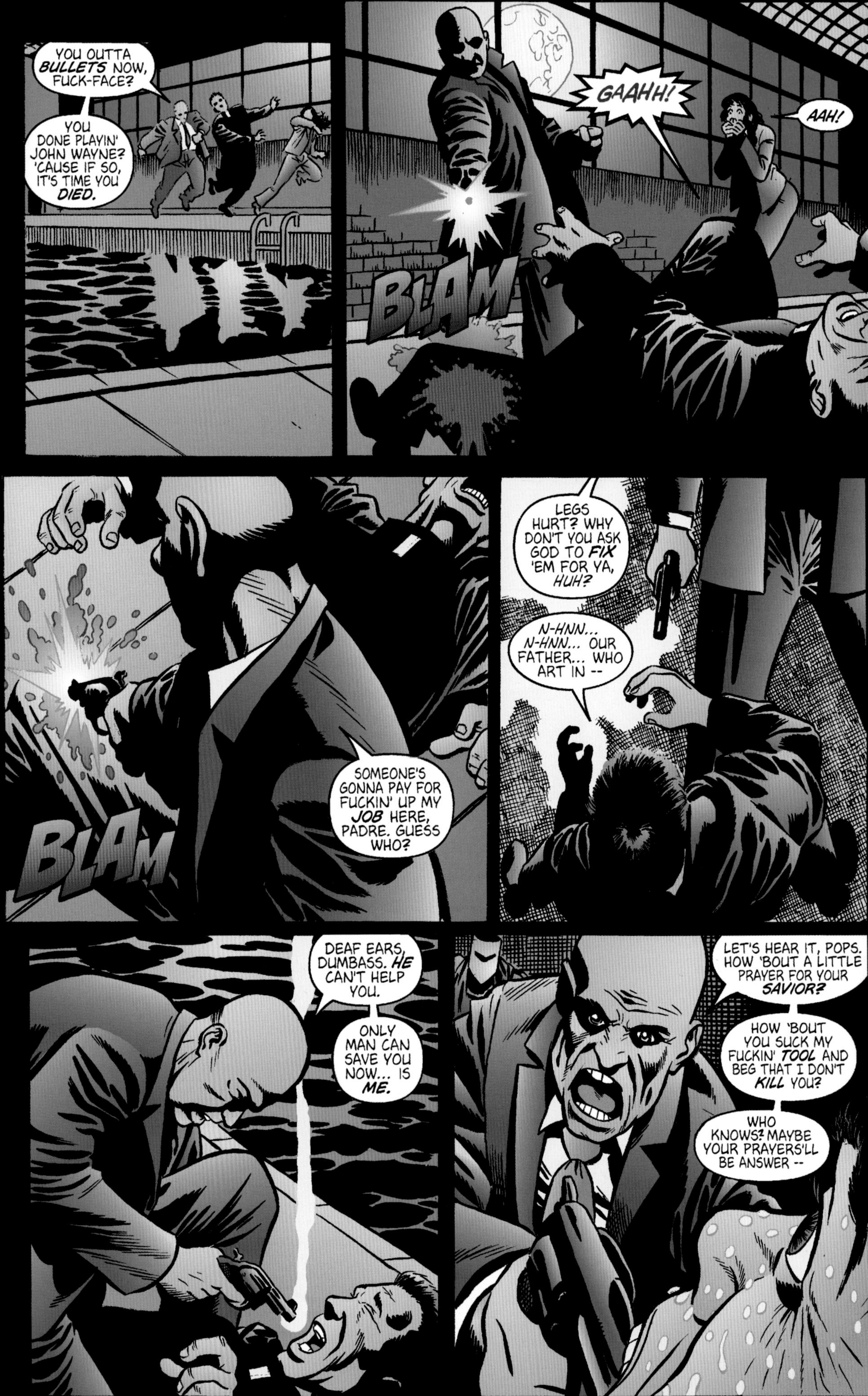
YOU OUTTA BULLETS NOW, FUCK-FACE?
YOU DONE PLAYIN' JOHN WAYNE? 'CAUSE IF SO, IT'S TIME YOU DIED.
GAAHH!
AAH!
BLAM
BLAM
SOMEONE'S GONNA PAY FOR FUCKIN' UP MY JOB HERE, PADRE. GUESS WHO?
LEGS HURT? WHY DON'T YOU ASK GOD TO FIX 'EM FOR YA, HUH?
N-HNN... N-HNN... OUR FATHER... WHO ART IN --
DEAF EARS, DUMBASS. HE CAN'T HELP YOU.
ONLY MAN CAN SAVE YOU NOW... IS ME.
LET'S HEAR IT, POPS. HOW 'BOUT A LITTLE PRAYER FOR YOUR SAVIOR?
HOW 'BOUT YOU SUCK MY FUCKIN' TOOL AND BEG THAT I DON'T KILL YOU?
WHO KNOWS? MAYBE YOUR PRAYERS'LL BE ANSWER --

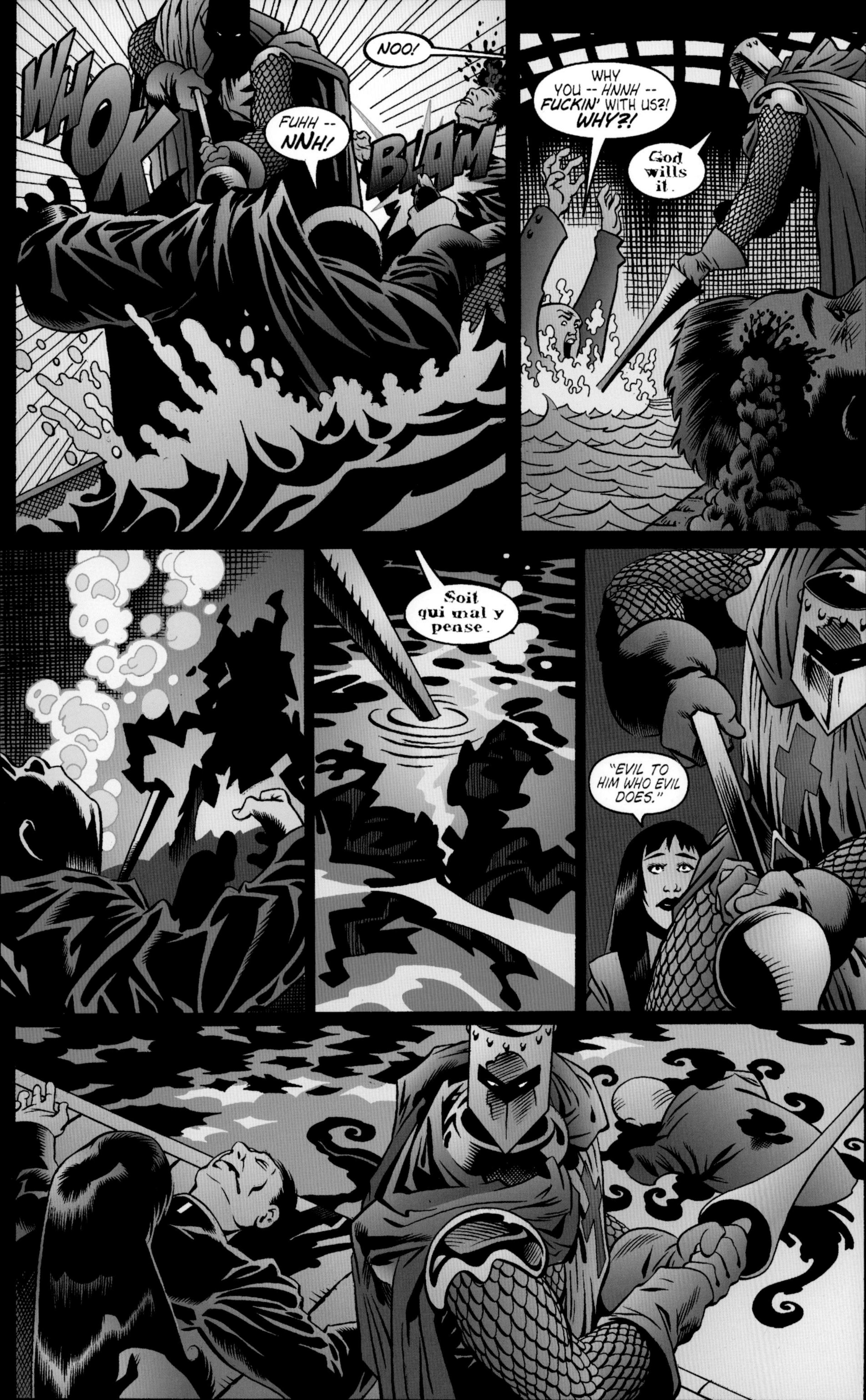
WHOK
NOO!
FUHH -- NNH!
BLAM
WHY YOU -- HNNH -- FUCKIN' WITH US?! WHY?!
God wills it.
Soit qui mal y pense.
"EVIL TO HIM WHO EVIL DOES."

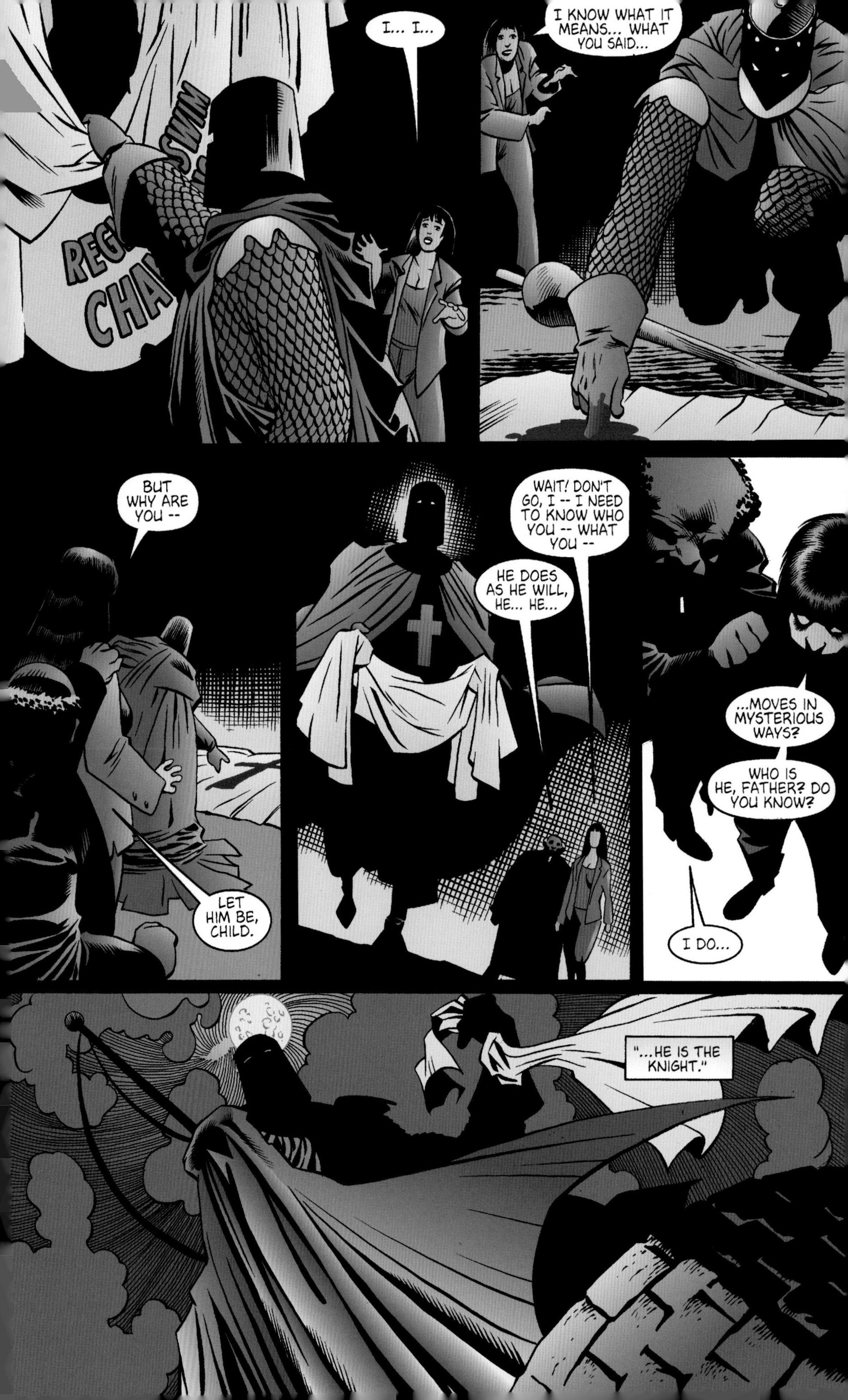
I... I...
I KNOW WHAT IT MEANS... WHAT YOU SAID...
BUT WHY ARE YOU --
LET HIM BE, CHILD.
WAIT! DON'T GO, I -- I NEED TO KNOW WHO YOU -- WHAT YOU --
HE DOES AS HE WILL, HE... HE...
...MOVES IN MYSTERIOUS WAYS?
WHO IS HE, FATHER? DO YOU KNOW?
I DO...
"...HE IS THE KNIGHT."

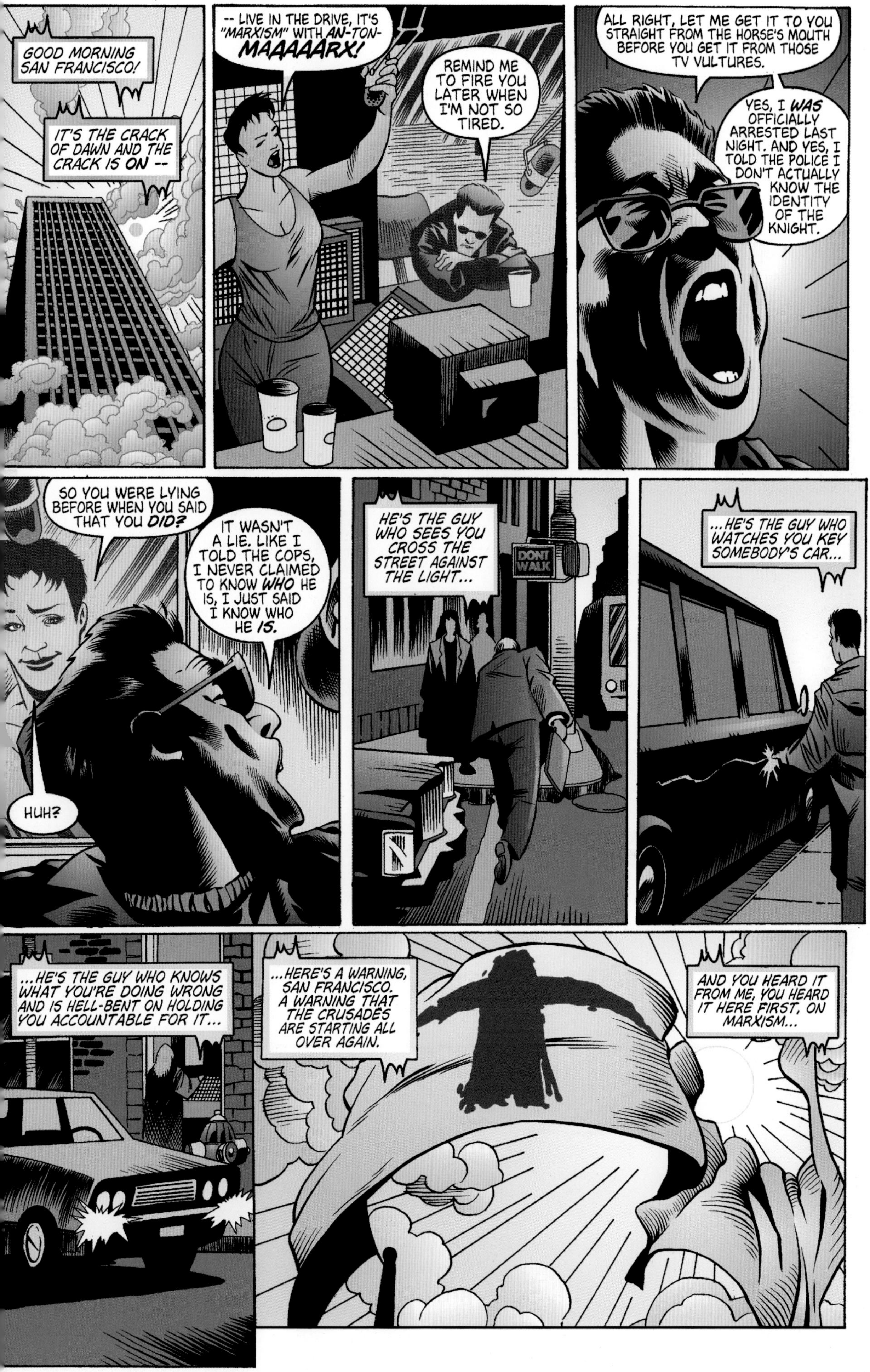
GOOD MORNING SAN FRANCISCO!
IT'S THE CRACK OF DAWN AND THE CRACK IS ON --
-- LIVE IN THE DRIVE, IT'S "MARXISM" WITH AN-TON-MAAAAARX!
REMIND ME TO FIRE YOU LATER WHEN I'M NOT SO TIRED.
ALL RIGHT, LET ME GET IT TO YOU STRAIGHT FROM THE HORSE'S MOUTH BEFORE YOU GET IT FROM THOSE TV VULTURES.
YES, I WAS OFFICIALLY ARRESTED LAST NIGHT. AND YES, I TOLD THE POLICE I DON'T ACTUALLY KNOW THE IDENTITY OF THE KNIGHT.
SO YOU WERE LYING BEFORE WHEN YOU SAID THAT YOU DID?
IT WASN'T A LIE. LIKE I TOLD THE COPS, I NEVER CLAIMED TO KNOW WHO HE IS, I JUST SAID I KNOW WHO HE IS.
HUH?
HE'S THE GUY WHO SEES YOU CROSS THE STREET AGAINST THE LIGHT...
DONT WALK
...HE'S THE GUY WHO WATCHES YOU KEY SOMEBODY'S CAR...
...HE'S THE GUY WHO KNOWS WHAT YOU'RE DOING WRONG AND IS HELL-BENT ON HOLDING YOU ACCOUNTABLE FOR IT...
...HERE'S A WARNING, SAN FRANCISCO. A WARNING THAT THE CRUSADES ARE STARTING ALL OVER AGAIN.
AND YOU HEARD IT FROM ME, YOU HEARD IT HERE FIRST, ON MARXISM...

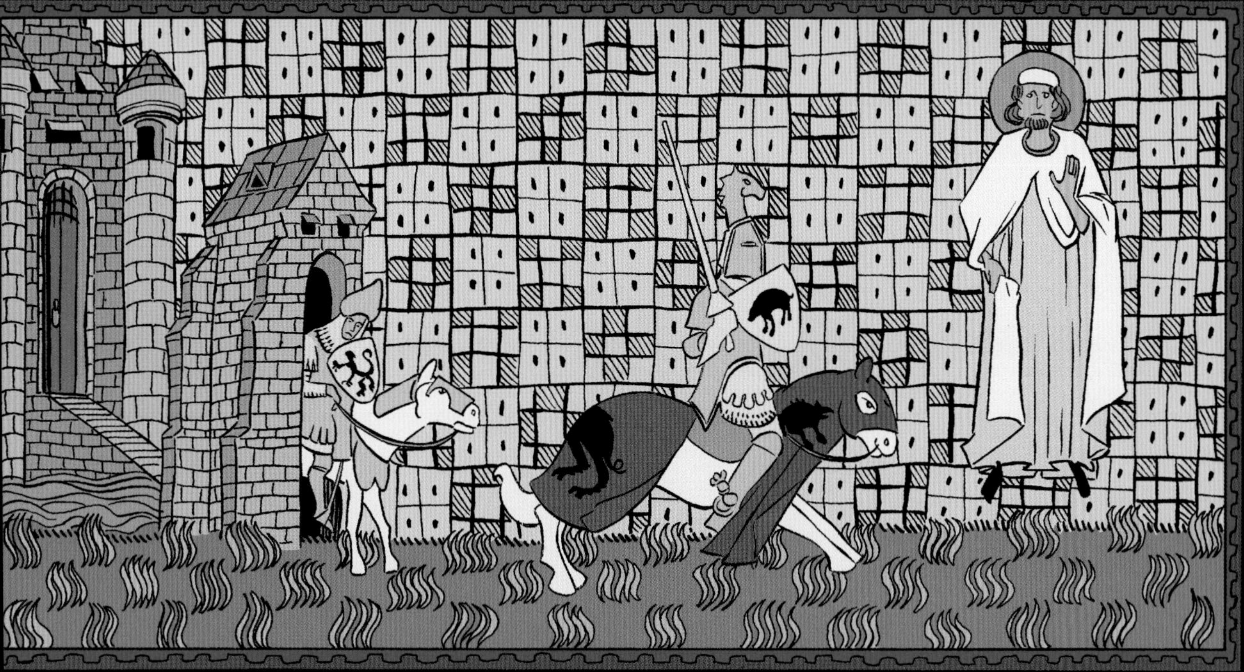

"He who does not fill his world
with phantoms remains alone."
-- Antonio Porchia

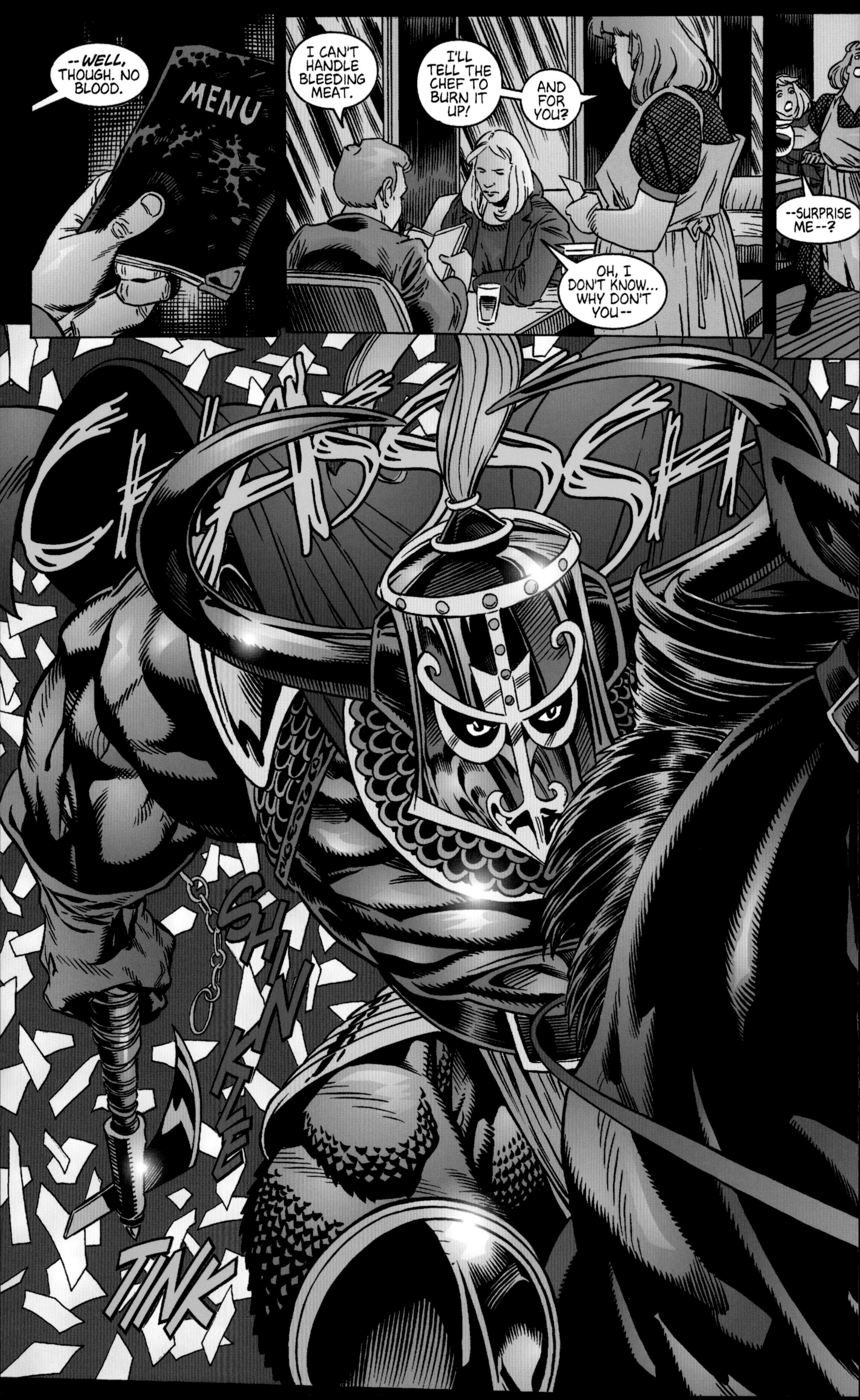

--WELL, THOUGH. NO BLOOD.
MENU
I CAN'T HANDLE BLEEDING MEAT.
I'LL TELL THE CHEF TO BURN IT UP!
AND FOR YOU?
OH, I DON'T KNOW... WHY DON'T YOU--
--SURPRISE ME--?
CHASSH
SHINKLE
TINK

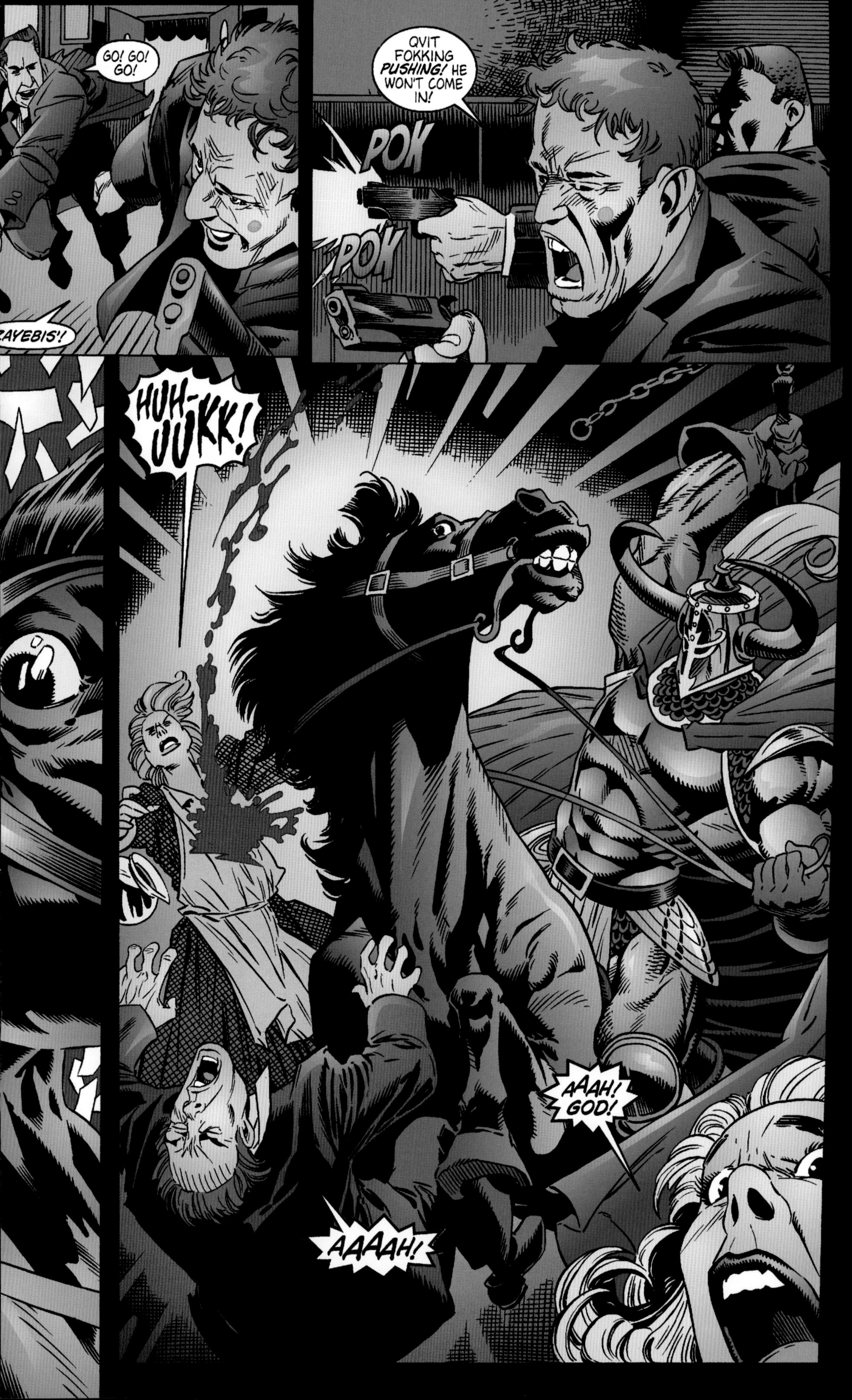
GO! GO! GO!
ZAYEBIS'!
QVIT FOKKING PUSHING! HE WON'T COME IN!
POK
POK
HUH-UUKK!
AAAH! GOD!
AAAAH!

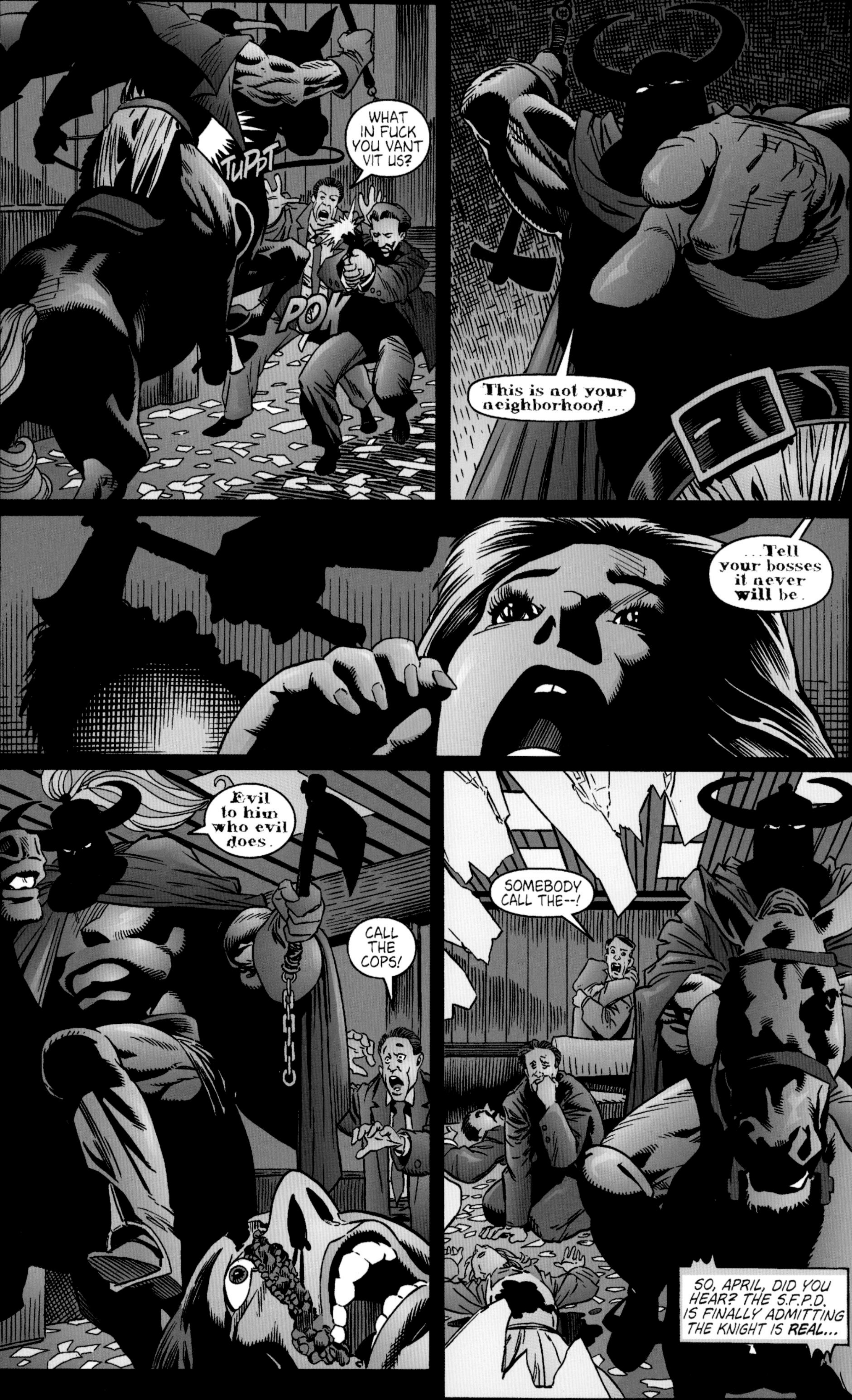
WHAT IN FUCK YOU VANT VIT US?
TUPPT
POK
This is not your neighborhood...
...Tell your bosses it never will be.
Evil to him who evil does.
CALL THE COPS!
SOMEBODY CALL THE--!
SO, APRIL, DID YOU HEAR? THE S.F.P.D. IS FINALLY ADMITTING THE KNIGHT IS REAL...

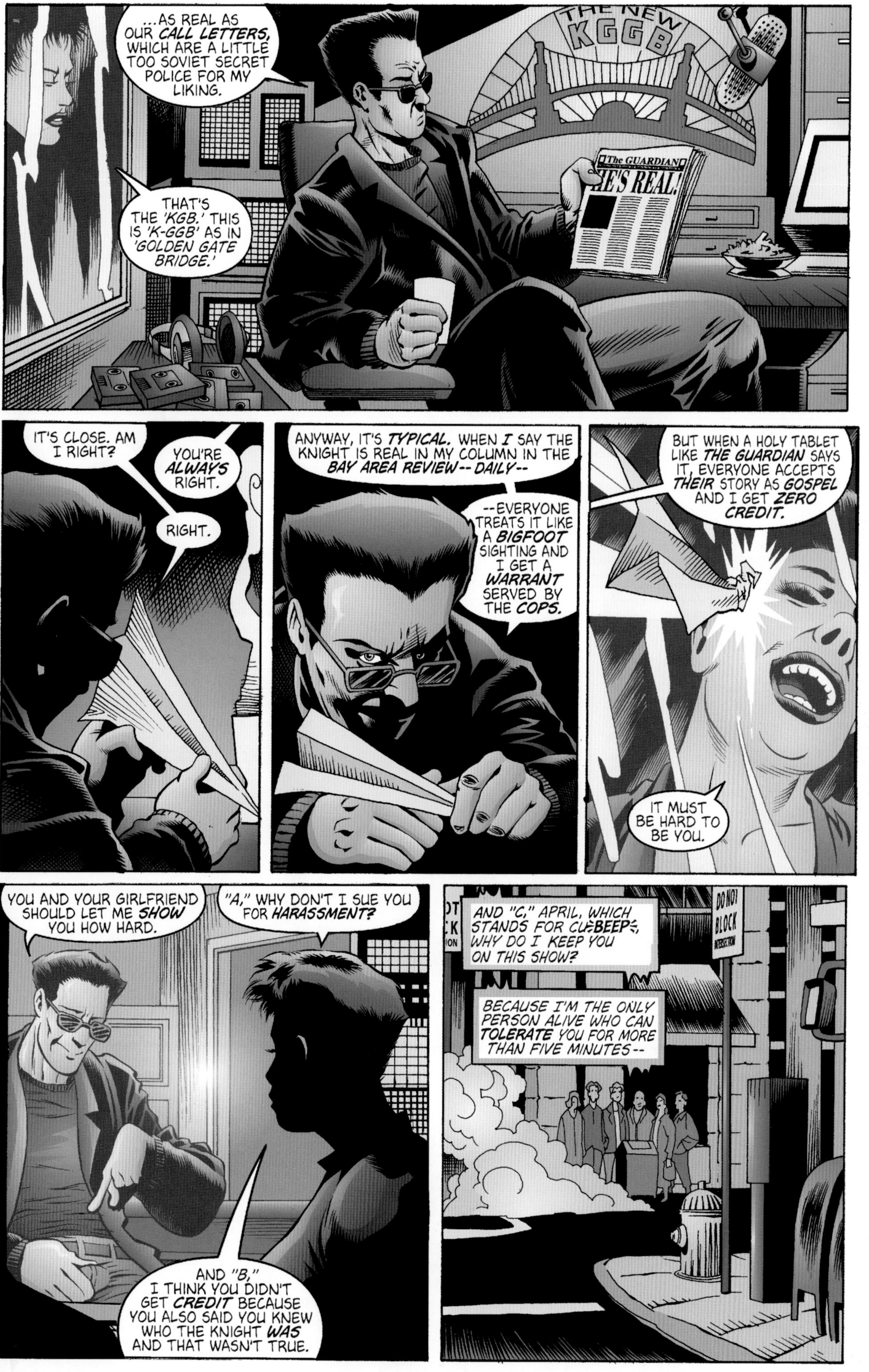
...AS REAL AS OUR CALL LETTERS, WHICH ARE A LITTLE TOO SOVIET SECRET POLICE FOR MY LIKING.
THE NEW KGGB
The GUARDIAN
HE'S REAL!
THAT'S THE 'KGB.' THIS IS 'K-GGB' AS IN 'GOLDEN GATE BRIDGE.'
IT'S CLOSE. AM I RIGHT?
YOU'RE ALWAYS RIGHT.
RIGHT.
ANYWAY, IT'S TYPICAL. WHEN I SAY THE KNIGHT IS REAL IN MY COLUMN IN THE BAY AREA REVIEW-- DAILY--
--EVERYONE TREATS IT LIKE A BIGFOOT SIGHTING AND I GET A WARRANT SERVED BY THE COPS.
BUT WHEN A HOLY TABLET LIKE THE GUARDIAN SAYS IT, EVERYONE ACCEPTS THEIR STORY AS GOSPEL AND I GET ZERO CREDIT.
IT MUST BE HARD TO BE YOU.
YOU AND YOUR GIRLFRIEND SHOULD LET ME SHOW YOU HOW HARD.
"A," WHY DON'T I SUE YOU FOR HARASSMENT?
AND "B," I THINK YOU DIDN'T GET CREDIT BECAUSE YOU ALSO SAID YOU KNEW WHO THE KNIGHT WAS AND THAT WASN'T TRUE.
AND "C," APRIL, WHICH STANDS FOR C=BEEP=, WHY DO I KEEP YOU ON THIS SHOW?
DO NOT BLOCK INTERSECTION
BECAUSE I'M THE ONLY PERSON ALIVE WHO CAN TOLERATE YOU FOR MORE THAN FIVE MINUTES--

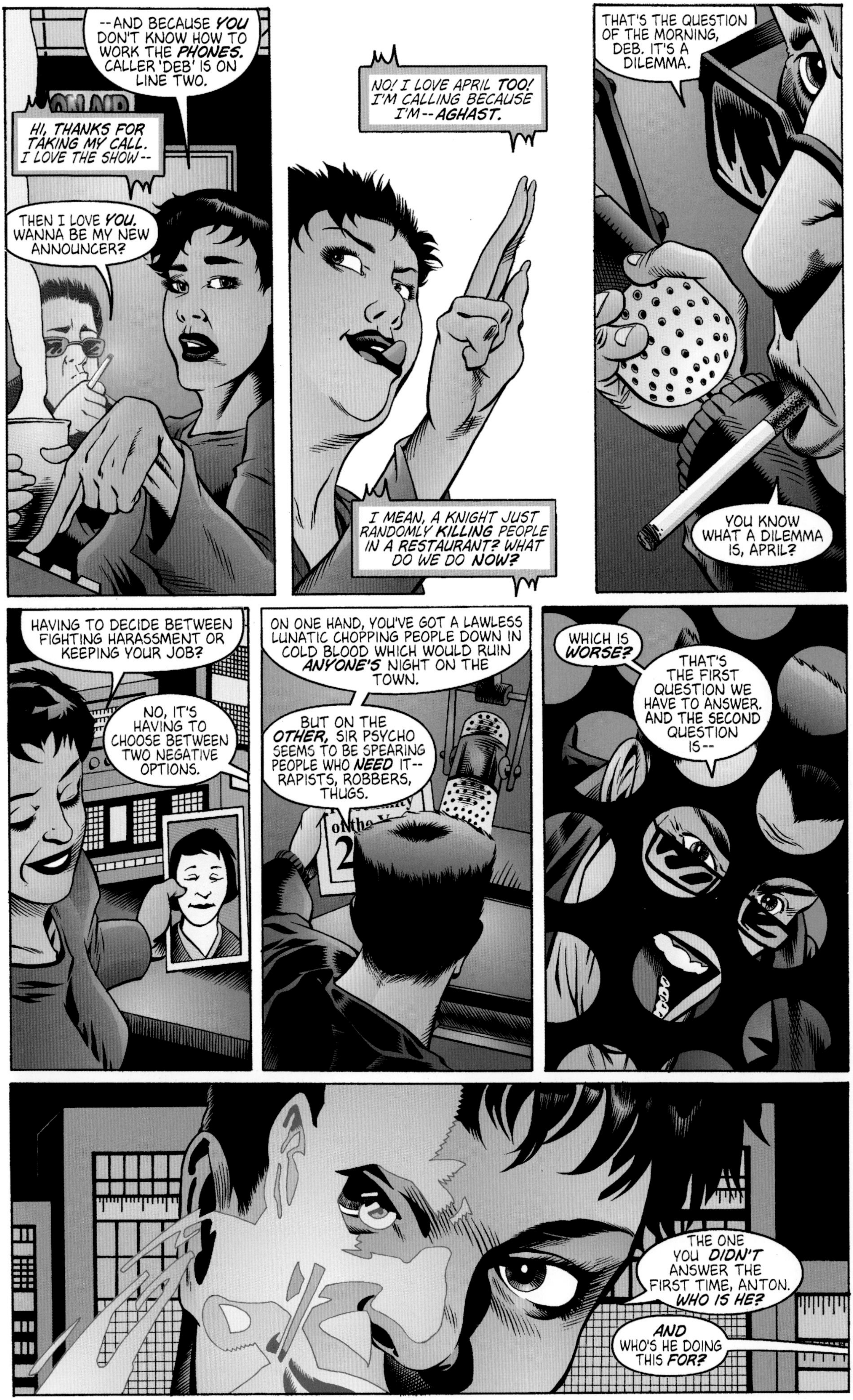
--AND BECAUSE YOU DON'T KNOW HOW TO WORK THE PHONES. CALLER 'DEB' IS ON LINE TWO.
HI, THANKS FOR TAKING MY CALL. I LOVE THE SHOW--
THEN I LOVE YOU. WANNA BE MY NEW ANNOUNCER?
NO! I LOVE APRIL TOO! I'M CALLING BECAUSE I'M--AGHAST.
I MEAN, A KNIGHT JUST RANDOMLY KILLING PEOPLE IN A RESTAURANT? WHAT DO WE DO NOW?
THAT'S THE QUESTION OF THE MORNING, DEB. IT'S A DILEMMA.
YOU KNOW WHAT A DILEMMA IS, APRIL?
HAVING TO DECIDE BETWEEN FIGHTING HARASSMENT OR KEEPING YOUR JOB?
NO, IT'S HAVING TO CHOOSE BETWEEN TWO NEGATIVE OPTIONS.
ON ONE HAND, YOU'VE GOT A LAWLESS LUNATIC CHOPPING PEOPLE DOWN IN COLD BLOOD WHICH WOULD RUIN ANYONE'S NIGHT ON THE TOWN.
BUT ON THE OTHER, SIR PSYCHO SEEMS TO BE SPEARING PEOPLE WHO NEED IT--RAPISTS, ROBBERS, THUGS.
WHICH IS WORSE?
THAT'S THE FIRST QUESTION WE HAVE TO ANSWER. AND THE SECOND QUESTION IS--
THE ONE YOU DIDN'T ANSWER THE FIRST TIME, ANTON. WHO IS HE?
AND WHO'S HE DOING THIS FOR?

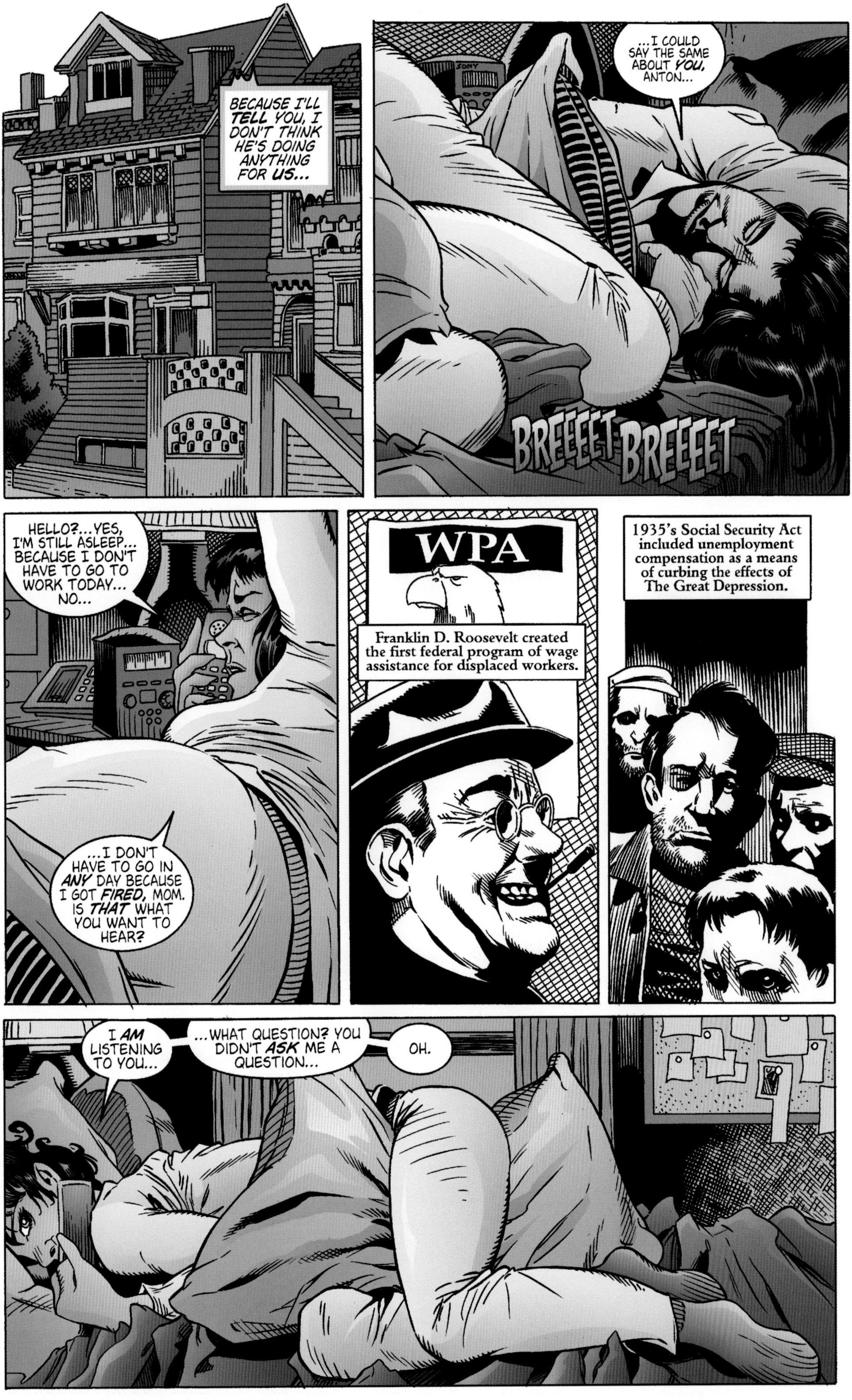
BECAUSE I'LL TELL YOU, I DON'T THINK HE'S DOING ANYTHING FOR US...
...I COULD SAY THE SAME ABOUT YOU, ANTON...
SONY
BREEEET BREEEET
HELLO?...YES, I'M STILL ASLEEP... BECAUSE I DON'T HAVE TO GO TO WORK TODAY... NO...
...I DON'T HAVE TO GO IN ANY DAY BECAUSE I GOT FIRED, MOM. IS THAT WHAT YOU WANT TO HEAR?
WPA
Franklin D. Roosevelt created the first federal program of wage assistance for displaced workers.
1935's Social Security Act included unemployment compensation as a means of curbing the effects of The Great Depression.
I AM LISTENING TO YOU...
...WHAT QUESTION? YOU DIDN'T ASK ME A QUESTION...
OH.

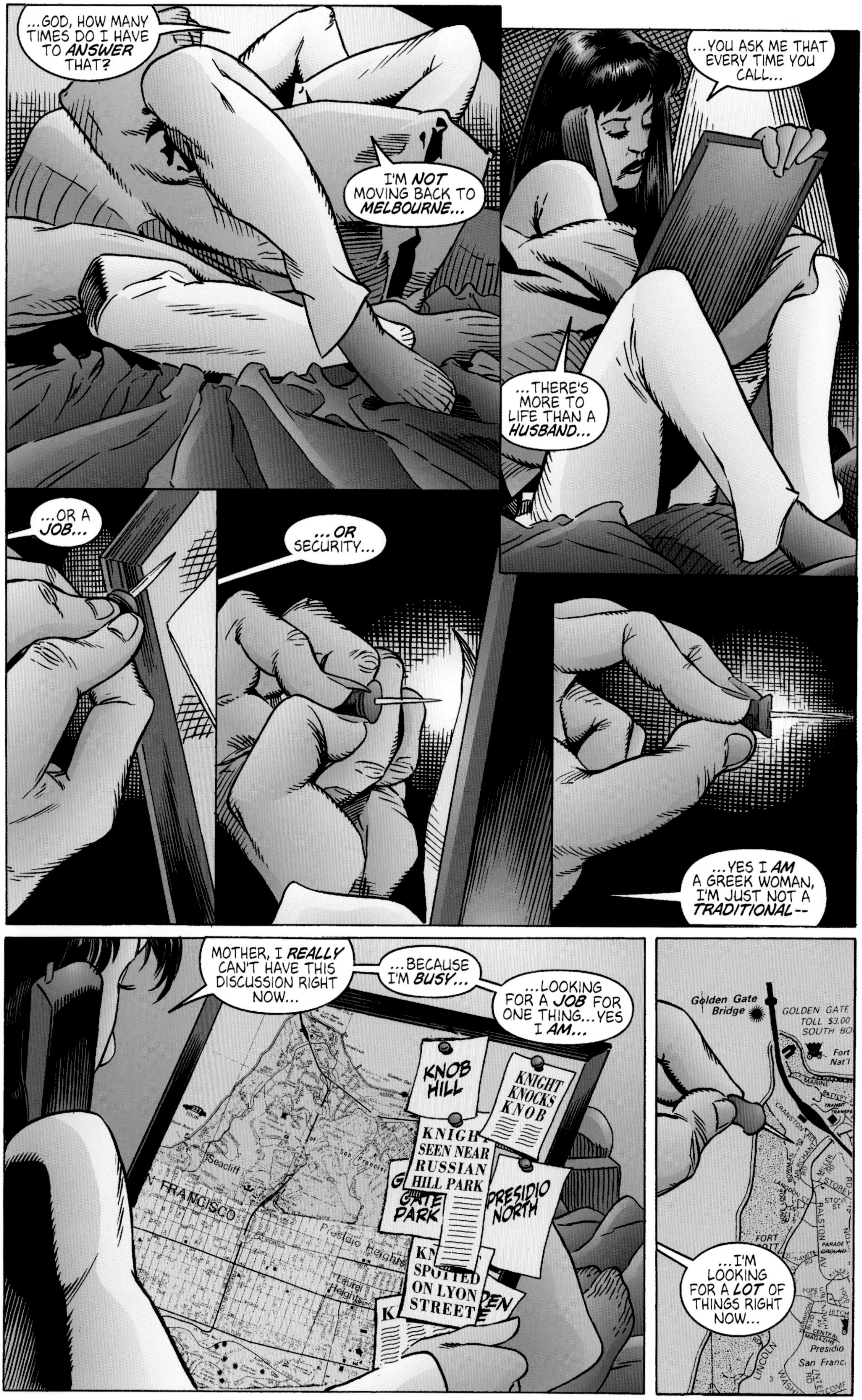
...GOD, HOW MANY TIMES DO I HAVE TO *ANSWER* THAT?
I'M *NOT* MOVING BACK TO *MELBOURNE...*
...YOU ASK ME THAT EVERY TIME YOU CALL...
...THERE'S MORE TO LIFE THAN A *HUSBAND...*
...OR A *JOB...*
...OR SECURITY...
...YES I *AM* A GREEK WOMAN, I'M JUST NOT A *TRADITIONAL--*
MOTHER, I *REALLY* CAN'T HAVE THIS DISCUSSION RIGHT NOW...
...BECAUSE I'M *BUSY...*
...LOOKING FOR A *JOB* FOR ONE THING...YES I *AM...*
KNOB HILL
KNIGHT KNOCKS KNOB
KNIGHT SEEN NEAR RUSSIAN HILL PARK
PRESIDIO NORTH
SPOTTED ON LYON STREET
Seacliff
SAN FRANCISCO
Presidio Heights
Laurel Heights
Golden Gate Bridge
GOLDEN GATE TOLL $3.00
Fort Nat'l
MARINE
LINCOLN
Presidio
...I'M LOOKING FOR A *LOT* OF THINGS RIGHT NOW...

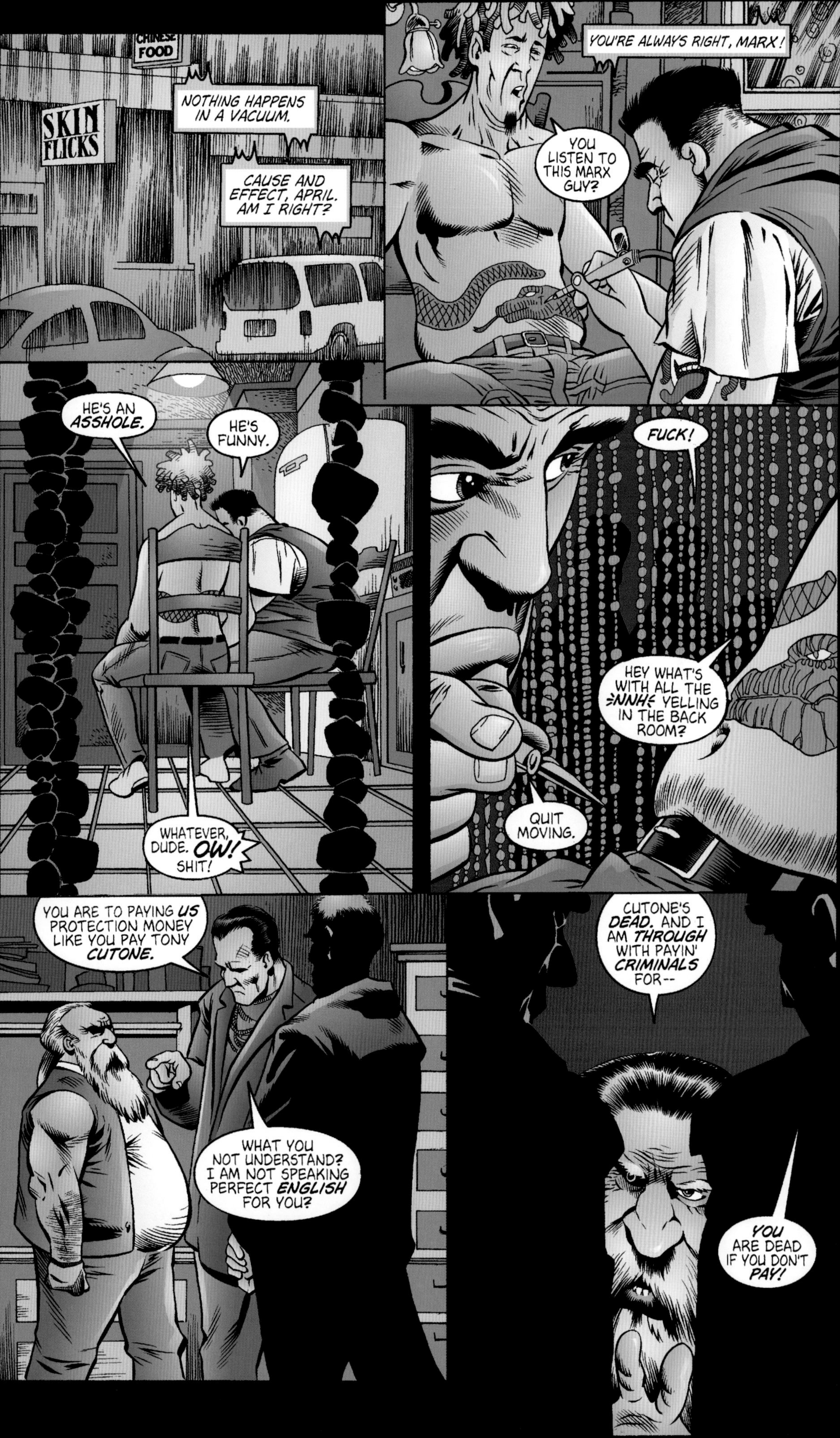
CHINESE FOOD
SKIN FLICKS
NOTHING HAPPENS IN A VACUUM.
CAUSE AND EFFECT, APRIL. AM I RIGHT?
YOU'RE ALWAYS RIGHT, MARX!
YOU LISTEN TO THIS MARX GUY?
HE'S AN ASSHOLE.
HE'S FUNNY.
WHATEVER, DUDE. OW! SHIT!
FUCK!
HEY WHAT'S WITH ALL THE NNH YELLING IN THE BACK ROOM?
QUIT MOVING.
YOU ARE TO PAYING US PROTECTION MONEY LIKE YOU PAY TONY CUTONE.
WHAT YOU NOT UNDERSTAND? I AM NOT SPEAKING PERFECT ENGLISH FOR YOU?
CUTONE'S DEAD. AND I AM THROUGH WITH PAYIN' CRIMINALS FOR--
YOU ARE DEAD IF YOU DON'T PAY!

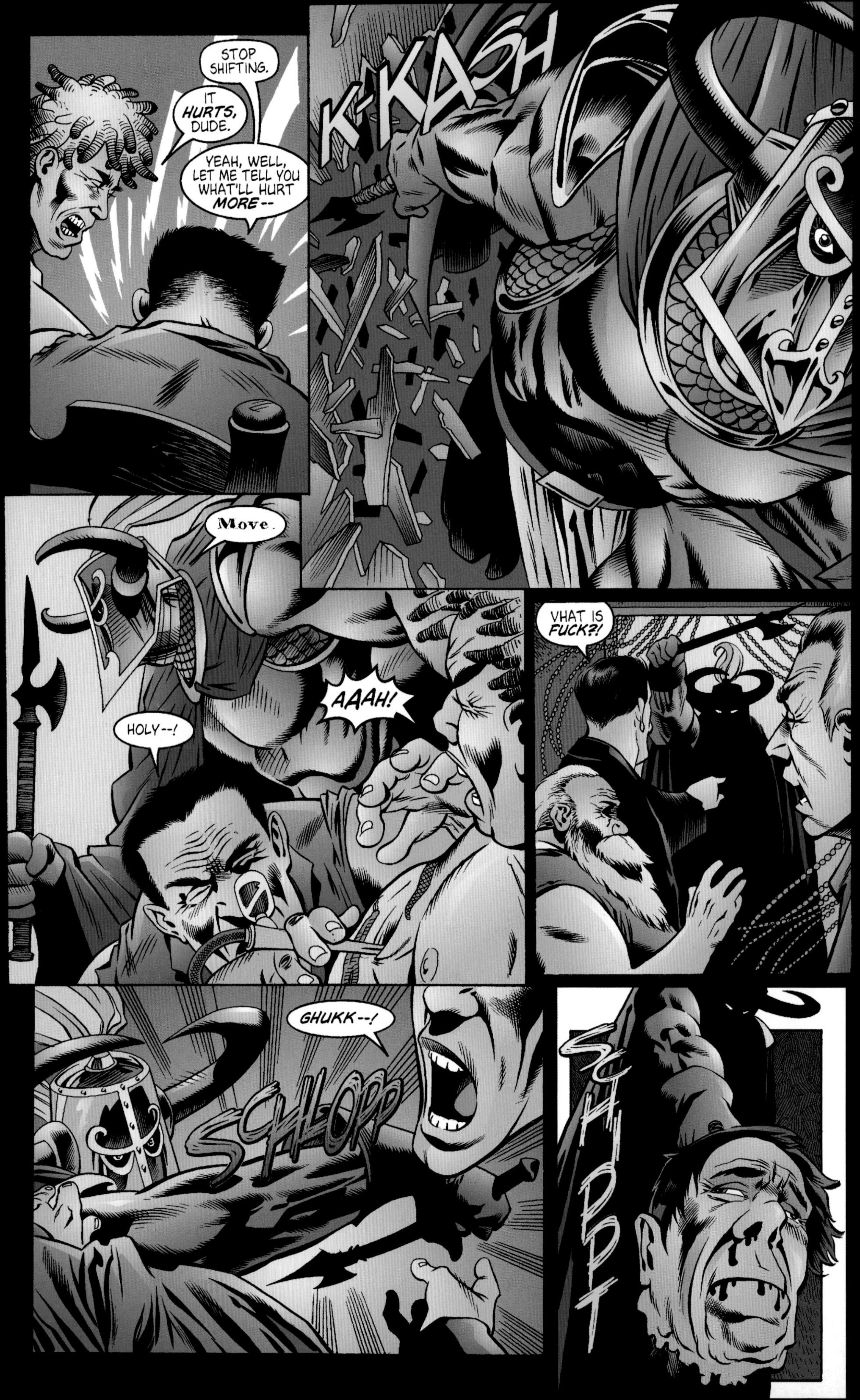
STOP SHIFTING.
IT HURTS, DUDE.
YEAH, WELL, LET ME TELL YOU WHAT'LL HURT MORE--
K-KASH
Move.
HOLY--!
AAAH!
VHAT IS FUCK?!
GHUKK--!
SCHLOPP
SCHHPPT

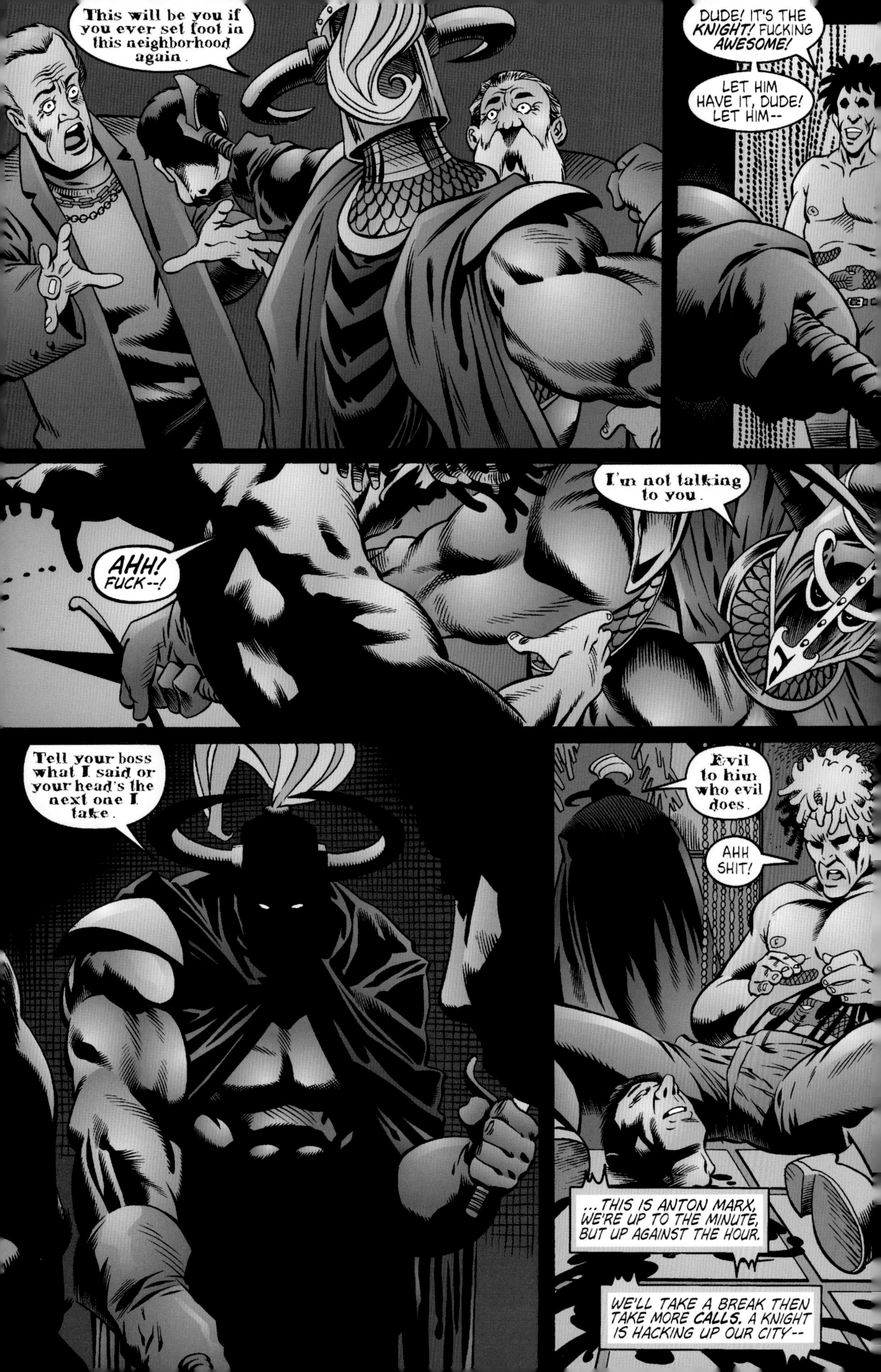
This will be you if you ever set foot in this neighborhood again.
DUDE! IT'S THE KNIGHT! FUCKING AWESOME!
LET HIM HAVE IT, DUDE! LET HIM--
I'm not talking to you.
AHH! FUCK--!
Tell your boss what I said or your head's the next one I take.
Evil to him who evil does.
AHH SHIT!
...THIS IS ANTON MARX, WE'RE UP TO THE MINUTE, BUT UP AGAINST THE HOUR.
WE'LL TAKE A BREAK THEN TAKE MORE CALLS. A KNIGHT IS HACKING UP OUR CITY--

-- WHAT DO *YOU* THINK ABOUT THAT?

I THINK THIS WAS A THREAT.

DETECTIVE? I RAN A PROFILE ON THE DEAD GUY. NADA.

HE MUS' BE AN ILLEGAL.

LIKE ALL YOUR *RELATIVES,* HORACE?

HEY, WHY DON' YOU GO FUCK YOURSELF, REEK?

IT'S *"RICK,"* WETBACK.

OH, SORRY. WHY DON' YOU GO FUCK YOURSELF, *"REEK WETBACK."*

YOU COULD BRING HIM UP ON DISCIPLINARY REVIEW FOR THAT.

NAH. EES JUS' A BUNCH OF SHIT TALK. NO BIGGIE.

SO YOU THINK THEESE WAS A *THREAT?*

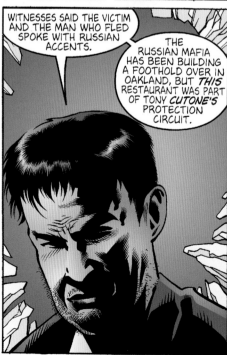

WITNESSES SAID THE VICTIM AND THE MAN WHO FLED SPOKE WITH RUSSIAN ACCENTS.

THE RUSSIAN MAFIA HAS BEEN BUILDING A FOOTHOLD OVER IN OAKLAND, BUT *THIS* RESTAURANT WAS PART OF TONY *CUTONE'S* PROTECTION CIRCUIT.

I THINK THE RUSSIANS ARE TRYING TO TAKE CUTONE'S TERRITORY.

THAT MEANS THE KNIGHT EESE KILLING OFF *MOBSTERS.*

SO WHAT DO WE DO? *STOP* HEEM? OR SEND HEEM A DOZEN *ROSES?*

HE'S A *MURDERER*, HORACE. WE DON'T *THANK* MURDERERS.

HEY, SOMETIMES THE *SHIT* NEEDS TO BE *FLUSHED.*

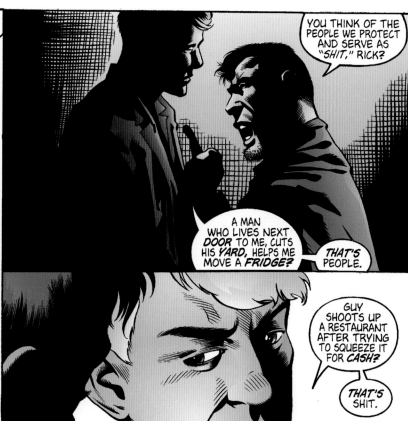

YOU THINK OF THE PEOPLE WE PROTECT AND SERVE AS *"SHIT,"* RICK?

A MAN WHO LIVES NEXT *DOOR* TO ME, CUTS HIS *YARD*, HELPS ME MOVE A *FRIDGE?*

THAT'S PEOPLE.

GUY SHOOTS UP A RESTAURANT AFTER TRYING TO SQUEEZE IT FOR *CASH?*

THAT'S SHIT.

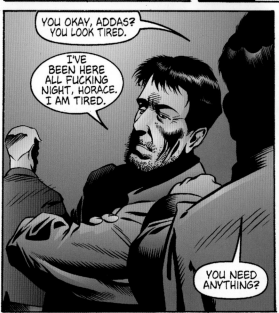

YOU OKAY, ADDAS? YOU LOOK TIRED.

I'VE BEEN HERE ALL FUCKING NIGHT, HORACE. I AM TIRED.

YOU NEED ANYTHING?

A WIFE. CHILDREN WHO RESPECT ME.

AN EARLY RETIREMENT PACKAGE --

A *CROSS*.

HUH? YOU WAN' TO *PRAY?*

THE *KNIGHT* LEAVES A *CROSS.*

LOOK AROUND OUTSIDE. SEE IF YOU CAN FIND ONE.

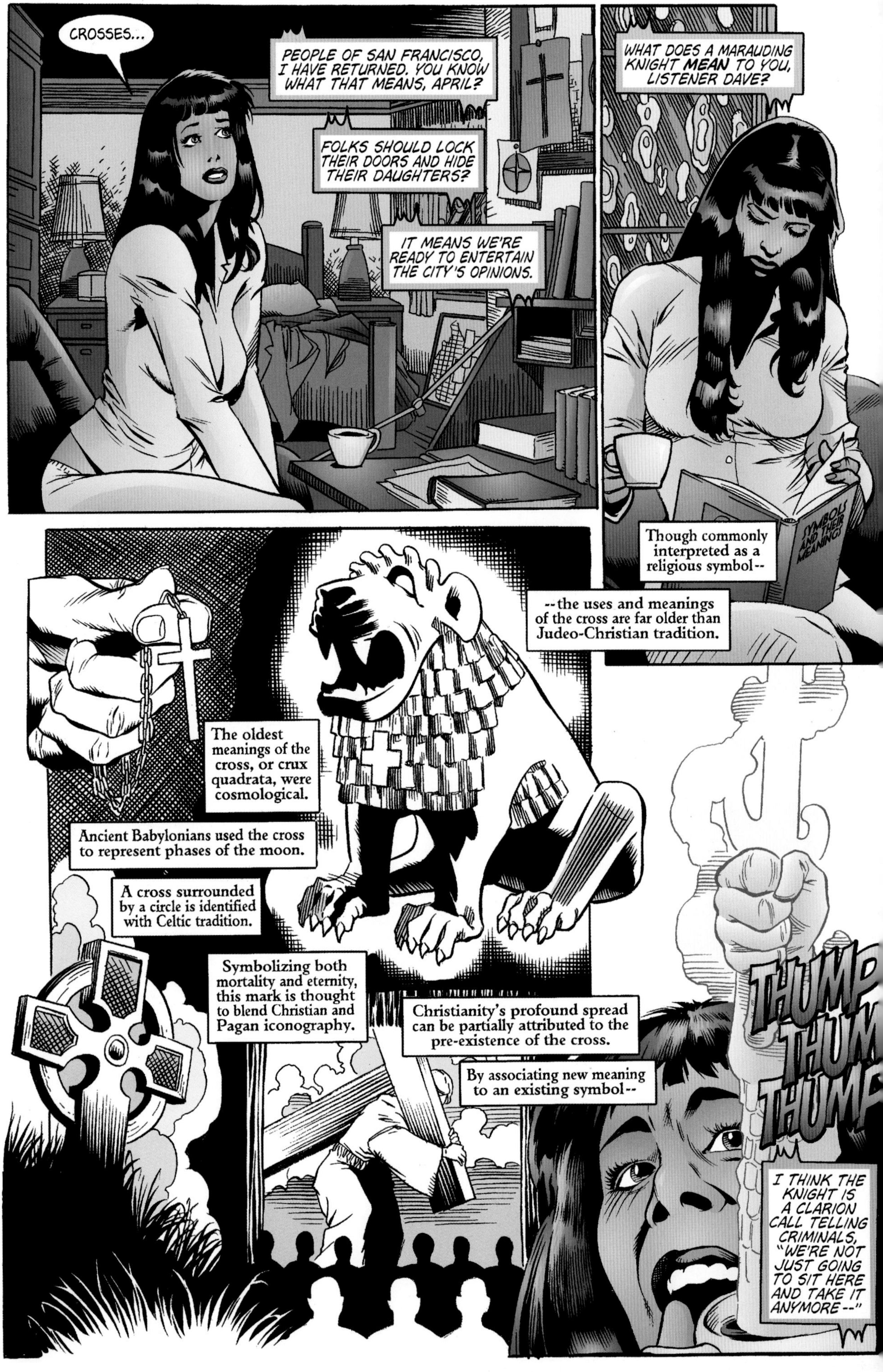

CROSSES...
PEOPLE OF SAN FRANCISCO, I HAVE RETURNED. YOU KNOW WHAT THAT MEANS, APRIL?
FOLKS SHOULD LOCK THEIR DOORS AND HIDE THEIR DAUGHTERS?
IT MEANS WE'RE READY TO ENTERTAIN THE CITY'S OPINIONS.
WHAT DOES A MARAUDING KNIGHT MEAN TO YOU, LISTENER DAVE?
SYMBOLS AND THEIR MEANINGS
Though commonly interpreted as a religious symbol--
--the uses and meanings of the cross are far older than Judeo-Christian tradition.
The oldest meanings of the cross, or crux quadrata, were cosmological.
Ancient Babylonians used the cross to represent phases of the moon.
A cross surrounded by a circle is identified with Celtic tradition.
Symbolizing both mortality and eternity, this mark is thought to blend Christian and Pagan iconography.
Christianity's profound spread can be partially attributed to the pre-existence of the cross.
By associating new meaning to an existing symbol--
I THINK THE KNIGHT IS A CLARION CALL TELLING CRIMINALS, "WE'RE NOT JUST GOING TO SIT HERE AND TAKE IT ANYMORE--"

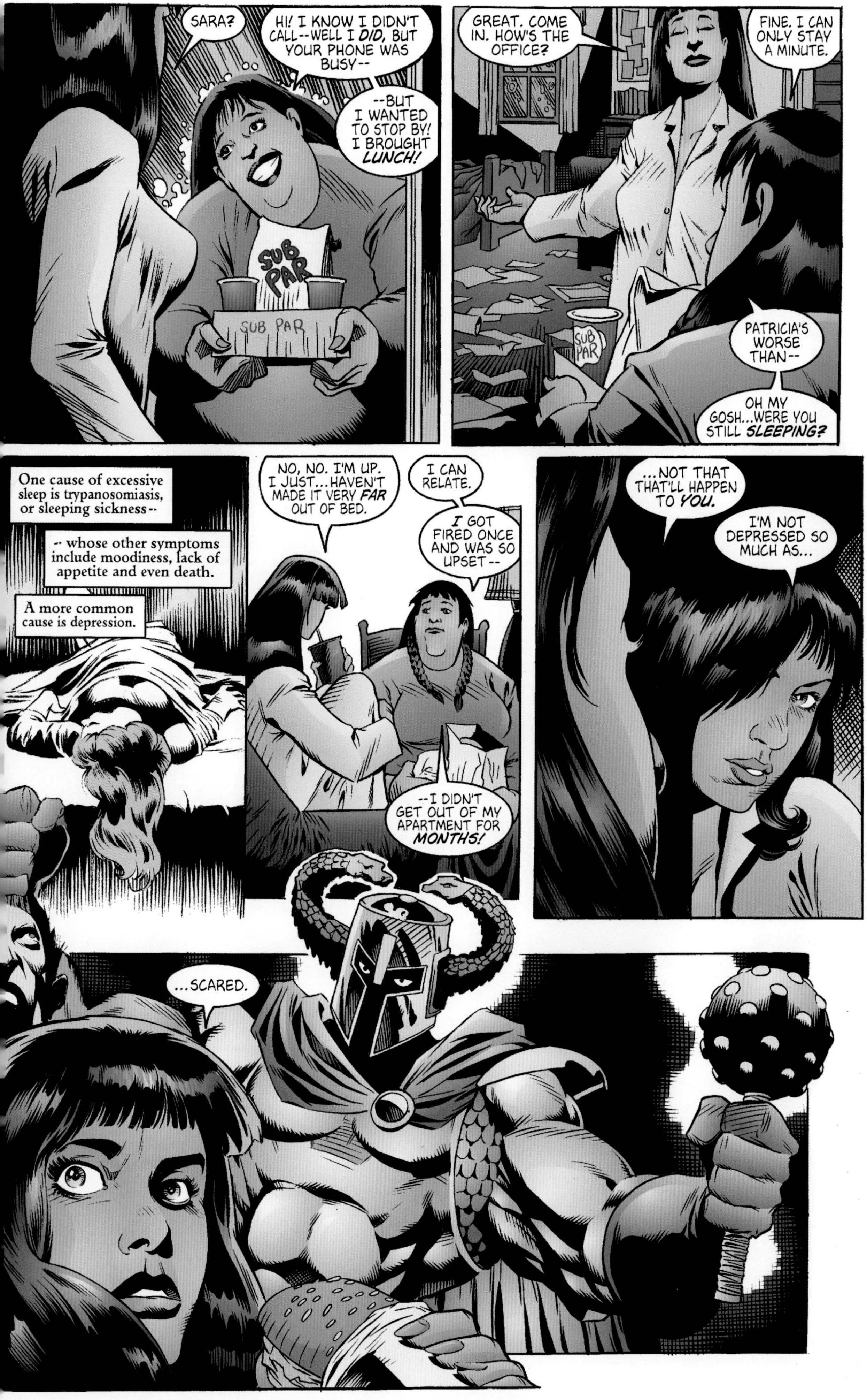
SARA?
HI! I KNOW I DIDN'T CALL--WELL I *DID*, BUT YOUR PHONE WAS BUSY--
--BUT I WANTED TO STOP BY! I BROUGHT *LUNCH!*
SUB PAR
SUB PAR
GREAT. COME IN. HOW'S THE OFFICE?
FINE. I CAN ONLY STAY A MINUTE.
SUB PAR
PATRICIA'S WORSE THAN--
OH MY GOSH...WERE YOU STILL *SLEEPING?*
One cause of excessive sleep is trypanosomiasis, or sleeping sickness--
--whose other symptoms include moodiness, lack of appetite and even death.
A more common cause is depression.
NO, NO. I'M UP. I JUST...HAVEN'T MADE IT VERY *FAR* OUT OF BED.
I CAN RELATE.
I GOT FIRED ONCE AND WAS SO UPSET--
--I DIDN'T GET OUT OF MY APARTMENT FOR *MONTHS!*
...NOT THAT THAT'LL HAPPEN TO *YOU.*
I'M NOT DEPRESSED SO MUCH AS...
...SCARED.

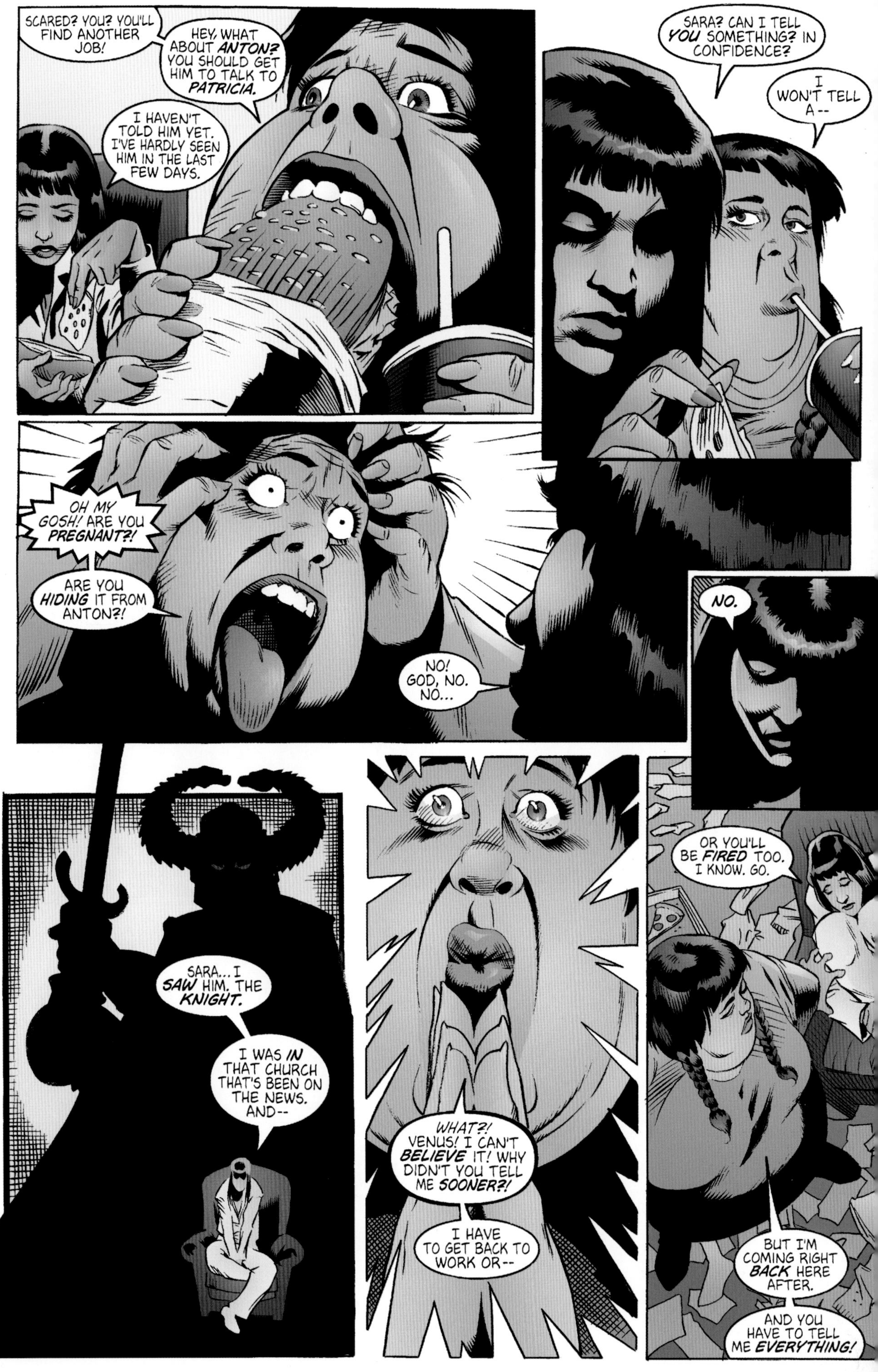

SCARED? YOU? YOU'LL FIND ANOTHER JOB!
HEY, WHAT ABOUT ANTON? YOU SHOULD GET HIM TO TALK TO PATRICIA.
I HAVEN'T TOLD HIM YET. I'VE HARDLY SEEN HIM IN THE LAST FEW DAYS.
SARA? CAN I TELL YOU SOMETHING? IN CONFIDENCE?
I WON'T TELL A --
OH MY GOSH! ARE YOU PREGNANT?!
ARE YOU HIDING IT FROM ANTON?!
NO! GOD, NO. NO...
NO.
SARA... I SAW HIM. THE KNIGHT.
I WAS IN THAT CHURCH THAT'S BEEN ON THE NEWS. AND--
WHAT?! VENUS! I CAN'T BELIEVE IT! WHY DIDN'T YOU TELL ME SOONER?!
I HAVE TO GET BACK TO WORK OR--
OR YOU'LL BE FIRED TOO. I KNOW. GO.
BUT I'M COMING RIGHT BACK HERE AFTER.
AND YOU HAVE TO TELL ME EVERYTHING!

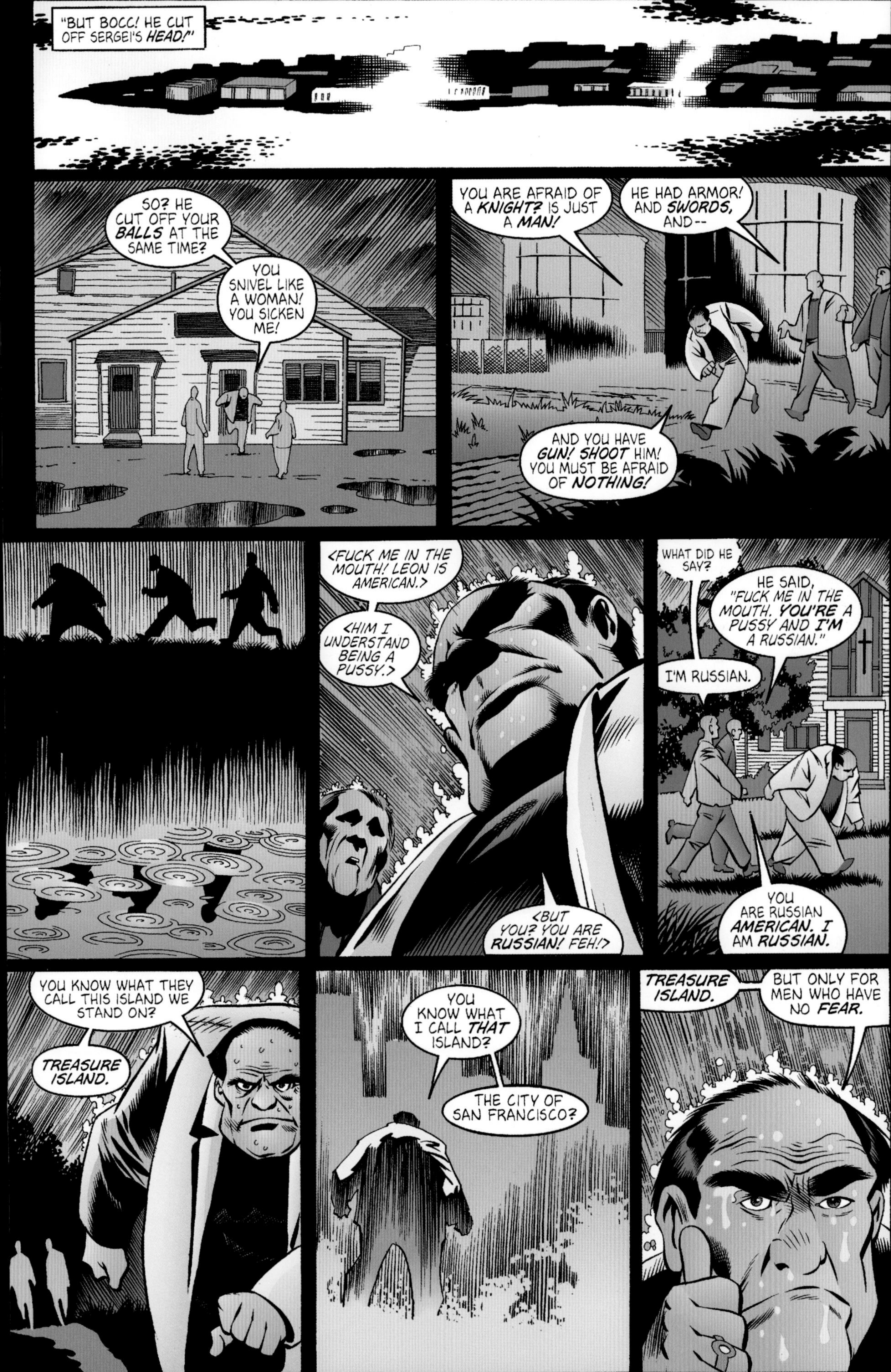
"BUT BOCC! HE CUT OFF SERGEI'S HEAD!"
SO? HE CUT OFF YOUR BALLS AT THE SAME TIME?
YOU SNIVEL LIKE A WOMAN! YOU SICKEN ME!
YOU ARE AFRAID OF A KNIGHT? IS JUST A MAN!
HE HAD ARMOR! AND SWORDS, AND--
AND YOU HAVE GUN! SHOOT HIM! YOU MUST BE AFRAID OF NOTHING!
<FUCK ME IN THE MOUTH! LEON IS AMERICAN.>
<HIM I UNDERSTAND BEING A PUSSY.>
<BUT YOU? YOU ARE RUSSIAN! FEH!>
WHAT DID HE SAY?
HE SAID, "FUCK ME IN THE MOUTH. YOU'RE A PUSSY AND I'M A RUSSIAN."
I'M RUSSIAN.
YOU ARE RUSSIAN AMERICAN. I AM RUSSIAN.
YOU KNOW WHAT THEY CALL THIS ISLAND WE STAND ON?
TREASURE ISLAND.
YOU KNOW WHAT I CALL THAT ISLAND?
THE CITY OF SAN FRANCISCO?
TREASURE ISLAND.
BUT ONLY FOR MEN WHO HAVE NO FEAR.

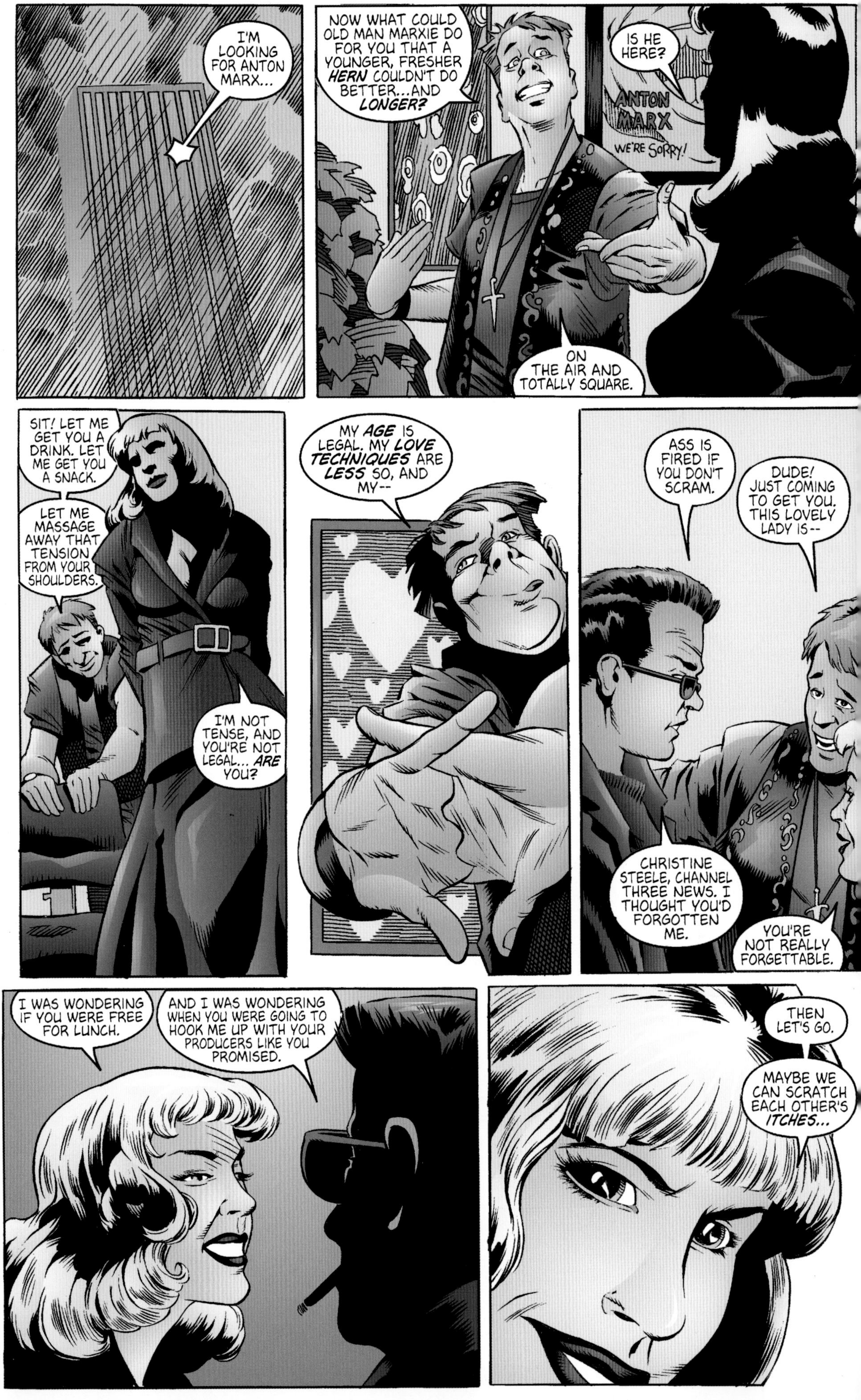
I'M LOOKING FOR ANTON MARX...
NOW WHAT COULD OLD MAN MARXIE DO FOR YOU THAT A YOUNGER, FRESHER HERN COULDN'T DO BETTER...AND LONGER?
IS HE HERE?
ANTON MARX
WE'RE SORRY!
ON THE AIR AND TOTALLY SQUARE.
SIT! LET ME GET YOU A DRINK. LET ME GET YOU A SNACK.
LET ME MASSAGE AWAY THAT TENSION FROM YOUR SHOULDERS.
I'M NOT TENSE, AND YOU'RE NOT LEGAL... ARE YOU?
MY AGE IS LEGAL. MY LOVE TECHNIQUES ARE LESS SO, AND MY--
ASS IS FIRED IF YOU DON'T SCRAM.
DUDE! JUST COMING TO GET YOU. THIS LOVELY LADY IS--
CHRISTINE STEELE, CHANNEL THREE NEWS. I THOUGHT YOU'D FORGOTTEN ME.
YOU'RE NOT REALLY FORGETTABLE.
I WAS WONDERING IF YOU WERE FREE FOR LUNCH.
AND I WAS WONDERING WHEN YOU WERE GOING TO HOOK ME UP WITH YOUR PRODUCERS LIKE YOU PROMISED.
THEN LET'S GO.
MAYBE WE CAN SCRATCH EACH OTHER'S ITCHES...

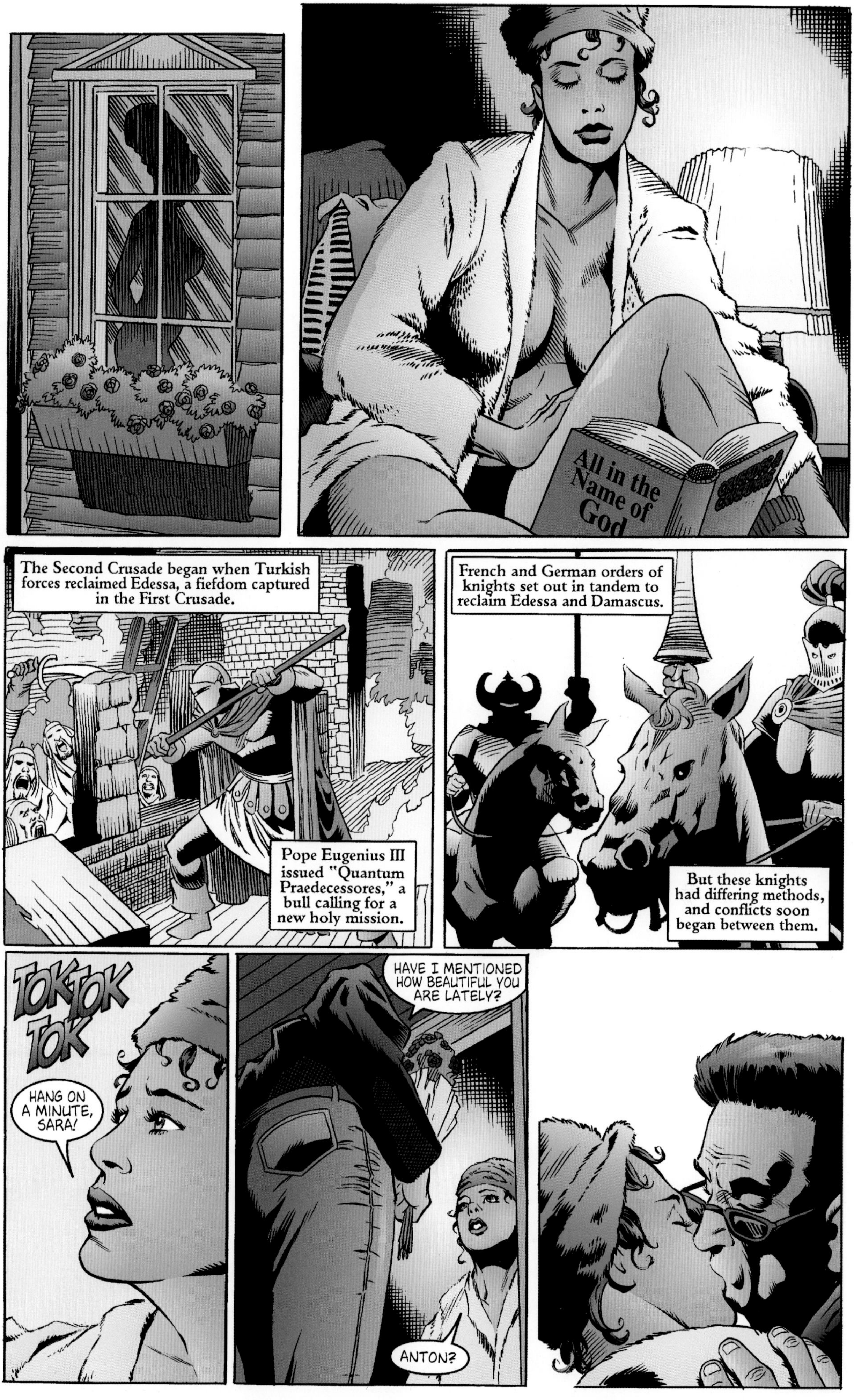
All in the Name of God
The Second Crusade began when Turkish forces reclaimed Edessa, a fiefdom captured in the First Crusade.
Pope Eugenius III issued "Quantum Praedecessores," a bull calling for a new holy mission.
French and German orders of knights set out in tandem to reclaim Edessa and Damascus.
But these knights had differing methods, and conflicts soon began between them.
TOK TOK TOK
HANG ON A MINUTE, SARA!
HAVE I MENTIONED HOW BEAUTIFUL YOU ARE LATELY?
ANTON?

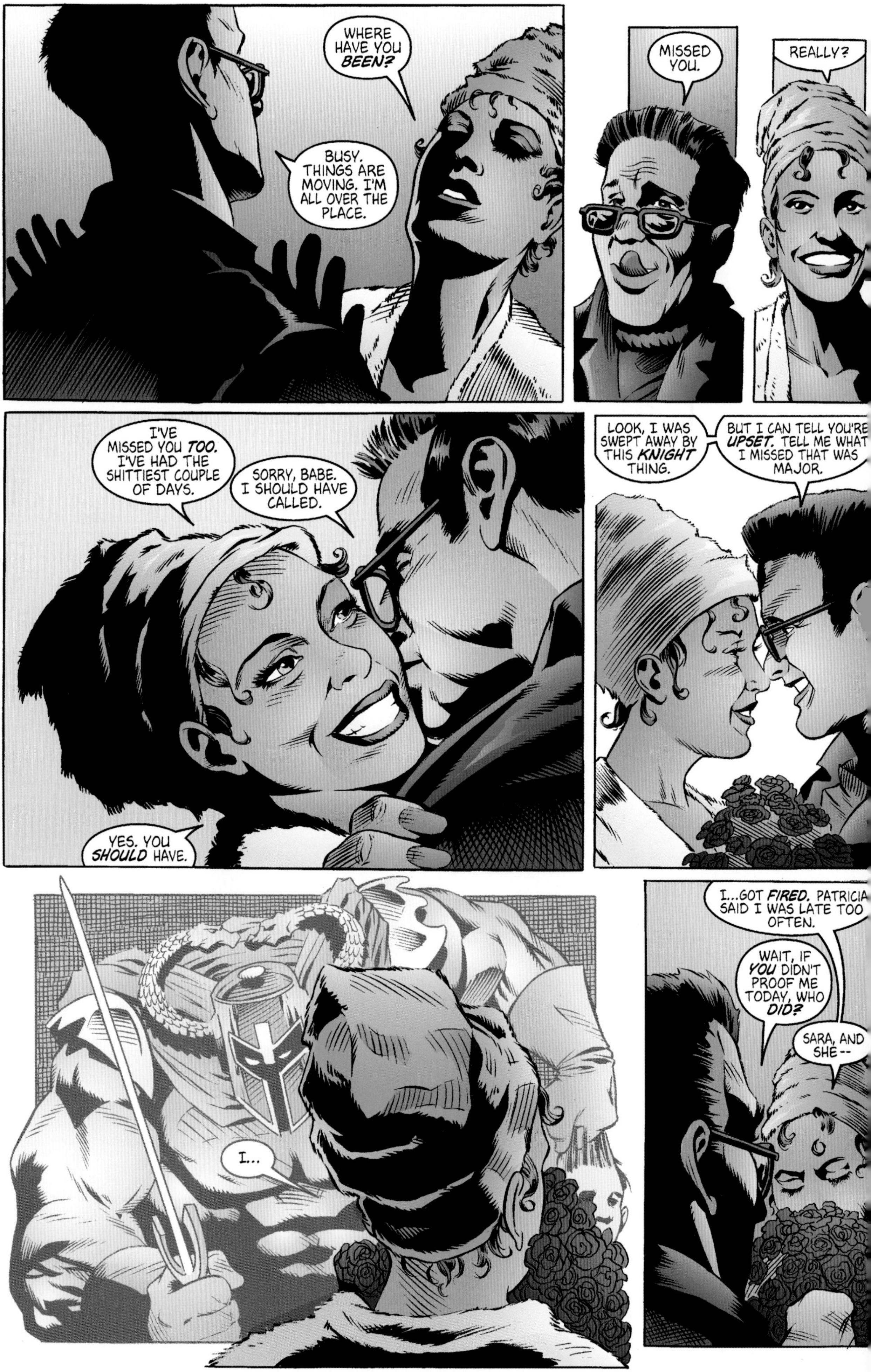
WHERE HAVE YOU BEEN?
BUSY. THINGS ARE MOVING. I'M ALL OVER THE PLACE.
MISSED YOU.
REALLY?
I'VE MISSED YOU TOO. I'VE HAD THE SHITTIEST COUPLE OF DAYS.
SORRY, BABE. I SHOULD HAVE CALLED.
YES. YOU SHOULD HAVE.
LOOK, I WAS SWEPT AWAY BY THIS KNIGHT THING.
BUT I CAN TELL YOU'RE UPSET. TELL ME WHAT I MISSED THAT WAS MAJOR.
I...
I...GOT FIRED. PATRICIA SAID I WAS LATE TOO OFTEN.
WAIT, IF YOU DIDN'T PROOF ME TODAY, WHO DID?
SARA, AND SHE --

OH! SHE'S COMING HERE WHEN SHE GETS DONE WITH IT!

YOU CAN'T STAY!

I CAN'T?

YOU CAN IF YOU DON'T MIND SARA *SEEING* YOU HERE WITH ME.

OH... UH...

"...I'LL STAY 'TIL SHE GETS HERE, THEN SNEAK OUT THE BACK."

...GOT IT FROM *BOCC*...

BAY AND TAYLOR

Vent you ANGER the DODG HATER CL

SHOW ME...

KLIPPAKLOP KLIPF

KLOP KLIPPAKLOPKL

HERE.

LOOK.

KLIPPA KLOP KLIPPA

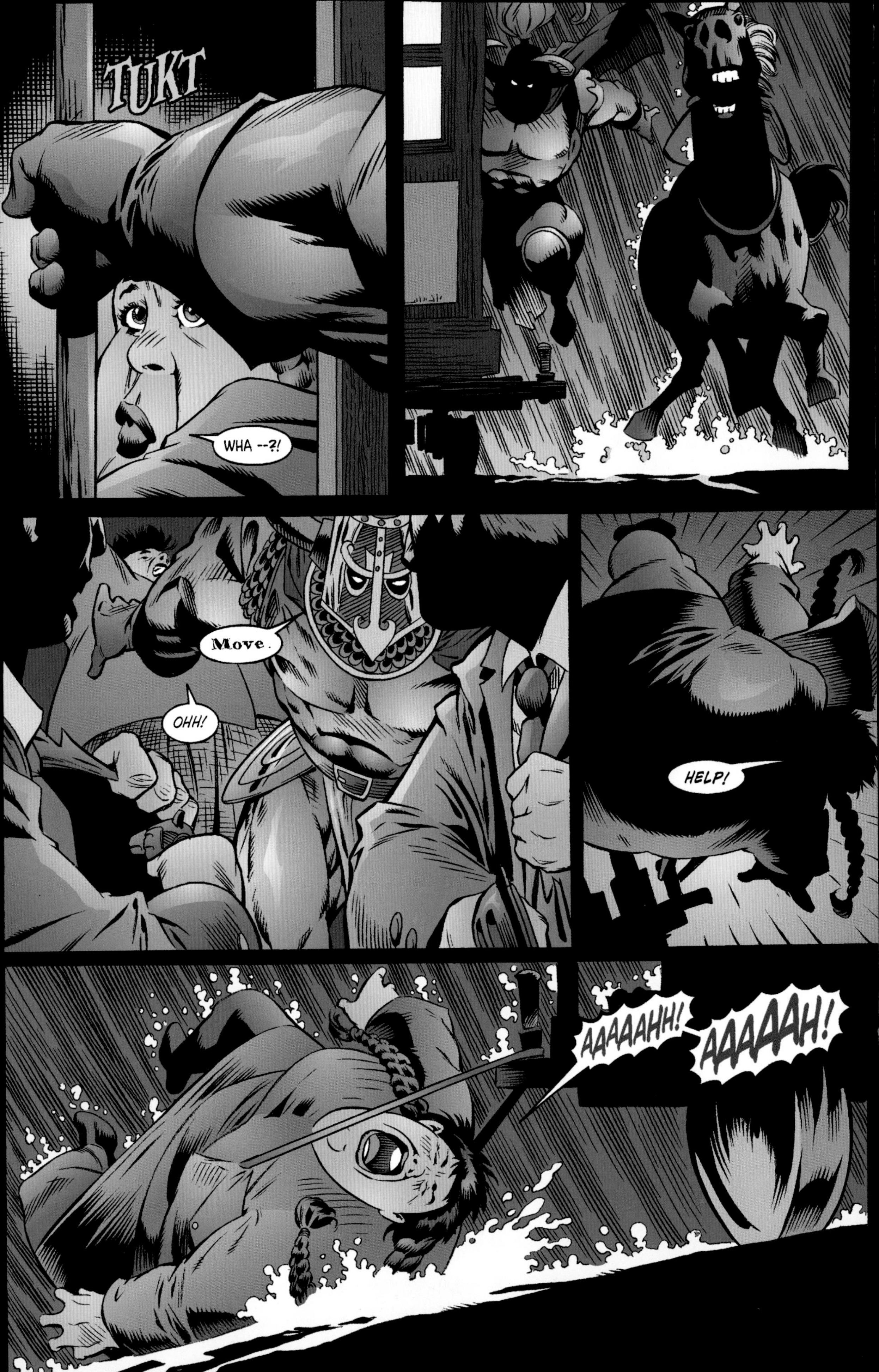
TUKT
WHA --?!
Move.
OHH!
HELP!
AAAAAHH!
AAAAAH!

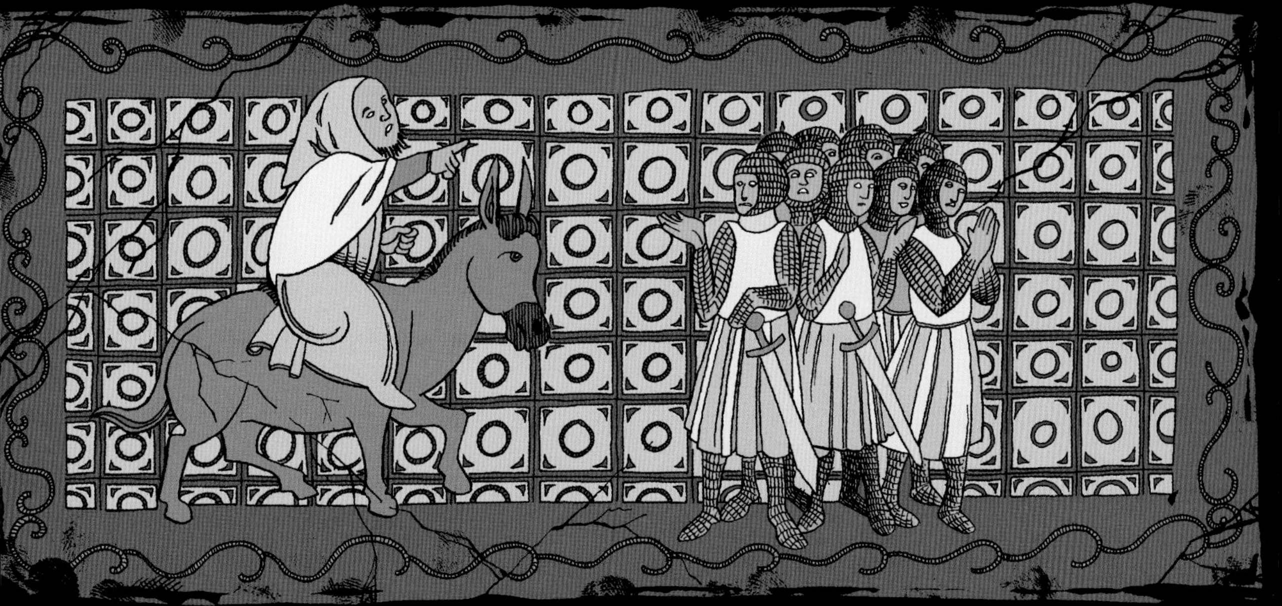

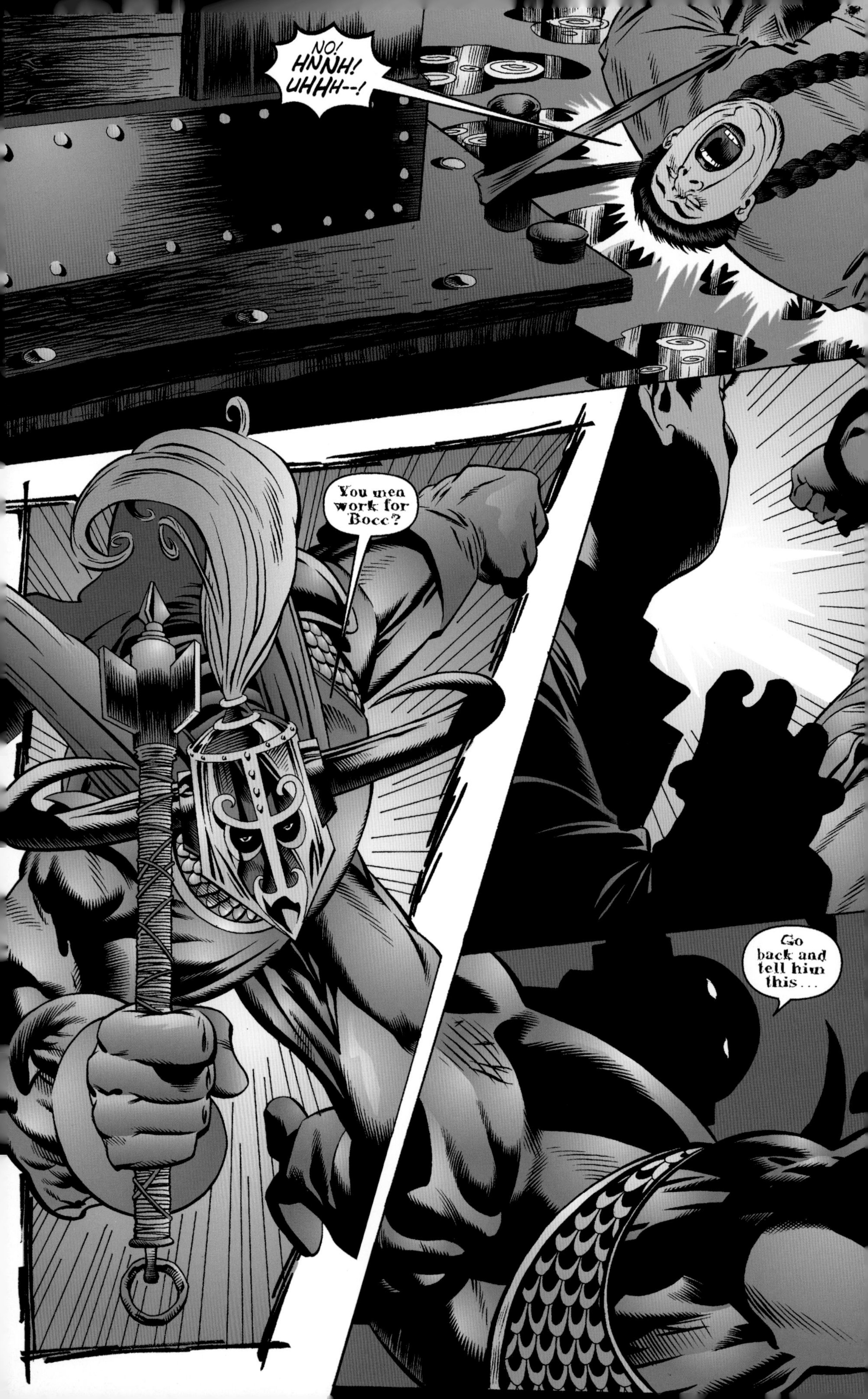
NO! HNNH! UHHH--!
You men work for Bocc?
Go back and tell him this...

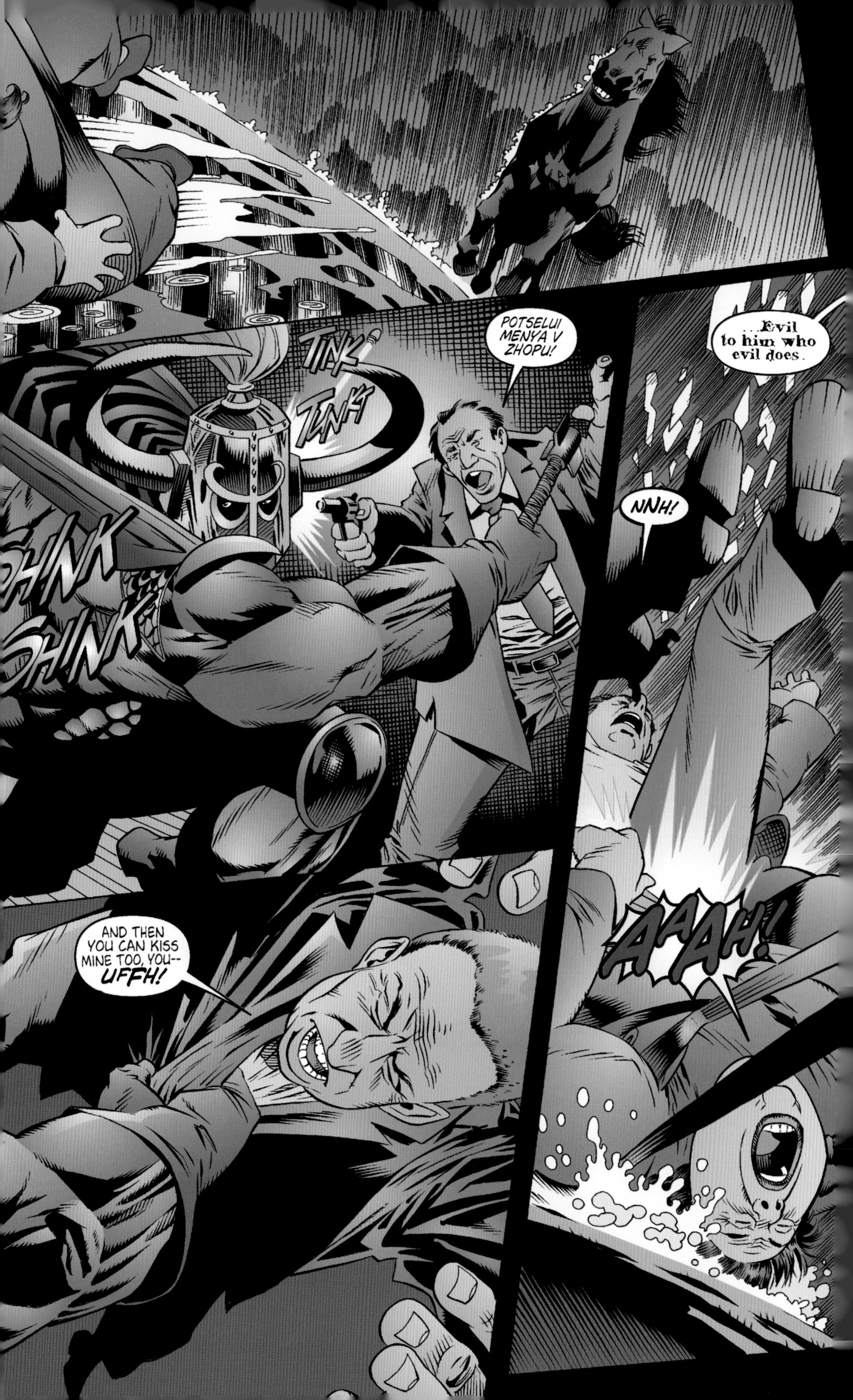

TINK
TUNK
POTSELUI MENYA V ZHOPU!
SHNK
SHNK
...Evil to him who evil does.
NNH!
AND THEN YOU CAN KISS MINE TOO, YOU-- UFFH!
AAAH!

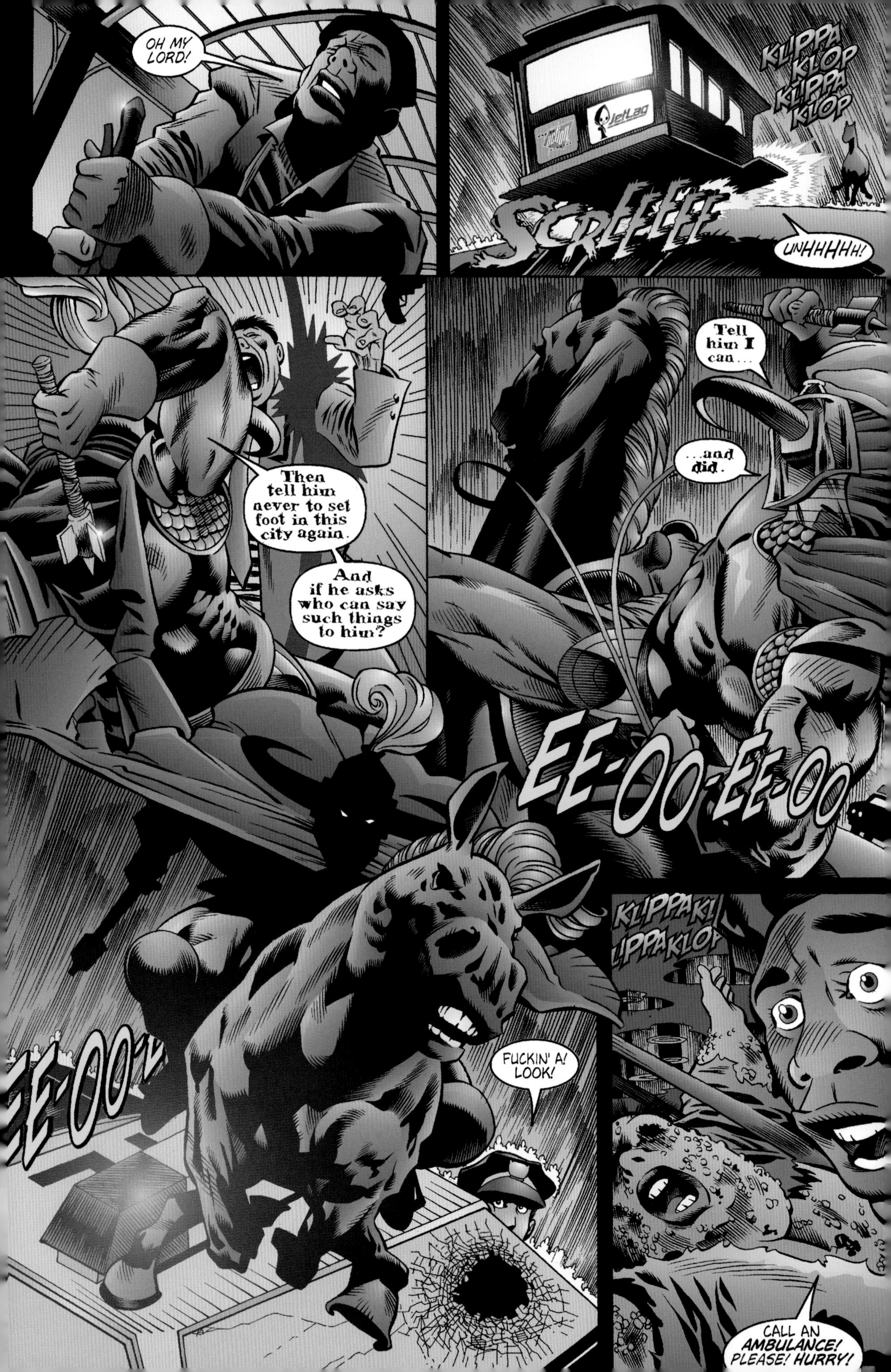
OH MY LORD!
KLIPPA KLOP KLIPPA KLOP
SCREEEEE
UNHHHHH!
Then tell him never to set foot in this city again.
And if he asks who can say such things to him?
Tell him I can...
...and did.
EE-OO-EE-OO
EE-OO
KLIPPA KLIPPA KLOP
FUCKIN' A! LOOK!
CALL AN AMBULANCE! PLEASE! HURRY!

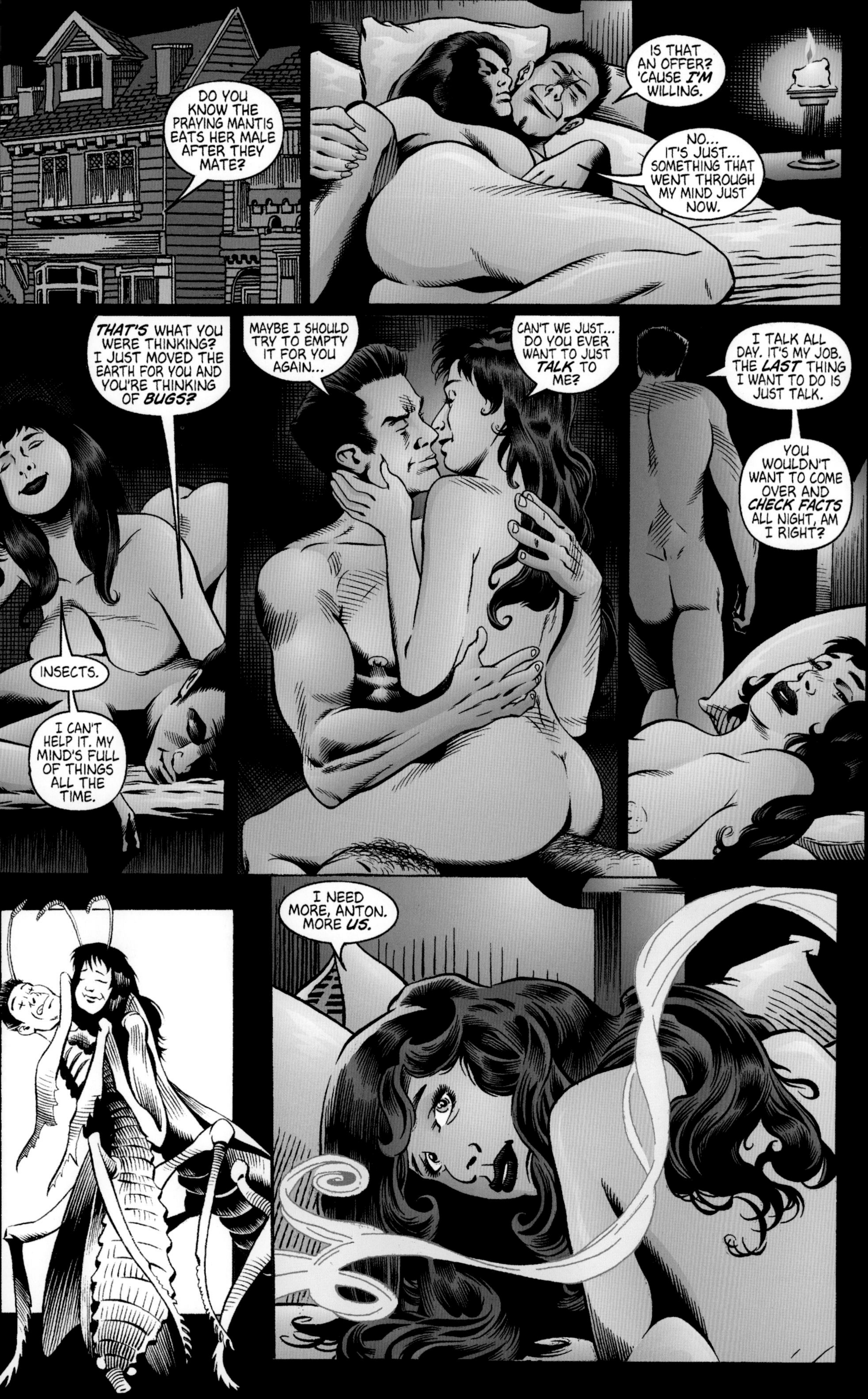
DO YOU KNOW THE PRAYING MANTIS EATS HER MALE AFTER THEY MATE?
IS THAT AN OFFER? 'CAUSE I'M WILLING.
NO... IT'S JUST... SOMETHING THAT WENT THROUGH MY MIND JUST NOW.
THAT'S WHAT YOU WERE THINKING? I JUST MOVED THE EARTH FOR YOU AND YOU'RE THINKING OF BUGS?
INSECTS.
I CAN'T HELP IT. MY MIND'S FULL OF THINGS ALL THE TIME.
MAYBE I SHOULD TRY TO EMPTY IT FOR YOU AGAIN...
CAN'T WE JUST... DO YOU EVER WANT TO JUST TALK TO ME?
I TALK ALL DAY. IT'S MY JOB. THE LAST THING I WANT TO DO IS JUST TALK.
YOU WOULDN'T WANT TO COME OVER AND CHECK FACTS ALL NIGHT, AM I RIGHT?
I NEED MORE, ANTON. MORE US.

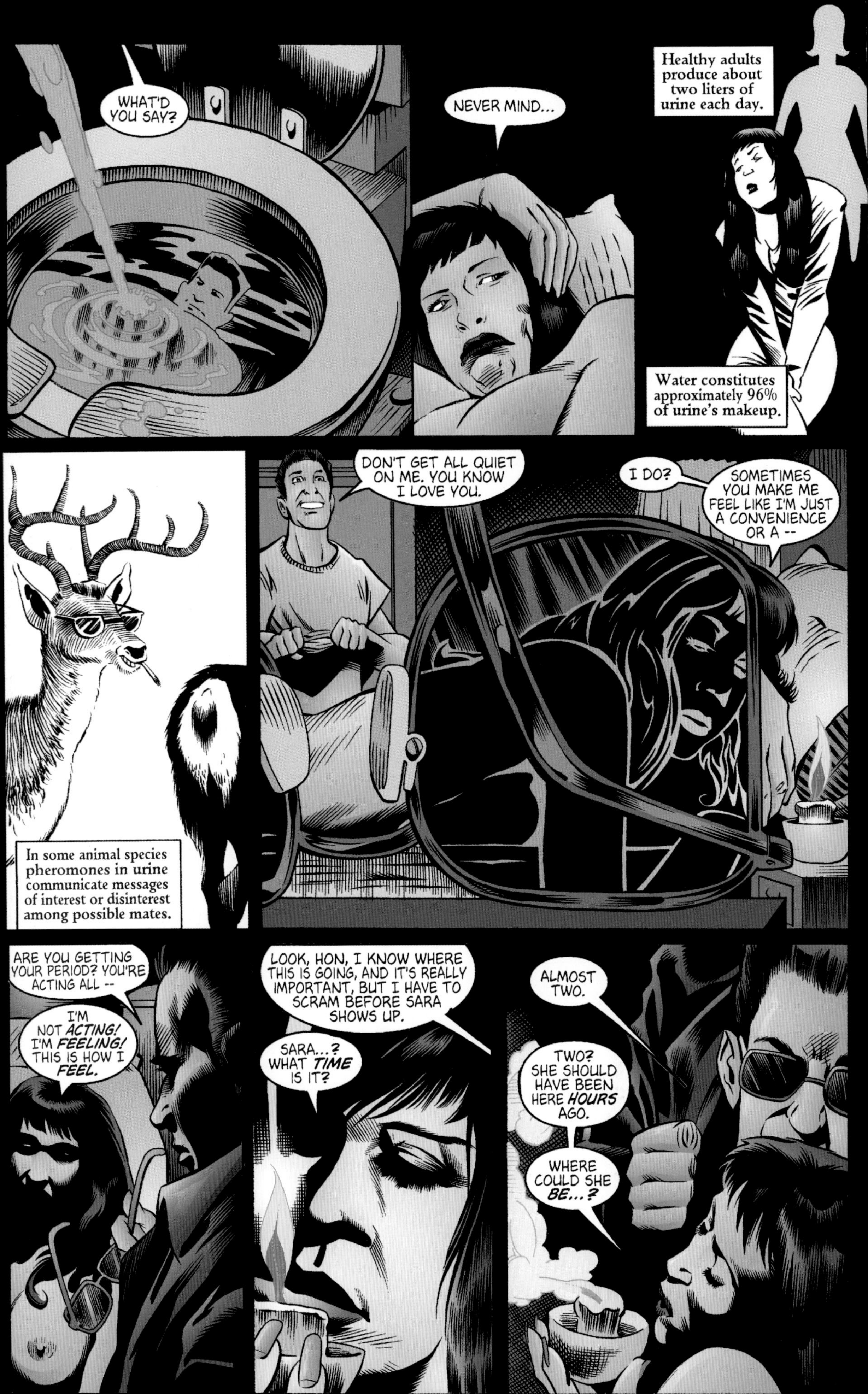
WHAT'D YOU SAY?
NEVER MIND...
Healthy adults produce about two liters of urine each day.
Water constitutes approximately 96% of urine's makeup.
In some animal species pheromones in urine communicate messages of interest or disinterest among possible mates.
DON'T GET ALL QUIET ON ME. YOU KNOW I LOVE YOU.
I DO?
SOMETIMES YOU MAKE ME FEEL LIKE I'M JUST A CONVENIENCE OR A --
ARE YOU GETTING YOUR PERIOD? YOU'RE ACTING ALL --
I'M NOT ACTING! I'M FEELING! THIS IS HOW I FEEL.
LOOK, HON, I KNOW WHERE THIS IS GOING, AND IT'S REALLY IMPORTANT, BUT I HAVE TO SCRAM BEFORE SARA SHOWS UP.
SARA...? WHAT TIME IS IT?
ALMOST TWO.
TWO? SHE SHOULD HAVE BEEN HERE HOURS AGO.
WHERE COULD SHE BE...?

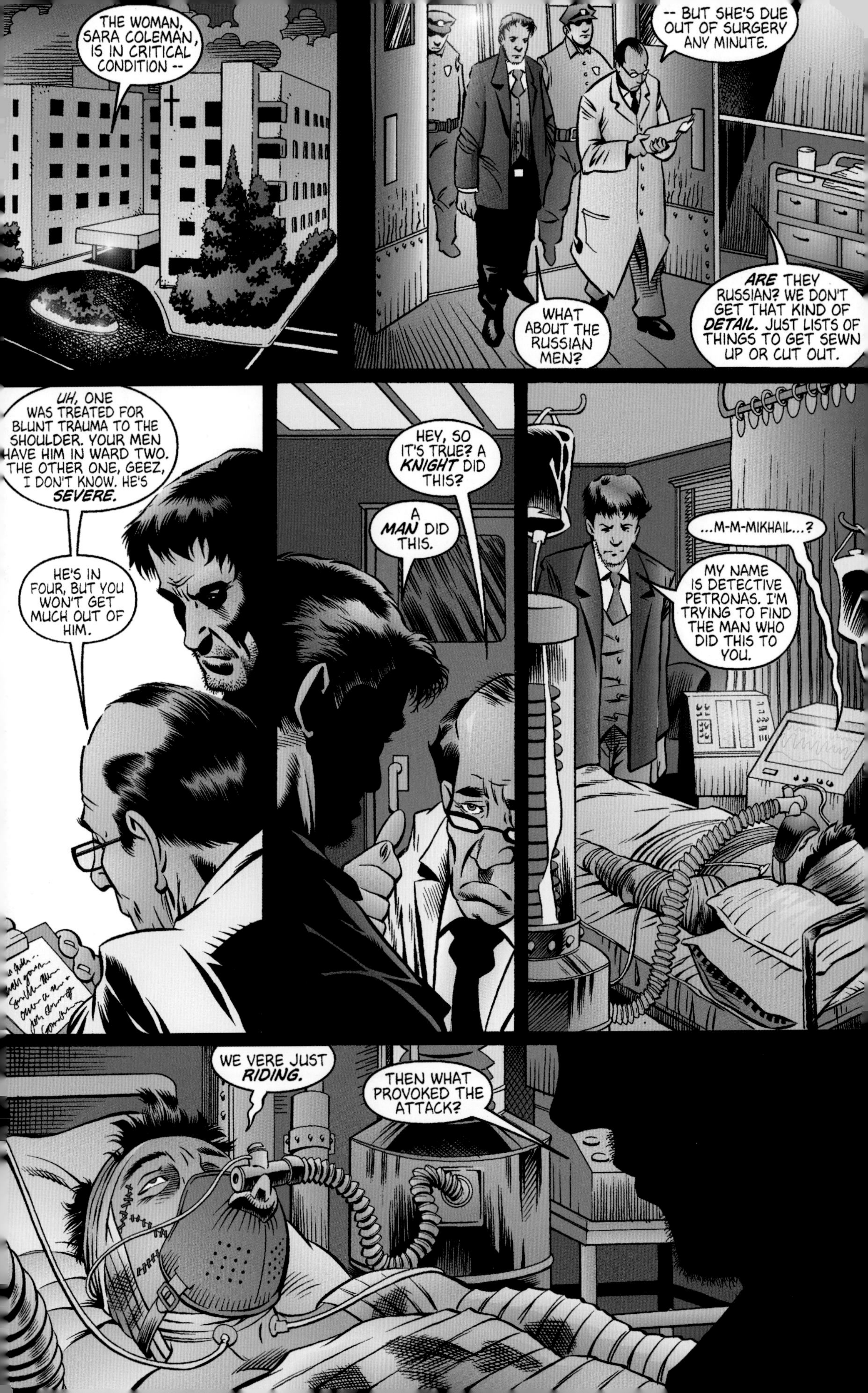
THE WOMAN, SARA COLEMAN, IS IN CRITICAL CONDITION --
-- BUT SHE'S DUE OUT OF SURGERY ANY MINUTE.
WHAT ABOUT THE RUSSIAN MEN?
ARE THEY RUSSIAN? WE DON'T GET THAT KIND OF DETAIL. JUST LISTS OF THINGS TO GET SEWN UP OR CUT OUT.
UH, ONE WAS TREATED FOR BLUNT TRAUMA TO THE SHOULDER. YOUR MEN HAVE HIM IN WARD TWO. THE OTHER ONE, GEEZ, I DON'T KNOW. HE'S SEVERE.
HE'S IN FOUR, BUT YOU WON'T GET MUCH OUT OF HIM.
HEY, SO IT'S TRUE? A KNIGHT DID THIS?
A MAN DID THIS.
...M-M-MIKHAIL...?
MY NAME IS DETECTIVE PETRONAS. I'M TRYING TO FIND THE MAN WHO DID THIS TO YOU.
WE VERE JUST RIDING.
THEN WHAT PROVOKED THE ATTACK?

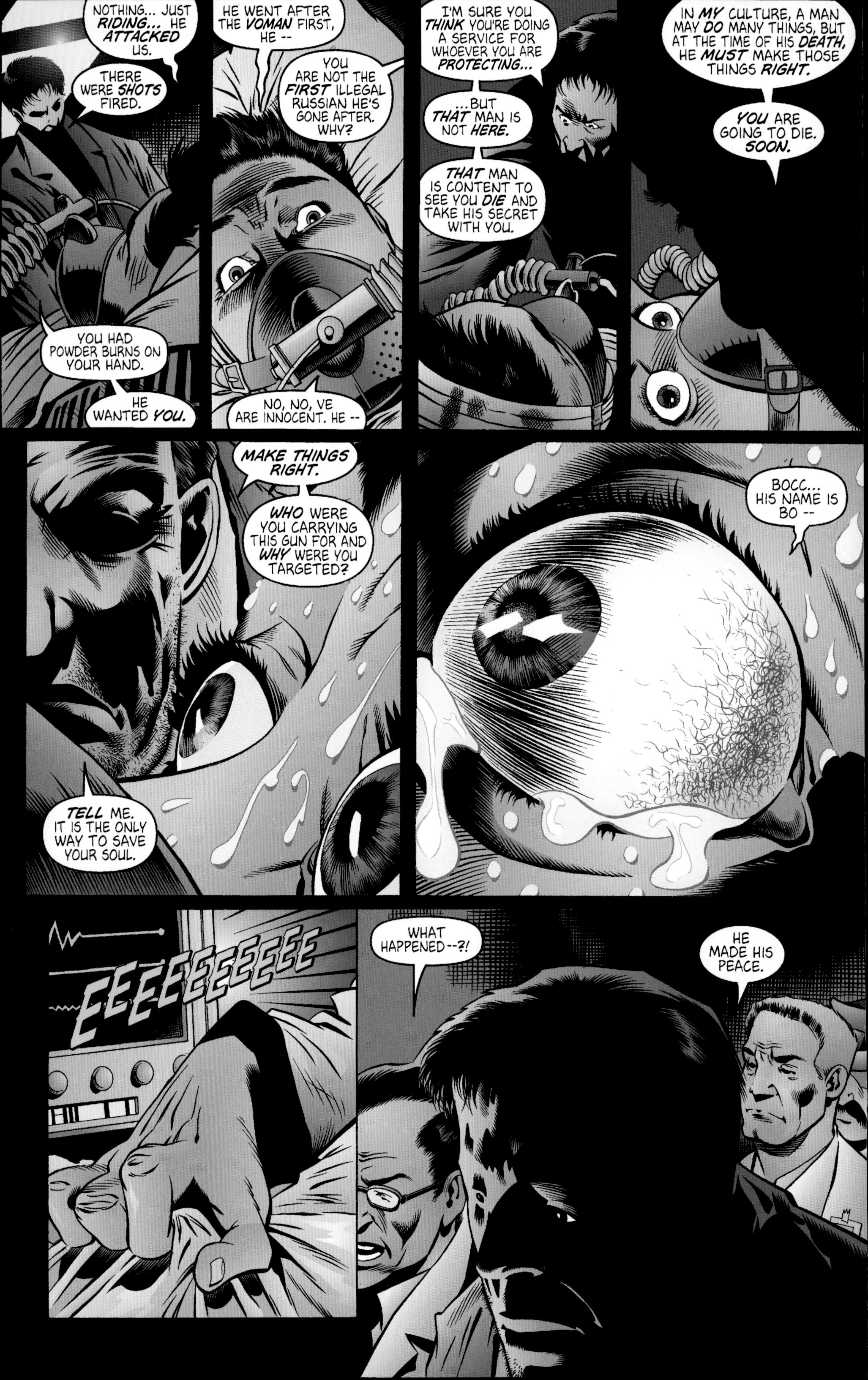
NOTHING... JUST RIDING... HE ATTACKED US.
THERE WERE SHOTS FIRED.
YOU HAD POWDER BURNS ON YOUR HAND.
HE WANTED YOU.
HE WENT AFTER THE VOMAN FIRST, HE --
YOU ARE NOT THE FIRST ILLEGAL RUSSIAN HE'S GONE AFTER. WHY?
NO, NO, VE ARE INNOCENT. HE --
I'M SURE YOU THINK YOU'RE DOING A SERVICE FOR WHOEVER YOU ARE PROTECTING...
...BUT THAT MAN IS NOT HERE.
THAT MAN IS CONTENT TO SEE YOU DIE AND TAKE HIS SECRET WITH YOU.
IN MY CULTURE, A MAN MAY DO MANY THINGS, BUT AT THE TIME OF HIS DEATH, HE MUST MAKE THOSE THINGS RIGHT.
YOU ARE GOING TO DIE. SOON.
MAKE THINGS RIGHT.
WHO WERE YOU CARRYING THIS GUN FOR AND WHY WERE YOU TARGETED?
TELL ME. IT IS THE ONLY WAY TO SAVE YOUR SOUL.
BOCC... HIS NAME IS BO --
EEEEEEEEEEE
WHAT HAPPENED--?!
HE MADE HIS PEACE.

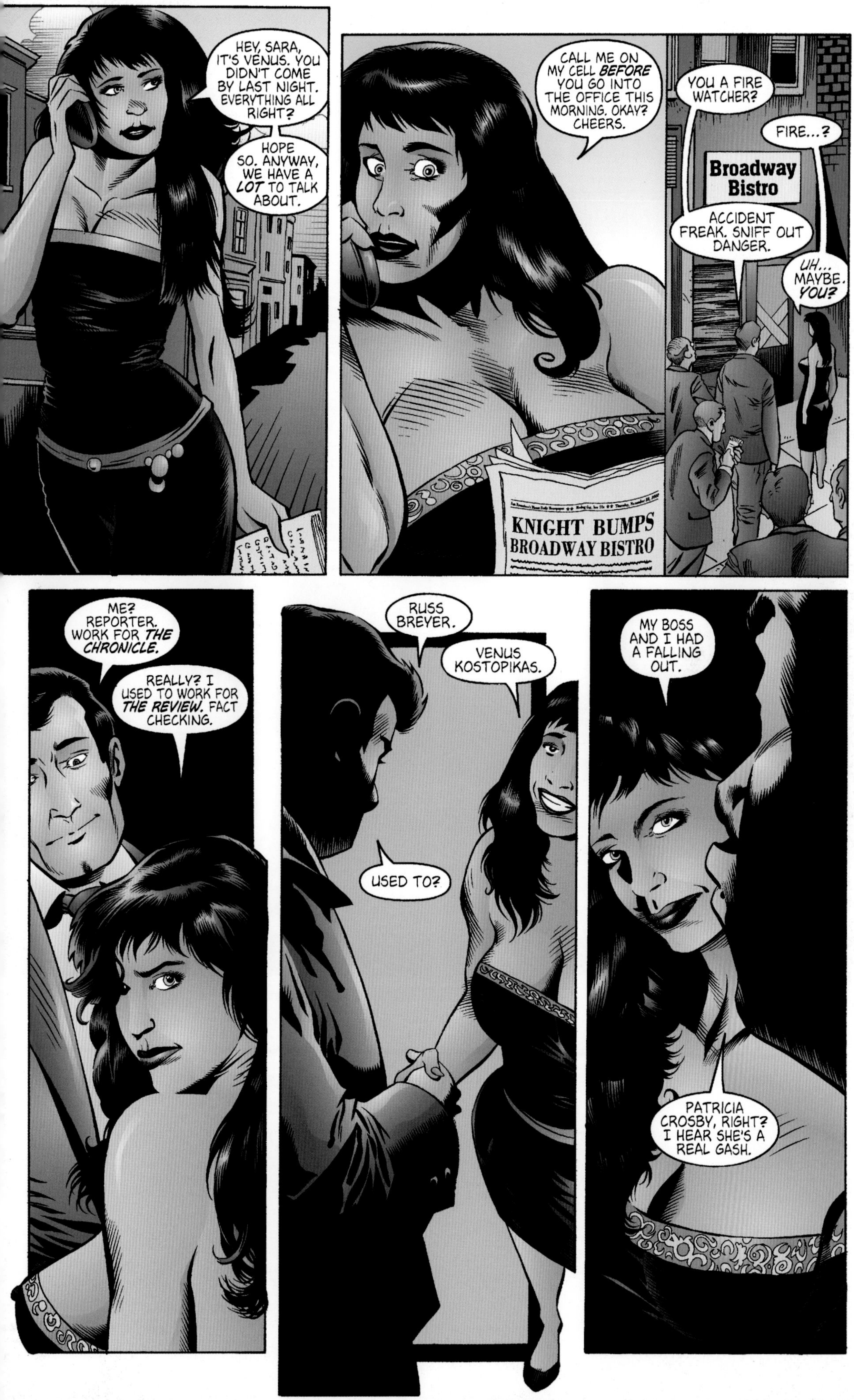
HEY, SARA, IT'S VENUS. YOU DIDN'T COME BY LAST NIGHT. EVERYTHING ALL RIGHT?
HOPE SO. ANYWAY, WE HAVE A *LOT* TO TALK ABOUT.
CALL ME ON MY CELL *BEFORE* YOU GO INTO THE OFFICE THIS MORNING. OKAY? CHEERS.
KNIGHT BUMPS
BROADWAY BISTRO
YOU A FIRE WATCHER?
FIRE...?
Broadway Bistro
ACCIDENT FREAK. SNIFF OUT DANGER.
UH... MAYBE. *YOU?*
ME? REPORTER. WORK FOR *THE CHRONICLE.*
REALLY? I USED TO WORK FOR *THE REVIEW.* FACT CHECKING.
RUSS BREYER.
VENUS KOSTOPIKAS.
USED TO?
MY BOSS AND I HAD A FALLING OUT.
PATRICIA CROSBY, RIGHT? I HEAR SHE'S A REAL GASH.

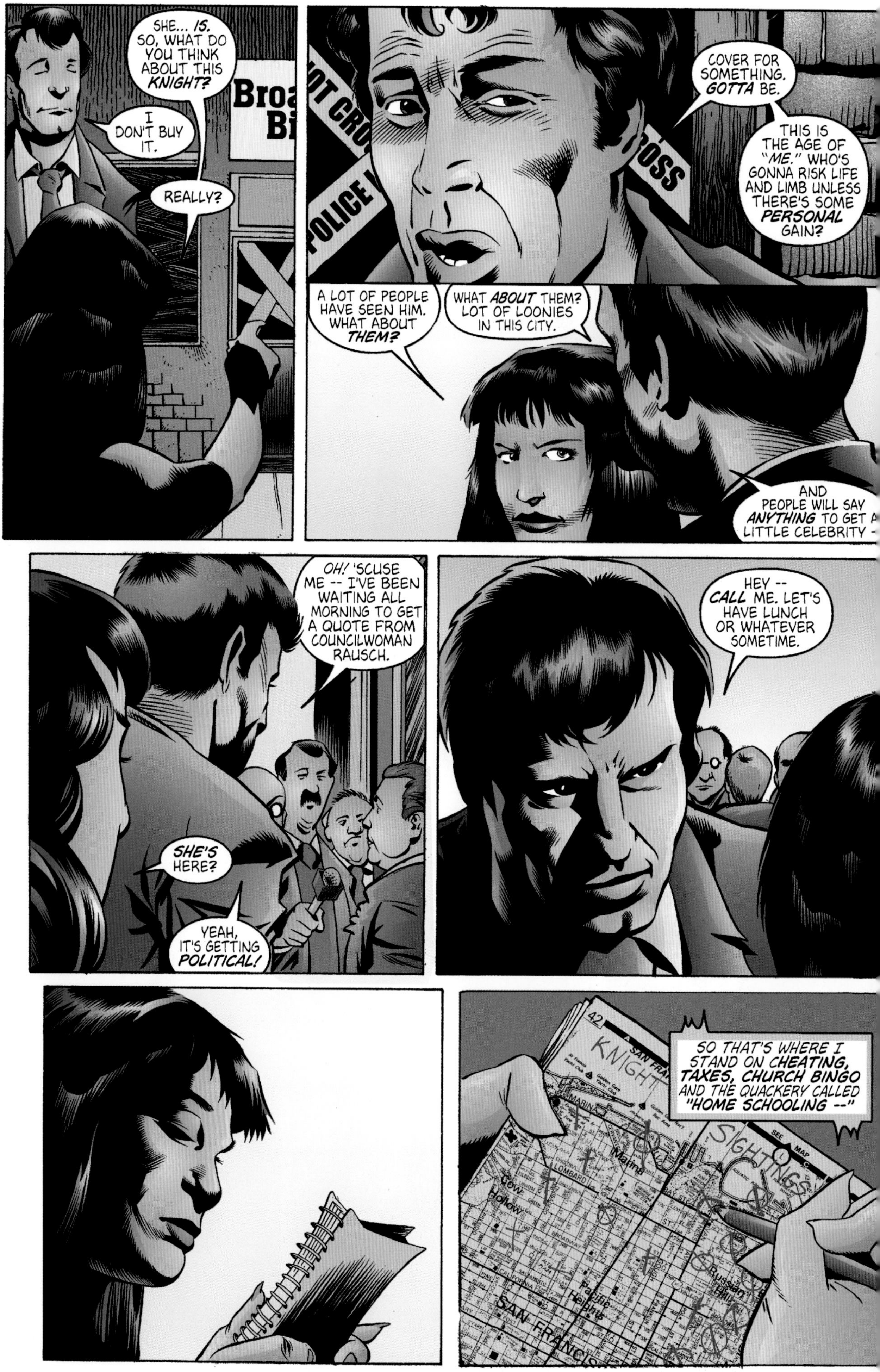
SHE... IS. SO, WHAT DO YOU THINK ABOUT THIS KNIGHT?
I DON'T BUY IT.
REALLY?
COVER FOR SOMETHING. GOTTA BE.
THIS IS THE AGE OF "ME." WHO'S GONNA RISK LIFE AND LIMB UNLESS THERE'S SOME PERSONAL GAIN?
A LOT OF PEOPLE HAVE SEEN HIM. WHAT ABOUT THEM?
WHAT ABOUT THEM? LOT OF LOONIES IN THIS CITY.
AND PEOPLE WILL SAY ANYTHING TO GET A LITTLE CELEBRITY --
OH! 'SCUSE ME -- I'VE BEEN WAITING ALL MORNING TO GET A QUOTE FROM COUNCILWOMAN RAUSCH.
SHE'S HERE?
YEAH, IT'S GETTING POLITICAL!
HEY -- CALL ME. LET'S HAVE LUNCH OR WHATEVER SOMETIME.
SO THAT'S WHERE I STAND ON CHEATING, TAXES, CHURCH BINGO AND THE QUACKERY CALLED "HOME SCHOOLING --"
KNIGHT
SIGHTINGS

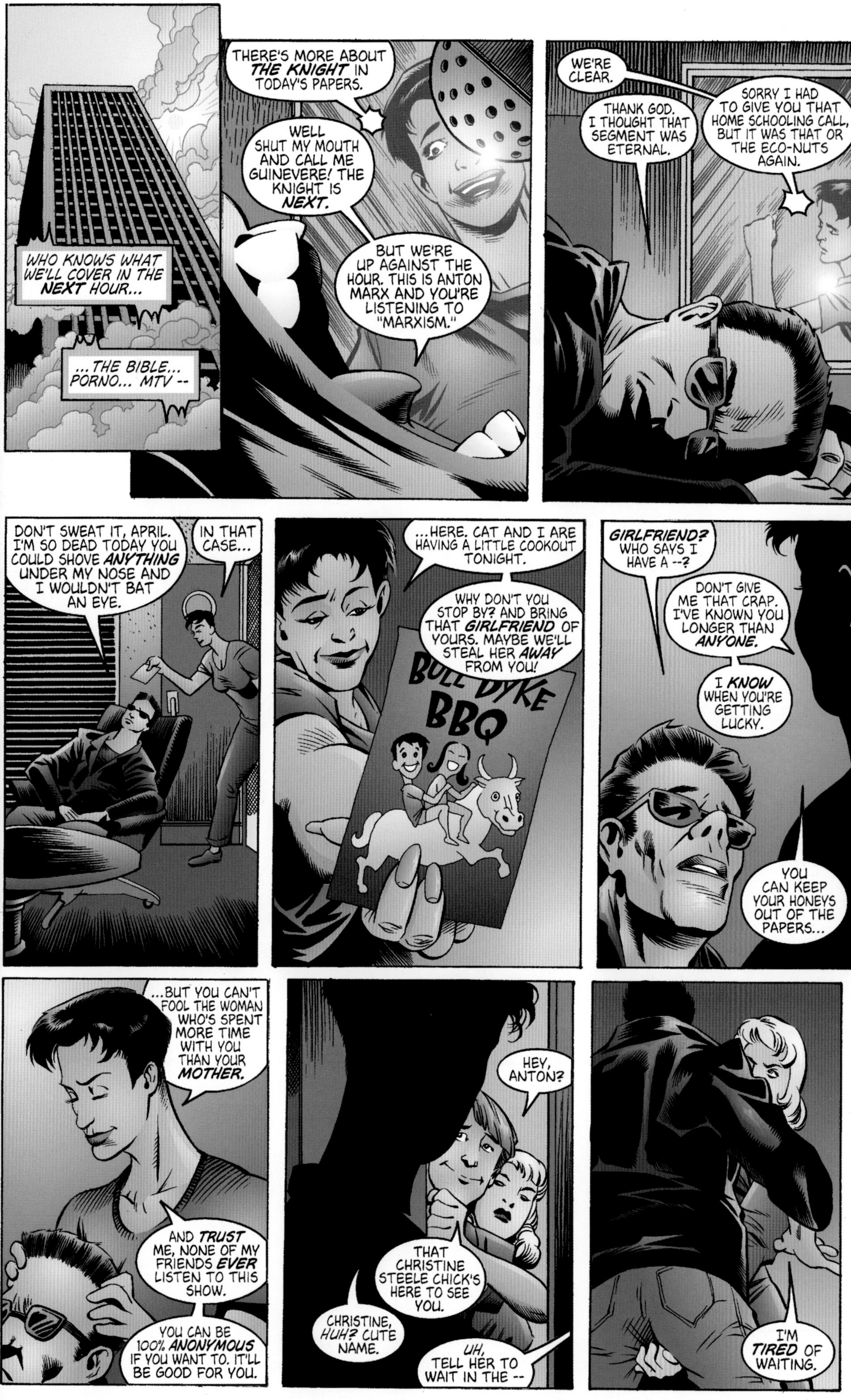
WHO KNOWS WHAT WE'LL COVER IN THE NEXT HOUR...
...THE BIBLE... PORNO... MTV --
THERE'S MORE ABOUT THE KNIGHT IN TODAY'S PAPERS.
WELL SHUT MY MOUTH AND CALL ME GUINEVERE! THE KNIGHT IS NEXT.
BUT WE'RE UP AGAINST THE HOUR. THIS IS ANTON MARX AND YOU'RE LISTENING TO "MARXISM."
WE'RE CLEAR.
THANK GOD. I THOUGHT THAT SEGMENT WAS ETERNAL.
SORRY I HAD TO GIVE YOU THAT HOME SCHOOLING CALL, BUT IT WAS THAT OR THE ECO-NUTS AGAIN.
DON'T SWEAT IT, APRIL. I'M SO DEAD TODAY YOU COULD SHOVE ANYTHING UNDER MY NOSE AND I WOULDN'T BAT AN EYE.
IN THAT CASE...
...HERE. CAT AND I ARE HAVING A LITTLE COOKOUT TONIGHT.
WHY DON'T YOU STOP BY? AND BRING THAT GIRLFRIEND OF YOURS. MAYBE WE'LL STEAL HER AWAY FROM YOU!
BULL DYKE BBQ
GIRLFRIEND? WHO SAYS I HAVE A --?
DON'T GIVE ME THAT CRAP. I'VE KNOWN YOU LONGER THAN ANYONE.
I KNOW WHEN YOU'RE GETTING LUCKY.
YOU CAN KEEP YOUR HONEYS OUT OF THE PAPERS...
...BUT YOU CAN'T FOOL THE WOMAN WHO'S SPENT MORE TIME WITH YOU THAN YOUR MOTHER.
AND TRUST ME, NONE OF MY FRIENDS EVER LISTEN TO THIS SHOW.
YOU CAN BE 100% ANONYMOUS IF YOU WANT TO. IT'LL BE GOOD FOR YOU.
HEY, ANTON?
THAT CHRISTINE STEELE CHICK'S HERE TO SEE YOU.
CHRISTINE, HUH? CUTE NAME.
UH, TELL HER TO WAIT IN THE --
I'M TIRED OF WAITING.

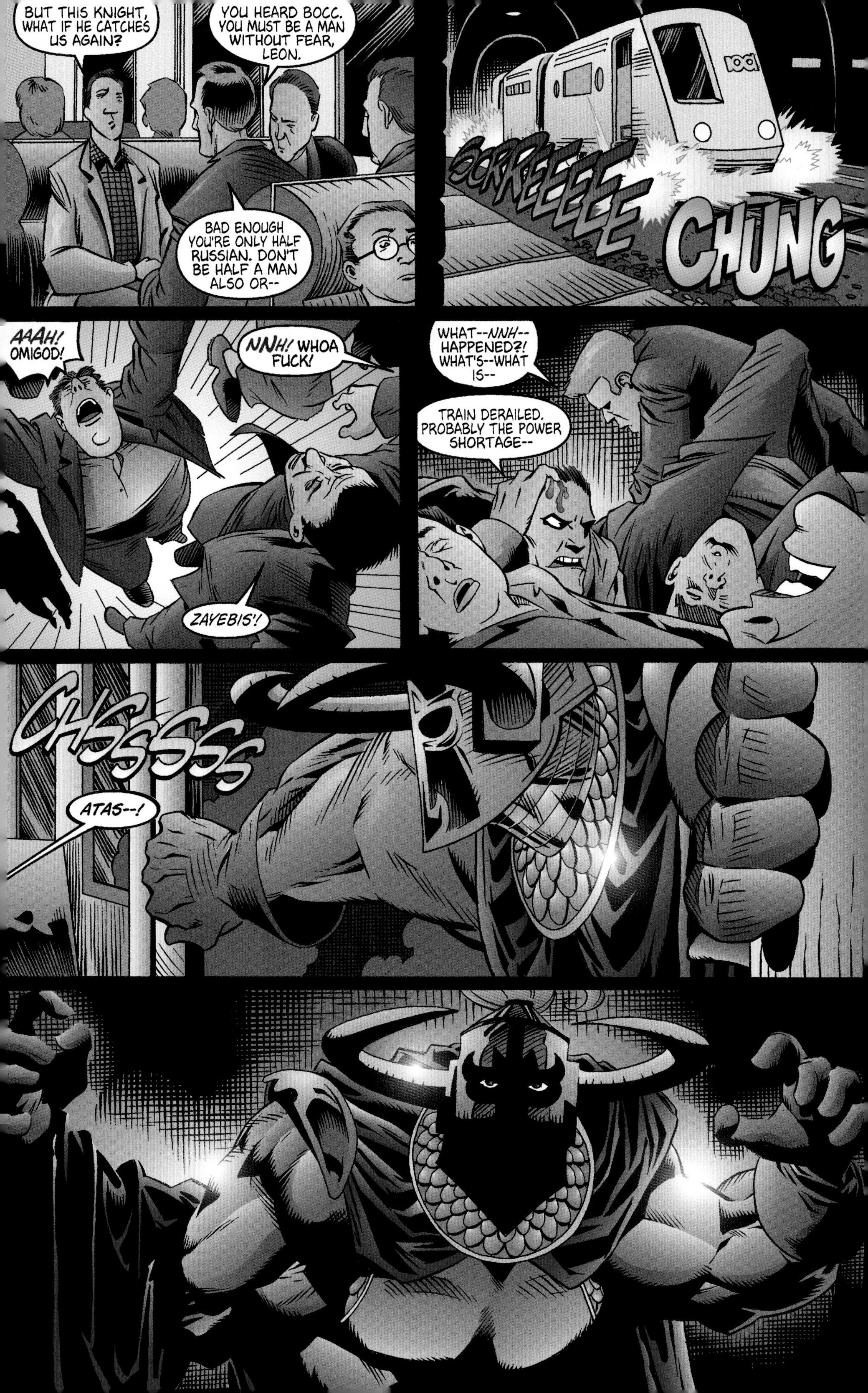
BUT THIS KNIGHT, WHAT IF HE CATCHES US AGAIN?
YOU HEARD BOCC. YOU MUST BE A MAN WITHOUT FEAR, LEON.
BAD ENOUGH YOU'RE ONLY HALF RUSSIAN. DON'T BE HALF A MAN ALSO OR--
SCRREEEEEE
CHUNG
AAAH! OMIGOD!
NNH! WHOA FUCK!
ZAYEBIS'!
WHAT--NNH--HAPPENED?! WHAT'S--WHAT IS--
TRAIN DERAILED. PROBABLY THE POWER SHORTAGE--
CHSSSSS
ATAS--!

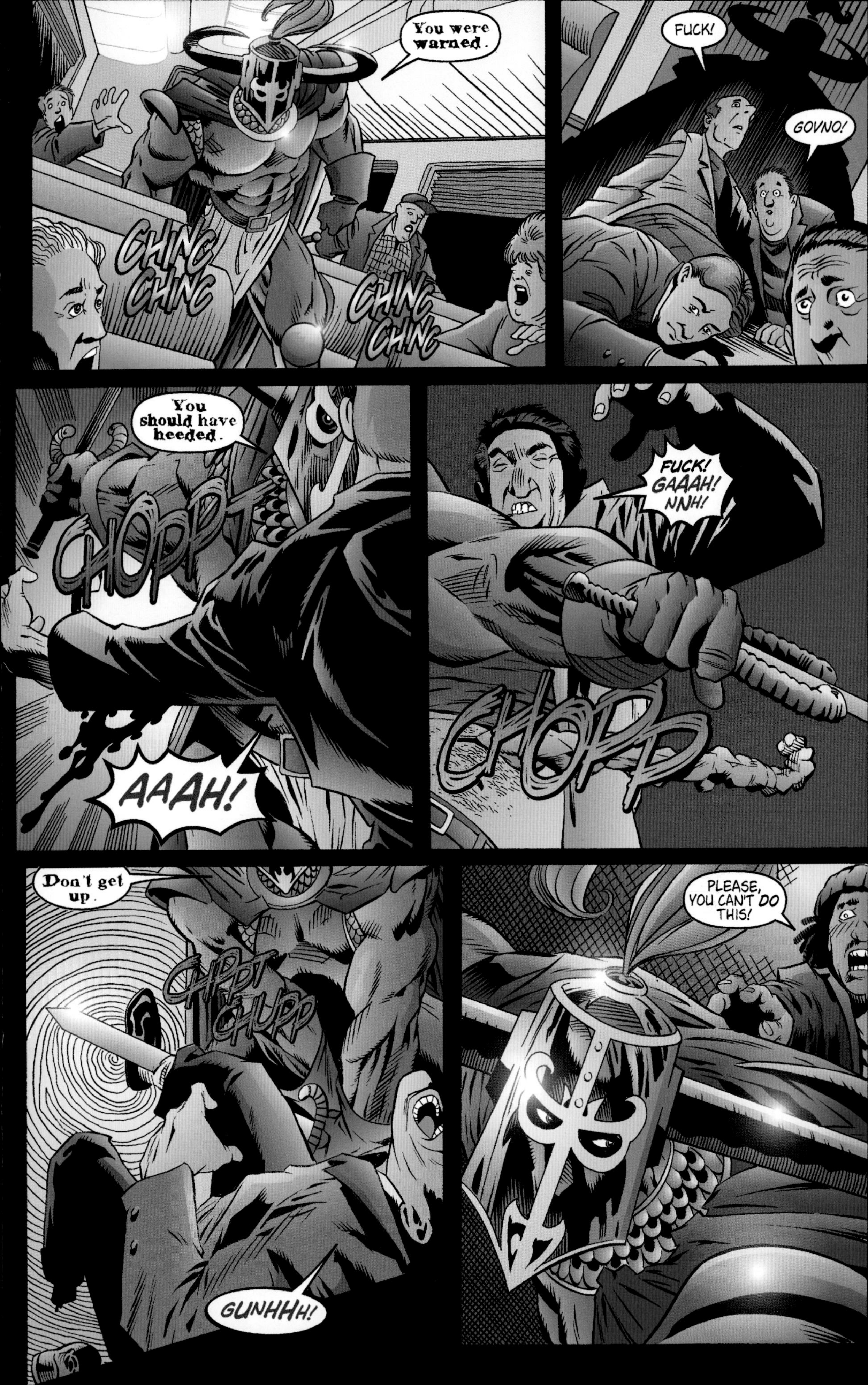
You were warned.
CHING CHING
CHING CHING
FUCK!
GOVNO!
You should have heeded.
CHOPP
AAAH!
FUCK! GAAAH! NNH!
CHOPP
Don't get up.
CHPPT CHUPP
GUNHHH!
PLEASE, YOU CAN'T DO THIS!

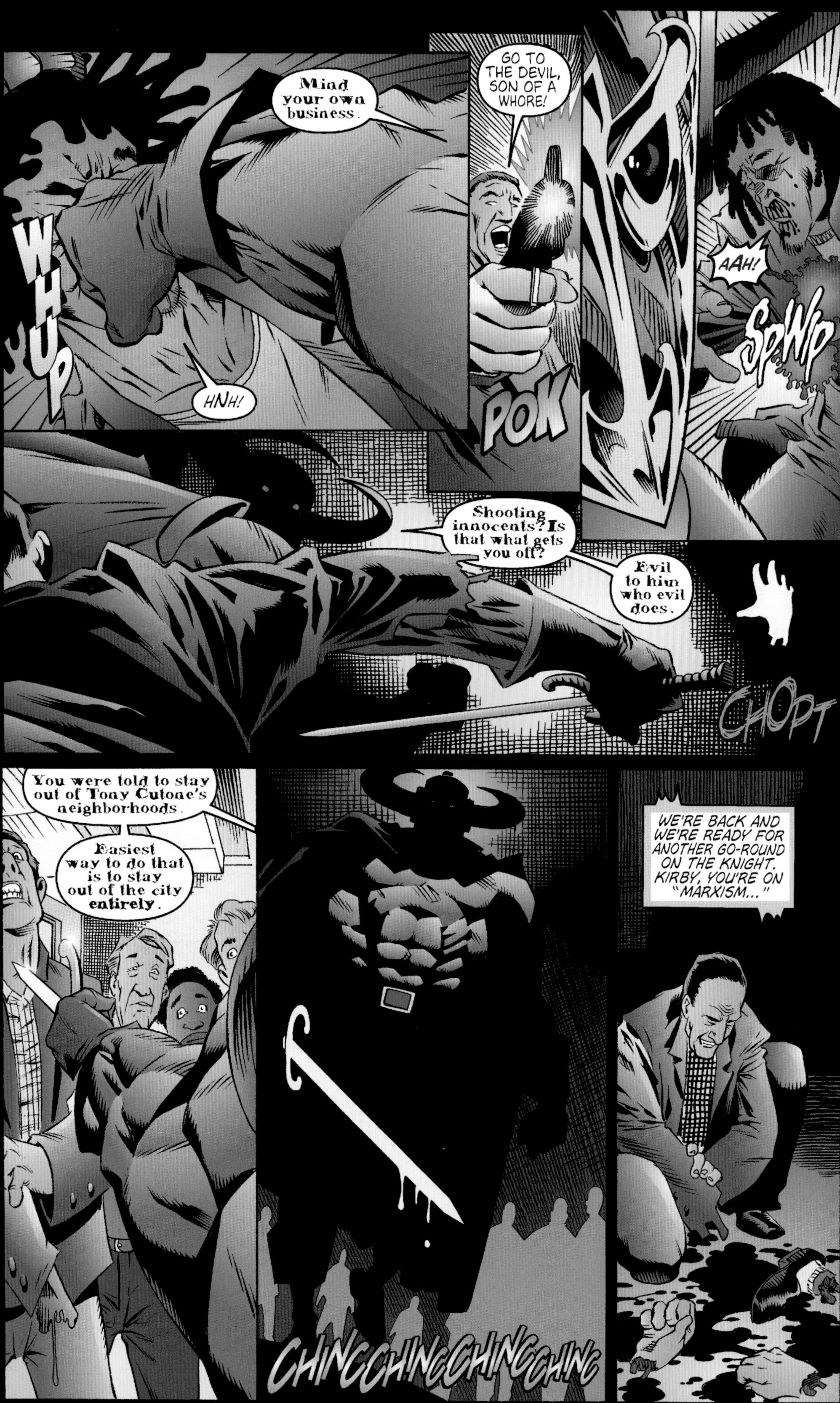

Mind your own business.
WHUP
HNH!
GO TO THE DEVIL, SON OF A WHORE!
POK
AAH!
SPWIP
Shooting innocents? Is that what gets you off?
Evil to him who evil does.
CHOPT
You were told to stay out of Tony Cutone's neighborhoods.
Easiest way to do that is to stay out of the city entirely.
CHINGCHINGCHINGCHING
WE'RE BACK AND WE'RE READY FOR ANOTHER GO-ROUND ON THE KNIGHT. KIRBY, YOU'RE ON "MARXISM..."

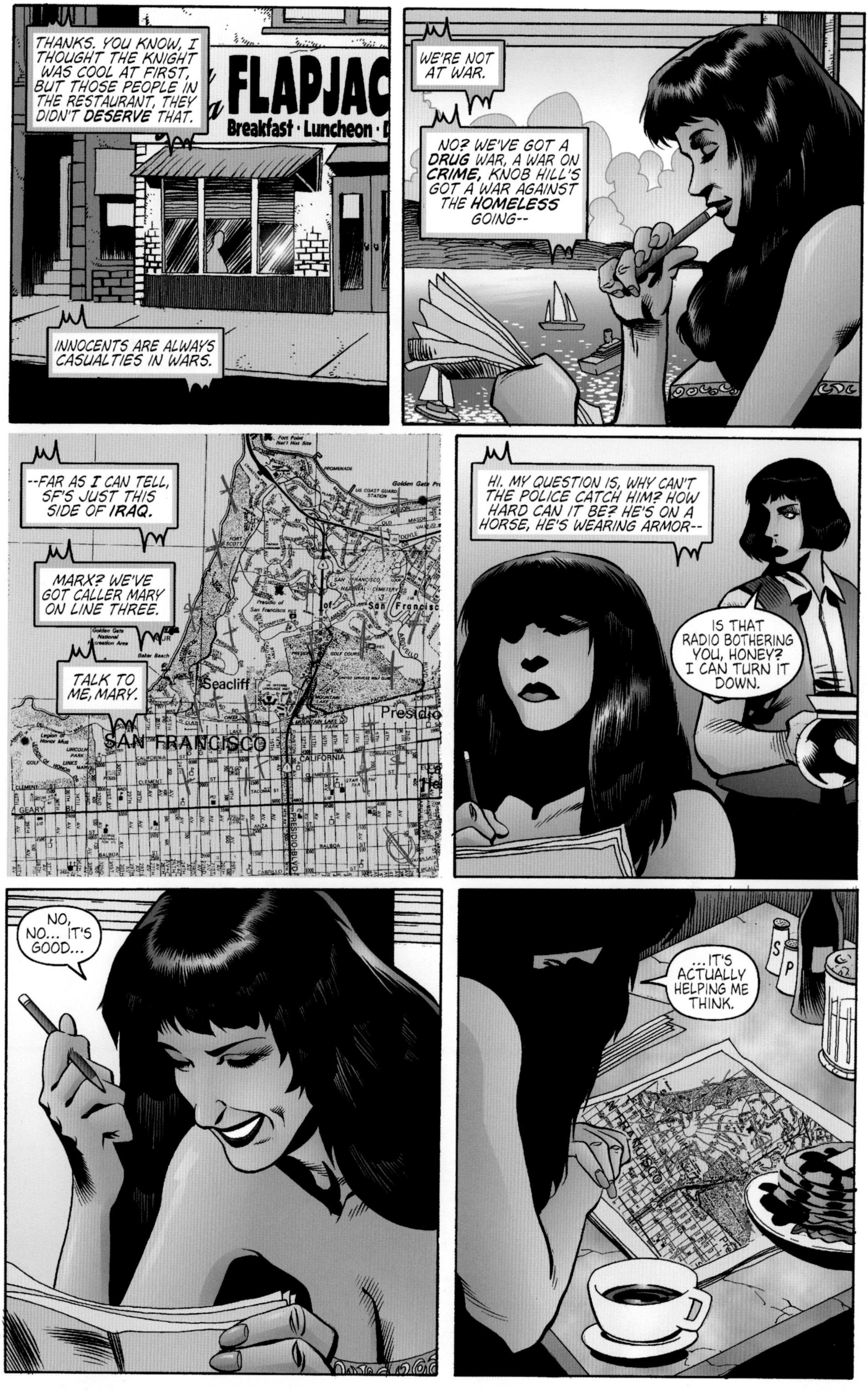

FLAPJAC
Breakfast · Luncheon · D
THANKS. YOU KNOW, I THOUGHT THE KNIGHT WAS COOL AT FIRST, BUT THOSE PEOPLE IN THE RESTAURANT, THEY DIDN'T DESERVE THAT.
INNOCENTS ARE ALWAYS CASUALTIES IN WARS.
WE'RE NOT AT WAR.
NO? WE'VE GOT A DRUG WAR, A WAR ON CRIME, KNOB HILL'S GOT A WAR AGAINST THE HOMELESS GOING--
--FAR AS I CAN TELL, SF'S JUST THIS SIDE OF IRAQ.
MARX? WE'VE GOT CALLER MARY ON LINE THREE.
TALK TO ME, MARY.
SAN FRANCISCO
Seacliff
Presidio
HI. MY QUESTION IS, WHY CAN'T THE POLICE CATCH HIM? HOW HARD CAN IT BE? HE'S ON A HORSE, HE'S WEARING ARMOR--
IS THAT RADIO BOTHERING YOU, HONEY? I CAN TURN IT DOWN.
NO, NO... IT'S GOOD...
...IT'S ACTUALLY HELPING ME THINK.
S
P

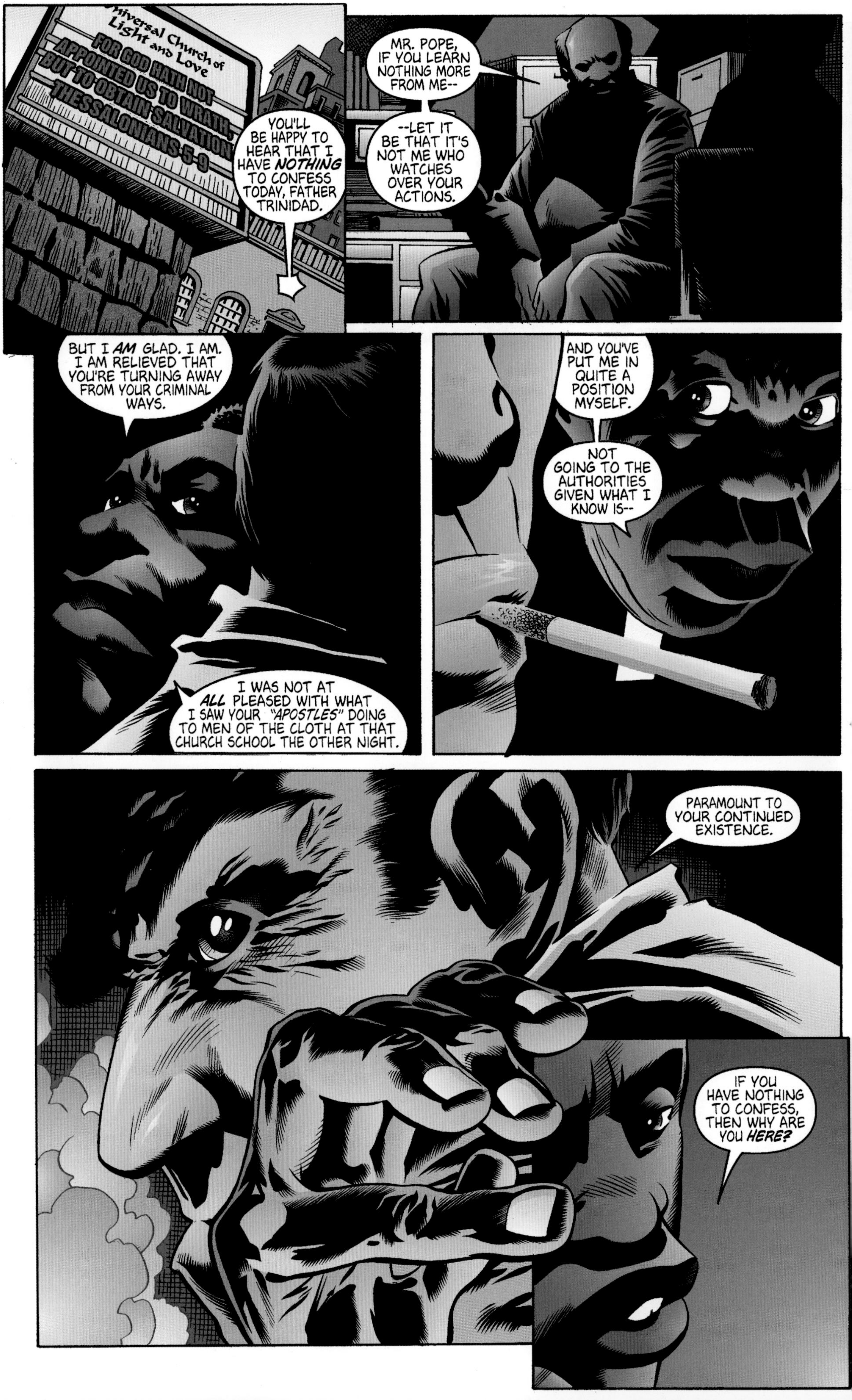
Universal Church of Light and Love
FOR GOD HATH NOT APPOINTED US TO WRATH, BUT TO OBTAIN SALVATION THESSALONIANS 5-9
YOU'LL BE HAPPY TO HEAR THAT I HAVE NOTHING TO CONFESS TODAY, FATHER TRINIDAD.
MR. POPE, IF YOU LEARN NOTHING MORE FROM ME--
--LET IT BE THAT IT'S NOT ME WHO WATCHES OVER YOUR ACTIONS.
BUT I AM GLAD. I AM. I AM RELIEVED THAT YOU'RE TURNING AWAY FROM YOUR CRIMINAL WAYS.
I WAS NOT AT ALL PLEASED WITH WHAT I SAW YOUR "APOSTLES" DOING TO MEN OF THE CLOTH AT THAT CHURCH SCHOOL THE OTHER NIGHT.
AND YOU'VE PUT ME IN QUITE A POSITION MYSELF.
NOT GOING TO THE AUTHORITIES GIVEN WHAT I KNOW IS--
PARAMOUNT TO YOUR CONTINUED EXISTENCE.
IF YOU HAVE NOTHING TO CONFESS, THEN WHY ARE YOU HERE?

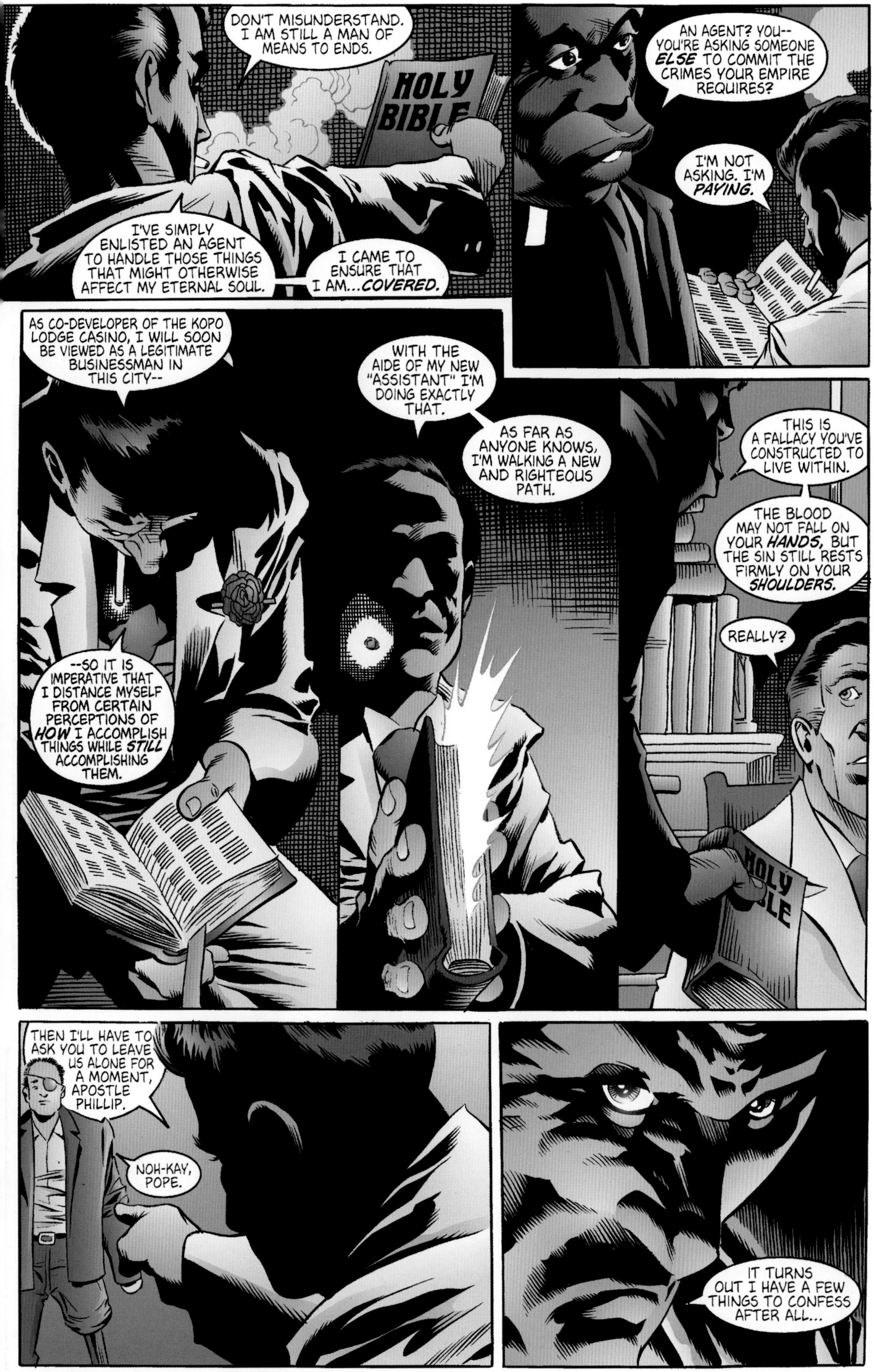
DON'T MISUNDERSTAND. I AM STILL A MAN OF MEANS TO ENDS.
HOLY BIBLE
I'VE SIMPLY ENLISTED AN AGENT TO HANDLE THOSE THINGS THAT MIGHT OTHERWISE AFFECT MY ETERNAL SOUL.
I CAME TO ENSURE THAT I AM...COVERED.
AN AGENT? YOU-- YOU'RE ASKING SOMEONE ELSE TO COMMIT THE CRIMES YOUR EMPIRE REQUIRES?
I'M NOT ASKING. I'M PAYING.
AS CO-DEVELOPER OF THE KOPO LODGE CASINO, I WILL SOON BE VIEWED AS A LEGITIMATE BUSINESSMAN IN THIS CITY--
--SO IT IS IMPERATIVE THAT I DISTANCE MYSELF FROM CERTAIN PERCEPTIONS OF HOW I ACCOMPLISH THINGS WHILE STILL ACCOMPLISHING THEM.
WITH THE AIDE OF MY NEW "ASSISTANT" I'M DOING EXACTLY THAT.
AS FAR AS ANYONE KNOWS, I'M WALKING A NEW AND RIGHTEOUS PATH.
THIS IS A FALLACY YOU'VE CONSTRUCTED TO LIVE WITHIN.
THE BLOOD MAY NOT FALL ON YOUR HANDS, BUT THE SIN STILL RESTS FIRMLY ON YOUR SHOULDERS.
REALLY?
HOLY BIBLE
THEN I'LL HAVE TO ASK YOU TO LEAVE US ALONE FOR A MOMENT, APOSTLE PHILLIP.
NOH-KAY, POPE.
IT TURNS OUT I HAVE A FEW THINGS TO CONFESS AFTER ALL...

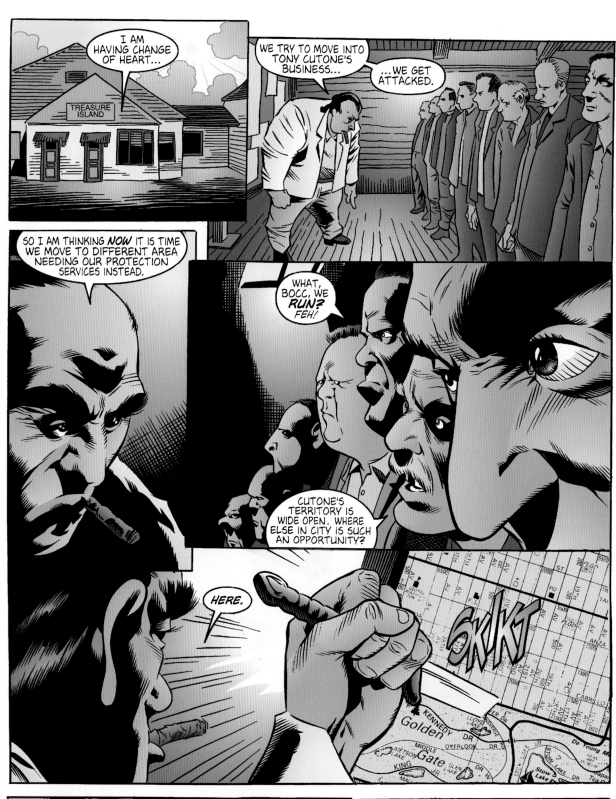

I AM HAVING CHANGE OF HEART...

TREASURE ISLAND

WE TRY TO MOVE INTO TONY CUTONE'S BUSINESS...

...WE GET ATTACKED.

SO I AM THINKING *NOW* IT IS TIME WE MOVE TO DIFFERENT AREA NEEDING OUR PROTECTION SERVICES INSTEAD.

WHAT, BOCC, WE *RUN?* FEH!

CUTONE'S TERRITORY IS WIDE OPEN. WHERE ELSE IN CITY IS SUCH AN OPPORTUNITY?

HERE.

SKIKT

KENNEDY DR
Golden
MIDDLE
Gate

THAT...THAT IS *THE POPE'S* TERRITORY.

IT IS UNTIL IT *ISN'T...*

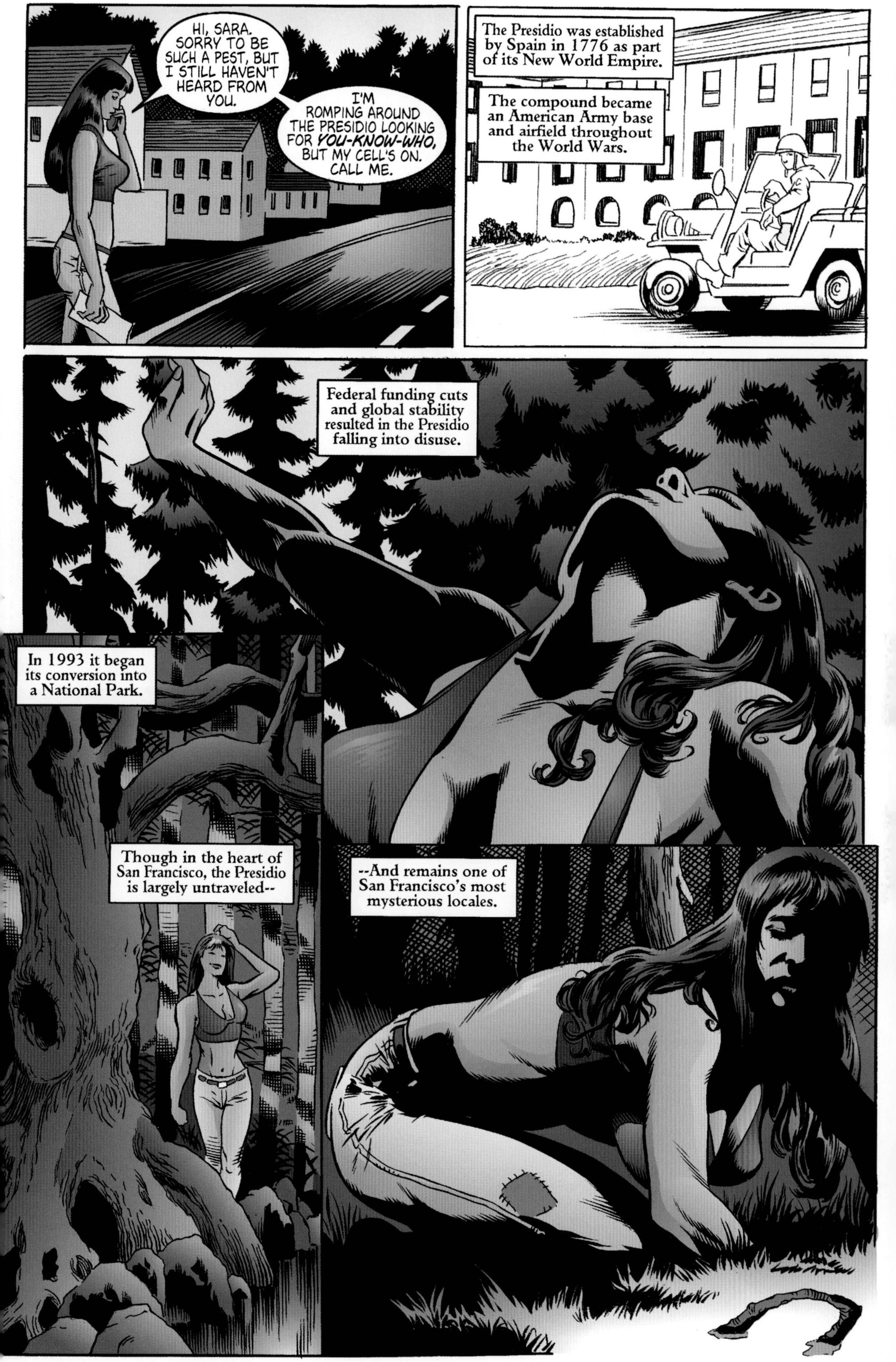
HI, SARA. SORRY TO BE SUCH A PEST, BUT I STILL HAVEN'T HEARD FROM YOU.
I'M ROMPING AROUND THE PRESIDIO LOOKING FOR YOU-KNOW-WHO, BUT MY CELL'S ON. CALL ME.
The Presidio was established by Spain in 1776 as part of its New World Empire.
The compound became an American Army base and airfield throughout the World Wars.
Federal funding cuts and global stability resulted in the Presidio falling into disuse.
In 1993 it began its conversion into a National Park.
Though in the heart of San Francisco, the Presidio is largely untraveled--
--And remains one of San Francisco's most mysterious locales.

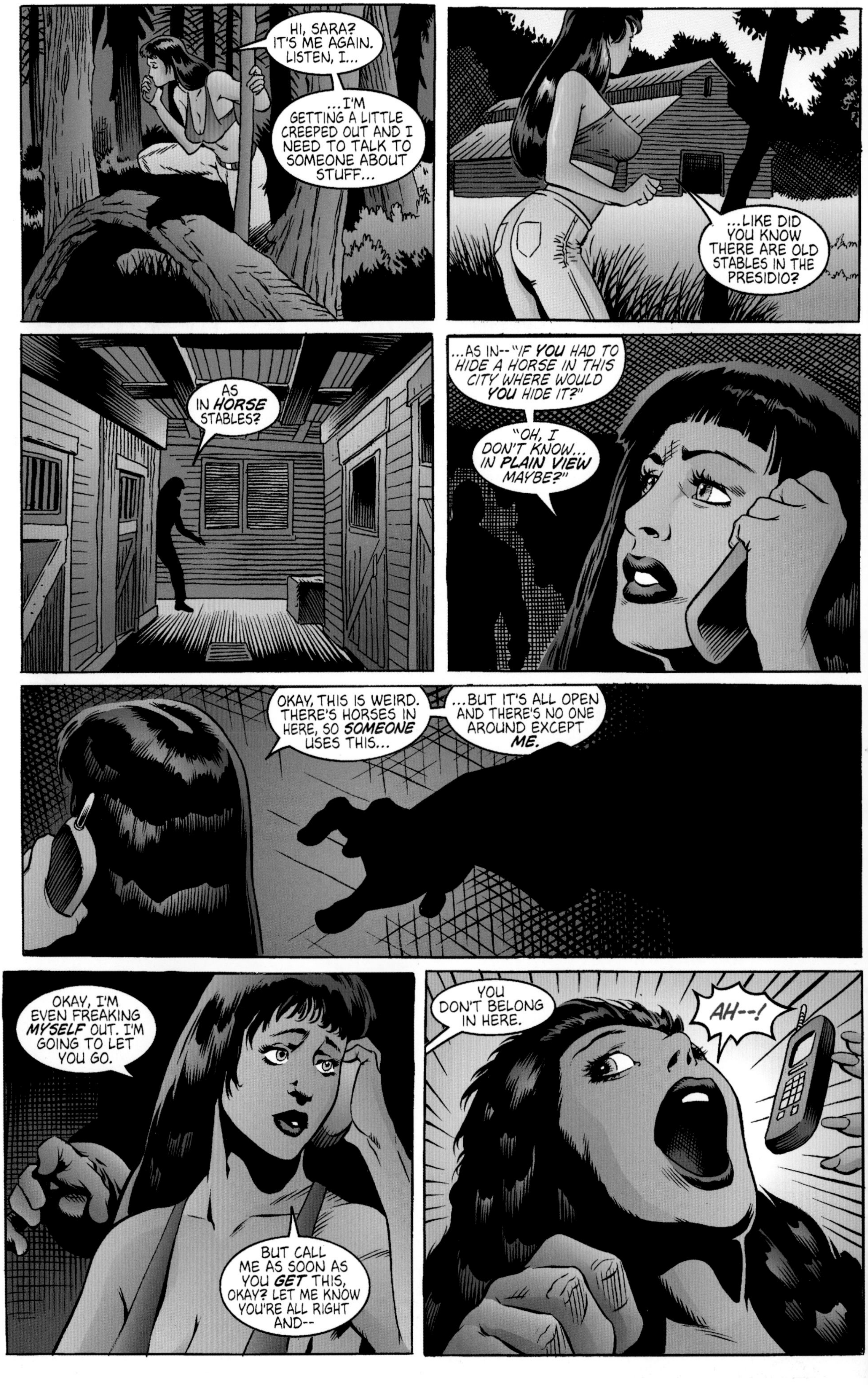
HI, SARA? IT'S ME AGAIN. LISTEN, I...
...I'M GETTING A LITTLE CREEPED OUT AND I NEED TO TALK TO SOMEONE ABOUT STUFF...
...LIKE DID YOU KNOW THERE ARE OLD STABLES IN THE PRESIDIO?
AS IN HORSE STABLES?
...AS IN--"IF YOU HAD TO HIDE A HORSE IN THIS CITY WHERE WOULD YOU HIDE IT?"
"OH, I DON'T KNOW... IN PLAIN VIEW MAYBE?"
OKAY, THIS IS WEIRD. THERE'S HORSES IN HERE, SO SOMEONE USES THIS...
...BUT IT'S ALL OPEN AND THERE'S NO ONE AROUND EXCEPT ME.
OKAY, I'M EVEN FREAKING MYSELF OUT. I'M GOING TO LET YOU GO.
BUT CALL ME AS SOON AS YOU GET THIS, OKAY? LET ME KNOW YOU'RE ALL RIGHT AND--
YOU DON'T BELONG IN HERE.
AH--!

...SURE, AND THERE'S A *LOT* MORE THAT NEEDS EXPLAINING, TOO.

LIKE WHY DON'T THE SIGHTINGS EXTEND BEYOND THE *INCIDENT* AREA? WHY DON'T PEOPLE *SEE* THE KNIGHT RIDING BACK *HOME* THROUGH--

--UH-- HANG ON--

POLICE SCANN KNIGHT JUST ATTA BART CAR IN AKLAND TUNNEL

MY LOYAL SUBJECTS, *THIS JUST IN*--

--THE KNIGHT HAS ATTACKED A *BART SUBWAY CAR* IN THE OAKLAND TUNNEL.

YOU HEARD IT HERE *FIRST.* THE KNIGHT HAS ATTACKED A SUBWAY CAR. SOME THINGS COME IMMEDIATELY TO MIND...

ONE--THIS IS GOING TO BE A *MAJOR EGG* ON THE FACE OF THE SFPD.

TWO--IT'S NO LONGER JUST SAN FRANCISCO *PROPER.* A TRAIN CROSSING THE *BAY?*

THAT'S A WHOLE NEW TARGET AREA. THE KNIGHT IS EXPANDING HIS CIRCLE.

THREE--YOUR EVENING COMMUTE IS GOING TO BE A *BITCH.*

AND *FOUR?* AN ATTACK IN BROAD DAYLIGHT ON MASS TRANSIT MEANS--

--THE GLOVES ARE *OFF.* IF HE'S ATTACKING TRAINLOADS OF PEOPLE, WE'RE *ALL* AT HIS MERCY NOW...

POLICE SCANNER -- IGHT JUST ATTACKED BA CA

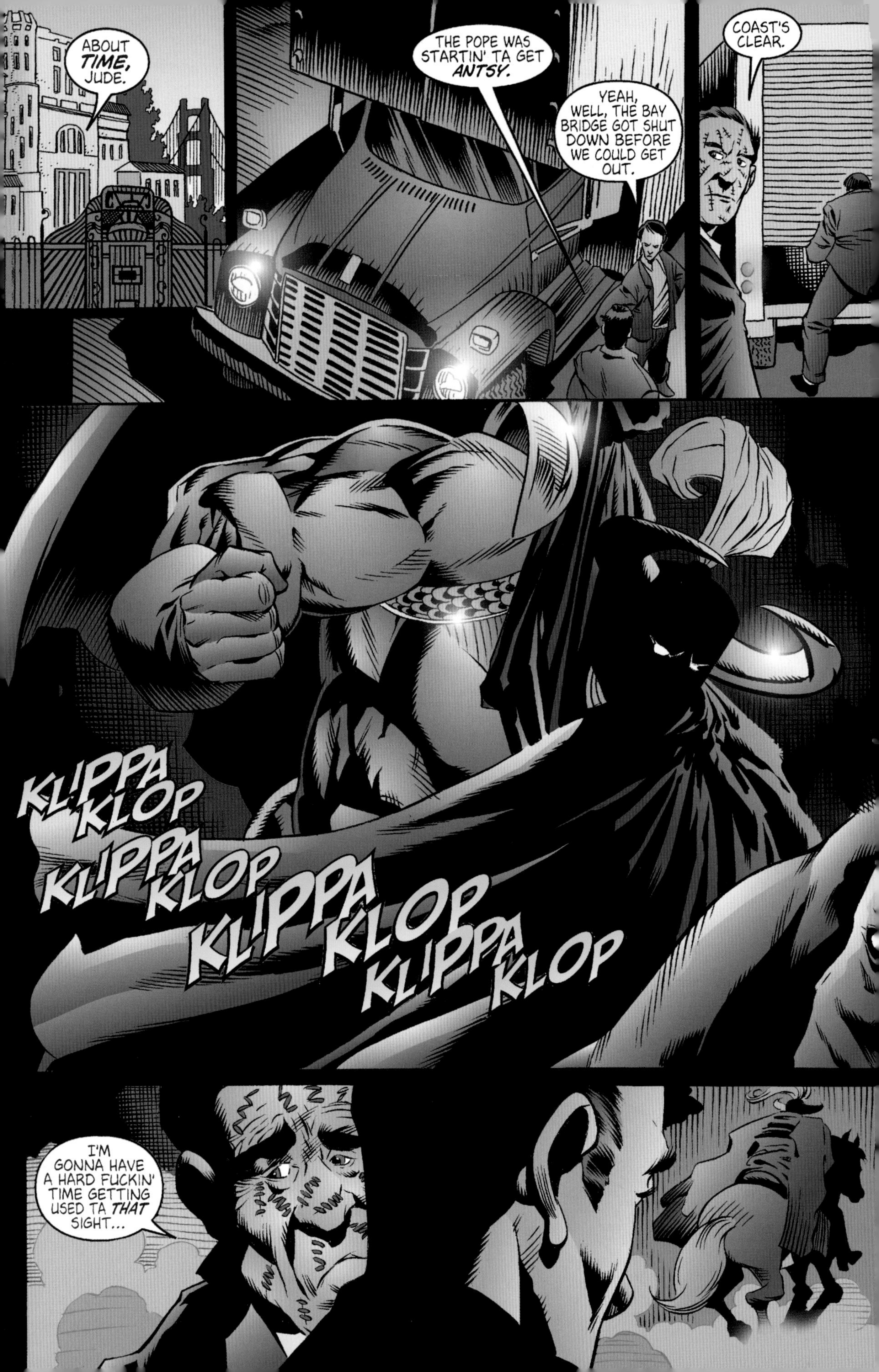
ABOUT TIME, JUDE.
THE POPE WAS STARTIN' TA GET ANTSY.
YEAH, WELL, THE BAY BRIDGE GOT SHUT DOWN BEFORE WE COULD GET OUT.
COAST'S CLEAR.
KLIPPA KLOP
KLIPPA KLOP
KLIPPA KLOP
KLIPPA KLOP
I'M GONNA HAVE A HARD FUCKIN' TIME GETTING USED TA THAT SIGHT...

"Liberation is not deliverance"
-- Victor Hugo

"YOU'RE NOT
ALLOWED
IN HERE..."

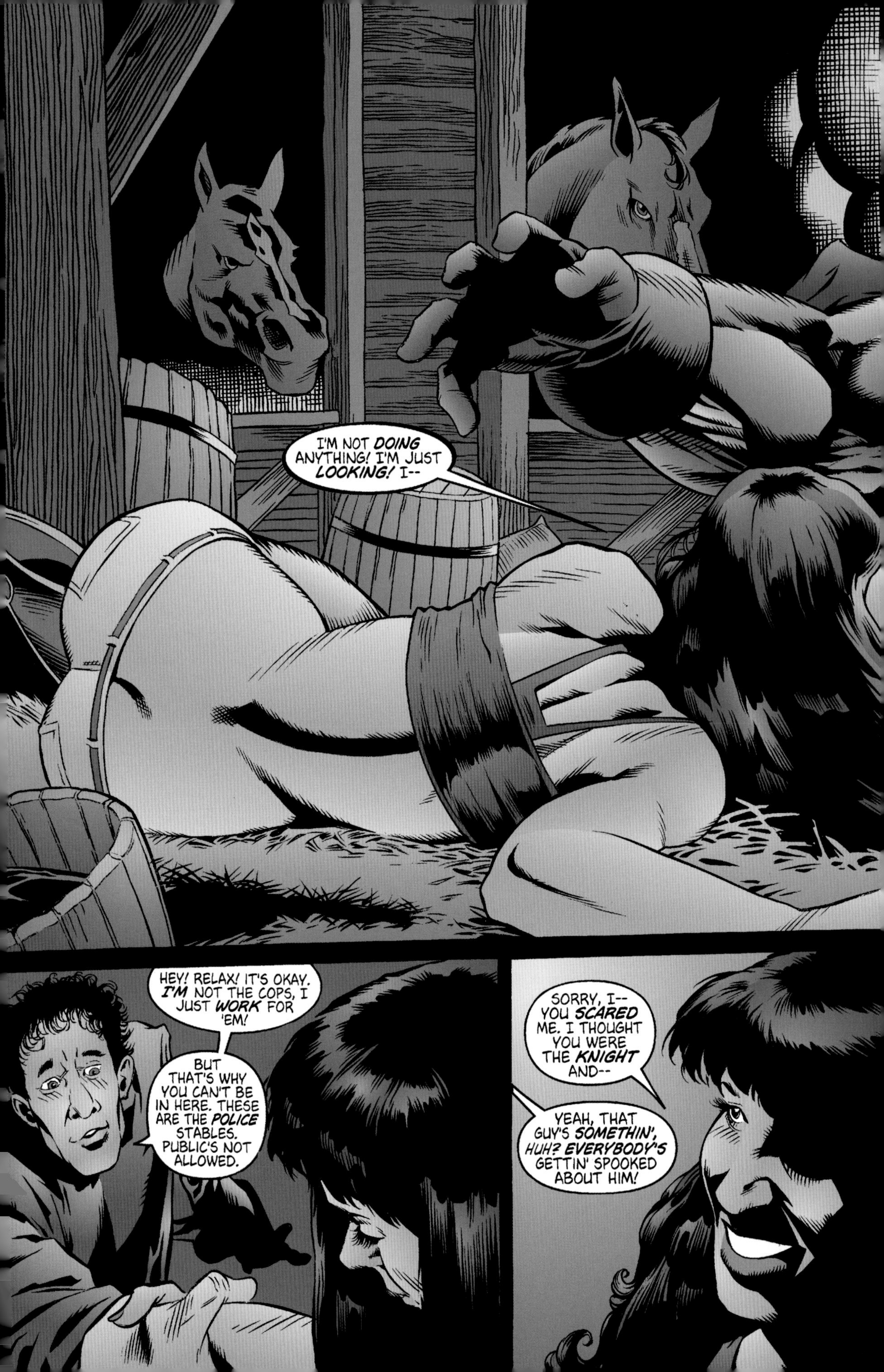
I'M NOT DOING ANYTHING! I'M JUST LOOKING! I--
HEY! RELAX! IT'S OKAY. I'M NOT THE COPS, I JUST WORK FOR 'EM!
BUT THAT'S WHY YOU CAN'T BE IN HERE. THESE ARE THE POLICE STABLES. PUBLIC'S NOT ALLOWED.
SORRY, I-- YOU SCARED ME. I THOUGHT YOU WERE THE KNIGHT AND--
YEAH, THAT GUY'S SOMETHIN', HUH? EVERYBODY'S GETTIN' SPOOKED ABOUT HIM!

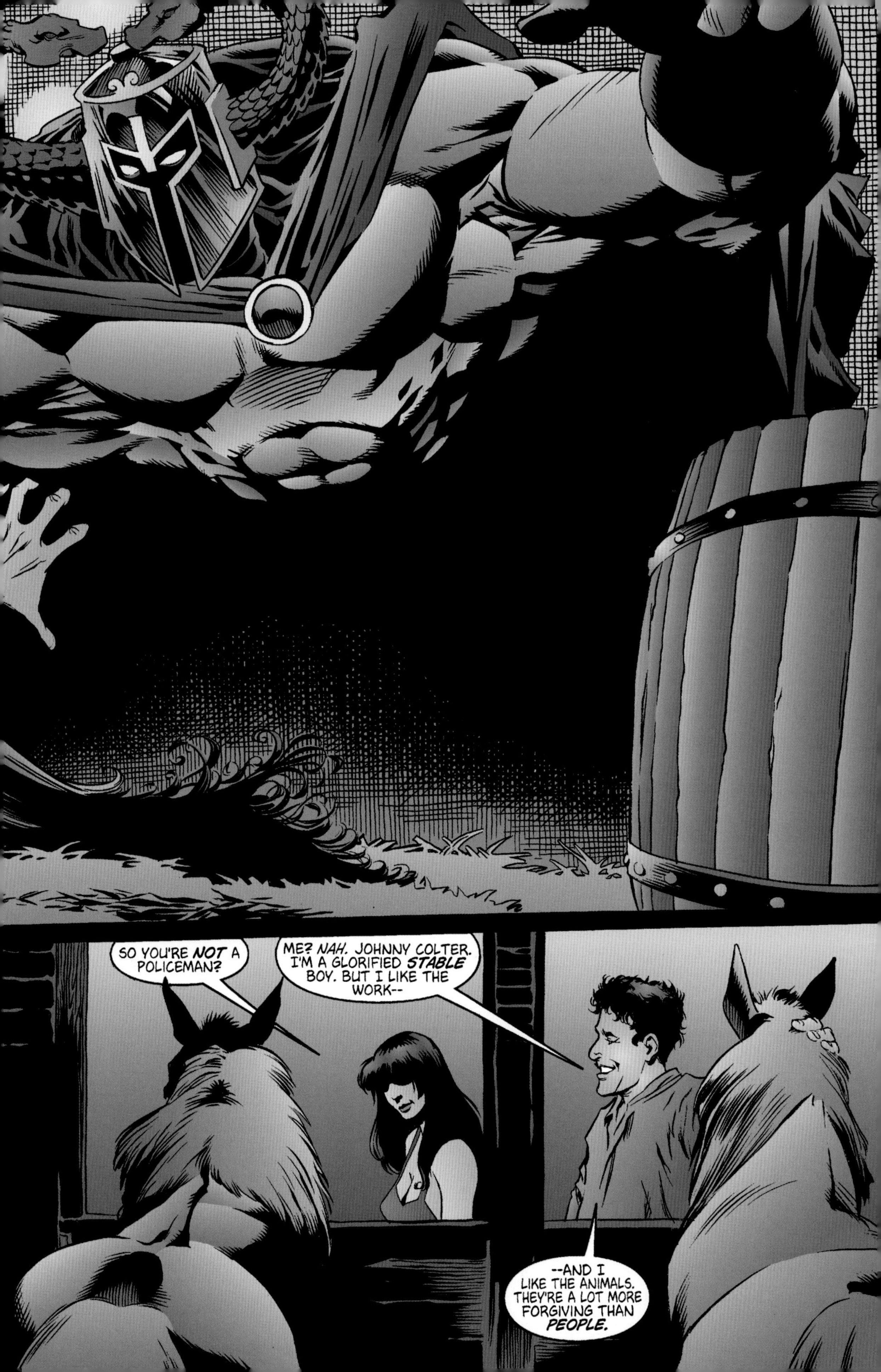
SO YOU'RE NOT A POLICEMAN?
ME? NAH. JOHNNY COLTER. I'M A GLORIFIED STABLE BOY. BUT I LIKE THE WORK--
--AND I LIKE THE ANIMALS. THEY'RE A LOT MORE FORGIVING THAN PEOPLE.

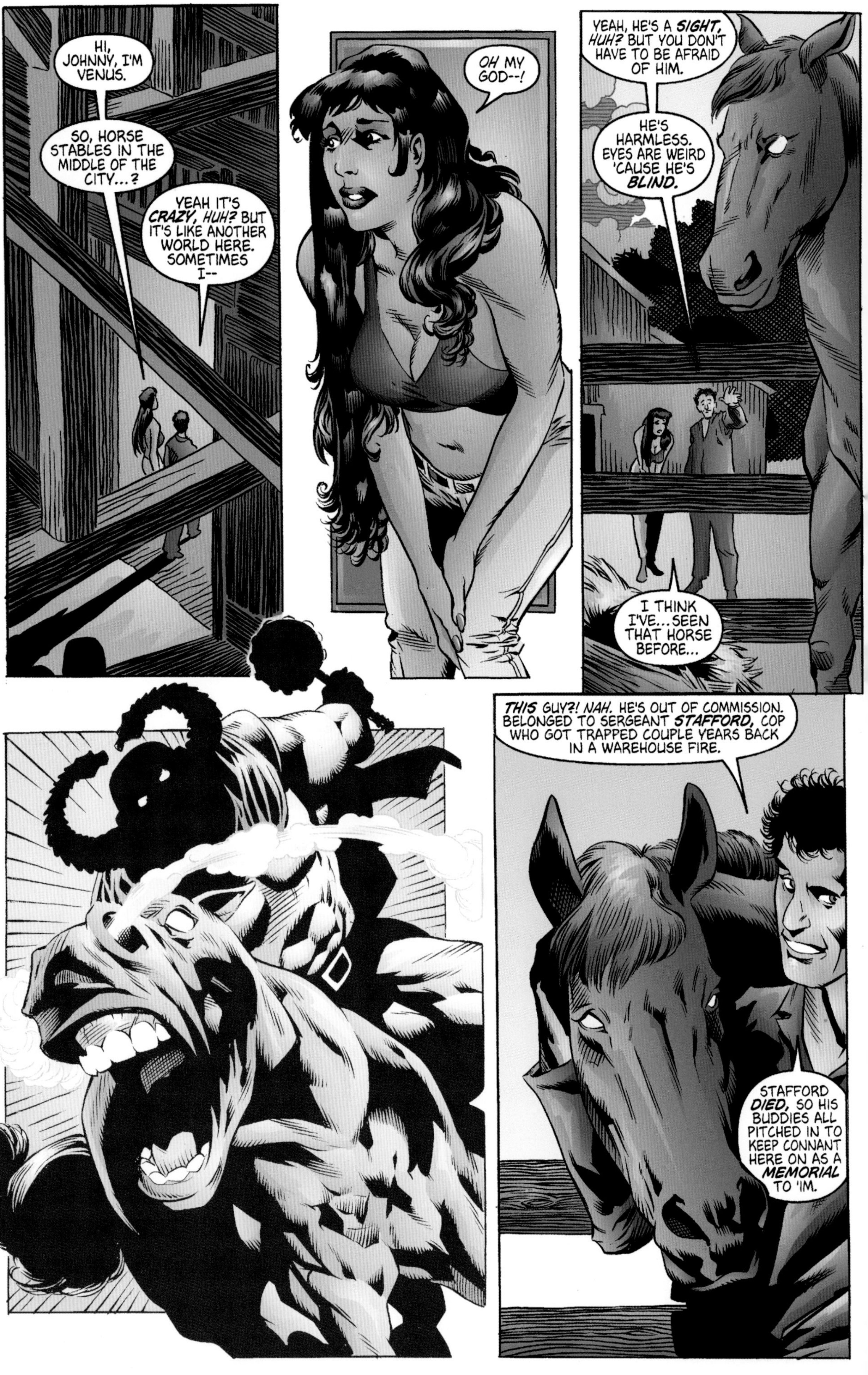
HI, JOHNNY, I'M VENUS.
SO, HORSE STABLES IN THE MIDDLE OF THE CITY...?
YEAH IT'S CRAZY, HUH? BUT IT'S LIKE ANOTHER WORLD HERE. SOMETIMES I--
OH MY GOD--!
YEAH, HE'S A SIGHT, HUH? BUT YOU DON'T HAVE TO BE AFRAID OF HIM.
HE'S HARMLESS. EYES ARE WEIRD 'CAUSE HE'S BLIND.
I THINK I'VE... SEEN THAT HORSE BEFORE...
THIS GUY?! NAH. HE'S OUT OF COMMISSION. BELONGED TO SERGEANT STAFFORD, COP WHO GOT TRAPPED COUPLE YEARS BACK IN A WAREHOUSE FIRE.
STAFFORD DIED, SO HIS BUDDIES ALL PITCHED IN TO KEEP CONNANT HERE ON AS A MEMORIAL TO 'IM.

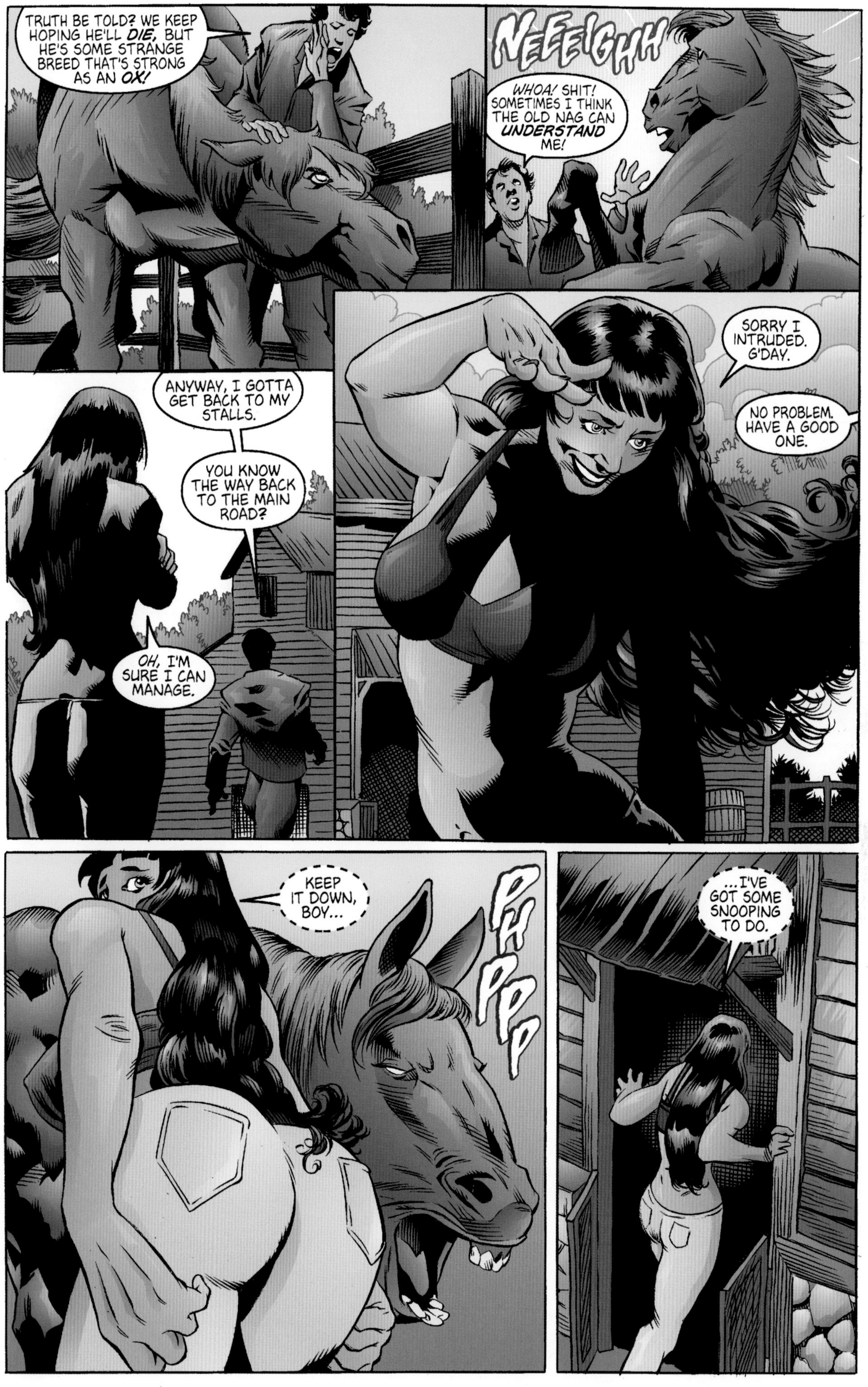
TRUTH BE TOLD? WE KEEP HOPING HE'LL DIE, BUT HE'S SOME STRANGE BREED THAT'S STRONG AS AN OX!
NEEEIGHH
WHOA! SHIT! SOMETIMES I THINK THE OLD NAG CAN UNDERSTAND ME!
ANYWAY, I GOTTA GET BACK TO MY STALLS.
YOU KNOW THE WAY BACK TO THE MAIN ROAD?
OH, I'M SURE I CAN MANAGE.
SORRY I INTRUDED. G'DAY.
NO PROBLEM. HAVE A GOOD ONE.
KEEP IT DOWN, BOY...
PHPPP
...I'VE GOT SOME SNOOPING TO DO.

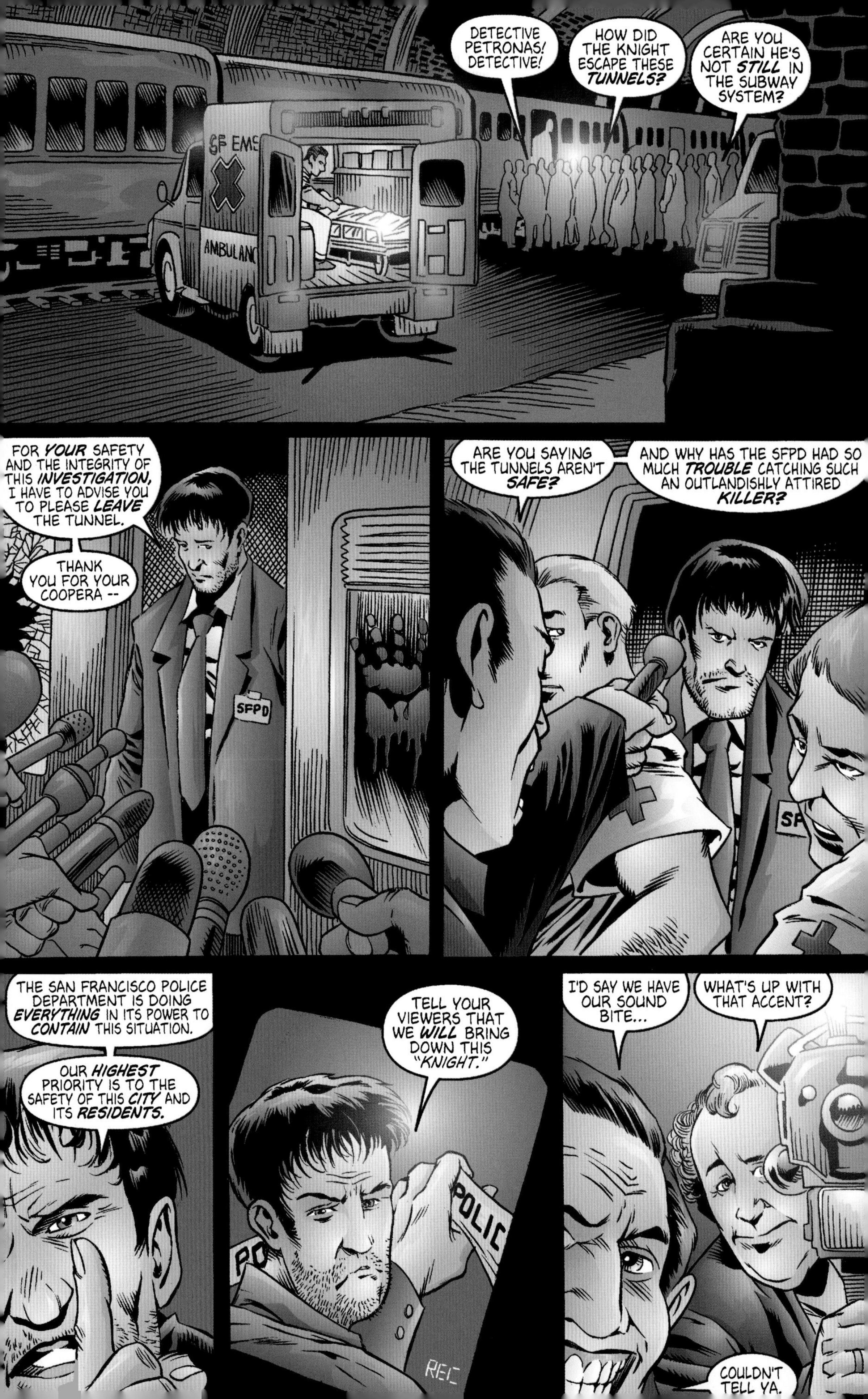

DETECTIVE PETRONAS! DETECTIVE!
HOW DID THE KNIGHT ESCAPE THESE TUNNELS?
ARE YOU CERTAIN HE'S NOT STILL IN THE SUBWAY SYSTEM?
SF EMS
AMBULANC
FOR YOUR SAFETY AND THE INTEGRITY OF THIS INVESTIGATION, I HAVE TO ADVISE YOU TO PLEASE LEAVE THE TUNNEL.
THANK YOU FOR YOUR COOPERA --
SFPD
ARE YOU SAYING THE TUNNELS AREN'T SAFE?
AND WHY HAS THE SFPD HAD SO MUCH TROUBLE CATCHING SUCH AN OUTLANDISHLY ATTIRED KILLER?
SF
THE SAN FRANCISCO POLICE DEPARTMENT IS DOING EVERYTHING IN ITS POWER TO CONTAIN THIS SITUATION.
OUR HIGHEST PRIORITY IS TO THE SAFETY OF THIS CITY AND ITS RESIDENTS.
TELL YOUR VIEWERS THAT WE WILL BRING DOWN THIS "KNIGHT."
POLIC
PO
REC
I'D SAY WE HAVE OUR SOUND BITE...
WHAT'S UP WITH THAT ACCENT?
COULDN'T TELL YA.

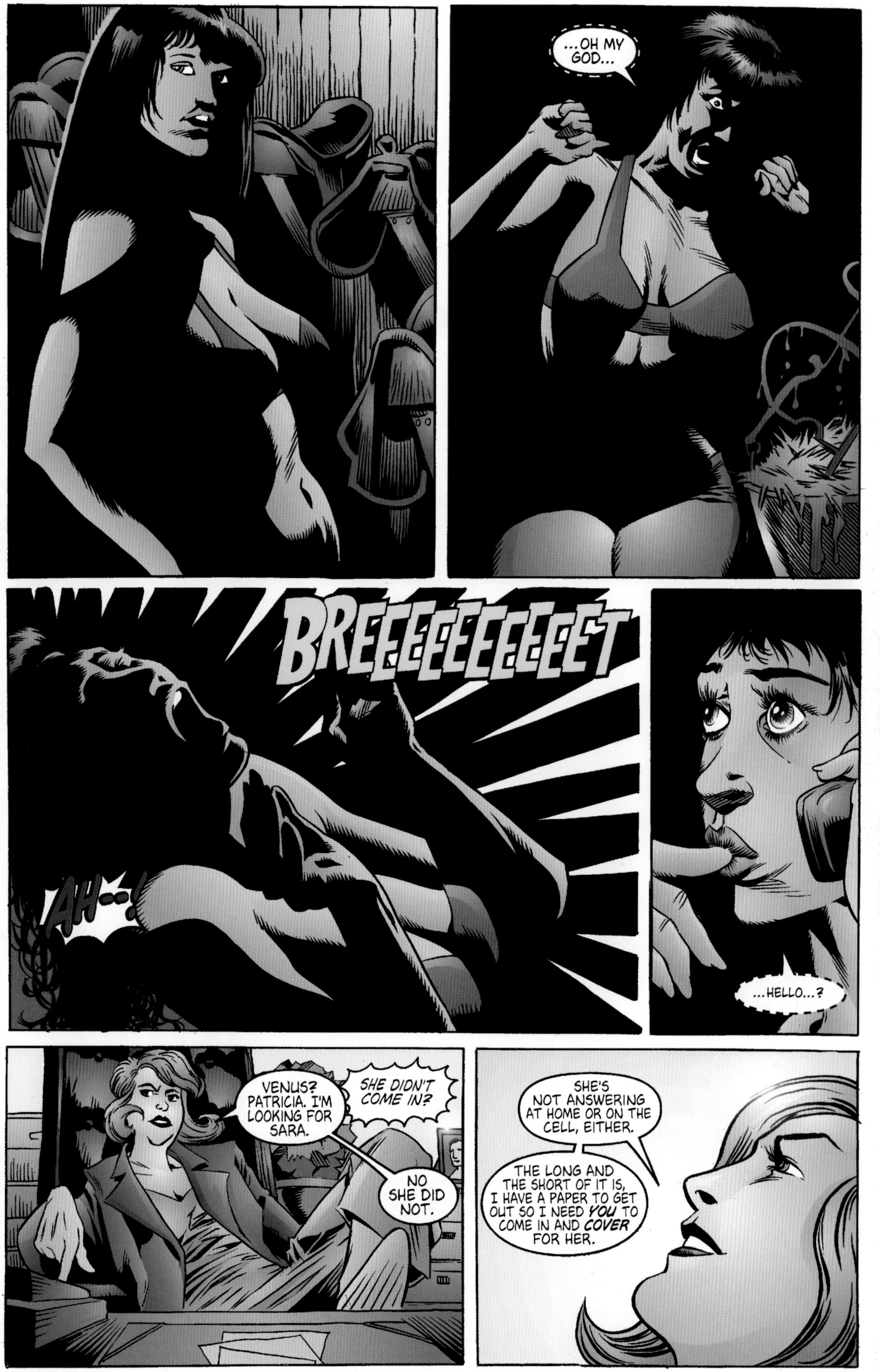
...OH MY GOD...
BREEEEEEEEEEET
AH--!
...HELLO...?
VENUS? PATRICIA. I'M LOOKING FOR SARA.
SHE DIDN'T COME IN?
NO SHE DID NOT.
SHE'S NOT ANSWERING AT HOME OR ON THE CELL, EITHER.
THE LONG AND THE SHORT OF IT IS, I HAVE A PAPER TO GET OUT SO I NEED YOU TO COME IN AND COVER FOR HER.

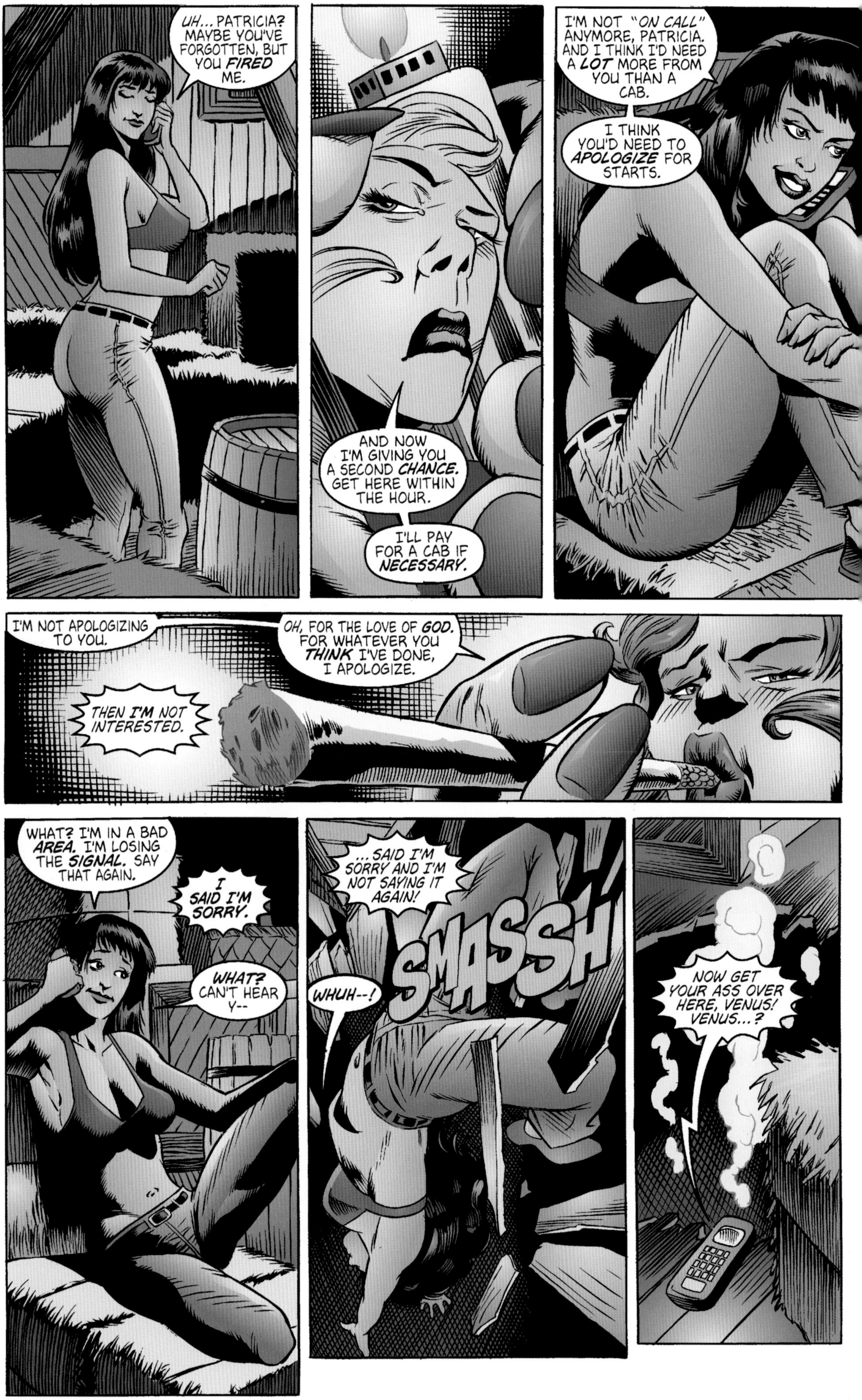
UH... PATRICIA? MAYBE YOU'VE FORGOTTEN, BUT YOU FIRED ME.
AND NOW I'M GIVING YOU A SECOND CHANCE. GET HERE WITHIN THE HOUR.
I'LL PAY FOR A CAB IF NECESSARY.
I'M NOT "ON CALL" ANYMORE, PATRICIA. AND I THINK I'D NEED A LOT MORE FROM YOU THAN A CAB.
I THINK YOU'D NEED TO APOLOGIZE FOR STARTS.
I'M NOT APOLOGIZING TO YOU.
OH, FOR THE LOVE OF GOD. FOR WHATEVER YOU THINK I'VE DONE, I APOLOGIZE.
THEN I'M NOT INTERESTED.
WHAT? I'M IN A BAD AREA. I'M LOSING THE SIGNAL. SAY THAT AGAIN.
I SAID I'M SORRY.
WHAT? CAN'T HEAR Y--
...SAID I'M SORRY AND I'M NOT SAYING IT AGAIN!
SMASSH
WHUH--!
NOW GET YOUR ASS OVER HERE, VENUS! VENUS...?

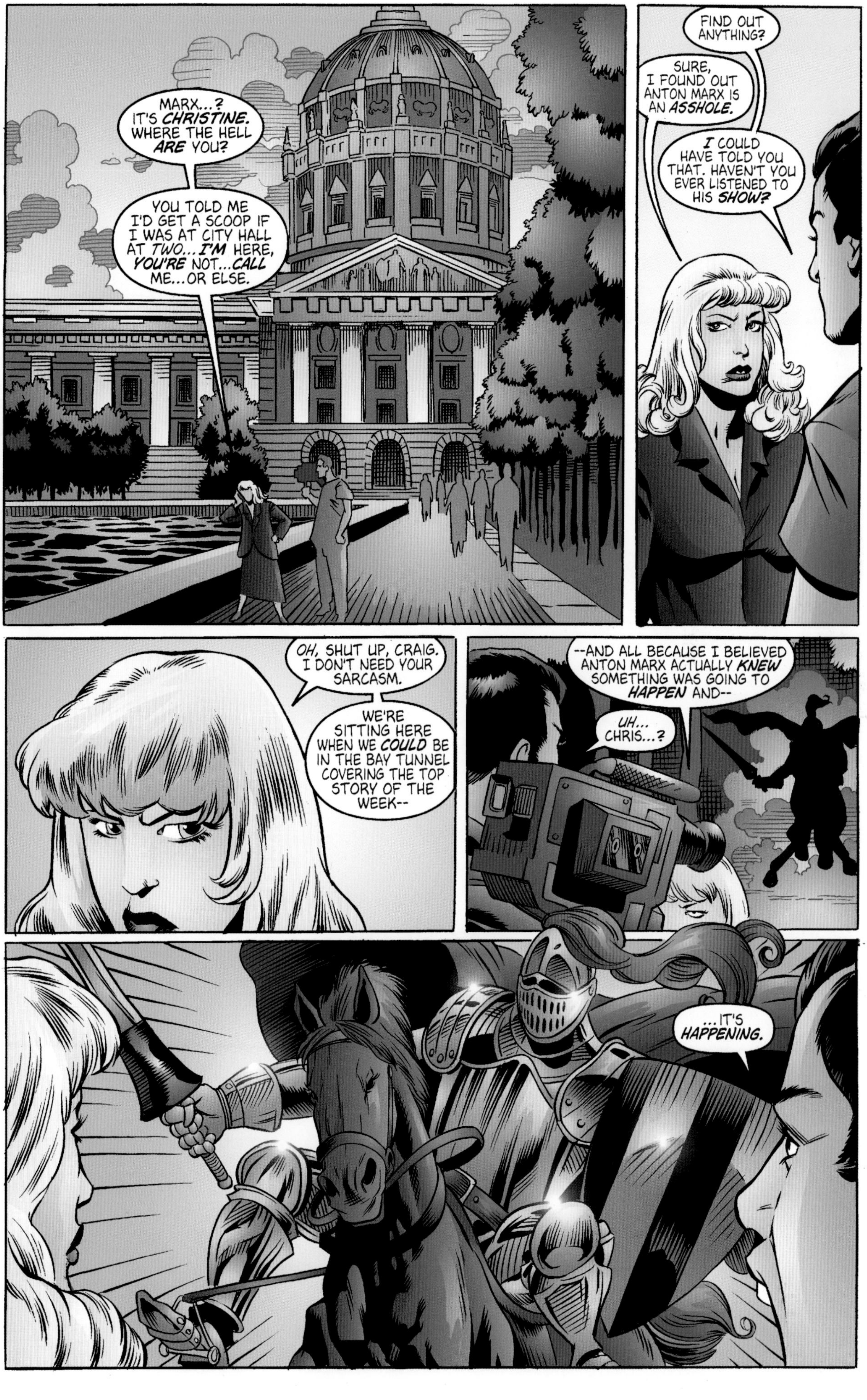
MARX...? IT'S CHRISTINE. WHERE THE HELL ARE YOU?
YOU TOLD ME I'D GET A SCOOP IF I WAS AT CITY HALL AT TWO... I'M HERE, YOU'RE NOT...CALL ME...OR ELSE.
FIND OUT ANYTHING?
SURE, I FOUND OUT ANTON MARX IS AN ASSHOLE.
I COULD HAVE TOLD YOU THAT. HAVEN'T YOU EVER LISTENED TO HIS SHOW?
OH, SHUT UP, CRAIG. I DON'T NEED YOUR SARCASM.
WE'RE SITTING HERE WHEN WE COULD BE IN THE BAY TUNNEL COVERING THE TOP STORY OF THE WEEK--
--AND ALL BECAUSE I BELIEVED ANTON MARX ACTUALLY KNEW SOMETHING WAS GOING TO HAPPEN AND--
UH... CHRIS...?
...IT'S HAPPENING.

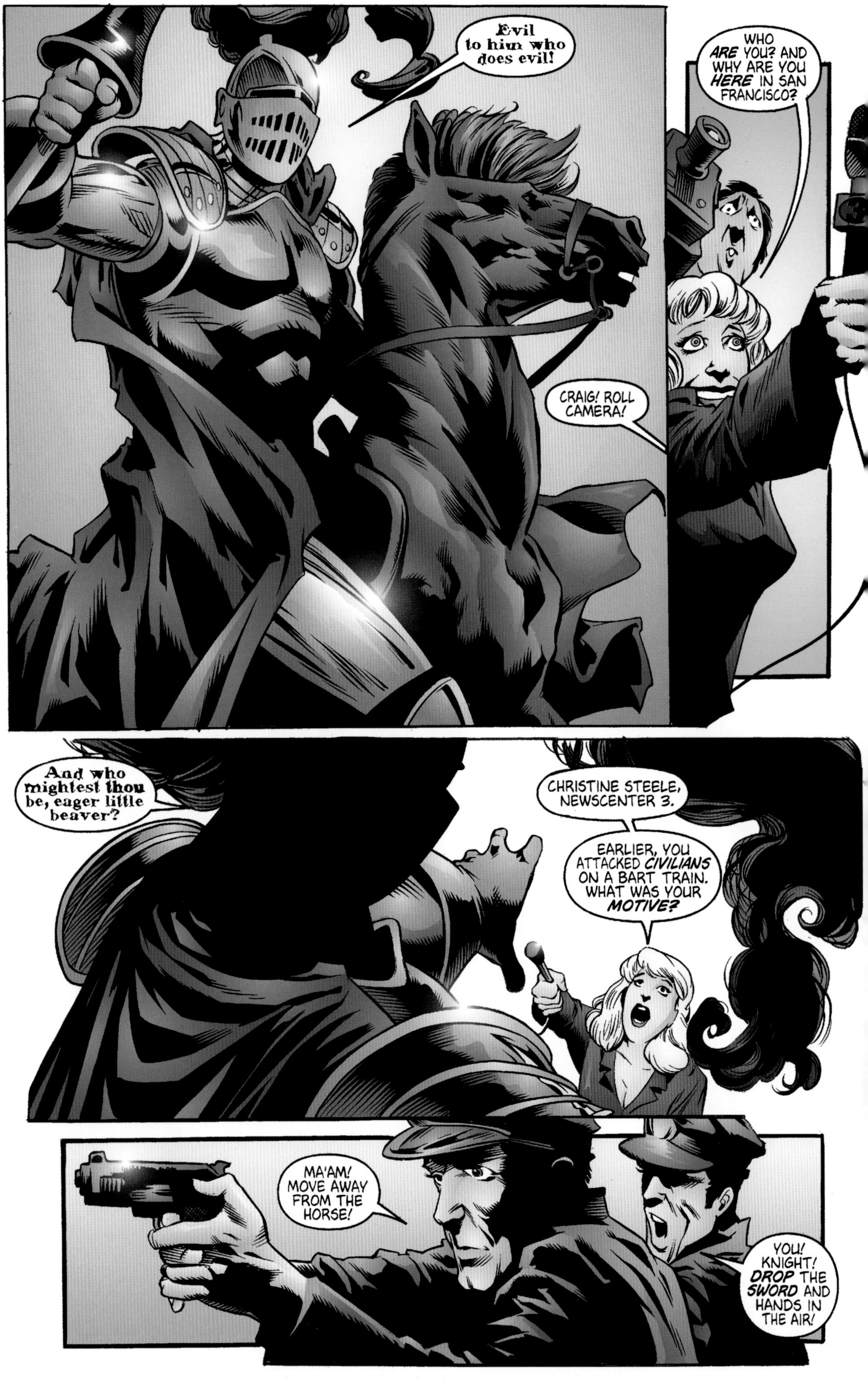
Evil to him who does evil!
WHO ARE YOU? AND WHY ARE YOU HERE IN SAN FRANCISCO?
CRAIG! ROLL CAMERA!
And who mightest thou be, eager little beaver?
CHRISTINE STEELE, NEWSCENTER 3.
EARLIER, YOU ATTACKED CIVILIANS ON A BART TRAIN. WHAT WAS YOUR MOTIVE?
MA'AM! MOVE AWAY FROM THE HORSE!
YOU! KNIGHT! DROP THE SWORD AND HANDS IN THE AIR!

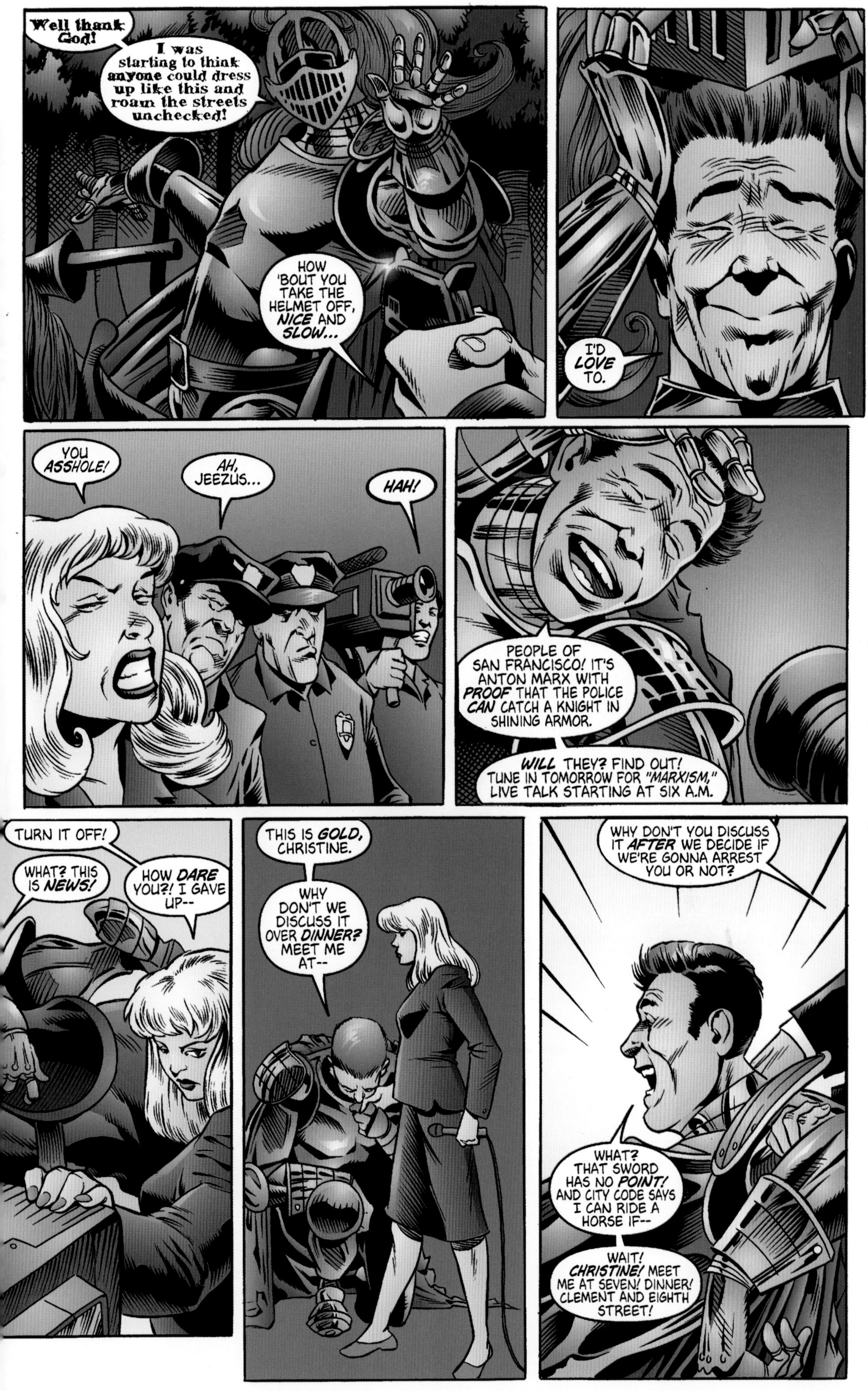
Well thank God!
I was starting to think anyone could dress up like this and roam the streets unchecked!
HOW 'BOUT YOU TAKE THE HELMET OFF, NICE AND SLOW...
I'D LOVE TO.
YOU ASSHOLE!
AH, JEEZUS...
HAH!
PEOPLE OF SAN FRANCISCO! IT'S ANTON MARX WITH PROOF THAT THE POLICE CAN CATCH A KNIGHT IN SHINING ARMOR.
WILL THEY? FIND OUT! TUNE IN TOMORROW FOR "MARXISM," LIVE TALK STARTING AT SIX A.M.
TURN IT OFF!
WHAT? THIS IS NEWS!
HOW DARE YOU?! I GAVE UP--
THIS IS GOLD, CHRISTINE.
WHY DON'T WE DISCUSS IT OVER DINNER? MEET ME AT--
WHY DON'T YOU DISCUSS IT AFTER WE DECIDE IF WE'RE GONNA ARREST YOU OR NOT?
WHAT? THAT SWORD HAS NO POINT! AND CITY CODE SAYS I CAN RIDE A HORSE IF--
WAIT! CHRISTINE! MEET ME AT SEVEN! DINNER! CLEMENT AND EIGHTH STREET!

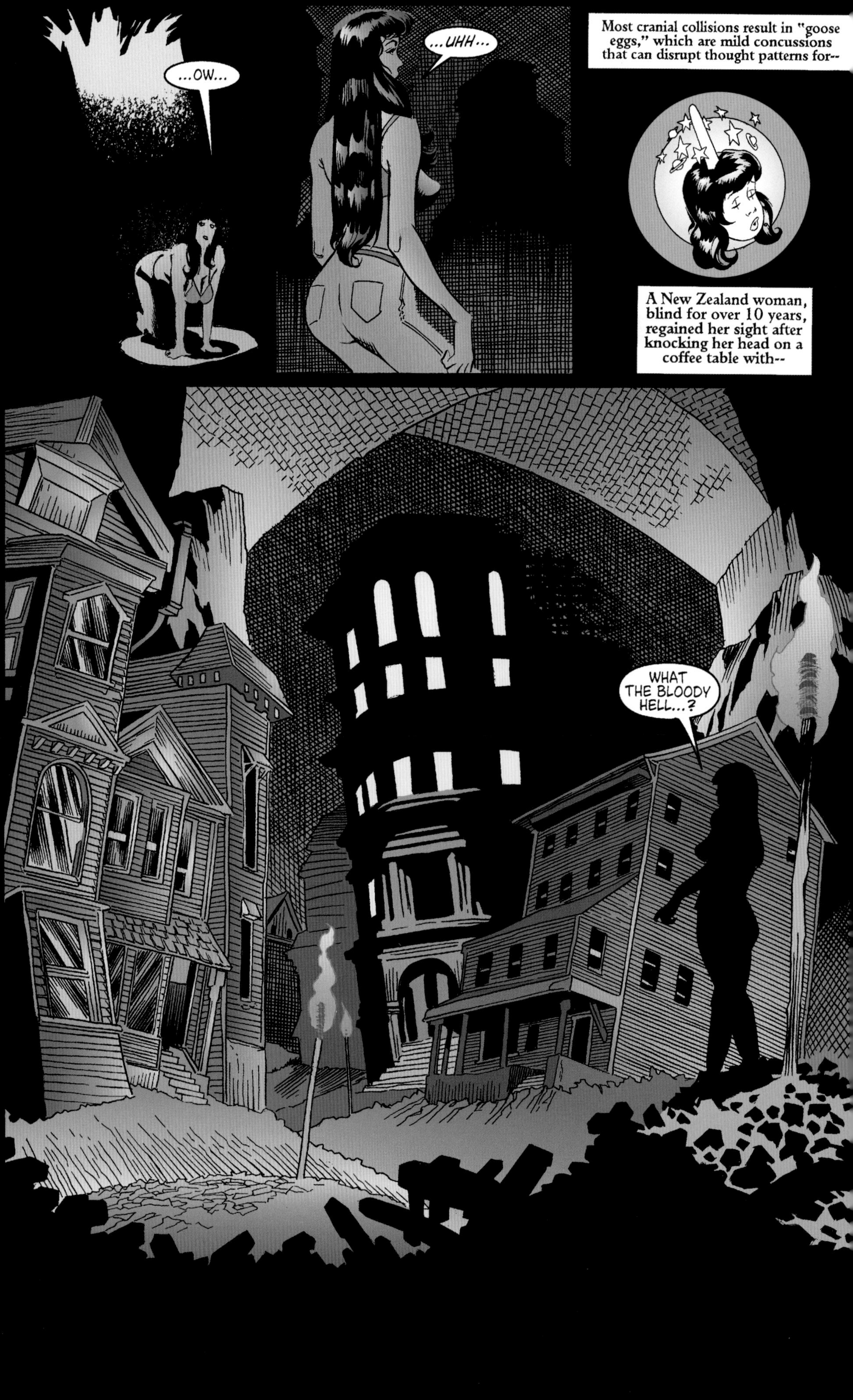
...OW...
...UHH...
Most cranial collisions result in "goose eggs," which are mild concussions that can disrupt thought patterns for--
A New Zealand woman, blind for over 10 years, regained her sight after knocking her head on a coffee table with--
WHAT THE BLOODY HELL...?

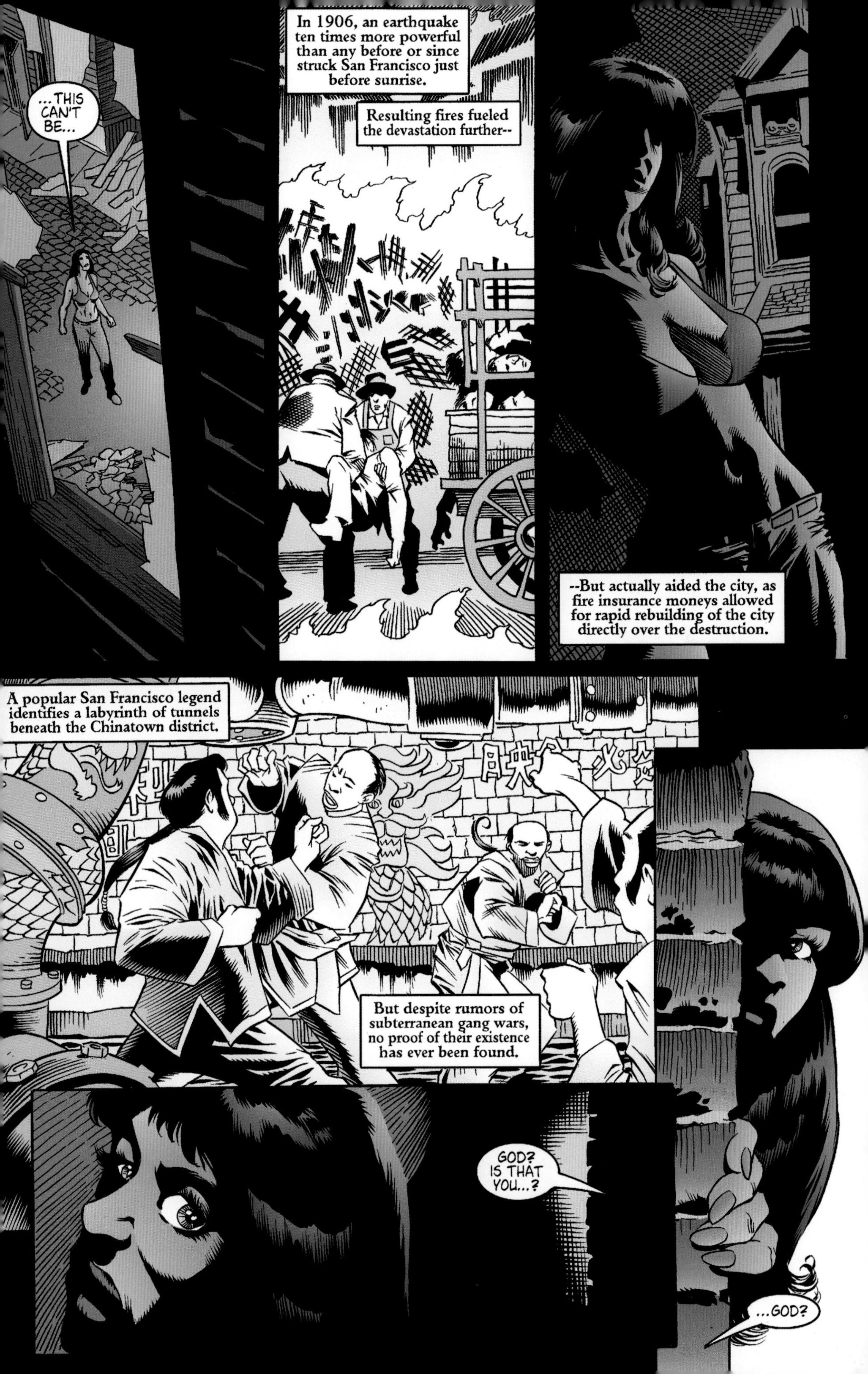

...THIS CAN'T BE...
In 1906, an earthquake ten times more powerful than any before or since struck San Francisco just before sunrise.
Resulting fires fueled the devastation further--
--But actually aided the city, as fire insurance moneys allowed for rapid rebuilding of the city directly over the destruction.
A popular San Francisco legend identifies a labyrinth of tunnels beneath the Chinatown district.
But despite rumors of subterranean gang wars, no proof of their existence has ever been found.
GOD? IS THAT YOU...?
...GOD?

NYET.

KEEP LOOKING.

BUT, BOCC. WE LOOK ALL MORNING AND SEE *NOTHING*.

I DON'T PAY FOR YOU TO *QUESTION* ME!

I PAY FOR YOU TO DO WHAT I *SAY*! WATCH POPE'S *HOUSE*!

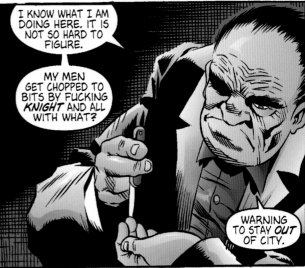

I KNOW WHAT I AM DOING HERE. IT IS NOT SO HARD TO FIGURE.

MY MEN GET CHOPPED TO BITS BY FUCKING *KNIGHT* AND ALL WITH WHAT?

WARNING TO STAY *OUT* OF CITY.

AND WHO WOULD NOT WANT VIRILE, YOUNG, RUSSIAN CRIME CZAR IN THE CITY? LIMP DICK, *OLD*, AMERICAN CRIME CZAR LIKE POPE.

SO WHERE TO BE *FINDING* THIS KNIGHT? THE COMPOUND OF *THE POPE*, IF --

BOCC, LOOK!

LOOK!

ZAYEBIS'... CALL THE OTHERS...

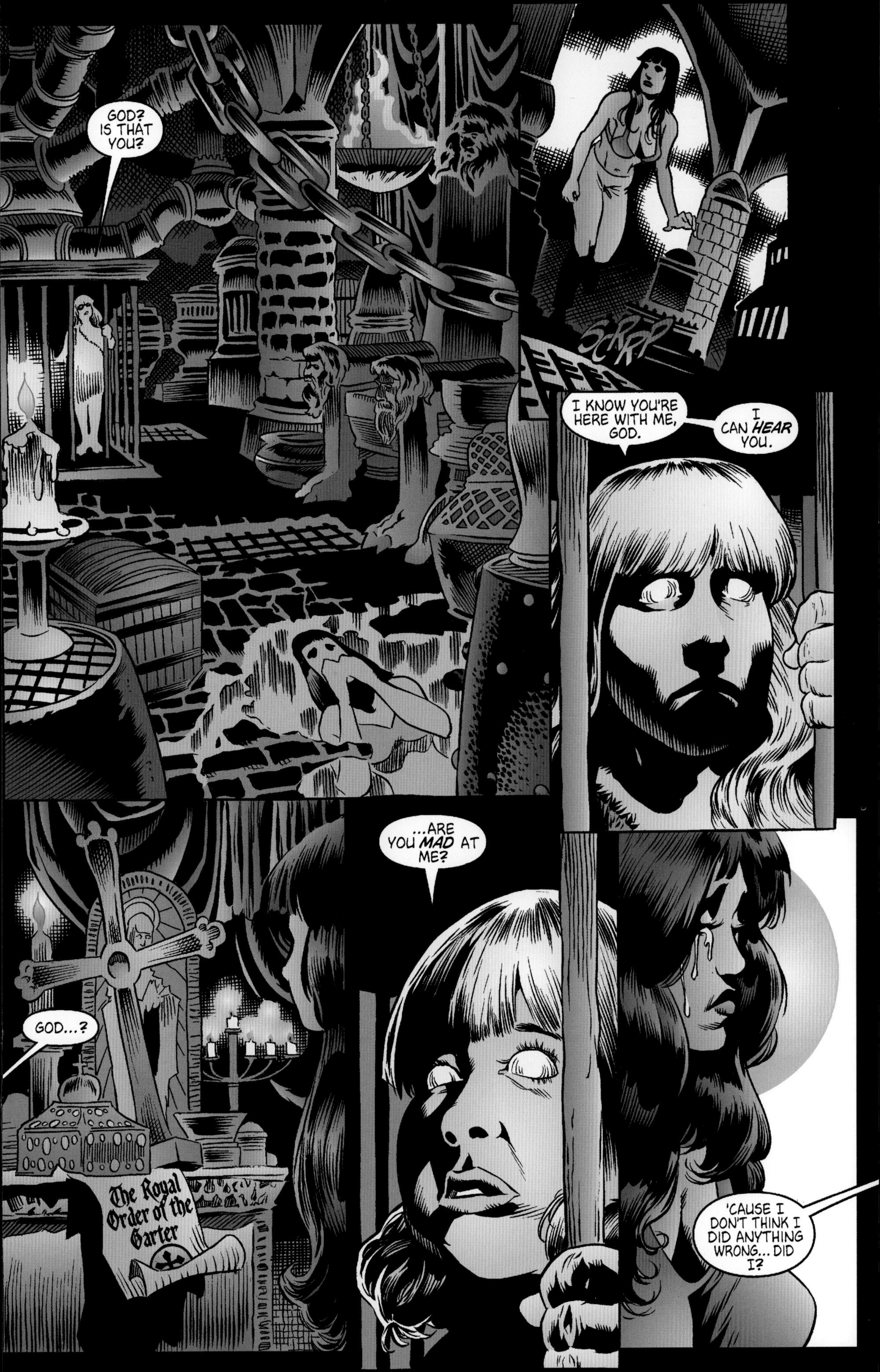
GOD? IS THAT YOU?
SCRPP
I KNOW YOU'RE HERE WITH ME, GOD.
I CAN HEAR YOU.
GOD...?
The Royal Order of the Garter
...ARE YOU MAD AT ME?
'CAUSE I DON'T THINK I DID ANYTHING WRONG... DID I?

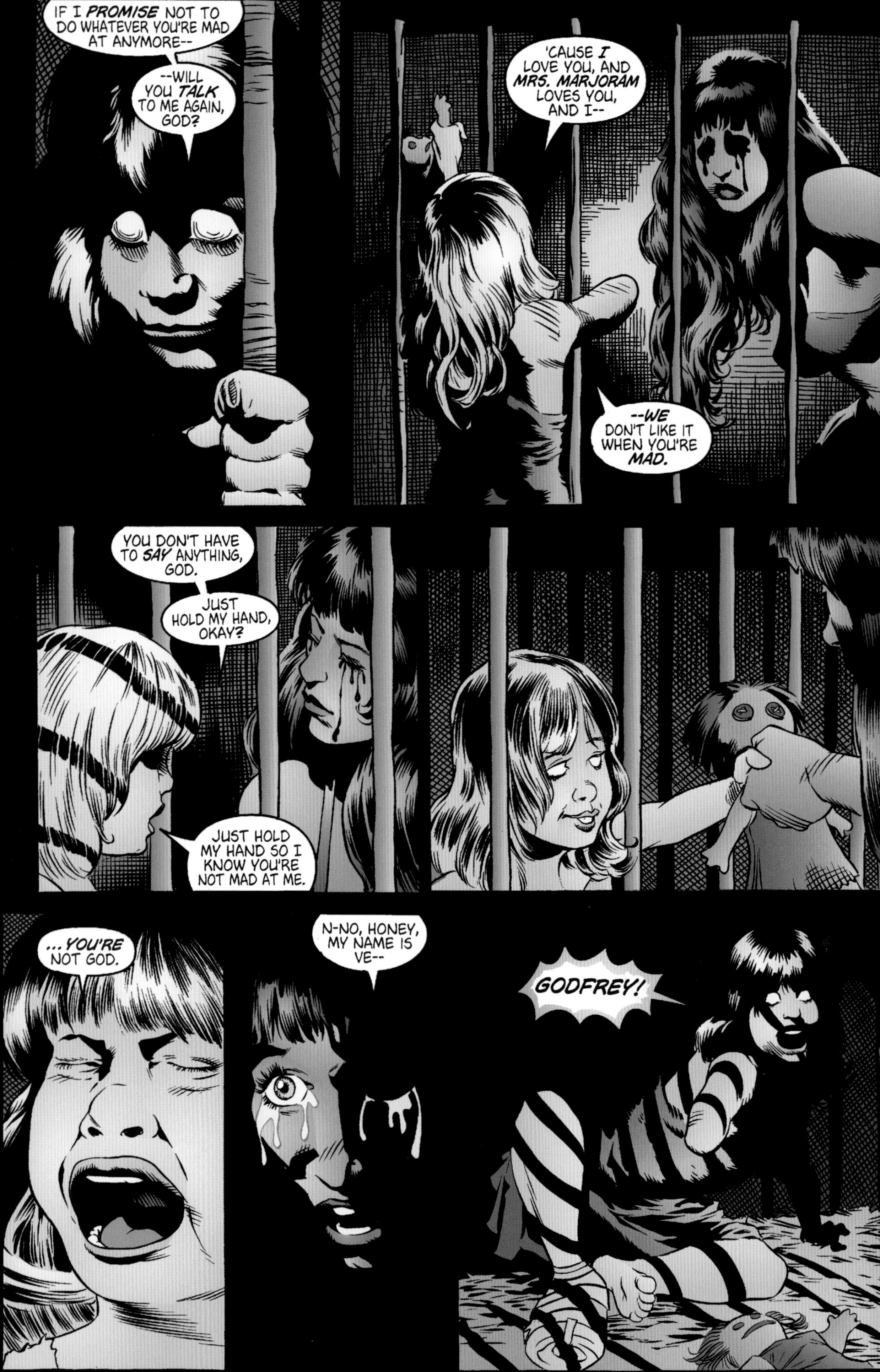

IF I PROMISE NOT TO DO WHATEVER YOU'RE MAD AT ANYMORE--
--WILL YOU TALK TO ME AGAIN, GOD?
'CAUSE I LOVE YOU, AND MRS. MARJORAM LOVES YOU, AND I--
--WE DON'T LIKE IT WHEN YOU'RE MAD.
YOU DON'T HAVE TO SAY ANYTHING, GOD.
JUST HOLD MY HAND, OKAY?
JUST HOLD MY HAND SO I KNOW YOU'RE NOT MAD AT ME.
...YOU'RE NOT GOD.
N-NO, HONEY, MY NAME IS VE--
GODFREY!

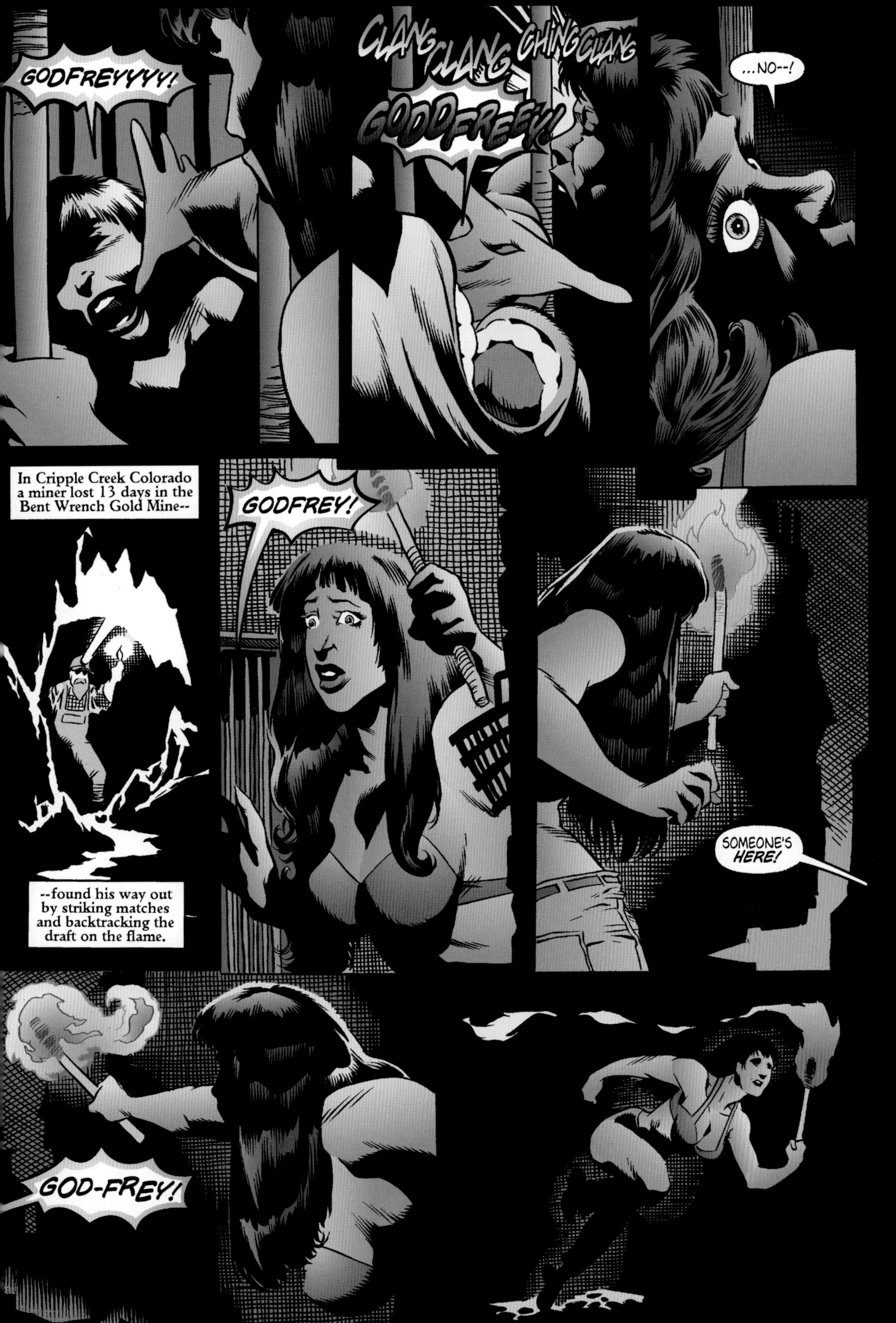
GODFREYYYY!
CLANG CLANG CHING CLANG
GODDFREEY!
...NO--!
In Cripple Creek Colorado a miner lost 13 days in the Bent Wrench Gold Mine--
--found his way out by striking matches and backtracking the draft on the flame.
GODFREY!
SOMEONE'S HERE!
GOD-FREY!

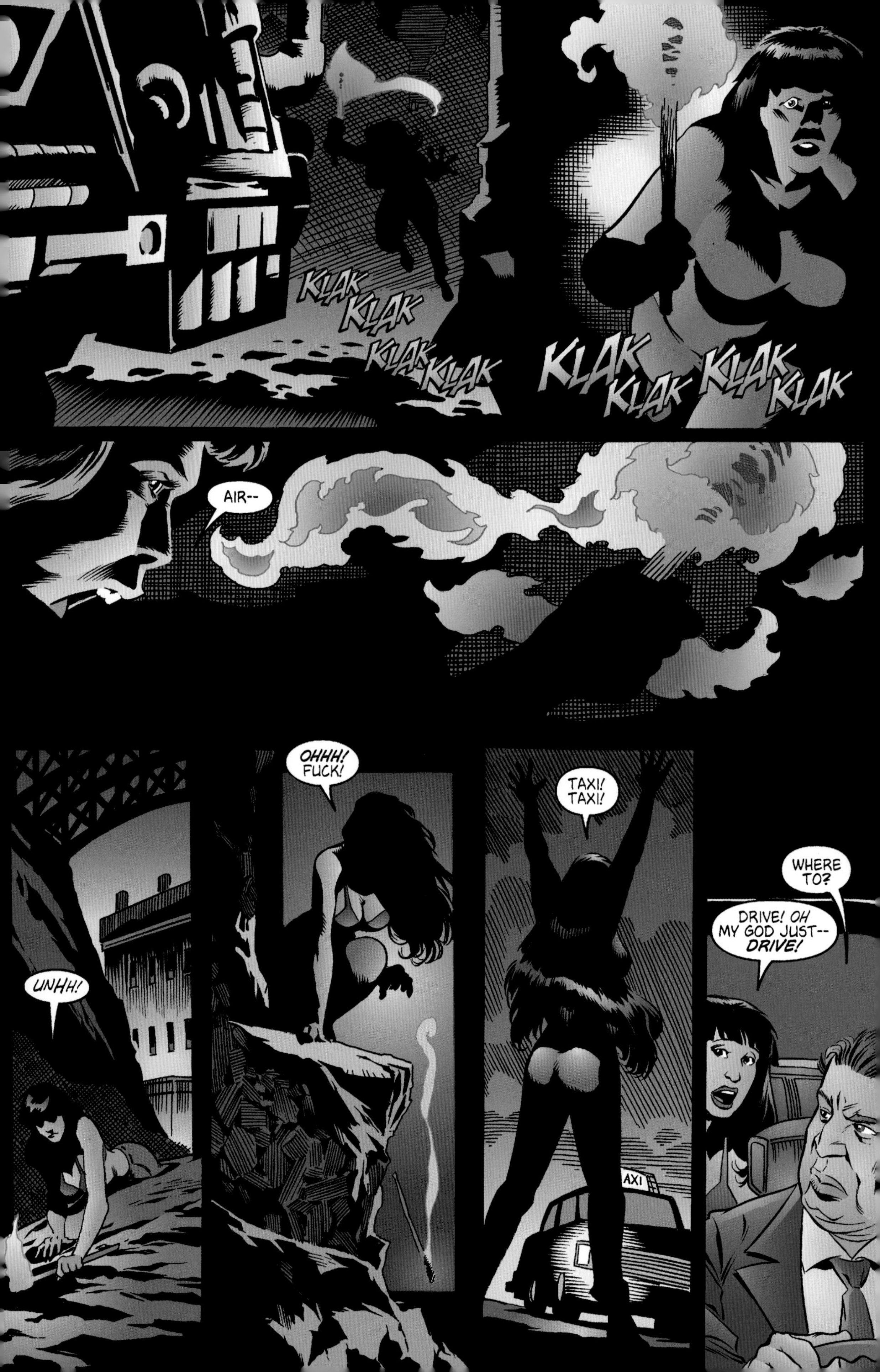
KLAK
KLAK
KLAK
KLAK
KLAK
KLAK
KLAK
KLAK
AIR--
UNHH!
OHHH! FUCK!
TAXI! TAXI!
AXI
WHERE TO?
DRIVE! OH MY GOD JUST-- *DRIVE!*

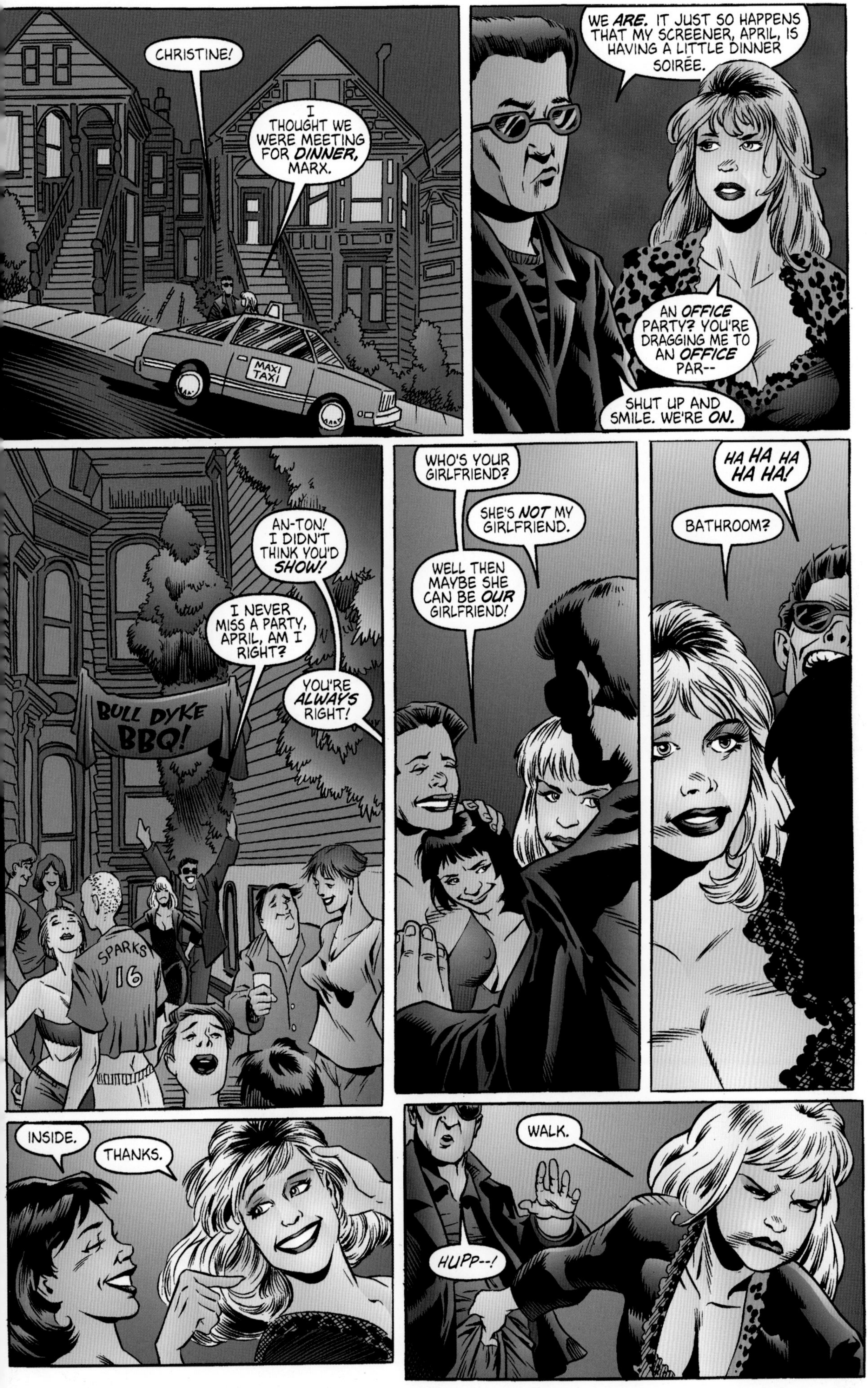
CHRISTINE!
I THOUGHT WE WERE MEETING FOR DINNER, MARX.
MAXI TAXI
WE ARE. IT JUST SO HAPPENS THAT MY SCREENER, APRIL, IS HAVING A LITTLE DINNER SOIRÉE.
AN OFFICE PARTY? YOU'RE DRAGGING ME TO AN OFFICE PAR--
SHUT UP AND SMILE. WE'RE ON.
AN-TON! I DIDN'T THINK YOU'D SHOW!
I NEVER MISS A PARTY, APRIL, AM I RIGHT?
YOU'RE ALWAYS RIGHT!
BULL DYKE BBQ!
SPARKS 16
WHO'S YOUR GIRLFRIEND?
SHE'S NOT MY GIRLFRIEND.
WELL THEN MAYBE SHE CAN BE OUR GIRLFRIEND!
HA HA HA HA HA!
BATHROOM?
INSIDE.
THANKS.
WALK.
HUPP--!

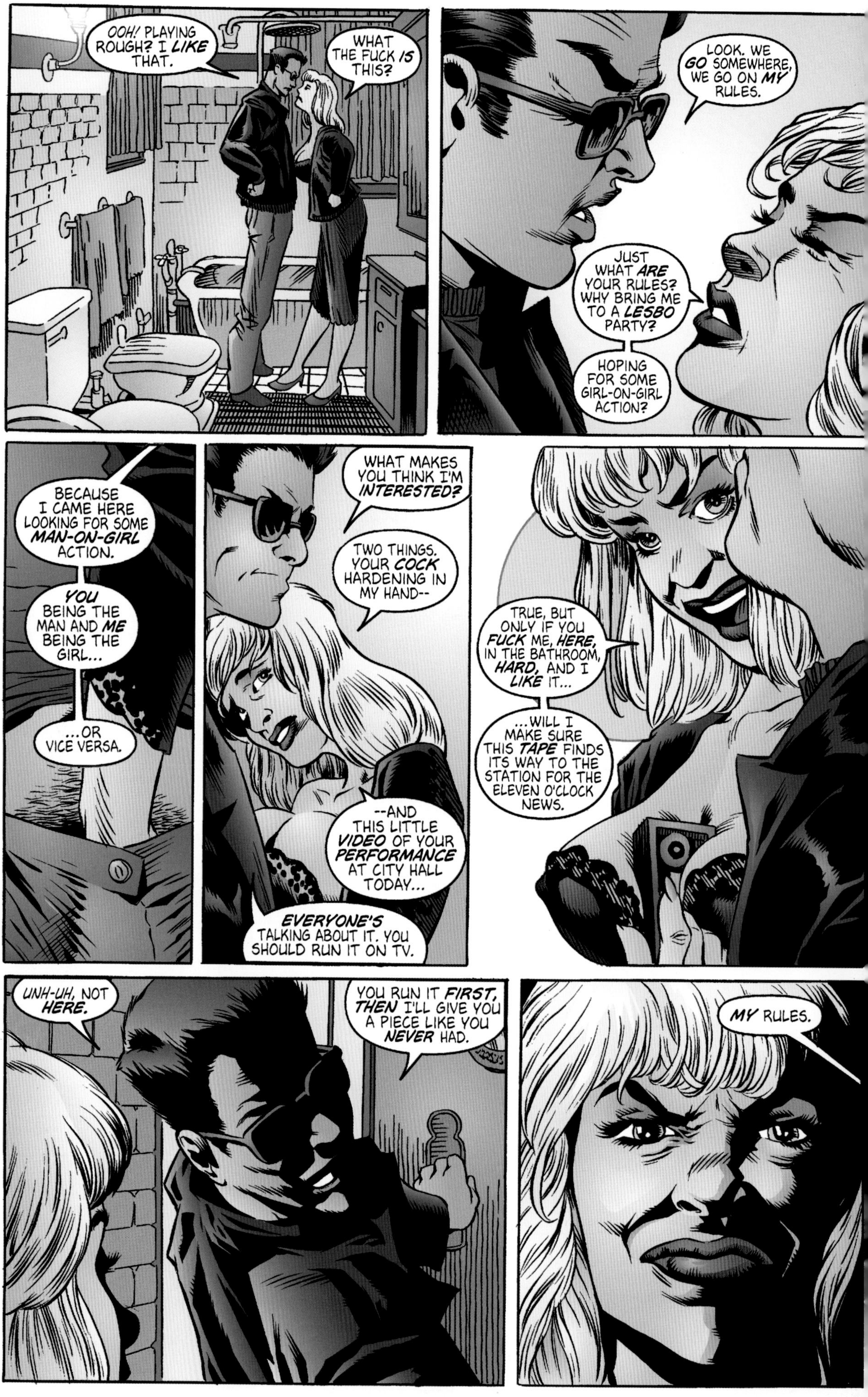
OOH! PLAYING ROUGH? I LIKE THAT.
WHAT THE FUCK IS THIS?
LOOK. WE GO SOMEWHERE, WE GO ON MY RULES.
JUST WHAT ARE YOUR RULES? WHY BRING ME TO A LESBO PARTY?
HOPING FOR SOME GIRL-ON-GIRL ACTION?
BECAUSE I CAME HERE LOOKING FOR SOME MAN-ON-GIRL ACTION.
YOU BEING THE MAN AND ME BEING THE GIRL...
...OR VICE VERSA.
WHAT MAKES YOU THINK I'M INTERESTED?
TWO THINGS. YOUR COCK HARDENING IN MY HAND--
--AND THIS LITTLE VIDEO OF YOUR PERFORMANCE AT CITY HALL TODAY...
EVERYONE'S TALKING ABOUT IT. YOU SHOULD RUN IT ON TV.
TRUE, BUT ONLY IF YOU FUCK ME, HERE, IN THE BATHROOM, HARD, AND I LIKE IT...
...WILL I MAKE SURE THIS TAPE FINDS ITS WAY TO THE STATION FOR THE ELEVEN O'CLOCK NEWS.
UNH-UH, NOT HERE.
YOU RUN IT FIRST, THEN I'LL GIVE YOU A PIECE LIKE YOU NEVER HAD.
MY RULES.

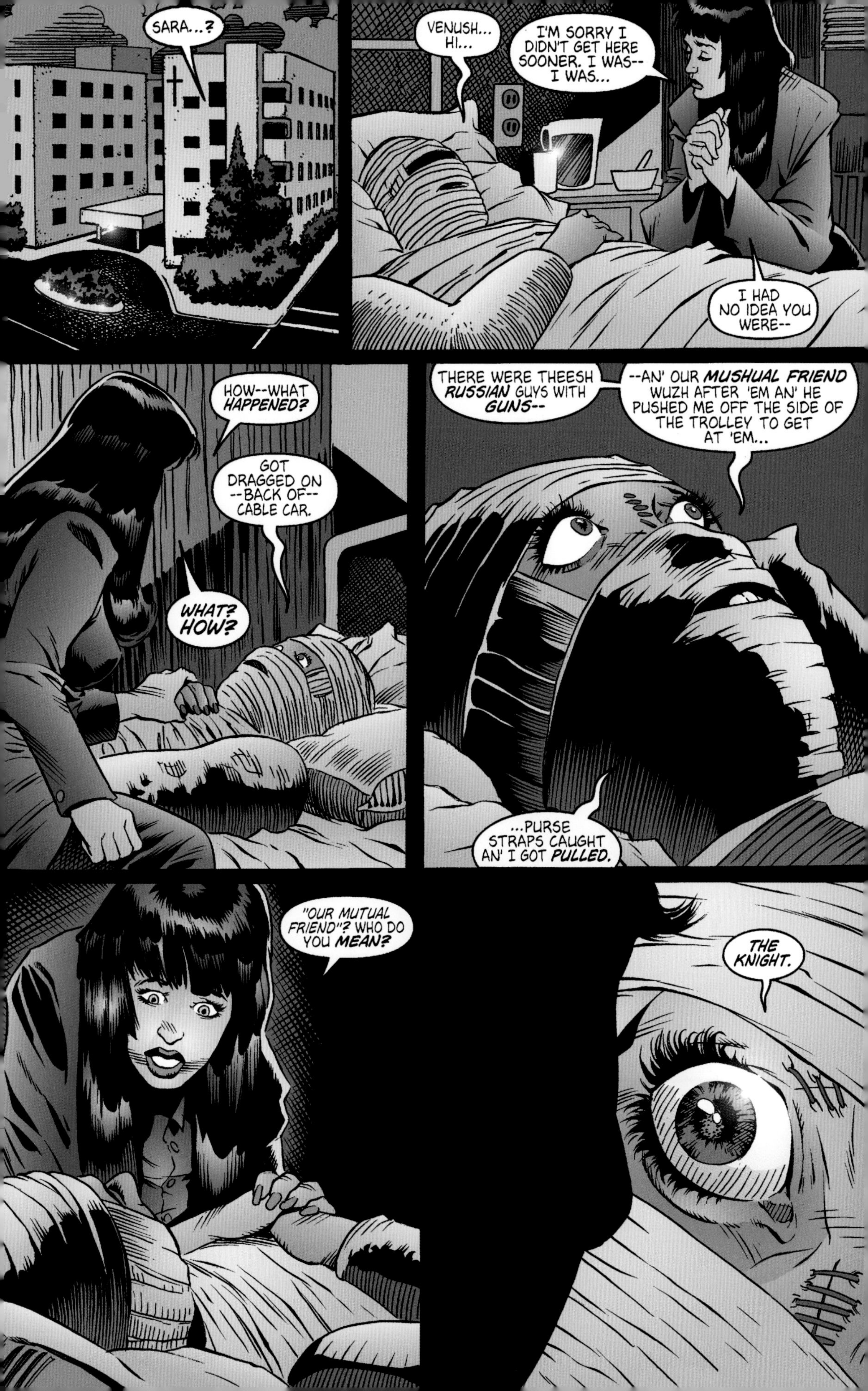
SARA...?
VENUSH... HI...
I'M SORRY I DIDN'T GET HERE SOONER. I WAS-- I WAS...
I HAD NO IDEA YOU WERE--
HOW--WHAT HAPPENED?
GOT DRAGGED ON --BACK OF-- CABLE CAR.
WHAT? HOW?
THERE WERE THEESH RUSSIAN GUYS WITH GUNS--
--AN' OUR MUSHUAL FRIEND WUZH AFTER 'EM AN' HE PUSHED ME OFF THE SIDE OF THE TROLLEY TO GET AT 'EM...
...PURSE STRAPS CAUGHT AN' I GOT PULLED.
"OUR MUTUAL FRIEND"? WHO DO YOU MEAN?
THE KNIGHT.

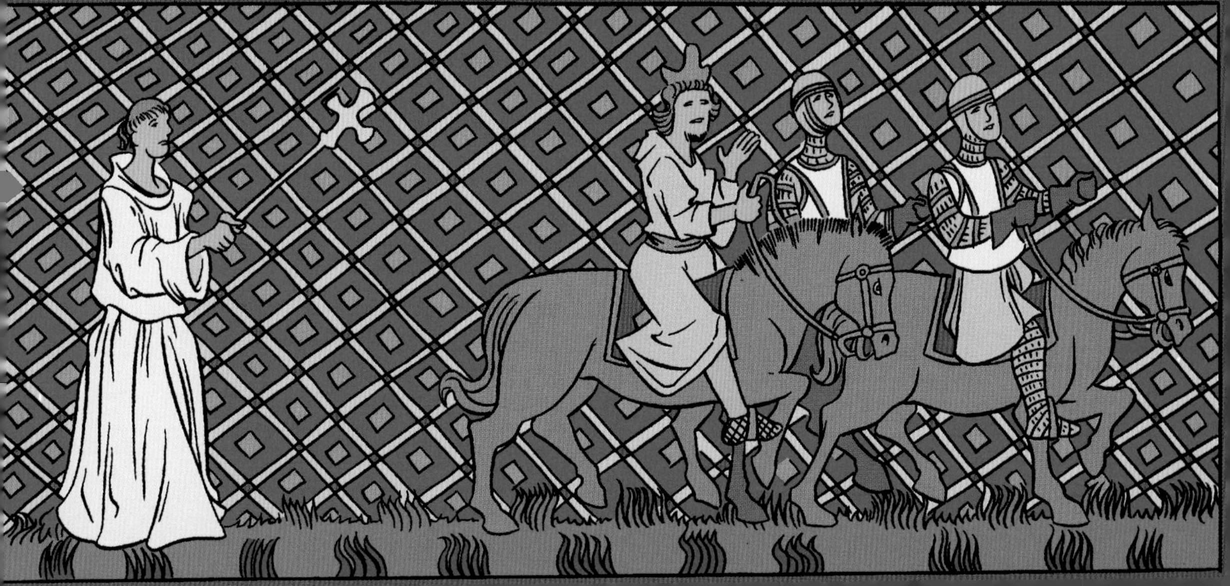

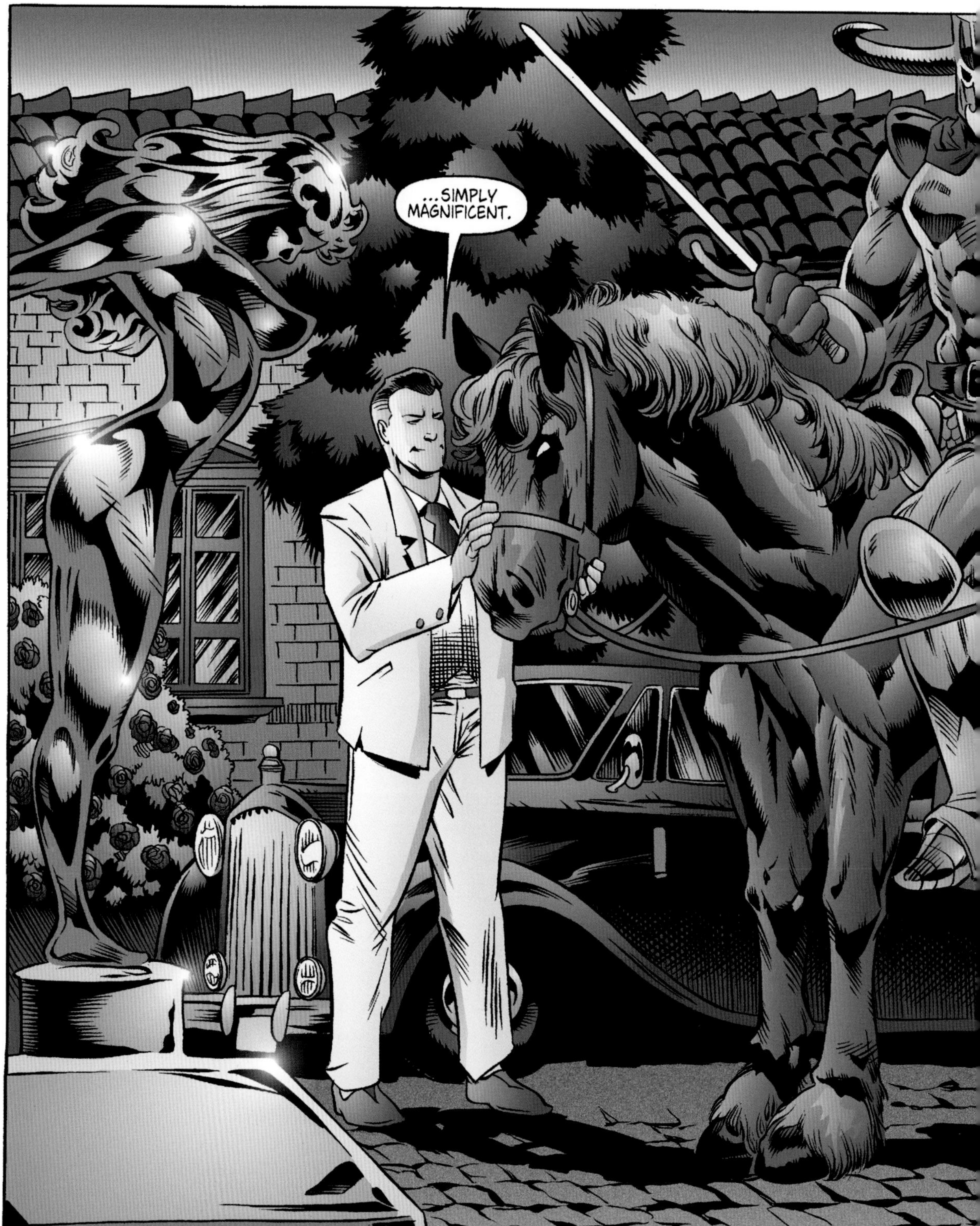
...SIMPLY MAGNIFICENT.

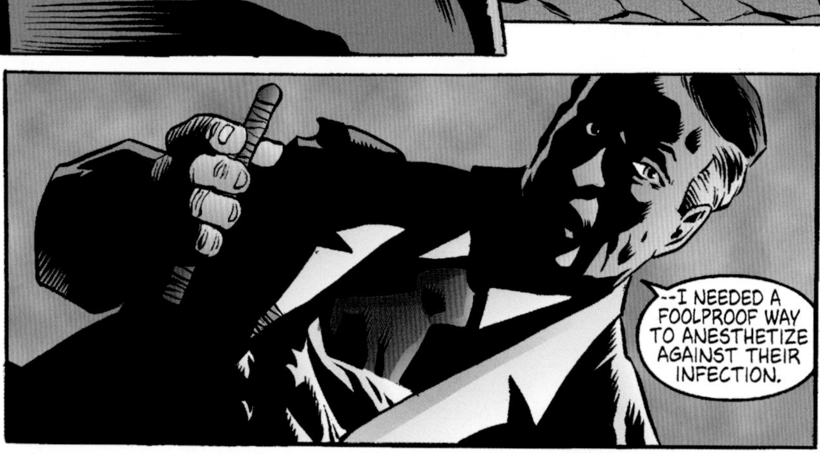
--I NEEDED A FOOLPROOF WAY TO ANESTHETIZE AGAINST THEIR INFECTION.

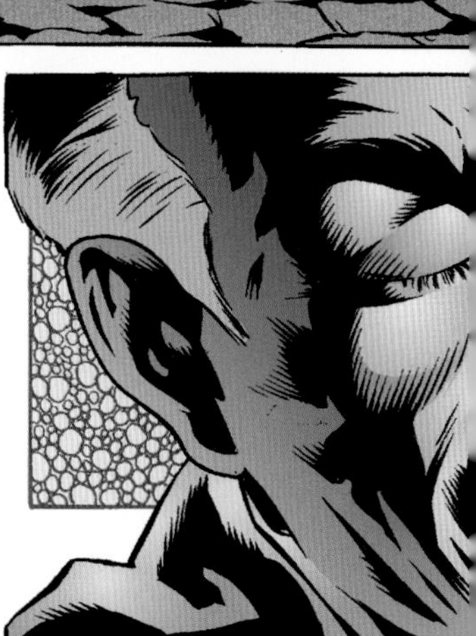

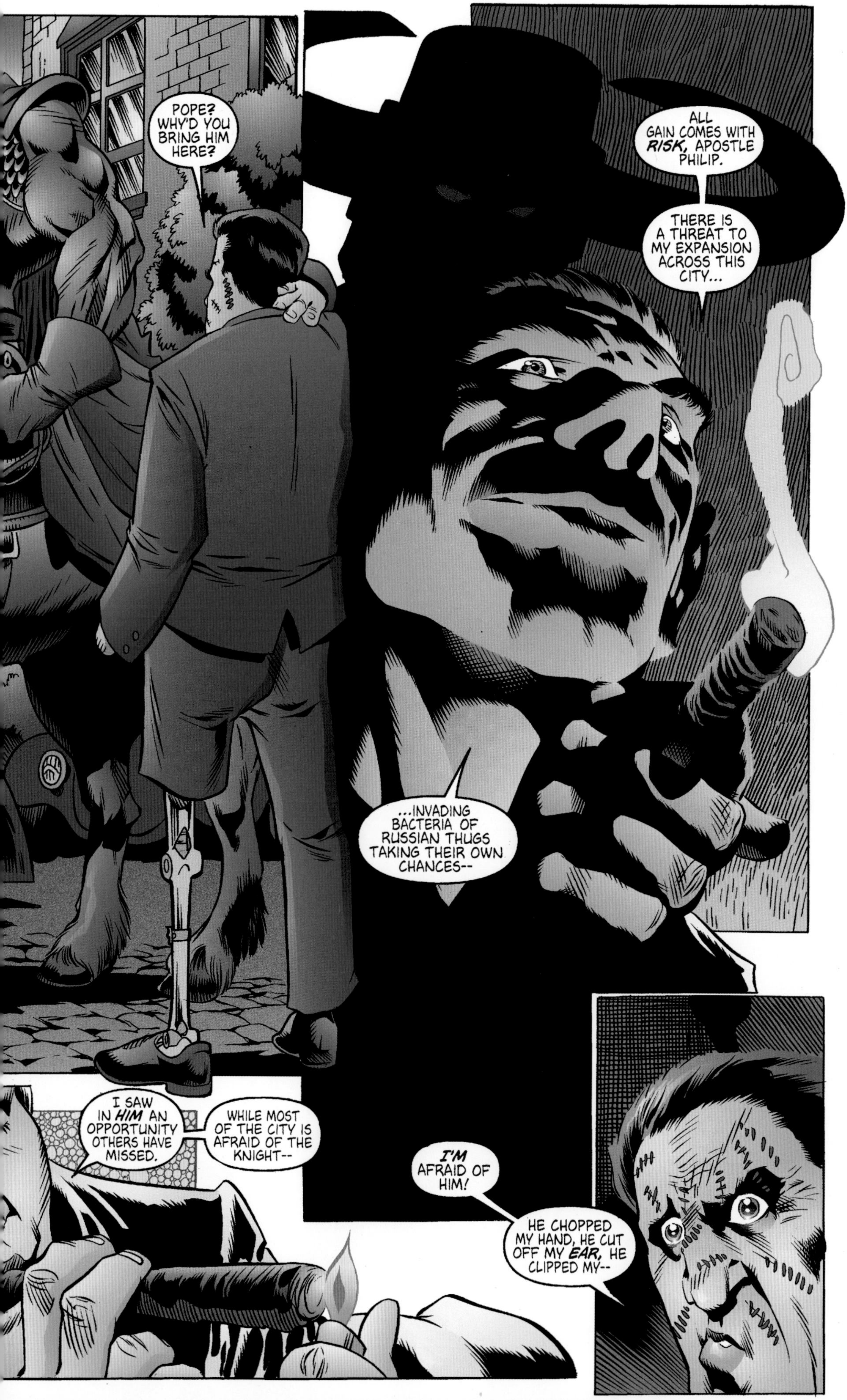
POPE? WHY'D YOU BRING HIM HERE?
ALL GAIN COMES WITH RISK, APOSTLE PHILIP.
THERE IS A THREAT TO MY EXPANSION ACROSS THIS CITY...
...INVADING BACTERIA OF RUSSIAN THUGS TAKING THEIR OWN CHANCES--
I SAW IN HIM AN OPPORTUNITY OTHERS HAVE MISSED.
WHILE MOST OF THE CITY IS AFRAID OF THE KNIGHT--
I'M AFRAID OF HIM!
HE CHOPPED MY HAND, HE CUT OFF MY EAR, HE CLIPPED MY--

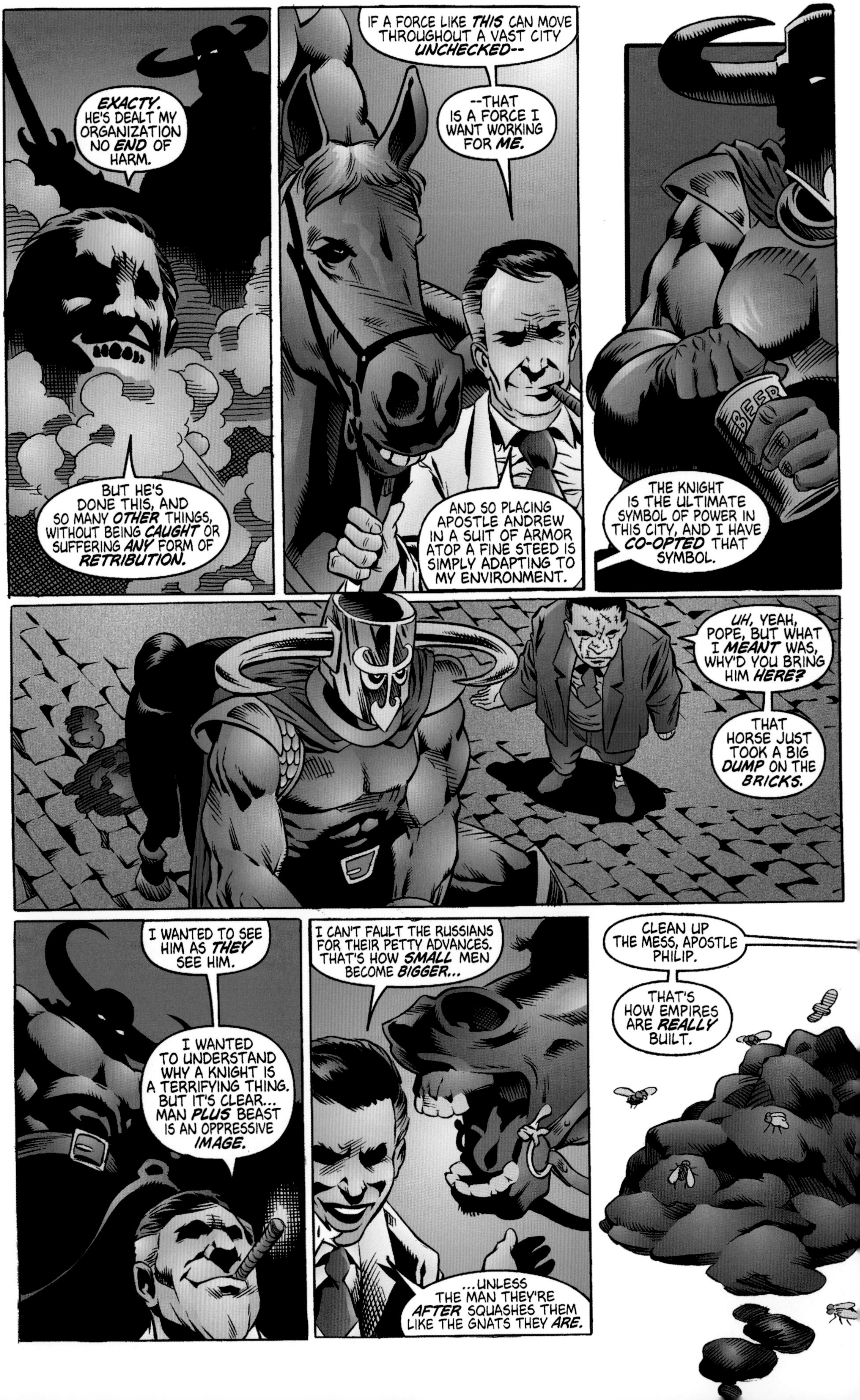
EXACTY. HE'S DEALT MY ORGANIZATION NO END OF HARM.
BUT HE'S DONE THIS, AND SO MANY OTHER THINGS, WITHOUT BEING CAUGHT OR SUFFERING ANY FORM OF RETRIBUTION.
IF A FORCE LIKE THIS CAN MOVE THROUGHOUT A VAST CITY UNCHECKED--
--THAT IS A FORCE I WANT WORKING FOR ME.
AND SO PLACING APOSTLE ANDREW IN A SUIT OF ARMOR ATOP A FINE STEED IS SIMPLY ADAPTING TO MY ENVIRONMENT.
BEER
THE KNIGHT IS THE ULTIMATE SYMBOL OF POWER IN THIS CITY, AND I HAVE CO-OPTED THAT SYMBOL.
UH, YEAH, POPE, BUT WHAT I MEANT WAS, WHY'D YOU BRING HIM HERE?
THAT HORSE JUST TOOK A BIG DUMP ON THE BRICKS.
I WANTED TO SEE HIM AS THEY SEE HIM.
I WANTED TO UNDERSTAND WHY A KNIGHT IS A TERRIFYING THING. BUT IT'S CLEAR... MAN PLUS BEAST IS AN OPPRESSIVE IMAGE.
I CAN'T FAULT THE RUSSIANS FOR THEIR PETTY ADVANCES. THAT'S HOW SMALL MEN BECOME BIGGER...
...UNLESS THE MAN THEY'RE AFTER SQUASHES THEM LIKE THE GNATS THEY ARE.
CLEAN UP THE MESS, APOSTLE PHILIP.
THAT'S HOW EMPIRES ARE REALLY BUILT.

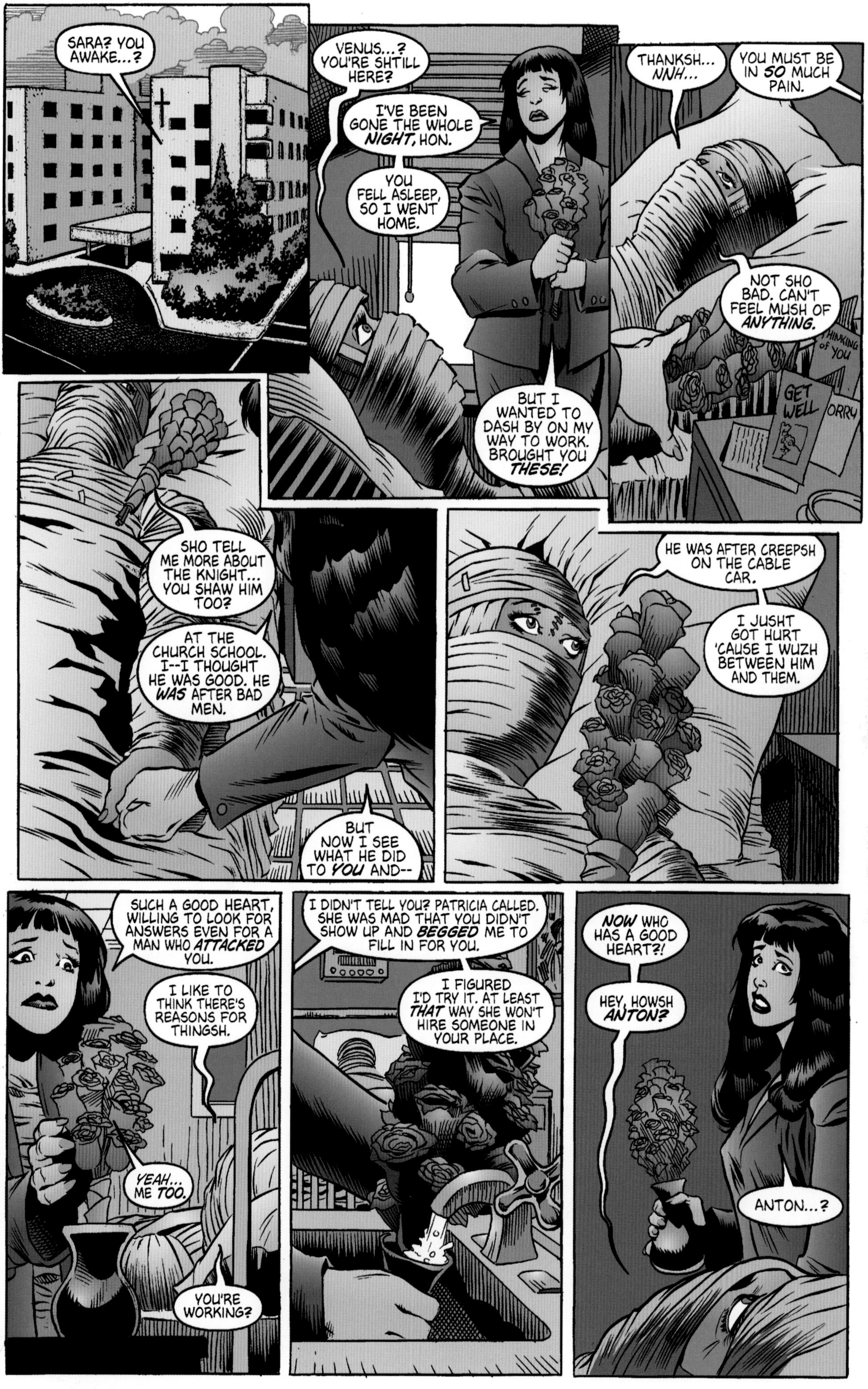
SARA? YOU AWAKE...?
VENUS...? YOU'RE SHTILL HERE?
I'VE BEEN GONE THE WHOLE NIGHT, HON.
YOU FELL ASLEEP, SO I WENT HOME.
BUT I WANTED TO DASH BY ON MY WAY TO WORK. BROUGHT YOU THESE!
THANKSH... NNH...
YOU MUST BE IN SO MUCH PAIN.
NOT SHO BAD. CAN'T FEEL MUSH OF ANYTHING.
THINKING of YOU
GET WELL
ORRY
SHO TELL ME MORE ABOUT THE KNIGHT... YOU SHAW HIM TOO?
AT THE CHURCH SCHOOL. I--I THOUGHT HE WAS GOOD. HE WAS AFTER BAD MEN.
BUT NOW I SEE WHAT HE DID TO YOU AND--
HE WAS AFTER CREEPSH ON THE CABLE CAR.
I JUSHT GOT HURT 'CAUSE I WUZH BETWEEN HIM AND THEM.
SUCH A GOOD HEART, WILLING TO LOOK FOR ANSWERS EVEN FOR A MAN WHO ATTACKED YOU.
I LIKE TO THINK THERE'S REASONS FOR THINGSH.
YEAH... ME TOO.
YOU'RE WORKING?
I DIDN'T TELL YOU? PATRICIA CALLED. SHE WAS MAD THAT YOU DIDN'T SHOW UP AND BEGGED ME TO FILL IN FOR YOU.
I FIGURED I'D TRY IT. AT LEAST THAT WAY SHE WON'T HIRE SOMEONE IN YOUR PLACE.
NOW WHO HAS A GOOD HEART?!
HEY, HOWSH ANTON?
ANTON...?

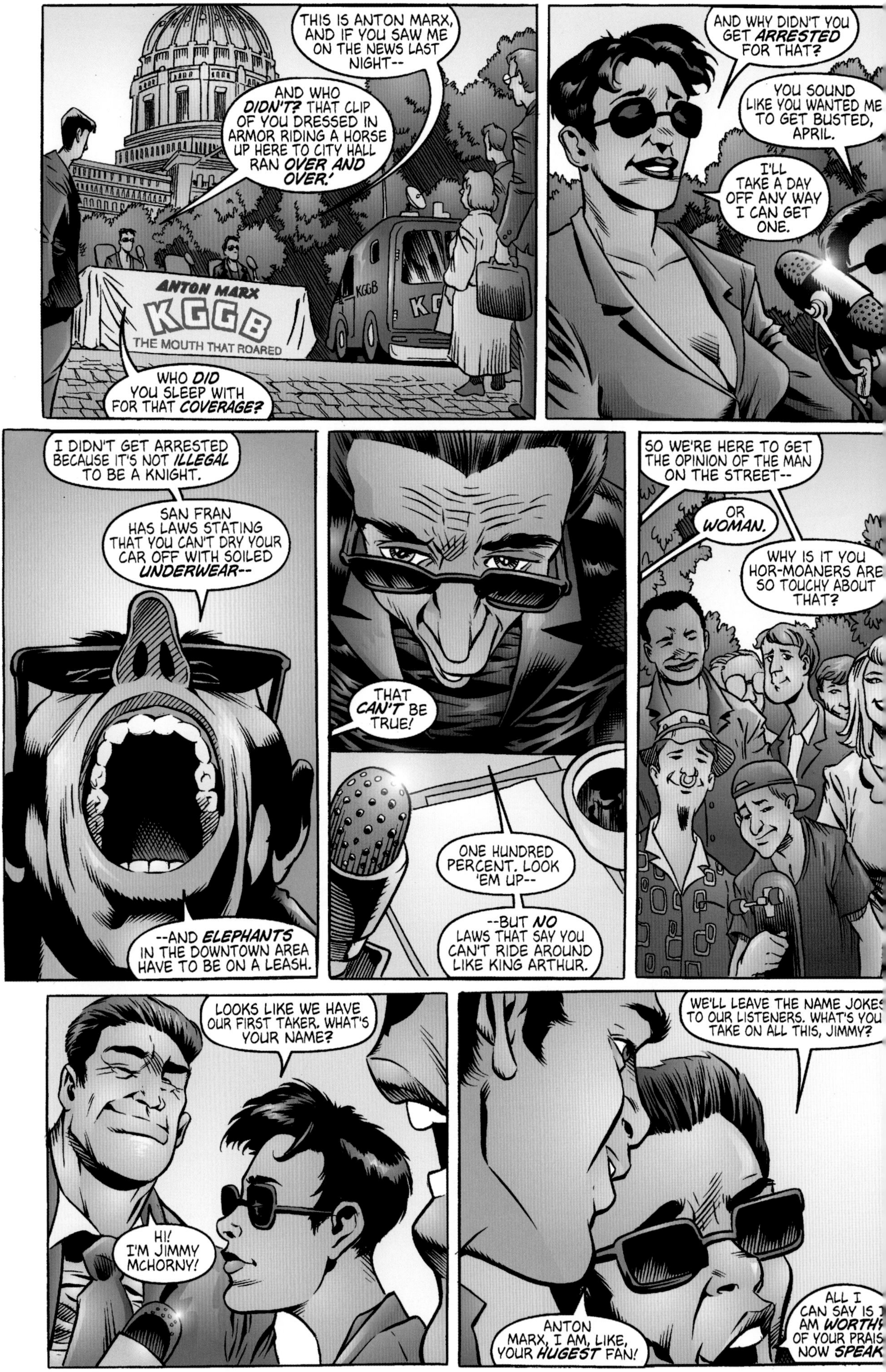
THIS IS ANTON MARX, AND IF YOU SAW ME ON THE NEWS LAST NIGHT--
AND WHO DIDN'T? THAT CLIP OF YOU DRESSED IN ARMOR RIDING A HORSE UP HERE TO CITY HALL RAN OVER AND OVER.'
ANTON MARX
KGGB
THE MOUTH THAT ROARED
KGGB
WHO DID YOU SLEEP WITH FOR THAT COVERAGE?
AND WHY DIDN'T YOU GET ARRESTED FOR THAT?
YOU SOUND LIKE YOU WANTED ME TO GET BUSTED, APRIL.
I'LL TAKE A DAY OFF ANY WAY I CAN GET ONE.
I DIDN'T GET ARRESTED BECAUSE IT'S NOT ILLEGAL TO BE A KNIGHT.
SAN FRAN HAS LAWS STATING THAT YOU CAN'T DRY YOUR CAR OFF WITH SOILED UNDERWEAR--
--AND ELEPHANTS IN THE DOWNTOWN AREA HAVE TO BE ON A LEASH.
THAT CAN'T BE TRUE!
ONE HUNDRED PERCENT. LOOK 'EM UP--
--BUT NO LAWS THAT SAY YOU CAN'T RIDE AROUND LIKE KING ARTHUR.
SO WE'RE HERE TO GET THE OPINION OF THE MAN ON THE STREET--
OR WOMAN.
WHY IS IT YOU HOR-MOANERS ARE SO TOUCHY ABOUT THAT?
LOOKS LIKE WE HAVE OUR FIRST TAKER. WHAT'S YOUR NAME?
HI! I'M JIMMY MCHORNY!
WE'LL LEAVE THE NAME JOKES TO OUR LISTENERS. WHAT'S YOU TAKE ON ALL THIS, JIMMY?
ANTON MARX, I AM, LIKE, YOUR HUGEST FAN!
ALL I CAN SAY IS I AM WORTHY OF YOUR PRAIS NOW SPEAK

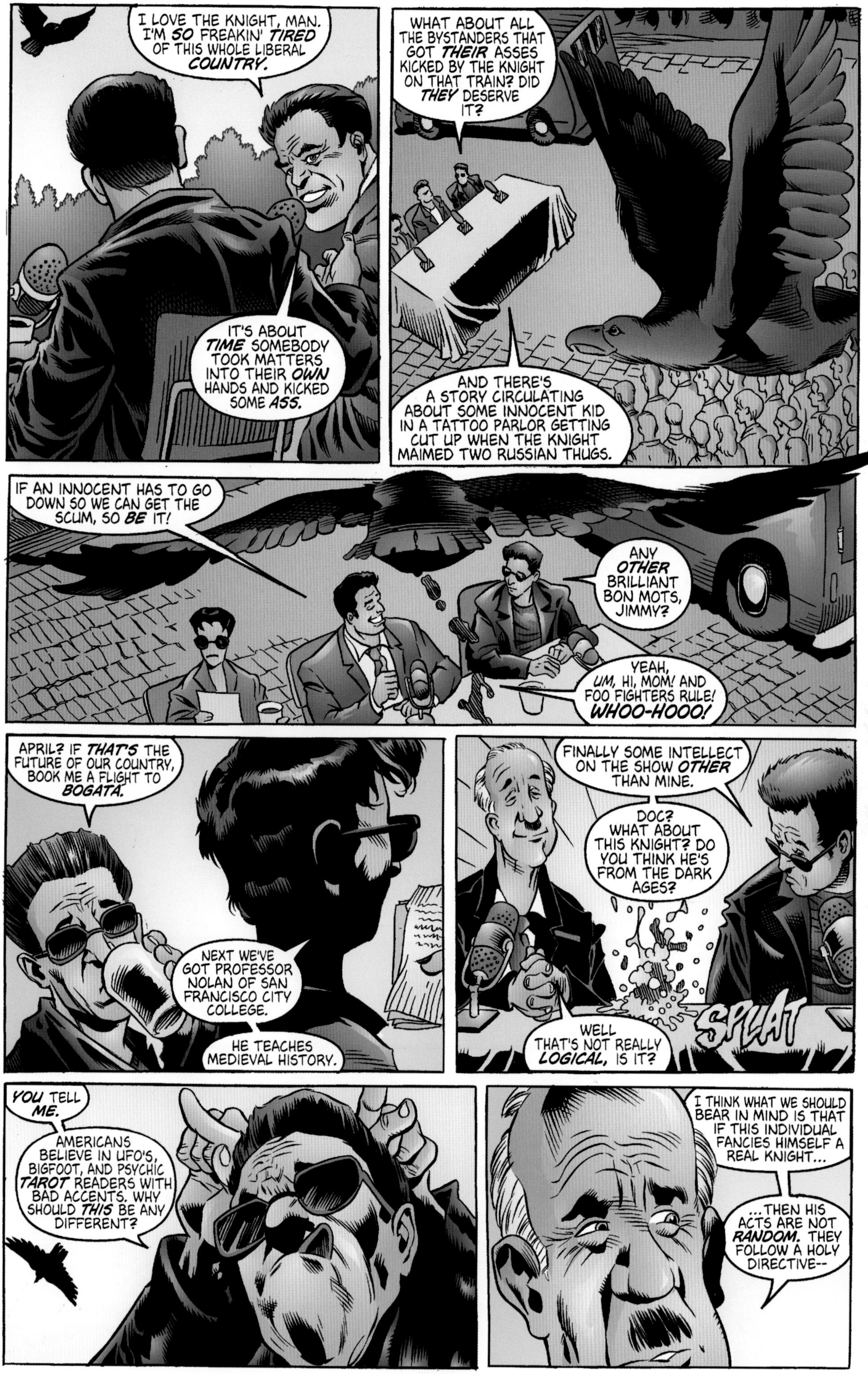
I LOVE THE KNIGHT, MAN. I'M SO FREAKIN' TIRED OF THIS WHOLE LIBERAL COUNTRY.
IT'S ABOUT TIME SOMEBODY TOOK MATTERS INTO THEIR OWN HANDS AND KICKED SOME ASS.
WHAT ABOUT ALL THE BYSTANDERS THAT GOT THEIR ASSES KICKED BY THE KNIGHT ON THAT TRAIN? DID THEY DESERVE IT?
AND THERE'S A STORY CIRCULATING ABOUT SOME INNOCENT KID IN A TATTOO PARLOR GETTING CUT UP WHEN THE KNIGHT MAIMED TWO RUSSIAN THUGS.
IF AN INNOCENT HAS TO GO DOWN SO WE CAN GET THE SCUM, SO BE IT!
ANY OTHER BRILLIANT BON MOTS, JIMMY?
YEAH, UM, HI, MOM! AND FOO FIGHTERS RULE! WHOO-HOOO!
APRIL? IF THAT'S THE FUTURE OF OUR COUNTRY, BOOK ME A FLIGHT TO BOGATA.
NEXT WE'VE GOT PROFESSOR NOLAN OF SAN FRANCISCO CITY COLLEGE.
HE TEACHES MEDIEVAL HISTORY.
FINALLY SOME INTELLECT ON THE SHOW OTHER THAN MINE.
DOC? WHAT ABOUT THIS KNIGHT? DO YOU THINK HE'S FROM THE DARK AGES?
WELL THAT'S NOT REALLY LOGICAL, IS IT?
SPLAT
YOU TELL ME.
AMERICANS BELIEVE IN UFO'S, BIGFOOT, AND PSYCHIC TAROT READERS WITH BAD ACCENTS. WHY SHOULD THIS BE ANY DIFFERENT?
I THINK WHAT WE SHOULD BEAR IN MIND IS THAT IF THIS INDIVIDUAL FANCIES HIMSELF A REAL KNIGHT...
...THEN HIS ACTS ARE NOT RANDOM. THEY FOLLOW A HOLY DIRECTIVE--

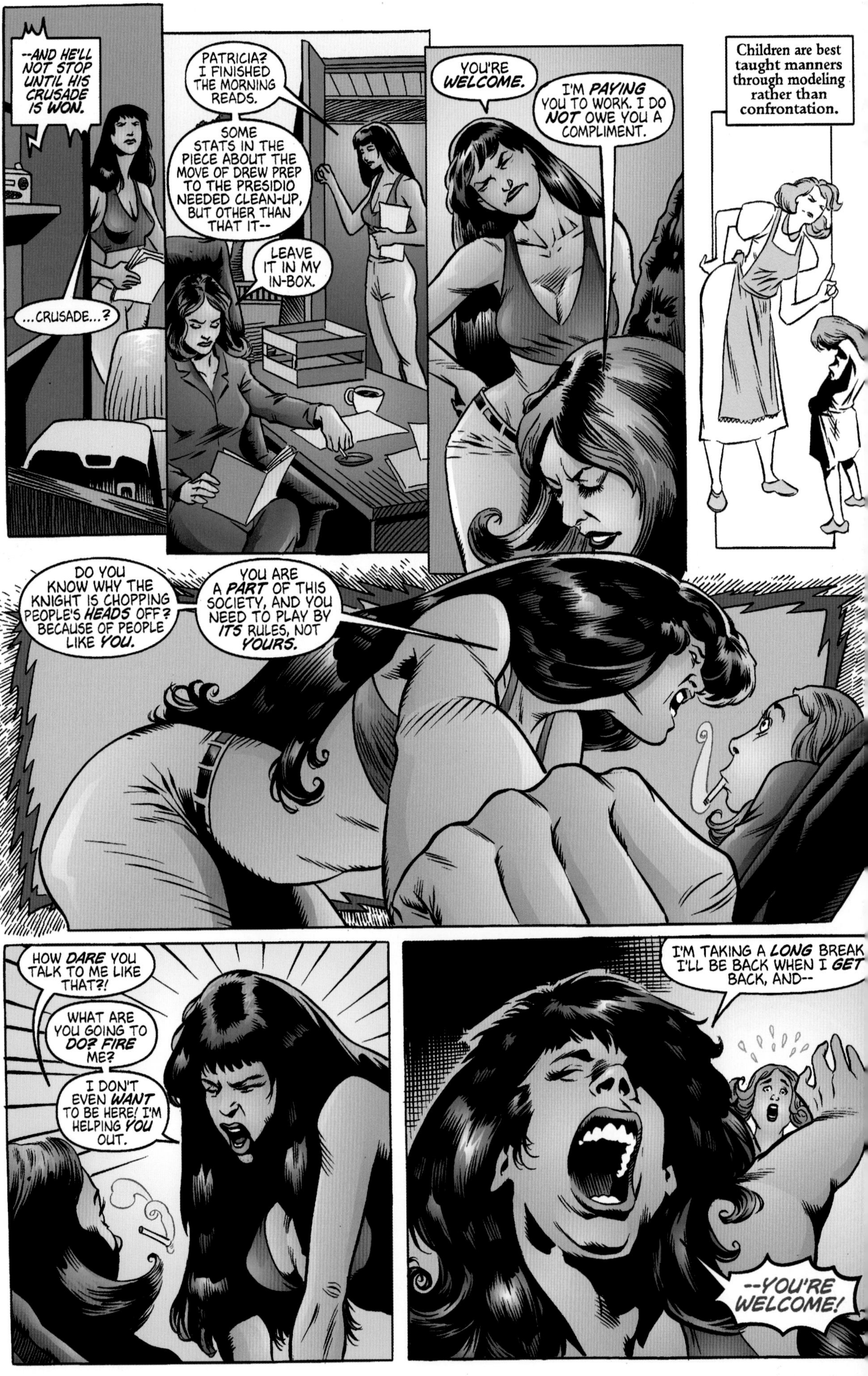
--AND HE'LL NOT STOP UNTIL HIS CRUSADE IS WON.
...CRUSADE...?
PATRICIA? I FINISHED THE MORNING READS.
SOME STATS IN THE PIECE ABOUT THE MOVE OF DREW PREP TO THE PRESIDIO NEEDED CLEAN-UP, BUT OTHER THAN THAT IT--
LEAVE IT IN MY IN-BOX.
YOU'RE WELCOME.
I'M PAYING YOU TO WORK. I DO NOT OWE YOU A COMPLIMENT.
Children are best taught manners through modeling rather than confrontation.
DO YOU KNOW WHY THE KNIGHT IS CHOPPING PEOPLE'S HEADS OFF? BECAUSE OF PEOPLE LIKE YOU.
YOU ARE A PART OF THIS SOCIETY, AND YOU NEED TO PLAY BY ITS RULES, NOT YOURS.
HOW DARE YOU TALK TO ME LIKE THAT?!
WHAT ARE YOU GOING TO DO? FIRE ME?
I DON'T EVEN WANT TO BE HERE! I'M HELPING YOU OUT.
I'M TAKING A LONG BREAK I'LL BE BACK WHEN I GET BACK, AND--
--YOU'RE WELCOME!

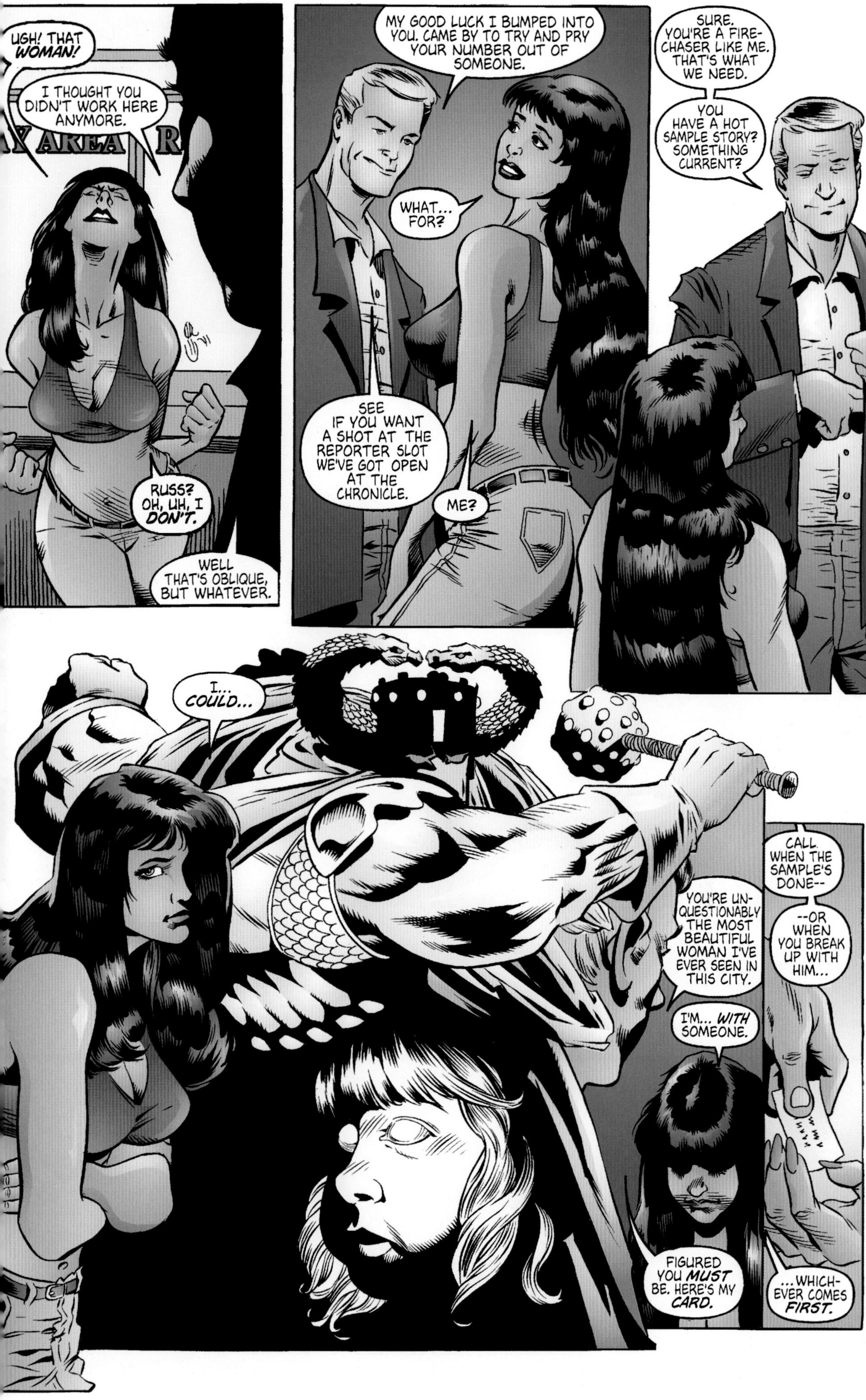

UGH! THAT WOMAN!
I THOUGHT YOU DIDN'T WORK HERE ANYMORE.
RUSS? OH, UH, I DON'T.
WELL THAT'S OBLIQUE, BUT WHATEVER.
MY GOOD LUCK I BUMPED INTO YOU. CAME BY TO TRY AND PRY YOUR NUMBER OUT OF SOMEONE.
WHAT... FOR?
SEE IF YOU WANT A SHOT AT THE REPORTER SLOT WE'VE GOT OPEN AT THE CHRONICLE.
ME?
SURE. YOU'RE A FIRE-CHASER LIKE ME. THAT'S WHAT WE NEED.
YOU HAVE A HOT SAMPLE STORY? SOMETHING CURRENT?
I... COULD...
YOU'RE UN-QUESTIONABLY THE MOST BEAUTIFUL WOMAN I'VE EVER SEEN IN THIS CITY.
I'M... WITH SOMEONE.
FIGURED YOU MUST BE. HERE'S MY CARD.
CALL. WHEN THE SAMPLE'S DONE--
--OR WHEN YOU BREAK UP WITH HIM...
...WHICH-EVER COMES FIRST.

...KNIGHTS BELIEVED THEY WERE FORGIVEN THEIR VIOLENT ACTIONS BY GOD AND--
TREASURE ISLAND
--AS A RESULT, THEY OFTEN FOUND--
LISTEN TO THIS FUCK! HE THINK HE KNOW WHERE KNIGHT IS?
BOCC KNOW WHERE KNIGHT IS.
HERE. IN THE HOME OF MY MOST HATED ENEMY. POPE.
FUCKING "VATICAN" OF THE POPE IS WHERE KNIGHT IS. I AND ROZMIK SAW HIM THERE, NO?
RICHMOND
SUNSET
FOREST HILL
WE SAW HIM, SO WHAT WE DO ABOUT THAT? TURN HIM INTO POLICE?
FUCK POLICE! THE POPE, HE WOULD CALL THE POLICE ON US.
HE WOULD LET SOMEONE ELSE DO HIS WORK FOR HIM.
THE ONLY WAY POPE KNOW TO GET THE FUCK OUT OF MY CITY-- GO BACK TO ROME--
--IS IF WE KICK HIM IN ASS WHILE LOOKING HIM IN EYE.
WHAT ABOUT THE KNIGHT?
HIS IS ONE MAN. WE ARE MANY.
WHICH IS MOST POWERFUL, ONE KNIGHT OR MANY MAN?
FOKKING SHIT! MANY MAN IS ANSWER! YOU ARE STUPID AS BRICKS!
GET UP, GET GUNS, AND GET READY! MOVE!

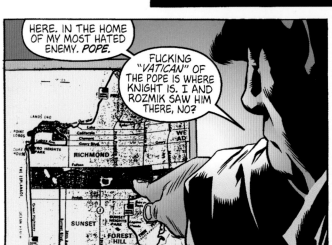

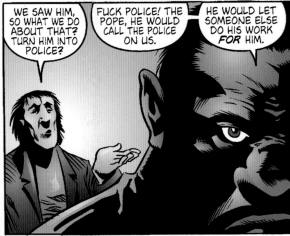

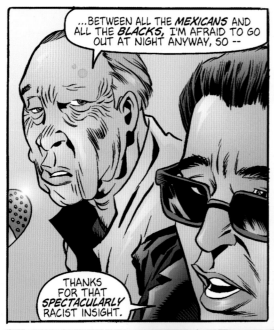

...BETWEEN ALL THE *MEXICANS* AND ALL THE *BLACKS*, I'M AFRAID TO GO OUT AT NIGHT ANYWAY, SO --

THANKS FOR THAT *SPECTACULARLY* RACIST INSIGHT.

WHO'S NEXT, APRIL?

WELL, WE'RE ALMOST OUT OF *TIME* ON THIS SEGMENT--

--BUT WE HAVE A LOVELY OFFICE WORKER NAMED--

VENUS.

VENUS?! *UH...* SO VENUS, WHAT DO *YOU* THINK OF THE KNIGHT?

I THINK HE'S HERE TO REMIND *CERTAIN PEOPLE* THEY'D BETTER RESPECT *CERTAIN OTHER PEOPLE* OR *THEY'LL GET THEIRS.*

WELL...*UH*...THERE YOU HAVE IT, PEOPLE OF FRISCO.

WE'RE UP AGAINST THE HOUR, SO, *UH,* WE'LL BREAK AND BE BACK WITH MORE! LIVE! AT CITY HALL!

VENUS! BABE! WAIT UP!

WHAT WAS THAT ALL ABOUT? AND DON'T SAY, *"THE KNIGHT."*

YOU WERE TALKING TO ME, WEREN'T YOU?

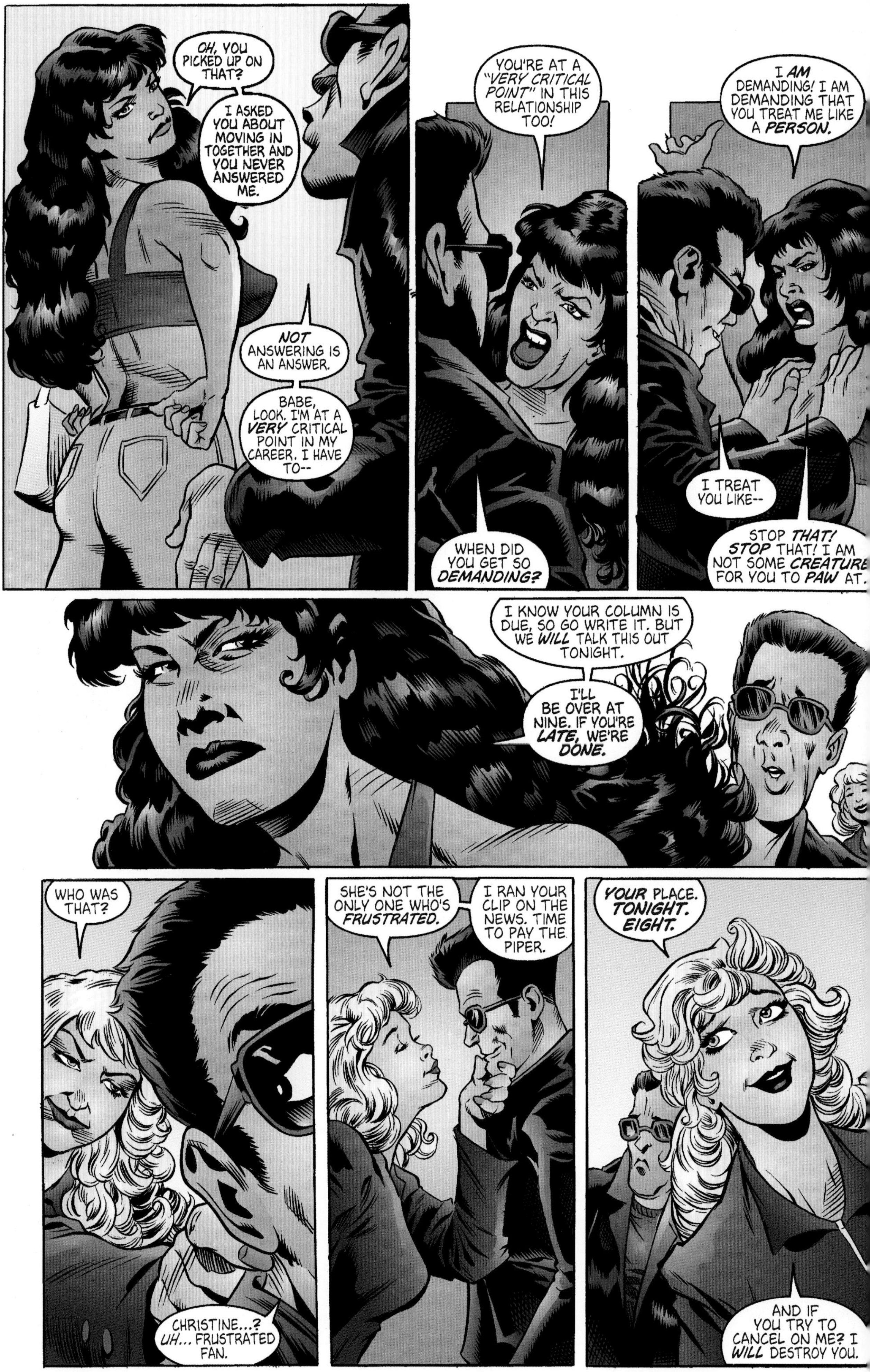
OH, YOU PICKED UP ON THAT?
I ASKED YOU ABOUT MOVING IN TOGETHER AND YOU NEVER ANSWERED ME.
NOT ANSWERING IS AN ANSWER.
BABE, LOOK. I'M AT A VERY CRITICAL POINT IN MY CAREER. I HAVE TO--
YOU'RE AT A "VERY CRITICAL POINT" IN THIS RELATIONSHIP TOO!
WHEN DID YOU GET SO DEMANDING?
I AM DEMANDING! I AM DEMANDING THAT YOU TREAT ME LIKE A PERSON.
I TREAT YOU LIKE--
STOP THAT! STOP THAT! I AM NOT SOME CREATURE FOR YOU TO PAW AT.
I KNOW YOUR COLUMN IS DUE, SO GO WRITE IT. BUT WE WILL TALK THIS OUT TONIGHT.
I'LL BE OVER AT NINE. IF YOU'RE LATE, WE'RE DONE.
WHO WAS THAT?
CHRISTINE...? UH... FRUSTRATED FAN.
SHE'S NOT THE ONLY ONE WHO'S FRUSTRATED.
I RAN YOUR CLIP ON THE NEWS. TIME TO PAY THE PIPER.
YOUR PLACE. TONIGHT. EIGHT.
AND IF YOU TRY TO CANCEL ON ME? I WILL DESTROY YOU.

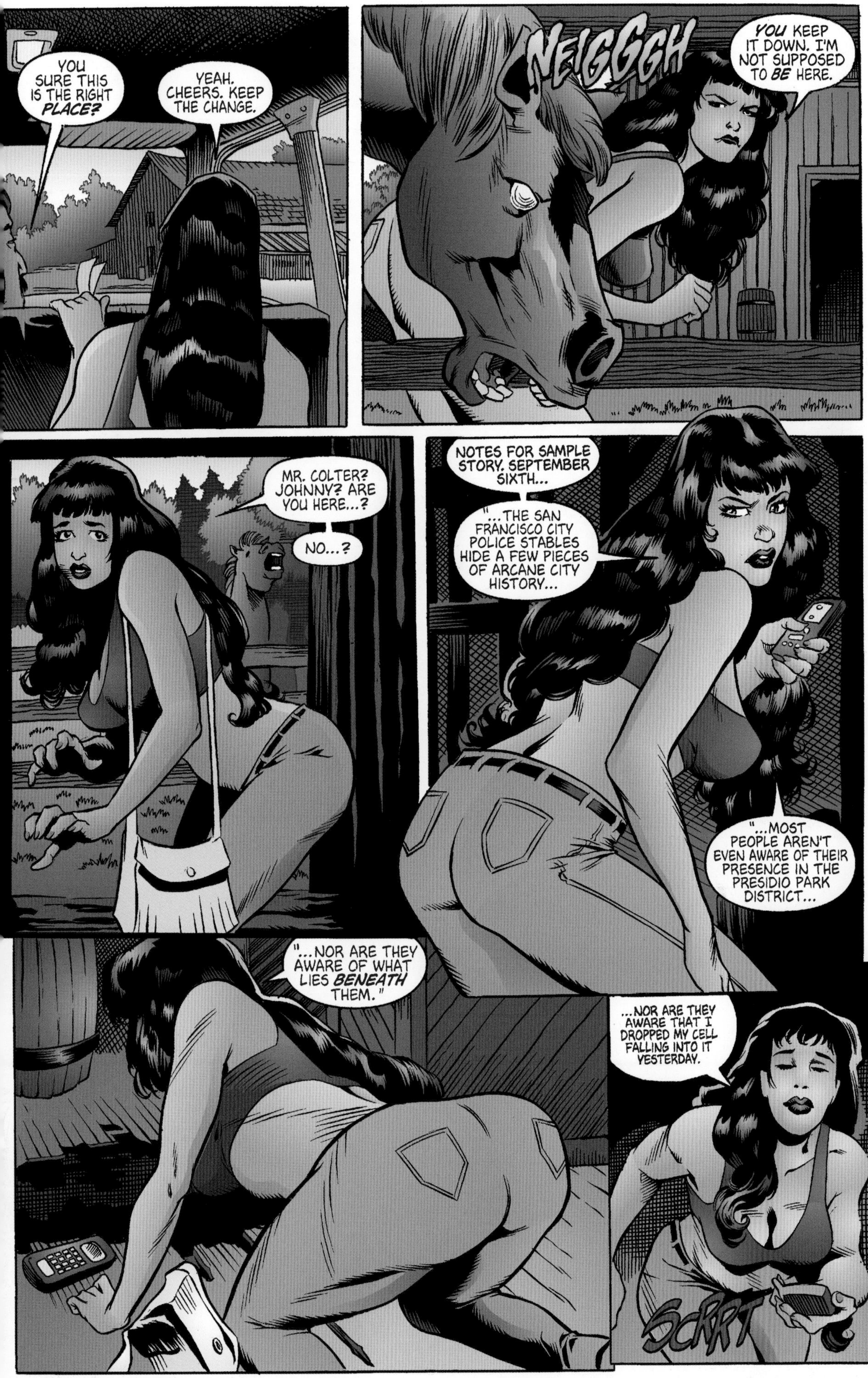

YOU SURE THIS IS THE RIGHT PLACE?
YEAH. CHEERS. KEEP THE CHANGE.
NEIGGGH
YOU KEEP IT DOWN. I'M NOT SUPPOSED TO BE HERE.
MR. COLTER? JOHNNY? ARE YOU HERE...?
NO...?
NOTES FOR SAMPLE STORY. SEPTEMBER SIXTH...
"...THE SAN FRANCISCO CITY POLICE STABLES HIDE A FEW PIECES OF ARCANE CITY HISTORY...
"...MOST PEOPLE AREN'T EVEN AWARE OF THEIR PRESENCE IN THE PRESIDIO PARK DISTRICT...
"...NOR ARE THEY AWARE OF WHAT LIES BENEATH THEM."
...NOR ARE THEY AWARE THAT I DROPPED MY CELL FALLING INTO IT YESTERDAY.
SCRRT

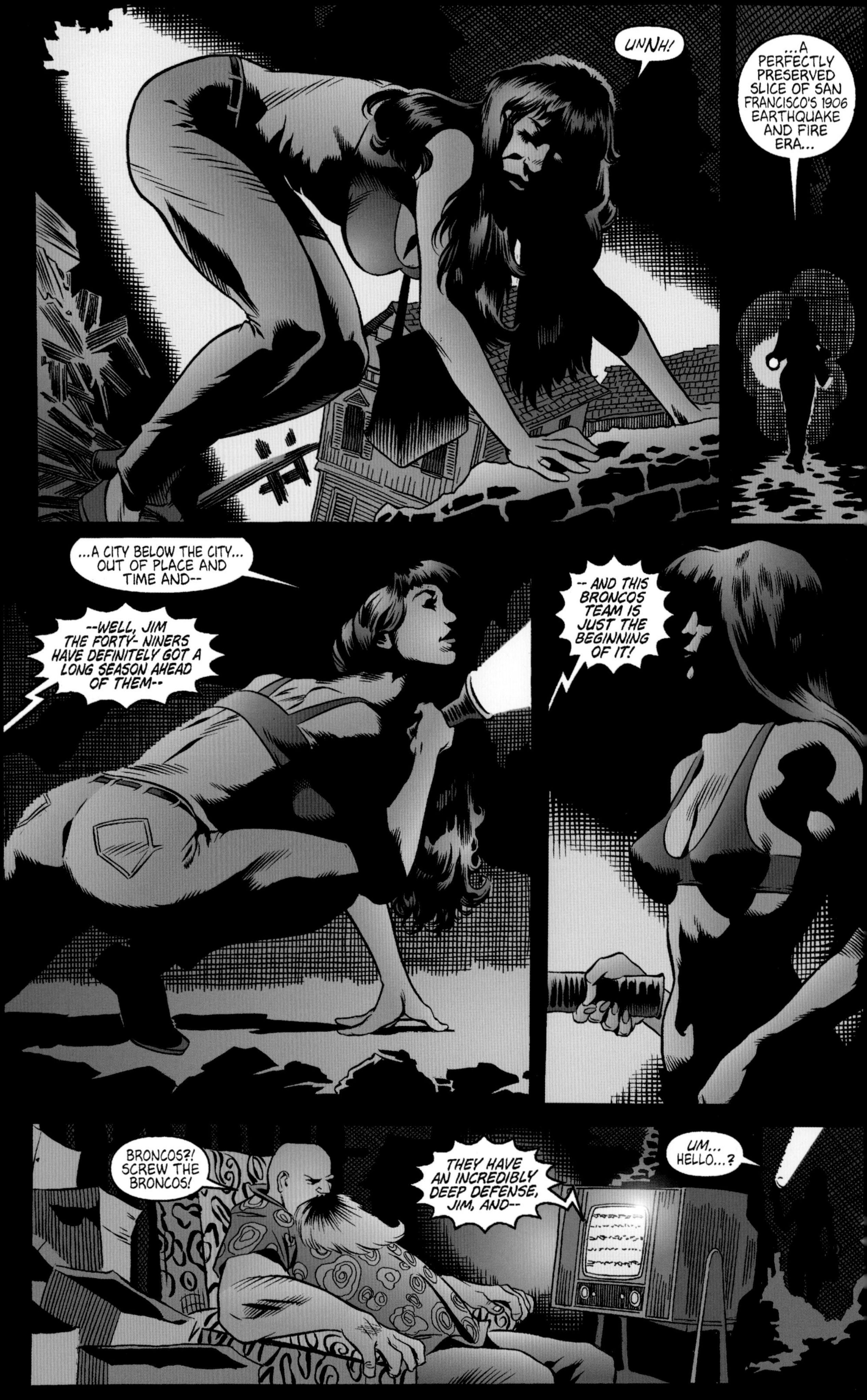
UNNH!
...A PERFECTLY PRESERVED SLICE OF SAN FRANCISCO'S 1906 EARTHQUAKE AND FIRE ERA...
...A CITY BELOW THE CITY... OUT OF PLACE AND TIME AND--
--WELL, JIM THE FORTY- NINERS HAVE DEFINITELY GOT A LONG SEASON AHEAD OF THEM--
-- AND THIS BRONCOS TEAM IS JUST THE BEGINNING OF IT!
BRONCOS?! SCREW THE BRONCOS!
THEY HAVE AN INCREDIBLY DEEP DEFENSE, JIM, AND--
UM... HELLO...?

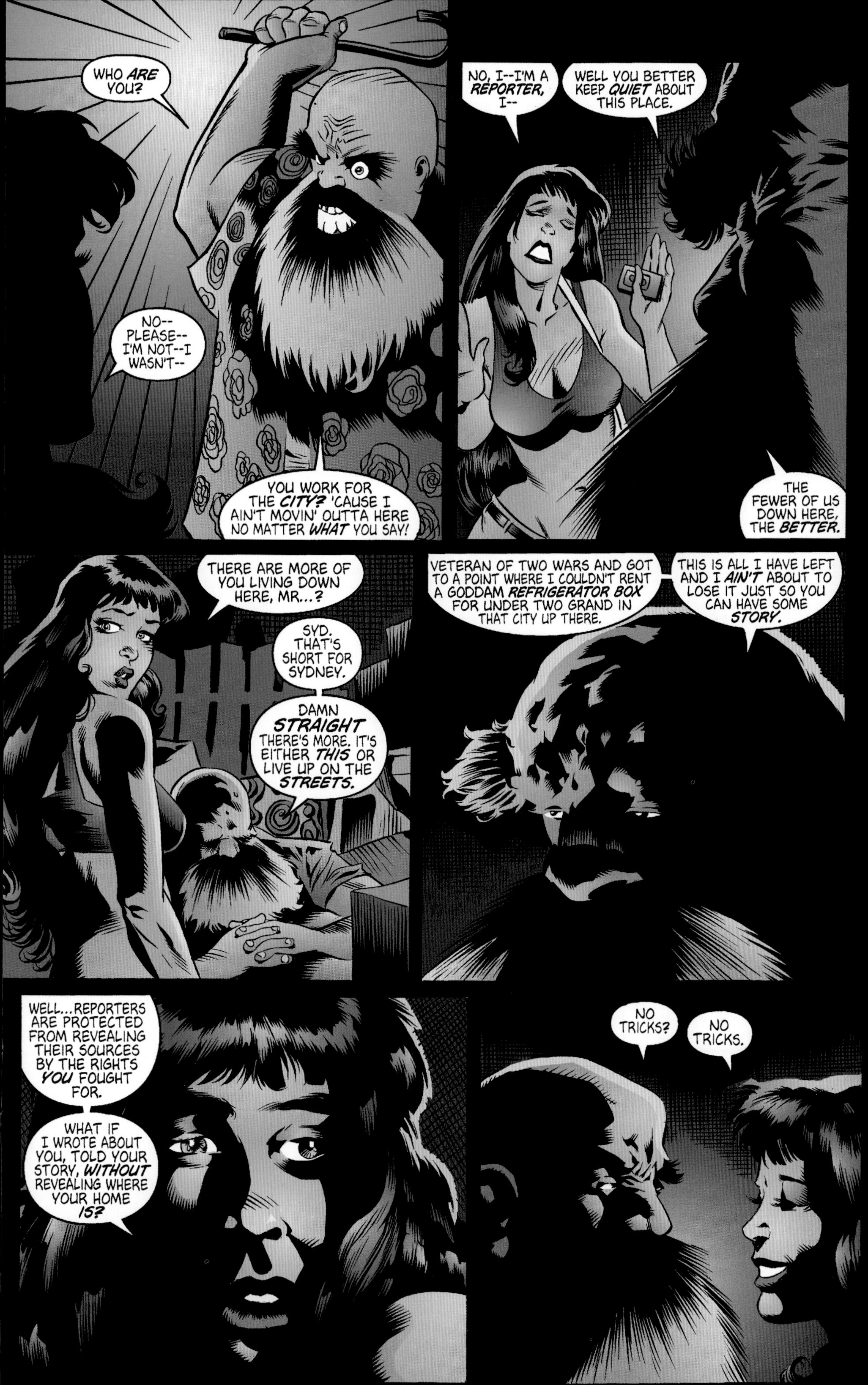
WHO *ARE* YOU?
NO-- PLEASE-- I'M NOT--I WASN'T--
YOU WORK FOR THE *CITY?* 'CAUSE I AIN'T MOVIN' OUTTA HERE NO MATTER *WHAT* YOU SAY!
NO, I--I'M A *REPORTER,* I--
WELL YOU BETTER KEEP *QUIET* ABOUT THIS PLACE.
THE FEWER OF US DOWN HERE, THE *BETTER.*
THERE ARE MORE OF YOU LIVING DOWN HERE, MR...?
SYD. THAT'S SHORT FOR SYDNEY.
DAMN *STRAIGHT* THERE'S MORE. IT'S EITHER *THIS* OR LIVE UP ON THE *STREETS.*
VETERAN OF TWO WARS AND GOT TO A POINT WHERE I COULDN'T RENT A GODDAM *REFRIGERATOR BOX* FOR UNDER TWO GRAND IN THAT CITY UP THERE.
THIS IS ALL I HAVE LEFT AND I *AIN'T* ABOUT TO LOSE IT JUST SO YOU CAN HAVE SOME *STORY.*
WELL...REPORTERS ARE PROTECTED FROM REVEALING THEIR SOURCES BY THE RIGHTS *YOU* FOUGHT FOR.
WHAT IF I WROTE ABOUT YOU, TOLD YOUR STORY, *WITHOUT* REVEALING WHERE YOUR HOME *IS?*
NO TRICKS?
NO TRICKS.

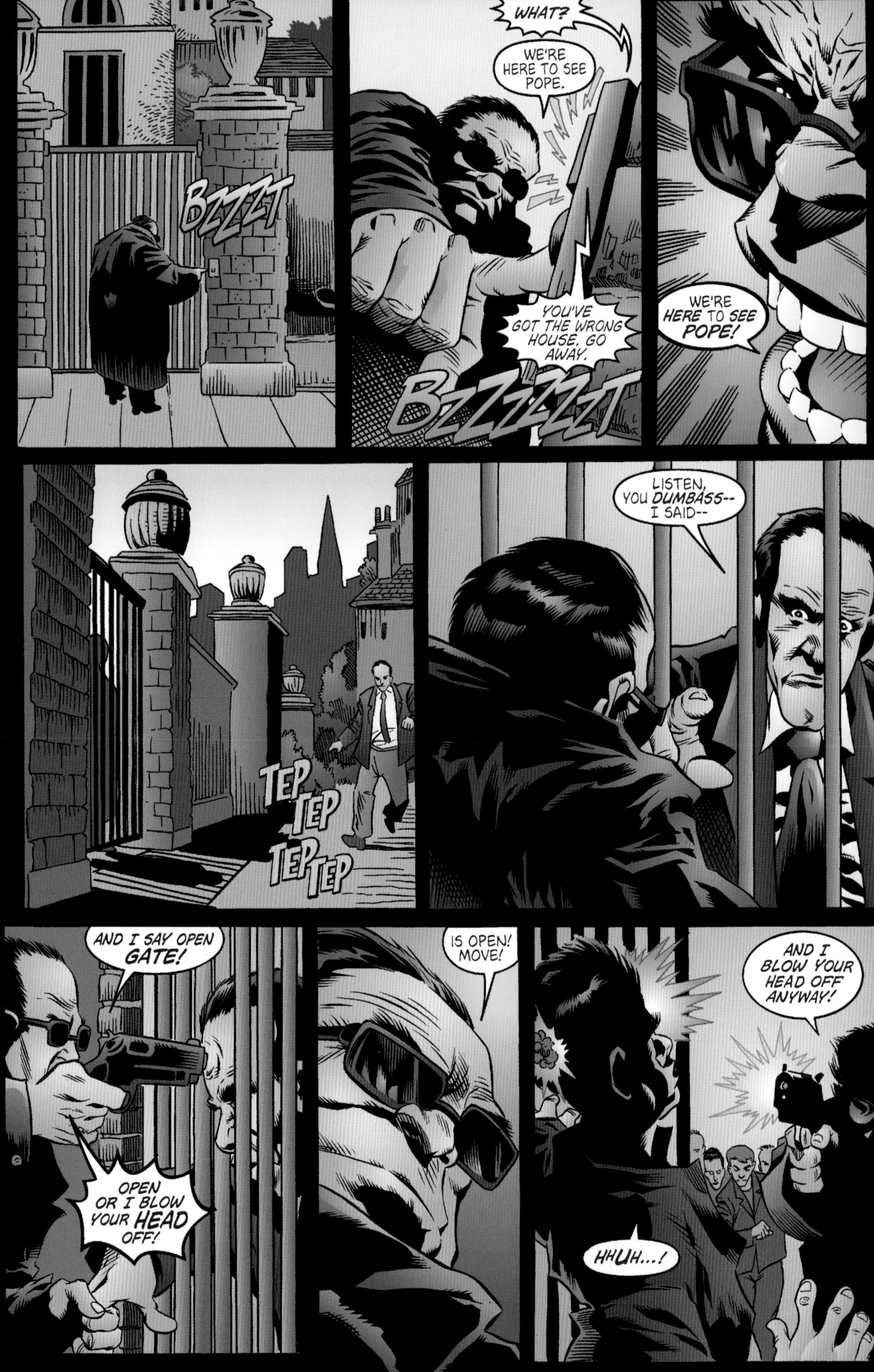
BZZZT
WHAT?
WE'RE HERE TO SEE POPE.
YOU'VE GOT THE WRONG HOUSE. GO AWAY.
BZZZZZZT
WE'RE HERE TO SEE POPE!
TEP TEP TEP TEP
LISTEN, YOU DUMBASS-- I SAID--
AND I SAY OPEN GATE!
OPEN OR I BLOW YOUR HEAD OFF!
IS OPEN! MOVE!
AND I BLOW YOUR HEAD OFF ANYWAY!
HHUH...!

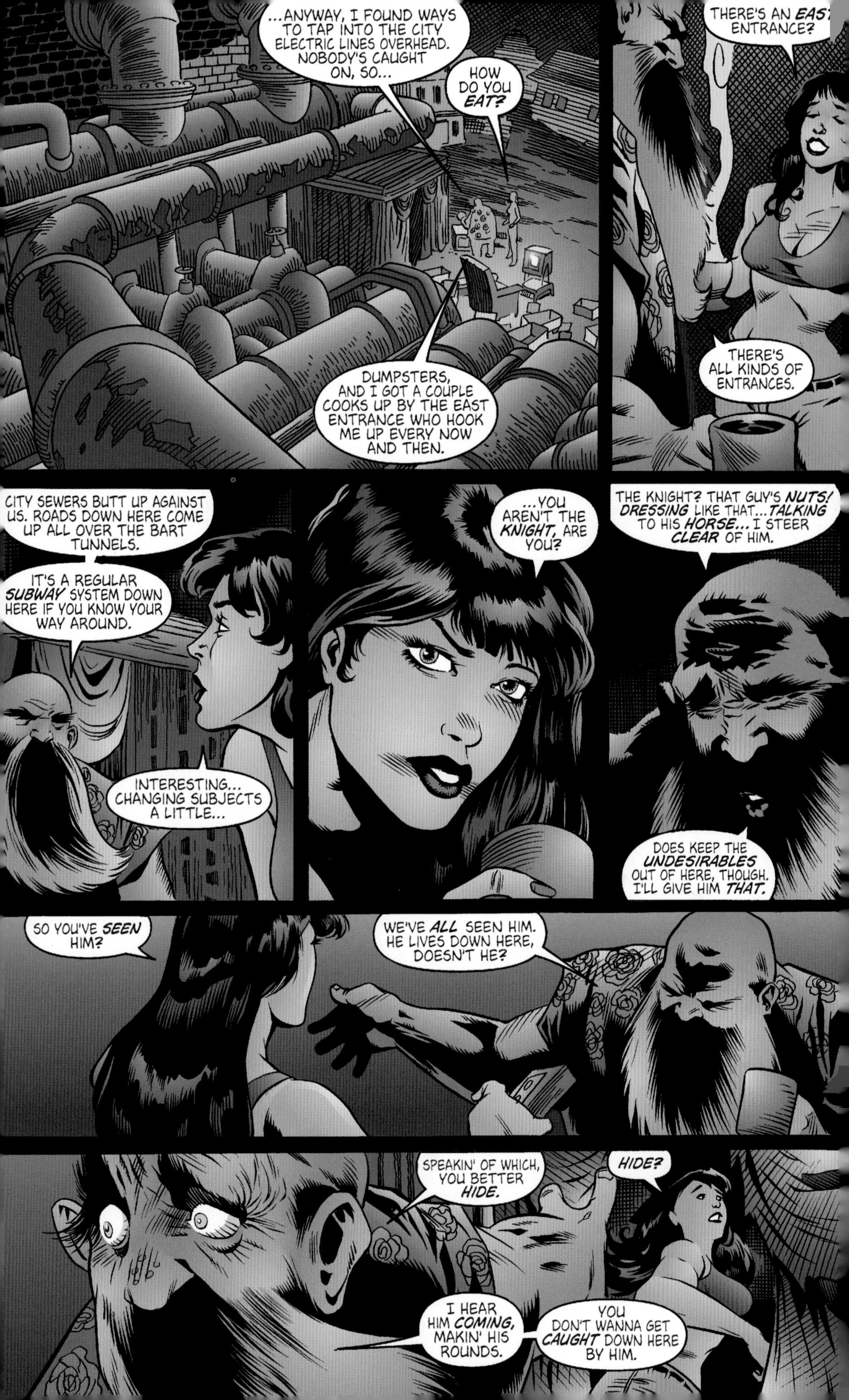
...ANYWAY, I FOUND WAYS TO TAP INTO THE CITY ELECTRIC LINES OVERHEAD. NOBODY'S CAUGHT ON, SO...
HOW DO YOU EAT?
DUMPSTERS, AND I GOT A COUPLE COOKS UP BY THE EAST ENTRANCE WHO HOOK ME UP EVERY NOW AND THEN.
THERE'S AN EAST ENTRANCE?
THERE'S ALL KINDS OF ENTRANCES.
CITY SEWERS BUTT UP AGAINST US. ROADS DOWN HERE COME UP ALL OVER THE BART TUNNELS.
IT'S A REGULAR SUBWAY SYSTEM DOWN HERE IF YOU KNOW YOUR WAY AROUND.
INTERESTING... CHANGING SUBJECTS A LITTLE...
...YOU AREN'T THE KNIGHT, ARE YOU?
THE KNIGHT? THAT GUY'S NUTS! DRESSING LIKE THAT...TALKING TO HIS HORSE... I STEER CLEAR OF HIM.
DOES KEEP THE UNDESIRABLES OUT OF HERE, THOUGH. I'LL GIVE HIM THAT.
SO YOU'VE SEEN HIM?
WE'VE ALL SEEN HIM. HE LIVES DOWN HERE, DOESN'T HE?
SPEAKIN' OF WHICH, YOU BETTER HIDE.
HIDE?
I HEAR HIM COMING, MAKIN' HIS ROUNDS.
YOU DON'T WANNA GET CAUGHT DOWN HERE BY HIM.

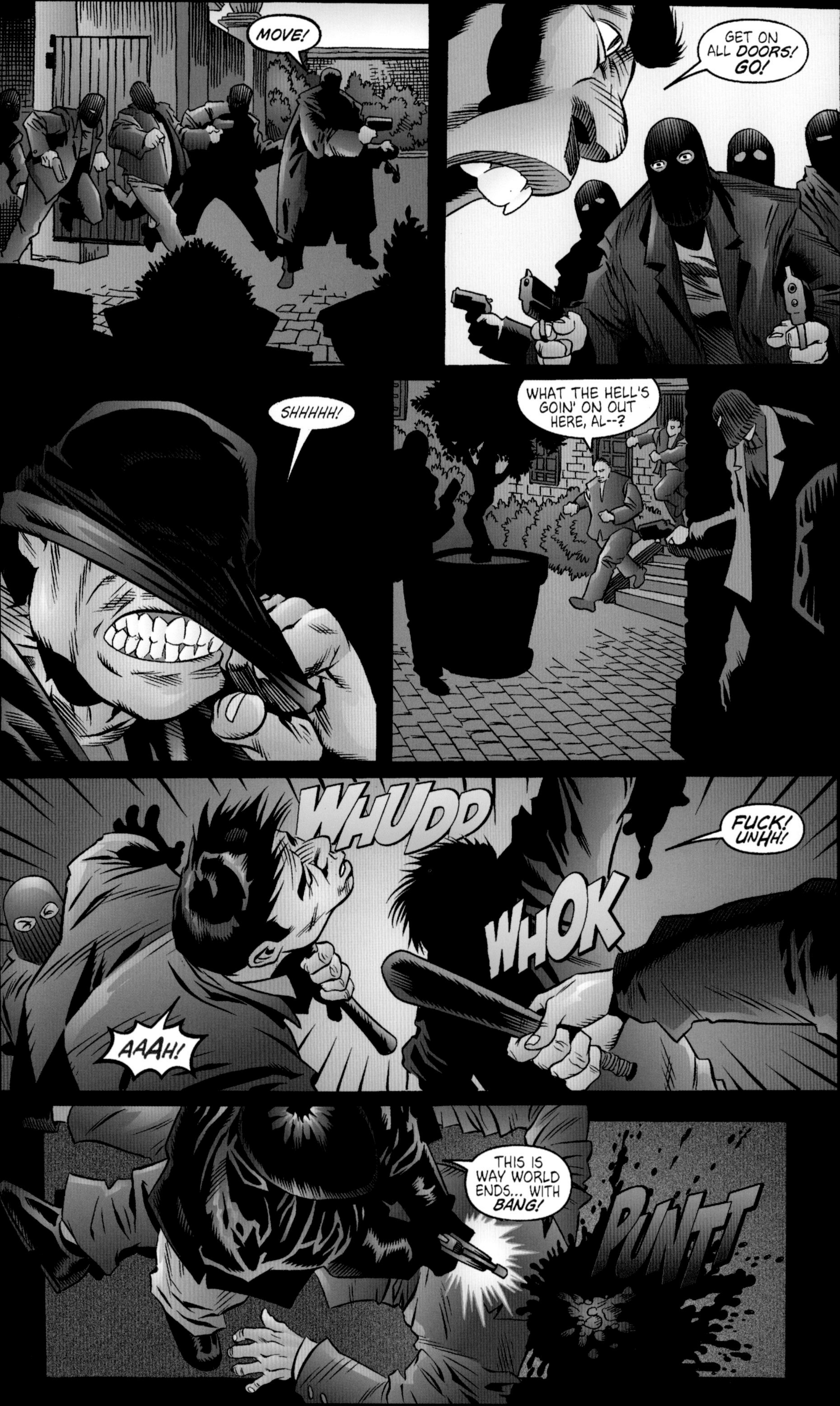
MOVE!
GET ON ALL DOORS! GO!
SHHHHH!
WHAT THE HELL'S GOIN' ON OUT HERE, AL--?
WHUDD
FUCK! UNHH!
WHOK
AAAH!
THIS IS WAY WORLD ENDS... WITH BANG!
PUNT T

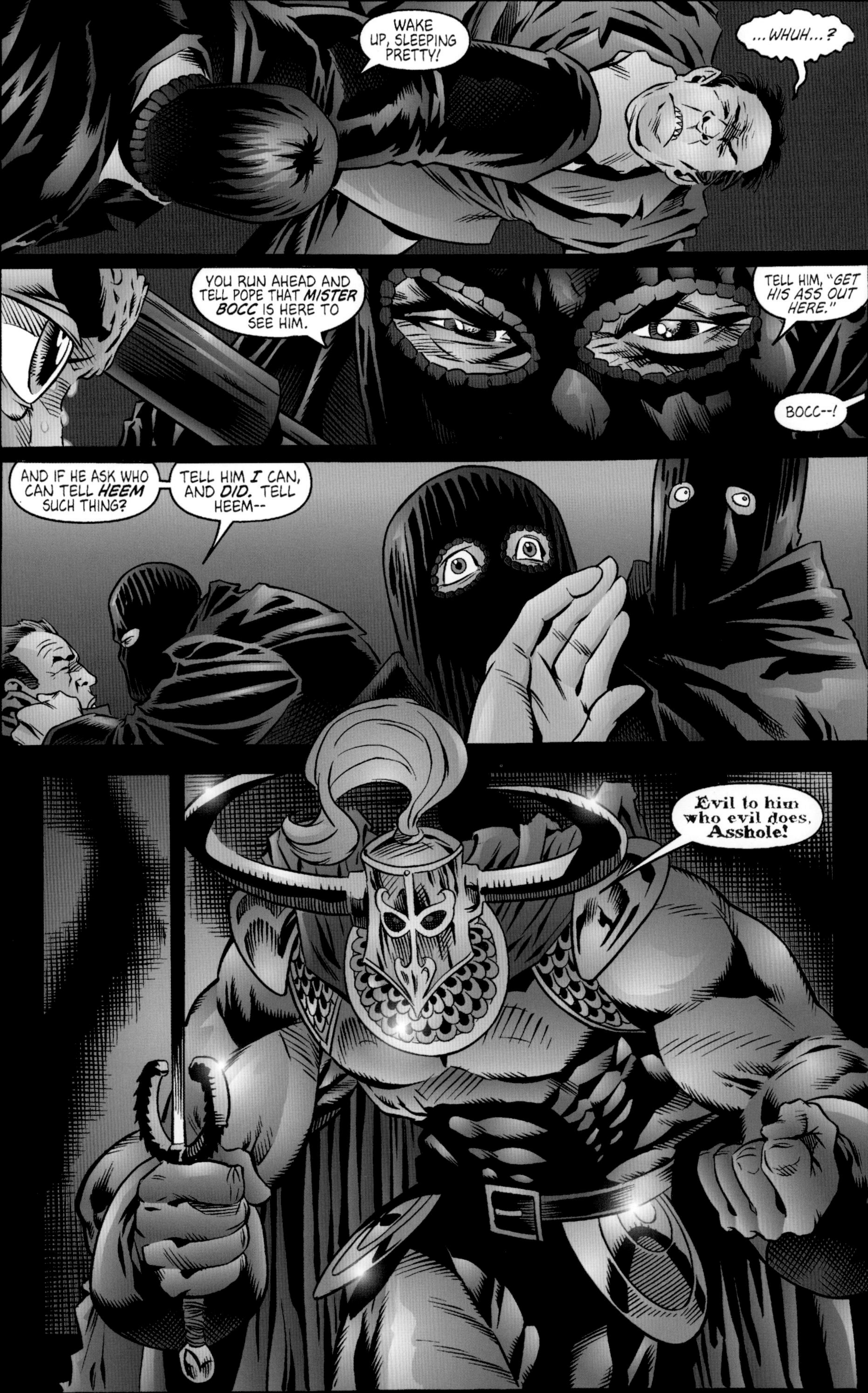
WAKE UP, SLEEPING PRETTY!
...WHUH...?
YOU RUN AHEAD AND TELL POPE THAT MISTER BOCC IS HERE TO SEE HIM.
TELL HIM, "GET HIS ASS OUT HERE."
BOCC--!
AND IF HE ASK WHO CAN TELL HEEM SUCH THING?
TELL HIM I CAN, AND DID. TELL HEEM--
Evil to him who evil does, Asshole!

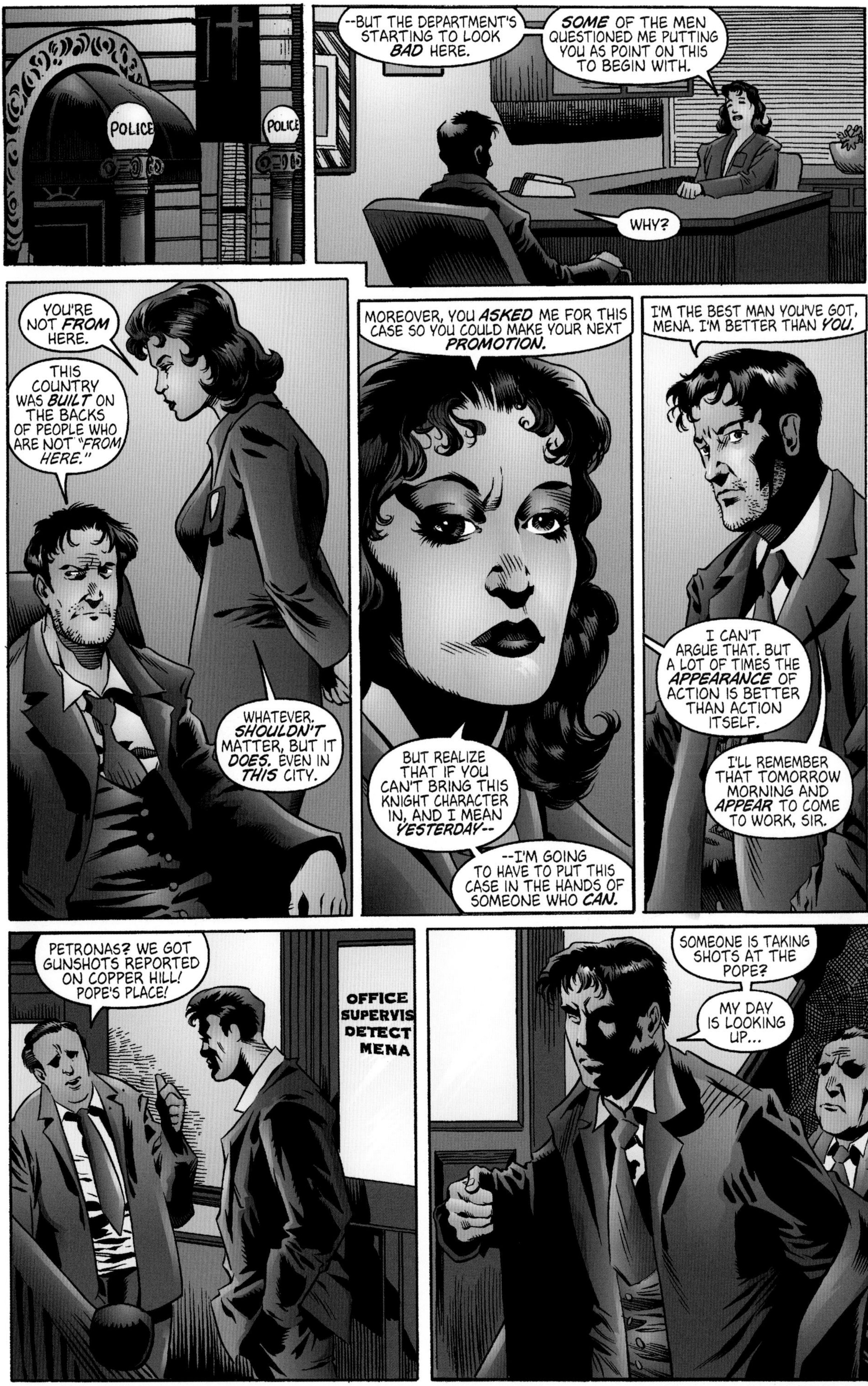
POLICE
POLICE
--BUT THE DEPARTMENT'S STARTING TO LOOK BAD HERE.
SOME OF THE MEN QUESTIONED ME PUTTING YOU AS POINT ON THIS TO BEGIN WITH.
WHY?
YOU'RE NOT FROM HERE.
THIS COUNTRY WAS BUILT ON THE BACKS OF PEOPLE WHO ARE NOT "FROM HERE."
WHATEVER. SHOULDN'T MATTER, BUT IT DOES. EVEN IN THIS CITY.
MOREOVER, YOU ASKED ME FOR THIS CASE SO YOU COULD MAKE YOUR NEXT PROMOTION.
BUT REALIZE THAT IF YOU CAN'T BRING THIS KNIGHT CHARACTER IN, AND I MEAN YESTERDAY--
--I'M GOING TO HAVE TO PUT THIS CASE IN THE HANDS OF SOMEONE WHO CAN.
I'M THE BEST MAN YOU'VE GOT, MENA. I'M BETTER THAN YOU.
I CAN'T ARGUE THAT. BUT A LOT OF TIMES THE APPEARANCE OF ACTION IS BETTER THAN ACTION ITSELF.
I'LL REMEMBER THAT TOMORROW MORNING AND APPEAR TO COME TO WORK, SIR.
PETRONAS? WE GOT GUNSHOTS REPORTED ON COPPER HILL! POPE'S PLACE!
OFFICE SUPERVIS DETECT MENA
SOMEONE IS TAKING SHOTS AT THE POPE?
MY DAY IS LOOKING UP...

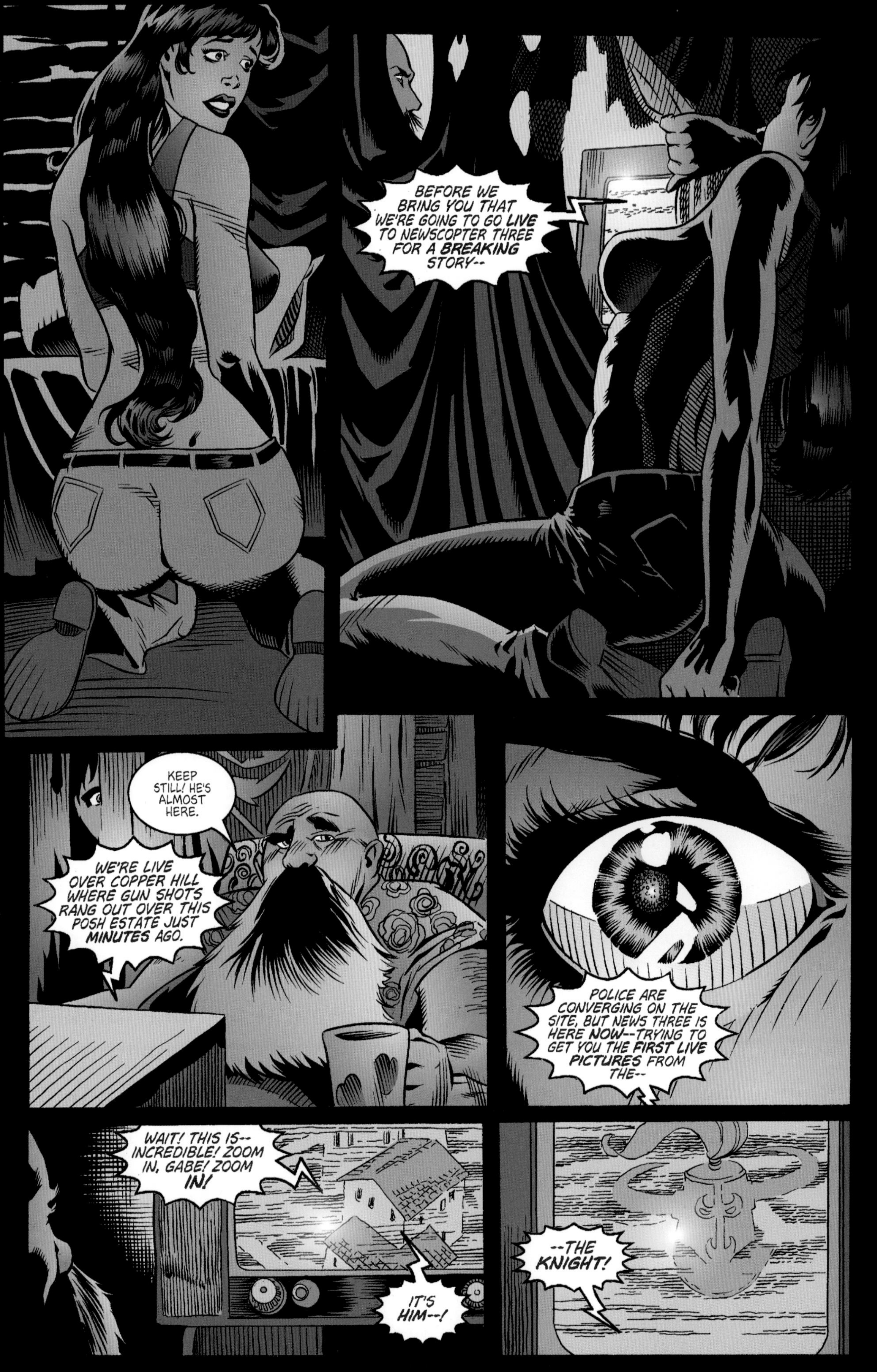
BEFORE WE BRING YOU THAT WE'RE GOING TO GO LIVE TO NEWSCOPTER THREE FOR A BREAKING STORY--
KEEP STILL! HE'S ALMOST HERE.
WE'RE LIVE OVER COPPER HILL WHERE GUN SHOTS RANG OUT OVER THIS POSH ESTATE JUST MINUTES AGO.
POLICE ARE CONVERGING ON THE SITE, BUT NEWS THREE IS HERE NOW--TRYING TO GET YOU THE FIRST LIVE PICTURES FROM THE--
WAIT! THIS IS--INCREDIBLE! ZOOM IN, GABE! ZOOM IN!
IT'S HIM--!
--THE KNIGHT!

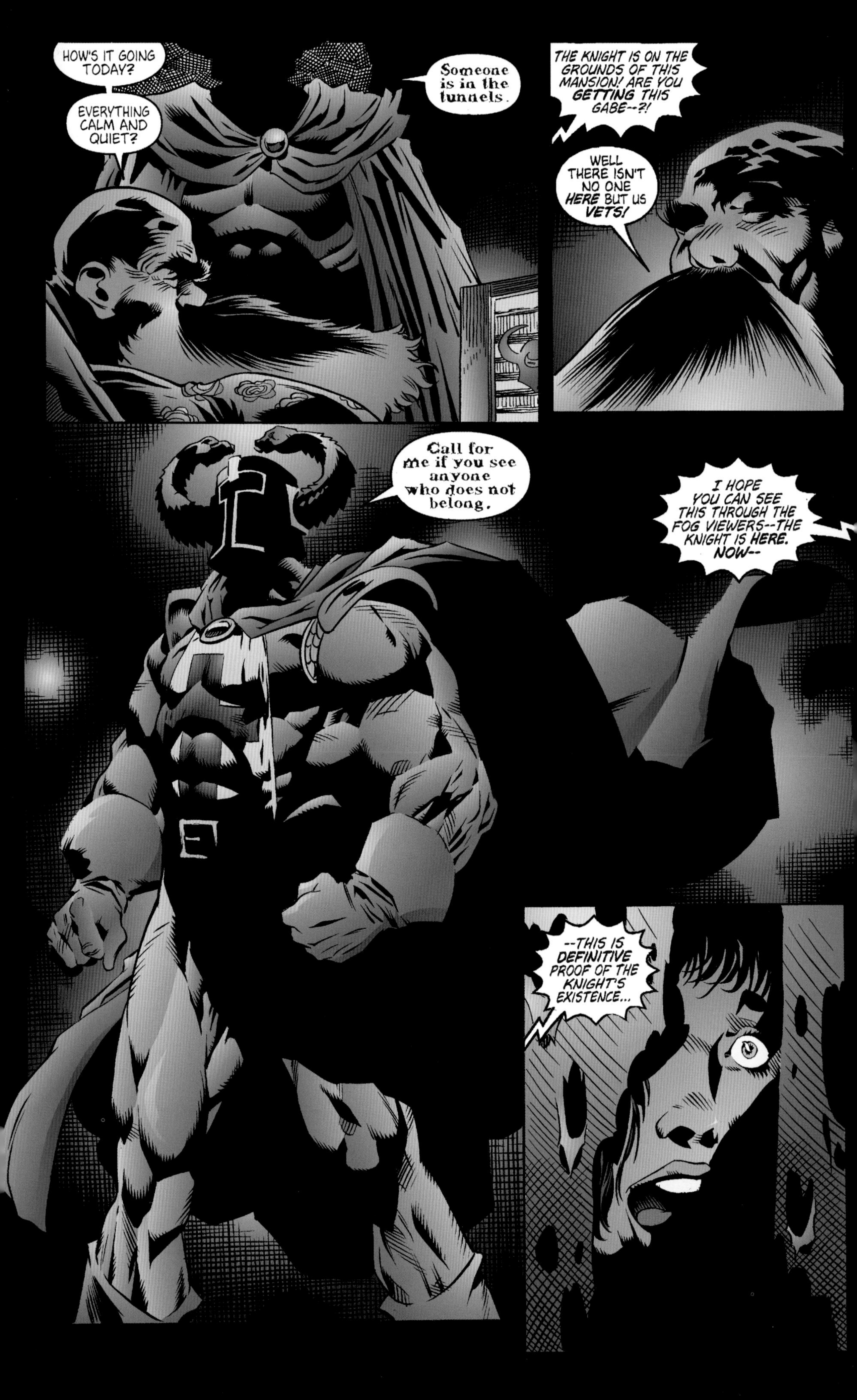
HOW'S IT GOING TODAY?
EVERYTHING CALM AND QUIET?
Someone is in the tunnels.
THE KNIGHT IS ON THE GROUNDS OF THIS MANSION! ARE YOU GETTING THIS GABE--?!
WELL THERE ISN'T NO ONE HERE BUT US VETS!
Call for me if you see anyone who does not belong.
I HOPE YOU CAN SEE THIS THROUGH THE FOG VIEWERS--THE KNIGHT IS HERE. NOW--
--THIS IS DEFINITIVE PROOF OF THE KNIGHT'S EXISTENCE...

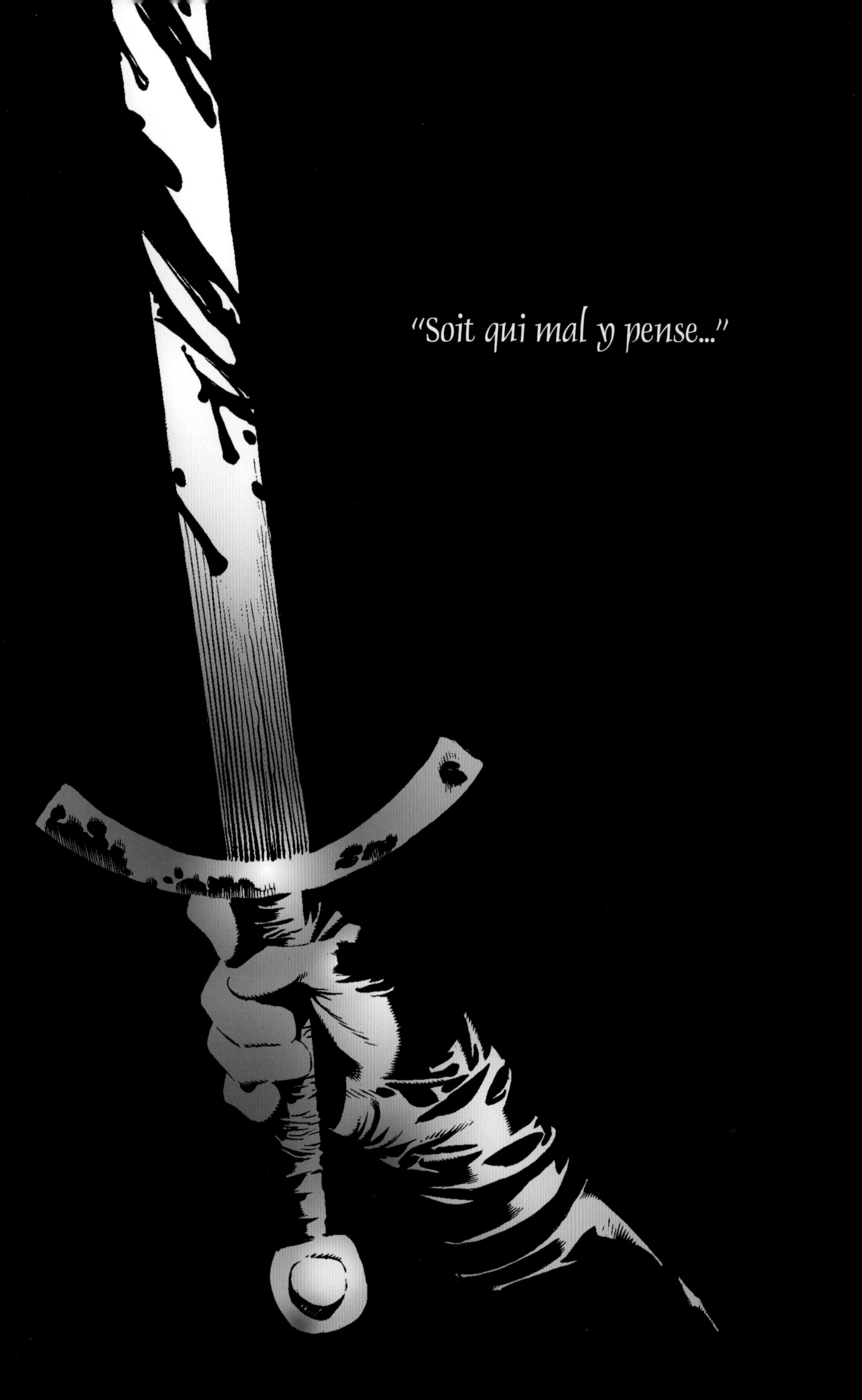
"Soit qui mal y pense..."

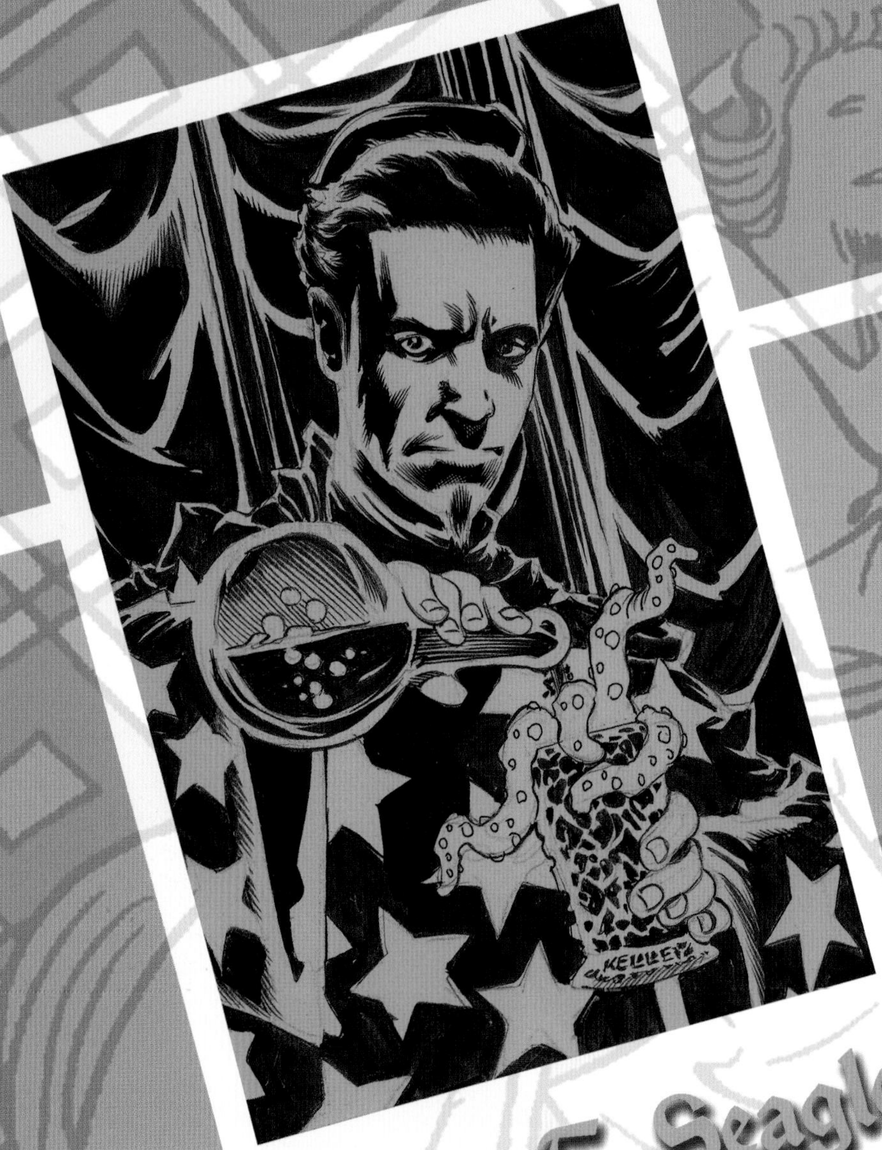
KELLEY

Steven T. Seagle

A partner in Man of Action Studios, creators of BEN 10 and GENERATOR REX (www.manofaction.tv), Steven has written numerous acclaimed graphic novels including SOLSTICE, it's a bird..., AMERICAN VIRGIN and SOUL KISS. His works for live stage can be found at www.speaktheaterarts.com.

Steven previously collaborated with Kelley on the comic adaptation of the SLEEPY HOLLOW film and to this day has no knowledge why anyone would adapt a two-hour film into a sixty-page comic book.

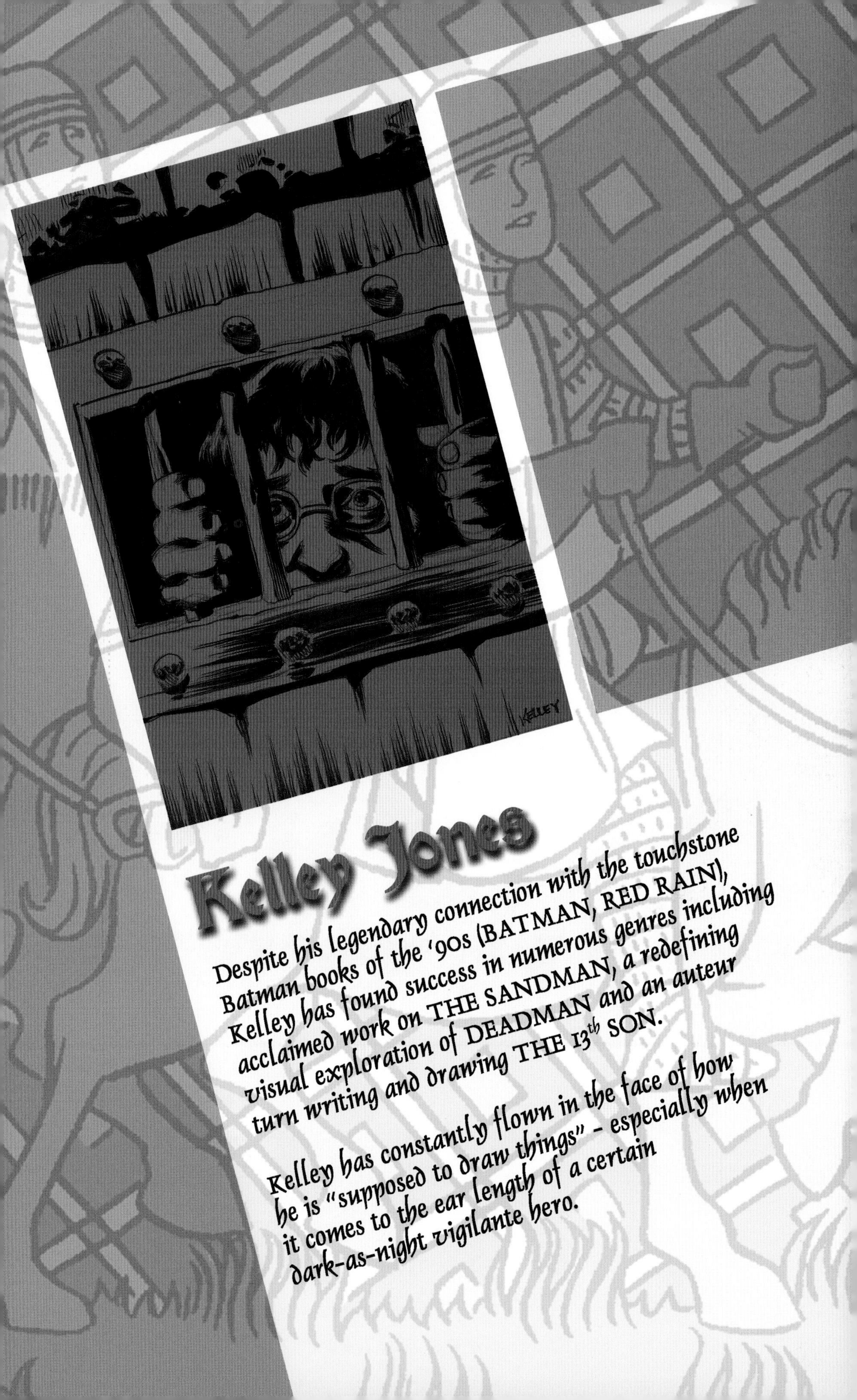
KELLEY

Kelley Jones

Despite his legendary connection with the touchstone Batman books of the '90s (BATMAN, RED RAIN), Kelley has found success in numerous genres including acclaimed work on THE SANDMAN, a redefining visual exploration of DEADMAN and an auteur turn writing and drawing THE 13th SON.

Kelley has constantly flown in the face of how he is "supposed to draw things" - especially when it comes to the ear length of a certain dark-as-night vigilante hero.

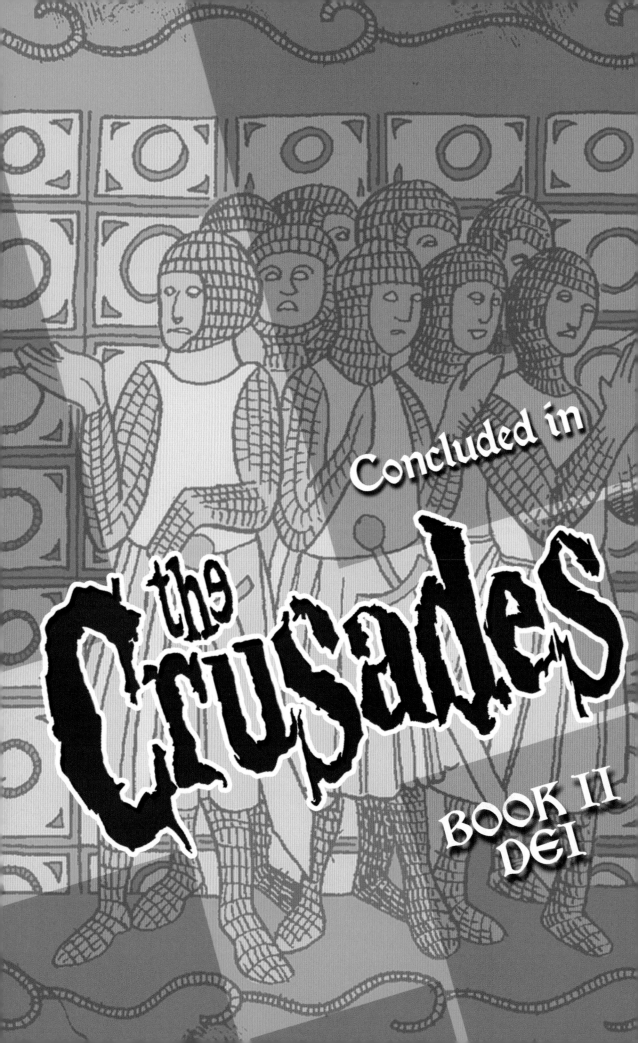

Concluded in

the Crusades

BOOK II
DEI